Cisco Exam Objectives
Exam 640-503: Routing 2.0

MW00747801

Routing Principles	
List the key information routers need to route data	
Describe classful and classless routing protocols and describe the use of the fields in a routing table	
Compare distance vector and link-state protocol operation	2
Given a preconfigured laboratory network, discover the topology, analyze the routing table, and test connectivity using accepted troubleshooting techniques	2

Extending IP Addresses	Chapter(s)
Given an IP address range, use VLSMs to extend the use of the IP addresses	3
Given a network plan that includes IP addressing, explain if route summarization is or is not possible	3
Configure an IP helper address to manage broadcasts	12

Configuring OSPF in a Single Area	Chapter(s)
Explain why OSPF is better than RIP in a large internetwork; how it discovers, chooses, and maintains routes; and how it operates in a single area NBMA environment	5
Configure OSPF for proper operation in a single area and verify OSPF operation in a single area	5
Configure a single-area OSPF environment and verify proper operation of your routers	5
Configure a single-area OSPF in an NBMA environment and verify proper operation of your routers	5

Interconnecting Multiple OSPF Areas	Chapter(s)
Describe the issues with interconnecting multiple areas and how OSPF addresses each	6
Explain the differences between the possible types of areas, routers, and LSAs	6
Explain how OSPF supports the use of VLSM, how it supports the use of route summarization in multiple areas, and how it operates in a multiple area NBMA environment	6
Configure a multi-area OSPF network and verify OSPF operation in multiple areas	6
Given an addressing scheme and other laboratory parameters, configure a multiple-area OSPF environment and verify proper operation (within described guidelines) of your routers	6

Configuring EIGRP	Chapter(s)
Describe Enhanced IGRP features and operation	7
Explain how EIGRP discovers, chooses, and maintains routes; how it supports the use of VLSM; how it operates in an NBMA environment; how it supports the use of route summarization; and how it supports large networks	7
Configure Enhanced IGRP and verify Enhanced IGRP operation	7
Configure an Enhanced IGRP environment and verify proper operation of your routers	7
Configure Enhanced IGRP in an NBMA environment and verify proper operation of your routers	7

Configuring Basic Border Gateway Protocol	Chapter(s)
Describe BGP features and operation	9
Describe how to connect to another autonomous system using an alternative to BGP, static routes	9
Explain how BGP policy-based routing functions within an autonomous system and how BGP peering functions	9
Describe BGP communities and peer groups	10
Describe and configure external and internal BGP, and describe BGP synchronization	9
Configure a BGP environment and verify proper operation of your routers	9

Implementing BGP in Scalable Networks	Chapter(s)
Describe the scalability problems associated with Internal BGP	10
Explain and configure BGP route reflectors	10
Describe and configure policy control in BGP using prefix lists, and describe methods to connect to multiple ISPs using BGP	10
Explain the use of redistribution between BGP and Interior Gateway Protocols (IGPs)	10
Configure a multihomed BGP environment and verify proper operation of your routers	10

Optimizing Routing Update Operation	Chapter(s)
Select and configure the different ways to control routing update traffic	13
Configure route redistribution in a network that does not have redundant paths between dissimilar routing processes and in a network that does have redundant paths	13
Resolve path selection problems that result in a redistributed network and verify route redistribution	13
Configure policy-based routing using route maps	13
Configure redistribution between different routing domains and verify proper operation of your routers	13
Configure policy-based routing within your pod and verify proper operation of your routers	13

Implementing Scalability Features in Your Internetwork	Chapter(s)
Given a set of network requirements, configure many of the features discussed in the course and verify proper operation (within described guidelines) of your routers	15

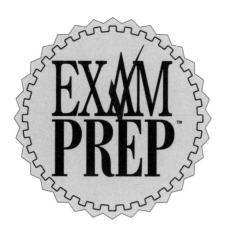

CCNP™ Routing

Robert E. Larson
Corwin S. Low
Paulden Rodriguez

The Coriolis Group, LLC
14455 N. Hayden Road, Suite 220
Scottsdale, Arizona 85260

(480)483-0192
FAX (480)483-0193
www.coriolis.com

Library of Congress Cataloging-in-Publication Data
Larson, Bob, 1949-
    CCNP routing / by Bob Larson, Corwin Low, and Paulden Rodriguez.
      p.   cm. -- (Exam prep)
    Includes index.
    ISBN 1-57610-778-7
    1. Electronic data processing personnel--
Certification.   2. Telecommunication--Switching systems--Examinations--Study guides. I. Low, Corwin S. II. Rodriquez, Paulden. III. Title. IV. Series.

QA76.3 .L38   2000
004.6'2--dc21
                                 00-064413
                                     CIP

President and CEO
Keith Weiskamp

Publisher
Steve Sayre

Acquisitions Editor
Shari Jo Hehr

Development Editor
Deborah Doorley

Product Marketing Manager
Brett Woolley

Project Editor
Stephanie Palenque

Technical Reviewer
Michael Jennings

Production Coordinator
Todd Halvorsen

Cover Designer
Jesse Dunn

Layout Designer
April Nielsen

CD-ROM Developer
Michelle McConnell

Printed in the United States of America
10 9 8 7 6 5 4 3 2 1

The Coriolis Group, LLC • 14455 North Hayden Road, Suite 220 • Scottsdale, Arizona 85260

ExamCram.com Connects You to the Ultimate Study Center!

Our goal has always been to provide you with the best study tools on the planet to help you achieve your certification in record time. Time is so valuable these days that none of us can afford to waste a second of it, especially when it comes to exam preparation.

Over the past few years, we've created an extensive line of *Exam Cram* and *Exam Prep* study guides, practice exams, and interactive training. To help you study even better, we have now created an e-learning and certification destination called **ExamCram.com**. (You can access the site at **www.examcram.com**.) Now, with every study product you purchase from us, you'll be connected to a large community of people like yourself who are actively studying for their certifications, developing their careers, seeking advice, and sharing their insights and stories.

I believe that the future is all about collaborative learning. Our **ExamCram.com** destination is our approach to creating a highly interactive, easily accessible collaborative environment, where you can take practice exams and discuss your experiences with others, sign up for features like "Questions of the Day," plan your certifications using our interactive planners, create your own personal study pages, and keep up with all of the latest study tips and techniques.

I hope that whatever study products you purchase from us—*Exam Cram* or *Exam Prep* study guides, *Personal Trainers*, *Personal Test Centers*, or one of our interactive Web courses—will make your studying fun and productive. Our commitment is to build the kind of learning tools that will allow you to study the way you want to, whenever you want to.

Help us continue to provide the very best certification study materials possible. Write us or email us at **learn@examcram.com** and let us know how our study products have helped you study. Tell us about new features that you'd like us to add. Send us a story about how we've helped you. We're listening!

Visit ExamCram.com now to enhance your study program.

Good luck with your certification exam and your career. Thank you for allowing us to help you achieve your goals.

Keith Weiskamp
President and CEO

Look for these other products from The Coriolis Group:

CCNP Routing Exam Cram
by Eric McMasters, Brian Morgan, and Mike Shroyer

CCNP Switching Exam Cram
by Richard Deal

CCNP Support Exam Cram
by Matthew Luallen

CCNP Switching Exam Prep
by Sean Odom and Doug Hammond

CCIE Routing and Switching Exam Cram
by Henry Benjamin and Tom Thomas

To my wife Jerri, my parents Lou and Elmer Larson,
and my four children Brett, Christopher, Jared, and Jade.
—Robert E. Larson

ॐ

To Henry & Rose Low and Rick & Lynette Locatelli.
—Corwin S. Low

ॐ

This book is dedicated to all aspiring IT professionals.
—Paulden Rodriguez

ॐ

About the Authors

Robert E. Larson has been involved in the computer industry since May 18, 1980, when Mt. St. Helens erupted stranding him with a friend, Darrel Smith, for 10 days with food, shelter, and two new TRS-80s. Since graduate school in 1984, Bob has worked full-time as a computer trainer, course developer, and consultant.

In 1985, Bob started Bob Larson and Associates initially to provide trainers, consultants, and course developers to the growing computer industry. He had the good fortune to be involved in some very large projects for organizations like The Boeing Company, US General Services Administration—Audit Division, Food Services of America, GTE, the Washington State Bar Association, and several community colleges and universities. BL&A trainers have presented courses in most states west of the Mississippi. In 1994, BL&A opened an independent computer-training center in central Washington State at Yakima.

In the last half of the 1990s the company, and Bob's interests shifted toward networking, network training, and consulting—initially Microsoft certification training. Bob owes a huge debt to Sue Loreen and Geri Nelson from Edmonds Community College who begged, pleaded, threatened, and cajoled him to go look at a 1997 presentation by Cisco Systems for a new training idea they had—Cisco Networking Academies to be run in community and technical colleges, as well as high schools. Edmonds opened their Academy in 1998 and Green River Community College followed the next year.

Bob was very fortunate in 1999 to be able work in South Africa with the first Cisco Academy developed in part as a Nelson Mandella/Cisco training initiative. The CCNA graduating class was the first on the continent with all 18 students certified on their first try—a reflection of their qualities and commitment. In February 2000, Bob was chosen, in part at least because of his South African experience, to do a three-week switch and router project in Ghana.

Bob is currently working on several CCNP training projects.

Corwin S. Low draws from a diverse cache of disciplines—both technical and creative. On the technical side, he has analyzed and engineered numerous security and performance profiles for large companies. While on the creative side, he has engineered and implemented numerous application-level programs. He has even won high acclaim from independent associations such as Ziff-Davis and the

Washington Software Alliance for content, usability, and creativity. Cory has been acknowledged for implementing solutions that are logical and work intelligently and intuitively, whether process-based or program-based.

In 1979, Cory got his start in the world of computing with a DEC PDP-11/03 running RT-11. In 1982 he got his first inkling of networking with the introduction of BITNET, the *Because It's Time Network,* and ARPANET, the predecessor to the Internet.

Along with fellow business partner Mr. Michael Simon and colleague Mr. Adam Engst, Cory penned the popular computer book, *The Internet Starter Kit for Windows.* This title sold in excess of 250,000 copies and went on to be translated into six different languages.

Cory is a cofounder of Conjungi Networks, a computer network and infrastructure design company. With his colleagues, Cory implemented one of the largest network security implementations ever designed in 1995. At that time, it enabled over 50,000 nodes within an organization to access the Internet securely—parts of which are still in use even today, as that number has grown to over 100,000. It is at Conjungi where Cory utilizes most of his Cisco skills.

Under the Conjungi name, Cory designed and project managed WebAdmin, Microsoft Corporation's first server-side HTML-based Internet standards application. It enabled IS professionals to manage and administer Windows NT and BackOffice Servers. It was so successful that it drew acclaim from Mr. Bill Gates himself and initiated an entirely new set of applications to be developed by Microsoft.

Prior to starting Conjungi, Cory designed, engineered, implemented, and project managed a very large-scale on-demand Audio and Video System that enabled over 40 individual locations and kiosks to select from a library of 2,500 hours of audio programming and 7,500 hours of video programming. The project had construction logistics as well, and spanned 4 buildings using traditional analog as well as digital (via fiber) media. An additional goal of this system was to make it easy to use as well as easy to understand. The system and parts of the system are still used even after 5 years of continuous use.

Proficient in many network devices including routers, bridges, firewalls, encryption devices as well as other network appliances, Cory is also very familiar with most desktop productivity applications, database applications and tools, development and engineering tools, diagnostic tools, as well as a diverse set of operating systems.

Cory is currently on a work sabbatical in Rome, Italy.

Paulden Rodriguez is a network consultant for Bob Larson & Associates. He is a Cisco Certified Design Professional and Cisco Certified Network Professional, as well as a specialist in the operation of network routing protocols. Paulden is also a technical reviewer for The Coriolis Group and a PC/Network Technician at Northshore Center of Shoreline Community College, located in Bothell, Washington.

Acknowledgments

I'd like to thank the following individuals for their support during the writing of this book:

Corwin Low and Paul Rodriguez for all the writing support.

Brett Larson, Chris Larson, Scott Wolfe, Dave Warner, Wes Clanton, and the other employees of Bob Larson & Associates for their support in giving me the time to work on this project and for putting up with me during that time.

Geri Nelson and the staff at Edmonds Community College's Business and Technology Center plus Bruce Riveland and the staff at Green Giver Community College's Education and Training Center for supporting me and allowing me the time to undertake this and my other "projects."

My Cisco students in South Africa: Mpafane Simani, Daniel Sedibeng, Setotolwane Phago, Bongani Sokudela, Mphekeleli Dhlamini, Tlatlaru Matemane, Maria Marakalla, Linda Princess Sithela, Leonard Nkosi, Herbert Sibeko, Gwendoline Lefifi, Emmarancia Nelwamondo, Charmaine Kefilwe Dube, Bongani Gasa, Aluwani Magidi, Trevor Fanafana Mabena, Nothemba Sonkwele, Mokgadi Mathekga, and Dumisani Sondlo, who taught me way too late in life that there is more to life than sitting behind a keyboard. A special thought for Sharin Badri who started the journey with us but whose early passing reminded all of us how much one person can touch and change our lives.

Thanks to all of my students over the years who continually remind me through their trials and successes that while we are in the technology field we are still a people world.

Special thanks to Bruce Smith, a business paper owner-publisher and friend, who has always encouraged me and helped me in many ways over the last 20 years.
—*Robert E. Larson*

I'd like to thank the following individuals for their support during the writing of this book:

Bob Larson and Paul Rodriguez for all their writing support.

Michael Simon, Julie Huffman, Sara Boddy, George Guempel, Molly Hegenderfer, Danny Tiongco, Raymond Pompon, Mark Schulstad, and Tammey Grable and all related to Conjungi Networks for their huge support and sacrifice in giving me the time and space to write this book. Special thanks to Mike for encouraging me to follow my heart.

Frs. Jerry Stookey, OP, Paulus Pascal, OP, Chrys Finn, OP, Michael O'Rourke, OP, Edmund Nantes, OP, Boyd Sulpico, OP, and the others at Santa Sabina for putting up and supporting me on a regular basis.

Frs. Michael Sweeney, OP, Allen Duston, OP, Robert Christian, OP, Michael Dodds, OP, Martin Badenhorst, OP, Scott Steinkerchner, OP, Peter Hunter, OP; and Srs. Judith Zoebelein, FSE, Catherine Mary Clarke, FSE, Veronica Raferty, OP, Barbara Gerace, FSP, and Beatrice Bigatau, FSP for more than just roadside assistance.

Elizabeth Heil and Sara Savoldello with the Vatican Patrons of the Arts, Luigi Salimbeni, Stefano Pasquini, and Francesca Reali with the Ufficio Internet della Santa Sede for letting me help out when this book was driving me crazy.

Mario, Giulia, Mauro, and Gaia Ottoviani as well as Garrett Boge, for helping me get by in the Eternal City—despite Telecom Italia.

Dan Cheely for providing a catalyst for me.

And finally to Richard, Jill, Taylor, Elliott, Abby, Garrett, Christina, Conrad, and Anselm Black for getting me on the road in the first place.
—*Corwin S. Low*

I'd like to thank the following individuals for their support during the writing of this book:

Corwin Low and Bob Larson for all their writing support and for allowing me the golden opportunity to be able to participate in this challenging and rewarding endeavor. Special thanks goes to Bob Larson for being a tremendously valuable contact in the field of Cisco internetworking.

Keith Edholm, Kenny Rosario, and the rest of the staff at Shoreline Community College's Northshore Center for introducing me to the IT field and for training me to become a respected IT professional. They are the best.

Lastly, I'd like to thank my family for giving me the support and encouragement that was necessary to succeed in the writing of this book.
—*Paulden Rodriguez*

Contents at a Glance

Table of Contents

Chapter 2
Routing Principles 21

Chapter 3
Extending IP Addresses 77

Chapter 4
Routing Protocols Overview 107

Chapter 5
OSPF in a Single Area 133

Chapter 6
Interconnecting Multiple OSPF Areas 187

Chapter 9
Border Gateway Protocol 293

Chapter 10
Implementing BGP in Scalable ISP Networks 343

Chapter 12
Managing Network and Device Access 419

Exam Insights

Welcome to *CCNP Routing Exam Prep*. This book aims to help you get ready to take—and pass—Cisco Certification Exam 640-503, titled "Building Scalable Cisco Networks," or BSCN. This Exam Insights section discusses exam preparation resources, the testing situation, Cisco's certification programs in general, and how this book can help you prepare for Cisco's certification exams.

Exam Prep books help you understand and appreciate the subjects and materials you need to pass Cisco certification exams. We have worked from Cisco's curriculum objectives to ensure that all key topics are clearly explained. Our aim is to bring together as much information as possible about Cisco certification exams.

Nevertheless, to completely prepare yourself for any Cisco test, we recommend that you begin by taking the Self-Assessment included in this book immediately following this Exam Insights section. This tool will help you evaluate your knowledge base against the requirements.

Based on what you learn from that exercise, you might decide to begin your studies with some classroom training or some background reading. You might decide to read The Coriolis Group's *Exam Prep* book that you have in hand first, or you might decide to start with another study approach. You may also want to refer to one of a number of study guides available from Cisco or third-party vendors.

We also strongly recommend that you configure and become comfortable with the Cisco IOS features on which you will be tested because nothing beats hands-on experience and familiarity when it comes to understanding the questions you are likely to encounter on a certification test. See Appendix C, "Study Resources," at the end of this book for information about how and where to get router experience. Book learning is essential, but hands-on experience is the best teacher of all.

How to Prepare for an Exam

Preparing for any Cisco-related test (including BSCN) requires you to obtain and study materials designed to provide comprehensive information about the Cisco IOS and its capabilities that will appear on your specific exam. The following list of materials will help you study and prepare:

➤ *Classroom Training*—Cisco Training Partners, Cisco Networking Academies (at selected community colleges), and third-party training companies all offer classroom training for Cisco Certified Networking Associate (CCNA) and Cisco Certified Networking Professional (CCNP) exams, including BSCN. These companies aim to help you prepare to pass the BSCN test. Although such training can run $450 (or more) per day in class, most of the individuals lucky enough to participate find them to be quite worthwhile.

➤ *Cisco Connection Online*—This is the name of Cisco's Web site (**www.cisco.com**), the most current and up-to-date source of Cisco information. You may have to fill out a questionnaire to get to some topics, and others are limited to Cisco partners and vendors.

➤ *The CCPrep Web site*—This Cisco certification Web site is the most well known in the world. You can find it at **www.ccprep.com** (formerly known as **www.CCIEprep.com**). Here, you can find exam preparation materials, practice tests, self-assessment exams, and numerous certification questions and scenarios. In addition, professional staff members are available to answer questions that you can post on the answer board.

➤ *Cisco training kits*—These kits are available only if you attend a Cisco class at a certified training facility or if a Cisco Training Partner in good standing gives you one.

Study guides—Several publishers, including The Coriolis Group, offer BSCN titles. The Coriolis Group series includes:

➤ *The Exam Cram series*—These books give you information about the material you need to know to pass the tests.

➤ *The Exam Prep series*—These books provide a greater level of detail than the *Exam Cram* books and are designed to teach you everything you need to know from an exam perspective. Each book comes with a CD that contains interactive practice exams in a variety of testing formats. *CCNP Routing Exam Prep* is the perfect learning companion to prepare you for Exam 640-503, "Building Scalable Cisco Networks."

Together, the two series make a perfect pair.

➤ *Multimedia*—These Coriolis Group materials are designed to support learners of all types—whether you learn best by listening, reading, or doing:

➤ *The Exam Cram Personal Trainer*—Offers a unique, personalized self-paced training course based on the exam.

➤ *The Exam Cram Personal Test Center*—Features multiple test options that simulte the actual exam, including Fixed-Length, Random, Review, and Test All. Explanations of correct and incorrect answers reinforce concepts learned.

➤ *The Exam Cram Audio Review series*—This series offers a concise review of key topics covered on the exam, as well as practice questions.

➤ *Other Resources*—Many materials about Cisco technologies and BSCN topics are available. The complete resource section in Appendix C at the back of this book should give you an idea of where you should look for further discussion.

By far, this set of required and recommended materials represents an outstanding collection of sources and resources for BSCN and related topics. We anticipate that you will find that this book belongs in this company.

Taking a Certification Exam

Once you have prepared for your exam, you need to register with a testing center. Each computer-based CCNP exam costs $100, and if you don't pass, you may retest for an additional $100 for each try. In the United States and Canada, tests are administered by Prometric Testing Centers.

You can sign up for a test through Prometric's Web site at **www.2test.com**, or you can register by phone at 800-204-EXAM (within the United States or Canada). The Web site will not allow you to schedule exams within 48 hours, so use the phone registration for shorter scheduling interval. Be forewarned you will have to listen to several minutes of messages including several directing you to the Web site. The Prometric company and exam information site is **www.prometric.com/**.

To sign up for a test, you must possess a valid credit card, or you may contact the company for mailing instructions to send them a check (in the United States). Prometric vouchers purchased through Prometric or a third-party reseller are nonreturnable, nonrefundable, and can be used for certification exams. To order a voucher, call 1–800–616–3926. Only when payment is verified, or a check has cleared, can you actually register for a test.

To schedule an exam, call the toll-free number or visit the Web page at least one day in advance. To cancel or reschedule an exam, you must call before 7 P.M. Central Standard Time the day before the scheduled test time (or you will be charged, even if you don't appear to take the test). When you want to schedule a test, have the following information ready:

➤ *Your name*—Enter it as you would like to have it appear on your certificate.

➤ *Your social security, social insurance, or Prometric number (SP)*

➤ *Contact telephone numbers*—If there is a problem, Prometric will use these numbers to reach you.

➤ *Mailing address*—The address to which you want your certificate mailed.

➤ *Exam number (640-503) and title (BSCN, or Advanced Routing)*

➤ *Email address*—Once again, this is used for contact purposes. This is often the fastest and most effective means of contacting you.

➤ *A method of payment*—As already mentioned, a credit card is the most convenient method, but alternate means can be arranged in advance, if necessary.

Once you sign up for a test, you will be informed as to when and where the test is scheduled. Try to arrive at least 15 minutes early.

You will need to bring two forms of identification to the testing site. One form must be a photo ID such as a driver's license or a valid passport. The other must have a signature. The test cannot be delivered without the appropriate forms of identification.

The Exam Situation

When you arrive at the testing center for your scheduled your exam, you will need to sign in with an exam coordinator. He or she will ask you to show two forms of signature identification, one of which must be a photo ID. After you have signed in and your time slot arrives, you will be asked to deposit any books, bags, pagers, calculators, Palm Pilots, or other items you brought with you. Then you will be escorted into a closed room.

All exams are completely closed book. In fact, you will not be permitted to take anything with you into the testing area, but you will be furnished with one or two blank sheets of paper and a pen or, in some cases, an erasable plastic sheet and an erasable pen. Before the exam, you should memorize as much of the important material as you can, so you can write that information on the blank sheet as soon as you are seated in front of the computer. You can refer to this piece of paper any time you like during the test, but you will have to surrender the sheet when you leave the room.

You will have some time to compose yourself, to record this information, and to take a sample orientation exam before you begin the real test. You will also be required to complete a computer-based survey to track demographics of the test candidates. Typically, if an exam has a 75 minute time limit, you will have 90 minutes to take the sample exam, complete the survey and take the actual exam. Once you start the actual exam you now have only the exam time limit. If this is your first Cisco exam, we suggest you take the orientation test before taking your first exam. Because they are all more or less identical in layout, behavior, and controls, however, you probably won't need to do this more than once.

Typically, the room will be furnished with anywhere from one to a dozen computers, and each workstation will be separated from the others by dividers designed to keep you from seeing what is happening on someone else's computer. Keep in mind that the people next to you could be taking a certification exam from an industry totally unrelated to yours, so don't be concerned if someone starts after you or finishes before you. Most test rooms feature a wall with a large picture window and/or closed circuit cameras. This permits the exam coordinator to monitor the room, to prevent exam-takers from talking to one another, and to observe anything out of the ordinary that might go on. The exam coordinator will have preloaded the appropriate Cisco certification exam—for this book, Exam 640-503—and you will be permitted to start as soon as you are seated in front of the computer.

All Cisco certification exams allow a certain maximum amount of time in which to complete the work (this time is indicated on the exam by an on-screen counter/clock, so you can check the time remaining whenever you like). All Cisco certification exams are computer generated and most use a multiple-choice format, often with six to eight choices. It is possible, if not likely, that several questions will refer to an exhibit containing dozens of commands from which you will be expected to select one as the answer to a specific question. Although this may sound quite simple, the questions not only are constructed to check your mastery of basic facts and skills about the subject material, but they also require you to evaluate one or more sets of circumstances or requirements. Often, you are asked to give more than one answer to a question, although you will be told how many to choose. You get only one pass through the questions—you cannot mark a question and return to it later. Taking the exam is quite an adventure, and it involves real thinking. This book shows you what to expect and how to deal with the potential problems, puzzles, and predicaments.

When you complete a Cisco certification exam, the software will tell you whether you have passed or failed. All test objectives are broken into several topic areas and each area is scored on a basis of 100 percent. Particularly if you do not pass the exam, we suggest you select the button on the screen that asks if you want to print the report. The test administrator will print for you. You can use this report to help you prepare for another go-around, if needed. Once you see your score, you have the option of printing additional copies of the score report. It is a good idea to print it twice.

Remember, if you need to retake an exam, you will have to schedule a new test with Prometric and pay another $100.

Note: The first time you fail a test, you can retake the test the next day. However, if you fail a second time, you must wait 14 days before retaking that test. The 14-day waiting period remains in effect for all retakes after the second failure.

The next section explains more about how Cisco test questions look and how they must be answered.

Exam Layout and Design

Whichever type of Cisco test you take, questions belong to one of five basic types:

➤ Multiple-choice with a single answer

➤ Multiple-choice with one or more answers (the question will indicate how many answers)

➤ Multipart with one or more answers (the question will indicate how many answers)

➤ CLI-based questions (many times, an exhibit will present a sample IOS configuration in which you are asked to choose the correct command or interpret the configuration's output, per the question's directions)

➤ A different format, such as fill in the blank, ordering, or matching

Always take the time to read a question at least twice before selecting an answer, and pay special attention to words such as "not" that can radically change the question.

Always look for an Exhibit button as you examine each question. The Exhibit button brings up graphics used to help explain a question, provide additional data, or illustrate network design or program behavior. An exhibit is usually a screen capture of program output or Graphical User Interface (GUI) information that you must examine to analyze the question's contents and formulate an answer. Before scheduling your test, make sure you understand the Windows interface—maximizing, restoring, moving, resizing, and tiling windows. One could argue this is a small body of information that you should have mastered before now—if not, do it now.

Not every question has only one answer; many questions require multiple answers. Therefore, it is important to read each question carefully to see how many answers are required. Look for additional instructions pertaining to the number of answers. Such instructions often occur in brackets immediately following the question itself (as they do for all multiple-choice questions in which one or more answers are possible).

Note: *Most Cisco exams do not allow you to return to questions, so you must make sure to answer the question as best you can before proceeding to the next one. The exam will clearly state before you start whether you can mark answers and return.*

The following multiple-choice question requires you to select a single correct answer. Following the question is a brief summary of each potential answer and why it is either right or wrong.

Question 1

Given the IP address 185.24.0.0 with the subnet mask 255.255.240.0, what would be the number of total subnets and host addresses?

○ a. Subnets 16 / hosts 4,096

○ b. Subnets 32 / hosts 2,046

○ c. Subnets 16 / hosts 4,094

○ d. Subnets 16 / hosts 14

The correct answer is c. Subnets 16 / hosts 4,094.

This sample question format corresponds closely to the Cisco certification exam format—the only difference on the exam is that answer keys do not follow questions. To select an answer, you would position the cursor over the radio button next to the answer. Then click the left mouse button to select the answer.

Let us examine a question for which one or more answers are possible. This type of question provides checkboxes rather than radio buttons for marking all appropriate selections.

Question 2

Which of the following BGP path attributes are used specifically to influence the path a router takes to reach a destination in another AS? [Choose two answers]

❑ a. Origin

❑ b. Local preference

❑ c. Weight

❑ d. Next-hop

Answers b and c are correct. The major difference between local preference and weight is that the former is propagated within the AS, whereas the latter remains local to the router on which it is configured; but both are used to influence the path taken to networks in external ASes. Answer a is incorrect because origin is a path attribute used specifically to define the source of routing information. Answer d is incorrect because the next hop attribute is used to identify the next hop router used to reach a destination network.

For this particular question, three answers are required. As far as the authors can tell (and Cisco won't comment), such questions are scored as wrong unless all the required correct selections are chosen. A partially correct answer does not result in partial credit when the test is scored. For Question 2, you have to check the boxes next to items b and c to obtain credit for a correct answer. Picking the right answers also means knowing why the other answers are wrong!

Cisco's Testing Format

Currently, Cisco uses a fixed-length testing format using a fixed number of questions. Although each candidate will get the same number of questions, the order of the questions can vary. There can be multiple exam question sets, so if you have to retake an exam do not assume it will be the same questions. From time to time, questions might be replaced and others may not be scored.

You will get only one pass through the questions. You cannot mark questions to return to them later. As you work your way through the exam, another counter that Cisco provides in the upper-right corner (near the remaining time) will come in handy—the number of questions completed and the number outstanding.

It is wise to budget your time by making sure that you have completed at least one-quarter of the questions one-quarter of the way through the exam period and three-quarters of the questions three-quarters of the way through (15 questions in 19 minutes).

If you are not finished when only five minutes remain, use that time to guess your way through any remaining questions. Remember, guessing is potentially more valuable than not answering because blank answers are always wrong, but a guess may turn out to be right. If you don't have a clue about any of the remaining questions, pick answers at random, or choose all a's, b's, and so on. The important thing is to submit an exam for scoring that has an answer for every question.

Tip: At the very end of your exam period, you are better off guessing than leaving questions unanswered.

Question-Handling Strategies

Based on the exams we have taken, some interesting trends have become apparent. For those questions that take only a single answer, usually two or three of the answers will be obviously incorrect, and a couple of the answers will be plausible. Of course, only one can be correct. Unless the answer leaps out at you, begin the process of answering by eliminating those answers that are most obviously wrong.

Note: If the answer seems immediately obvious, reread the question to look for a trap; sometimes those are the ones you are most likely to get wrong.

Cisco exams are generally pretty straightforward and not intended to beat you out of your certification, but then again they are not designed to be a walk in the park. You must pay attention, particularly with syntax. Knowing the difference between **access–list 75 deny any** and **access list 75 deny any** should be assumed (note the hyphen).

Almost always, at least one answer out of the possible choices for a question can be eliminated immediately because it matches one of these conditions:

➤ The answer does not apply to the situation.

➤ The answer describes a nonexistent issue, an invalid option, or an imaginary state.

After you eliminate all answers that are obviously wrong, you can apply your retained knowledge to eliminate further answers. Look for items that sound correct but refer to actions, commands, or features that are not present or not available in the situation that the question describes.

If you are still faced with a blind guess among two or more potentially correct answers, reread the question. Try to picture how each of the possible remaining answers would alter the situation. Be especially sensitive to terminology; sometimes the choice of words (e.g., "remove" instead of "disable") can make the difference between a right answer and a wrong one.

Only when you have exhausted your ability to eliminate answers, but remain unclear about which of the remaining possibilities is correct, should you guess at an answer. An unanswered question offers you no points, but guessing gives you at least some chance of getting an answer right. Keep in mind that the clock is ticking and you cannot come back later, but don't be too hasty when making a blind guess.

Numerous questions assume that the default behavior of a particular command or option is in effect. If you know the defaults and understand what they mean, this knowledge will help you cut through many Gordian knots.

Mastering the Inner Game

In the final analysis, knowledge breeds confidence, and confidence breeds success. If you study the materials in this book carefully, review all the practice questions at the end of each chapter and do the practice exams on the CD-ROM, you should become aware of those areas where additional learning and study are required. After you have worked your way through this book, take the practice exam in the back of the book and the practice exams on the CD-ROM. This will provide a reality check and help you identify areas for further study. Make sure you follow up and review materials related to the questions you miss on the practice exams before scheduling a real exam. Only when you have covered that ground and feel comfortable with the whole scope of the practice exams should you set an exam appointment (otherwise, obtain some additional practice tests so you can keep trying until you hit the magic number of 80 percent correct).

Tip: If you take a practice exam and don't score at least 80 percent correct, you will want to practice further. If you are more ambitious or better funded, you might want to purchase a practice exam from a third-party vendor.

Armed with the information in this book and with the determination to augment your knowledge, you should be able to pass the certification exam. However, you need to work at it or you will spend the exam fee more than once before you finally pass. If you prepare seriously, you should do well. Good luck!

The next section covers the exam requirements for the various Cisco certifications.

The Cisco Certification Program

The Cisco Certification Program currently includes the following separate certificates with various specialty tracks, each of which boasts its own special acronym (as a certification candidate, you need to have a high tolerance for alphabet soup of all kinds). You should become familiar with and visit regularly Cisco's Web site at **www.cisco.com/go/certifications/**. The major certifications are:

Note: *The number of questions and time limits for the following exams were accurate at the time this book was written. Cisco reserves the right to change either as it sees fit. Cisco generally tries to keep this information confidential, although you can check either figure when you register for an exam.*

Note: *Within the certification program, specific specializations exist. For the purposes of this book, we focus only on the Routing and Switching track. Visit* ***www.cisco.com/warp/public/10/wwtraining/certprog/index.html*** *for information on the other specializations.*

- *CCNA (Cisco Certified Networking Associate)*—Exam 640-507 is a 65-question, 75-minute exam. The cost is $100. The CCNA certification demonstrates the ability to install, configure, and operate simple-routed local area network (LAN), routed wide area network (WAN), and switched LAN. Topics include: Ethernet, Token-Ring, TCP/IP, IPX/SPX, IP RIP, IGRP, IPX RIP, access lists, switches VLANs, Serial Communications, ISDN, Frame-Relay, and Point-to-Point Protocol (PPP). The CCNA is a solid foundation for pursuing advanced Cisco certifications. It is a prerequisite for the Cisco Certified Network Professional (CCNP) and Cisco Certified Design Professional (CCDP), and is suggested for Cisco Certified Internetwork Expert (CCIE). It covers concepts and skills vital to the operation of modern computer networks, and would be valuable to network administrators, network engineers, and students preparing for these roles.

- *CCDA (Cisco Certified Design Associate)*—Exam 640-441 is a 72-question, 120-minute exam. The cost is $100. The Cisco Network Design Career certification

Table 1   Cisco Routing and Switching CCNA, CCNP, and CCIE Requirements

CCNA

Only 1 exam required	
Exam 640-507	Cisco Certified Network Associate 2.0

CCNP*

All 4 of these are required	
Exam 640-503	Routing 2.0
Exam 640-504	Switching 2.0
Exam 640-505	Remote Access 2.0
Exam 640-506	Support 2.0

* You need to have your CCNA before you become a CCNP.

CCIE

1 written exam and 1 lab exam required	
Exam 350-001	CCIE Routing and Switching Qualification
Lab Exam	CCIE Routing and Switching Laboratory

track is designed for people who want to design Cisco-based networks that predominantly include routed LAN, routed WAN, and switched LAN networks. The focus here is on developing hierarchical network design skills that enable you to know when, where, and how to employ routers and LAN switches, along with the appropriate design methods that relate to your company's specific needs. CCDA is the design alternative to CCNA, offering more case studies but fewer hands-on configuration projects. This path is often selected for sales and support staff.

➤ *CCNP 2.0 (Cisco Certified Networking Professional)*—The CCNP 2.0 replaces the older CCNP 1.0 certification, reflecting the changes in technology and Cisco's position within the industry. CCNP is a comprehensive internetworking skills certification that requires successfully passing four exams. The cost of each exam is $100. The number of questions and time limit for each should be confirmed by checking with your testing center or by calling Prometric. The four exams are:

➤ *BSCN (Building Scalable Cisco Networks)*—Exam 640-503 is a 61-question, 75-minute exam. This exam replaces the Advanced Cisco Router Configuration (ACRC) version 11.3. BSCN includes those activities that network administrators must perform when managing access and controlling overhead traffic in dynamic, routed networks. Router capabilities are used to control traffic over LANs and WANs, as well as to provide connections for corporate networks to Internet Service Providers (ISPs). BSCN includes extensive coverage of Classless Inter Domain Routing (CIDR), Open Shortest Path First (OSPF), Enhanced Interior Gateway Routing Protocol (EIGRP), and Border Gateway Protocol (BGP).

➤ *BCMSN (Building Cisco Multilayer Switching Networks)*—Exam 640-504 is a 64-question, 75-minute exam. This exam replaces the Cisco LAN Switch Configuration (CLSC) exam. It covers the knowledge and skills necessary to build campus networks using multilayer switching technologies over high-speed Ethernet. It includes using routing and switching technologies, concepts, and implementations to work together to solve the growing network needs of the modern organization.

➤ *BCRAN (Building Cisco Remote Access Networks)*—Exam 640-505 is a 62-question, 75-minute exam. This exam replaces the Configuring, Monitoring, and Troubleshooting Dialup Services (CMTD) exam. It covers the knowledge and skills necessary to build a remote access network to interconnect central sites to branch offices and home office/telecommuters. It includes the technologies to control access to the central site, as well as to maximize bandwidth utilization over the remote links.

➤ *CIT (Cisco Internetwork Troubleshooting)*—Exam 640-506 is a 61-question, 75-minute exam. This exam replaces the Cisco Internetwork Troubleshooting (CIT) exam 640-406. CIT includes how to baseline and troubleshoot an environment using Cisco routers and switches for multiprotocol client hosts and servers connected with the following: Ethernet, Fast Ethernet, and Token Ring LANs; Serial, Frame-Relay, and ISDN BRI WANs.

An alternative to taking all four exams involves taking the single Foundation Exam 640-509 (cost is $200), which can be substituted for BSCN Exam 640-503, BCMSN Exam 640-504, and BCRAN Exam 640-505. You must still take CIT Exam 640-506, however.

➤ *CCDP (Cisco Certified Design Professional)*—The CCDP 2.0 replaces the older CCDP 1.0 certification, reflecting the changes in technology and Cisco's position within the industry. CCDP is a comprehensive internetworking design skills certification that requires successfully passing four exams. The cost of each exam is $100. The number of questions and time limit for each should be confirmed by checking with your testing center or calling Prometric. The four exams are:

  ➤ *BSCN*—Exam 640-503 is a 61-question, 75-minute exam. This exam replaces ACRC version 11.3. BSCN includes those activities that network administrators must perform when managing access and controlling overhead traffic in dynamic, routed networks. Router capabilities are used to control traffic over LANs and WANs, as well as to provide connects for corporate networks to ISPs. BSCN includes extensive coverage of CIDR, OSPF, EIGRP, and BGP.

  ➤ *BCMSN*—Exam 640-504 is a 64-question, 75-minute exam. This exam replaces the CLSC exam. It covers the knowledge and skills necessary to build campus networks using multilayer switching technologies over high-speed Ethernet. It includes using routing and switching technologies, concepts, and implementations to work together to solve the growing network needs of the modern organization.

➤ *BCRAN*—Exam 640-505 is a 62-question, 75-minute exam. This exam replaces the CMTD exam. It covers the knowledge and skills necessary to build a remote access network to interconnect central sites to branch offices and home offices/telecommuters. It includes the technologies to control access to the central site, as well as to maximize bandwidth utilization over remote links.

➤ *CID (Cisco Internetwork Design)*—Exam 640-025 is a 100-question, 120-minute exam. It covers the knowledge and skills necessary to troubleshoot internetworks that include Cisco equipment. It develops a functional understanding of the standard problem-solving model, common network troubleshooting tools, and the diagnostic tools provided with Cisco software to analyze and resolve network problems in modern dynamic internetworks. It covers the range from needs analysis to identifying key technical, business, and administrative issues that drive the design to using different technology options to meet identified needs including media, internetworking equipment, topologies, and internetworking system software. It covers the use of Cisco hardware and software products to develop a complete internetwork design solution.

An alternative to taking all four exams involves taking the single Foundation Exam 640-509 (cost is $200), which can be substituted for BSCN Exam 640-503, BCMSN Exam 640-504, and BCRAN Exam 640-505. You must still take CID Exam 640-025, however.

➤ *CCIE (Cisco Certified Internetwork Expert)*—The CCIE certification is possibly the most influential in the internetworking industry today. It is famous (or infamous) for its difficulty and for how easily it holds its seekers at bay. The certification requires only one written exam (350-001); passing that exam qualifies you to schedule time at a Cisco campus to demonstrate your knowledge in a two-day practical laboratory setting. You must pass this lab with a score of at least 80 percent to become a CCIE. Recent statistics have put the passing rates at roughly 20 percent for first attempts and 35 through 50 percent overall. Once you achieve CCIE certification, you must recertify every two years by passing a written exam administered by Cisco.

➤ *CCSI (Certified Cisco Systems Instructor)*—To obtain status as a CCSI, you must be employed (either permanently or by contract) by a Cisco Training Partner in good standing, such as GeoTrain Corporation. That training partner must sponsor you through Cisco's Instructor Certification Program, and you must pass the two-day program that Cisco administers at a Cisco campus. You can build on CCSI certification on a class-by-class basis. Instructors must demonstrate competency with each class they are to teach by completing the written exam that goes with each class. Cisco also requires that instructors maintain a high customer satisfaction rating, or they will face decertification.

At the time this book is being written, Cisco is evaluating a requirement to periodically recertify for the various programs. The best place to keep tabs on the Cisco Career Certifications program and its related requirements is on the Web. The URL for the program is **www.cisco.com/go/certifications/**. Note that Cisco's Web site changes often, so if this URL doesn't work, try using Cisco's site **www.cisco.com** and follow the Training/Certification links.

Tracking Cisco Certification Status

As soon as you pass any Cisco exam (congratulations), you must complete a certification agreement. To do this, go to Cisco's Web site **www.cisco.com/go/certifications/** and select the Tracking System link, or go directly to the Certification Tracking Web site (**www.galton.com/~cisco/**). You can also mail a hard copy of the agreement to Cisco's certification authority. You will not be certified until you complete a certification agreement and Cisco receives it in one of these forms.

The Certification Tracking Web site also allows you to view your certification information. Cisco will contact you via email and explain your certification and its use. Once you are registered into one of the career certification tracks, you will be given a login on this site, which is administered by Galton, a third-party company that has no in-depth affiliation with Cisco or its products. Galton's information comes directly from Sylvan Prometric, the exam-administration company for much of the computing industry.

Once you pass the necessary certification exam(s) and agreed to Cisco's nondisclosure terms, you will be certified. Official certification normally takes from four to six weeks, so don't expect to get your credentials overnight. When the package for a qualified certification arrives, it includes a welcome kit that contains a number of elements:

➤ A graduation letter

➤ Official certificate (suitable for framing)

➤ A laminated wallet card

➤ A license to use the Cisco certification logo, thereby allowing you to use the logo in advertisements, promotions, documents, resumes, letterhead, business cards, and so on

➤ Access to the online Tracking System

Many people believe that the benefits of Cisco certification go well beyond the perks that Cisco provides to newly anointed members of this elite group. We are starting to see more job listings that request or require applicants to have certification for CCNA, CCNP, and so on, and many individuals who complete the program can qualify for increases in pay and/or responsibility. As an official recognition of hard work and broad knowledge, one of the Cisco credentials is a badge of honor in many IT organizations.

About this Book

Career opportunities abound for well-prepared IT professionals, including those who are Cisco networkers. If you are new to the field of networking, this book is designed to be your gateway toward becoming a Cisco Certified Network Professional or Cisco Certified Design Professional. This book will provide you with the knowledge you need to study and prepare for BSCN Exam 640-503. Those who may already have prior Cisco networking experience will find that the book adds depth and breadth to that experience.

Cisco routers are at the heart of many of the world's networks, both large and small. The skills developed for this exam will help to make you a more useful and marketable member of the industry. If you know how to configure the industry standard (de facto), employers know that you can work with any other technology—or learn the skills necessary to do so.

When you complete this book, you will be at the threshold of an Internet/intranet networking career that can be very fulfilling and challenging. This is a rapidly advancing field that offers ample opportunity for personal growth and for making a contribution to your business or organization. This book is intended to provide you with knowledge that you can apply right away and a sound basis for understanding the changes that you will encounter in the future. It also is intended to give you the hands-on skills you need to be a valued professional in your organization.

This book is filled with real-world projects that cover every aspect of installing and configuring Cisco routers. The projects are designed to make what you learn come alive through actually performing the tasks. Also, every chapter includes a range of practice questions to help prepare you for the Cisco certification exam. All of these features are offered to reinforce your learning so you will feel confident in the knowledge you have gained from each chapter.

Features

The features listed on the next page are designed to improve this book's value in aiding you to fully understand advanced router concepts.

➤ *Chapter objectives*—Each chapter in this book begins with a detailed list of the test objectives to be mastered within that chapter. This list provides you with a quick reference to the contents of that chapter as well as a useful study aid.

➤ *Illustrations and tables*—Numerous illustrations of screenshots and components aid you in the visualization of common setup steps, theories, and concepts. In addition, many tables provide details and comparisons of both practical and theoretical information.

➤ *Notes, tips, and warnings*—*Notes* present additional helpful material related to the subject being described. *Tips* from the authors' experience provide extra information about how to attack a problem, how to configure routers for a particular need, or what to do in certain real-world situations. *Warnings* are included to help you anticipate potential mistakes or problems so you can prevent them from happening.

➤ *Real-world projects*—Although it is important to understand the theory behind router and networking technology, nothing can improve upon real-world experience. To this end, along with theoretical explanations, each chapter provides hands-on projects aimed at providing you with real-world implementation experience.

➤ *Chapter summaries*—Each chapter contains a summary of the concepts it has introduced. These summaries provide a helpful way to recap and revisit the ideas covered in each chapter.

➤ *Review questions*—End-of-chapter assessment begins with a set of review questions that reinforce the ideas introduced in each chapter. These questions ensure that you have mastered the concepts, and they are written to help prepare you for the Cisco certification examination. Answers to these questions are found in Appendix A.

➤ *Sample tests*—Use the sample test and answer key in Chapters 16 and 17 to test yourself. Then move on to the two interactive practice exams found on the CD-ROM.

Where Should You Start?

This book is intended to be read in sequence, from beginning to end. Each chapter builds upon those that precede it, to provide a solid understanding of Building Scalable Cisco Networks—Advanced Routing. After completing the chapters, you may find it useful to go back through the book and use the review questions and projects to prepare for Cisco Certification Exam 640-503. Readers are also encouraged to investigate the many pointers to online and printed sources of additional information that are cited throughout this book.

Please share your feedback on the book with us, especially if you have ideas about how we can improve it for future readers. We will consider everything you say carefully, and we will respond to all suggestions. Send your questions or comments to us at **learn@examcram.com**. Please remember to include the title of the book in your message; otherwise, we will be forced to guess which book you are writing about. And we do not like to guess—we want to *know*. Also, be sure to check out the Web page at **www.examcram.com**, where you'll find information updates, commentary, and certification information. Thank you, and enjoy the book.

Self-Assessment

We include a Self-Assessment in this *Exam Prep* to help you evaluate your readiness to tackle Cisco Certified Networking Professional (CCNP) certification. It should also help you understand what you need to master the topic of this book—namely, Exam 640-503, Building Scalable Cisco Networks (BSCN). But before you tackle this Self-Assessment, let us talk about concerns you may face when pursuing CCNP certification, and what an ideal CCNP candidate is like.

CCNPs in the Real World

In the next section, we describe an ideal CCNP candidate, knowing full well that only a few real candidates will meet this ideal. In fact, the description of that ideal candidate might seem downright scary. But take heart—although the requirements to obtain CCNP certification may seem formidable, they are by no means impossible. However, you should be keenly aware that it does take time and it requires some expense and substantial effort to get through the process.

First, understand that CCNP certification is an attainable goal. You can get all the real-world motivation you need from knowing that many others have done so before, so you will be able to follow in their footsteps. If you are willing to tackle the process seriously and do what it takes to obtain the necessary experience and knowledge, you can take—and pass—all the certification tests involved to become a CCNP. In fact, we have designed these *Exam Preps*, and the companion *Exam Crams*, to make it as easy on you as possible to prepare for these exams. But prepare you must!

The same, of course, is true for all Cisco career certifications, including:

➤ *Cisco Certified Networking Associate (CCNA), which is the first step on the road to CCNP certification*—This involves a single exam that covers information from Cisco's Introduction to Cisco Router Configuration (ICRC) class and the Cisco LAN Switch Configuration (CLSC) class. Cisco also has developed a class geared to CCNA certification, known as Cisco Routing and LAN Switching (CRLS).

➤ *Cisco Certified Design Associate (CCDA), which is the first step on the road to CCDP certification*—This involves a single exam that covers the basics of design theory. To prepare for it, you should attend the Designing Cisco Networks (DCN) class and/or the Cisco Internetwork Design (CID) class.

➤ *CCNP, which is an advanced certification regarding internetwork design, implementation, and troubleshooting*—This certification consists of multiple exams. You can obtain CCNP certification in two ways: (1) You could pass the individual exams for BSCN, BCMSN (Building Cisco Multilayer Switching Networks), BCRAN (Building Cisco Remote Access Networks), and CIT (Cisco Internetwork Troubleshooting). (2) If you are not one for taking a lot of exams, you can take the Foundation Routing/Switching exam and the CIT exam. Either combination will complete the requirements.

➤ *Cisco Certified Design Professional (CCDP), which is an advanced certification regarding internetwork design*—This certification consists of multiple exams. You can attain the CCDP in two ways: (1) You could pass the individual exams for BSCN, BCMSN, BCRAN and CID. (2) If you are not one for taking a lot of exams, you can take the Foundation Routing/Switching exam and the CID exam. Either combination will complete the requirements.

➤ *Cisco Certified Internetwork Expert (CCIE), which is commonly referred to as the "black belt" of internetworking*—This is considered the single most difficult certification to attain in the internetworking industry. First you must take a qualification exam. Once you pass the exam, the real fun begins. You will need to schedule a two-day practical lab exam to be held at a Cisco campus, where you will undergo a "trial by fire" of sorts. Your ability to configure, document, and troubleshoot Cisco equipment will be tested to its limits. Do not underestimate this lab exam.

The Ideal CCNP Candidate

Just to give you some idea of what an ideal CCNP candidate is like, we present some relevant statistics about the background and experience of such an individual. Don't worry if you don't meet or come close to meeting these qualifications now—this is a far from ideal world, and where you fall short is simply where you will have to do more work.

➤ *Academic or professional training in network theory, concepts, and operations*—This includes everything from networking media and transmission techniques through network operating systems, services, and applications.

➤ *Three-plus years of professional networking experience*—This includes experience with Ethernet, token ring, modems, and other networking media. This experience must include installation, configuration, upgrading, and troubleshooting.

➤ *Two-plus years in a networked environment*—This includes hands-on experience with Cisco routers, switches, and other related equipment. A solid understanding of each system's architecture, installation, configuration, maintenance, and troubleshooting is also essential.

➤ *A thorough understanding of key networking protocols, addressing, and name resolution, including TCP/IP and IPX/SPX.*

➤ *Familiarity with key TCP/IP-based services*—These include ARP, BOOTP, DNS, FTP, SNMP, SMTP, Telnet, TFTP, and other relevant services for your internetwork deployment.

Fundamentally, this boils down to a bachelor's degree in computer science plus three years of work experience in a technical position involving network design, installation, configuration, and maintenance. We believe that well under half of all certification candidates meet these requirements; in fact, most meet less than half of these requirements—at least, when they begin the certification process. But because thousands of people have survived this ordeal, you can survive it too—especially if you heed what our Self-Assessment can tell you about what you already know and what you need to learn.

Put Yourself to the Test

The following series of questions and observations is designed to help you figure out how much work you must do to pursue Cisco career certification and what kinds of resources you should consult on your quest. Be absolutely honest in your answers, or you will end up wasting money on exams you are not yet ready to take. There are no right or wrong answers here, only steps along the path to certification. Only you can decide where you really belong in the broad spectrum of aspiring candidates. Two things should be clear from the outset, however:

➤ Even a modest background in computer science will be helpful.

➤ Extensive hands-on experience with Cisco products and technologies is an essential ingredient to certification success.

1. Have you ever taken any computer-related classes? [Yes or No]

   If Yes, proceed to question 2; if No, proceed to question 4.

2. Have you taken any classes included in Cisco's curriculum? [Yes or No]

   If Yes, you will probably be able to handle Cisco's architecture and system component discussions. If you are rusty, brush up on basic router operating system concepts, such as RAM, NVRAM, and flash memory. You will also want to brush up on the basics of internetworking, especially IP subnetting, access lists, and WAN (wide area network) technologies.

If No, consider some extensive reading in this area. We strongly recommend instructor-led training offered by a Cisco Training Partner or at any of the growing number of Cisco Networking Academies at select community and technical colleges. However, you may want to check out a good general advanced routing technology book, such as *Cisco CCIE Fundamentals: Network Design and Cast Studies* by Andrea Cheek, H. Kim Lew, and Kathleen Wallace (Cisco Press, Indianapolis, IN, 1998; ISBN: 1-57870-066-3). If this title doesn't appeal to you, check out reviews for other, similar titles at your favorite online bookstore.

3. Have you taken any networking concepts or technologies classes? [Yes or No]

If Yes, you will probably be able to handle Cisco's internetworking terminology, concepts, and technologies. If you are rusty, brush up on basic internetworking concepts and terminology, especially networking media, transmission types, the OSI reference model, and networking technologies such as Ethernet, token ring, FDDI, and WAN links.

If No, you might want to read one or two books in this topic area. Check the section at the end of each chapter for a selection of resources that will give you additional background on the topics covered in this book.

4. Have you done any reading on routing protocols and/or routed protocols (e.g., IP, IPX, AppleTalk)? [Yes or No]

If Yes, review the requirements stated in the paragraphs after Questions 2 and 3. If you meet those requirements, move on to the next question.

If No, consult the recommended reading for both topics. A strong background will help you prepare for the Cisco exams better than just about anything else.

The most important key to success on all of the Cisco tests is hands-on experience with Cisco routers and related equipment. If we leave you with only one realization after taking this Self-Assessment, it should be that there is no substitute for time spent installing, configuring, and using the various Cisco products upon which you will be tested repeatedly and in depth. We cannot stress enough that quality instructor-led training will benefit you greatly and give you additional hands-on configuration experience with the technologies upon which you are to be tested.

5. Have you installed, configured, and worked with Cisco routers? [Yes or No]

If Yes, make sure you understand basic concepts as covered in the classes Introduction to Cisco Router Configuration(ICRC) or Cisco Certified Network Associate(CCNA) before progressing into the materials covered here because this book expands on the basic topics taught there.

Tip: You can download objectives and other information about Cisco exams from the company's Training and Certification page on the Web at www.cisco.com/training.

If No, you will need to find a way to get a good amount of instruction on the intricacies of configuring Cisco equipment. You need a broad background to get through any of Cisco's career certifications. You will also need to have hands-on experience with the equipment and technologies on which you will be tested.

Tip: If you have the funds, or your employer will pay your way, consider taking a class at a Cisco Training Partner (preferably one with "distinguished" status for the highest quality possible) or at any of the growing number of Cisco Networking Academies at select community and technical colleges. In addition to classroom exposure to the topic of your choice, you will get a good view of the technologies being widely deployed and will be able to take part in hands-on lab scenarios with those technologies.

Before you even think about taking any Cisco exam, make sure you have spent enough time with the related Cisco IOS to understand how it may be installed and configured, how to maintain such an installation, and how to troubleshoot that software when things go wrong. This will help you in the exam as well as in real life.

Whether you attend a formal class on a specific topic to get ready for an exam or use written materials to study on your own, some preparation for the Cisco career certification exams is essential. At $100 to $200 (depending on the exam) per try—pass or fail—you want to do everything you can to pass on your first try. That is where studying comes in.

6. Have you taken a practice exam on your chosen test subject? [Yes or No]

If Yes, and you scored 80 percent or better, you are probably ready to tackle the real thing. If your score isn't above that crucial 80 percent threshold, keep at it until you break that barrier. Keep in mind that practice tests should match the version and objectives of the exam for which you are prepping. Many of the tests downloaded from the Internet include questions from other exams or older versions with different objectives.

If No, obtain all the free and low-budget practice tests you can find and get to work. Keep at it until you can break the passing threshold comfortably.

We have included a practice exam in this book so you can test yourself on the information and techniques you have learned. If you don't hit a score of at least 70 percent after this test, you will want to investigate the other practice test resources mentioned in this section.

For any given subject, consider taking a class if you have tackled self-study materials and have taken the test, but failed anyway. The opportunity to interact with an instructor and fellow students can make all the difference in the world, if you can afford that privilege. For information about Cisco classes, visit the Training and Certification page at **www.cisco.com/training** (use the Locate a Course link), or the Cisco Networking Academy site **www.cisco.com/warp/public/779/edu/ academy/**.

If you cannot afford to take a class, visit the Training and Certification page anyway because it also includes pointers to additional resources and self-study tools. Even if you cannot afford to spend much at all, you may still want to invest in some low-cost practice exams from commercial vendors to help you assess your readiness to pass a test. The following Web sites offer some practice exams online:

➤ CCPrep.com at **www.ccprep.com** (requires membership)

➤ Boson Software at **www.boson.com/**

➤ Network Study Guides at **www.networkstudyguides.com** (pay as you go)

Tip: When it comes to assessing your test readiness, there is no better way than to take a good-quality practice exam and pass with a score of 70 percent or better. When we are preparing ourselves, we shoot for 80-plus percent, just to leave room for the "weirdness factor" that sometimes shows up on Cisco exams.

Assessing Readiness for Exam 640-503

In addition to the general exam-readiness information in the previous section, you can do several things to prepare for the BSCN exam. A great source of questions and related information is available at the CCPrep Web site at **www.ccprep.com**. This is a good place to ask questions and get good answers, or simply to watch the questions that others ask (along with the answers, of course).

You should also cruise the Web to look for "braindumps" (recollections of test topics and experiences recorded by others) to help you anticipate topics you are likely to encounter on the test.

Tip: When using any braindump, it is okay to pay attention to information about questions, but you can't always be sure that a braindump's author will also be able to provide correct answers. Thus, use the questions to guide your studies, but don't rely on the answers in a braindump to lead you to the truth. Double-check everything you find in any braindump.

For BSCN preparation in particular, we also recommend that you check out one or more of these resources as you prepare to take Exam 640-503:

➤ Cisco Connection Online (CCO) Documentation (**www.cisco.com/ univercd/home/home.htm**). From the CCO Documentation home page you can select a variety of topics, including but not limited to Troubleshooting Internetwork Systems and Internetwork Troubleshooting guides, as well as Internetwork Technologies Overviews and Design Guides.

➤ *Cisco IOS 12.0 Solutions for Network Protocols, Volume 1: IP.* Cisco Press, Indianapolis, IN, 1999; ISBN: 1-57870-154-6.

➤ Andrew Bruce Caslow (CCIE #3139). *Cisco Certification: Bridges, Routers and Switches for CCIEs*, Prentice Hall, Upper Saddle River, NJ, 1999; ISBN: 0-13-082537-9.

Stop by the Cisco home page, your favorite bookstore, or an online bookseller to check out the many resources available. CCO Documentation provides a wealth of great material.

One last note: hopefully, it makes sense to stress the importance of hands-on experience in the context of the BSCN exam. As you review the material for that exam, you'll realize that hands-on experience with the Cisco IOS with various technologies and configurations is invaluable.

Onward, through the Fog!

Once you have assessed your readiness, undertaken the right background studies, obtained the hands-on experience that will help you understand the products and technologies at work, and reviewed the many sources of information to help you prepare for a test, you will be ready to take a round of practice tests. When your scores come back positive enough to get you through the exam, you are ready to go after the real thing. If you follow our assessment regime, you will know what you need to study, and when you are ready, you can make a test date at Prometric. Good luck!

CHAPTER ONE

Scaling Growing Internetworks

After completing this chapter, you will be able to:

✓ Identify the key requirements of a scalable internetwork

✓ Describe the features and strengths of the Cisco three-layer model

✓ Compare the strengths and weaknesses of segmenting with bridges, switches, and routers

✓ Given an internetwork requirement, select the key requirements

This chapter reviews some basics of internetworks and the issues that impact their implementation and expansion. It also introduces some terms and concepts to provide a common point of reference for future discussions. This chapter also defines some of the problems and issues faced in the workplace as well as in taking the certification exam. Later chapters provide detailed solutions to these problems and issues.

Internetworks

One of the first definitions for *internetworking* described it as the connection of two or more local area networks (LANs) to function somewhat as a single network. Internetworking was probably never really as simple as that implies, and it clearly isn't simple today. Not only do we now need to consider connecting LANS and wide area networks (WANs), we also have growing numbers of metropolitan area networks (MANs) and campus networks, each with its own characteristics, strengths, and weaknesses.

The picture becomes more complex when we recognize that we are no longer dealing just with traditional data. Businesses of all sizes are moving toward incorporating many of the following technologies that use the same systems as their data:

➤ Voice-over IP for local and/or long distance communication

➤ Video conferencing and collaborative work processes

➤ Client/server applications internally and with customers

➤ Router multicasts for training and internal/external communications

➤ High-definition imaging for industries ranging from health care to publishing

➤ Telemetry to monitor critical processes and procedures

➤ Various forms of E-commerce

Many of these technologies also incorporate the use of the Internet as an alternative to the private and more traditional methods of connectivity. With this blend of technologies, however, come new concerns about and new ways of looking at securing our data as well as our networks.

The increase of these technologies will mean that we are going to be called on to provide ever-increasing levels of support for:

➤ Greater bandwidth

➤ Bandwidth on demand

➤ Quality of service (QoS)

➤ Class of service (CoS)—prioritization

To be scalable, a network must be able to grow as the organization's requirements change with a minimum of disruption and loss of resources. Although a fully meshed network may provide high levels of reliability, it often cannot be expanded without considerable reconfiguration and resulting reductions in service.

A network that is well designed, implemented, funded, and maintained should be able to grow as quickly as needed to meet the requirements of the organization. The alternative is increased network congestion or too much traffic for the available bandwidth. This is always inefficient, and in the worst case it can mean a complete collapse in the data network and considerable losses in revenue, reputation, and future growth for the organization. Many retailers new to E-commerce learned this lesson during the Christmas season in 1999. This is clearly not a resume item for the information technology (IT) professionals involved, many of whom needed those resumes sooner than they expected.

Cisco's Hierarchical Network Model

Cisco uses a three-layer hierarchical model to define the data distribution process. It maintains that even the largest networks can be reduced to these three layers. The Cisco model includes the following layers:

➤ Core layer

➤ Distribution layer

➤ Access layer

If properly implemented, this model allows for orderly address assignment, efficient transmission of data, increased scalability, and more structured device configuration. It simplifies device management and configuration because devices in the same layer perform the same tasks. To understand the model, one must recognize that each layer represents a change in filtering implemented by a router or layer 3 switch. An example of the three-layer model is shown in Figure 1.1.

The three-layer model represents an enterprise-type network with smaller networks not requiring all three layers until they grow or are assimilated by another organization. For this reason the model should be considered in plans for even new start-ups to avoid the inefficiency and disruptions that could occur during periods of rapid network growth or when the network is being assimilated into another larger system.

The Core Layer

The core layer represents the site-to-site connection within the enterprise network. As such, it represents critical links that, if lost, would mean entire sites would be cut off from the rest of the organization. Therefore, at this layer, reliability and performance are most important. Although redundant links would be appropriate at this

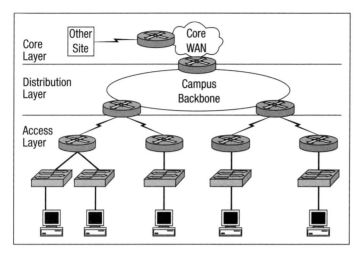

Figure 1.1 The Cisco basic three-layer model.

layer, filtering of any type would not. Any necessary filtering should be done at lower levels so the core layer can concentrate exclusively on fast delivery.

The Distribution Layer

The distribution layer—the campus backbone—connects network segments possibly representing departments or buildings with core layer services. Filtering with access lists is used to control traffic and implement quality of service and class of service prioritization within the network. This is where policy-based traffic control, which will be discussed a later chapter, occurs.

In larger networks, such as campus networks, this layer often includes:

➤ Virtual LAN (VLAN) routing

➤ Departmental/building access

➤ Address or area aggregation

➤ Internet and remote user access to the network

➤ Security for outside access (Internet/remote users)

Improved performance of switches and developing VLAN standards and technologies is pushing switches, both layer 2 and layer 3, up into the distribution layer. Switching technologies are addressed in the Building Cisco Multilayer Switching Networks (BCMSN) certification.

The Access Layer

The end users connect to the network in the access layer. Filtering could be through the use of access lists or MAC layer filtering with bridges and switches. In smaller

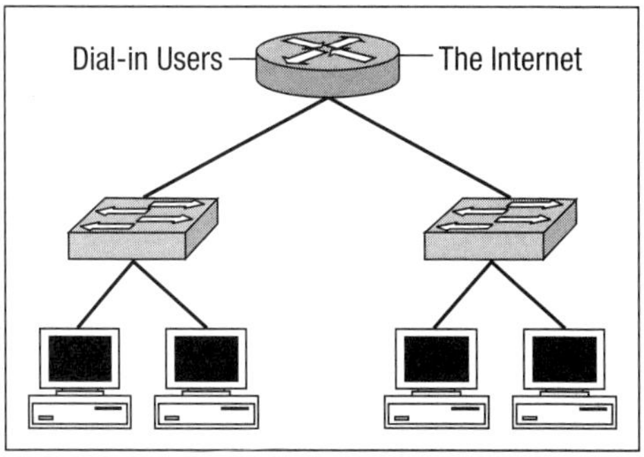

Figure 1.2 A single-layer network model.

noncampus networks, remote sites or users and the Internet may connect at this layer and would then require the increased security of technologies such as user authentication and firewalls. An example of the single-layer model is shown in Figure 1.2.

Routers within the Hierarchy

Following the model provides a topology wfõÆ three distinct layers and distinct functionality for the routers in each layer. Although switching technologies are becoming a consideration in this model, this course and exam concentrates only on the router's role.

➤ Core layer routers are responsible for site-to-site connectivity and must therefore be optimized for availability and reliability. Loss of service at this layer can be catastrophic. Maintaining connectivity of LAN and WAN circuits at this layer is critical.

➤ Distribution layer routers must implement QoS requirements through policy-based traffic control. Preserving bandwidth and maintaining network security need to be considerations at this level.

➤ Access layer routers keep workgroup or departmental traffic from getting into upper layers. Routers at this level often need to manage access of dial-up users.

Redundant Links and the Three-Layer Model

Each layer should link only to the layer above or below it. Any links between devices in the same layer will compromise the hierarchical design and may make future expansion more difficult. An example of redundant links between layers is shown in Figure 1.3.

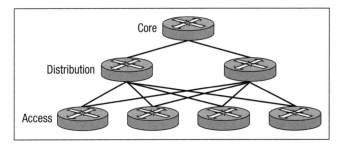

Figure 1.3 Redundant links between layers.

LANS, MANS, WANS, and Campus Networks

Let us start with some simple definitions for each of the common networks distilled from various Cisco sources.

Local Area Network

A LAN is a high-speed, low-error data network covering a relatively small geographic area, typically up to a few thousand meters and more typically within a single building or cluster of buildings. LANs connect workstations, peripherals, terminals, and other devices in a single building or other geographically limited area. LAN standards specify cabling and signaling at the physical and data link layers of the OSI model. Ethernet, Fast Ethernet, Gigabit Ethernet, FDDI, token ring, and Asynchronous Transfer Mode (ATM) switching are widely used LAN technologies.

Metropolitan Area Network

A MAN is a network that spans a metropolitan area. Generally, a MAN spans a larger geographic area than a LAN, but a smaller geographic area than a WAN. MANs typically need to use common carriers, often a single carrier, to connect sites and WAN technologies.

Wide Area Network

A WAN is a data communications network that serves users across a broad geographic area, both national and international, and often uses transmission devices provided by common carriers. ISDN, Frame-Relay, SMDS, and X.25 are examples of WAN technologies.

Campus Network

A campus is a building or group of buildings connected into one enterprise network that consists of multiple LANs. A campus is all or part of a company network located at a single physical location. Campus networks can use either LAN or WAN technologies.

Common Network Overview

Our main interest here is to recognize the implications for bandwidth for each network. Both MANs and WANs use common carriers such as phone companies for connectivity, and therefore they pay for bandwidth on some form of metered basis. This leads to strategies that try to reduce bandwidth cost. In the case of LANs and campus networks—even those using wide area technologies—the organization usually owns the media and therefore tends to treat bandwidth as if it were free. The decision to increase bandwidth will then be different for LANs and campus networks than for MANs and WANs.

A campus network that owns or leases the land between the buildings will have considerably more freedom to install additional connections than those same buildings located on city streets. This also makes it possible for switching technologies, such as VLANs, to move into the distribution layer.

Network Growth Scaling Problems

A network that fails or is unable to grow with demands put on it by a changing organization will suffer network congestion. Initially, congestion may appear as slow service during peak periods within the day, week, or month. But congestion can cause many problems and eventually may bring the whole system down. Obviously, monitoring the network's performance and responding effectively to the warning signs are critical functions.

Results of Congestion

Congestion, or too much traffic for the infrastructure, can result in any of the following conditions:

➤ Increased data collisions

➤ Dropped packets

➤ Retransmission of dropped or lost packets

➤ Incomplete routing updates if update packets are lost

➤ Overrun device buffers and capabilities

Congestion Warning Signs

Unfortunately, the warning signs of congestion tend to be intermittent and elusive. When excessive congestion leads to lost packets, the results may vary, depending on the services being used during that time. The three most common warning signs are:

➤ Applications time-out or become unavailable.

➤ Users cannot connect to services.

➤ The network crashes—you waited too long.

Dealing with Congestion

Clearly, other parts of the network can contribute to congestion. Increasing server central processing unit (CPU) power, memory, and disk access can and should all be addressed, but for our purposes we will concentrate here on layer 2 and 3 solutions.

Reducing the number of users in a collision domain will increase available bandwidth and reduce congestion. Because reducing the number of total users isn't really an option, we break the network into multiple collision domains through segmentation. An example of single collision domain LAN with hubs is shown in Figure 1.4.

The three ways to clear up network congestion through segmentation are:

➤ Segmenting with bridges

➤ Segmenting with LAN switches

➤ Segmenting with routers

Segmenting with Bridges

A bridge can be used to break a network into multiple collision domains. Bridges work at the data link layer of the OSI model and use MAC addresses to determine

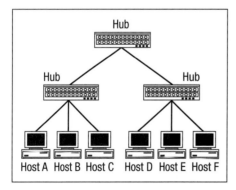

Figure 1.4   A single collision domain network with hubs.

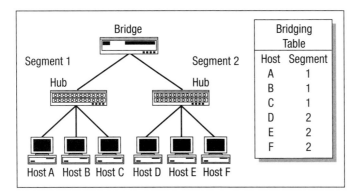

Figure 1.5   A network segmented by a bridge.

whether to forward data frames across the bridge. An example of the network segmented by a bridge is shown in Figure 1.5.

Each segment is now a separate collision domain, reducing congestion and potential collisions. Note that the actual table would have port numbers and MAC addresses for each host.

An additional plus is that bridges have buffering (memory) to hold packets from one segment destined for another segment until the media is clear on the destination segment. This effectively eliminates intersegment traffic collisions at least to the extent the buffer can hold all necessary packets. One analogy is the way railroads use siding tracks to allow trains to pass each other safely.

Bridges have a couple of weaknesses that must be addressed:

➤ A bridge forwards broadcast and multicast packets, so even though we now have two collision domains, we still have only one broadcast domain. Any host going haywire can still bring down the entire network.

➤ Bridges forward packets to all segments except the source when they get a data frame with an unknown MAC address.

➤ Increased latency, the delay between the time when a device receives a data frame and the time that frame is forwarded out the destination port, is an issue with bridges. Estimates of latency rates are up to 30 percent while forwarding decisions are made. Buffering to prevent intersegment collisions can also increase latency.

➤ If memory set aside for buffering is exceeded, packets will be discarded, requiring retransmission of the lost data.

Segmenting with LAN Switches

LAN switches are conceptually multiport bridges, which can microsegment the network into a separate collision domain for each switch port. As with bridges, forwarding is done using MAC addresses and port numbers. An example of the network segmented with LAN switching is shown in Figure 1.6.

LAN switches share all of the strengths and weaknesses of bridges, as discussed in the preceding section, including the single broadcast domain. As switch technology evolves, some strengths unique to LAN switches are greatly improving network performance. Some of the more notable enhancements include:

➤ With adequate buffering, multiple segments can be transmitting at the same time.

➤ Switching, unlike hubs, does not share bandwidth, thereby increasing resources to users. In a fully switched segment, each user could get 100 percent of the available bandwidth.

➤ Switched segments can use full duplex if both devices support the technology, thereby increasing bandwidth to almost double the normal. To reach double bandwidth would assume equal volumes of traffic going each way, so the real increase will be somewhat less.

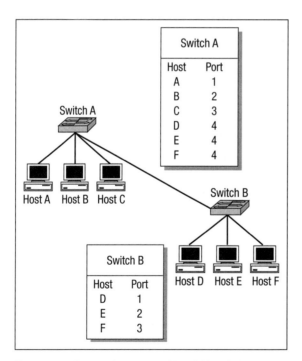

Figure 1.6 A network segmented by a LAN switch.

➤ Many switches support auto sensing, which allows a single switch to support both 10Mb and 100Mb devices on a per-port basis.

➤ Switches can be introduced incrementally into existing Ethernet networks because they are compatible with IEEE 802.3 standards, thereby protecting the investment in older technology until it can be upgraded.

➤ Cell-switching (ATM) has lead to a line of devices that can work in both the WAN and LAN environments. This technology involves using a simpler data structure with a uniform data size, called a "cell." An analogy compares containerized shipping with general trucking. Devices can run much faster because they handle only a single-size container.

➤ Layer 3 switches can offer both layer 2 and layer 3 capabilities, providing MAC layer segmentation as well as routing. The real power of these devices will be with VLANs. Layer 2 switches using VLAN technology can already segment a network into multiple collision and broadcast domains. What they cannot do is bring them back together so they can communicate; therefore, a router is still required in the mix. The layer 2/layer 3 switch can consolidate this into a single device in some implementations. This technology is covered in the BCMSN certification.

➤ Switch manufacturers are introducing many new features, such as port-trunking, Fast IP, and learned VLANs, among numerous others. Some manufacturers have moved the switching logic out of the IOS and directly into the circuitry, with significant increases in performance. These technologies are covered in the BCMSN certification.

Switching technology has evolved to reduce the latency problems of bridges through several methods of forwarding frames. The trade-off is reduced quality control checks.

Store-and-Forward Switching

Store-and-forward switching captures the entire frame into a buffer, checks to make sure the data is neither a runt nor a giant, runs the **cyclic redundancy check** (CRC), and if everything checks out, it uses the destination MAC for address forwarding. This is the slowest method, but it does not forward bad data frames.

Fragment-Free Switching

Fragment-free switching captures the entire frame into buffer, checks to make sure the data is neither a runt nor a giant, and then uses the destination MAC address forwarding. This is somewhat faster than store-and-forward switching because it doesn't run the CRC, but it has an increased chance of forwarding bad data frames.

Fast-Forward, or Cut-Through, Switching

Fast-forward switching, or cut-through switching, reads the frame as it passes through just long enough to check the destination MAC address before forwarding. This is the fastest method, but it performs no checks for bad data frames.

Segmenting with Routers

Unlike bridges and switches, which create logical segments with separate collision domains but maintain a single broadcast domain, routers create separate physical segments that are each collision and broadcast domains. Routers by default do not forward broadcasts or unknown addresses.

Whereas bridges and switches use MAC, or layer 2, addresses to keep track of every host and make forwarding decisions, routers use network, or layer 3, addresses to keep track of networks only (not hosts) for forwarding decisions. An example of segmenting the network with routers is shown in Figure 1.7.

Furthermore, whereas bridges and switches must learn about each host by monitoring the source addresses of packet traffic, routers use routing protocols to exchange data to update each other.

Given the appropriate IOS, routers can maintain separate routing tables for multiple network protocols such as IP, IPX, and AppleTalk.

Routers can select from multiple paths to a destination network by using various metrics based on the routing protocol(s) in use. From simply counting routers (hops) to assigning a cost to each path, the administrator can predict and control flows.

All of these great features come at a cost in the form of latency rates greater than either bridges or switches, often ranging from 20 to 40 percent.

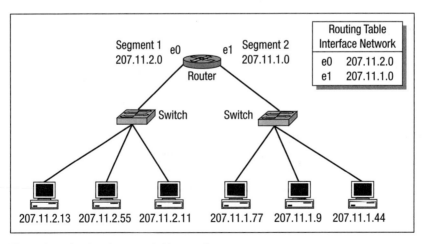

Figure 1.7   A network segmented by a router.

Network Scaling Key Requirements

Five requirements must be met in designing networks to ensure scalability in the future. The nature of the business and possibly its level of development will assign different levels of importance to each network. With some businesses, a loss of network resources (reliability) for a day would be an inconvenience, whereas with others it could be a financial catastrophe from which recovery might be difficult.

The five key requirements are:

➤ Reliability and availability

➤ Responsiveness

➤ Efficiency

➤ Adaptability

➤ Accessibility and security

Reliability and Availability

The reliability and availability requirement refers to the network's availability to users 365 days per year around the clock, as advertised. Each business will have to determine how important reliability is. Business size is not always a good predictor. A one-person ticket agency is out of business during the time his or her computer is offline.

In the three-layer network model, the higher the layer the more important reliability and availability become. Reduced reliability at the core layer will impact many users and significant portions of the network.

Responsiveness

Latency is a source of frustration for all users. The greater the latency, the greater the frustration. This would be particularly true in time-sensitive transactions, such as stock purchases. The key is to strike a balance between QoS requirements and responding to user needs. As an example, although not exactly the same thing, remember the feeling the last time your credit card transaction was slow because the card reader couldn't connect to the host?

Efficiency

Designing a network to efficiently allocate resources often involves restricting unnecessary traffic to preserve bandwidth for the necessary traffic. Access lists and other technologies can be used to reduce the number and complexity of routing updates and other forms of broadcast traffic. At the extreme, entire types of services can be denied to preserve bandwidth. I recently worked at a site in Africa where 85 users had to share a single 64K ISDN connection to the Internet—any reduction in efficiency literally meant total loss of service to everyone.

Adaptability

In addition to integrating different network technologies, protocols, and legacy systems, we must create an environment that can incorporate technologies that may be unknown today. Although we cannot always predict with great accuracy the course a network will take over the next few years, we should plan for many likely scenarios. Beyond that, we need to incorporate a design and devices that increase our chances of responding to the unknown. From following accepted standards to devices and applications that support interoperability, we hedge our bets.

Accessibility and Security

A properly designed network must have capabilities to support the industry standard WAN technologies efficiently and with a reliable level of security. As companies open their networks to remote users using dial-up services and to the two-way exposure of connecting to the Internet, it becomes increasingly important to be able to secure company resources.

Cisco IOS Features: Solutions for Specific Internetwork Requirements

Reliability and Availability Features

Critical to all layers, but particularly at the core, routers must be able to deal quickly with changes and failures in the network. Scalable protocols, such as Enhanced Interior Gateway Routing Protocol (EIGRP) and Open Shortest Path First (OSPF), provide the following features:

➤ Fast convergence time due to rapid failure detection and each router's stored network topology map.

➤ Reachability strength due to multiple metrics as a basis for routing decisions.

Responsiveness Features

Scalable protocols such as EIGRP and OSPF maintain the entire network topology map locally in each router, providing the following features:

➤ Choice among alternative paths.

➤ Load-balancing between multiple paths.

Dial-up backups for WAN links make critical links more reliable and provide possible extra capacity during periods of congestion.

Efficiency Features

IOS optimizes network efficiency by preserving bandwidth and critical routing data while reducing update traffic over WAN links. Scalable protocols such as EIGRP and OSPF provide the following features:

➤ Access lists to control network traffic due to normal data, broadcasts, and routing protocol updates.

➤ Routing table updates reduced by using route summarization and incremental routing updates only when network changes occur.

➤ Dial-on-demand routing (DDR), which creates connections only when "interesting" traffic is detected, thereby saving cost over full-time dedicated links.

➤ Switched access using packet switched networks such as Frame-Relay to reach remote sites around the world.

➤ Snapshot routing, which allows initial and periodic updates of full distance-vector routing information while freezing tables between updates.

➤ Compression over WAN connections to reduce network traffic using both header and data compression.

Adaptability Features

Due to frequent modifications and growth in the network, scalable networks must be able adjust to changes such as:

➤ Mixing routable and nonroutable protocols.

➤ Balancing the varying requirements when multiple protocols are supported.

➤ Integrating "island" networks.

Cisco IOS features that support network adaptability include:

➤ EIGRP support of multiple network protocols such as IP, IPX, and AppleTalk.

➤ Redistribution to exchange routing data between different routing protocols.

Accessibility and Security Features

The networks, particularly at the distribution layer, need to provide a variety of secure WAN connections, including support for telecommuters and remote sites. Cisco IOS features that support network accessibility include:

➤ Dedicated and switched WAN support to create a basic WAN infrastructure of telephone and digital links that are augmented by Frame-Relay, ATM, SMDS, and X.25 switches.

➤ Exterior protocol support such as Border Gateway Protocol (BGP) for strong connections to Internet Service Providers (ISPs).

Cisco IOS features supporting network security include:

➤ Access lists to prevent selected users from accessing network resources.

➤ Authentication protocols on WAN links using Point-to-Point Protocol (PPP) to challenge user connections.

Chapter Summary

This chapter provided a basic overview of Cisco's idea of scalable internetworks. It also provides a foundation on which the later chapters are built. The following were topics and key points that you may want to remember:

➤ Internetworking, the connection of two or more LANs to function as a single network, and an organization's skills at designing and implementing these systems affects the ability of the businesses to adapt to new technologies.

➤ Cisco has defined a three-layered hierarchical network model to separate network functions to facilitate the selection of equipment and the implementation of processes like policy-based traffic control. The three layers are core, distribution, and access. The core layer represents the site-to-site connection within the enterprise network, the critical links where reliability and performance are most important. Redundancy would be appropriate, but filtering should be avoided. The distribution layer, the campus backbone, connects network segments with core layer services. Policy-based traffic control occurs at this layer. The access layer is where the end users connect to the network. Filtering could be through the use of access lists or MAC layer filtering with bridges and switches.

➤ Congestion is the result of increasing demand on a network. How effectively and efficiently a network design can be expanded to meet growth and the associated congestion is its scalability. The hierarchical model can be quickly expanded, whereas a fully meshed network provides a high degree of reliability but limited scalability.

➤ Generally we combat congestion with segmenting. In this section we compared segmenting with bridges, LAN switches, and routers. Bridges and switches, layer 2 devices, are faster (less latency) but can only segment collision domains. They forward broadcast packets and unknown destination packets so cannot segment broadcast domains. Routers offer absolute physical segmentation, both collision and broadcast domain, but they also increase latency.

➤ The five key requirements of a scalable internetwork are: reliability and availability; responsiveness; efficiency; adaptability; and accessibility and security. In this section we summarized the Cisco IOS features to meet each one of these key requirements. We will look at these IOS features and their and implementation in detail in the chapters of this book. As you learn more about protocols like OSPF, EIGRP, and BGP and features like policy-based traffic control in later chapters, you will see that each meets one or more of these key requirements.

Review Questions

1. Which of the following are part of the three-layer Cisco network hierarchy model?

   a. User

   b. Distribution

   c. Resource

   d. Core

   e. Access

2. Which one of the following is not a weakness of segmenting a network with bridges?

   a. Broadcasts are forwarded

   b. Increased latency exists over hubs or repeaters

   c. Unknown IP addresses are forwarded to all segments except the source

   d. When buffering capacity is exceeded, packets are discarded

3. Which three are forwarding methods within Cisco switches?

   a. Store-and-forward

   b. Fast-forward

   c. Layer-2 forwarding

   d. Fragment-free

4. At which layer of the three-layer model does policy-based traffic control occur?

   a. Core

   b. Distribution

   c. Access

5. Loss of connectivity at the core layer primarily impacts which key requirement of scalable networks?

   a. Reliability and availability

   b. Responsiveness

   c. Efficiency

   d. Adaptability

   e. Accessibility and security

6. EIGRP support for multiple network protocols, such as IP, IPX, and AppleTalk, meets which key requirement of scalable networks?

   a. Reliability and availability

   b. Responsiveness

   c. Efficiency

   d. Adaptability

   e. Accessibility and security

7. Border Gateway Protocol (BGP) meets which key requirement of scalable networks?

   a. Reliability and availability

   b. Responsiveness

   c. Efficiency

   d. Adaptability

   e. Accessibility and security

8. Packet switched networks such as Frame-Relay meet which key requirement of scalable networks?

   a. Reliability and availability

   b. Responsiveness

   c. Efficiency

   d. Adaptability

   e. Accessibility and security

9. Fast convergence time due to rapid failure detection meets which key requirement of scalable networks?

   a. Reliability and availability

   b. Responsiveness

   c. Efficiency

   d. Adaptability

   e. Accessibility and security

1

10. Snapshot routing meets which key requirement of scalable networks?

    a. Reliability and availability

    b. Responsiveness

    c. Efficiency

    d. Adaptability

    e. Accessibility and security

11. Mixing routable and nonroutable protocols meets which key requirement of scalable networks?

    a. Reliability and availability

    b. Responsiveness

    c. Efficiency

    d. Adaptability

    e. Accessibility and security

12. Compression over WAN connections meets which key requirement of scalable networks?

    a. Reliability and availability

    b. Responsiveness

    c. Efficiency

    d. Adaptability

    e. Accessibility and security

CHAPTER TWO

Routing Principles

After completing this chapter, you will be able to:

✓ Describe classful and classless routing protocols

✓ List the key information routers need to route data

✓ Describe the use of the fields in a routing table

✓ Compare distance-vector and link-state protocol operations

✓ Given a preconfigured laboratory network, discover the topology, analyze the routing table, and test connectivity using accepted troubleshooting techniques

The topics of this chapter include binary basics, IP addressing, subnetting, and routing basics. We compare distance-vector and link-state routing protocols, pointing out the strengths and weaknesses of each. We also compare common interior routing protocols—Routing Information Protocol (RIP), Interior Gateway Routing Protocol (IGRP), Enhanced IGRP, and Open Shortest Path First (OSPF)—for convergence issues.

This chapter defines some of the problems and issues we face in the workplace as well as in taking the certification exam. Later chapters provide the detailed solutions.

IP Address and Subnet Basics

Transmission Control Protocol/Internet Protocol (TCP/IP) uses 32-bit (binary) IP addresses to create a network addressing system that identifies both the network and the specific host (node) on the network. TCP/IP is the protocol for the Internet, Windows NT/2000, Unix, and even Novell version 5.

IPv4 addresses are usually displayed as decimal values (e.g., 207.161.57.143), called *dotted decimal notation*. This works well for humans who are comfortable with base-10 numbers and using symbols such as periods or commas as data separators. To understand how routing works, it is necessary to understand that the actual values look more like this: 11001111.10100001.00111001.10001111. Again, the decimals are for the humans.

Before we look at IP addressing, IP address classes, routing masks, and subnet masks, we investigate some simple techniques for converting binary to decimal and decimal to binary. Although the following discussion is quite basic, it is nevertheless critical to understanding how routers process addresses.

Binary-to-Decimal Conversion Basics

Binary data is made up of ones and zeros representing switches in the on (1) and off (0) positions. Although binary data can be grouped in any increment, such as three or four digits (110 or 1011), in TCP/IP, it is usually grouped in eight-digit groups, each called a *byte* (equal to 8 bits). IP addresses are then 32 bits, or 4 bytes, in length.

A byte can be any combination of eight zeros and ones ranging from 00000000 to 11111111, creating 256 unique combinations with decimal values ranging from 0 to 255. Figure 2.1 shows the value of binary numbers that equal 0 through 8 in decimal values.

We can see that a 1 in the rightmost column is equal to 1 (decimal value). A 1 in the second column yields a value of 2—see the third row in Figure 2.1. Note also that the fourth row equals 3, with a 1 in both rightmost columns. A 1 in the third

```
0  0  0  0  =  0
0  0  0  1  =  1
0  0  1  0  =  2
0  0  1  1  =  3
0  1  0  0  =  4
0  1  0  1  =  5
0  1  1  0  =  6
0  1  1  1  =  7
1  0  0  0  =  8
```

Figure 2.1   Table calculating 4-bit binary numbers.

column from the right equals 4, and a 1 in the fourth column equals 8. The column values are 8, 4, 2, and 1—doubling each position going to the left. It seems a pattern is developing.

Elaborate mathematical explanations exist for converting binary to decimal. Everything becomes an exponential power of 2. A summary of eight bits numbered right to left beginning with 0, the formula for each position, and the resulting values are shown in Figure 2.2.

Many books and Web sites present the mathematics behind binary; however, there is a very simple table that can be used to convert binary to decimal, decimal to binary, and even to assist in various subnet calculations. As in Figure 2.2, we will number the positions right to left, but we will start with 1 and stop with 8. To calculate the values, start at the right with the same 1, and then double the value of each position as you go to the left. The resulting two-row table is shown in Figure 2.3.

To begin, enter the binary bits (for example 10111001) in the third row on Figure 2.3. Now put the decimal values in the fourth row only for the third-row ones.

Position	7	6	5	4	3	2	1	0
Calculation	2^7	2^6	2^5	2^4	2^3	2^2	2^1	2^0
Value	128	64	32	16	8	4	2	1

Figure 2.2   Calculating the value of an 8-bit binary number.

Position	8	7	6	5	4	3	2	1
Value	128	64	32	16	8	4	2	1

Figure 2.3   Simple tool for converting 8-bit binary numbers.

Position	8	7	6	5	4	3	2	1	
Value	128	64	32	16	8	4	2	1	
	1	0	1	1	1	0	0	1	
	128		32	16	8			1	= 185

Figure 2.4 Sample conversion of an 8-bit binary number.

Some students like to think they are multiplying the number in row 3 times the value in row 2—not technically correct, but it works. Finally, just sum the values in the fourth row. The result of converting 10111001 is shown in Figure 2.4.

Tip: At each exam, use one of the two sheets of paper and the pencil provided to sketch out the above table before the pressure is on. In the BSCN exam, you probably won't be asked to convert binary to decimal, but the table will be useful in creating and/or verifying subnets, host numbers, and so forth. Even if you can "see" the correct answer, there is no excuse for math errors when it is so easy to check your work.

If you are at all unsure of the process, take a moment to sketch out the table and convert the following binary values to decimals:

a. 01110101 _____

b. 10001111 _____

c. 11101001.00011011.10000000.10100100 _____._____._____._____

d. 10101010.00110100.11100110.00010111 _____._____._____._____

Answers: (a) 117, (b) 143, (c) 233.27.128.164, (d) 170.52.230.23

Decimal-to-Binary Basics

We can use our conversion table (Figure 2.3) and a series of simple divisions to help us convert decimal values to binary.

Assume we want to convert 207 to binary. The steps are shown in Figure 2.5.

The steps would be:

1. Start with the leftmost value (128) in the table and see if the 227 can be divided by it. It will go once, so we put a 1 in the first box in row three of the table. Calculate the remainder (79).

2. The remainder can be divided by the next value (64), so we put a 1 in row three of our table. Calculate the remainder (15).

3. Because the remainder cannot be divided by either 32 or 16, we put 0s in row three of our table.

4. Continue until there is no remainder. You can use row four to check your work.

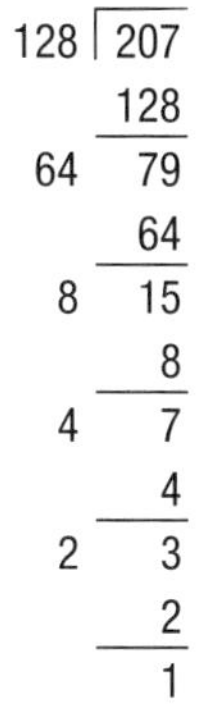

Position	8	7	6	5	4	3	2	1
Value	128	64	32	16	8	4	2	1

Position	8	7	6	5	4	3	2	1	
Value	128	64	32	16	8	4	2	1	
	1	1	0	0	1	1	1	1	
	128	64			8	4	2	1	= 207

Figure 2.5 Converting 207 to a binary value.

If you are at all unsure of the process, take a moment to sketch out the table and convert the following decimal values to binary:

a. 252 ______________________

b. 91 ______________________

c. 116.127.71.3 __________.__________.__________.__________

d. 255.255.255.0 __________.__________.__________.__________

Answers: (a) 11111100, (b) 01011011, (c) 01110100.01111111.01000111.00000011, (d) 11111111.11111111.11111111.00000000

Working with the Table Relationships

The more you work with the table, the more you will see relationships within the table that can be used to speed up your calculations, and you will gain the ability to visualize the results without doing the calculations. The same process we used to build the eight-bit table can be extended, if necessary. A table extended to 12 bits is shown in Figure 2.6.

With binary numbers that are made up primarily of ones, it may be quicker and easier to subtract the zero bit values from 255. Converting the binary 11101101 is shown in Figure 2.7.

Position	12	11	10	9	8	7	6	5	4	3	2	1
Value	2048	1024	512	256	128	64	32	16	8	4	2	1

Figure 2.6 A 12-bit conversion table.

Position	8	7	6	5	4	3	2	1	
Value	128	64	32	16	8	4	2	1	
		1	1	1	0	1	1	0	1	255
				16			2		-18
									237

Figure 2.7 Converting a binary number by subtracting the zero values.

If you select any position in the value row, the sum of all digits to the right being ones is the position value minus 1. Figure 2.8, for example, uses the eight-bit table (Figure 2.3) and the value 64. Calculating the value of all ones to the right yields 63.

This method works for all positions. Looking at the first bit in our eight-bit table, we can see that having all ones to the right of that position would equal 127. We know this is true because all eight bits set to 1 equals 255 (128 + 127).

Class Address System

IP addresses have been traditionally broken into five classes based on the value of the first octet. It is common to memorize the three classes that are used for host connections: 1 to 126 are class A, 128 to 191 are class B, and 192 to 223 are class C. But why the strange ranges? What happened to 127? Why not break it into increments of 25 to make it easier to remember? One of my early network instructors told me that each point was the number assigned when they decided they needed to refine the system—seemed reasonable at the time.

The reality is that we need to look at the binary values to see the reason for the break points. All class A networks have a 0 as the first bit. All class B networks start with 10 as the first two bits. Class C starts with 110. Figure 2.9 shows the pattern and details for all five classes of addresses.

This method of determining IP address classes is referred to as the *first octet rule*. In addition to defining the classes, it provides an efficient way for layer 3 devices to start interpreting the address. Any address beginning with a zero can be forwarded only to an interface that connects directly or indirectly to a class A network.

Position	8	7	6	5	4	3	2	1	
Value	128	**64**	32	16	8	4	2	1	
			1	1	1	1	1	1	
			32	16	8	4	2	1	= 63

Figure 2.8 Demonstrating the value of all ones to the right of a bit location.

Class	Starts With	Binary Range	Decimal Value Range	Maximum Subnets	Maximum Hosts
A	0	00000000-01111111	0-127	127	16,777,214
B	10	10000000-10111111	128-191	16,384	65,534
C	110	11000000-11011111	192-223	2,097,152	254
D	1110	11100000-11101111	224-239		
E	1111	11110000-11111111	240-255		

Figure 2.9 IP address class definitions and related properties.

Note these important exclusions:

➤ Class D addresses are reserved exclusively for router multicasts, and class E is reserved for future expansion and research.

➤ First octet 0 (00000000) is not allowed.

➤ First octet 127 (01111111) is reserved for loopback and is used for internal testing. Using the **ping** command with the loopback address confirms properly installed and functioning TCP/IP on the local machine (e.g., **ping 127.0.0.1** at the command line).

The following IP address ranges are set aside as private addresses to be used by any organization within their internal networks. Routers within your network will forward them normally, whereas routers out in the Internet will drop them. The ranges are:

➤ 10.0.0.0 to 10.255.255.255—A full class A network

➤ 172.16.0.0 to 172.31.255.255—16 contiguous class B networks

➤ 192.168.0.0 to 192.168.255.255—255 contiguous class C networks

It is not necessary (or even possible) to register these addresses with any registration body such as Network Solutions.

Class Default Routing Masks

Routing masks allow the layer 3 devices to separate the network portion of the address from the host portion. Routing masks are made up of a series of contiguous binary ones beginning at the left. The point where the mask changes from ones to zeros represents the boundary, or break point, between the network portion of the address and the host portion. Once the mask pattern changes to zeros, there can be only zeros to the 32nd bit. All devices in the network will share the same network portion of the address, but each must have a unique host portion.

Doing a binary bit-wise **AND** on the IP address and the subnet mask results in the network address. In the **AND** process, a 1 and a 1 equal 1, anything else equals 0. In nonmathematical terms, anything with a 1 under it is brought down, and everything else is a 0. Table 2.1 demonstrates distilling the network portion of the address.

Class default routing masks are even octets of eight ones, which each equate to 255 in decimal values. Table 2.2 shows the default routing masks.

Class networks and their resulting network/host relationships are often represented using dot/letter notation, such as n.h.h.h for a class A, n.n.h.h for a class B, and n.n.n.h for a class C network. Another representation is net.host.host.host for A, net.net.host.host for B, and net.net.net.host for C.

In a classful network, one need look only at the first octet to know both the class and therefore the default routing mask. For example, the IP address 171.15.12.112 falls in the class B range (128-191), and therefore the default routing mask must be 255.255.0.0, indicating that the 171.15 portion of the number is the network.

Another notation representing this address and routing mask is 171.15.12.112/16, indicating that the mask is 16 bits long (or two octets). In a classful environment, the only values that can appear after the IP address for default masks are /8, /16, and /24, representing full octets.

Subnet Basics

Classful addressing, or using only default classes, can lead to inefficiencies in the use of IP addresses or lead to network congestion due to too many devices on a network. We can increase the routing mask by adding more binary ones to the default mask. This effectively breaks up our network into subnetworks or subnets. We could choose to break up a class A, B, or C network into two or more subnets to suit our purposes.

Table 2.1 IP using the bit-wise AND to derive the network address.

Binary Form	Decimal Form	Description
10110111.00110011.00011011.00011011	183.51.27.27	IP address
11111111.11111111.00000000.00000000	255.255.0.0	Routing mask
10110111.00110011.00000000.00000000	183.51.0.0	Network

Table 2.2 IP class address default routing masks.

Decimal Form	Binary Form
255.0.0.0	11111111.00000000.00000000.00000000
255.255.0.0	11111111.11111111.00000000.00000000
255.255.255.0	11111111.11111111.11111111.00000000

2

Before we get into the possible numbers of subnets and hosts, let us look just at how many possible subnet values there are. At first glance, it might seem that there could be dozens or even hundreds, but in fact there can be only eight. Sometimes realizing how few possibilities there really are helps make this task seem less daunting. First, we need to remember that subnet masks can be created only by adding contiguous ones to the right end of a default routing mask. Each one we add to the routing mask reduces the number of zeros representing the host by one so that we stay within our 32-bit total. Second, each octet is only 8 bits long, so even if we want a subnet mask of 9 or 10 bits, we consider them only in groups of 8; that is, 10 bits becomes 8 bits plus 2 bits. In Figure 2.10, the upper sample shows us that adding a single one defines our first subnet mask, which is 128. The lower sample shows that adding a second one creates the next subnet mask, which is 192.

If we continue the process until all eight bits are used, we see that the only possible subnet mask values are as shown in Table 2.3.

Table 2.3 shows that there are only eight possible subnet mask values. Knowing how they are derived in binary prevents us from even considering a faulty decimal subnet

Position	8	7	6	5	4	3	2	1	
Value	128	64	32	16	8	4	2	1	
	1	0	0	0	0	0	0	0	
	128								= 128

Position	8	7	6	5	4	3	2	1	
Value	128	64	32	16	8	4	2	1	
	1	1	0	0	0	0	0	0	
	128	64							= 192

Figure 2.10   Adding a single one and then two ones to the routing mask.

Table 2.3   Possible subnet mask values using up to eight bits.

Binary Form	Decimal Form	Example
10000000	128	255.255.128.0
11000000	192	255.255.192.0
11100000	224	255.255.224.0
11110000	240	255.255.240.0
11111000	248	255.255.248.0
11111100	252	255.255.252.0
11111110	254	255.255.254.0
11111111	255	255.255.255.0

Position	8	7	6	5	4	3	2	1	
Value	128	64	32	16	8	4	2	1	
	1	1	0	1	0	1	1	1	
	128	64		16		4	2	1	= 215

Figure 2.11 Converting 215 to binary to see if it is a valid subnet value.

mask. For example, the subnet mask 255.255.255.215 is clearly not valid when we convert the 215 to binary. Figure 2.11 shows that the resulting binary value will not work because routing masks must be contiguous ones from left to right.

The zero values of the third and fifth bits violate the rule of contiguous ones, so 215 cannot be a valid subnet mask value. Being able to convert from decimal to binary kept us from accepting a bad default mask. In the field, you could use a PC-based subnet calculator or even the simple calculator that comes with all versions of Windows to quickly convert decimal to binary, but in most exams you won't have either tool.

Looking at Table 2.3, the possible subnet values, we see that the eighth possibility works only in subnetting a class A from 255.0.0.0 to 255.255.0.0 or a class B from 255.255.0.0 to 255.255.255.0. With a class C, the subnetting wouldn't leave any bits for the host address (255.255.255.255).

If we wanted to subnet a class B network with 10 bits, the binary result would be 11111111.11000000, or 255.192, as in 255.255.*255.192.* The same process would work with additional bits up to subnetting a class A with, say, 22 bits, which creates a binary subnet mask of 11111111.11111111.11111100, or 255.255.252. The resulting mask would be 255.*255.255.252.*

Calculating the Number of Subnets

Another reason for knowing how to convert decimal subnet mask values to binary is that the number of bits in the subnet mask is used to calculate the number of subnets created. The formula is 2^n, where n equals the number of bits beyond the default mask.

Tip: For nonmath majors, just start with 2 and double it n times. For example 2^4 would yield 2, 4, 8, 16, with 16 being the right answer. Even 2^8, which might seem intimidating to some, would yield 2, 4, 8, 16, 32, 64, 128, 256, with 256 being the right answer. Even if you are sure you know the right answer, it is a quick and reliable check—remember, it is foolish to blow a question if the math can be verified.

Given a subnet mask of 255.255.255.240 for a class C network, we can use our conversion table to determine that 240 requires four bits. We then calculate 2^4, which is 16 subnets created. Figure 2.12 shows the conversion for 240.

Position	8	7	6	5	4	3	2	1	
Value	128	64	32	16	8	4	2	1	
	1	1	1	1	0	0	0	0	
	128	64	32	16					= 240

2

Figure 2.12 Converting 240 to binary to see the number of bits required.

This becomes only slightly more difficult with longer subnet masks, such as 255.255.255.192 on a class B network. We know the third octet is eight ones, and we can use our techniques from the last exercise to see that 192 requires two bits. Therefore, our mask requires 10 bits, or 2^{10}, yielding 1,024 subnets (2, 4, 8, 16, 32, 64, 128, 256, 512, 1,024).

If you are unsure of the process, take a moment to calculate the number of subnets for each of the following examples:

a. 201.112.95.1 subnet mask: 255.255.255.128

b. 201.112.95.1 subnet mask: 255.255.255.252

c. 101.202.95.1 subnet mask: 255.255.224.0

d. 161.92.115.1 subnet mask: 255.255.255.252

Answers: (a) 2, (b) 16, (c) 2,048, (d) 16,384 (2, 4, 8, 16, 32, 64, 128, 256, 512, 1,024, 2,048, 4,096, 8,192, 16,384)

What about Valid Subnets?

Many programs, vendors, and Requests For Comments RFC 950 and 1878 use a different formula for calculating what are referred to as *valid subnets*. The formula 2^n-2 eliminates the first and last subnet because they are composed of all zeros or all ones, respectively. The rule states that subnets cannot be made up exclusively of either zeros or ones. This leads to significant losses of IP addresses from the invalid subnets. For example, a class C network with a subnet mask of 255.255.255.192 requires two bits, so 2^2-2 yields two subnets, and half of the IP host addresses are lost. Figure 2.13 shows the possible bit combinations using two bits.

Position	8	7	6	5	4	3	2	1	
Value	128	64	32	16	8	4	2	1	
	0	0							= 0
	0	1							= 64
	1	0							=128
	1	1							= 192

Figure 2.13 Possible bit combinations using two bits.

Note that the first value is 00, or the zero subnet, and the last one is 11, or 192 (the subnet value). Under RFC 950 and 1878, these two and their host addresses would have to be discarded. Cisco IOS version 12 and beyond assumes that you will use these subnets, so no configuration is required. In versions 11.3 up to 12, IOS requires the **ip subnet-zero** command to use these subnets.

Using the ip subnet-zero feature assumes that all layer 3 devices in the network will also accept these subnets—one rationale for an all-Cisco network with current IOS versions. Routers in the Internet or wide area network (WAN) won't be an issue because they use only the network portion of the address to forward packets. The local routers, however, will need to agree to use these subnets. Figure 2.14 uses our earlier conversion table (Figure 2.3) to compare the number of total subnets versus the valid subnets (before version 12).

We revisit this topic later in the section "Route Summarization," when we discuss variable-length subnet masks (VLSMs), but for now, assume we will use the zero subnet features to maximize our IP address usage.

Determining Number of Host Addresses per Subnet

There are several ways to figure out the number of addresses and hosts in a subnet, but it might be useful to look at what is happening in binary. Assume that we have a class C network 201.11.92.0 with a subnet mask of 255.255.255.224. We determine that 224 will require three bits, and therefore we calculate the possible combinations of three bits. Figure 2.15 uses our conversion table to calculate the subnet combinations of three bits and their decimal values.

Position	8	7	6	5	4	3	2	1
Value	128	64	32	16	8	4	2	1
Subnets 2^n	2	4	8	16	32	64	128	256
Subnets 2^n-2	0	2	6	14	30	62	126	254

Figure 2.14 Comparing total subnets to valid subnets.

Position	8	7	6	5	4	3	2	1		
Value	128	64	32	16	8	4	2	1		
	0	0	0	=	0				201.11.92.0
	0	0	1	=	32				201.11.92.32
	0	1	0	=	64				201.11.92.64
	0	1	1	=	96				201.11.92.96
	1	0	0	=	128				201.11.92.128
	1	0	1	=	160				201.11.92.160
	1	1	0	=	192				201.11.92.192
	1	1	1	=	224				201.11.92.224

Figure 2.15 Determining binary combinations of subnet mask 224.

If we calculate the number of subnets using 2^n, or 2^3, we get 8, confirming that we have all of the possible combinations. The decimal value then becomes the first IP address for each subnet.

Our second subnet then begins with 201.11.92.32. To get exactly 32 in the last octet, the five remaining bits for host addresses must all be zeros (001**00000**). But the RFCs say that we cannot have a host address of all zeros, so our first address is the subnet address—identifying the entire subnet.

The largest value that can be created with the first three bits set to 001 is 001**11111**, or 63 in decimal form. Because the RFCs say that we cannot have a host address of all ones, our last address is the subnet broadcast. Figure 2.16 shows a partial list of the binary values with the first three bits set to 001 (32).

A similar pattern will appear if we look at each of the values created from our three bits—the first one is the subnet address (all zeros in the host) and the last one is the broadcast (all ones in the host). Figure 2.17 summarizes the subnets with the first three bits set to 001 (32).

Position	8	7	6	5	4	3	2	1		
Value	128	64	32	16	8	4	2	1		
	0	0	1	0	0	0	0	0	= 32	Subnet Address
	0	0	1	0	0	0	0	1	= 33	
	0	0	1	0	0	0	1	0	= 34	
	0	0	1	0	0	0	1	1	= 35	
	0	0	1	1	1	1	0	1	= 61	
	0	0	1	1	1	1	1	0	= 62	
	0	0	1	1	1	1	1	1	= 63	Broadcast Address

Figure 2.16   Examples of binary values beginning with 001.

Position	8	7	6	Subnet Value	Broadcast Value	Host Range
Value	128	64	32			
	0	0	0 =	0	31	1-30
	0	0	1 =	32	63	33-62
	0	1	0 =	64	95	65-94
	0	1	1 =	96	127	97-126
	1	0	0 =	128	159	129-158
	1	0	1 =	160	191	161-190
	1	1	0 =	192	223	193-222
	1	1	1 =	224	255	225-254

Figure 2.17   Subnet details with first 3 bits set to 001.

Note that the broadcast address is always one less than the next subnet address. Recognizing this fact saves having to calculate it. The host addresses, then, are the range between the subnet and the broadcast addresses. The number of host addresses can then be calculated using 2^n-2, where n is the number of bits set aside for host addresses and the –2 subtracts the subnet and broadcast addresses.

Figure 2.17 shows that the increment between subnets is 32. There are at least two simple ways to calculate this without having to build the table:

➤ If you know the decimal value of the subnet mask (e.g., 224), subtract that value from 256. The result is the increment between subnets.

➤ If you know the number of bits used in the subnet, using our conversion table, take the value in the rightmost bit location. Looking at Figure 2.17, we see that with three bits used, the value in the third bit column is 32.

Either way, we now need only to start with 0 and continue to add the increment until the subnets have all been identified—stopping when we get to the subnet mask value (0, 32, 64, 96, 128, 160, 192, 224).

Note: If we are not using the zero subnet feature (valid subnets only), we would start with the increment value and stop excluding the subnet mask value (32, 64, 96, 128, 160, 192).

To summarize, the number of subnets equals 2^n, where n equals the number of bits used in the subnet. If we weren't using zero subnets, it would be 2^n-2, to remove the first and last subnets, which are all zeros or all ones, respectively. The number of host addresses is 2^n-2 where n is the number of bits set aside for the host address and the –2 removes the subnet and broadcast addresses that cannot be assigned to a host. To determine the total number of hosts, multiply the number of subnets by the number of hosts in each subnet.

Extending our logic up to class A and B networks is pretty simple. Our formula of 2^n-2 still works, but in the case of 171.16.0.0 with 255.255.192.0, we are using 2 bits of the third octet for the subnet, leaving 14 bits for the hosts. Therefore, $2^{14}-2$ would be 16,382. We could use our doubling technique: 2, 4, 8, 16. . . . until we have the 14th one.

We can also calculate the 2^n as if it were a class C and multiply the result times 256 for each additional octet. For a class B, the formula would be $(2^n \times 256)-2$; a class A would be $(2^n \times 256 \times 256)-2$. The 256 is for each octet in the mask with a zero. Using the example from the previous paragraph, n would be 6, so our formula would be $(2^6 \times 256)-2$, or $(64 \times 256)-2$, which equals 16,382. For the class A 255.192.0.0, it would be $(2^6 \times 256 \times 256)-2$, or $(64 \times 256 \times 256)-2$, which equals 4,194,302. You just need to decide if this is easier than 2, 4, 8, 16. . . . for 22 times. Figure 2.18 summarizes the subnets for a class B network with the first three bits set to 001 (32).

Network: 171.16.0.0 with subnet mask 255.255.224.0

Position	8	7	6	Subnet	Subnet	Broadcast	
Value	128	64	32	Value	Address	Value	Host Range
	0	0	0 =	0	171.16.0.0	171.16.31.255	171.16.1.1 = 171.16.31.254
	0	0	1 =	32	171.16.32.0	171.16.63.255	171.16.32.1 = 171.16.63.254
	0	1	0 =	64	171.16.64.0	171.16.95.255	171.16.64.1 = 171.16.95.254
	0	1	1 =	96	171.16.96.0	171.16.127.255	171.16.96.1 = 171.16.127.254
	1	0	0 =	128	171.16.128.0	171.16.159.255	171.16.128.1 = 171.16.159.254
	1	0	1 =	160	171.16.160.0	171.16.191.255	171.16.160.1 = 171.16.191.254
	1	1	0 =	192	171.16.192.0	171.16.223.255	171.16.192.1 = 171.16.223.254
	1	1	1 =	224	171.16.224.0	171.16.255.255	171.16.224.1 = 171.16.255.254

Figure 2.18 Class B subnet details with first three bits equaling 001.

Note: We know that in the real world you will use a subnet calculator or the calculator that comes with Windows or even Excel—but in the exam, none of those tools will be available to you.

Before dismissing the data in the table in Figure 2.18, look at the broadcast address for any subnet—it should be exactly one bit less than the next subnet address. The host range is one larger than the subnet address to one less than the broadcast address—just like in our class C.

Determining the Subnet Mask for a Given Number of Subnets

Assume that you know that you want nine subnets. One easy way to determine the subnet mask is to use the conversion table of Figure 2.3 and convert the desired number of subnets to binary. The number of bits required is the number of bits in your subnet mask. From there, we can calculate the decimal value. Figure 2.19 demonstrates using the conversion table to determine a subnet mask.

Position	8	7	6	5	4	3	2	1	
Value	128	64	32	16	8	4	2	1	
					1	0	0	1	
					8			1	= 9

Position	8	7	6	5	4	3	2	1	
Value	128	64	32	16	8	4	2	1	
	1	1	1	1	0	0	0	0	
	128	64	32	16					= 240

Figure 2.19 Determining the subnet mask required to create nine subnets.

The upper table of Figure 2.19 shows that it takes four bits to create the binary value equal to 9. The lower table shows that using four bits as the subnet mask yields a subnet mask value of 240, as in 255.255.255.240. We can confirm this by calculating 2^4, which equals 16. This is much larger than we need, but 2^3, which equals 8, confirms that three bits won't work. Because we have the number of bits in our subnet mask (4), we also know the number of bits left for hosts (4), and we can calculate the number of hosts per subnet using 2^4-2, which equals 14.

Had we needed nine subnets in a class B address, the subnet mask would have been 255.255.240.0. We now would have 12 bits for hosts, or 2^{12}-2, which equals 4,094.

Creating subnets by extending the default routing mask allows us to segment our network and thereby reduce congestion and increase security, group users, and so forth. But this comes at the cost of lost host addresses. At a minimum, you lose the subnet and broadcast address for each subnet over the single network design. At worst, you can lose large numbers of hosts when you need a number of subnets that doesn't associate closely to a subnet mask, such as in our example of needing nine. A full 7 of our 16 host addresses are lost—or reserved for future growth, if you prefer. With careful planning, we can manage this loss. We will also see, in the section "Route Summarization," that techniques such as VLSMs can help reduce this loss.

The subnet zero feature in IOS v12 salvages two subnets of host addresses over the RFC standard for valid subnets. This is particularly critical when only a few subnets are required.

Router, Routed, Routable, and Routing

The term "router," and its many derivatives, like so many terms in the computer industry, was taken from our common usage language and has come to mean different things in different contexts. This leads to some confusion when one party tries to narrowly define a term—particularly if it varies much from common usage. In general terminology, the process of forwarding an item from one location to another location is called *routing*. Routing, of course, is not limited to computer networks. A postal worker, for example, will be part of a lengthy process to route a letter from a sender to a recipient. Similarly, in computer networks, packets are delivered or routed to a logical destination.

Variations of the term "route" are also applied to protocols. We have rout*ed*, or rout*able*, protocols, such as TCP/IP and IPX, as compared to *non*routable protocols, such as NetBEUI and DLC. On the other hand, rout*ing* protocols, such as RIP, IGRP, OSPF, refer to protocols that allow routers to share information, and, in the process, learn the topology and status of the internetwork.

Router Functions: Routing vs. Switching

It is important to know that routers perform two major functions: routing and switching. Routers act as relay devices and must understand the logical topology of the computer network and thus must communicate with neighboring devices. In this context, *routing* refers to the process of communicating with other routers to learn about the topology and status of the systems. *Switching* in this context refers to the forwarding of packets from an incoming interface to the appropriate outbound interface. Switching uses the end product of the routing process—the *routing table*—to make its decisions.

Basic Switching Functions

The term "switching" in this context is the same as layer 2 switching in that packets are being forwarded from an inbound interface (port) to an outbound interface. On layer 2 devices, the switching is based on a table of physical (MAC) addresses of end devices. In layer 3, this switching is based on a table of network addresses. An important distinction is that the device is performing switching—not working as a switch, the common term for a layer 2 device.

Switching within a router follows four steps:

1. The packet will be accepted by an inbound interface only if the data frame's destination address (MAC) matches one of the router interfaces. The frame will then be buffered in memory to wait for further processing. The specific memory is dependent on the device model.

2. The network portion of the destination logical address is checked against the routing table. If successful, the switching process associates the packet with a next-hop device and an outbound interface. The next-hop device could be an end node if the final destination is local to one of the router's interfaces. If the address cannot be found and no default route is set, the packet will be discarded and an Internet Control Message Protocol (ICMP) packet will be sent to the sender indicating the packet is undeliverable.

3. The physical address of the next-hop device is now determined using Address Resolution Protocol (ARP) for a local area network (LAN) or a map table for a WAN.

4. The data frame is modified to overwrite the destination physical address to that of the next-hop device and the source physical address to that of the router. The data frame is now moved out of the buffer to the outbound interface. As it is put on the media, the CRC and end delimiter are added to the frame for verification by the next device.

Basic Routing Function

The goal is to develop a routing table that reflects a loop-free network topology with "best" routes for each destination network so that the switching function can properly forward packets within the router.

Note: The word "best" as used in this context means "lowest rating" on the routing table.

After a router is started, has performed its self-test, and loaded the configuration, it attempts to communicate with and identify neighboring routing devices to determine the network topology and begin sharing routing information. The method of discovering the other routing devices varies, depending on the routing protocol, but usually begins with broadcasts. As the devices respond, the physical layer addresses (MAC) are learned and used. One method, the hello protocol, is a layer 3 (OSI) protocol that some devices can use to identify each other and verify functional connections. Each device derives the MAC addresses of its neighbors by analyzing the source address of the hello packets.

As the network topology becomes known, the device can start comparing alternative routes with the ultimate goal of creating a table listing only best route choices. Different routing protocols use different methods of determining the best route by assigning *metrics* to one or more criteria. Simple protocols such as RIP may use only the number of routers (hops) a packet has to pass through to its destination as the metric, whereas others such as IGRP use several criteria (e.g., bandwidth, delay, reliability). Multiple routes to the same network will be maintained in the routing table only if they have basically equal metrics.

This routing table is then used by the switching function discussed in the previous section to determine how to forward packets through the router. The routing function must be complete and stable before switching can be effectively carried out.

Routing Requirements

For effective loop-free routing to occur, three requirements must be met:

1. The appropriate protocol suite must be enabled and configured on the network.

2. The destination network must be known and accessible to this device.

3. Which outbound interface provides the best connection must be determined.

Appropriate Protocol Enabled and Configured

For the device to recognize the destination's logical (network) address, the right routing protocol, such as IP or IPX, must be enabled and properly activated. Just as IP's 32-bit addressing system means nothing to IPX devices, the 80-bit IPX address is unfathomable to an IP device. Multiple protocols can be enabled on the same interface.

```
router#config t
router(config)#int e0
router(config-if)#ip address 192.168.10.1 255.255.255.0
```

This code sets an IP address of 192.168.10.1 to the first Ethernet interface. By setting the IP address, the IP is automatically bound to the interface. For routing to occur, a similar entry must be made on at least a second interface or subinterface.

```
router#config t
router(config)#int s0
router(config-if)#ip address 192.168.11.1 255.255.255.0
```

This code sets an IP address of 192.168.11.1 to the first serial interface. With this simple configuration, the router can now pass packets between the two networks (192.168.10 and 192.168.11). Figure 2.20 shows the router with these two interfaces configured.

In addition, any encapsulation method, clock rate, or other configuration options that need to be completed to provide a connection to the network should be done at this point.

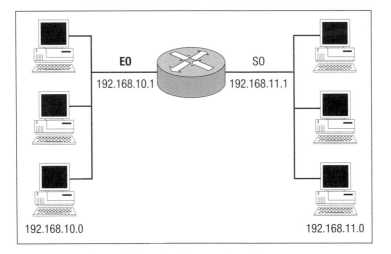

Figure 2.20 Router with two interfaces configured.

Destination Network Known and Accessible

In our example, the route table consists of only the two networks. Traffic destined to networks beyond them is undeliverable. This is true unless we let the router know of alternate destinations by one of the following means:

➤ Add a default route.

➤ Add one or more static routes.

➤ Add a routing protocol so that routes can be dynamically added.

If a router does not know about a destination network, it will drop the packet. It will also send an ICMP packet back to the source address informing it of its failure to deliver.

We can see the existing routes (or lack of them) using the **show ip route** command:

```
router#show ip route
Codes: C - connected, S - static, I - IGRP, R - RIP, M - mobile, B - BGP
       D - EIGRP, EX - EIGRP external, O - OSPF, IA - OSPF inter area
       E1 - OSPF external type 1, E2 - OSPF external type 2, E - EGP
       i - IS-IS, L1 - IS-IS level-1, L2 - IS-IS level-2, * - candidate
default
       U - per-user static route

Gateway of last resort is not set

C    192.168.10.0/24 is directly connected, Ethernet0
C    199.168.11.0/24 is directly connected, Serial0
```

Without using these techniques, our router would be limited to passing packets between the two adjacent subnets. In small networks, we could create static routes or a default route to which packets with unknown destination logical address would be sent. Otherwise, we would enable a routing protocol using a command such as **router rip** or **router igrp n**, where n is the autonomous network number. This would be followed by a series of **network** commands listing the adjacent networks to be advertised to neighboring routers.

```
router rip
 network 192.168.10.0
 network 192.168.11.0
```

The router will send and receive routing updates only on the interfaces of the networks included in a **network** command. Any adjacent networks not included in a **network** command will not be advertised in any routing updates.

Interface Selection for the Best Path

Assuming the protocol and interfaces are properly configured and the routing table contains the destination address, the packet should be directed to the outbound interface with the best path. Routing protocols use various metrics to determine the best path. From as simple as counting router hops in RIP to incorporating bandwidth or delay in more advanced protocols, the metrics are measured and the interface with the lowest rating will be the only listing in the routing table. If two or more interfaces have the same metric, some protocols will allow for load-balancing between them.

The packet is now forwarded to the selected outbound interface for encapsulation appropriate to the network path.

Routing Table Information

The *routing table* contains the information used in deciding which is the best interface to forward the packets. The **show ip route** command demonstrates how this information is displayed. Note that each route is listed on a separate row below the *Codes:* section, which works as a legend for the first code in each row.

```
Router#show ip route
Codes: C - connected, S - static, I - IGRP, R - RIP, M - mobile, B - BGP
       D - EIGRP, EX - EIGRP external, O - OSPF, IA - OSPF inter area
       N1 - OSPF NSSA external type 1, N2 - OSPF NSSA external type 2
       E1 - OSPF external type 1, E2 - OSPF external type 2, E - EGP
       i - IS-IS, L1 - IS-IS level-1, L2 - IS-IS level-2, * - candidate
       U - per-user static route, o - ODR

Gateway of last resort is not set

C    204.204.8.0/24 is directly connected, Serial0
C    204.204.7.0/24 is directly connected, Serial1
I    223.8.151.0/24 [100/8576] via 204.204.7.1, 00:00:11, Serial1
I    199.6.13.0/24 [100/10476] via 204.204.7.1, 00:00:11, Serial1
S    201.100.11.0/24 [1/0] via 204.204.8.2
C    210.93.105.0/24 is directly connected, Ethernet0
```

Let us look at each element separately, using the shaded row as an example, and, when appropriate, compare it to the others.

➤ *Method used to learn about the route*—The *I* in our example indicates using the IGRP protocol. The *Codes:* section at the top of the display deciphers the codes for use.

➤ *Destination network address*—The next element, *199.6.13.0* in our example, indicates the logical network or subnetwork. The */24* indicates the routing mask using 24 bits; in this case, the default class C mask.

➤ *Administrative distance*—Indicates the reliability of the method used to learn about this network. The smaller the number the better. *100* is the default for IGRP, which is considerably higher than for the static routes, which are rated as ones. Note that the directly connected routes C are not assigned an administrative overhead because their reliability should be absolute. We will look at administrative distance in more detail at the end of this section.

➤ *Routing metric*—Combines the entire path cost using methods specified by the routing protocol. For example, RIP would show the cumulative hop count (number of routers) to the destination network. Again, the smaller the number, the better. In our example, the *10476* is determined using metrics specified by IGRP. Note that the entry above it is lower; both are included because they go to different networks. If they had both gone to the same network, only the upper one would be included in the routing table because of the lower metric.

Note also that the static route has a metric of zero and the directly connected networks have no metric at all—they are local.

➤ *Logical address of the next layer 3 device (204.204.7.1)*—Will forward our packet on toward the final destination. We don't know how far away the network is, but we know that it is at least one router away.

➤ *Age of the routing table entry*—Information is given in hours, minutes, and seconds. The *00:00:11* in our example indicates the data was refreshed just 11 seconds ago.

➤ *Outbound interface (Serial1)*—To send the packet for forwarding to the next relay device in our example.

Administrative Distance Factors

Administrative distance, a somewhat arbitrary rating of reliability of the method of learning about routes, is one of the factors used in selecting a best path. The smaller the administrative distance, the more attractive the method of learning about a route. Manual entries, which get low scores, are considered the most reliable, whereas simple metrics are considered the least reliable and therefore are assigned higher values. Protocols with multiple metrics are rated somewhere between these two. Table 2.4 summarizes this relationship.

Routing Metrics

Routing metrics are used to help determine the best route to every destination network. The method of creating the metric value is set by the routing protocol. From

Table 2.4   Common administrative distances ranked smallest to largest.

Routing Information Source	Default Distance
Connected routes	0
Static routes for local interface	0
Static routes to next-hop router	1
Enhanced IGRP summary route	5
External BGP-derived routes	20
EIGRP-derived routes	90
IGRP-derived routes	100
OSPF-derived routes	110
RIP (v1 & v2)-derived routes	120
IS-IS-derived routes	115
EGP-derived routes	140
External EIGRP-derived routes	170
Internal BGP-derived routes	200
Unknown	255

as simple as using a single criterion such as router hop count to a composite of several factors, these metrics are the sum of the various metrics for each link to the destination network. The goal is to use these metrics to select the shortest, fastest, or most reliable route to a specific network.

In this section, we compare the RIP and IGRP routing metrics, saving the more advanced protocols, such as OSPF, EIGRP, and BGP, for later chapters.

RIP

The Routing Information Protocol is a relatively simple to implement distance-vector interior gateway protocol (IGP). RIP is the most commonly used protocol in the global Internet, particularly in small to medium networks. As an IGP, it is used within a single autonomous system or administrated system.

TCP/IP is defined in RFCs 1058 and 1723. Many network protocols such as IPX, AppleTalk, and Banyon Vines have their own derivations of RIP. Not all can exchange information. Microsoft Windows NT uses RIP on multihomed servers to perform routing between multiple network segments.

RIP uses hop count as its only metric to measure the distance to a destination network. Each router is typically assigned a value of 1, so passing through three routers would create a metric of 3. As a final safeguard against data loops circulating data forever, RIP sees any hop count greater than 15 as being unreachable. Figure 2.21 demonstrates an oversimplification of a RIP network in which Router A sees two paths to Router F.

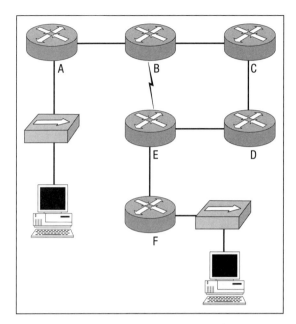

Figure 2.21　A RIP network with two alternative paths between Routers A and F.

Data routed from Router A through B and E to F will have a hop count of 4. But if it takes the longer, but real, route from A through B, C, D, and E to F, it will have a hop count of 6. RIP will then always use the former. But what if all links are Ethernet except B to E, which is a modem link? It is possible that the shorter route may be considerably slower—RIP may not return the fastest route.

IGRP

Cisco's proprietary Interior Gateway Routing Protocol uses a composite metric that can incorporate indicators of bandwidth, reliability, load, internetwork delay, and Maximum Transfer Unit (MTU). By default, IGRP incorporates only bandwidth and delay in the metric.

Reliability and load can have values ranging from 1 to 255, delay can range from 1 to 2^{24}, and bandwidth can range from 1,200bps to 10Gbps. The administrator can manipulate these metrics by assigning weights to each factor to influence link decisions.

IGRP supports multiple paths, allowing equal bandwidth links to perform load-balancing with up to six links. If one link fails, the other(s) can take over routing. The metrics do not have to be exactly equal as long as they fall within a predefined range. Load-balancing can then be performed relative to the metrics.

Referring to Figure 2.21, IGRP could choose the longer route from A through B, C, D, and E to F after considering the bandwidth of the modem connection between B and E.

Interior vs. Exterior Routing Protocols

For many reasons (e.g., size issues, complexity, and different administrative strategies), no single routing protocol works efficiently and effectively within and between all internetworks. We separate them into interior (within) and exterior (between) to focus on their purpose.

Interior Routing Protocols

Interior routing protocols are designed to exchange routing information within an autonomous system or internetwork. An autonomous system is independently administered and follows its own routing strategy. Examples of interior routing protocols are RIP, IGRP, and OSPF. Figure 2.22 shows both interior and exterior gateway routers. The routers connected with the thin lines are using interior routing protocols. The heavier lines indicate those using exterior gateway protocols.

IGRP is a Cisco proprietary protocol developed in the mid-1980s to overcome the shortcomings of RIP as networks got larger. RIP's reliance on a hop-count limit of 16 was limiting the growth of networks and its usefulness for internetworks. Enhanced IGRP is covered in Chapter 7.

OSPF, an interior routing protocol developed by the Internet Engineering Task Force (IETF), was another effort to replace RIP and deal with growing internetworks. OSPF is covered in Chapters 5 and 6.

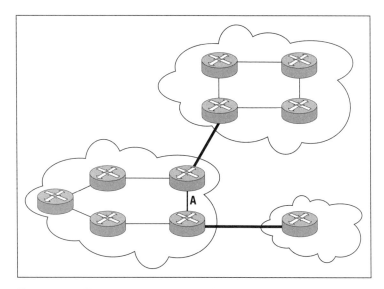

Figure 2.22   Three autonomous systems linked by exterior gateway protocols.

Exterior Routing Protocols

Exterior gateway routing protocols perform interdomain routing between multiple autonomous systems, such as a business's connection to an Internet Service Provider (ISP). Exterior gateway routers in each system share route and accessibility information. Border Gateway Protocol (BGP) replaces the older, less-scalable exterior gateway protocol (EGP) as the standard for exterior gateway routing protocols.

The link marked *A* in Figure 2.22 is an example of pass-through routing, which occurs between BGP peer routers within a network that is running an interior routing protocol. The details of BGP are covered in Chapters 8 and 9.

Classful vs. Classless Routing Protocols

Routing protocols can be differentiated in several ways. One such method is whether they support classless addresses. We discussed earlier in this chapter (in the section "IP Address and Subnet Basics") the class A, B, and C addressing schemes and how subnetting worked. Now we will look at how classful addressing limits a protocol when working in large internetworks.

Classful Routing

Classful routing protocols (RFC 950), such as RIPv1 and IGRP, exchange routing information within the internetwork without including the subnet mask with the IP address. When the routing is established and networks are advertised, there is no indication of a subnet mask. Attempts to include a subnet mask will return an error. The following code demonstrates both protocols for example purposes only.

```
router rip
 network 210.93.105.0
 network 204.204.7.0
 network 167.111.0.0

router igrp 100
 network 210.93.105.0
 network 204.204.7.0
 network 167.111.0.0
```

Classful routing protocols, or fixed-length subnet mask (FLSM) environments, must follow two rules. First, all subnets must use a single subnet mask for all network addresses in a given classful network (the network address assigned by InterNIC or another registering body). Restated simply, all interfaces within the classful network must have the same subnet mask. This single-mask requirement allows routers to share information with other routers within the system because each device interprets the addresses the same way. Because this is within a single network system, the network administrator must make sure of compliance.

One drawback to the single subnet mask rule is that it can lead to inefficient use of IP addresses, particularly in router-to-router links. Figure 2.23 shows two routers with a series of class C subnets wasting 28 addresses in connecting the two routers.

A problem arises when attempts are made to connect to routers that are not a part of the autonomous system and therefore have no assurance that they will be using the same subnet mask. This leads to the second rule: All subnets must be contiguous and cannot be separated by other networks. Unless default class masks are used, the subnetting will be lost in route summarization, as discussed in the next section. Separated subnets can appear to routers as two alternative routes to the same subnet.

In classful networks, route summarization occurs automatically when routes are exchanged with networks that use different subnet masks. If the network is not on an interface of both routers, where a subnet mask was defined, then the routes are summarized to the default routing mask when they are advertised to neighboring networks. They are summarized using the first octet rule. No other route summarization is allowed in classful networks. The following code uses RIP to demonstrate how classful routes are summarized.

```
router rip
 network 210.93.105.0
 network 167.111.0.0
```

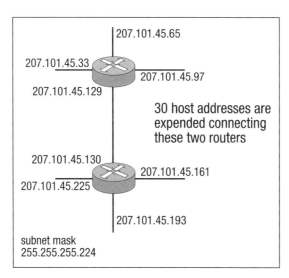

Figure 2.23   Seven subnets on two routers.

What is lost is that our interfaces are configured to and our **network** commands include e0: 210.93.105.33, e1: 210.93.105.65, e2: 210.93.105.97, and s0: 167.111.101.98, all with 255.255.255.224 as the subnet mask. The summarization of our 210.93.105.0 network isn't really a problem if there are no other subnets anywhere else. In that case, all packets will come to our router and it can do the final distributions. If there are other subnets (such as 210.93.105.128 or 210.93.105.160) out in the internetwork somewhere, though, routers can see it as two alternative paths to the same network and include only the best one in the routing tables.

Classless Routing

Classless routing (RFCs 1517-1520) allows for assignments of addresses without regard to the old classes, opting instead for a prefix mask made up of contiguous binary ones. This means that a portion of a class C or a contiguous group of class Cs could be assigned to an organization using a single mask and therefore a single entry in the Internet routing tables. For example, /25 or 255.255.255.128 would assign one-half of a class C, whereas /23 or 255.255.254.0 would include two class Cs with 508 total hosts.

Whereas classful default masks identify the network number, prefix masks represent the network/host boundary. This process is covered in Chapter 3.

The biggest difference is that classless routing protocols, such as RIPv2, EIGRP, OSPF, IS-IS, and BGP, can include the subnet mask in all routing exchanges. This allows multiple masks within a network and therefore better utilization of available IP addresses. The use of different length masks is called variable-length subnet masking. Figure 2.24 shows two routers with a series of subnets each with 30 host addresses but only expending two host addresses in connecting the two routers.

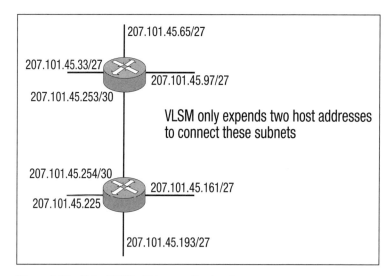

Figure 2.24 Using VLSM within a small network.

Classless Inter Domain Routing (CIDR), VLSM, EIGRP, OSPF, and BGP are all covered in detail in later chapters.

Distance-Vector vs. Link-State Protocols

How protocols share routing information within a network falls into two categories: distance-vector and link-state protocols. Each has its own attributes and stability features, as well as strengths and weaknesses. Enhanced IGRP is a hybrid protocol incorporating features of both classes.

Distance-Vector Protocols

Distance-vector routing protocols, such as RIPv1, RIPv2, IGRP, and EIGRP, exchange routing data only with adjacent routing devices using broadcast or multi-cast packets. These routing updates include the complete routing table, which is then used to update and confirm the next router's entries. Each router's routing table then is only as dependable as its neighbor's understanding of the network. This is sometimes referred to as "routing by rumor."

Routing updates are on regular intervals—as short as 30 seconds for RIP. This can mean considerable network traffic for updates on a network, particularly if the network is stable. Figure 2.25 shows how distance-vector routing updates are forwarded.

Router A sends its routing table to both B and D, who then update their own routing tables. Router B forwards its table to both C and A. Router C learns A's perception of the network, including the existence of networks linked to Routers D and E. Router D forwards its table to Routers E and A. Similarly, Router E learns A's perception of the network, including the existence of networks linked to Routers B and C.

Distance-vector protocols generally use the Bellman-Ford algorithm to generate a shortest-path spanning tree. Although the entire routing table gets transmitted, it is

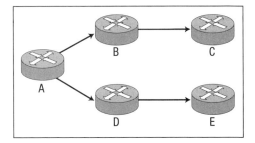

Figure 2.25   Distance-vector routing.

sent only to adjacent routers. Distance-vector is a simpler protocol then link-state, requiring less router resources (central processing unit [CPU] and memory), but it is more prone to routing loops.

Note that EIGRP is a hybrid protocol that includes attributes of link-state protocols and is often compared in both categories. EIGRP is covered in detail in Chapter 7.

Distance-vector protocols incorporate several techniques to increase the stability of the process. These include count to infinity, holddown timers, split-horizon updates, and poison-reverse updates. Table 2.5 describes each technique. More detailed information can be obtained from any basic CCNA text.

Table 2.5   Routing protocol stability techniques.

Technique	Description
Count to infinity	Each protocol has a critical number of hops that, once the distance to a destination network exceeds that point, it is determined that the network is unreachable and the packet is killed off. This reduces the impact of "loops," particularly in protocols that are slow to converge or networks with incomplete router tables. The "hops" count in the table at the end of this section (Figure 2.26) shows the maximum number of hops for each protocol.
Hold-down timers	The router will neither advertise nor listen to updates until the hold-down period has elapsed (e.g., three updates for RIP). This technique is used to flush bad information about a route from all routers and is usually triggered by a link failure within the route.
Split-horizon updates	Used to help prevent routing loops, split-horizon updates prevent an interface from being used to advertise routing information that was learned from that interface. Router A will not advertise to Router B any routing information that it learned about from B.
Poison-reverse updates	These updates are often used with split-horizon updates to tag a network or subnet as unreachable. Rather than merely omitting the information from the update, the metric is set so that every device will see it as unreachable (e.g., setting the hop count to 16 in a RIP network). Although this increases the size of the update (compared to just ignoring it), it reduces the chance of routing loops, particularly larger loops involving several routers.
Scheduled updates	Routing updates occur on a schedule regardless of changes in the network. This can be augmented by event-triggered updates.
Event-triggered updates	Changes in the network that cause a change in a device's routing table can trigger a routing update. The link-state protocols tend to use this technique exclusively, whereas distance-vector protocols will use flash (nonscheduled) updates in addition to regular updates, often combined with other techniques such as holddown timers.
Hierarchical topology required	To localize the distribution of link-state updates, a hierarchical design can be broken into areas, thereby reducing update traffic throughout the entire network.
Route summarization	This is the consolidation of advertised routes to reduce the number of routing table entries required to define the network. This is automatic with classful networks; later chapters show how classless networks use CIDR to handle route summarization.
Knowledge of entire topology	Link-state protocols lead to a consistent view of the network by all routing devices and thereby reduce the chance of routing loops. This requires more resources (e.g., CPU, memory) on the routers.

(continued)

Table 2.5   Distance-vector protocol techniques *(continued)*.

Technique	Description
Load-balancing (equal paths)	If there are routes with equal metrics, the routed traffic can be split equally between the routes on a round-robin basis. Failure in one route can lead to shifting traffic to the other(s).
Load-balancing (unequal paths)	If there are routes with unequal metrics within an acceptable range, the routed traffic can be split proportionally between the routes.

Similarly, link-state protocols also use stability techniques to prevent routing loops and increase routing integrity and efficiency. The techniques described briefly in Table 2.5 will be covered in detail in later chapters.

Link-State Protocols

Link-state protocols, such as OSPF and IS-IS, multicast or broadcast updates to all routing devices but forward only the portion of their routing tables reflecting their interface links. Although link-state advertisements (LSAs) flood the network, they are smaller in size than distance-vector updates, reducing bandwidth requirements on each link.

Unlike distance-vector protocols, link-state protocols update only when changes occur in the network, thereby reducing network traffic in a stable network. The device that detects the network change generates the LSA. This LSA is a multicast, which is copied by the adjacent routers to be used for updating their local routing tables. The LSA is then forwarded to the next device. Note that the protocol may still send periodic packets (30 minutes for OSPF) to keep the links synchronized.

This flooding of updates is mitigated by protocols such as OSPF that require a hierarchical network design and logical update areas rather than the entire network. This can reduce the scope of any change and the time it takes the network to converge. This process is covered in Chapters 5 and 6 on OSPF.

Link-state protocols use more complex algorithms, such as Dijkstra's algorithm. They generally require greater router resources, such as CPU usage and memory, than distance-vector protocols and are therefore often more expensive to implement. Link-state protocols are less vulnerable to routing loops and converge more quickly than distance-vector protocols. Figure 2.26 shows a comparison of the attributes of the distance-vector and link-state routing protocols.

Convergence Issues

Convergence is the time required for a group of routers running the same protocol to agree on the network topology (synchronize) after a change. The process can be triggered by route status change or the addition of a new route. The network is said to be *converged* when the process is complete. The convergence process varies with the protocol in use.

Attribute	Distance-Vector			Hybrid	Link-State	
	RIPv1	RIPv2	IGRP	EIGRP	OSPF	IS-IS
Event triggered updates			X	X	X	X
Scheduled updates	X	X	X			
Count to infinity x	X	X	X	X	X	
Holddown timersx	X	X				
Split horizon updates	X	X	X			
Poison-reverse updates	X	X	X	X		
Heirarchical topology required					X	X
Route summarization – manual				X	X	X
Route summarization – automatic	x^1	x^1	x^1	X		
Knowledge of entire topology				X	X	X
VLSM support	X		X	X	X	
Load-balancing – equal paths	X	X	X	X	X	X
Load-balancing – unequal paths			X	X		
Metric used Hops	Hops	Comp	Comp	Cost	Cost	
Hop count limit 15	15	100-255	100	200	1024	
Scalability	Medium	Medium	Large	Large	Large	V Large
Routing algorithim	B-F^2	B-F^2	B-F^2	Dual	Dijkstra	IS-IS

[1]Classful summarization only
[2]Bellman-Ford algorithim

Figure 2.26 Comparing distance-vector and link-state routing protocols.

The time for convergence within a network varies, depending on how the change was detected. It could be when the interface fails to receive three consecutive keep-alive packets or when the transport layer fails to receive three consecutive hello packets or routing updates. Other factors, such as network size, the algorithm used, and holddown timers that some protocols use, limit the network's ability to converge—it cannot possibly converge faster than the holddown period.

Figure 2.27 shows an example of simple network with a link down between Routers C and E. We then use this figure for an overview comparison of RIP, IGRP, EIGRP, and OSPF convergence processes. Details are covered in later chapters.

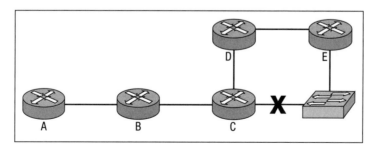

Figure 2.27 A simple network topology with a broken or discontinued link.

RIP

The steps for RIP convergence are as follows:

1. Router C detects the failure and triggers a flash update with the poisoned route to Routers D and B. Router C purges any routes learned from that interface from its routing table.

2. Router B sends a flash to Router A. A holddown timer is set.

3. Router C sends a broadcast query (RIP version 1) to Routers B and D. Router D responds with an alternative route, which is added to Router C's routing table. Router B responds with a poisoned route. Note that RIP version 2 would use a multicast to address 224.0.0.9.

4. As long as Router B is in holddown, updates from Router C about this new route will be ignored. Furthermore, Router B will continue to send poisoned route packets to Router C.

5. As the holddown timers for Routers B and A expire, the new route update from Router C will be added to their routing tables. The larger the network, the more holddown timers that have to be waited for.

Expected time to convergence would be 3.5 to 4 minutes.

IGRP

The steps for IGRP convergence are as follows:

1. Router C detects the failure and triggers a flash update with the route poisoned to Routers D and B. Router C purges any routes learned from that interface from its routing table.

2. Router B sends a flash update to Router A. A holddown timer is set.

3. Router C sends a broadcast query to all of its neighbors, including the downed route. Router D responds with an alternative route, which is added to Router C's routing table. Router B responds with a poisoned route.

4. As long as Router B is in holddown, updates from Router C about this new route will be ignored. Furthermore, Router B will continue to send poisoned route packets to Router C.

5. As the holddown timers for Routers B and A expire, the new route update from Router C will be added to their routing tables. The larger the network, the more holddown timers that have to be waited for.

Expected time to convergence would be 5.5 to 6 minutes.

Enhanced IGRP

The steps for EIGRP convergence are as follows:

1. Router C detects the failure between Routers C and E. It checks the topology table for an alternative route (feasible successor); because it can't find one, it enters an active convergence state.

2. Router C sends a broadcast query, looking for an alternative route to all of its neighbors. The neighboring routers acknowledge the query.

3. Router D responds with an alternative route with a higher feasible distance. Router B responds with no alternative route.

4. Router C updates the topology table and adds the new route with the higher metrics to its routing table.

5. Router C sends an immediate update of the new route to all interfaces. The adjacent routers update their routing tables and forward the updates to the next routers. Every router receiving the update acknowledges the update to the sender, thereby synchronizing and validating the new topology.

The time to convergence would take just a couple of seconds.

OSPF

The steps for OSPF convergence are as follows:

1. Router C detects and confirms the failure between Routers C and E. It deletes the route from its routing table. It then sends an LSA out all interfaces.

2. Routers B and D copy the LSA and forward it out all other interfaces.

3. All routers wait 5 seconds after receiving the LSA and then start the shortest path first (Dijkstra) algorithm. When the algorithm finishes, Router C adds the route to its routing table, and the others update the metric in their own routing tables.

4. After Router E ages out the topology table entry originated by Router C showing the failed link, it sends an LSA, which is forwarded throughout the network.

5. All routers wait 5 seconds after receiving the LSA; then they start the shortest path first algorithm again and then make final updates to their routing tables that reflect the new route from C through D to E.

The time to convergence would take just 5 to 6 seconds, depending on the size of the topology table. When the final LSA is considered, total time to stability within the network could take 30 to 45 seconds.

IOS Commands

In this section, we look at the IOS commands necessary to discover the topology of a network, analyze the routing table, display the router configuration, and test connectivity within the network.

Cisco Discovery Protocol

Cisco Discovery Protocol (CDP) commands allow you to gather information about the routers and switches that are directly connected to your routers and can be used to build a logical diagram of the network. Hubs, as layer 1 devices, are invisible to the CDP command, whereas Cisco switches are, by default, seen by the CDP commands. The following code is an example of the **show cdp neighbors** command:

```
Lab-C>show cdp neighbors
Capability Codes: R - Router, T - Trans Bridge, B - Source Route Bridge
                  S - Switch, H - Host, I - IGMP, r - Repeater

Device ID       Local Intrfce   Holdtme   Capability  Platform  Port ID
Lab-B               Ser 1        130          R         1601     Ser 0
Lab-D               Ser 0        146          R         1601     Ser 1
```

This code tells us that Router Lab-C is bordered by two Cisco 1601 routers. Lab-B is connected to Lab-C's Serial 1 interface via its own Serial 0 interface. Compare this code to the following code, in which we substituted a Cisco 1900 switch for the hub between Lab-D and Lab-E:

```
Lab-D>show cdp neighbors
Capability Codes: R - Router, T - Trans Bridge, B - Source Route Bridge
                  S - Switch, H - Host, I - IGMP, r - Repeater

Device ID       Local Intrfce   Holdtme   Capability  Platform  Port ID
Lab-C               Ser 1        136          R         1601     Ser 0
RouterLabSwitch     Eth 0        143         T S        1900     5
```

The **show cdp neighbors detail** command displays more information about each adjacent device. The following code is the Cisco 1900 switch between Lab-D and Lab-E:

```
Lab-D>show cdp neighbors detail
-------------
Device ID: Lab-C
Entry address(es):
  IP address: 204.204.7.1
Platform: cisco 1601, Capabilities: Router
```

```
Interface: Serial1,  Port ID (outgoing port): Serial0
Holdtime : 129 sec

Version :
Cisco Internetwork Operating System Software
IOS (tm) 1600 Software (C1600-BNSY-L), Version 11.2(18)P,  Rel Software
(fc1)
Copyright (c) 1986-1999 by cisco Systems, Inc.
Compiled Mon 12-Apr-99 14:46 by ashah

- - - - - - - - - - - - -
Device ID: RouterLabSwitch
Entry address(es):
  IP address: 10.2.2.9
Platform: cisco 1900,  Capabilities: Trans-Bridge Switch
Interface: Ethernet0,  Port ID (outgoing port): 5
Holdtime : 136 sec

Version :
V5.34
```

Note that the **show cdp neighbors detail** command gives us the IP address and the version of the IOS (routers), whereas the **show cdp neighbors** command does not.

The **show cdp ?** (help) command will display other CDP options:

```
Lab-D>show cdp ?
  entry     Information for specific neighbor entry
  interface  CDP interface status and configuration
  neighbors  CDP neighbor entries
  traffic    CDP statistics
  <cr>
```

The **show cdp interface** command reports the status and encapsulation of each interface. We could use **show cdp interface serial 0** (or **s0**) to get the information on only one interface. It also tells us that CDP is generating traffic every 60 seconds.

```
Lab-D>show cdp interface
Ethernet0 is up, line protocol is up
  Encapsulation ARPA
  Sending CDP packets every 60 seconds
  Holdtime is 180 seconds
Serial0 is administratively down, line protocol is down
  Encapsulation HDLC
  Sending CDP packets every 60 seconds
  Holdtime is 180 seconds
```

2

```
Serial1 is up, line protocol is up
  Encapsulation HDLC
  Sending CDP packets every 60 seconds
  Holdtime is 180 seconds
```

We now know something about the devices immediately adjacent to ours. We can now sketch those devices. We also know a single interface IP address for each neighbor device. With this information, we could Telnet to that device (we would need the passwords) and run the **show cdp** commands to discover the next adjacent device(s). Given the above results, our **telnet** command would be:

```
Lab-D>telnet 204.204.7.1
```

Display the Running Configuration

The **show running-config** (or **sho run**) command will display the current configuration of the router, including the interface addresses and subnet masks.

```
2504Router#show running-config
Building configuration...

Current configuration:
!
version 12.0⁽¹⁾
service timestamps debug uptime
service timestamps log uptime
no service password-encryption
!
hostname 2504Router
!
enable secret 5 $1$ySCk$ApJ5KAWDOWKL75BBRfXSsO
!
ip subnet-zero⁽²⁾
ip host 2504Router 192.168.11.2 192.168.10.1
ip host 4000Router 192.168.100.100 192.168.10.2
ip host 2501Router 192.168.12.2 192.168.11.3
!
interface Serial0
 ip address 192.168.11.1 255.255.255.0⁽³⁾
 clockrate 56000
 bandwidth 56
 no shutdown
!
interface Serial1
 ip address 192.168.12.1 255.255.255.0⁽³⁾
 no shutdown
!
```

```
interface TokenRing0
 ip address 192.168.10.1 255.255.255.0(3)
 ring-speed 4
 no shutdown
!
interface BRI0
 no ip address
 no ip directed-broadcast
 shutdown
!
router rip(4)
 network 192.168.10.0(5)
 network 192.168.11.0(5)
 network 192.168.12.0(5)
!
ip http server
no ip classless(6)
!
line con 0
 password cisco
 login
 transport input none
line aux 0
 password cisco
 login
line vty 0 4
 password cisco
 login
!
```

The notes in the output tell us the following pertinent information about our router:

[1] This designates the version of the IOS, but not the build or incremental version upgrade.

[2] We are using the subnet-zero option, allowing us to use all subnets.

[3] This designates the subnet mask associated with the interface.

[4] RIP routing is enabled.

[5] This shows the networks being advertised; it also determines the interfaces that updates will be sent out and listened to.

[6] IP classless routing is disabled. The router is using classful only.

Display the Routing Table

The routing table contains the best route to each network and the interface to forward the packets. The **show ip route** command demonstrates how this information is displayed. Note that each route is listed on a separate row below the *Codes:* section, which works as a legend for the first code in each row.

```
Lab-D#show ip route
Codes: C - connected, S - static, I - IGRP, R - RIP, M - mobile, B - BGP
       D - EIGRP, EX - EIGRP external, O - OSPF, IA - OSPF inter area
       N1 - OSPF NSSA external type 1, N2 - OSPF NSSA external type 2
       E1 - OSPF external type 1, E2 - OSPF external type 2, E - EGP
       i - IS-IS, L1 - IS-IS level-1, L2 - IS-IS level-2, * - candidate
       U - per-user static route, o - ODR

Gateway of last resort is not set

C    204.204.7.0/24 is directly connected, Serial1
R    223.8.151.0/24 [120/1] via 204.204.7.1, 00:00:26, Serial1
R    199.6.13.0/24 [120/1] via 204.204.7.1, 00:00:26, Serial1
C    210.93.105.0/24 is directly connected, Ethernet0
S    201.100.11.0/24 [1/0] via 199.6.13.1
R    192.168.100.0/24 [120/1] via 192.168.10.2, 00:00:25, TokenRing0
Lab-D#
```

Display IP Protocols Running

The **show ip protocols** command displays valuable information about what routing protocols are running, the interfaces that are associated with the protocol, the update cycle, when the next update is scheduled, and how long data will be held before it is flushed. The following code is for example purposes only, to show the results for both RIP and IGRP.

```
Lab-D#show ip protocols
Routing Protocol is "rip"
  Sending updates every 30 seconds, next due in 9 seconds
  Invalid after 180 seconds, hold down 180, flushed after 240
  Outgoing update filter list for all interfaces is not set
  Incoming update filter list for all interfaces is not set
  Redistributing: rip
  Default version control: send version 1, receive any version
    Interface       Send   Recv    Key-chain
    Ethernet0        1      1 2
    Serial1          1      1 2
  Routing for Networks:
    210.93.105.0
    204.204.7.0
```

```
    Routing Information Sources:
      Gateway         Distance      Last Update
      204.204.7.1          120      00:00:00
      210.93.105.2         120      18:05:40
    Distance: (default is 120)


Routing Protocol is "igrp 100"
  Sending updates every 90 seconds, next due in 69 seconds
  Invalid after 270 seconds, hold down 280, flushed after 630
  Outgoing update filter list for all interfaces is not set
  Incoming update filter list for all interfaces is not set
  Default networks flagged in outgoing updates
  Default networks accepted from incoming updates
  IGRP metric weight K1=1, K2=0, K3=1, K4=0, K5=0
  IGRP maximum hopcount 100
  IGRP maximum metric variance 1
  Redistributing: igrp 100
  Routing for Networks:
    210.93.105.0
    204.204.7.0
  Routing Information Sources:
    Gateway         Distance      Last Update
  Distance: (default is 100)
```

Debugging Routing Protocols

The Cisco **debug** command can be used to monitor in real time the process of
sharing routing information between routers. The following example demonstrates
debugging IGRP; similar commands exist for RIP and other protocols.

To start the debug process, type the **debug ip igrp events** (or **transactions**) command and then wait long enough for the next update cycle. Note the difference
between the **events** and **transactions** options. Type the command preceded by **no**
to turn off the debugging or use the **no debug all** command to stop all debugging
(or **undebug all** which can be shortened to **u all**).

```
Lab-D#debug ip igrp events
IGRP event debugging is on
Lab-D#
IGRP: sending update to 255.255.255.255 via Ethernet0 (210.93.105.1)
IGRP: Update contains 0 interior, 3 system, and 0 exterior routes.
IGRP: Total routes in update: 3
IGRP: sending update to 255.255.255.255 via Serial1 (204.204.7.2)
IGRP: Update contains 0 interior, 1 system, and 0 exterior routes.
IGRP: Total routes in update: 1
IGRP: received update from invalid source 223.8.151.1 on Ethernet0
IGRP: received update from 204.204.7.1 on Serial1
```

```
IGRP: Update contains 0 interior, 2 system, and 0 exterior routes.
IGRP: Total routes in update: 2

Lab-D#no debug ip igrp events (Note: undebug all would also work)
IGRP event debugging is off

Lab-D#debug ip igrp transactions
IGRP protocol debugging is on
Lab-D#
IGRP: received update from invalid source 223.8.151.1 on Ethernet0
IGRP: received update from 204.204.7.1 on Serial1
      network 223.8.151.0, metric 8576 (neighbor 1100)
      network 199.6.13.0, metric 10476 (neighbor 8476)
IGRP: sending update to 255.255.255.255 via Ethernet0 (210.93.105.1)
      network 204.204.7.0, metric=8476
      network 223.8.151.0, metric=8576
      network 199.6.13.0, metric=10476
IGRP: sending update to 255.255.255.255 via Serial1 (204.204.7.2)
      network 210.93.105.0, metric=1100

Lab-D#no debug ip igrp transactions
IGRP protocol debugging is off
Lab-D#
```

Type the **debug ip rip** command to start the debug process and then type the
show ip route command. After the initial IP route display, it will show all RIP
activity as it occurs.

```
Lab-D#debug ip rip
RIP protocol debugging is on
Lab-D#
RIP: sending v1 update to 255.255.255.255 via Ethernet0 (210.93.105.1)
     network 204.204.7.0, metric 1
     network 223.8.151.0, metric 2
     network 199.6.13.0, metric 2
RIP: sending v1 update to 255.255.255.255 via Serial1 (204.204.7.2)
     network 210.93.105.0, metric 1
RIP: ignored v1 update from bad source 223.8.151.1 on Ethernet0
RIP: received v1 update from 204.204.7.1 on Serial1
     223.8.151.0 in 1 hops
     199.6.13.0 in 1 hops
Lab-D#no debug ip rip
RIP protocol debugging is off
Lab-D#
```

Note the metric calculations.

Testing Connectivity

To test connectivity with other routers in the network, use the following commands in order:

➤ **telnet** (RFC 854), a TCP/IP terminal emulation protocol, tests connectivity between devices up to layer 7 (OSI model). If it can connect to this level, the connection is working at all levels.

➤ **ping** (packet internet gopher) checks connectivity at the network layer. ICMP echo messages are sent to indicate the reliability of the connection and time required.

➤ **trace ip** or **trace** (**tracert** in DOS/NT) not only checks connectivity like **ping**, but displays the routers it passed through to make the connection. Whereas **ping** is limited to 15 hops, **trace** will try 30 before giving up.

➤ **show interfaces** verifies the line and protocol status.

Telnet

You can Telnet with either the IP address or the host name of the other router. Example: **telnet 210.93.105.2** or **telnet Lab-C**. To Telnet to another router, you will need to know the password(s). Typing the **exit** command when you are done will close the session.

```
2504Router#telnet 4000router
Trying 4000Router (192.168.100.100)... Open

User Access Verification
Password:
4000Router>exit

[Connection to 4000router closed by foreign host]

2504Router#telnet 192.168.100.100
Trying 192.168.100.100 ... Open

User Access Verification
Password:
4000Router>exit

[Connection to 192.168.100.100 closed by foreign host]
2504Router#
```

To Telnet to a host name, naming resolution, such as a name server or an IP host table in your router's configuration, must be in place. The IP host table associates the host name with up to eight IP addresses. To display the IP host table, use the **show hosts** or **show run** commands.

```
2504Router#show hosts
Default domain is not set
Name/address lookup uses domain service
Name servers are 255.255.255.255


Host                     Flags        Age Type   Address(es)
2504Router               (perm, OK)   2   IP     192.168.11.1  192.168.10.1
4000Router               (perm, OK)   0   IP     192.168.100.100
192.168.10.2
2504Router#


2504Router#show run
!
ip host 2504Router 192.168.11.1 192.168.10.1
ip host 4000Router 192.168.100.100 192.168.10.2
!
```

Ping and Enhanced Ping

You can ping with either the IP address or the host name of the other router. Example: **ping 210.93.105.2** or **ping Lab-C**.

```
Lab-B#ping 204.204.7.1

Type escape sequence to abort.
Sending 5, 100-byte ICMP Echos to 204.204.7.1, timeout is 2 seconds:
!!!!!
Success rate is 100 percent (5/5), round-trip min/avg/max = 40/42/44 ms
```

Note that the escape sequence mentioned is Ctrl+Shift+6.

We now know the following from the output:

1. The five exclamation (*!*) marks indicate a successful ping. A period (.) would indicate a failure.

2. *Sending 5* indicates how many ICMP echos were sent.

3. *100-byte* is the size of the packets.

4. *2 seconds* is the time-out duration, before it gives up.

5. The success rate is *100 percent*, or five for five attempts (*5/5*).

6. *40/42/44 ms* is the minimum, average, and maximum round-trip time.

To ping a device name, type the command **ping lab-C**.

In the user mode, **ping** allows us only two choices: an IP address or a host name. At the privilege mode, we can control many of the settings of our **ping** command. Go to the privilege mode and type **ping?**. The result should look like this:

```
Lab-B#ping ?
  WORD       Ping destination address or hostname
  appletalk  Appletalk echo
  ip         IP echo
  ipx        Novell/IPX echo
  <cr>
```

Assuming we don't know the full structure of the commands, type **ping** and press Enter. You will be asked each of the following, one at a time:

```
Lab-B#ping
Protocol [ip]:
Target IP address: 199.6.13.2
Repeat count [5]: 15
Datagram size [100]: 1000
Timeout in seconds [2]: 5
Extended commands [n]:
Sweep range of sizes [n]:
```

The defaults are shown in square brackets. Pick any appropriate IP address and then make the above choices. If you answer *y* to either of the last two questions, you will get more choices. *Repeat count* changes the number of ICMP packets. *Datagram size* changes the packet size.

Trace IP or Trace

Type **trace ip** or **trace** and the IP address of the target destination, for example, **trace ip 223.8.151.1**. The following output would be the result of tracing a route from Lab-E to a port on Lab-B:

```
Lab-B#trace ip 219.17.100.1

Type escape sequence to abort.
Tracing the route to Lab-B (219.17.100.1)

  1 Lab-D (210.93.105.1) 4 msec 4 msec 0 msec
  2 Lab-C (204.204.7.1) 24 msec 24 msec 24 msec
  3 Lab-B (199.6.13.1) 44 msec *  44 msec
```

Note that the escape sequence is: Ctrl+Shift+6.

We now know:

1. The routing path to the target IP address.

2. The round-trip time for each of the three probe packets at each step of the trace.

To trace IP to a host name, the entry would be, for example, **trace ip Lab-C**.

Show Interfaces

The **show interfaces** and **clear counters** commands are very important in solving network problems. The router keeps very detailed statistics about data traffic it has sent and received on its interfaces. It also keeps track of bad data packets. With this data you can see if a problem exists on the network that a router interface services. More important to us, the **show interfaces** command tells us the status of our line connection and protocol. If either is down, we have no connection to that network.

Run the **show interfaces** command. The statistics for all interfaces should appear. Remember that Shift+Ctrl+6 will abort the display. To display a single Ethernet interface, type the abbreviated command **sho int e0**. The first screen of the result might look something like this:

```
Lab-E>show interfaces
Ethernet0 is up, line protocol is up
  Hardware is QCC Ethernet, address is 00e0.1eec.7a0b (bia 00e0.1eec.7a0b)
  Internet address is 210.93.105.2/24
  MTU 1500 bytes, BW 10000 Kbit, DLY 1000 usec, rely 255/255, load 1/255
  Encapsulation ARPA, loopback not set, keepalive set (10 sec)
  ARP type: ARPA, ARP Timeout 04:00:00
  Last input 00:00:00, output 00:00:00, output hang never
  Last clearing of "show interface" counters never
  Queueing strategy: fifo
  Output queue 0/40, 0 drops; input queue 0/75, 0 drops
  5 minute input rate 0 bits/sec, 0 packets/sec
  5 minute output rate 0 bits/sec, 0 packets/sec
     1416 packets input, 194827 bytes, 0 no buffer
     Received 703 broadcasts, 0 runts, 0 giants, 0 throttles
     0 input errors, 0 CRC, 0 frame, 0 overrun, 0 ignored, 0 abort
     0 input packets with dribble condition detected
     2361 packets output, 189912 bytes, 0 underruns
     0 output errors, 0 collisions, 2 interface resets
     0 babbles, 0 late collision, 1 deferred
     0 lost carrier, 0 no carrier
     0 output buffer failures, 0 output buffers swapped out
```

Note particularly that the first line tells us both the line and the protocol are up. It also shows the IP address/subnet mask on line three and the MAC address on line two.

Chapter Summary

In this chapter we reviewed IP addressing and subnet masks with special interest in classful networks in which the first octet rule determines the address class. Figure 2.28 summarizes the classful system in both decimal and binary, including the default routing mask.

Routers perform two separate and distinct functions: routing and switching. *Routing* is the process of learning the network topology and then creating a routing table that shows the best route to each network through an associated interface. *Switching* is the process of moving packets from an inbound interface to an outbound interface based on the routing table. Switching uses the end product of the routing function.

Three requirements are necessary for effective routing to occur. First, the appropriate protocol must be active, both enabled and configured, on the interfaces of the router. Second, the destination network must be known and accessible to the router. Third, the routing table must reflect the best path to the desired network via one of the router's interfaces. This last requirement often involves selecting from multiple routes using metrics that are recognized by the routing protocol.

The *routing table* contains the information used in deciding which is the best interface to forward the packets. The **show ip route** command displays each best route on a separate row. The information includes:

➤ The method used to learn about the route.

➤ The destination network address with a notation that indicates the routing mask (for example, 201.115.17.0/24).

➤ An administrative distance, which indicates the reliability of the method used to learn about this network.

➤ A routing metric, which combines the entire path cost using methods specified by the routing protocol. The metric can be as simple as hop count for RIP to a metric derived from bandwidth, delay, and so forth in more dynamic protocols.

Class	Starts With	Binary Range	Decimal Value Range	Maximum Subnets	Maximum Hosts	Subnet Mask
A	0	00000000-01111111	0-127	127	16,777,214	255.0.0.0
B	10	10000000-10111111	128-191	16,384	65,534	255.255.0.0
C	110	11000000-11011111	192-223	2,097,152	254	255.255.255.0
D	1110	11100000-11101111	224-239			
E	1111	11110000-11111111	240-255			

Figure 2.28   A summary of the IP classful address system.

➤ The logical address of the next routing device, which will forward our packet toward the final destination.

➤ Age of the routing table entry in hours, minutes, and seconds.

➤ The outbound interface to use to send the packet to the next relay device.

Interior routing protocols, such as RIPv1, RIPv2, IPRP, EIGRP, and OSPF, are used for routing packets within an autonomous system—one that is under a single administrative control and routing strategy. The autonomous system uses a set of IP addresses that are assigned by one of the registering agencies, such as InterNIC. Exterior routing protocols, such as BGP, are used for routing packets between autonomous systems.

Classful routing protocols, such as RIPv1 and IGRP, do not exchange subnet masks and therefore require that all interfaces within the autonomous system must use the same subnet mask. Additionally, all subnets must be contiguous, that is, not separated by any other networks. The single subnet mask allows the network routers to properly route packets within the network without an accompanying mask. When classful networks exchange routing data with other networks, the advertised networks are summarized using the default subnet mask. Generally, this is not a problem because the default mask will get the data to the network and the network routers can deal with the subnets. Classful routing can lead to inefficient use of IP addresses, particularly when connecting two routers, because a full subnet must be committed even though as few as two host addresses will be used.

Classless networks, on the other hand, can use variable-length subnet masking, which more efficiently allocates host addresses. Classless routing allows for assignments of addresses without regard to the old classes, opting instead for a prefix mask made up of contiguous binary ones to designate the network/host boundary. This means that a contiguous group of subnets can be assigned with a single entry in the Internet routing tables. Classless protocols, such as RIPv2, EIGRP, and OSPF, not only use VLSM, they also exchange subnet masks with their routing data.

Distance-vector routing protocols, such as RIPv1, RIPv2, IGRP, and EIGRP, exchange complete routing tables on regular intervals—as short as 30 seconds for RIP. These protocols generate considerable network traffic doing updates on a stable network and require less router resources (CPU and memory) than link-state protocols, but they are more prone to routing loops. EIGRP is a hybrid protocol that includes attributes of link-state protocols and is often compared in both categories.

Link-state protocols, such as OSPF and IS-IS, use LSAs to flood updates through the network. These updates are smaller than distance-vector updates, and thus reduce bandwidth requirements on each link. This flooding of updates is mitigated by protocols such as OSPF, which use a hierarchical network design and logical update areas rather than the entire network. This reduces the scope of any change and the time it takes the network to converge. Unlike distance-vector protocols, link-state protocols update only when changes occur in the network, thereby reducing network traffic in a stable network.

Link-state protocols use more elaborate algorithms that require greater router resources (e.g., CPU usage and memory) than do distance-vector protocols, and are therefore often more expensive to implement. Link-state protocols are less vulnerable to routing loops and tend to converge more quickly than distance-vector protocols.

One consideration in choosing a routing protocol is the time to convergence—the time it takes all routers to agree on the topology and route status of the network. Generally, distance-vector networks, such as RIP and IGRP, are the slowest to converge, whereas the hybrid EIGRP and link-state protocols are the fastest. This speed comes from using more complex routing algorithms, and therefore requires greater investment in router resources such as the CPU and memory.

The following IOS commands are used to discover the topology of the network, analyze the routing table, and test connectivity:

➤ **show cdp neighbors** identifies the other Cisco devices on a network. This command will give us the host name, interface, and device type information.

➤ **show cdp neighbors detail** tells us the host name, IOS version, and IP addresses of the devices.

➤ **show running-config** displays the current configuration of the router including the interface addresses, subnet masks, and routing protocols.

➤ **show ip route** displays the routing table. The fields are covered earlier in this summary.

➤ **show ip protocols** displays the routing protocols, the interfaces associated with each protocol, the update cycle, when the next update is scheduled, and how long data will be held before it is flushed.

➤ **debug ip (*protocol*)** can be used to monitor in real time the process of sharing routing information between routers.

➤ **telnet** tests connectivity between devices up to layer 7 (OSI model).

➤ **ping** checks connectivity at the network layer.

➤ **trace** checks connectivity and displays the routers it passed through to make the connection.

➤ **show interfaces** verifies the line and protocol status.

Review Questions

1. Given the IP host address 201.11.200.177 and the default gateway 201.11.200.190, which two of the following subnet masks will work?

    a. 255.255.255.240

    b. 255.255.255.248

    c. 255.255.255.192

    d. 255.255.240.0

2. Given the private address 172.16.0.0, determine the subnet mask necessary to create six subnets, each with at least 5,000 host addresses.

    Subnet mask: _____

3. Calculate the information for the first six subnets in Question 2.

Subnet Value	Subnet Address	Broadcast Value	Host Range

4. Given the IP address 185.24.0.0 with the subnet mask 255.255.240.0, what would be the number of total subnets and host addresses?

    a. Subnets 16; hosts 4,096

    b. Subnets 32; hosts 2,046

    c. Subnets 16; hosts 4,094

    d. Subnets 16; hosts 14

5. The two basic router functions are _____ and _____.

6. Which of the following is *not* part of the switching function within a router?

    a. Create framing and forward the packet

    b. Associate destination logical address with the next-hop logical device and outbound interface

    c. Determine the best route from all of the choices in the routing table

    d. Associate the next-hop logical device with its physical address for inclusion in the frame header

    e. Check framing and buffer the packet

7. Which three items represent requirements for effective routing?

   a. The destination network must be known and accessible to the router

   b. The metric must be the lowest available

   c. The appropriate protocol must be active on the interfaces of the router

   d. The routing table must reflect the best path to the desired network via one of the router's interfaces

   e. The subnet mask must match the network class

8. In the routing table, the larger the metric, the more desirable the route. True or false?

9. In the routing table, the larger the administrative distance, the more desirable the route. True or false?

10. In classful routing, the routes are summarized on the receiving router using the default mask. True or false?

11. Link-state routing protocols use more sophisticated algorithms than distance-vector protocols and therefore rely less on router resources. True or false?

12. RIP reaches convergence faster than IGRP in a similar network. True or false?

13. Match the protocols (RIPv1, RIPv2, IGRP, EIGRP, and OSPF) to the following protocol characteristics. Note that there may be more than one answer per characteristic.

   a. _____ Has a hop count limitation of 15.

   b. _____ Has an administrative distance of 120.

   c. _____ Uses a composite metric to determine the best path.

   d. _____ Supports VLSMs.

   e. _____ Has an administrative distance of 100.

   f. _____ Requires hierarchical network topology.

   g. _____ Allows manual route summarization.

   h. _____ Summarizes routes using default class masks.

   i. _____ Uses holddown timers to avoid routing loops.

   j. _____ Maintains a knowledge of the entire topology.

   k. _____ Uses poison-reverse updates.

   l. _____ Has a zero administrative distance.

   m. _____ Routing updates include entire routing tables.

   n. _____ Subnet mask is not included in routing updates.

   o. _____ Subnet mask is included in routing updates.

   p. _____ Uses a multicast to exchange updates.

14. Which of the following commands displays the routing table?

    a. **show routes all**

    b. **show ip routing table**

    c. **show ip routes**

    d. **show routes ip**

15. Which of the following is not displayed with the **show cdp neighbors** command?

    a. Host name of neighbor device

    b. IP address of neighbor device

    c. Interface connection of neighbor device

    d. Interface connection of local device

    e. Whether neighbor device is a router or switch

16. Which three of these commands display a local interface's IP address?

    a. **show run**

    b. **show CDP neighbors detail**

    c. **show IP protocols**

    d. **show interfaces**

    e. **show IP routes**

17. Which commands display the order for troubleshooting connectivity?

    a. **show interfaces**, **trace**, **ping**, **show cdp neighbors**

    b. **show interfaces**, **trace**, **ping**, **telnet**

    c. **telnet**, **ping**, **trace**, **show interfaces**

    d. **telnet**, **show interfaces**, **ping**, **trace**

Real-World Projects

In this project, you will need at least two routers with any type of common connection. Figure 2.29 shows a simple two-router configuration that will work. Any larger configuration with more Cisco routers and switches will work equally as well.

Project 2.1

In this project, we cover the techniques for capturing the results of your HyperTerminal (or Telnet) session in a text file, which can be viewed and/or printed using Notepad, WordPad, or Microsoft Word. Mastering this technique can save you time and typing in later projects and on the job. You will need a floppy disk on which to store your output.

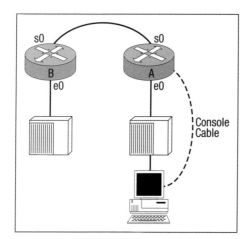

Figure 2.29 A basic two-router configuration for the real-world project.

Note: This feature will capture your future screens—not what is currently on the screen. You are in essence turning on a recording session. You will later "stop" the session, at which time it will be written to a text file.

1. Start a console session and go to the Enable (Privilege) mode.

2. Make sure that you have a floppy disk in the A: drive.

To start a capture session: Choose Transfer|Capture Text... from the menu.

We want our results stored on our floppy disk, so change the File: box to *A:\FirstCapture.txt.*

Note: Telnet users: The command is Terminal|Start Logging. The document you will create will have LOG as the extension. Otherwise the concepts are the same.

3. Click on the Start button. Anything that appears on the screen after this point will be copied to the file.

4. Access the Help feature by typing a question mark (?).

Press the Spacebar if prompted for More until you are through.

5. Try typing Show followed by a space and a question mark (?).

Press the Spacebar if prompted for More.

6. Choose Transfer|Capture Text|Stop from the menu. *This is probably one of the most important and most easily forgotten steps. If you forget it, your Capture file will probably be empty.*

Note: Telnet users: Use Terminal|Stop Logging to end the session.

7. Use Start|Programs|Windows Explorer from the taskbar to launch the Explorer program.

8. In the left-side panel, select the 3_ Floppy (A:) drive. The right side should list your text document. Double-click on your document's icon. The results should look something like this:

```
?
Exec commands:
  access-enable     Create a temporary Access-List entry
  clear             Reset functions
  connect           Open a terminal connection
  disable           Turn off privileged commands
  disconnect        Disconnect an existing network connection
  . . . .   (rows skipped by author)
  rlogin            Open an rlogin connection
  show              Show running system information
  slip              Start Serial-line IP (SLIP)
  systat            Display information about terminal lines
  telnet            Open a telnet connection
  —More— _____         _____  terminal        Set
  terminal line parameters
  traceroute        Trace route to destination
  tunnel            Open a tunnel connection
```

Note the gibberish appearing after *telnet*. That is where we had to press the Spacebar to see the rest of the list. Use basic word processing techniques to clean that up.

9. Return to your HyperTerminal session by clicking on the HyperTerminal button on the taskbar.

10. Start another capture session using any name of your choice, and then execute a couple of familiar commands.

11. When done, stop the capture and look over the results. Repeat the process until you are comfortable with capturing on demand.

Project 2.2

In this project, we use the CDP commands discussed in the chapter to define the topology of our network.

To discover the network:

1. Sketch the network devices large enough so that you can come back later and label the interfaces. Include any interfaces and cables that you can see.

2. Start a console session on your router and go to the enable mode. If you like, start a capture session to record your results.

3. Type the **sho run** (**show running-config**) command and document the local interfaces, IP addresses, and subnet masks on the sketch.

4. Type the **show cdp neighbors** command to see what Cisco devices are adjacent to you. Update your sketch.

5. Type the **show cdp neighbors details** command to get the IOS version and IP address information about your neighbors. Update your sketch.

6. Telnet to one of your neighbor routers with **telnet (ip address)**. You will need the passwords.

7. Repeat Steps 3 to 6 until your sketch of the network is complete.

Project 2.3

In this project we use the connectivity commands discussed in the chapter to test the topology of our network.

To test the network:

1. Use the sketch of the network from Project 2.2.

2. Start a console session on your router and go to the enable mode. If you like, start a capture session to record your results.

3. Use the **telnet (ip address)** command to start a Telnet session on another router from your sketch.

If you get the password prompt, you know you have full seven-layer connectivity to that device—you have hardware- and software-level connectivity. If you don't get the password prompt there are many possible reasons. If you connect to the other device, type **Exit** to end the Telnet session.

4. Type **ping (ip address)** to test physical connectivity to another router from your sketch. Note the results.

Were you successful? If not, continue trying closer devices until you are successful. You should at least be able to reach an adjacent device. If not, ping your own interfaces. If you are successful with pinging another device, continue until you can ping all devices.

5. Type **trace ip (ip address)** to test physical connectivity to another router from your sketch. Note the results.

Were you successful? If not, continuing trying closer devices until you are successful. You should at least be able to reach an adjacent device. If not, trace your own interfaces. If you are successful with pinging another device, continue until you can ping all devices.

6. Type **show interfaces** to verify that all relevant interfaces are functioning with both lines and protocols up.

Try typing **show int e0** to see just the Ethernet interface. Try any other interfaces.

7. If you cannot ping or trace past the adjacent devices, a routing protocol may not have been activated. Type **show ip routes** to see any networks beyond the interface shared with any adjacent routers. If you cannot, type **show run** to see if routing has been activated. Look for something like the following:

```
router rip
 network 199.6.13.0
 network 223.8.151.0
 network 204.204.7.0
 !
```

It will be necessary to start routing on each device if you want end-to-end connectivity. If you like, set up RIP or IGRP on each router and retry the commands from this project.

Project 2.4

In this project, we use the IP routing commands discussed in the chapter.

To view the IP routing tables:

1. Use the sketch of the network from Project 2.3.

2. Start a console session on your router and go to the enable mode. If you like, start a capture session to record your results.

3. Type **show ip routes** to see the routing table. Can you see any networks beyond the interface shared with any adjacent routers?

4. Type **show ip protocols** and look over the information.

5. *If IGRP is running*, type **debug ip igrp events** and then wait long enough for the next update cycle (up to 90 seconds). Type **no debug all** to stop all debugging.

6. Type **debug ip igrp transactions** and then wait long enough for the next update cycle. Type **no debug all** to stop all debugging.

7. *If RIP is running*, type **debug ip rip** and then wait long enough for the next update cycle. Type **no debug all** to stop all debugging. You can also use **undebug all** which can be shortened to **u all**.

8. Experiment with the features until you are comfortable with the techniques.

CHAPTER THREE

Extending IP Addresses

After completing this chapter, you will be able to:

✓ Discuss the history and evolution of IP addressing

✓ List many mechanisms to slow the depletion of IP addresses

✓ Reduce the number of route table entries by enabling hierarchical layers in an IP address

✓ Use variable-length subnet masks (VLSMs) to increase the number of available networks

✓ Determine which types of routing protocols are suitable for VLSMs

✓ Determine when and if route summarization can be implemented

S ay what you will about the problems of Internet protocol (IP) addressing, but remember that it was all started without the knowledge or even inkling of a prediction that its growth would explode exponentially. Most of us can remember the first NCSA Web browser because it wasn't really that long ago, but IP has been around far longer (in Internet time).

There is nothing to be done now concerning history. Information technology (IT) administrators must deal with the consequences. Many solutions to IP problems have cropped up over the years—some with foresight, some without. These comprise the myriad different ways that exist to improve traffic flow and decrease the burden on routers. This chapter reviews these methods—many of which truly help and assist.

Addressing in the IP Network

Some of the information in this chapter is review, even for the most junior of IT administrators. It is important, however, to understand the context prior to jumping headfirst into the topic of IP address extension.

IP addresses are logical addresses of devices that operate at layer 3 of the OSI network model. They were first defined in 1981 as a 32-bit number. Because 32-bit numbers are intimidating, even in decimal form, a dotted octet format was adopted. The common-use form is a set of four 8-bit numbers represented as decimal numbers separated by three periods.

For example, the 32-bit address 10101100000100000010000000000001 is just too frightening a number to use. Even if we separate the number into four 8-bit numbers with periods, it still comes out 10101100.00010000.00100000.00000001. So we commonly convert the binary octets into decimal values, yielding the less daunting 172.16.32.1.

Note: Even dotted octets are far too difficult to use and remember. Thus came the Domain Name Service (DNS), which mapped host names and domains into their IP address equivalents.

In the very beginning, the designers separated the address space into class A, B, and C. Later, class D and E arose. Because the IP protocol was efficient, simple, and did not lend itself to a lot of overhead, it won out over other rivals in terms of scalability. But it was not without its own problems.

➤ *Finite address space*—Assuming we do not count addresses that cannot be used for broadcasts, a 32-bit address represents at most 4,294,967,296 (2^{32}) unique addresses. That may seem like an overly large number of hosts, but keep in mind that we waste a substantial number of addresses in maintaining reasonable routing tables. That is, subnetting with one subnet mask may not be suitable for a specific network topology.

➤ *Routing table growth*—Nearly 100,000 unique routes exist as of the year 2000. For routers to efficiently pass packets from one network to another, they must compare destination addresses with the route table. Consider how much processing is required to match each packet with a table of this many entries.

There has been much talk (and many Requests For Comments, RFCs) about the so-called IPv6 next generation of addressing. However, IPv4 (the current level) is here to stay and has the support of every router on the market. Inertia alone will probably prevent IPv6 from being adopted for quite a while.

3

IP Addressing Solutions

Since the inception of IP addresses, many mechanisms have developed to slow their allocation and to reduce the number of route table entries by enabling more hierarchy in an IP address. These solutions include:

➤ Subnet masking

➤ Private networks

➤ Network Address Translation (NAT)

➤ Hierarchical addressing

➤ Variable-length subnet masks (VLSMs)

➤ Route summarization

➤ Classless Inter Domain Routing (CIDR)

Subnet Masking

Subnet masking was introduced in RFCs 950 (August 1985) and 1812 (June 1995). It was developed to add a level of hierarchy to an IP address. This level allows for extending the number of addresses derived from a single IP address—that is, the division of an address into a network portion and a host portion. Subnet masking is covered in detail in Chapter 2.

Private Networks

Prior to the Internet revolution, large corporations still had the need to develop and scale their internetworks. Early on, it was relatively easy to grab a class B network, thus allowing as many as 65,533 hosts to be allocated to a single company.

Note: Now you can understand why addresses started to deplete so quickly. Almost no companies, even large ones, have a need for 65,533 hosts, so a substantial number of host addresses went unused.

Table 3.1   Private internetworks.

Network	Range
10.0.0.0/8	10.0.0.0 through 10.255.255.255
172.16.0.0/12	172.16.0.0 through 172.31.255.255
192.168.0.0/16	192.168.0.0 through 192.168.255.255

The Internet Assigned Numbers Authority (IANA) therefore decided to allocate an entire class A network, 32 class B networks, and 256 class C networks to private addressing. They documented this in RFC 1918 (February 1996). Essentially, these networks should not appear in any Internet routing table. Without an entry, Internet routers will simply drop the packets. These addresses are described in Table 3.1.

Note: This information was introduced in Chapter 2 as part of the class system. However, it is reintroduced here in this form, which will become more clear in the section "Variable-Length Subnet Masks."

Of course, this doesn't prevent a single entity, such as a corporation, from using these addresses within their own internetwork router. Indeed, this is one reason that the IP protocol has had such an easy time penetrating large-scale enterprises.

Note: With these networks alone, a company can implement a huge internetwork without using a single public address, thus freeing up public address space for other uses.

Because Internet routers are instructed to drop packets in these privately addressed networks, it would be very difficult for hosts that fall within any of these networks to participate with the global Internet. A client using one of these addresses can likely send a packet to a target server on the Internet, but the response would never make it back because an Internet router would drop all packets. One-way communication is essentially no communication at all. Similarly, a client on the Internet cannot reach a server with one of these addresses because the first Internet router that one of its packets reaches will drop it.

Note: The private internetwork address space acts as a crude security device. Even though a private internetwork might be attached to the public Internet, it is difficult (although not impossible) for a meaningful connection to occur between any client and any server on each network.

Network Address Translation

The truth of the matter is that companies do need to communicate on the public Internet. A few good examples of such communication, but by no means all of them, follow:

➤ Business-to-business communication via the Internet

➤ Electronic mail

➤ Marketing via a Web site

➤ Internetworking via a Virtual Private Network (VPN)

➤ Remote access to corporate resources

➤ Research and development

If a company utilizes an addressing scheme from the pool of private internetworks, how then can communication occur? The answer lies with *Network Address Translation (NAT)*. RFC 1631 (May 1994) describes the use of a router or other network appliance to take a packet and change either its source or destination address.

Note: Most organizations implement NAT in an active proxy firewall. Most consumer devices implement NAT either in a border computer, or in an inexpensive router.

Packets traveling from a private network to a public network pass through a NAT router. The router then changes the source address to its public address on the public network and then forwards it to its destination. The return address is, of course, the public address on the public network. The router must keep track of the outbound communication so it can then change the destination address to the actual address of the host that has the private address when inbound packets return.

Figure 3.1 presents a simple NAT configuration. A workstation has an address of 192.168.1.10. To access a Web server at IBM, it needs to pass packets through a series of routers—not only its perimeter NAT router, but also any routers within the Internet. Because 192.168/16 falls under the private internetwork space, traffic will not pass back. The NAT router then must change the source address of the packet to its public address, 198.133.219.25, which it then passes to the Internet until it eventually gets to its destination at IBM. When the IBM server needs to pass packets back to the workstation, it really passes it back to the NAT router—specifically the public address. When this router receives the packet, it translates the destination address to 192.168.1.10 and forwards it onto its destination within the private network.

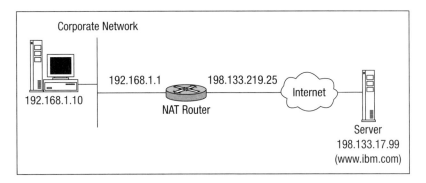

Figure 3.1 Simple NAT network.

It is not necessary for a NAT router to translate packets between a private network and a public network. Network designers can also utilize NAT to simply isolate traffic between private networks or between public networks. NAT between private and public networks is the most common implementation, and is one of the functions of most firewalls on the market.

Note: The NAT router has to keep track of the traffic going in and going out. It cannot just change the address and be done with it. In fact, it builds a table for each source and destination for each connection. This router, therefore, has to have sufficient memory not only for route tables but also for NAT connections.

Hierarchical Addressing

This section discusses hierarchical addressing and how its implementation drastically affects the decision-making mandate of routers.

What Is Hierarchical Addressing?

The best analogy for hierarchical addressing is the existing telephone network. Telephone numbers can be broken down into some very important components. The typical seven-digit number that we use to make calls in our own city has two parts: a three-digit number and a four-digit number, usually separated by a hyphen. The hyphen in fact is not dialed; it is there merely as a memory device. The three-digit number represents the local exchange, and the four-digit number is the actual number. It is easy to see that a local exchange has a maximum of 9,999 different numbers.

Note: The telephone analogy isn't completely historically correct, but for the most part it works for this example and illustrates the points.

AT&T introduced area codes to enable telephone dialing outside local areas. After that, they added country codes to enable the global community to communicate. What we have now for a local address is illustrated in Figure 3.2, which shows a complete telephone number for an address in the greater Seattle area.

Figure 3.2 A typical telephone number in Seattle.

Local residents of Seattle need dial only 555-1234, whereas other residents of North America must to dial 1 plus 206 plus the local number. The 1 tells the local exchange that the call is outside its area, and the 206 forwards it to the telephone equipment in Seattle.

Figure 3.3 shows a complete telephone number for an address in Rome, Italy. Notice that the template for a U.S. number is drastically different from its counterpart in Italy. In fact, the U.S. telephone systems do not have to have any information concerning the system in Italy.

To call Rome from the Seattle number, you must dial 011 to make an international call, 39 for Italy, 06 for Rome, 1234 for the local exchange, and 5678 for the number. The central office in the United States first sees the 011 and recognizes it as an international call. It then passes it to an international long-distance carrier. That carrier (AT&T, for example) sees the 39 and passes it to its counterpart in Italy. The local central office in Seattle doesn't know where the Italian numbers go, nor does it have to. It merely passes the number to a carrier that does know. Notice also that the Italian carrier must then route the call to Rome, where local carriers would pass it to the correct exchange and then the correct number.

The point here is that at no time does any exchange office know exactly where a call should be routed. Think of the ramifications if an exchange office had to know all the routing. It would have to track in real time all the changes all over the world all the time. If someone moved from one Rome neighborhood to another Rome neighborhood, the Seattle office would have to know about it. That would be an absurdity.

The Internet, although it doesn't have exactly the same refined hierarchical structure that the telephone switching system has (telephony has its own set of problems, by the way), is working for a similar goal. To minimize the amount of information that an individual router must have (in the form of a route table), a structure is put into place so that Internet addresses are parsed similar to telephone numbers. When certain patterns are matched on the most significant bits of an IP address—similar to the 011-39 for an international telephone call to Italy—an entire packet is forwarded to a neighboring router that knows about the remaining numbers.

Figure 3.3 A typical telephone number in Rome, Italy.

In this telephone analogy, think of the 011-39-06 of the Rome telephone number as a summary number. If you dial this combination of numbers, any subsequent numbers will reach anywhere in the greater Rome area. These summary numbers will be very important in their similar role for hierarchical addressing for routers.

Advantages of Hierarchical Addressing

Hierarchical addressing has two major benefits:

1. The routing table has a reduced number of entries.

2. Addresses are efficiently allocated.

Routing Tables

Recall in our telephone example that we represented Rome (from Seattle) as 011-39-06. Assuming that Roman telephone numbers uniformly are eight digits in length (which is not necessarily true), this means that traffic destined to as many as 100,000,000 (10^8) numbers can be represented with a single route entry. Similarly, 100,000,000 addresses can be routed to Paris, France, by simply changing the route summarization code to 011-33-1 (33 is the country code for France and 1 is the city code for Paris).

Note: Unlike IP addresses, telephone number lengths vary from country to country (and even sometimes within the same country), which doesn't matter much because of the way the telephone switching systems work. This is where the similarity between telephony and IP routing ends. IP addresses under IPv4 are always 32 bits.

In any case, with a hierarchical addressing system, route summarization is a way of having a single IP address represent a collection of IP addresses. The following benefits come from summarizing these routes:

➤ *More efficient routing*—A single route can be used for thousands of hosts.

➤ *Fewer central processing unit (CPU) cycles devoted to navigating a routing table for a match*—Imagine the difference in effort in traversing 10 items versus 10,000 items, for example.

➤ *Routing tables taking up less memory*—A route takes up finite space. Ten items take up a lot less memory than 10,000 items.

➤ *Easier to troubleshoot*—It is much easier to figure out problems when there are fewer variables. Ten variables are much easier to deal with than 10,000 variables.

Allocation of Addresses

By grouping addresses contiguously, hierarchical addressing can take advantage of all the possible addresses. Better yet, it is easy to see which addresses are available because they are all in the same sequence. If the addresses were random, it would be possible to waste huge numbers due to addressing conflicts.

For example, the classful routing protocols automatically create summary routes at a network boundary. They don't support discontiguous addressing, so some addresses would be completely unusable if not assigned contiguously. This topic is covered in the following section, under "Discontiguous Addressing."

Variable-Length Subnet Masks

3

This section introduces the concept of VLSMs, why they are useful, and how to set them up. We also discuss the use of VLSMs with classless and classful routing protocols.

Using Variable-Length Subnet Masks

VLSMs provide the ability to include more than one subnet mask within a network as well as the ability to subnet an already subnetted network address. The benefits of using VLSM include:

➤ Efficient use of IP addresses.

➤ Capability to utilize route summarization (described in the section "Route Summarization" in this chapter).

Figure 3.4 is a complex example of VLSMs. In this example, the subnet 172.16.0.0/16 is further subnetted at /24, /27, and /30.

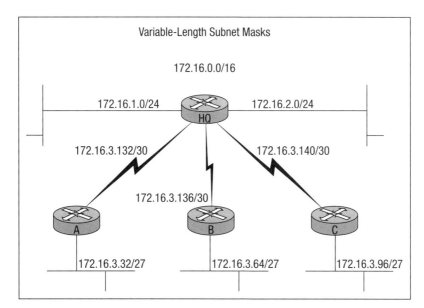

Figure 3.4   Variable-length subnet masks.

The 172.16.0.0./16 network has successfully been divided into subnets using a /24 masking. One of the subnetworks in this range, 172.16.3.0/24, has been further divided into smaller subnets with a /27 masking. These smaller subnets range from 172.16.3.0/27 to 172.16.3.224/27. In Figure 3.4, we have used 172.16.3.32/27, 172.16.3.64/27, and 172.16.3.96/27 for the three remote local area networks (LANs), and we have taken 172.16.3.128 and have broken it down further using a /30 masking.

Recall that a /30 masking leaves two bits—or four addresses—for the host. In most cases, however, only two of these host addresses are usable because the network address and the broadcast address take the upper and lower bounds. The taken networks are 172.16.3.132/30, 172.16.3.136/30, and 172.16.3.140/30.

Keep in mind that we have not utilized four entire networks in the 172.16.14.0/27 span and four entire networks in the 172.16.128/30 span. So there is typically some waste. However, it doesn't come close to the waste that would occur if you had tossed the entire class C space.

Note: Waste is somewhat relative. Our example uses the RFC 1918 private network addresses, so it is somewhat like wasting sunshine—it is a renewable source. On the other hand, real, routable network space would not be wasted so frivolously.

Understanding Variable-Length Subnet Masks

The previous paragraphs have presented a significant amount of numbers. It may not be completely obvious how we arrived at them. Unfortunately, when we do not use class addressing, it is very difficult to visualize why network addresses look so odd.

To understand VLSMs, we need the following:

1. A base network.

2. An estimate of the number of individual networks.

3. An estimate of the number of hosts.

Tip: You have an opportunity to deal with expansion of the number of networks if you don't use up the entire address space on hosts. All IT professionals know that renumbering IP networks is a lot worse than planning ahead of time. It is a delicate balance of whether to maximize hosts and minimize networks or to minimize hosts and maximize networks. But often you have enough play to give breathing room to both.

Our example started with a class B network, a network that is masked at /16. In this case, it is 172.16.0.0/16. Our network topology has two local networks and three remote networks. The local networks (serviced by the HQ Router) need an address space to accommodate up to 253 (2^8-2) hosts each, whereas the remote networks (serviced by Routers A, B, and C), need an address to accommodate up to

30 (2^5-2) hosts each. There is nothing magical about these numbers. Rather, it is why netmasks of /24 and /27, respectively, were chosen.

Let us return now to the question of the number of networks. A network with a netmask of /16 can support as many as 65,534 individual hosts. Clearly, this is overkill for what we want to accomplish (or for what nearly any company might want to accomplish). We also can extend the subnet mask 8 bits and functionally have 255 networks that each can accommodate 253 hosts. We need 253 hosts on two of our networks and 30 hosts on three of our networks. Because 30×3 is 90, this can all fit into a single /24 network with plenty of room to spare.

Accommodating the first two networks is easy—we just subnet assign 172.16.1.0/24 and 172.16.2.0/24 for those nets. Figure 3.5 shows these netmasks.

Notice that the host portion is 8 bits in length, meaning that we have room for up to 253 different hosts, thus meeting our requirement.

Let us attempt now to figure out the remote networks. We know that they need up to 30 different hosts, or at least five bits in the host. If we take one of the /24 networks, we would have three bits to extend the netmask for eight additional networks. Figure 3.6 shows this breakdown.

Table 3.2 shows the eight different networks in dotted binary and dotted decimal notation. The dotted binary reveals something extra. It shows precisely where the networks on Figure 3.4 come from. Note that with the binary representation we can show the extent of the /27 netmask.

In our example, we used only the .32, .64, and .96 decimal representations. But now we want to address the wide area network (WAN) links. Between the routers,

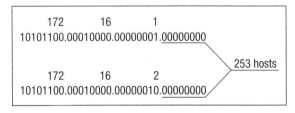

Figure 3.5 Netmasks for 172.16.1.0/24 and 172.16.2.0/24.

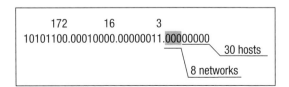

Figure 3.6 Extending the netmask for eight additional networks.

Table 3.2   Dotted binary and decimal representations of the eight /27 networks.

Dotted Binary	Dotted Decimal
10101100.00010000.00000011.00000000	172.16.3.0
10101100.00010000.00000011.00100000	172.16.3.32
10101100.00010000.00000011.01000000	172.16.3.64
10101100.00010000.00000011.01100000	172.16.3.96
10101100.00010000.00000011.10000000	172.16.3.128
10101100.00010000.00000011.10100000	172.16.3.160
10101100.00010000.00000011.11000000	172.16.3.192
10101100.00010000.00000011.11100000	172.16.3.224

only two address are needed—one for each end of the pipe. This means that we need, at a maximum, a /30 netmask. We can take one of the /27 networks and further subnet it.

The next one in sequence, 172.16.3.128, is a fine candidate. We also know that we have to support a minimum of three networks. Remarkably (as with most examples), we can extend the /27 network by three bits, allowing for eight networks, and make a /30 netmask. Figure 3.7 provides a visualization of this process.

Table 3.3 shows the eight different networks in dotted binary and decimal form. Once again, the binary form reveals precisely where the LAN links on Figure 3.4 come from. Note that with the binary representation we can show the extent of the /30 netmask.

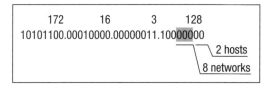

Figure 3.7   Extending the network for 172.16.3.128/27 by three more bits.

Table 3.3   Dotted binary and decimal representations of the eight /30 networks.

Dotted Binary	Dotted Decimal
10101100.00010000.00000011.10000000	172.16.3.128
10101100.00010000.00000011.10000100	172.16.3.132
10101100.00010000.00000011.10001000	172.16.3.136
10101100.00010000.00000011.10001100	172.16.3.140
10101100.00010000.00000011.10010000	172.16.3.144
10101100.00010000.00000011.10010100	172.16.3.148
10101100.00010000.00000011.10011000	172.16.3.152
10101100.00010000.00000011.10011100	172.16.3.156

Note: *Cisco field engineers will recognize that subnetting for these WAN links is mostly unnecessary. They would normally use the* **ip unnumbered** *command on these interfaces, so they would not have to use any IP address between the routers.*

Classless and Classful Routing Updates

VLSMs can be used when routing protocols send subnet masks with a network address. If the protocols don't support this, then you will be limited to networks that fall on eight-bit boundaries—or class boundaries.

Classless Routing Protocols

Routing protocols that include a subnet mask are *classless* routing protocols. These include:

➤ Routing Information Protocol, version 2 (RIPv2)

➤ Open Shortest Path First (OSPF)

➤ Enhanced Interior Gateway Routing Protocol (EIGRP)

➤ Border Gateway Protocol (BGP)

➤ Intermediate-System to Intermediate-System (IS-IS)

Figure 3.8 presents a network in which routers provide updates via OSPF. Because the routers piggyback any network with a subnet mask, as routing updates get sent from Routers A, B, and C, Router D will build a complete routing table with all the networks and subnet masks.

Classful Routing Protocols

Routing protocols that do not send subnet mask information with a network address are known as *classful* routing protocols. Because of this, they do not support VLSMs.

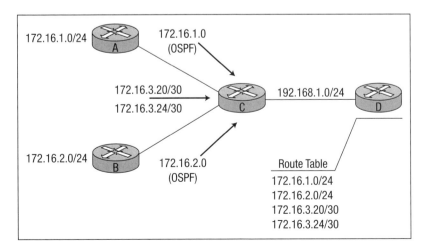

Figure 3.8 Routing updates using classless routing protocols.

These protocols include:

➤ RIPv1

➤ Interior Gateway Routing Protocol (IGRP)

These networks support only one subnet mask per network address because any information gathered in a routing update does not include a subnet mask field. The subnet mask is assumed on the basis of its class. Therefore, a class A network has a /8 netmask, a class B network as a /16 netmask, and so forth.

Figure 3.9 shows a network diagram that is similar to Figure 3.8 with an important difference—there is no Router B, nor are there any networks associated with this router. Routing would not behave correctly given the similar IP addressing scheme. Why? Because Router C cannot get router updates from both Router A and Router B with VLSMs. Router C will assume a /16 netmask because of the 172.16 in the first two octets of the IP address. It cannot build a table with two 172.16s—one to Router A and another to Router B. Therefore, it will use whichever update came in *last,* and traffic destined to the other network would go to the wrong router. This is precisely why the networks associated with Router B are missing, and it is why network topologies with VLSMs are not a good idea when classful routing protocols are used.

Note that Router D in both RIPv1 and OSPF scenarios does build correct routing tables, even though the sizes of the tables are substantially different. The route table has a single entry for 172.16 in the RIPv1 scenario, whereas it has four entries for 172.16 in the OSPF scenario. From Router D's perspective, 172.16's traffic all goes to router C, so even though 172.16 is further subnetted back up to Router A, Router D doesn't care because it would have already passed any packet to Router C.

A large degree of efficiency is gained in having a route table that is smaller and more compact. Not only does the router require less memory to actually hold the

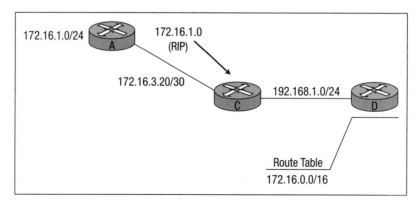

Figure 3.9   Routing updates using classful routing protocols.

table, the CPU requires less processing time to direct packets as well. The reduction of routes is called *route summarization* and is the topic of the next major section of this chapter.

Calculating VLSMs

Previously, we talked about how VLSMs allow you to subnet an already subnetted address. Now let us work on building one from scratch as network design engineers rather than reverse engineering a network diagram (as we did in the previous discussion). Consider the following hypothetical requirements:

➤ You have the subnet address 172.16.224.0/21.

➤ You want to address five hosts.

A 21-bit network leaves 11 bits for the number of hosts. This represents 2,046 ($2^{11}-2$) individual hosts. Because our requirement is to address five hosts, more than 2,000 addresses are wasted. By subnetting 172.16.244.0/21 further, we not only address these five hosts (and likely more), but also create future networks with similar capacities.

To deal with five hosts, we need at least three bits. This gives us six (2^3-2) unique hosts, leaving room for only one additional host. But note that practical experience has shown that leaving room for only one device is sets you up for the requirement for two extra devices within a week. So, instead of using three bits, we use four bits here. This gives us 14 (2^4-2) unique hosts. Although that is not a huge number, it does fulfill the requirement with some grace.

Note: Do not forget the practical wisdom outlined above. However, examinations do not always take the practical route. If there is a question that specifically asks to cover a number of hosts, respond with the number of bits that fulfill this requirement. Being practical in this case might be the wrong answer.

We started with a netmask of /21 and we require four bits for hosts, so this leaves seven bits for the new VLSM subnet. Seven bits represent 128 different networks. A good application for this environment is a corporate office that has many (more than 100) small satellite offices, such as an insurance company or a bank.

Figure 3.10 shows the 172.16.224.0/21 network converted to dotted binary, a small sampling of the 128 different networks, the host field, and the entire network address converted back to decimal.

The first 21 bits comprise the 16 bits in a normal classful network plus the 5 bits that make up the subnet specified in the original requirements. The next seven bits comprise the VLSM subnet that we just calculated. Finally, the last four bits are the

Ordinal	Network / Subnet / VLSM Subnet / Host	
1st	10101100 . 00010000 . 11100000 . 00000000	= 172.16.224.0
2nd	10101100 . 00010000 . 11100000 . 00010000	= 172.16.224.16
3rd	10101100 . 00010000 . 11100000 . 00100000	= 172.16.224.32
4th	10101100 . 00010000 . 11100000 . 00110000	= 172.16.224.48
.	. . . .	.
.	. . . .	.
16th	10101100 . 00010000 . 11100000 . 11110000	= 172.16.224.240
17th	10101100 . 00010000 . 11100001 . 00000000	= 172.16.225.0
18th	10101100 . 00010000 . 11100001 . 00010000	= 172.16.225.16
19th	10101100 . 00010000 . 11100001 . 00100000	= 172.16.225.32
.	. . . .	.
.	. . . .	.
127th	10101100 . 00010000 . 11100111 . 11100000	= 172.16.231.224
128th	10101100 . 00010000 . 11100111 . 11110000	= 172.16.231.240
	← 21-bits → ← 7-bits → ↔ 4-bits	

Figure 3.10 Worksheet for calculating a VLSM.

host field. This, of course, adds up to the 32 bits in an IP address. The netmask is /28, which is the original 21-bit network plus the 7 bits in the VLSM subnet.

The following items can be readily elucidated from Figure 3.10:

- The *Ordinal* column shows that there are indeed 128 separate networks that can be represented in seven bits. Rather than waste reams of paper with a useless 128-entry table, only a few networks are shown.
- The block in the middle is the most interesting because it shows a transition that crosses the traditional classful octet boundary. This is a good example that all but the last octet *do not* remain constant. The third octet actually spans from 224 to 231.
- Indeed, the networks travel chunks of 16 hosts—which is why the fourth octet increments by 16.

Let us now add a small monkey wrench to the mix. Let us suppose the corporate office has taken the five above addresses and allocated them to a remote office. In addition, the company has decided to open 2 additional offices and has plans to open more than 75 remote offices. Kudos to you for your planning because your design has room for more than one network. Figure 3.11 shows how this design can be realized using this newly created VLSM.

Note: *Did you notice that the remote LANs are utilizing the table from the beginning and that the WAN links work back from the end of the table? This isn't a mandate at all. However, it is good practice to separate the types because it makes for easier identification later.*

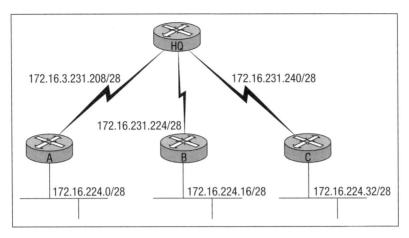

172.16.3.231.208/28   172.16.231.240/28

172.16.231.224/28

172.16.224.0/28   172.16.224.16/28   172.16.224.32/28

Figure 3.11   Implementing the VLSM in a remote network environment.

Figure 3.11, however, still displays some inefficiency. Because the remote LANs are likely using point-to-point serial lines, only two host addresses are actually required: one for the HQ router and one for the remote router (e.g., Router A). We have allocated one of our subnetted /28 networks for each of these links. Yet, a network with a netmask of /28 provides for 14 individual hosts. We have wasted 12 addresses needlessly. Our second mandate of providing 75 remote offices means we will run out of networks if we follow this path. To fix this, let us subnet the *last* network further. As we need more networks, we can continue to peel off more networks in the /28 space and subnet them further. Figure 3.12 shows this subnetting.

By taking the last network that had capacity, we have subdivided it to acquire four additional networks. Better yet, we know that in a point-to-point link, we will never need any more addresses (good thing, because there is no room for expansion). Figure 3.13 replaces the WAN links with the new networks.

Note: Remember that subnets that are unused can be further subnetted. If you use any address from a subnet, that entire subnet is now exempted from being subnetted. This is yet another reason why the example has networks starting from low numbers and increasing, whereas the subnetted networks start from high numbers and decrease.

Ordinal	Network	VLSM Subnet	Subnet	Host
1st	10101100 . 00010000 . 11100111 . 11110000 = 172.16.231.240
2nd	10101100 . 00010000 . 11100111 . 11110100 = 172.16.231.244
3rd	10101100 . 00010000 . 11100111 . 11111000 = 172.16.231.248
4th	10101100 . 00010000 . 11100111 . 11111100 = 172.16.231.252

Figure 3.12   Further subnetting.

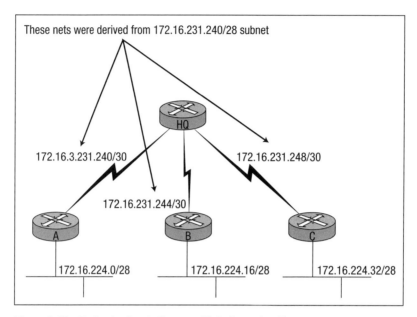

These nets were derived from 172.16.231.240/28 subnet

HQ

172.16.3.231.240/30   172.16.231.248/30

172.16.231.244/30

A   B   C

172.16.224.0/28   172.16.224.16/28   172.16.224.32/28

Figure 3.13   Revised network diagram with further subnetting.

Even though one net has been further subnetted, don't forget about the new net-mask. It is now /30 instead of /28 and is reflected in the network diagram.

Note: Although VLSMs are a terrific way of utilizing IP address space, do not go overboard with them. A well-thought-out design that accommodates with two or even three different netmasks is sufficient. Using more than three will likely add a bunch of confusion. Also, it will make a network more difficult to diagnose when problems crop up.

Discontiguous Addressing

A network utilizes *discontiguous addressing* when two different subnets of the same network (or subnet) are separated by a different network address. Keep in mind that although this is a valid practice, some routing protocols, particularly the classful ones, are incompatible with this scheme.

It is possible to have two networks, say, 172.16.1.0/24 and 172.16.2.0/24 (note the subnet mask length), separated by a different network, 192.168.1.0/24. A problem crops up, however, when we use a classful routing protocol because the routers do not send the subnet mask information. In this case, the networks 172.16.1.0/24 and 172.16.2.0/24 are assumed to be part of the class B space, and they become 172.16.1.0/16 and 172.162.2.0/16, respectively. Do you see the problem here?

The network between 192.168.1.0/24 has now learned two different routes, but they enter into the routing table identically. At this stage, routing to one of the two networks will not occur, but you will not be able to predict which one it will be. If you use discontiguous addressing, make sure that you are using a routing protocol that is classless, or one of the following protocols: RIPv2, OSPF, EIGRP, BGP, or IS-IS. You cannot use either RIPv1 or IGRP because they are classful.

Route Summarization

We have already touched on route summarization several times in this chapter. This section discusses some of the design and implementation considerations of route summarization. Summarization is described fully in RFC 1518 (September 1993), entitled *An Architecture for IP Address Allocation with CIDR*.

What Can Route Summarization Do?

In large internetworks, we can have thousands of network addresses. The Internet is an example of such a large-scale internetwork. For each router to maintain these routes, network performance could be drastically curtailed. Some of the drawbacks include the following:

➤ Larger routing tables mean more processing time to validate and forward packets.

➤ Larger tables mean more storage space on the part of the router.

Route summarization, also called *supernetting,* reduces the number of routes in a routing table because it takes a series of networks and consolidates them into a single summary address. Not all networks can be consolidated. Otherwise, we might just summarize routes down to a single entity and be done with it. Only careful planning and design can lead to effective route summarization.

Figure 3.14 shows two routers, A and B. Whereas Router A needs to know routes to all its peers, it can summarize the three subnetted networks to Router B, which needs only a single-route table entry. Without route summarization, Router B will

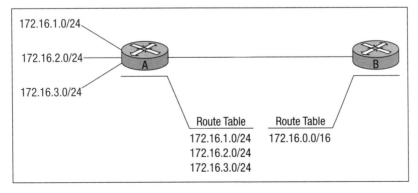

Figure 3.14   Route summarization.

have all three routes in its route table. Yet all of them route through Router A—clearly an inefficiency.

Be very careful when you try to summarize routes. They may not all be completely valid. Figure 3.15 shows a network for which summarization is not possible. Router B cannot summarize the 172.16.0.0/16 network because part of the traffic in this network must go to Router A and part of the traffic in this network must go to Router C.

Because summary masks are binary masks, just like subnet masks, summarization must take place on binary boundaries. Summarization always involves a smaller netmask. In the example in Figure 3.14, our summary mask is 16 bits and it comprises a number of networks that use a 24-bit netmask. Route summarization is most effective when the blocks are contiguous.

Recall the discussion on hierarchical addressing. Route summarization is just such a system, and it inherits the benefits of hierarchical addressing. That is, individual changes to some of the networks do not necessarily imply that they have to propagate to all the routers in the system because the summarization would not change. Remember the example of the telephone system? The telephone office in Seattle does not have to be aware of any movement in Rome because all traffic still gets routed to 011-39-06, regardless.

Routing protocols do support routing summarization with a couple of restrictions, as we discovered earlier in this chapter. Classful routing protocols (e.g., RIPv1 and IGRP) are limited to summarizations that occur on class network boundaries. This makes them somewhat inflexible because it is not always convenient for the summarizations to occur on these boundaries. Classless routing protocols (e.g., RIPv2, OSPF, and EIGRP) work much better. The reason for this is that subnet masks accompany the network address in classless routing protocols, whereas subnet masks are assumed based on the network address.

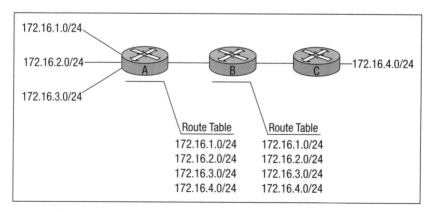

Figure 3.15   Network that cannot have route summarization.

Summarizing within an Octet

Exactly how beneficial can router summarization be? Let us examine its usefulness, for example, for the following list of eight networks that are connected to a router:

➤ 172.16.0.0/24

➤ 172.16.1.0/24

➤ 172.16.2.0/24

➤ 172.16.3.0/24

➤ 172.16.4.0/24

➤ 172.16.5.0/24

➤ 172.16.6.0/24

➤ 172.16.7.0/24

Can we summarize these networks? If so, what is the most efficient method for doing so? Table 3.4 shows each network converted into its dotted binary equivalent.

Although there are many summary routes in this configuration, the one that comprises the largest number of networks will be the best because it minimizes the number of route table entries. You can acquire the summary route by looking at the number of bits that match in all of the addresses. In this example, the first 21 bits of each of these networks are identical. Anything longer than that will require multiple summary routes. Therefore, the best summary route is 172.16.0.0/21.

If you plan your IP addressing scheme using this hierarchical nature, you will be able to have route summarization work to your advantage. This becomes most important when summarizing VLSMs.

Summarization works when the number of addresses is a power of two. If it isn't, divide the addresses into groups and summarize separately. Limited summarization is much better than no summarization.

Table 3.4   Summarization of a set of networks.

Network	Dotted Binary Equivalent
172.16.0.0/24	10101100.00010000.00000000.00000000
172.16.1.0/24	10101100.00010000.00000001.00000000
172.16.2.0/24	10101100.00010000.00000010.00000000
172.16.3.0/24	10101100.00010000.00000011.00000000
172.16.4.0/24	10101100.00010000.00000100.00000000
172.16.5.0/24	10101100.00010000.00000101.00000000
172.16.6.0/24	10101100.00010000.00000110.00000000
172.16.7.0/24	10101100.00010000.00000111.00000000

Summarizing VLSMs

Just as we were able to keep dividing networks into subnets to suit our needs, we can also benefit from summarization in the reverse direction. Each time we subdivide a network, the routes can be summarized so that downstream routers have absolutely no idea that traffic within a single network may go down drastically different paths. Although Figure 3.16 doesn't actually show any breakthrough information, it does show the route summaries that can come out of merging multiple networks.

In Figure 3.16, two summarizations are taking place:

1. Router A summarizes the 172.16.1.0/26 network with the 172.16.1.64/26 and 172.16.1.128/26 networks. It then can pass a single update with these combined networks to Router D.

2. Router D summarizes the 172.16.128.0/18 network with the 172.16.64.0/18 network as well as with the summarized update from Router A. It will then consolidate these into a single update that it can pass farther downstream, perhaps to a corporate router. The summarized network in this case coincidentally is a Class B subnet mask.

Note: Just because using VLSMs happen to fall on classful boundaries doesn't suddenly mean that it is appropriate to start using a routing protocol that supports only classful networks. On the contrary, you should stick with a classless protocol. Imagine what would happen if you tried to scale the network later and you had forgotten this tidbit of information. You would be faced with a problem of why router updates were occurring in some segments but not in other segments. In an age where 24-hour/7-day uptime is not just mandatory but critical, you will get a lot more sleep if you heed these words—or at least you get to keep your job.

Implementation Considerations

There is absolutely no question about the importance of route summarization. The benefits can be staggering, especially if you consider that the entire Internet makes

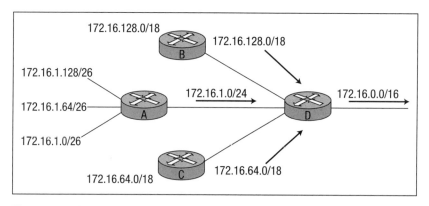

Figure 3.16 Router summarization in a VLSM network.

significant use of this technique. If it didn't, many routers would be taxed in terms of processing (of course, Cisco could always release more powerful models).

To take advantage of route summarization, the following rules must be followed:

1. Multiple IP addresses must share the same high-order bits or the networks must be somewhat contiguous. The more subnetted networks that get absorbed, the greater the benefit. You cannot simply merge random networks or the benefits go away.

2. Routing protocols, for maximum flexibility, must also deliver the subnet mask with the network. Otherwise, summarization will be limited to the classful boundaries. Although there is always some advantage to summarization, this is not optimal.

3. Routing tables must have the capacity to support classless routing.

There is some risk to summarization or oversummarization. If there is any routing failure, no packets will be able to find their way back to their destination. This is where having specific detailed routes would be better than having a generalized route.

Route Summarization and Cisco Routers

Until now, our discussions have been general. Each router manufacturer implements certain protocols, and Cisco is no different. However, due to Cisco's widespread acceptance in the industry, it has matured far beyond many other router manufacturers. As such, it makes sense to briefly discuss the specifics of Cisco routing and summarization. The particulars for individual protocols will be covered in their respective chapters.

Cisco IOS software on routers manage route summarization two ways:

➤ Sending route summaries

➤ Selecting routes from route summaries

Sending Route Summaries

For the RIP, IGRP, and EIGRP routing protocols, routing information is automatically summarized at classful network address boundaries. Summarization is automatic for all routes that have classful network addresses that differ from the major network address of the interface doing the advertising. You must manually configure OSPF for summarization.

Automatic summarization is not a solution in all cases. In fact, summarization may be undesirable. For instance, you would not want it to occur where address space is discontiguous. The routers wouldn't necessarily know that there are other networks elsewhere. For the EIGRP and RIPv2 routing protocols, auto summarization can be disabled.

Selecting Routes from Route Summaries

A router may acquire multiple routes to a particular destination. If this occurs, the router will keep the match that has the longest prefix. This is not unusual because it chooses the path that has the most specific information.

Summarizing and Discontiguous Networks

Figure 3.17 shows an example of a discontiguous network.

Classful routing protocols summarize at their network boundaries automatically. This is not changeable with RIPv1 or IGRP (because the fundamental protocol would then change). It does, however, have a couple of important consquences:

➤ Subnets are not advertised, only the classes are.

➤ Discontiguous subnets are not visible to each other. This is usually very bad.

Figure 3.17 shows that Router A will advertise to Router B that its route to 172.16.0.0/16 is available, and Router C will advertise to Router B that it has a route to 172.16.0.0/16 as well. This is because RIPv1 will not advertise subnets (it cannot). Router B will not be able to reliably route packets to either network.

Classless protocols such as RIPv2, OSPF, and EIGRP can resolve this situation only if they do not do summarization. In this case, the routers would advertise the individual networks. Router B would distinguish the difference between packets destined for 172.16.1.0/24 through Router A and 172.16.4.0/24 through Router C.

Classless Inter Domain Routing

CIDR creates blocks of multiple class C addresses. These blocks can be combined to create larger classless sets of addresses. ISPs acquire these blocks, which in turn allocate the subblocks to their customers. For the United States, the American Registry for Internet Numbers (ARIN) issues IP addresses.

Note: ARIN, as its name implies, is associated only with the Americas. Other organizations exist for other geographic areas, including RIPE NCC for Europe and APNIC for the Asia Pacific region.

As of May 2000, ARIN no longer issues IP addresses in blocks of less than 20 bits. At one time, organizations could "order" a class C address from ARIN, which would route packets to the company's selected Internet Service Provider (ISP). This is no longer true. Twenty bits, of course, represents 16 class C networks.

Figure 3.18 shows a WHOIS query with ARIN.

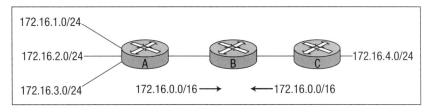

Figure 3.17   Discontiguous network.

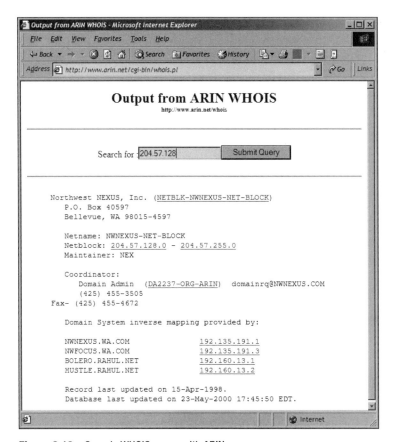

Figure 3.18   Sample WHOIS query with ARIN.

The range from 204.57.128.0 through 204.57.255.0, or 128 class C networks, was allocated to the ISP Northwest NEXUS. Northwest NEXUS will summarize this entire block and pass it for propagation to the Internet. This, of course, means that only one route summarization was sent, not 128 routes for these C classes. While we were praising the benefits of minimizing route tables and mini-mizing processing time, we ignored the benefit of the traffic associated with the routing protocols.

RFC 1518 (September 1993) and RFC 2050 (November 1996) describe CIDR in detail.

Chapter Summary

This chapter has addressed the following topics:

1. The finite number of IP addresses. At some point, this number will be exhausted and the Internet will no longer be able to accommodate the addition of new networks. The NIC has created several mechanisms to slow the consumption of IP networks.

2. Subnet masks. The subnet mask and its relationship to classless and classful routing protocols is explored.

3. Hierarchical addressing. Hierarchical addressing reduces the amount of knowledge and information that routers must maintain to deliver packets to their ultimate destination.

4. How to use variable-length subnet masks. VLSMs provide the ability to specify a different subnet mask for the same network number on different subnets. Their use can help optimize available address space.

5. How to create variable-length subnet masks. Creating VLSMs is a fairly easy process, but careful attention must be paid to the number of hosts that are required because often it must balance with the number of new networks that are created. It is also best to draw out the binary representation because the decimal representation does not do a good job of showing shifts in bits.

6. Route summarization. With route summarization, a single summary route, rather than multiple routes, is advertised to other areas. This saves bandwidth and route table space, as well as processing time.

7. Classless Inter Domain Routing. Many of this chapter's topics deal with curbing the consumption of IP addresses. CIDR is the effective method for creating large blocks of address space to be distributed to downstream ISPs. By doing so, it can make very effective use of route summarization.

Review Questions

1. Which of the following are solutions to the rapid consumption of IP addresses (not all solutions are listed)?

    a. Network Address Translation

    b. Hierarchical addressing

    c. Address allocation from the IANA

    d. Classless Inter Domain Routing

2. We are given the following network: 192.168.1.0/24. We want to subnet this network to provide seven WAN links that each remote up to 30 users. How many bits should be in the new netmask?

  a. 25

  b. 26

  c. 27

  d. 28

3. How many hosts are possible if we have a VLSM subnet mask of /29?

  a. 6

  b. 8

  c. 14

  d. 16

4. We are given the following network: 192.168.1.0/24. How can we subnet it to provide eight WAN links that each support up to 30 users?

  a. You cannot because not enough bits are available to deal with these networks.

  b. Subnet by adding three bits to the netmask, leaving five bits for the hosts.

  c. You must shrink the number of bits in the host field and increase the number of bits in the network field.

  d. Because the router can deal with multiple networks, assign the same address space from remote LAN networks to the WAN networks. The routing protocols should be able to forward the packets to the correct LAN.

5. Which of the following routing protocols support classless routing updates?

  a. RIPv1

  b. RIPv2

  c. OSPF

  d. IGRP

6. Which of the following addresses are not parts of the NIC's private address space?

  a. 172.32.0.0/16

  b. 10.5.25.0/24

  c. 192.168.254.0/24

  d. 172.0.0.0/8

7. When can or should route summarization be used? (Choose all answers that apply.)

   a. When a corporate router has several contiguous subnets that share the same high-order bits.

   b. When the router is capable of IP classless routing.

   c. When the routing protocols are capable of transmitting the network and the subnet mask.

   d. Router summarization should occur only at IANA facilities.

8. Given the following Cisco IOS configuration lines, is route summarization possible?

```
interface Ethernet 0
    ip address 172.16.20.1 255.255.255.0
interface Ethernet 1
    ip address 172.16.21.1 255.255.255.0
!
router eigrp 100
    network 172.16.0.0
!
```

   a. Yes

   b. No

9. What are the benefits of using a hierarchical IP addressing scheme? (Choose all answers that are correct.)

   a. A reduction in the size of route tables

   b. Better utilization of IP addresses

   c. More routes to the destination network

   d. Elimination of all local routes

10. With the network 192.168.1.0, what step should be taken to make more efficient use of this address space?

   a. Assign multiple masks to the network

   b. Assign a netmask of /8

   c. Assign a netmask of /16

   d. Assign a netmask of /24

Real-World Projects

The two projects listed in this section are not related. They separately involve VLSMs and route summarization. This is because we are looking at things from the design stage. Typically, when you work on something such as VLSMs, you automatically create the route summarization as you continue to create the new subnets. This would, in effect, defeat the exercise for examining a network and determining whether route summarization is possible.

Project 3.1 involves the task of creating a number of networks using VLSMs, whereas Project 3.2 involves the task of determining whether a set of networks can be summarized in a single routing entry.

Project 3.1

Amy Smith is given the network address 172.16.100.0/22 and is asked to create a subnet that can handle three individual networks of 100 hosts each.

1. Amy starts by investigating whether this is even possible. She writes some basic information down in the form of a worksheet.

2. What is the minimum number of bits required to represent 3 and the minimum number of bits to represent 100? Amy converts the bits to binary and figures out that she needs two bits for the network field and seven bits for the host field.

Decimal	Binary	Bits Needed	Maximum in Decimal
3	11	2	4
100	1100100	7	128

3. To accommodate the network and host fields (in addition to the original subnet), Amy adds the number of bits together and gets nine (two network + seven host).

4. Amy then compares this number to the number of hosts that are available to her. Her original subnet mask was 22, and an IP address is 32 bits long. She therefore has 10 bits at her disposal (32-22 = 10).

5. At this stage, Amy can increase the number of host bits or subnet bits, meaning she will have as many as eight networks and 128 hosts, or four networks and 256 hosts. She decides to go with eight networks because it has the least amount of headroom (and probably is a wiser engineering decision because of this).

Note: Amy has four networks available, but she needs only three. She has 128 hosts available, but she needs only 100. In expansion terms, she may or may not be able to predict whether the growth will occur in the number of networks or the number of hosts. But, clearly, if the network grows by one, she will be at capacity. By increasing the network field to three bits, she will have plenty of room to grow.

It is possible that Amy will be wrong, but the odds are that she will be correct. Any sort of planning done when possible can only reap better rewards later.

6. Amy creates the new subnet mask by adding the three VLSM bits onto the original value. The subnet mask is /25. She then fills out the networks by writing them out in dotted binary form to make them more obvious. She also writes the networks in decimal form (she zeroed out the host portion). She then writes down the three required networks with the new subnet mask.

Network	Binary	Decimal
1.	10101100.00010000.01100100.00000000	172.16.100.0/25
2.	10101100.00010000.01100100.10000000	172.16.100.128/25
3.	10101100.00010000.01100101.00000000	172.16.101.0/25

Note: *Two bits represent four networks, so there will be a leftover network. In addition, the networks are designed to fall on 128 host boundaries. Each of the networks, therefore, can have 128 individual hosts on them, giving a headroom of 28 hosts over the requirement of 100.*

Project 3.2

Calvin White is given a set of networks. He is asked to see if he can make things more efficient by using router summarization.

Calvin is given the following networks:

➤ 172.16.12.0/24

➤ 172.16.13.0/24

➤ 172.16.14.0/24

Calvin takes the following steps to determine if he can summarize the networks:

1. Calvin writes the networks on a worksheet and converts the networks to their dotted binary equivalents:

   172.16.12.0/24 = 10101100.00010000.00001100.00000000

   172.16.13.0/24 = 10101100.00010000.00001101.00000000

   172.16.14.0/24 = 10101100.00010000.00001110.00000000

2. Calvin then scans the networks from the left side of the bit field, remembering to look for the common high-order bits. He notices that the bits are the same all the way up until the 22nd bit, so, he writes down this number and zeros out the rest. The number of bits in the netmask is 22.

   10101100 . 00010000 . 00001100 . 00000000 = 172.16.12.0/22

3. Calvin can then use this summarization to publish these networks to downstream routers.

CHAPTER FOUR

Routing Protocols Overview

After completing this chapter, you will be able to:

✓ Characterize distance-vector and link-state routing protocols

✓ Understand how routers build their routing tables

✓ Understand how routers select the best route to a destination

✓ Describe the scalability problems associated with distance-vector routing protocols

✓ Introduce the scalable routing protocols OSPF, EIGRP, and BGP

✓ Compare and contrast the major features of OSPF, EIGRP, and BGP

Routing protocols are used to ensure that data packets get from their source to their destination. For a variety of reasons, it is difficult to imagine that packets do not always take the same route. In fact, it is better to state that packets often might not take the same route.

The path from source to destination depends on the switching abilities and states of the individual routers. The routers themselves monitor the traffic on their immediate links as well as links of their neighbors. Various factors, including bandwidth and physical cost of a link, can cause paths to be dynamically desirable or undesirable. The routers involved communicate this information, and the protocol is called a *routing protocol*.

Routing and the Need for Routing Protocols

Routing is the process of transferring an item from one location to another. For building a scalable computer network, we'll be discussing routers, the devices that perform the function of moving data between locations.

Keep in mind that a single router or equivalent entity participates in the process of routing. In very small cases, it may be the entire process. In a scalable environment, however, a group of routers make up the routing process. With large corporate environments, the control may lie with the IT staff; but on a global scale, where public networks such as the Internet are involved, only partial control may lie with the IT staff.

Key Information Required to Begin Routing

To route an object or data packet—or anything else for that matter—the router needs to know the following information:

➤ The destination network-layer address

➤ A valid path to the destination

➤ Sources to acquire routes or paths to the destination

➤ The outbound interface used to reach the destination

➤ The best path or paths to the destination

Before the router can begin routing, the first essential piece of information it needs to have is the logical network-layer address of the destination. Generally, this will be an IP address, but it can also be an address from another protocol suite, such as IPX or OSI.

When the router has the destination address in hand, it must next be able to know how to reach the destination address. This is accomplished by communicating with neighboring routers via a routing protocol to gather information about the networks these neighboring routers are aware of. This information is stored in the routing table, which lists all the networks that a router has learned about. If a network listed in the routing table is valid, then it can be used.

The routing table also specifies the interface used to reach the network. This item is required by the router because it has no other way to know which interface should be used to reach the destination. In addition to the outbound interface, the router must also know the network-layer address of the router from whom the network was learned. This router is always referred to as the *next hop* because it is usually directly connected.

Even though the router could at this point successfully reach the destination, simply being able to reach the destination is not enough. The router must be able to reach it as quickly and efficiently as possible. A path that meets such requirements is said to be the *best path*. To determine the best path, the router uses its routing protocol's metric. Because each routing protocol uses a different metric, however, there are different ways to determine the best path. Usually, though, the smallest metric for a destination equates to the best path.

For example, Routing Information Protocol (RIP) is a routing protocol that uses a metric called *hop count*. Hop count refers to the number of routers that are traversed to reach a destination. When the router learns of multiple paths to the same destination, it chooses the path with the least number of routers (i.e., the smallest hop count). This route is considered the best path. If multiple paths had the same hop count, the router would consider up to six of these to be equally best paths and would use them simultaneously to forward user traffic.

Other examples of metrics include cost, which is used by the Open Shortest Path First (OSPF) routing protocol and is based on media bandwidth, and composite, which is used by Interior Gateway Routing Protocol (IGRP) and Enhanced IGRP (EIGRP) and is based on several media properties (including bandwidth and delay, which are the only properties used, by default).

Understanding the Need for Routing Protocols

A network is a dynamic entity, and as such it changes throughout its life (which is hopefully long). As companies add and retire network segments, new routes are added or deleted. Manually adding and subtracting routes from each and every router is a ridiculous task; in addition, it impedes traffic for the duration of the manual update. In a large network that spans even a small regional area, this could take hours, if not days—clearly an unacceptable undertaking.

Routing protocols provide a mechanism to automatically provide routers with the critical information they need. Routing protocols may use different mechanisms to acquire the information, but the goal is essentially the same. Some routing protocols are proprietary to specific manufacturers, some have historic anomalies that reveal an era when computer networks were substantially smaller, and some are incredibly flexible in their ability to adapt to changing network environments.

This chapter introduces the prominent routing protocols and compares and contrasts their strengths and weaknesses. Individual chapters are devoted to the modern protocols.

A Comparison of Protocol Types

Surprisingly, all the routing protocols can be grouped into two distinct categories: *distance-vector* and *link-state,* which are really meant for small networks and large networks, respectively. Distance-vector protocols came first because early computer networks were small and somewhat autonomous. Because computer networks are always growing (or we'd like them to), and something called the Internet came around and made networks very large, link-state protocols arose from the need to be much more flexible. They incorporated many of the newer, more efficient features to overcome the deficiencies inherent in distance-vector protocols. Table 4.1 summarizes these two categories.

Note: Outside of the IP protocol suite, there are equivalent distance-vector and link-state protocols for IPX and AppleTalk, as well as any other network protocol suite. Cisco Systems has since relegated these protocols to other examinations. To be consistent with the outline of the Building Scalable Cisco Networks objects, only the IP protocol suite is covered by this book.

This chapter describes the differences in how each protocol category, distance-vector and link-state, exchange the following information:

➤ Hierarchical addressing

➤ Neighboring routers

➤ Path discovery

➤ Selecting a route or path

➤ Maintaining routing tables

Table 4.1   Routing Protocol Categories.

Category	Protocol	Characteristic
Distance-vector	RIP, IGRP	Small networks
Link-state	OSPF, IS-IS	Large networks

Hierarchical Addressing

We covered hierarchical addressing extensively in Chapter 3. When used in the context of route summarization, or the collection of multiple networks in a single network route, less information is passed around to the individual routers.

For example, suppose you had a network expanding throughout the globe but also had a significant presence in the major cities of the United Kingdom: London, Manchester, Edinburgh, Glasgow, Birmingham, Newcastle, Cardiff, and Belfast. Rather than deal with all the individual routes to each of these cities from each and every router in the United States, Canada, Mexico, France, and so forth, you could have a single route leading to a major hub router in London, the most probable location for a centralized connection point. Therefore, when a router anywhere in the world needed to reach the UK region, it would simply use the route leading to the major hub router in London. Figure 4.1 shows how this works.

4

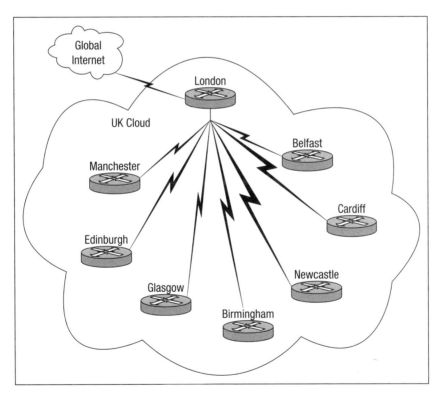

Figure 4.1   Global network to the United Kingdom via London.

Neighboring Routers

In a small network environment, a downed router is likely detectable whenever someone calls the help desk and complains of an inability to access a remote or semi-remote resource. But because it is a small network, the impact is commensurately small. On the other hand, in a large network, a downed critical router can drastically affect hundreds, thousands, or even more users. Depending on the types of applications—real-time, mission-critical, and so forth—the results could be disastrous. For the help desk to wait for the wave of support calls is not only absurd, it can cost an organization thousands or even millions of dollars.

Link-state protocols have a process to identify neighboring routers, to periodically poll them, and to potentially take action if a neighbor is not reachable (i.e., either the neighbor is down or the link to the neighbor is down—the same result). The next two sections show the key differences in how the distance-vector and link-state categories of protocols deal with neighbors.

Distance-Vector Method of Identifying Neighbors

Following are some data points regarding the methods that distance-vector routing protocols use to identify neighbors:

➤ Has no formal method of learning about neighbors.

➤ Detects when a neighbor is not available only when a routing update from a neighbor is not received during a regular update interval.

➤ Interval for detecting the availability of a neighbor ranges from 10 to 90 seconds, depending on the protocol.

Link-State Method of Identifying Neighbors

Following are some data points regarding the methods that link-state routing protocols use to identify neighbors:

➤ Formally establishes a connection (hence the term link-state) between each and every neighbor using a special protocol.

➤ Detects when a neighbor is down when the link protocol is breached, that is, when communication is not received within a predetermined amount of time.

➤ Interval for detecting the availability of a neighbor is typically 10 seconds.

Path Discovery

For small networks with just a few routers, distance-vector protocols can use the "hearsay" method for communication because the relative amount of traffic for the routing protocol itself is small (hopefully) in comparison to the data that the network would ordinarily carry. Besides, in a small network, the entire routing table should take up no more than a few small packets.

However, in a very large network with more than 100 routers, a route table could potentially become significant. With each router sending tables to all its neighbors, especially across slow wide area network (WAN) links, bandwidth on certain links may devote much of their capacity just for the routing protocol—clearly a waste of space and time.

Routers that support the link-state routing protocols send information for specific links, not their entire link-state table. This has the advantage of reducing network overhead as well as speeding convergence times. Also, because each router receives the link-state information firsthand, there is less chance for routing errors to be propagated throughout the network—a clearly desirable side effect.

Distance-Vector Method of Path Discovery

Following are some data points regarding the methods that distance-vector routing protocols use to discover paths:

➤ Every router creates a routing table to all directly connected networks. The routing table is then sent to each of its immediate neighbors.

➤ Routers incorporate all the routing tables from each neighbor.

Link-State Method of Path Discovery

Following are some data points regarding the methods that link-state routing protocols use to discover paths:

➤ Every router creates a link-state table that includes information about the entire network.

➤ Every router sends update packets with information about links to all other routers in the internetwork.

➤ Routers receive update packets from their neighbors, acquire the contents, and then pass the information to other neighbors.

Selecting a Path or Route

Small networks may be implemented with the same networking technologies, such as purely 100Mbps Fast Ethernet. However, as companies grow, they may have legacy wiring systems (e.g., 4Mbps and 16Mbps Token Ring), backbones (e.g., CDDI or FDDI), WAN links (e.g., T1, fractional DS3, or ISDN), or any combination of these. Some links are inherently faster than others. Distance-vector routing protocols typically use the hop count, but often this isn't the best path. For instance, you may

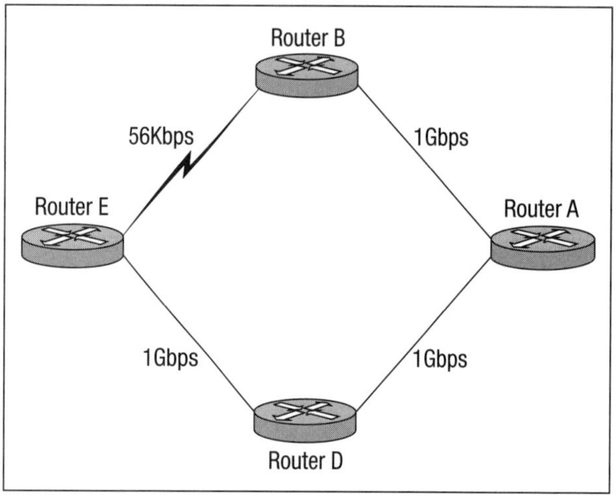

Figure 4.2 Which route would you choose to get from Router E to Router B?

have a single WAN link or a multihop of Gigabit Ethernet. Which one would likely pass more data? Which one would have the smallest metric? Figure 4.2 illustrates this situation.

All things being equal, you can probably intuit that the best path from Router E to Router B would be the path through the multiple Gigabit Ethernet links rather than the path through the 56Kbps link. In this case, hop count would not be a reliable indicator of the best path. You would need to choose a routing protocol that instead took into account link speed (media bandwidth).

Link-state protocols use bandwidth to determine the actual "distance" to a destination. Therefore, they work much better in real-world, large-scale internetworks.

Distance-Vector Method of Selection

Following are some data points regarding the methods that distance-vector routing protocols use to select routes:

➤ Typical metric method used is the number of routers, or hops, between the source and destination.

➤ The path with the lowest number of hops is declared the best path.

➤ The maximum number of hops usually doesn't exceed 15 (for RIP and RIPv2).

➤ The Bellman-Ford algorithm is used to determine the shortest path.

➤ Routing tables can include multiple equal cost routes, which are used for route redundancy and load balancing.

Link-State Method of Selection

Following are some data points regarding the methods that link-state routing protocols use to select routes:

➤ Metric used is a calculation based on the bandwidth of the link. This is called the *cost*.

➤ The path with the lowest total cost is the best path.

➤ Shortest Path First (SPF), sometimes called Dijkstra's algorithm, is the algorithm used to determine the lowest cost.

➤ Routing tables can include multiple equal cost routes, which, like distance-vector methods, are used for route redundancy and load balancing.

4

Maintaining Routing Tables

In small networks, distance-vector routing protocols typically exchange their routing tables in periodic intervals. This is acceptable because the routing tables are relatively small and the amount of traffic generated is less significant relative to normal network traffic. In a large network, however, the routing tables can be gigantic, so transmitting entire tables to every router can be disastrous. Periodically updating all the routers with all the tables can lead to a saturation of the links with just the traffic due to the routing protocol, not even considering the ability to pass actual data. Once again, link-state protocols address this issue.

Distance-Vector Method of Routing Table Maintenance

Following are some data points regarding the methods that distance-vector routing protocols use to maintain routing tables:

➤ When a single router determines that the internetwork has changed (either by its own configuration or through an update from a neighbor) it updates its own routing table and then sends the *entire* routing table to its neighbors.

➤ When a router incorporates a routing table from a neighboring router, it recalculates the cost via the Bellman-Ford algorithm. The resulting table is then forwarded to its neighbors.

➤ When the routing tables converge, the routers reach a steady state.

➤ Every update interval (30 seconds for RIP; 90 seconds for IGRP), each router once again sends its routing table to its own neighbors.

Link-State Method of Routing Table Maintenance

Following are some data points regarding the methods that link-state routing protocols use to maintain routing tables:

➤ When a single router determines that the internetwork has changed, it updates its link-state table and sends *only* the changed entries to all routers in the internetwork.

➤ When a router receives an update from a neighbor, it adds it to its own link-state table.

➤ Routers run the SPF algorithm to determine the best path(s).

➤ During steady state, or if the internetwork has not changed, routers send updates only on route entries that have not been updated in a specific interval. This interval is determined by the protocol and can last anywhere from 30 minutes to 2 hours.

Scalability and Routing Protocols

With the number of growing dot-com companies, as well as with consolidation in virtually every industry, scalability is not a matter of "will it happen?" but a matter of "when will it happen?" Therefore, scalability is a critical issue. An IT manager may suddenly encounter a network that has grown to three times its original size. Therefore the scalability of a network demands a scalable routing protocol.

In addition, interoperability may become an issue. Not every network consists of solely Cisco or Nortel equipment. And it isn't often practical to replace $100,000 of hardware for the convenience of a routing protocol, so choosing a standardized instead of a proprietary protocol goes a long way.

Distance-Vector Scalability Limitations

A smaller network, or one that has fewer than 100 individual routers, is far more forgiving of nondata or nonapplication data. This is usually because there is so much bandwidth available that it hardly shows up as a significant portion of the traffic. For IT managers, it is often easier to throw a network device, such as a switch to replace a hub, than to sit down and evaluate congestion problems (not to mention that it requires a lot less time).

However, as the network grows, the amount of traffic due to the routing protocols starts to grow. With it come a number of problems, noticeable in the fact that data takes longer to get from its source to its destination throughout the network. There are three obvious problems that occur:

➤ Increased bandwidth utilization

➤ Increased central processing unit (CPU) utilization

➤ Network convergence or steady-state delay

Increased Bandwidth Utilization

Remember that distance-vector routing protocols periodically send their entire routing tables to all their neighbors. The larger the network (with more and more routers), the larger the table. In addition, each router acquires a table from its neighbor and then passes it to all of its other neighbors. Although this may not seem like a lot of traffic, it is very easy to see that this is an exponential model. With fixed bandwidths on links (100Mbps for Fast Ethernet down to 56Kbps for a relatively slow frame-relay link), the pipes can soon fill up with just router protocol traffic.

Increased CPU Utilization

For a router to accept an update from a neighbor, recalculate routing and cost tables, and then pass an entirely new update to all neighbors requires processing power. Again, as a network scales (and routers are added), routing tables increase in size as the number of neighbors increases. Accommodating the growth and dealing with decisions to route packets to the best destinations are increasingly problematic issues with distance-vector protocols.

Network Convergence Delay

Recall that a change in a routing table causes a recalculation and then a forwarding of the table to neighbors. Neighbors must then take the new table into account and do the same recalculation and pass it on to their neighbors. These calculations take time, and because the routing packets also take time to pass from router to router (depending on the link performance), it takes a calculable amount of time for the network to converge. By induction, the more routers in an internetwork, the more time is required before network convergence can occur. Prior to network convergence, real data packets may take longer to get to their destination or make take less optimal routes, decreasing the user experience dramatically.

Link-State Scalability Features

Link-state routing protocols address each deficiency in the distance-vector routing protocols.

Bandwidth Utilization

Link-state protocols send an update that concerns only new information, not the entire routing table. Even though updates are needed because of changing environments (downed links, at-capacity links, and so on), the amount of traffic required to advertise the changes throughout the entire internetwork is minimized in the link-state protocol.

In addition, when there are no changes in an internetwork, updates can be sent out at predefined intervals rather than at arbitrarily small intervals. Some protocols allow as much as two hours between updates.

CPU Utilization

In general, the smaller number of packets sent out for routing updates requires less work on the part of the CPU for each router. In addition, working on routing table deltas rather than an entire routing table substantially reduces the amount of CPU processing. Furthermore, with less time working on updates and more time actually routing packets, the capacity of individual routers to handle a scaling environment is increased.

Network Convergence

Routers that implement distance-vector routing protocols do not maintain a formal relationship with their neighbors. Routers that implement link-state routing protocols, on the other hand, do establish a formal neighbor relationship. This relationship is established and maintained by the use of the *hello* protocol. Hello protocol packets are sent at short intervals (e.g., every 10 seconds for OSPF). When a router fails to receive a hello from a neighbor, it assumes that the link with the neighbor is down and proceeds to flood its other interfaces with this update information. This proactive procedure of maintaining tables is far quicker than the method used by distance-vector routing protocols and thus minimizes the network convergence times.

Summarizing Distance-Vector and Link-State Characteristics

Table 4.2 provides a useful chart for comparing and contrasting distance-vector and link-state routing protocol characteristics.

Table 4.2   Comparison of distance-vector and link-state attributes.

Distance-Vector	Link-State
Routing protocol examples: RIP, RIPv2, IGRP	Routing protocol examples: OSPF, IS-IS
Broadcasts entire routing table at periodic intervals	Multicasts selected information only when a topology change is detected
Uses a metric based on distance and direction	Uses a metric based on media bandwidth (in OSPF's case)
The best path is typically the path with the least number of hops	The best path is typically the fastest path
Maximum number of supported hops is typically 15	Maximum number of supported hops is 65,535 (in theory)
Establishes no formal peer relationships with neighbors	Establishes formal peer relationships with neighbors using the hello protocol

(continued)

Table 4.2   Comparison of distance-vector and link-state attributes *(continued)*.

Distance-Vector	Link-State
When a router detects a directly connected link failure, the router immediately poisons the attached network, broadcasts a triggered update, and removes the network from its routing table	When a router learns of a directly connected link failure, the router multicasts a routing update to selected neighbors
When a router receives an update indicating a failed network, the router immediately sends out a triggered update and goes into holddown for the route	When a router receives an update indicating a failed network, the router processes the update and, if it is valid, copies it to its topological database and multicasts an update to selected neighbors
Must maintain complete knowledge of the internetwork	Can maintain partial knowledge of the internetwork
Classful	Classless
Supports equal-cost load balancing	Supports equal-cost load balancing
Slow convergence	Fast convergence
Does not scale	Scales very well

Introduction to the Scalable Routing Protocols OSPF, EIGRP, and BGP

Now that we have addressed the major scalability issues with classic distance-vector routing algorithms and have seen how link-state algorithms offer a scalable alternative solution, we are now ready to introduce the routing protocols that empower many of today's Internet routing infrastructures. Specifically, we will be taking a brief yet detailed look at the following routing algorithms:

➤ Open Shortest Path First (OSPF)

➤ Enhanced Interior Gateway Routing Protocol (EIGRP)

➤ Border Gateway Protocol (BGP)

Note that whereas OSPF is a true link-state routing protocol, EIGRP and BGP are considered advanced distance-vector routing protocols. However, even though EIGRP and BGP are stigmatized with a distance-vector designation, they are no less capable of meeting a network's scalability requirements. In fact, as we will see in this chapter as well as later ones, both of these routing protocols have been shaped tremendously by link-state characteristics.

Open Shortest Path First

OSPF is a link-state routing algorithm that was designed to address the scalability issues that classic distance-vector routing algorithms such as RIP encountered in growing enterprise networks during the 1980s. Defined in Request For Comments

(RFC) 2178, OSPF has become the Internet's standard interior gateway protocol due to its support of the following scalable features:

➤ *Robust metric*—OSPF uses a cost metric based on media speed or bandwidth. Because a cost metric has no hop count constraint, OSPF implementations are allowed to stretch across thousands of routers.

➤ *Incremental routing updates*—Routing updates are sent out immediately when topology change occurs. In addition, topology changes do not cause entire routing tables to be advertised.

➤ *Fast convergence*—Topology changes are allowed to affect only certain areas of the OSPF internetwork.

➤ *CIDR, VLSM, and route summarization*—These features are supported in a hierarchically designed internetwork. Routing protocols that support such features are considered classless.

➤ *Minimum resource consumption*—OSPF has the potential to consume sub-stantial router and network resources, but the application of OSPF's scalability features compensates for this problem extremely well.

➤ *Support for various WAN topologies*—OSPF can be configured to operate over various WAN topologies in multiple modes.

An OSPF router operates with other OSPF routers in what is called an *area*. Each router residing within the same area maintains the same routing information in a topological database. This topological database contains all the routes within an area but only certain routes from outside the area. The reason an OSPF router is able to omit certain routes from outside its area becomes apparent when we consider that OSPF is a classless routing protocol that supports VLSM and route summarization. Both are features that allow networks to be aggregated into only a single route, a *summary route*, and advertised to OSPF neighbors. The summary route is what the OSPF neighbors would refer to in lieu of having several individual routes. Figure 4.3 provides an illustrative example of route summarization.

In Figure 4.3, the router from Area 1 is aggregating several networks into a single route. This summary route is propagated to the rest of the OSPF areas. As a result, routers outside Area 1 are able to reach any network within this area without having explicit knowledge of all the networks therein.

In addition to advertising routes, OSPF must also calculate the best path for each route it knows of. The topological database has all the routes known to the OSPF router, but these may not necessarily be the best routes available. As a result, OSPF uses the *shortest path first (SPF)* algorithm, also called the *Dijkstra* algorithm, to calculate the best path for each network listed in the topology table. These best paths are then placed in the router's routing table.

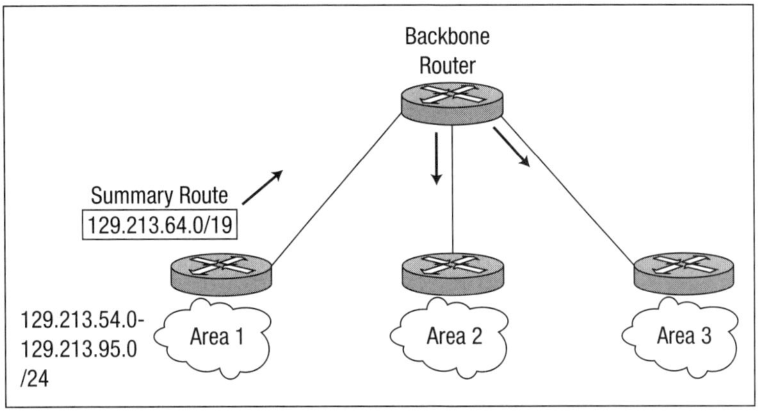

Figure 4.3 Route summarization eliminates the need to know of every single possible route in the internetwork.

Whenever an OSPF router joins the network, the OSPF router will go through a series of stages in which the router must converge with the rest of the network. These stages in OSPF operation can be summarized as follows:

1. Discover and maintain neighbor relationships.

2. Elect designated routers (DRs) and backup designated routers (BDRs).

3. Build and synchronize the topological database.

4. Choose the best path.

5. Notify the OSPF internetwork of topology changes whenever they occur.

OSPF routers accomplish these stages using various link-state advertisement (LSA) packets. These packets are designed to facilitate communications between OSPF routers and to support hierarchical OSPF features, such as route summarization, in the internetwork.

OSPF has, in fact, many hierarchical features besides route summarization, such as area designation, load balancing, and virtual links. All these features have been designed for the purpose of allowing OSPF to scale with large internetworks. Without these features, OSPF would not be able to manage escalating resource-consumption problems or deal with the diminishing network performance that occurs as result of these resource-consumption issues. It is therefore necessary to use OSPF's hierarchical features whenever a single area has outstripped its capacity to adequately meet critical scalability requirements.

Enhanced Interior Gateway Routing Protocol

EIGRP is a hybrid routing algorithm that was designed to blend the best characteristics of distance-vector and link-state algorithms together to create a highly scalable routing platform. Designed by Cisco Systems to be a successor to IGRP, EIGRP supports the scalability requirements of large, multiprotocol enterprise networks. As a result, EIGRP supports the following scalable features:

➤ *Composite metric*—EIGRP uses a metric based on several media attributes, including bandwidth and delay. The use of a composite metric allows routers to more accurately assess the feasibility of any given network path.

➤ *Incremental updates*—Updates are multicast to neighbors only when a topology change occurs. In addition, only those routers that need to be informed of the topology change are notified.

➤ *Fast convergence*—Like OSPF, EIGRP convergence occurs very fast with the help of its scalable routing features.

➤ *Multiprotocol support*—Unlike OSPF, EIGRP supports additional network-layer protocols besides IP, such as IPX and AppleTalk.

➤ *Unequal-cost load balancing*—Unlike most routing protocols, EIGRP supports load balancing across unequal-cost links.

➤ *CIDR, VLSM, and route summarization*—Unlike OSPF, route summarization can occur at arbitrary network boundaries.

➤ *Reduced resource consumption*—EIGRP allows minimal consumption of router and network resources, such as bandwidth and CPU utilization.

➤ *Traffic bounding*—EIGRP can be configured to limit the range of EIGRP packets.

➤ *Support for NBMA networks*—Nonbroadcast multiaccess (NBMA) networks are supported by EIGRP. EIGRP bandwidth utilization can be controlled on these networks to prevent EIGRP from consuming the entire bandwidth of oversubscribed links.

EIGRP uses the *Distributed Update Algorithm (DUAL)* to perform all route computations and to select the best path through the use of EIGRP's composite metric. DUAL allows all routers involved in a topology change to synchronize at the same time and also guarantees a loop-free topology.

When a topology change occurs, the router that detected the change looks in its topology table (a storage component similar to OSPF's topological database) to find an alternative path to the network. If a valid alternative path is available, then the router places this route in its routing table and sends out a multicast update to the EIGRP internetwork. However, if an alternative path is not found in the router's topology table, then an EIGRP *query* packet is sent to ask neighboring routers for an alternative path. The process of querying is an efficient method that EIGRP employs to discover if neighboring routers have a path for the failed route. Once the router has received all replies to its queries, the router decides what to do with the queried route, based on these replies, and subsequently multicasts a routing update to the EIGRP internetwork that informs all routers of the decision it made.

Just as for OSPF, this convergence process is affected by the range that updates and other such routing information packets have in the EIGRP internetwork. That is, such hierarchical features as route summarization and EIGRP *traffic bounding* have a direct impact on the extent and impact that topology changes have on the routers in an EIGRP autonomous system.

EIGRP does not use the concept of areas to facilitate any hierarchical routing schemes. Instead, EIGRP uses the concept of autonomous systems (although EIGRP does not use autonomous systems for the same purposes that OSPF uses areas).

EIGRP can scale to thousands of routers and is able to support numerous complex local area network (LAN) and WAN topologies. The scalability features that EIGRP provides to growing enterprise networks allows them to meet technical goals and requirements with the assurance of knowing that EIGRP will always deliver without fail.

Border Gateway Protocol

BGP is an interautonomous routing algorithm that was designed as a replacement for the now-obsolete Exterior Gateway Protocol. Specified in RFC 1771, BGP has become the standard exterior routing protocol for the current Internet and is used extensively therein to connect enterprise networks to Internet Service Providers (ISPs) and to connect ISPs with other ISPs. The current version of BGP is BGP4.

Following are some of BGP's more salient features:

➤ Policy-based routing

➤ Fast convergence

➤ Robust metrics called path attributes

➤ Unsurpassed scalability

➤ Support for CIDR and route summarization

➤ Reliable and incremental routing updates

The primary function of BGP is to communicate network reachability information between *autonomous systems* (ASs). An autonomous system is defined as a group of routers under the same technical administration, using an interior gateway protocol (IGP) to route packets within the AS, and using an exterior gateway protocol (EGP) to route packets between ASs (RFC 1771). An IGP is a routing protocol that is used within an AS, and an EGP is a routing protocol that is used between ASs. Both terms can apply to BGP, because BGP is used both within and between ASs. When BGP is used within an AS, it is termed Internal BGP, or IBGP, and when used between ASs it is termed External BGP, or EBGP. It is common—and highly recommended—for BGP to run with another IGP within an AS. This is because BGP was not really designed to be an IGP; it was designed to be an exterior routing protocol. As a result, many BGP implementations require that OSPF, EIGRP, or some other scalable IGP run within the AS along with BGP (see Figure 4.4).

This cohabitation between BGP and a different IGP generally means that redistribution will be occurring on some of the AS's routers. Redistribution is a configurable process that allows a router running two different protocols to exchange routing information between its two protocols. This is necessary because two different routing protocols cannot communicate information with each other any other way. It is similar to two people speaking different languages—an interpreter is needed to translate between the languages. This is essentially what redistribution is: a translation between two different routing protocol languages. In a BGP environment, the process of redistribution generally occurs from BGP into an IGP (such as from BGP into OSPF or BGP into EIGRP). That is, BGP-learned routes are translated (redistributed) into the IGP so that the router's IGP can advertise these routes to other IGP-speaking peers. As a result, there is no need to run BGP on all routers within the AS as long as the routers are running some IGP. It is therefore quite common for BGP routers to be placed only on the AS borders where there are connections to external ASs.

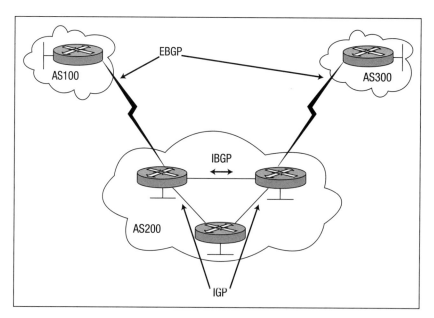

Figure 4.4   The operating domains of EBGP, IBGP, and IGP.

As we previously mentioned, the primary purpose of BGP is to exchange network reachability with other BGP routers. When two directly connected BGP routers initialize, the first thing they do is open up a TCP connection with each other. The TCP connection allows both routers to become what are known as *BGP peers* or *BGP neighbors*. Two BGP peers initially exchange their full routing tables with each other and thereafter exchange only incremental routing updates whenever a topology or configuration change occurs. All BGP updates are sent reliably, meaning that their delivery is guaranteed.

4

BGP updates contain network reachability information, and they also contain what are called *path attributes*. Path attributes are the metrics that BGP uses. These path attributes are not really similar to the metrics that we have thus far become accustomed to seeing. This is because BGP path attributes are a different breed of metric. They are metrics bred from what is termed *policy-based routing*. BGP is a policy-based routing protocol. This means that BGP bases its routing decisions not on technical metrics, such as hop count, bandwidth, or cost, but rather on policy-based metrics, such as AS-path, weight, and MED, to name a few. These policy-based metrics allow BGP routers within an AS to *control* the routing information that enters and leaves the AS. This policy for defining how traffic is controlled is a policy born from the enterprise network's *administrative rules* for defining exactly with which external ASs and external networks the enterprise should be allowed to communicate. If, for example, a certain external network was not trusted, then an administrative rule would be drawn up stating what the exact policy regarding this untrusted network should be. Once this policy was formulated, network engineers could proceed to choose the appropriate *BGP policy*, using BGP's path attributes, and program the routers accordingly. Chapters 9 and 10 cover BGP policy and path attributes in greater depth.

Summarizing OSPF, EIGRP, and BGP Features

Table 4.3 presents a useful chart for comparing and contrasting the scalable routing protocols introduced in this chapter.

Table 4.3   Comparing scalable routing protocol features.

Routing Protocol	Distance-Vector or Link-State	IGP or EGP	Metric	Unique Features
OSPF	Link-state	IGP	Cost (a function of bandwidth)	Supports areas; operates in multiple modes on WAN topologies
EIGRP	Advanced distance-vector	IGP	Composite (generally a function of bandwidth and delay)	Multiprotocol support; unequal-cost load balancing; EIGRP bandwidth modification
BGP	Advanced distance-vector	Either	Path attributes	Policy-based routing

Chapter Summary

IT professionals must implement routing protocols to ensure consistent network connectivity for their growing networks. Distance-vector routing protocols are appropriate for smaller networks, whereas link-state protocols are appropriate for larger networks.

Whereas the scalable routing protocol OSPF serves to uphold the link-state stereotype, the scalable routing protocols EIGRP and BGP are shattering the distance-vector stereotype by incorporating such link-state features as fast convergence and reduced resource consumption. In the next chapter, we will explore in depth the first of these three scalable routing protocols, OSPF.

Review Questions

1. Which are link-state protocols?

   a. RIP

   b. OSPF

   c. IGRP

   d. EIGRP

2. Which statements are true of distance-vector protocols? Choose two.

   a. Uses the Shortest Path First (SPF) algorithm.

   b. Typically determines the best path by the lowest hop count.

   c. Is the toughest type of routing protocol to configure.

   d. Sends out updates periodically regardless of network change.

3. Which statements are true of link-state protocols? Choose two.

   a. Learns about neighbors to ensure bidirectional communication before sending routing information.

   b. Sends out multicast updates when network changes occur.

   c. Uses the Bellman-Ford algorithm for calculating the best path.

   d. Has slower convergence compared to distance-vector routing protocols.

4. Which two of the following items are required to route an object?

   a. The source address

   b. The destination address

   c. At least two possible routes to the destination

   d. The best path(s) to the destination

   e. A routing protocol

   f. The neighbor's incoming interface

5. How do distance-vector routing protocols respond after detecting a directly connected link failure?

   a. They go into holddown and send out a multicast update.

   b. They issue a broadcast update to neighbors indicating that the route has been placed in a steady state.

   c. They poison the network, broadcast a triggered update, and remove the route from their routing table.

   d. They poison the network, multicast a triggered update, and remove the route from their routing table.

6. What is hop count?

   a. The number of servers with which the router can communicate.

   b. The ratio of neighboring routers to remote routers.

   c. The number of networks that are traversed along a path to a destination.

   d. The number of routers that are traversed along a path to a destination.

7. How does a link-state protocol respond to a remote topology change?

   a. It waits until the holddown interval has passed before sending an update.

   b. It notes the accepted topology change and multicasts a routing update to selected neighbors.

   c. The router must respond with a broadcast routing update to all neighboring routers.

   d. The router never responds to remote topology changes because its neighbors respond for the router.

8. Which one of the following is not a scalability problem associated with distance-vector routing protocols?

   a. Bandwidth utilization

   b. Supported number of routers

   c. Small routing tables

   d. CPU utilization

9. How does a link-state routing protocol learn of neighbors?

   a. It senses their carrier-detect signal.

   b. It learns via a routing update.

   c. It learns via the hello protocol.

   d. The link-state protocol does not learn of neighbors, only networks.

4

10. Which of the following are reasons why convergence is slower with distance-vector protocols than with link-state protocols? Choose two.

    a. Every router must be informed of topology changes.

    b. A TCP connection must be established with neighbors before routing information can be exchanged.

    c. Entire routing tables are sent out.

    d. The router can notify its neighbors of a failed link only at the next scheduled update.

11. Which of the following are features of the OSPF protocol? Choose four.

    a. Slow convergence due to broadcast routing tables

    b. Metric based on media bandwidth

    c. Support for various WAN topologies

    d. No support for route summarization

    e. Unequal-cost load balancing

    f. Incremental updates

    g. Support for multiple areas

    h. Use of the Bellman-Ford algorithm

12. Which of the following are features of the EIGRP protocol? Choose four.

    a. Unequal-cost load balancing

    b. Metric based on hop count

    c. Support for multiple network-layer protocols

    d. Use of the Shortest Path First (SPF) algorithm

    e. Inefficient use of network resources

    f. Sending of full routing tables to every router in the internetwork

    g. Use of query packets to ask neighbors if they have an alternative path

    h. Ability to limit the range of EIGRP traffic

13. What is the essential purpose of BGP?

    a. To exchange network reachability information with other BGP routers.

    b. To exchange periodic routing updates with all directly connected neighbors.

    c. To be an interior gateway routing protocol.

    d. To communicate only with BGP routers that lay outside the autonomous system.

14. What is BGP policy-based routing?

    a. The use of technical-based metrics, such as bandwidth and hop count.

    b. When routers are unaware that they can reach certain remote networks.

    c. The use of policy-based metrics to control the traffic that passes through an autonomous system.

    d. A type of routing in which the routers themselves choose the policy-based metrics that will implement network policy.

15. What is the first thing two BGP routers must do before they can exchange routing information?

    a. Exchange neighbor information

    b. Establish a TCP connection

    c. Find out if the neighbor's routing information is valid

    d. Clear their BGP routing tables

4

Real-World Projects

Networks come in many shapes and sizes. You may have networks that contain two computers hooked up with a null modem cable or you may have networks that expand across thousands of routers and contain millions of users. Most networks will generally fall somewhere between these two extremes.

Networks vary not only in physical design but in technical requirements as well. Some networks expect growth to be static, other networks expect minimal growth, and still other networks expect dramatic growth. Some networks expect user traffic to increase only slightly, whereas others expect user traffic to increase substantially.

These types of conditions and requirements shape the decisions network engineers make when determining the best products, technologies, and protocols to select for their networks. Sound decisions will always be made when the best options are chosen for the established requirements.

In the following scenario, we examine a network and analyze its technical requirements for such features as scalability and performance. Based on the requirements set forth, we proceed to figure out which class of routing protocol—distance-vector or link-state—is most suited to meeting the network's requirements.

Characterizing Our Network

Figure 4.5 depicts the logical topology of a LAN comprising five routers. Each link in this Ethernet LAN has a bandwidth of 10Mbps.

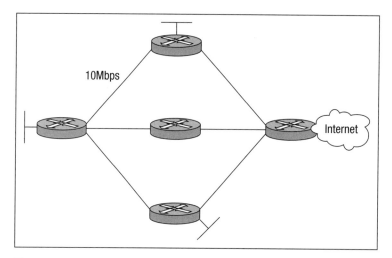

Figure 4.5 Example of an Ethernet LAN.

Business and technical administrators for the LAN expect the network to grow by three or four routers within the next five years. They also expect that user traffic within the network will remain well within the handling capacity for routers and media bandwidth, so traffic congestion is not an issue.

The administrators have also stated two more requirements for the LAN. The first is that any routing protocol chosen for the network should be easy to configure and should not be too difficult to troubleshoot. The second is that topology changes should be dealt with as quickly as possible.

All the LAN's requirements, whether conditional or arbitrary, have equal priority.

As the network administrator, you have been delegated the task of figuring out which routing protocol class, distance-vector or link-state, would best meet the needs of this network. You began first by gathering the information on which you will base your decision:

Project 4.1

To assess your network's requirements:

1. First determine how much future growth is expected in your network.

Based on the expected requirements you have been given, you find that the network is expected to grow only by three or four routers within the next five years.

2. Determine if network traffic is expected to be an issue with your network.

Based on the expected requirements you have been given, you find that the network is not expected to have any issues with traffic congestion.

3. Determine if any other requirements will influence your selection of the routing protocol class.

You find that the routing protocol for the network must be easy to configure and not too difficult to troubleshoot. In addition, fast convergence is required.

Project 4.2

To determine which routing protocol class best meets your network's requirements:

4

1. Match your network's scalability requirement with the best class.

Because your network will not achieve a hop count over 15, the best class is distance-vector. Link-state is best suited for large networks.

2. Match your network's traffic requirement with the best class.

Traffic in the network is expected to always be minimal, so it does not matter which routing protocol class is chosen to meet this requirement. You may therefore match it with both classes.

3. Match your network's other requirements with the appropriate routing protocol class.

For the requirement that the routing protocol be easy to configure and not too difficult to troubleshoot, distance-vector would be the best class. Link-state is comparatively more difficult to configure and troubleshoot.

For the requirement that convergence should be fast, the best class would be link-state. Link-state has a comparatively faster convergence time than distance-vector.

4. Choose the routing protocol class that had the most matches.

The distance-vector class matched three out of four of the network's requirements, whereas the link-state class matched two out of four (technically speaking, of course). You therefore choose the distance-vector class for your network.

CHAPTER FIVE

OSPF in a Single Area

After completing this chapter, you will be able to:

✓ Describe the benefits that OSPF offers over distance-vector routing protocols

✓ Discuss the five OSPF stages of operation in a single-area broadcast topology

✓ Discuss OSPF operation in single-area nonbroadcast topologies

✓ Configure OSPF for the appropriate network topology

✓ Monitor and troubleshoot OSPF in a single area

This chapter offers a high-level overview of Open Shortest Path First (OSPF) operation, configuration, and verification within a single area. It discusses the primary network topologies over which this scalable routing protocol is capable of running, including the broadcast multiaccess and nonbroadcast multiaccess networks, as well as some of the issues that arise with OSPF's implementation within these environments. Finally, the hands-on project at the end of this chapter involves an OSPF case study, which will allow you to practice and solidify some of the concepts and skills you have gained from this chapter's presentation of the Internet's most valued interior gateway protocol.

Introduction to OSPF

OSPF is a link-state routing algorithm that was designed in 1988 as an open-standard solution to the scalability problems that Routing Information Protocol (RIP) was encountering in large internet-works. RIP, as a distance-vector routing protocol, was limited in its operation to 15 router hops and would consume costly bandwidth by broadcasting full routing tables every minute to an entire network. For a growing corporate enterprise seeking to expand and optimize its data infrastructure, RIP no longer stood as a viable solution to meeting Internet scalability requirements. It was quite clear that a new interior gateway protocol (IGP) was needed that could address these critical needs. Consequently, OSPFv1 was created in 1988, although it was never deployed due to its experimental status. It wasn't long, however, before an optimized version, OSPFv2, found deployment and subsequently ushered in OSPF as the Internet's premier IGP for meeting technical requirements in performance, availability, and security.

Some of OSPF's most salient features include the following:

➤ *Robust metric*—OSPF uses a cost metric based on media speed or bandwidth. Because such a metric does not use hop count to make the routing decision, OSPF has virtually no limitation to the number of routers it can cross. Additionally, having a speed-based metric means that this link-state protocol can more accurately assess a link's capacity to handle traffic loads and therefore choose the path that offers the best bandwidth performance.

➤ *Fast convergence*—When a topology change occurs, OSPF immediately responds by flooding the entire internetwork with multicast link-state advertisements (LSAs) that apprise all routers of the topology change and simultaneously let all routers recompute the best path. This is in stark contrast to traditional distance-vector algorithms, which require full routing tables to be broadcast only at scheduled intervals.

➤ *Hierarchical routing*—OSPF follows a hierarchical approach to routing by dividing an internetwork into what are known as areas and defining the functions that these areas perform, analogous to the Cisco three-layer model, which defines the traffic that occurs at each layer and hence the functions that each layer's routers perform. Likewise, in an OSPF environment, routers situated within certain areas are responsible for generating and receiving certain types of OSPF traffic. The benefits of having this design are that you can cut down on the amount of traffic (and thereby minimize router workloads and free up network bandwidth) by minimizing the number of routers that are involved in dealing with the various types of OSPF traffic.

➤ *Route summarization*—A design strategy that incorporates the concepts of areas and hierarchical traffic flow also facilitates route summarization by obviating the need for any one router to have to keep track of all possible routes in an entire OSPF internetwork. With route summarization, area routes can be aggregated and advertised to other areas as a single route.

➤ *Variable Length Subnet Masks (VLSMs)*—The ability of OSPF to summarize routes coincides with its ability to advertise subnet masks along with routes. This feature is necessary for Classless Inter Domain Routing (CIDR), in which the traditional class A, B, and C default routing prefixes no longer need identify the network portion of an IP address.

➤ *Load-balancing*—OSPF has the capacity to maintain up to six equal-cost paths in its routing table for a destination, thereby allowing traffic to load-share across multiple links.

➤ *Authentication*—OSPF has the ability to use clear-text passwords and MD5 cryptography for the purpose of validating routing updates to ensure that the source of updates is in fact a legitimate source and not a hacker possibly attempting to corrupt routing information.

➤ *TOS-based routing*—An application that practices type of service (TOS) routing can set the IP TOS bit in its data packet's IP header to specify the type of route over which the traffic should be sent. There are five types of service that IP packets can request: best effort delivery, minimal delay, minimal cost, maximum reliability, and maximum throughput. Based on the TOS an application requests, OSPF can choose the path that best meets this traffic's specified requirement. For example, when OSPF receives a packet that specifies minimal delay, it will choose the path with the least delay and route the packet on this path.

Along with these essential features, OSPF maintains three types of routing repositories that each store information peculiar to an aspect of OSPF behavior, ranging from statistics on discovered neighbors, to maps of the internetwork, to entries stating the best routing paths in the internetwork. However, these information warehouses do not operate mutually exclusively from one another because they all evolve from the same information-gathering processes and all depend on each other to manage information necessary to sustaining OSPF's behavioral diversity.

OSPF's three data repositories are:

➤ The neighbor database

➤ The topological database

➤ The routing table

The Neighbor Database

The neighbor database contains all of a router's known neighbors that reside within the same area. An OSPF router is considered a neighbor if it has established bi-directional communication with another OSPF router. This process of establishing bidirectional communication to achieve neighborship will be covered in a later section.

The Topological Database

The second type of repository for OSPF data is called the topological database (also known as the link-state database), which stores all routes in the OSPF internetwork and indicates how these routes are interconnected. All routers in the same area maintain identical topological databases. A router that belongs to multiple areas will maintain a topological database for each area of membership.

The topological database is initially constructed from the neighbor database of each area router in a process in which OSPF packets known as LSAs are exchanged between adjacent routers. These LSAs are the essential ingredients for the topological database, as well as the primary mechanism for communicating routing information, and contain such items as:

➤ LSA type

➤ Router ID of the LSA's source

➤ Route(s) being advertised

➤ Cost of route(s)

Note that there are seven types of LSAs, each distinguished based on the information they contain and the routers that originate them. Despite these distinguishing features, however, all LSAs share one common purpose: serving as the encapsulation for OSPF routing information.

Table 5.1 provides an overview of the seven LSA types. For this chapter, we will deal with only the first two of these LSA types, the router-LSA and the network-LSA.

The Routing Table

The third and final repository for OSPF information is the routing table. The routing table lists the best routes in an internetwork based on the least-cost criterion, and

Table 5.1   LSA types.

Type	Name	Description
Type 1	router-LSA	Each router within an area advertises a single router-LSA that describes all of the router's active interfaces and neighbors.
Type 2	network-LSA	A router that gets elected to be a designated router (DR) will advertise a network-LSA that describes all attached routers on the DR's segment.
Type 3	network-summary-LSA	A router that lays on the border between two areas (called an area border router, or ABR) advertises network-summary-LSAs that describe routes to various areas within the OSPF internetwork.
Type 4	ASBR-summary-LSA	Using this type of LSA, an ABR will let areas know how to reach the ASBR (a router that lays on the border between the OSPF internetwork and an external autonomous system).
Type 5	AS-external-LSA	Using this type of LSA, an ASBR will let areas know how to reach external autonomous systems.
Type 6	group-membership-LSA	This LSA is used in Multicast Open Shortest Path First (MOSPF) to locate multicast group members.
Type 7	NSSA-LSA	This LSA is used in NSSAs (not-so-stubby areas).

is constructed from the topological database. Unlike the topological database, each router's routing table is unique because the path calculation is a function of each router's unique location within the internetwork.

As mentioned at the beginning of this chapter, there are unique types of OSPF network topologies. The four most common of these are stated as follows:

➤ Broadcast multiaccess

➤ Nonbroadcast Multiaccess (NBMA)

➤ Point-to-multipoint

➤ Point-to-point

Each of these networks has a unique operational and design consideration. The following sections of this chapter will explore in depth these considerations and present the fundamental router IOS commands necessary for defining and configuring these OSPF environments.

OSPF over Broadcast Multiaccess Networks

An IP broadcast multiaccess network is an environment in which all devices that reside on the same layer-three segment listen and react to packets transmitted among each other. The obvious example of this type of network would be an 802.3 Ethernet, pictured in Figure 5.1.

As seen in Figure 5.1, host A transmits a packet that, no matter what the destination is, will be seen by all nodes that attach through a hub directly to the physical cabling

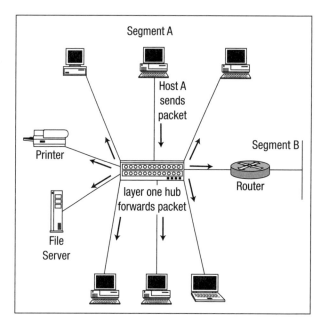

Figure 5.1   Ethernet network.

of segment A. Remember that a layer-one hub does not offer any segmentation capabilities, which means that when a hub receives a frame it automatically forwards the frame out all ports without checking the contents to make an intelligent forwarding decision. However, devices situated outside segment A would not receive host A's transmission unless the router that encloses segment A determines that the destination is remote (that is, on another segment). The router is therefore the device that restricts the automatic propagation of signal transmissions, and in doing so always defines the extent that broadcast networks cover.

Referring once again to Figure 5.1, after receiving the packet sent by host A, all devices would consequently rip the packet open just enough for their Ethernet adapter's interface processor to examine the Ethernet MAC address and decide whether to continue processing the packet. If the destination MAC address happened to match a receiver's own MAC address, the interface processor could immediately relay the packet to the receiver's central processing unit (CPU) for further processing. All other devices on host A's segment would consequently have discarded the unicast packet on determining that the MAC address did not match one of their own. For these devices, no CPU cycles would have been consumed.

There are conditions, though, in which a packet that does not have a matching data-link address undergoes CPU processing. One such circumstance is found when a packet is destined for a broadcast address, represented in Ethernet as 0xffffffffffff. A device that receives one of these broadcast packets will automatically deliver the packet over to its CPU to determine whether the packet is destined for its own segment, because the packet could be destined for another segment instead. The receiver would not know for sure until the CPU examined the layer-three IP address (recall that a Network Interface Card's [NIC] interface processor operates only up to the data-link layer, which means it does not understand IP addresses). But no matter to which particular network a broadcast packet is addressed, the packet is necessarily processed by all CPUs residing on the sender's segment.

As discussed earlier, distance-vector routing protocols, such as RIP, use this broadcast method for transmitting routing updates. OSPF, however, takes a much more efficient approach by utilizing multicasts in its hierarchical operations. Multicasts are transmissions that devices use to specify a subset of hosts on an internetwork that have been configured to receive the multicast transmission. A host that wishes to receive a multicast transmission must be configured either manually or dynamically with the IP multicast address of the multicast application in which the host wishes to participate. In OSPF, multicasting happens to be an entirely dynamic process that requires no manual configuration other than the commands for initializing the OSPF routing process.

To illustrate the basic multicast process, Figure 5.2 shows a common OSPF broadcast topology in which multiple routers connect to each other through a shared local area network (LAN) segment. From a layered perspective, this topology is the same as your run-of-the-mill Ethernet segment; that is, the topology still conforms to Ethernet 802.3 specifications and still represents one layer-three IP subnet. The only difference is that instead of populating the network segment with workstations and servers, the segment is now composed of routers and an interconnecting device, which, for the purposes of this diagram, is a hub router.

In Figure 5.2, the non-OSPF routers will immediately drop the OSPF packets as soon as they discover the MAC address is an unrecognized one. No CPU work is

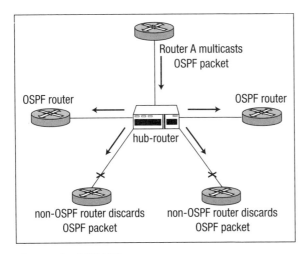

Figure 5.2   OSPF LAN.

wasted in the process. (There are, though, some NICs that pass all multicasts to the CPU, regardless of whether they are recognized.)

OSPF multicasting processes occur differently over the various types of OSPF networks; however, the essential purposes of OSPF multicasting remain unchanged. These essential purposes are most clearly brought out in the broadcast multiaccess environment, where OSPF multicasting is used to carry out the following tasks that represent the five stages of OSPF operation:

➤ Discover and maintain neighbor relationships

➤ Elect designated routers and backup designated routers (DR/BDRs)

➤ Build and synchronize the topological database

➤ Choose the best path

➤ Notify the internetwork of topology changes

The following sections explore these stages of OSPF operation, as well as OSPF configuration procedures in the single-area broadcast network. Then, we will take a look at how OSPF modifies some of these operational parameters to integrate with the nonbroadcast environments of NBMA, with point-to-multipoint, and with point-to-point.

Neighbor Discovery

Whenever OSPF routers first initialize, they join the IP multicast group of 224.0.0.5, the AllSPFRouters address. Using this address, each OSPF router will multicast hello packets onto the subnetwork and also listen for replies to these hellos. The result of this hello procedure is a bidirectional establishment of communication between all OSPF neighbors. Following are the typical contents of a hello packet:

➤ *Router ID*—This is the highest IP address of the router's active loopback interfaces; if there are none, then the router will use the highest IP address of its other interfaces. For instance, if no loopback interface was configured, and if ethernet 0 was 136.108.4.19 and serial 0 was 136.108.7.1, the router ID would be chosen from serial 0. The router ID is the designation by which the router is known to the OSPF internetwork.

➤ *Hello and dead timers*—Not only are hello packets used to discover neighbors, hellos are also used to make sure that these neighbor relationships stay active. Every hello interval, which is by default 10 seconds, neighbors will multicast each other. If a neighbor is not heard from within 40 seconds (the default dead interval), that neighbor will be considered down.

➤ *Neighbors*—All neighbors with which the router has established bidirectional communication will be listed in the hello packet.

➤ *Area ID*—This is an administratively defined designation that is shared by all router interfaces within the same area.

➤ *Router priority*—A router's priority value is the criteria for choosing a DR and BDR.

➤ *DR and BDR*—To centralize routing functions within an OSPF seg-ment, a DR and BDR are chosen during OSPF's initialization process. Their router IDs are listed in the hello.

➤ *Authentication password*—This encrypted password authenticates two OSPF routers that wish to communicate with each other. The passwords on both peer routers must match if a communication session is to occur.

➤ *Stub area flag*—There are several types of OSPF areas, one of which is a stub area. A router that belongs to a stub area will carry this flag in its hello packet to announce its stub area membership.

The following three steps describe the neighbor discovery process and identify the OSPF states that occur during this beginning stage in OSPF operation:

1. An OSPF router in a down state initializes its internal OSPF data processes and proceeds to multicast a hello packet out all interfaces to the AllSPFRouters address 224.0.0.5.

2. All OSPF routers residing on the same segments as the transmitting router receive the hello packet and examine it to determine whether neighborship can be established. A hello packet's timer intervals, area ID, password (if configured), and stub flag (if configured), as well as the subnet mask must match exactly on both OSPF routers if neighborship is to occur. If these criteria have been met, the routers receiving the hello packet will subsequently add the sender to their neighborship database. This is Init state.

3. All neighboring routers respond to a sender's hello by unicasting a hello packet of their own to the sender, who would then go through the same procedure of examining the packet's contents to ensure matching parameters. There is now, in addition, another criterion for acceptance, which is that a sender's router ID must appear among the neighbors listed in the received unicast hello packet. If the sender does not locate its own address in the reply, it does not add that responding router to its own neighborship database and hence does not establish neighborship with the router. If, on the other hand, the sender's examination criteria have been met, the sender will proceed to add the respondent router to its neighborship database. In this case, the sender is now in two-way state.

To summarize the neighbor discovery process, an OSPF router in a down state comes online and multicasts a hello packet to all OSPF routers on all directly attached segments. All OSPF routers then check on the packet's contents and, upon meeting acceptance criteria, add the sender to their neighborship databases. The OSPF routers also unicast hello packets back to the sender, which then goes through the same content verification process and adds the replying routers to its neighborship database. This condition is known as a two-way state.

Once bidirectional communication has been established between OSPF neighbors, the next stage that must occur is election of a DR and BDR. The following section will explore this next stage in OSPF's operation in a broadcast multiaccess environment.

DR/BDR Discovery

Early in the creation of OSPF, designers realized that two major technical problems could occur with each OSPF router multicasting routing information to each and every OSPF router lying on the same directly attached segments. The first problem dealt with the potentially enormous amount of traffic such a routing method would generate; the second problem concerned keeping routing databases synchronized.

This latter concern was an issue in OSPF's design because it was recognized that having multiple sources of routing updates on a broadcast network could lead to a problem in which routers that are out of sync performance-wise advertise conflicting information that results in unsynchronized routing databases.

The solution was therefore to find some method of making OSPF routers synchronize their databases with only one router on each directly attached segment. This would ensure not only that all routers on the segment would be working with the same link-state databases but also a reduction in the quantity of traffic because instead of having all routers on a segment multicast information to each other, they would need to send the information only to a router that would be designated to receive and forward multicasts for the segment (Figure 5.3).

Consequently, OSPF designers proposed the DR/BDR solution. Each segment, during the neighbor discovery process, would elect a DR and BDR using a priority-based selection criterion by which the router with the highest priority in its hello packet would become the DR and the runner-up would serve in a fault-tolerance capacity as a backup to the DR. The BDR would not, however, respond to any OSPF transmissions that it received on this multicast address unless it detected that the DR was not responding.

Furthermore, after the neighbor discovery process had elected a DR and BDR, each OSPF router would then establish relationships called adjacencies with the DR and BDR. This adjacency relationship would thereby allow all routers on a segment to synchronize their topological database only with the DR and send routing updates only to the DR, which would then be responsible for forwarding the routing updates to the rest of the area. The multicast address chosen for exclusive communication with the DR/BDR was 224.0.0.6, known as the AllDR/BDR address.

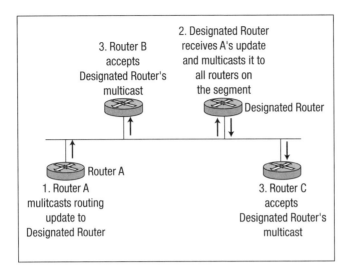

Figure 5.3   Designating a router.

Internetwork Discovery

Discovering the internetwork is the next stage in OSPF operation over broadcast networks. As soon as the DR and BDR have been elected for each segment and adjacencies have been established with the DR and BDR, routers can then proceed to discover the internetwork through a process in which all DRs exchange summaries of their link-state database (which at this stage contains only information gathered from the neighbor database) with all their neighbors in order to build complete link-state databases. The sequence of steps in this internetwork discovery process is accomplished through the Exchange protocol, which involves the following steps:

1. During what is known as the *Exstart* state, a router establishes a master/slave relationship with each attached segment's DR by examining the DR's router ID and comparing it to its own router ID. The router with highest ID becomes master, and the loser becomes slave.

   The purpose of defining this master/slave relationship between a router and its DRs is simply to determine who first initiates the exchange of database information. The master takes the initiative.

2. Following the *Exstart* state is the *Exchange* state, wherein the master begins to send a summary of its link-state database packaged in database description packets (DDPs), which are essentially packets that contain 20-byte LSA headers. In the topological database, LSA headers belong to complete LSA entries and contain such fields as LSA type, LSA aging timer, router ID, and a sequence number used to indicate how current an LSA is.

The purpose of sending only summaries of link-state databases as opposed to sending the full database is that both routers in the master/slave exchange already share some link-state information due to the neighbor discovery process. Therefore, instead of exchanging the entire link-state database (at this stage built from the neighbor discovery process), a router could simply send a summary of database information in the form of LSA headers, which provide just enough data for the receiver to determine whether it needs to request more information on a particular LSA header. If the receiving router did require more information on an LSA, either because there was no entry for this LSA in its database or because the LSA's sequence number was more current than its own, the sender would go ahead and submit the complete LSA packet.

3. A slave acknowledges receipt of a DDP packet with a link-state acknowledgment (LSAck) and proceeds to examine the DDP to determine whether more information is needed. If the slave discovers that it requires a complete LSA, the slave will transmit a link-state request (LSR) to the master. The master would, in turn, respond with the requested information in a link-state update (LSU) packet multicast to the slave's segment. This response characterizes the *Loading* state.

4. The exchanges of LSRs and LSUs between masters and slaves continue until both entities have synchronized their topological databases, a condition that characterizes the *Full* state. At this point all routers within an area share the same topological database and hence share a synchronized view of the internetwork. Subsequently, routing can now occur.

Best Path Discovery

Upon constructing an entire map of the internetwork from its topological database, a router will next proceed to build its routing table. The OSPF routing table contains categorical elements common to all protocol routing tables, including destination, metric value, next-hop, and age of entry. As might be expected, there are some differences in the manner in which these pieces of information are presented. One difference that distinguishes an OSPF routing table is its capacity to refer to destinations by router IDs instead of traditional network numbers, such as 132.6.18.0. But the most significant difference relates to OSPF's cost metric, where cost in OSPF is a value based on the speed or bandwidth of a link (interface); the lower the cost, the more desirable the link. The default cost for OSPF interfaces can be calculated by using the formula 100,000,000 bits per second (bps) divided by BW, where BW is equivalent to a link's bandwidth (also expressed in bps). For example, a 100BaseT link (100Mbps = 100,000,000bps) would have a cost of 1, which is 100,000,000bps divided by 100,000,000bps. Table 5.2 lists some common default cost values for OSPF links.

Table 5.2   OSPF default costs.

Bandwidth	OSPF Cost
56Kbps	1785
T1 (1.544Mbps)	64
10Mbps	10
16Mbps	6
100Mbps	1

To calculate the best path, OSPF uses Dijkstra's Shortest Path First (SPF) algorithm, which works by adding up the cost for each link that a packet would traverse to reach a given destination. If there are several possible paths to a destination, the SPF algorithm chooses the path with the least cost (Figure 5.4). An entry in the routing table is consequently made for the least-cost destination.

In cases where there happen to be multiple equal-cost paths for a destination, the routing table would be able to list up to six of these. This feature is useful for managing traffic congestion because having multiple equal-cost paths in a routing table allows traffic to load balance across these links. However, unlike Interior Gateway Routing Protocol (IGRP) and Enhanced IGRP (EIGRP), load-balancing in an OSPF environment is not possible with unequal-cost paths.

Convergence

Routing tables, topological databases, and neighborship databases are not static entities that never change once they are created. An internetwork is always in a

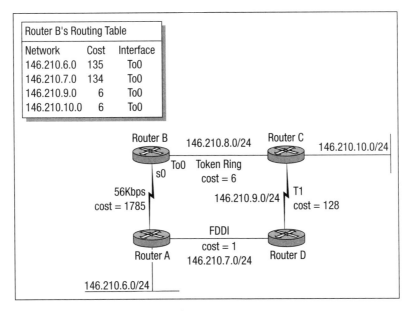

Figure 5.4   Calculating the best path.

state of flux as new routers come online, old routers go offline, new links get added, and old links change state. These topology changes necessarily change the way in which OSPF routers view the internetwork and, as a result, shape the information that they maintain to represent this view.

In a single OSPF area, this view of the internetwork is always aimed at synchronization, which means that any topology changes within the area must get reflected identically and accurately within the area databases. This process of synchronization is referred to as *convergence*—whenever a topology change occurs, convergence becomes the goal for all OSPF routers. But because routers cannot detect changes in a network that is not directly connected, there must be a way for routers to communicate these topology changes to their areas and beyond while maintaining the scalability and efficiency that are OSPF's distinguishing traits. The method that routers use to notify one another of topology changes is known as *flooding*. Flooding, as will be seen shortly, defies its connotation of complete and clumsy saturation by instead defining a discrete manner in which topological updates flow selectively and expediently from router to router.

When a link change occurs, which could be caused, for instance, by a new link/router coming online or a current link/router going down, OSPF routers that are directly impacted by the change will immediately construct an LSU packet that contains one or more updated LSAs and will then multicast this LSU out to their respective designated routers at 224.0.0.6 (Figure 5.5).

As shown in Figure 5.5, when router A goes down, all neighbors attached to router A's segment fail to hear any periodic hellos. After 40 seconds pass without hearing a

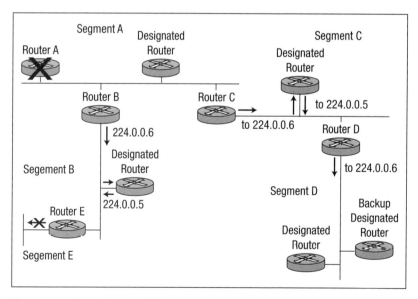

Figure 5.5 Multicasting an LSU.

hello from router A, the neighbors on segment A would consider this unresponsive peer dead and would subsequently remove its link-state entry from their router-LSA. These neighbors would then proceed to construct an LSU with the updated router-LSA and flood it to 224.0.0.6 out all OSPF interfaces except the interface on which the topology change was detected. This means router B will flood the LSU to segment B, and router C will flood the LSU to segment C, but neither of these routers flood to segment A, nor does the DR on segment A flood an LSU to 224.0.0.5. The reason neither router B, router C, nor the DR flood segment A with the topology change is due to the adherence to *Split Horizon rules*, which state that a topology change learned of on an interface should not be advertised back out that same interface.

Once the designated routers on segments B and C receive the LSU, they will acknowledge receipt with an LSAck and will then flood the LSU out to segments B and C, respectively, using the AllSPFRouters address 224.0.0.5. All routers on these segments receive the LSU and will consequently respond according to the following algorithm:

1. The router verifies that the LSU's contents are acceptable. That is, the LSA must have a valid checksum, be of known type and of a type that can be accepted, and not have aged out.

2. After verifying content validity, the router then looks in its topological database to determine if the LSA entry is inside. If the entry is not found inside the database, then the router will copy the LSA to its database, acknowledge the LSA with an LSAck (sent to the DR/BDR), and will flood the LSU out all its OSPF interfaces that have established adjacencies (except, of course, the interface on which the LSU was received).

3. If, on the other hand, the LSA entry is found in its topological database, the router proceeds to determine if the received LSA's sequence number matches its own LSA's sequence number. Recall that the sequence number is an LSA header element that indicates how current the LSA is. If the sequence number received by the router is the same as its own, then the router simply discards the LSA.

    In Figure 5.5, this first occurs when routers B and C receive the LSU from their respective DRs on segments B and C.

4. However, if the sequence number is not the same, a determination is made as to whether the sequence number is newer or older than what is in the database. A newer sequence number would signify that the received information was more current and would hence cause the router to (1) send an LSAck to the DR, (2) copy the new information to its database, and (3) flood the LSU containing this updated LSA out the OSPF interfaces that have established adjacencies.

In Figure 5.5, when router D receives the LSU from its adjacent DR on segment C, router D proceeds to flood the LSU to segment D's DR/BDR. Router E on segment E, however, would not flood the LSU it received because, even though the segment E interface may be configured for OSPF, it has not established any adjacency on that segment.

One final component to OSPF convergence remains: updating the routing table. Whenever an entry is added to or removed from the topological database, the SPF algorithm is rerun on the database to see if a better route is available. It should be emphasized that during convergence the SPF algorithm is always executed after, never prior to, flooding an LSU.

Figure 5.6 displays an algorithmic flowchart depicting the decision-making process in OSPF convergence.

To summarize OSPF convergence, when a router first detects a topology change, it constructs an LSU that contains one or several LSAs noting the change and proceeds to multicast it to each segment with which it has established adjacencies with a DR. The DR, in turn, forwards the LSU to each of its attached segments using the 224.0.0.5 AllOSPFRouters multicast address. Upon receiving this LSU, a router then runs through an algorithmic decision process to determine if the LSU contents are valid. A valid LSU causes the router to copy the contents to its topological database, flood the LSU out to any attached segments with established adjacencies, and finally execute the SPF algorithm on its database to determine if there is possibly a better path. Through this efficient and expedient flooding process, an entire OSPF area becomes synchronized with the same topological data.

The following section discusses basic OSPF configuration procedures within our single-area broadcast network.

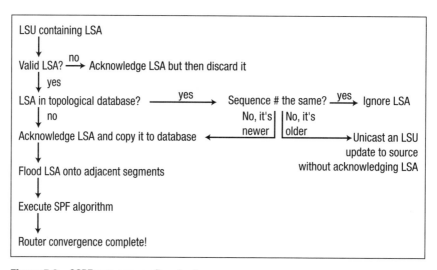

Figure 5.6 OSPF convergence flowchart.

Configuration

Initial configuration of a router for OSPF begins with enabling the OSPF process. The following command is used:

```
Router(config)#router ospf  process-id
```

As you can see, the OSPF router command differs syntactically from that of RIP by including a *process-id* parameter. The *process ID* is a numeric value that distinguishes multiple OSPF processes running within the router. Each process can be thought of as a separate instance of OSPF operation/configuration.

5

Warning: Running multiple OSPF processes within a single router is not recommended due to the additional resources required by the router to sustain this type of operation.

Once the OSPF process has been initiated, the router must have some way of identifying the interfaces that will be sending and receiving OSPF packets as well as identifying the area in which these interfaces will reside. The following command is used for fulfilling these two purposes:

```
Router(config-router)#network address wildcard-mask area area-id
```

Before exploring this command's interpretation we would benefit in first understanding how the **network** command works in classful routing protocols such as RIP. This is because OSPF's method of identifying networks is an evolution from RIP's method. Insofar as we understand the mechanics behind RIP's interpretation of the **network** command, we are equipped with a frame of reference that will help facilitate an understanding of OSPF's interpretation.

Understanding the network Command

Usually we think of a routing protocol's **network** command only as identifying the major classful network (for example, 24.0.0.0, 128.17.0.0, 195.100.7.0, and so forth) for which the router's routing protocol will send and receive routing updates. This is the case with protocols such as RIP and IGRP, which only have the inherent capacity to work with network numbers that abide by classful rules of addressing.

So how exactly does the router use a configured classful network address to determine whether routing updates will be sent or received on an interface? First, the router takes the interface's IP address, converts it to binary 1's and 0's, and then checks the high-order bits to ascertain the address's class (either A, B, or C). Based on this ascertained class the router knows which default mask (255.0.0.0 for class A, 255.255.0.0 for class B, or 255.255.255.0 for class C) to associate with the interface. The router then proceeds to run a Boolean **AND** with the default mask and the interface's IP address (Figure 5.7).

1 AND 0 = 0	Address	130.4.100.1	10000010 00000100 01100100 00000001
0 AND 1 = 0	Mask	255.255.0.0	11111111 11111111 00000000 00000000
1 AND 1 = 1	Result	130.4.0.0	10000010 00000100 00000000 00000000
0 AND 0 = 0			

Note that the result of this Boolean AND is a classful network number

Figure 5.7 ANDing.

The result of the Boolean AND is a major classful network number that the router then takes and compares with the major classful network that was configured via the **network** command. If the two numbers match, the router then knows that this interface can send or receive routing updates. A mismatch, on the other hand, would indicate that this interface could not be a routing protocol participant for this network.

OSPF's **network** command can similarly specify a major classful network number that identifies which OSPF interfaces are authorized to send or receive routing updates, but OSPF's **network** command can also use a wildcard mask to specify classless types of addresses—that is, addresses that do not follow the class A, B, and C format but instead refer to addresses such as subnets, interfaces, and summary networks. As was the case with our classful routing protocols, an OSPF interface that belonged to one of these classless addresses would consequently be authorized to send or receive routing updates. Moreover, in addition to receiving this authorization, an interface would also receive an area ID, as specified in the OSPF **network** command. Thus, the OSPF **network** command serves a dual purpose: specifying authorized OSPF interfaces and specifying the area to which they belong.

The following examples describe how the wildcard mask is used in generating the classless address with which an interface IP address will be compared.

In our first example, a router with several interfaces has been enabled for OSPF with the **router ospf** command. The network administrator doing the configuration has decided that because only one of these interfaces will be doing OSPF routing, the **network** command should specify only this particular interface's address. Specifying only a unicast address would force the router to allow only the interface with the matching address to be able to route OSPF packets. The following command was therefore used:

```
Router(config-router)#network 134.16.139.1 0.0.0.0 area  0
```

A 0 in the wildcard mask indicates a match with the corresponding octet for an address. In this instance, the wildcard mask indicates a match for each byte in 134.16.139.1, which means that whatever interface address gets compared to

134.16.139.1 must be matched identically byte for byte. An interface that matches 134.16.139.1 will be allowed to participate in area 0. An interface that does not match will not be able to route OSPF for area 0.

The next example presents a scenario in which three interfaces (132.16.8.1, 132.16.12.1, and 132.16.16.1) become enabled for OSPF with the **router ospf** command. In this scenario, the administrator wants only the interfaces 132.16.8.1 and 132.16.12.1 to route OSPF in the same area; 132.16.16.1 will be placed in another area. To accomplish these objectives, the administrator determines that an address that could summarize only 132.16.8.1 and 132.16.12.1 would be an efficient alternative to specifying a **network** command for each these individual interfaces. The following commands were consequently used:

```
Router(config-router)#network 132.16.0.0 0.0.15.255 area 1
Router(config-router)#network 132.16.16.1 0.0.0.0 area 0
```

Looking at the wildcard mask for 132.16.0.0, we know that the first two 0's indicate where a match must occur with 132.16.0.0 and an interface IP address. But how are the last two octet values in 0.0.15.255 to be interpreted?

To achieve an interpretation, let us convert 0.0.15.255 and 132.16.0.0 into binary notation:

```
0.0.15.255 = 00000000.00000000.00001111.11111111
132.16.0.0 = 10000100.00010000.00000000.00000000
```

Here we see that the wildcard mask carries a stream of 1's. Each 1 indicates a "do not match" or "do not care." This signifies that whenever a wildcard mask (in binary) has a 1, the corresponding bit on an address is of no consequence because no match needs to be made for that bit.

In this scenario, we therefore see that 0.0.15.255 means that the first 20 bits of 132.16.0.0 must match an address's corresponding first 20 bits but that the last 12 bits of 132.16.0.0 are irrelevant. Table 5.3 shows what occurs when our three interface IP addresses are matched up with 132.16.0.0 0.0.15.255.

Table 5.3   Qualifying the OSPF interfaces.

Interface	Interface Compared to 132.16.0.0 0.0.15.255	Match?
132.16.8.1	132.16.8.1 = 10000100.00010000.0000|1000.00000001	Yes
	132.16.0.0 = 10000100.00010000.0000|0000.00000000	
132.16.12.1	132.16.12.1 = 10000100.00010000.0000|1100.00000001	Yes
	132.16.0.0 = 10000100.00010000.0000|0000.00000000	
132.16.16.1	132.16.16.1 = 10000100.00010000.0001|0000.00000001	No
	132.16.0.0 = 10000100.00010000.0000|0000.00000000	

As seen in Table 5.3, the interfaces 132.16.8.1 and 132.16.12.1 both match the first 20 bits of 132.16.0.0 and are therefore inducted into area 1. However, 132.16.16.1 does not match because of its 20th high-order bit. As a result, this last interface is disqualified from participating in area 1.

Optional OSPF Configuration

Once OSPF has been initialized and participating interfaces have been identified, several optional commands become available for tuning OSPF operation:

➤ **interface loopback**

➤ **ip ospf cost**

➤ **ip ospf priority**

➤ **ip ospf hello-interval**

➤ **ip ospf dead-interval**

The Loopback Interface

A router ID, as mentioned earlier, is an address that identifies a router to the OSPF domain. By default, a router chooses its highest active IP interface address to fulfill this purpose. However, if a router's highest interface happened to go down, OSPF operation would subsequently be disrupted. Network administration as well would be adversely affected if the router ID is used in OSPF fault, performance, accounting, or configuration management. To address reliability and manageability requirements, therefore, a network administrator may choose to configure a fixed router ID that is not susceptible to availability problems. The mechanism that Cisco introduces to achieve this purpose is the *loopback interface*, which is a software interface with a virtual address that can never go down. The loopback interface address will automatically override a router's highest active IP interface address to become the default router ID.

The following commands are used in configuring the loopback interface:

```
Router(config)#interface loopback interface-number
Router(config-if)#ip address ip-address subnet-mask
```

The loopback interface can be a real subnet address or it can be a fake address. An administrator may opt for a fake address if network requirements dictated a need to conserve IP address space or perhaps meet reliability concerns. However, if trouble-shooting were an important issue (a fake address cannot be pinged because it has no routing table entry), then an administrator might opt instead for a real loopback interface address. The decision is almost always based on the weight of these network requirements.

Modifying OSPF Cost

There are certain occasions in which the cost of an OSPF interface should be modified. One of these occasions may occur when an environment is using routers from multiple vendors. The issue here is with the manner in which each vendor calculates a link's cost. As seen earlier, Cisco routers use the 100,000,000bps/bandwidth formula. But another vendor may have a method of calculation that would cause disagreement with the Cisco router on the cost of a mutually shared link. To facilitate interoperability, therefore, the cost of an interface would need to be synchronized on all routers attached to the same broadcast network.

Another occasion that may necessitate cost modification occurs when a network administrator needs to influence the path that traffic takes to reach a given destination. In such an instance, the administrator should first identify network performance and availability goals and then characterize network traffic to arrive at a complete and accurate understanding of where, how, and why the cost modifications would need to happen. This network analysis and the subsequent decision making that ensues will always be based on the network's technical goals and the priority given to each of these goals.

The following command modifies the cost of an OSPF interface, where *cost* is a value from 1 to 65535.

```
Router(config-if)#ip ospf cost cost
```

Modifying the Priority of an OSPF Interface

An interface's priority determines whether it will become a DR, a BDR, or neither. The higher the value, the better chance an interface has of becoming elected DR or BDR for a given segment. By default, all Cisco router interfaces have a priority value of 1. Because this presents a scenario in which multiple routers share the same default priority, Cisco allows the router ID to be a tie-breaker. As a result, whichever router has the highest router ID is elected DR, and the second highest router ID becomes BDR.

The primary reason for modifying OSPF priority is to handpick which router gets elected DR and which gets elected BDR. The criteria an administrator follows in making this decision are basically router capacity/performance logistics. That is, a router with more memory and processing speed and with the capacity to adequately handle DR/BDR functions would be a better choice for the job of DR/BDR than would a comparatively weaker router.

Priority modification occurs with this command:

```
Router(config-if)#ip ospf priority priority
```

where *priority* is a value that ranges from 0 to 255. A *priority* of 0 indicates that an interface cannot be chosen as DR or BDR.

Configuring the Hello and Dead Timers

The hello-interval timer specifies how often hello packets are sent to neighbors. An administrator may choose to increase the default of 10 seconds to reduce the amount of hello traffic on the network. Or the administrator may choose to decrease the interval to speed up the time it takes for topology changes to be detected. Whatever the reason, it is imperative that all routers on the same segment be configured with the same hello-interval timer; otherwise, neighbors that disagree on the timer value will not communicate with each other.

The following command is used to modify the hello interval:

```
Router(config-if)#ip ospf hello-interval seconds
```

Another timer that can be modified on an OSPF interface is the dead-interval timer, which specifies the amount of time that can elapse without hearing a hello from a neighbor before that neighbor is declared dead. The default is four times the default hello interval, or 40 seconds.

Use this command to modify the dead-interval timer:

```
Router(config-if)#ip ospf dead-interval seconds
```

This concludes our section on OSPF operation and configuration within a single area broadcast multiaccess network. The next sections explore OSPF operation and configuration within the nonbroadcast networks. As we will see, configuration of these OSPF networks plays an integral role in determining how neighbor discovery, DR/BDR discovery, and convergence occur in environments in which traditional multicasts are no longer allowed to fulfill these tasks.

OSPF over NBMA, Point-to-Multipoint, and Point-to-Point Networks

Broadcast media, such as Ethernet, Token Ring, and FDDI, are not the only media over which OSPF can run. OSPF also recognizes the traditionally nonbroadcast media, which can include such wide area network (WAN) technologies as ATM, SMDS, X.25, Frame-Relay, PPP, HDLC, and T1/E1. Each of these media support various topologies and configurations to which OSPF must be able to adapt to

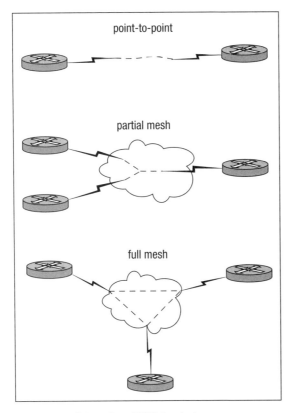

point-to-point

partial mesh

full mesh

Figure 5.8   Categories of WAN topologies.

maintain its essential broadcast functions. These WAN topologies can be categorized into the following three designs, as pictured in Figure 5.8:

➤ *Full mesh*—In a full mesh topology, every router is connected to every other router through virtual circuits, which can be either SVCs or PVCs. This topology allows for complete redundancy and minimal delay between all routers. However, this design also becomes subject to cost and scalability concerns when the fully meshed network begins to assimilate more links.

The number of links in a full mesh design can be calculated with the following formula: $(N \times (N-1))/2$, where N is the number of routers. Hence, a full mesh network with 10 routers would have $(10 \times (10-1)/2 = 45$ links.

➤ *Partial mesh*—In a partial mesh topology, not all routers are directly connected to each other through virtual circuits. A router that needs to reach another peer router that is not directly connected must therefore traverse one or more links. This design is less expensive than full mesh because it requires fewer virtual circuits. However, there can also be an increased delay in router-to-router communication because multiple links may need to be traversed. This design category includes a limitless variety of configurations, including the so-called star, hub-and-spoke, point-to-multipoint, multipoint, and multipoint-to-multipoint configurations.

➤ *Point-to-point*—A point-to-point topology connects two routers together.

Based on which topology and configuration a WAN is using, OSPF classifies WAN technologies into three types of networks (Figure 5.9):

➤ *Nonbroadcast multiaccess networks*—These are networks that connect multiple routers together but do not *by default* support a broadcast capability. An NBMA network is generally configured in full mesh. Examples of media found in this class include SMDS, X.25, and Frame-Relay.

➤ *Point-to-multipoint networks*—These are networks that connect multiple routers in a partial mesh configuration. Point-to-multipoint networks do not *by default* support a broadcast capability. Examples of media that are in this class include those found in NBMA networks.

➤ *Point-to-point networks*—These are networks that connect only two routers together. Each point-to-point network is its own subnet. In addition, broadcasts are supported. Examples of media in this class include PPP, HDLC, and T1/E1.

In addition to this topology-based classification, NBMA and point-to-multipoint networks can be further classified according to whether they are configured as

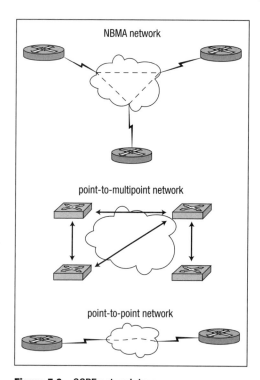

Figure 5.9 OSPF network types.

broadcast or nonbroadcast. By default, both network types are configured as nonbroadcast, which means that in this case there is no support for a broadcast capability such as is found in Ethernet. Although OSPF can operate in this nonbroadcast environment, OSPF nonbroadcast networks can also be configured to support the broadcast capability. The two possible modes for an NBMA and point-to-multipoint network running OSPF are:

➤ Broadcast mode

➤ Nonbroadcast mode

One other mode is supported by NBMA and point-to-multipoint networks, as well as by point-to-point networks: the subinterface mode. In a Frame-Relay environment, subinterfaces can be either point-to-point or multipoint. An OSPF network that is in point-to-point subinterface mode contains multiple subnets that are created by dividing an interface into multiple subinterfaces and linking individual PVCs to their own subinterfaces. Each subinterface is on its own subnet and will hence behave like a physical point-to-point network. A multipoint subinterface, on the other hand, works by linking multiple PVCs to a single subinterface that is on one subnet (Figure 5.10).

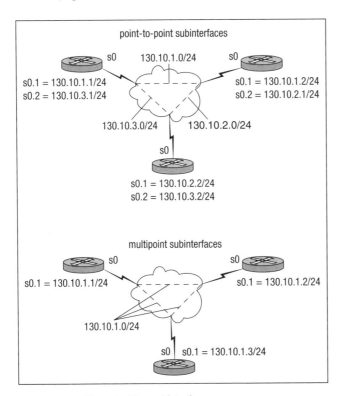

Figure 5.10 Characterizing subinterfaces.

Table 5.4 OSPF modes.

Network Type	Supported Modes	Proprietary or RFC?
NBMA	nonbroadcast mode (also called NBMA mode)	RFC
	broadcast mode	proprietary
	multipoint subinterface mode	proprietary
Point-to-multipoint	nonbroadcast mode	RFC
	broadcast mode	proprietary
	point-to-point subinterface mode	proprietary

Table 5.4 summarizes the common OSPF modes in which NBMA and point-to-multipoint networks can run. Note that Table 5.4 also states whether each mode is standards-based (RFC) or is proprietary to Cisco.

For this chapter, we use Frame-Relay as our primary example when explaining the characteristics and configurations of each of the three OSPF network types covered in this section. As will be seen, Frame-Relay's ability to support various topologies makes it an ideal example for exploring OSPF operation in a broadcast and non-broadcast WAN environment.

OSPF over NBMA Networks

A nonbroadcast multiaccess network is, by definition, a network that supports multiple routers but does not by default support an Ethernet-like broadcast capability. Some examples of NBMA networks include Frame-Relay, X.25, SMDS, and ATM. (To qualify as an NBMA network, ATM must be using either SVCs or fully meshed PVCs.) The reason an NBMA network does not allow broadcasts becomes evident when we take a look at a partial-mesh topology (see Figure 5.11).

In Figure 5.11, router 0 has three PVCs connected to its serial interface. When router 1 sends a broadcast routing update to router 0, the routing update cannot be forwarded out to routers 2 and 3. This circumstance is due to the Split Horizon problem, which states that a routing update received on an interface cannot be sent out that same interface. It makes no difference that the PVCs each attach to a separate destination because Split Horizon sees only one interface rather than multiple PVCs.

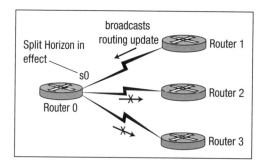

Figure 5.11 Partial-mesh NBMA network.

Likewise, consider a scenario in which all routers in Figure 5.11 have been configured to run OSPF as if they were all on a normal broadcast network. When one of these routers discovers a topology change, the first thing it will do is send a multicast hello packet to the DR/BDR address 224.0.0.6. Figure 5.11 shows a topology that forms one subnet; all routers on the segment would need be informed of this topology change. However, complete neighbor notification is not possible in this topology because when a router, say router 1, sends a multicast LSU to 224.0.0.6, the receiving designated router, router 0, cannot forward the LSU out to routers 2 and 3. The reason is once again due to Split Horizon, which does not differentiate between multicasts or broadcasts when stating its rule. As a result, any complete communication between OSPF neighbors in this NBMA environment is subsequently shackled.

OSPF in NBMA Mode

OSPF solutions developers have been able to rectify the Split Horizon problem by coming up with a way for OSPF to allow full communication in an NBMA network. This solution, referred to as OSPF in NBMA mode, would allow OSPF to emulate operation over a broadcast network. This means that such activities as neighbor discovery, DR/BDR election, and convergence could occur without the shackling effects of Split Horizon looming nearby. To implement this solution, however, OSPF solutions developers realized that two requirements would first need to be met:

➤ Full mesh topology

➤ Supporting configuration

The requirement for full mesh topology is aimed at allowing all routers to communicate directly with each other in an NBMA network. To understand why a full mesh requirement is imposed on an NBMA network, recall how OSPF routers in a broadcast network react when they detect a topology change. One of the first actions the router will take is to send out an LSU to its DR. The DR will, in turn, forward the LSU to all other routers on the same segment. Now imagine this same scenario in a fully meshed NBMA network. In a fully meshed NBMA network, pictured in Figure 5.12, a router that detects a link failure (assume the failed link is not on the NBMA network) will notify its DR (we will see how later). The DR will in turn notify each router on the NBMA network of the topology change; however, a router that was for some reason disconnected from the DR would not be able to receive any notification.

This example explains why a DR must have complete connections with each router on an NBMA network, but it does not sufficiently explain why a full mesh is needed. Therefore, recall once again what happens in a broadcast network when the DR goes down. The BDR will kick in and carry out the functions that the DR has just abdicated, which means that now the BDR has to have direct connectivity with

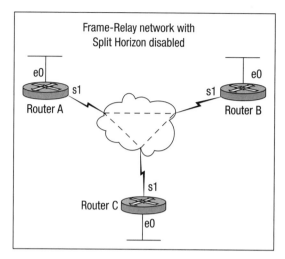

Figure 5.12 Full mesh NBMA topology.

each router. In an NMBA network, the BDR functions in exactly the same capacity as on a broadcast network. The BDR would consequently need to be directly connected to each router in the event that the DR is no longer able to fulfill its functions.

We now know why the DR and BDR need to have direct connectivity with all routers on an NBMA network, but we still have not explained why non-DR/BDR routers would need to be able to communicate with each other. Moving along toward a full explanation, then, consider what the DR/BDR election process means for routers that have not been banned from participating (by being configured with a zero priority). It means that all these routers are potential DRs and BDRs, and must therefore be able to have full connectivity with each and every router on the NBMA network.

But what about the zero-priority routers? This is another reason why fully meshed routers are a requirement in an NBMA network. Besides being able to establish adjacencies (or have the potential to establish adjacencies) with all routers on a network, all routers must be able to communicate with each other because indirect routing is not supported if a link failure occurs between two routers on an NBMA network. For example, consider a scenario in which router A was elected DR (see Figure 5.12). If the link between router B and router C were to fail, then communication between both routers would also fail. However, neither router would be able to use router A to patch up communication because NBMA routers consider each other directly connected and hence are unable to understand that they can route through another router on the same network to reach around a failed link.

Although the full mesh requirement is necessary in an NBMA network running OSPF, there are, of course, partial mesh networks that do not follow a full mesh topology. These networks will be subsequently configured according to the *point-to-multipoint* model.

The second requirement for running OSPF in NBMA mode has to do with configuring the router with the appropriate commands. The first command lets a router know it is in NBMA mode. This command is on by default on an NBMA interface (e.g., a Frame-Relay interface):

```
Router(config-if)#ip ospf network non-broadcast
```

Note: NBMA mode can also be referred to as NBMA non-broadcast mode.

An OSPF router that is configured with an NBMA interface, such as a Frame-Relay interface, will by default operate in NBMA mode. This means the router will carry out its usual OSPF tasks of discovering neighbors, electing a DR/BDR, and so forth, but because it is on an NBMA network, it will behave accordingly. "Behaving accordingly" means that routers cannot send multicasts, at least not while in NBMA mode. So by what means do OSPF routers communicate hellos, LSUs, DDPs, and all other such OSPF packets? The answer is by replicating packets and sending them individually to each neighbor as unicasts.

Due to this lack of a multicast capability, an OSPF router must have some way of being able to identify its neighbors (because they cannot be dynamically discovered). The NBMA solution to this problem comes through manual configuration of neighbors via the **neighbor** command. In an NBMA network, only DRs, BDRs, and all routers that are eligible to become DR or BDR need to be configured with neighbor statements. The reason only designated routers and potential designated routers need to be configured with neighbors is that these are the routers that will (or will possibly) need to begin establishing adjacencies on the NBMA segment. Having established adjacencies with the DR, all routers on an NBMA network will learn of each other.

Following is the command used to achieve this neighbor identification:

```
Router(config-router)#neighbor ip-address [priority priority] [poll-inter-
val seconds] [cost cost]
```

➤ *ip-address*—This is the neighbor's interface IP address.

➤ *priority*—This optional parameter is a value from 0 to 255 that denotes the neighbor's eligibility to become DR or BDR. The router with the highest priority becomes DR and the router with the second highest priority becomes DR. A router's default priority is 0.

This parameter also dictates the manner in which a router sends hello packets. If the router is eligible to become DR, as indicated by a nonzero priority, the router sends periodic hellos to its DR and BDR as well as all neighbors that are eligible to become DR/BDR, but the router does not send hellos to neighbors that are not eligible. In addition, noneligible routers send hellos to the DR and BDR and will respond to hellos sent by eligible routers. DRs and BDRs always send periodic hello packets to all routers.

➤ *poll-interval*—This is an optional parameter that specifies how often a DR and BDR will send hellos to neighbors that have gone down, to see whether these neighbors have come up. The default poll interval is 120 seconds.

➤ *cost*—This is an optional parameter from 1 to 65535 that specifies the cost to reach a neighbor. In an NBMA network, there is (or should be) full mesh connectivity between OSPF routers, which means that the cost for an interface is the same for all interfaces on the same network. This parameter is therefore unnecessary in a full mesh NBMA network.

OSPF in Broadcast Mode

We have seen how OSPF can operate over an NBMA network by being configured in a nonbroadcast mode over a full mesh topology. However, Cisco solutions developers have come up with another mode—*broadcast mode*—that can actually turn an NBMA network into a broadcast network. In simulated broadcast mode, all routers behave just as if they were still on a NBMA broadcast network such as Ethernet. That is, not only would neighbor discovery, DR/BDR election, database synchronization, and convergence occur in a broadcast network-like fashion, but multicasting would be supported as well. These routers would therefore no longer need to be configured with **neighbor** commands because they could use multicasts to dynamically discover their neighbors. However, the full mesh requirement would still need to be in effect for all routers to be able to communicate directly with each other. In addition, the underlying data-link technology, for instance Frame-Relay, would need to be configured to allow this broadcast capability to work.

The following command is used to configure an NBMA interface in broadcast mode:

```
Router(config-if)#ip ospf network broadcast
```

Figure 5.13 depicts a fully meshed Frame-Relay network. This network has been configured with the **ip ospf network broadcast** command to allow multicasting

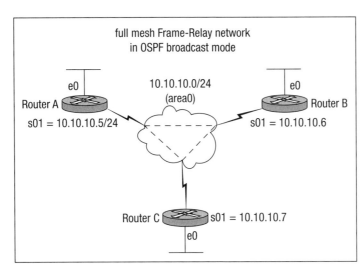

full mesh Frame-Relay network
in OSPF broadcast mode

10.10.10.0/24
(area0)

e0
Router A
s01 = 10.10.10.5/24

e0
Router B
s01 = 10.10.10.6

Router C s01 = 10.10.10.7
e0

5

Figure 5.13   NBMA broadcast network with multipoint subinterfaces.

to occur over this otherwise nonbroadcast network. Here are the initial configurations for each of the three routers in Figure 5.13:

Router A

```
Router_A(config)#interface Serial0.1 multipoint
Router_A(config-if)#encapsulation frame-relay
Router_A(config-if)#ip address 10.10.10.5 255.255.255.0
Router_A(config-if)#ip ospf network broadcast
Router_A(config-if)#frame-relay map ip 10.10.10.6 101 broadcast
Router_A(config-if)#frame-relay map ip 10.10.10.7 100 broadcast
Router_A(config-if)#exit
Router_A(config)#router ospf 1
Router_A(config-router)#network 0.0.0.0 255.255.255.255 area 0
```

Router B

```
Router_B(config)#interface Serial0.1 multipoint
Router_B(config-if)#encapsulation frame-relay
Router_B(config-if)#ip address 10.10.10.6 255.255.255.0
Router_B(config-if)#ip ospf network broadcast
Router_B(config-if)#frame-relay map ip 10.10.10.5 101 broadcast
Router_B(config-if)#frame-relay map ip 10.10.10.7 102 broadcast
Router_B(config-if)#exit
Router_B(config)#router ospf 1
Router_B(config-router)#network 0.0.0.0 255.255.255.255 area 0
```

Router C

```
Router_C(config)#interface Serial0.1 multipoint
Router_C(config-if)#encapsulation frame-relay
Router_C(config-if)#ip address 10.10.10.7 255.255.255.0
Router_C(config-if)#ip ospf network broadcast
Router_C(config-if)#frame-relay map ip 10.10.10.5 100 broadcast
Router_C(config-if)#frame-relay map ip 10.10.10.6 102 broadcast
Router_C(config-if)#exit
Router_C(config)#router ospf 1
Router_C(config-router)#network 0.0.0.0 255.255.255.255 area 0
```

Note in these configurations that the **broadcast** keyword has been appended to each **frame-relay map** statement. This keyword allows Frame-Relay routers to forward broadcast/multicast traffic across each specified link. OSPF and Frame-Relay are now in agreement as to how broadcast/multicast traffic is handled.

Note also in these configurations that multipoint subinterfaces have been used. This is not a requirement for OSPF operation. Subinterfaces are commonly used in Frame-Relay networks to support multiple networks on the same router, as well as to provide reliability in the event that a PVC failure occurs (with subinterfaces, a link failure would not bring down an interface because the PVC would be associated with a subinterface that would take the fall instead). Because supporting multiple OSPF networks on the same interface in a full mesh Frame-Relay environment is a complicated practice that is usually avoided, we are subsequently left with the latter reason for explaining the subinterface presence in OSPF NBMA networks.

Another possible reason for the presence of subinterfaces is to address Split Horizon issues. Split Horizon is mainly a loop prevention mechanism that is relevant only in distance-vector-based networks that are vulnerable to this problem. OSPF has built-in processes that prevent the formation of loops. The necessity for Split Horizon is therefore nonexistent. Subinterfaces, as a means to address the loop prevention issue, are also therefore of no consequence to OSPF.

Note: The Cisco IOS defaults to disable Split Horizon on Frame-Relay interfaces when (1) no subinterfaces are used, and (2) multipoint subinterfaces are used. Split Horizon is enabled by default only when point-to-point subinterfaces are used.

OSPF over Point-to-Multipoint Networks

When a network is not able to meet the full mesh requirement or is subject to continual link failures, the alternative is to run OSPF in a point-to-multipoint configuration. A point-to-multipoint network is, by definition, a network that supports multiple routers in a partial mesh. A router on a point-to-multipoint network can have one or several neighbors connecting on the same interface. OSPF sees each of these directly connected neighbors as a point-to-point link, which means that each pair of directly connected routers will automatically establish adjacencies with each other. There is therefore no DR/BDR election. But the absence of a DR and BDR does not mean that database synchronization and LSU convergence no longer occur. These roles are assumed by each router in the point-to-multipoint network. In addition, neighbor discovery will also occur, in a manner depending on the OSPF mode of the point-to-multipoint network.

There are several benefits that point-to-multipoint networks offer over their NBMA counterparts. One benefit arises from the fact that a partial mesh topology uses a smaller number of virtual circuits than an NBMA full mesh topology, making point-to-multipoint networks a cost-effective and scalable alternative to NBMA networks. Dropping the NBMA full mesh topology also allows OSPF to support a practically unlimited number of WAN topologies that can be designed to maximize network efficiency at minimal cost.

Furthermore, a point-to-multipoint OSPF network is more resilient than an OSPF NBMA network. The latter's requirement for complete router connectivity means that a DR link failure could cripple OSPF operation because a router that could no longer communicate with its DR could also no longer communicate with the rest of the network. With the point-to-multipoint model, however, the fact that DRs no longer exist means that the no-link failure would have the capacity to disrupt a router's communication with the rest of its neighbors. This is because all routers on a point-to-multipoint network treat each neighbor equally as point-to-point communication partners.

Interestingly, a point-to-multipoint network can be configured on a full mesh topology. Although this configuration is not recommended (due to the increased workload that would result from each router having to maintain $(N \times N(N-1))/2$ adjacencies), it may be necessary when the WAN infrastructure is subject to reliability concerns. Running OSPF in point-to-multipoint mode over a full mesh network should, however, be a last resort. A better solution to the problem of reliability in a full mesh topology would be to upgrade the WAN network by either choosing new media or reinforcing current media. This solution would involve negotiating with a service provider that could meet the network's requirements for reliability.

Fortunately, the current trend in global internetworking infrastructures is toward improving reliability. Today's fiber-optic-based Internet backbones are utilizing fault-tolerant media solutions as well as redundant hardware/software platforms that are designed with maximum performance and availability.

OSPF in Point-to-Multipoint Nonbroadcast Mode

In a nonbroadcast point-to-multipoint network, there is no support for OSPF multicasting. As a result, multicasts that would be sent intact by a broadcast router are instead replicated and sent individually to OSPF neighbors. This method of flooding is the same emulated method we saw in NBMA networks.

The command that lets OSPF operate in point-to-multipoint nonbroadcast mode is as follows:

```
Router(config-if)#ip ospf network point-to-multipoint non-broadcast
```

In a nonbroadcast point-to-multipoint environment, OSPF neighbors must be identified with **neighbor** commands. The **neighbor** command is necessary in this case because a router cannot discover neighbors' identities through multicasts.

But there is another reason why the **neighbor** command is used: to specify the cost of a neighbor. In a full mesh topology, the cost of the network interface is the same for all routers, but in a partial mesh topology, not all neighbors are directly connected to each other. Therefore, the cost to these neighbors is not the same as the cost of a router's interface to the network, as it happened to be with full meshes. The cost to reach these neighbors must be made to reflect the actual cost of all links that are traversed to reach them. The following command achieves this purpose:

```
Router(config-router)#neighbor ip-address [priority priority]
  [poll-interval seconds] [cost cost]
```

This **neighbor** command is the same one we used in our NBMA network. The only difference here is that the **cost** parameter now takes effect.

Following is a sample configuration of a router that was configured in point-to-multipoint nonbroadcast mode:

```
Router(config)#interface Serial0
Router(config-if)#ip address 10.0.1.1 255.255.255.0
Router(config-if)#ip ospf network point-to-multipoint non-broadcast
Router(config-if)#encapsulation frame-relay
Router(config-if)#no keepalive
Router(config-if)#frame-relay local-dlci 200
Router(config-if)#frame-relay map ip 10.0.1.3 202
Router(config-if)#frame-relay map ip 10.0.1.4 203
Router(config-if)#frame-relay map ip 10.0.1.5 204
Router(config-if)#no shutdown
Router(config-if)#exit
Router(config)#router ospf 1
Router(config-router)#network 10.0.1.0 0.0.0.255 area 0
Router(config-router)#neighbor 10.0.1.3 cost 5
Router(config-router)#neighbor 10.0.1.4 cost 10
Router(config-router)#neighbor 10.0.1.5 cost 15
```

In this configuration, a Frame-Relay interface is configured to support three OSPF neighbors that each have unique costs. An OSPF point-to-multipoint interface, such as the one shown in the above example, is by definition a numbered point-to-point interface that supports either one or more neighbors. Because this is also a non-broadcast network, all neighbors reside on only one subnet.

OSPF in Point-to-Multipoint Broadcast Mode

When OSPF operates in broadcast mode over a point-to-multipoint network, multicasts are subsequently supported. This means that **neighbor** statements are no longer necessary because neighbors can be dynamically discovered with multicasts. The following command is issued to enable OSPF in point-to-multipoint broadcast mode:

```
Router(config-if)#ip ospf network point-to-multipoint
```

Following are sample configurations for four routers configured in a point-to-multipoint Frame-Relay network that is running OSPF in broadcast mode. The network topology for this configuration is shown in Figure 5.14:

Router_A's Configuration

```
router(config)#hostname Router_A
Router_A(config)#interface serial 2
Router_A(config-if)#ip address 10.0.0.3 255.0.0.0
Router_A(config-if)#ip ospf network point-to-multipoint
Router_A(config-if)#encapsulation frame-relay
Router_A(config-if)#clock rate 2000000
Router_A(config-if)#frame-relay map ip 10.0.0.2 301 broadcast
Router_A(config-if)#exit
Router_A(config)#router ospf 1
Router_A(config-router)# network 10.0.0.0 0.0.0.255 area 0
```

Router_B's Configuration

```
router(config)#hostname Router_B
Router_B(config)#interface serial 1
Router_B(config-if)#ip address 10.0.0.2 255.0.0.0
Router_B(config-if)#ip ospf network point-to-multipoint
Router_B(config-if)#encapsulation frame-relay
Router_B(config-if)#frame-relay map ip 10.0.0.1 201 broadcast
Router_B(config-if)#frame-relay map ip 10.0.0.3 202 broadcast
Router_B(config-if)#frame-relay map ip 10.0.0.4 203 broadcast
Router_B(config-if)#exit
Router_B(config)#router ospf 1
Router_B(config-router)#network 10.0.0.0 0.0.0.255 area 0
```

5

Router_C's Configuration

```
router(config)#hostname Router_C
Router_C(config)#interface serial 0
Router_C(config-if)#ip address 10.0.0.1 255.0.0.0
Router_C(config-if)#ip ospf network point-to-multipoint
Router_C(config-if)#encapsulation frame-relay
Router_C(config-if)#frame-relay map ip 10.0.0.2 101 broadcast
Router_C(config-if)#frame-relay map ip 10.0.0.4 102 broadcast
Router_C(config-if)#exit
Router_C(config)#router ospf 1
Router_C(config-router)#network 10.0.0.0 0.0.0.255 area 0
```

Router_D's Configuration

```
router(config)#hostname Router_D
Router_D(config)#interface serial 3
Router_D(config-if)#ip address 10.0.0.4 255.0.0.0
Router_D(config-if)#ip ospf network point-to-multipoint
Router_D(config-if)#encapsulation frame-relay
Router_D(config-if)#clock rate 1000000
Router_D(config-if)#frame-relay map ip 10.0.0.1 401 broadcast
Router_D(config-if)#frame-relay map ip 10.0.0.2 402 broadcast
Router_D(config-if)#exit
Router_D(config)#router ospf 1
Router_D(config-router)#network 10.0.0.0 0.0.0.255 area 0
```

In these configurations, we see that neighbor statements have not been issued for any of the routers, which are all running in OSPF broadcast mode within the same subnet. Note also that the **broadcast** keyword has been appended to all the **frame-relay map** statements.

OSPF in Point-to-Multipoint Point-to-Point Subinterface Mode (Optional)

Point-to-point subinterface mode is another mode in which OSPF can run over a point-to-multipoint network. In this mode, OSPF sees each subinterface as a unique

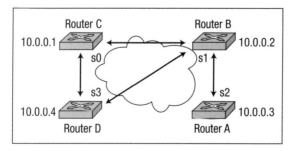

Figure 5.14 Point-to-multipoint broadcast network.

subnet with all the properties of a normal point-to-point interface. That is, multicasting is supported and adjacencies are automatically established between directly connected neighbors. There is therefore no DR/BDR election. Additionally, multicasts use the address 224.0.0.5.

There are a couple of benefits to opting for this type of configuration. First, because multicasting is supported in point-to-point subinterface mode, neighbors do not need to be manually configured via the **neighbor** command. Second, when a subinterface virtual circuit (VC) goes down, the physical interface remains up. This is in contrast to a configuration in which all VCs terminate on a physical interface that is not using subinterfaces. In such a configuration, any VC failure will bring the entire interface down.

The following command is used to create a point-to-point subinterface:

```
Router(config-if)#interface serial interface-number.subinterface-number
  point-to-point
```

The *interface-number* parameter that precedes the *subinterface-number* parameter is the physical interface's number. The *subinterface-number* can be any value in the range 1 to 4294967293.

Following is a sample configuration for a point-to-multipoint network configured with point-to-point subinterfaces. The diagram for this network is seen in Figure 5.15. Note that although the topology is *physically* point-to-point, a point-to-multipoint configuration can still apply.

Router A

```
Router_A(config)#interface Loopback0
Router_A(config-if)#ip address 3.3.3.3 255.255.255.255
Router_A(config-if)#interface Serial0
Router_A(config-if)#no ip address
Router_A(config-if)#encapsulation frame-relay
Router_A(config-if)#no keepalive
Router_A(config-if)#interface Serial0.1 point-to-point
Router_A(config-if)#ip address 1.1.1.2 255.255.255.0
Router_A(config-if)#ip ospf network point-to-multipoint
Router_A(config-if)#frame-relay map ip 1.1.1.1 16 broadcast
Router_A(config-if)#exit
Router_A(config)#router ospf 1
Router_A(config-router)#network 1.1.1.0 0.0.0.255 area 0
```

Router B

```
Router_B(config)#interface Loopback0
Router_B(config-if)#ip address 2.2.2.2 255.255.255.255
Router_B(config-if)#interface Serial0
```

```
Router_B(config-if)#no ip address
Router_B(config-if)#encapsulation frame-relay
Router_B(config-if)#no keepalive
Router_B(config-if)#clockrate 2000000
Router_B(config-if)#interface Serial0.1 point-to-point
Router_B(config-if)#ip address 1.1.1.1 255.255.255.0
Router_B(config-if)#ip ospf network point-to-multipoint
Router_B(config-if)#frame-relay map ip 1.1.1.2 16 broadcast
Router_B(config-if)#exit
Router_B(config)#router ospf 1
Router_B(config-router)#network 1.1.1.0 0.0.0.255 area 0
```

OSPF over Point-to-Point Networks

The last OSPF media classification is the point-to-point network, which is by definition a network that connects two routers together. Examples of WAN technologies found in this classification include PPP, HDLC, and T1. In these media, the broadcast concept no longer carries the significance it had in multirouter designs, where broadcasts were used to address all routers and where multicasts were used to address a subset of all routers. In a point-to-point network, however, broadcast/multicast messages still serve a purpose of identifying the router on the other side without having to identify that router individually. As a result, the OSPF multicast address 224.0.0.5 becomes a supported tool for implementing OSPF operations, excluding DR/BDR discovery; because adjacencies are automatically established between routers, there is no need for a DR or BDR. Database synchronization and flooding are consequently the domain of each point-to-point router.

The configuration of a point-to-point OSPF network is nearly identical to that of a broadcast mode. The only difference is that it now becomes possible to use an unnumbered interface instead of a numbered interface. That is, instead of specifying a unique IP address on an OSPF interface, you can use the **ip unnumbered** command to specify that an interface use an already existing address from the router.

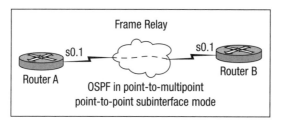

Figure 5.15   Point-to-multipoint network with point-to-point subinterfaces.

The following commands shows how an unnumbered interface works:

```
Router(config)#interface serial 1
Router(config-if)#ip unnumbered ethernet 0
```

The router will use ethernet 0's IP address whenever a packet is transmitted out serial 1; that is, the packet's source address will be that of Ethernet 0.

The primary reason for using an unnumbered interface is to conserve network addresses. There are, however, a few disadvantages to going with this approach, one of which is that you cannot ping an unnumbered interface.

This concludes our discussion of OSPF operation and implementation within the NBMA, point-to-multipoint, and point-to-point networks. As we have seen, OSPF maintains its characteristic features within traditionally nonbroadcast environments by employing configurations that allow OSPF routers to identify the mode in which they will be operating over various topologies. These modes, including NBMA mode, NBMA broadcast mode, point-to-multipoint broadcast mode, point-to-multipoint nonbroadcast mode, and the various subinterface modes, determine whether neighbors are manually configured, as is the case with all the nonbroadcast modes, or whether neighbors are discovered dynamically, which is the case with all the broadcast modes. These modes determine whether DRs and BDRs are elected, which they are in NBMA and networks but not in point-to-multipoint networks. They also determine how convergence occurs, meaning whether a topology update gets flooded by a network's DR, which is the case in NBMA and networks, or whether topology updates get flooded by all routers, as is the method in point-to-multipoint networks. Table 5.5 summarizes the common OSPF modes and the OSPF operations that these modes affect.

Table 5.5 Summarizing OSPF modus operandi.

Network Type	Modes	Topology	Multicasting?	DR Election?	Neighbors
NBMA	NBMA	Full mesh	No	Yes	Statically defined
	Broadcast	Full mesh	Yes	Yes	Dynamically discovered
	Multipoint subinterface	Full mesh	Supported	Yes	Dynamically discovered
Point-to-multipoint	Nonbroadcast	Partial mesh	No	No	Statically defined
	Broadcast	Partial mesh	Yes	No	Dynamically discovered
	Point-to-point subinterface	Partial mesh	Yes	No	Dynamically discovered
Point-to-point		Point-to-point	Yes	No	Dynamically discovered

Verifying and Troubleshooting OSPF in a Single Area

Verifying and troubleshooting OSPF in a single area first involves understanding what each of the following **show** and **debug** commands tell us about OSPF's configuration and status:

➤ **show ip protocol**

➤ **show ip route**

➤ **show ip ospf interface**

➤ **show ip ospf**

➤ **show ip ospf neighbor**

➤ **show ip ospf neighbor detail**

➤ **show ip ospf database**

➤ **debug ip ospf events**

The show ip protocol Command

The **show ip protocol** command displays the configuration parameters for all routing protocols on the router. With it you can view routing protocol timers, metric info, whether access lists have been set for routing updates, what protocols are being redistributed, which networks are being routed for, and from which routing peers the router is receiving updates. Following is sample output from this useful command:

```
Router# show ip protocols
Routing Protocol is "igrp 109"
  Sending updates every 90 seconds, next due in 44 seconds
  Invalid after 270 seconds, hold down 280, flushed after 630
  Outgoing update filter list for all interfaces is not set
  Incoming update filter list for all interfaces is not set
  Default networks flagged in outgoing updates
  Default networks accepted from incoming updates
  IGRP metric weight K1=1, K2=0, K3=1, K4=0, K5=0
  IGRP maximum hopcount 100
  IGRP maximum metric variance 1
  Redistributing: igrp 109
  Routing for Networks:
    198.92.72.0
```

```
Routing Information Sources:
  Gateway         Distance     Last Update
  198.92.72.18        100      0:56:41
  198.92.72.19        100      6d19
  198.92.72.22        100      0:55:41
  198.92.72.20        100      0:01:04
  198.92.72.30        100      0:01:29
Distance: (default is 100)
```

Following are some of the more important fields in the **show ip protocols** output:

➤ *Routing Protocol is "igrp 109"*—This field specifies the routing protocol used.

➤ *Outgoing update filter list . . .*—This field tells us if outgoing routing updates are being filtered.

➤ *Incoming update filter list . . .*—This field tells us if incoming routing updates are being filtered.

➤ *Default networks*—This field indicates how default networks are handled in both incoming and outgoing updates.

➤ *Redistributing*—This indicates the protocol(s) being redistributed. If the routing protocol states that it is redistributing into itself, then this means that no redistribution is occurring.

➤ *Routing*—These are the networks for which the router is sending and receiving routing updates.

➤ *Routing Information Sources*—These are all the routers from which this router is receiving routing information. This peer's IP address and administrative distance are specified, as well how long ago its last routing update was received.

The show ip route Command

The **show ip route** command displays the routing table. This command is an invaluable tool for getting a concise and detailed overview of all routes that the router knows about. Each entry in the routing table includes an indication of the route's address, how the route was learned, the route's advertised distance and cost, the next hop, how long ago the route was last updated, and the interface used to reach the route.

Following is a sample routing table for a router running OSPF in point-to-multipoint mode within a single area. The diagram for this routing table is shown in Figure 5.16:

```
Router_B#show ip route
Codes: C - connected, S - static, I - IGRP, R - RIP, M - mobile, B - BGP
```

```
          D - EIGRP, EX - EIGRP external, O - OSPF, IA - OSPF inter area
          E1 - OSPF external type 1, E2 - OSPF external type 2, E - EGP
          i - IS-IS, L1 - IS-IS level-1, L2 - IS-IS level-2, * -candidate
default
Gateway of last resort is not set
          200.200.10.0 255.255.255.255 is subnetted, 1 subnets
O    200.200.10.1 [110/65] via 128.213.10.1,  Serial0
          128.213.0.0 is variably subnetted, 3 subnets, 2 masks
O    128.213.10.3 255.255.255.255 [110/128] via 128.213.10.1, 00:00:00,
   Serial0
O    128.213.10.1 255.255.255.255 [110/64] via 128.213.10.1, 00:00:00,
   Serial0
C    128.213.10.0 255.255.255.0 is directly connected, Serial0
```

In router B's routing table, the O indicates an OSPF intra-area route. Note that all three OSPF-derived routes are host addresses instead of subnet addresses. This is because OSPF is a classless routing protocol that can refer to routes by host address instead of by subnetwork number. Even so, we can still interpret a host entry as an indication that the host's subnet is reachable. In the case of host routes that have a 255.255.255.255 mask, which is the case in router B's table, the subnet consists of only one router and generally indicates an interface IP address.

Also note that router A has two entries in the routing table, one for its router ID and another for its interface. This interesting circumstance is due to the fact that A's router ID is its loopback interface address. Recall that the loopback interface is a separate network number and can hence be listed in a routing table.

The show ip ospf interface Command

The **show ip ospf interface** command is used to examine OSPF statistics for an interface. These statistics include an indication as to whether the OSPF interface is

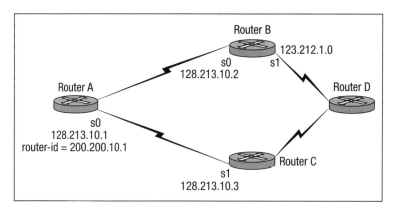

Figure 5.16 Point-to-multipoint OSPF network.

up, its IP address, area ID, router ID, network type (e.g., broadcast, nonbroadcast, point-to-multipoint), cost, state (e.g., DR, BDR, DROTHER), and timer intervals.

This command additionally identifies who the segment's DR and BDR are, as well as how many neighbors are on the segment. If the interface is a DR or BDR, then the command will also indicate all routers with which the DR/BDR has established adjacency.

Following is sample output from the **show ip ospf interface** command. The **ethernet 0** parameter was appended so that the output would list statistics only for Ethernet 0:

```
Router# show ip ospf interface ethernet 0
Ethernet 0 is up, line protocol is up
Internet Address 131.119.254.202, Mask 255.255.255.0, Area 0.0.0.0
Process ID 1, Router ID 192.77.99.1, Network Type BROADCAST, Cost: 10
Transmit Delay is 1 sec, State DROTHER, Priority 1
Designated Router (ID) 131.119.254.10, Interface address 131.119.254.10
Backup Designated Router (ID) 131.119.254.28, Interface address
131.119.254.28
Timer intervals configured: Hello 10, Dead 60, Wait 40, Retransmit 5
Hello due in 0:00:05
Neighbor Count is 8, Adjacent neighbor count is 2
  Adjacent with neighbor 131.119.254.28  (Backup Designated Router)
  Adjacent with neighbor 131.119.254.10  (Designated Router)
Suppress hello for 0 neighbor(s)
```

There are a few items to point out with this command's output:

➤ *Area 0.0.0.0*—This is a dotted decimal representation of the number 0.

➤ *Transmit Delay is 1 sec*—This is the amount of time OSPF waits before sending an LSA. Before sending the LSA, the link-state age is incremented by this number.

➤ *State DROTHER*—A router can be in one of several states, including DR, BDR, DROTHER (neither DR or BDR), WAITING (indicates the interface is in the election stage), point-to-point (indicates the interface is point-to-point for OSPF), and point-to-multipoint (indicates the interface is point-to-multipoint for OSPF).

➤ *Designated Router . . .* —This field indicates the DR's router ID, followed by the DR's interface IP address.

➤ *Wait 40*—This timer indicates how many seconds a router spends in the election stage before running out of patience and choosing a DR.

➤ *Retransmit 5*—This timer indicates how many seconds a router waits before retransmitting a DDP packet that has not been acknowledged.

➤ *Hello due in 0:00:05*—This is the number of seconds left until the next hello packet is sent out.

The show ip ospf Command

The **show ip ospf** command presents information on the OSPF routing process, which applies to the entire router. This command indicates such parameters as the router ID, number of areas, LSA intervals, and how many times the SPF algorithm has been executed.

```
Router#show ip ospf
Routing Process "ospf 201" with ID 192.42.110.200
Supports only single TOS(TOS0) route
It is an area border and autonomous system boundary router
Summary Link update interval is 0:30:00 and the update due in 0:16:26
External Link update interval is 0:30:00 and the update due in 0:16:27
Number of areas in this router is 3
Area 192.42.110.0
 Number of interfaces in this area is 1
 Area has simple password authentication
 SPF algorithm executed 6 times
 Area ranges are
 Link State Update Interval is 0:30:00 and due in 0:16:55
 Link State Age Interval is 0:20:00 and due in 0:06:55
```

The show ip ospf neighbor Command

The **show ip ospf neighbor** command is a highly useful tool for determining who a router's neighbors are. There are several variations to this command, the first of which is presented here:

```
Router#show ip ospf neighbor
    ID          Pri    State         Dead Time    Address         Interface
199.199.199.137  1    FULL/DR        0:00:31      160.89.80.37    Ethernet0
192.31.48.1      1    FULL/DROTHER   0:00:33      192.31.48.1     Fddi0
192.31.48.200    1    FULL/DROTHER   0:00:33      192.31.48.200   Fddi0
199.199.199.137  5    FULL/DR        0:00:33      192.31.48.189   Fddi0
```

As can be seen, the **show ip ospf neighbor** command presents us with six categories of information:

➤ *ID*—This is the neighbor's router ID.

➤ *Pri*—This is the neighbor's priority.

➤ *State*—This is the neighbor's state. FULL state means that the neighbor is adjacent. An adjacent neighbor is indicated as either a DR, BDR, or DROTHER.

➤ *Dead Time*—This is the amount of time remaining that the router waits to receive an OSPF hello packet from the neighbor before declaring the neighbor down.

➤ *Address*—This is the neighbor's directly connected interface IP address.

➤ *Interface*—This is the interface used to reach the neighbor.

The show ip ospf neighbor detail Command

The **show ip ospf neighbor detail** command presents us with the most information about a router's neighbors:

```
Router#show ip ospf neighbor detail
Neighbor 160.89.96.54, interface address 160.89.96.54
    In the area 0.0.0.3 via interface Ethernet0
    Neighbor priority is 1, State is FULL
    Options 2
    Dead timer due in 0:00:38
 Neighbor 160.89.103.52, interface address 160.89.103.52
    In the area 0.0.0.0 via interface Serial0
    Neighbor priority is 1, State is FULL
    Options 2
    Dead timer due in 0:00:31
```

Several new parameters have been added with this command:

➤ *In the area . . .*—This is the area in which the neighbor is known. The local router's interface is also specified.

➤ *Options 2*—These are options found in a hello packet: 2 indicates the area is not a stub; 0 indicates the area is a stub.

➤ *Dead timer due in 0:00:31*—This is the countdown (in hours, minutes, and seconds) to a neighbor's death.

The show ip ospf database Command

The **show ip ospf database** command displays a router's topological database, which is a collection of LSAs that describe all routes known in the OSPF internetwork. Following is the output from **show ip ospf database**:

```
Router#show ip ospf database
OSPF Router with id(190.20.239.66) (Process ID 300)
```

```
                Displaying Router Link States(Area 0.0.0.0)

     Link ID        ADV Router       Age       Seq#     Checksum   Link count
   155.187.21.6    155.187.21.6     1731    0x80002CFB    0x69BC        8
   155.187.21.5    155.187.21.5     1112    0x800009D2    0xA2B8        5
   155.187.1.2     155.187.1.2      1662    0x80000A98    0x4CB6        9
   155.187.1.1     155.187.1.1      1115    0x800009B6    0x5F2C        1
   155.187.1.5     155.187.1.5      1691    0x80002BC     0x2A1A        5
   155.187.65.6    155.187.65.6     1395    0x80001947    0xEEE1        4
   155.187.241.5   155.187.241.5    1161    0x8000007C    0x7C70        1
   155.187.27.6    155.187.27.6     1723    0x80000548    0x8641        4
   155.187.70.6    155.187.70.6     1485    0x80000B97    0xEB84        6

                 Displaying Net Link States(Area 0.0.0.0)

     Link ID        ADV Router       Age       Seq#     Checksum
   155.187.1.3    192.20.239.66     1245    0x800000EC    0x82E
```

The above categories of information are explained next:

➤ *Displaying Router Link States*—This designates the router-LSA section. All entries here indicate the router's attached neighbors discovered via the hello protocol.

➤ *Link ID*—This is the neighbor's router ID.

➤ *ADV Router*—The router that advertised this information.

➤ *Age*—This is the number of seconds since the last update.

➤ *Seq#*—This is the LSA entry's sequence number.

➤ *Checksum*—This is the **checksum** value for the LSA received from the neighbor.

➤ *Link count*—This is the number of OSPF links that the neighbor has configured.

The debug ip ospf events Command

One very useful OSPF troubleshooting command is the **debug ip ospf events** command. This command is used when an OSPF router is not seeing a neighbor on an attached segment. It will tell us whether the router and its neighbor have the same IP mask, OSPF hello interval, and OSPF dead interval. These three parameters, in addition to area ID and stub-status, must be identical for neighborship to occur.

The following output shows us that a neighbor was not visible because its dead interval did not match what was configured on the router:

```
Router#debug ip ospf events
OSPF:hello with invalid timers on interface Ethernet0
hello interval received 10 configured 10
net mask received 255.255.255.0 configured 255.255.255.0
dead interval received 40 configured 30
```

Chapter Summary

OSPF is a supremely scalable link-state protocol that can be configured to operate efficiently and expediently over many different broadcast and nonbroadcast network environments, including broadcast networks (such as Ethernet), NBMA networks (such as Frame-Relay), point-to-multipoint networks (again such as Frame-Relay), and point-to-point networks (such as T1/E1). Depending on the topology and mode of configuration, OSPF can go through five stages of operation:

1. Neighbor discovery, in which a router exchanges hello packets to discover neighbors that are on directly attached segments.

2. DR/BDR election, a process that involves establishing a type of neighbor relationship called an adjacency with a router that will flood topology updates to and for a segment and also synchronize topological databases for the segment's routers.

3. Internetwork discovery, the stage in which a router and its adjacent DR will exchange information to build their topological databases, which are repositories that store all known routes within the OSPF internetwork.

4. Best path discovery, during which a router runs the SPF algorithm on its topological database to calculate the fastest path, based on media bandwidth.

5. Convergence, which involves flooding multicasts out to the OSPF internetwork when a topology change occurs.

This concludes our discussion on OSPF within a single area. The next chapter takes a look at how a network that is on the precarious path toward expanding its data infrastructure will use OSPF to meet the challenges that this complex process of scaling a network entails. Upon completing the next chapter, we will finally understand why OSPF has at times been deservedly called the Internet's most powerful IGP.

Review Questions

1. Which of the following is not an advantage that OSPFv2 has over RIP?

   a. Support for route summarization

   b. Increased maximum hop count

   c. Support for multiple network-layer protocols

   d. Faster convergence

2. What information does an OSPF hello packet contain? Choose two.

   a. Router ID

   b. MAC address of DR

   c. LSA type

   d. IP address of DR

3. What is the first step a router takes when it receives an LSA?

   a. Copies it to its topological database

   b. Checks to see if the LSA is in its topological database

   c. Acknowledges the LSA

   d. Verifies that the LSA is acceptable

4. How is the topological database built during the stage of internetwork discovery?

   a. A router floods its segment with multicasts.

   b. A router establishes an adjacency with a DR and exchanges DDPs.

   c. The DR floods the internetwork with multicasts.

   d. The DR sends hello packets to each adjacency.

5. When does a router send out a link-state request (LSR)?

   a. When the router needs the IP address of the DR

   b. When the router receives a hello packet from a neighbor

   c. When the router needs more information from a DDP

   d. When the router is detects a failed link

6. Which of the following is a reason why multicasts are preferred over broadcasts?

   a. Multicasts are able to reach more hosts.

   b. Multicasts that are not addressed to hosts do not interrupt their CPU.

   c. Broadcasts are able to reach more hosts.

   d. Multicasts are supported by all devices.

7. In what state can routers begin to route information?

   a. Exchange state

   b. Exstart state

   c. Two-way state

   d. Full state

8. How does OSPF choose the best path?

   a. The SPF algorithm calculates the path with the least delay.

   b. The SPF algorithm chooses the path with the least hops.

   c. The SPF algorithm chooses the path with the least cost.

   d. The SPF algorithm calculates the path with the most reliability.

9. Which of the following is not a characteristic of an OSPF network in NBMA mode?

   a. Multicasting occurs.

   b. Neighbors are statically defined.

   c. Routers establish adjacencies.

   d. Multicasting does not occur.

10. Which of the following is the most important requirement for an OSPF network configured in either NBMA or NBMA broadcast mode?

    a. No multicasting

    b. Statically defined neighbors

    c. Full mesh

    d. Frame-Relay

11. What is the Split Horizon rule?

    a. Routing updates are required to use multicasts instead of broadcasts.

    b. Routing updates cannot be forwarded out interfaces that are not using subinterfaces.

    c. Routing updates can be sent out only an interface that is abiding by Split Horizon.

    d. A routing update received on an interface cannot be sent back out that same interface.

12. What command specifies the OSPF network type?

    a. **ip ospf network type**

    b. **ip ospf type**

    c. **ip ospf network**

    d. **ip ospf mode**

5

13. When would you most likely choose to configure OSPF in point-to-multipoint nonbroadcast mode instead of NBMA mode?

    a. When you need support for dynamic neighbor discovery

    b. When an NBMA network can no longer meet the full mesh requirement

    c. When using multicasts

    d. When a broadcast configuration is used with Frame-Relay

14. In what OSPF mode does a DR/BDR election not occur?

    a. Point-to-multipoint

    b. NBMA

    c. Broadcast

    d. NBMA broadcast

15. Which of the following would most likely be an advantage that a partial mesh topology has over a full mesh topology?

    a. A partial mesh is not subject to link failure.

    b. A partial mesh is more redundant than a full mesh.

    c. A partial mesh always supports more bandwidth.

    d. A partial mesh scales better.

16. What happens when you configure a full mesh NBMA network in NBMA broadcast mode?

    a. The network will fail due the increased bandwidth utilization.

    b. Multicasting is subsequently supported.

    c. Nothing happens.

    d. An error message would appear on the router indicating that this configuration is not possible.

17. What command would not give you the DR's router ID?

    a. **show ip ospf neighbor**

    b. **show ip ospf database**

    c. **show ip ospf**

    d. **show ip ospf interface**

18. What does the **show ip protocol** command do?

    a. It tells you all the routes in the network that the router knows about.

    b. It tells you how many routing updates are being sent and received.

    c. It gives you the status of an interface.

    d. It lets you know if redistribution is occurring.

19. What does the following configuration indicate:

```
Router(config)#interface Serial0
Router(config-if)#ip address 10.0.1.1 255.255.255.0
Router(config-if)#ip ospf network point-to-multipoint non-broadcast
Router(config-if)#encapsulation frame-relay
Router(config-if)#no keepalive
Router(config-if)#frame-relay local-dlci 200
Router(config-if)#frame-relay map ip 10.0.1.3 202
Router(config-if)#frame-relay map ip 10.0.1.4 203
Router(config-if)#frame-relay map ip 10.0.1.5 204
Router(config-if)#no shutdown
Router(config-if)#exit
Router(config)#router ospf 1
Router(config-router)#network 10.0.1.0 0.0.0.255 area 0
Router(config-router)#neighbor 10.0.1.3 cost 5
Router(config-router)#neighbor 10.0.1.4 cost 10
Router(config-router)#neighbor 10.0.1.5 cost 15
```

a. The network will support multicasting because the **neighbor** command is being used.

b. Not all neighbors are directly connected.

c. Multiple subnets are being used.

d. Frame-Relay is configured to support broadcasts.

20. What can we likely infer from the following configuration:

```
Router_A(config)#interface Serial0
Router_A(config-if)#encapsulation frame-relay
Router_A(config-if)#ip address 10.10.10.5 255.255.255.0
Router_A(config-if)#ip ospf network broadcast
Router_A(config-if)#frame-relay map ip 10.10.10.6 101 broadcast
Router_A(config-if)#frame-relay map ip 10.10.10.7 100 broadcast
Router_A(config-if)#exit
Router_A(config)#router ospf 1
Router_A(config-router)#network 0.0.0.0 255.255.255.255 area 0
```

a. The physical topology is a partial mesh.

b. The physical topology is a full mesh.

c. The absence of neighbor statements indicates that neighbor discovery does not occur.

d. DRs are not supported.

Real-World Project

A branch office network has recently been installed with a router that will be connecting with two other routers over a full mesh Frame-Relay network. This network will be running OSPF in NBMA broadcast mode. As the network administrator for this new branch office it is your task to get the router up and running on the network. After configuring the router with the basic initialization commands, you are now ready to complete the following steps to begin routing OSPF over the Frame Relay network in NBMA broadcast mode:

1. Configure the OSPF routing process with process ID 1.

   ```
   Router(config)#router ospf 1
   ```

2. In router configuration mode, specify that OSPF will be routing for network address 196.27.100.3 within area 0. Use the appropriate wildcard mask.

   ```
   Router(configrouter)#network 196.27.100.3 0.0.0.0 area 0
   ```

3. Configure a loopback interface with the address 200.10.197.1 255.255.255.255.

   ```
   Router(config)#interface loopback 1
   Router(config-if)#ip address 200.10.197.1 255.255.255.255
   ```

4. Enter interface configuration mode for the serial 0 interface.

   ```
   Router(config-if)#interface serial 0
   ```

5. On the same interface, configure Frame-Relay encapsulation.

   ```
   Router(config-if)#encapsulation frame-relay
   ```

6. On the same interface, specify a multipoint subinterface with subinterface number 1 and configure address 196.27.100.3 255.255.255.240. Also specify that this router will not be allowed to get elected DR or BDR.

   ```
   Router(config-if)#interface serial0.1 multipoint
   Router(config-if)#ip address 196.27.100.3 255.255.255.240
   Router(config-if)#ip ospf priority 0
   ```

7. In subinterface configuration mode, specify the OSPF network type that will let the router operate in broadcast mode over the Frame-Relay network.

```
Router(config-if)#ip ospf network broadcast
```

8. In subinterface configuration mode, configure **frame-relay map** statements with the **broadcast** keyword.

```
Router(config-if)#frame-relay map ip 196.27.100.1 20 broadcast
Router(config-if)#frame-relay map ip 196.27.100.2 30 broadcast
```

9. Verify that your router has visibility on the network with other OSPF routers.

```
Router#show ip ospf neighbors
```

10. If OSPF cannot see both neighbors, then run the appropriate debugging command to determine if each each neighbor is configured with the same hello and dead intervals and same mask.

```
Router#debug ip ospf events
```

5

CHAPTER SIX

Interconnecting Multiple OSPF Areas

After completing this chapter, you will be able to:

✓ Describe the problems that single-area networks encounter during growth and explain how OSPF addresses each of these problems

✓ Compare and contrast the various types of OSPF areas, LSAs, and routers found in a multi-area network

✓ Configure routers for operation in the appropriate area

✓ Describe OSPF packet flow in a multi-area network

✓ Explain how route summarization occurs in a multi-area network

✓ Configure both inter-area and external route summarization on the appropriate routers

✓ Describe and configure virtual links

✓ Verify OSPF operation and configuration in a multi-area network

✓ Given a set of network specifications, configure and verify a multi-area network

This chapter covers the operation and configuration of OSPF within multiple areas. It discusses what some of the issues are with scaling a single-area network and explains how OSPF has been able to address these issues by offering a hierarchical solution that can meet the requirements of a scalable OSPF internetwork. As we will see, this hierarchical solution entails interconnecting multiple areas and optimizing the flow of traffic both within and between these interconnected areas. The tools that OSPF utilizes to bring about this optimized interconnection include such instruments as area designation, LSA handling, route summarization, and virtual links. Finally, this chapter shows how these hierarchical tools are configured and verified to demonstrate how OSPF's multi-area solution actually works in a production environment.

Issues with Scaling Single-Area OSPF Networks

As an OSPF network grows, so do the requirements of its network resources. OSPF routers, for instance, must be able to handle the increasing load that results from processing traffic received from new neighbor routers and newly installed networks. As these new neighbors begin sending OSPF hellos, routing updates, and additional network traffic, an OSPF router must subsequently establish neighbor relationships, run its SPF algorithm to calculate new routes, and process and respond to all the traffic received from these newly acquired neighbors.

All these activities consume a router's CPU cycles. The more activities on which the router is working, the more CPU cycles that will be consumed. Eventually, a router's performance will begin to buckle as a result of the increasing workload it is processing. Exactly when this performance degradation begins to occur is a function of the router's resource capacities—for example, its throughput and CPU speed—and of the traffic load placed on the router.

Warning: As a rule of thumb, a router's average five-minute CPU utilization level should never be above 75 percent. To view a router's average CPU utilization levels, issue the **show processes** command.

In addition to processing an increased amount of OSPF traffic, an OSPF router must also be able to store much of this traffic in its routing repositories. Information on new neighbors will need to be entered into the router's neighbor table, new routes will need to be entered into the topological database, and new optimal routing entries will need to be listed in the routing table.

All these entries consume a router's memory. The more neighbors and routes the router learns of, the more memory that is consumed. These events will therefore leave less memory available for other router processes besides OSPF.

*Note: Use the **show memory** command to view how much memory a router has and how much is being used.*

As a result of the consequences that network growth has on OSPF routers, there are certain warning signs that can alert a network administrator to the likelihood that an OSPF area is beginning to outgrow its environment's resources. These warning signs are as follows:

➤ *SPF algorithm is being frequently executed.* In an area with, say 300 routers, there is an increased likelihood that topology changes will occur often. Each topology change would cause an update to be flooded throughout the OSPF area so that each router could then recompute its best paths.

This warning sign can also arise in the event that topology changes are occurring at a rate greater than or equivalent to the rate at which the SPF algorithm is being calculated. Such an event could occur, for instance, when a router's link-state changes rapidly (a process known as *flapping*). Because any change in link-state causes an update to be flooded throughout the area, all routers would subsequently be forced to run their SPF algorithm each time a flapping update was received, or at an interval specified by the **spf holdtime** command, which states the minimum amount of time that must pass between two executions of the SPF algorithm.

In an area with 300 routers, average rates of link-state change are already high enough. Now with the added probability of router flapping, the problem of frequent algorithmic execution would only intensify.

*Note: To view how many times the SPF algorithm has been executed, use the **show ip ospf** command. You will need to issue the command at specific time intervals because the value is not stated with respect to time.*

➤ *Topological database is getting large.* Every route that the router knows of gets listed in this database. For a 300-router area with 300 networks, the number of entries would be 300. In addition, all redundant paths for each destination would also be entered into the topological database.

➤ *The routing table is getting large.* For 300 networks, 300 routing entries would be listed. If there were multiple equal-cost paths for any destination, then these would also be listed. Although an entire routing table is not sent out during a link-state update, the SPF algorithm would take longer to compute the best path for a larger routing table. This is one issue with maintaining large routing tables. And, of course, memory limitations would also be an issue.

OSPF's Hierarchical Solution

In anticipation of these problems with scaling a single OSPF area, OSPF designers created a routing protocol with the capacity to support multiple areas. With such a capacity, a single area could be divided into multiple areas, each maintaining its own unique topological database. No two areas would need to carry identical routing information in their databases because all areas would operate independently of one another. As a result, it was possible for each area to have an independent view of the OSPF internetwork. This meant that instead of a router viewing each area as a collection of networks, the router could instead view an area as a *single route*.

However, simply dividing an OSPF internetwork into multiple areas would not, by itself, cause routers to maintain unique topological databases that represented unique views of the OSPF internetwork. A tool was needed that would allow all of an area's networks to be seen as only one or a few network routes. This tool was *route summarization*. With it, several network addresses could be aggregated into a single *summary route*. This summary route would implicitly represent a contiguous series of network numbers, allowing a topological database to maintain its routing integrity and at the same time facilitate OSPF's hierarchical solution for resource consumption.

Route summarization had the beneficial effect of lessening the load on OSPF routers by freeing them from having to maintain explicit information about all routes in the internetwork. Another advantage of this tool was reducing the frequency with which the SPF algorithm needed to be calculated. Now that all routes were not explicitly known to the router but were instead masked within summary routes, any topology change that involved a hidden route would consequently have no effect on the router. (Actually, such topology changes would not even be advertised outside the event's originating area.) Thus, no route calculation would occur.

Route summarization proved to be one of the major tools that allowed OSPF designers to justify the efficacy of their multiple-area solution for scaling single-area networks. Summarization alone, though, was not a sufficient enough means for implementing the hierarchical solution that OSPF designers wanted. Eventually, the hierarchical solution was built upon to include different *types* of areas that would each be responsible for originating and flooding certain *types* of OSPF traffic. These traffic types would be carried in different types of link-state advertisements (LSAs), and only certain types of routers would be able to generate these various routing advertisements. The results of these developments further proved to be of tremendous utility in tackling resource consumption issues in single-area networks.

Types of OSPF Areas, Routers, and LSAs in a Multi-Area Internetwork

A multi-area OSPF internetwork is an eclectic mixture of various areas, routers, and LSAs. Together, these components create a highly efficient routing infrastructure that is quickly adaptive and responsive to network topology changes. Tables 6.1, 6.2, and 6.3 offer an overview of these components, which will be explored more fully in the coming sections.

Table 6.1   OSPF areas.

Area Type	Description
Standard Area	Is the single-area environment covered in Chapter 5. It accepts all types of OSPF traffic.
Backbone Area	Interconnects all areas. All areas, no matter which type, must connect to the backbone area. It accepts all types of OSPF traffic.
Stub Area	Accepts all types of OSPF traffic except AS-external-LSAs (type 5 LSAs). To communicate with external autonomous system (AS) routes, the stub area must have a default route.
Totally Stub Area	Does not accept any inter-area OSPF traffic (type 3, 4, and 5 LSAs). To communicate with outside areas and external AS routes, the totally stub area must have a default route.
Not-So-Stubby Area (NSSA)	Is a stub area that connects to an external AS. To accept routes from the external AS, this area utilizes type 7 LSAs.

Table 6.2   OSPF routers.

Router Type	Description
Internal Router	Has all interfaces connected to the same area. All internal routers within the same area maintain identical topological databases.
Backbone Router	Has at least one interface connected to the backbone area.
Area Border Router (ABR)	Connects multiple areas and maintains a topological database for each one. ABRs act as gateways in that they are responsible for forwarding traffic both to and from their attached areas.
Autonomous System Boundary Router (ASBR)	Has at least one interface connected to an external AS. This router is responsible for redistributing routing information from an external AS and injecting it into the OSPF domain.
Stub Router	Resides in a stub area.
Totally Stub Router	Resides in a totally stub area.
NSSA Router	Resides within an NSSA.

6

Table 6.3   LSA types.

LSA Type	Description
Type 1: Router-LSA	Each router within an area advertises a single router-LSA that describes all of the router's active interfaces and neighbors.
Type 2: Network-LSA	A router that gets elected designated router (DR) will advertise a network-LSA that describes all attached routers on the DR's segment.
Type 3: Network-summary-LSA	Network-summary-LSAs describe routes to various areas within the OSPF internetwork. Only an ABR can originate these types of LSAs.
Type 4: ASBR-summary-LSA	By using this type of LSA, an ABR will let areas know how to reach the ASBR.
Type 5: AS-external-LSA	By using this type of LSA, an ASBR will let areas know how to reach external autonomous systems.
Type 6: Group-membership-LSA	This LSA is used in Multicast Open Shortest Path First (MOSPF) to locate multicast group members. We will not cover this LSA.
Type 7: NSSA-LSA	This LSA is used only in NSSAs to describe external AS routes. NSSA-LSAs are propagated only within the NSSA.

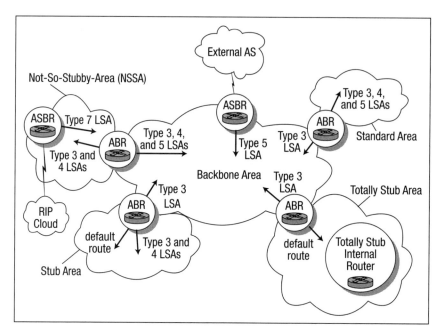

Figure 6.1   A multi-area OSPF internetwork.

To understand how these multi-area components work together, we will cover the router and LSA types in the context of the areas in which they function. Figure 6.1 provides a visual representation of how these components interconnect hierarchically.

Standard Areas

Standard areas were the first type of area defined and were the subject of Chapter 5. These areas support LSAs 1 through 5.

The most common type of router found within a standard area is the internal router, which is a router that has all interfaces connected to the same area. Although internal routers can accept all summary and external LSAs, these routers cannot generate them. The only LSAs that internal routers can generate are type 1 and 2 LSAs.

The other type of OSPF router found in a standard area is the area border router. The ABR connects the standard area to the backbone area and to any other areas. This router is the gateway for the standard area. As such, any traffic that goes out from or comes in to this area must necessarily cross the ABR.

Due to its unique location, an ABR is the only device allowed to advertise routing information for the standard area to the rest of the internetwork. It docs this by generat-ing type 3 LSAs, which are routing updates that list all of the routes in a standard area that the ABR knows of. However, if the ABR is configured to summarize routes, then the type 3 LSA would hide some or all of the routes in

one or more summary routes. Note, therefore, that a network-summary-LSA (type 3) is not required to summarize routes in order to be called a network-summary-LSA. A later section of this chapter fully explores how route summarization occurs in
a multi-area environment.

The reason for having the ABR solely advertise a standard area's routes to the OSPF internetwork is that there is absolutely no need for all internal routers to waste resources advertising their area's routes when there is one router that can sufficiently address this task. All routers belonging to the same area maintain the same link-state information in their topological databases, so only one router is necessary to communicate the area's routes to other areas. Because the ABR's location best qualifies it for this purpose, the ABR is consequently the most logical choice.

The ABR forwards routing information and topology updates for its standard area, and it forwards other area's network-summary-LSAs into its standard area as well. These type 3 LSAs are generated by ABRs in other areas and are flooded to each ABR in the backbone area. When the summary-LSA is received by a standard area ABR, the LSA is forwarded intact to the standard area. Each router subsequently makes an entry in its topological database and runs the SPF algorithm. Figure 6.2 shows the progression of type 3 LSAs throughout the multi-area internetwork.

In addition to flooding its standard area with type 3 LSAs, the ABR will also flood this area with type 4 and type 5 LSAs. The ASBR-summary-LSA (type 4) lets an internal router know how to reach the ASBR (or ASBRs, as the case may be), which is the router that connects an OSPF autonomous system (AS) to external networks or external autonomous systems. The AS-external-LSA (type 5), on the other hand, lets an internal router know how to reach the actual external networks. For example, consider Figure 6.3.

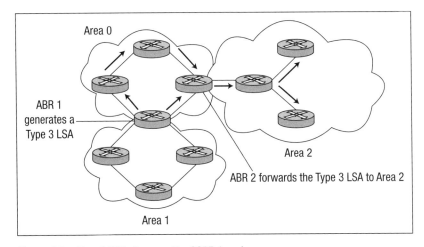

Figure 6.2   Type 3 LSAs traverse the OSPF domain.

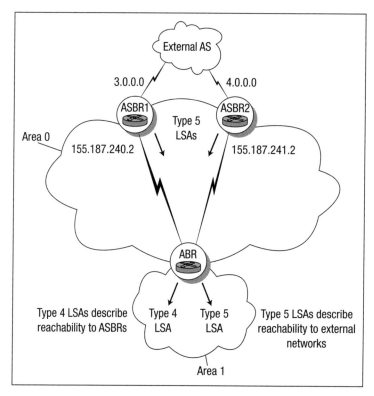

Figure 6.3 An external autonomous system (AS).

In Figure 6.3, we see that there are two ASBRs that each connect to an external network. Each of these ASBRs will advertise a type 5 LSA that contains its respective external route. ASBR 1 will advertise network 3.0.0.0, and ASBR 2 will advertise network 4.0.0.0. When the ABR for Area 1 receives the type 5 LSAs, it will flood them to Area 1. Each internal router would then add these LSAs to its topological database and routing table.

The following code shows the topological database for Area 1:

```
Router#show ip ospf database
OSPF Router with id(190.20.239.66) (Process ID 1)
 .
 .
 .


                Displaying Summary ASBR Link States(Area 1)
      Link ID         ADV Router        Age       Seq#         Checksum
  155.187.240.2   155.187.240.2     1245      0x800009B6   0x5F2C
  155.187.241.2   155.187.241.1     1245      0x8000007C   0x7C70
```

```
                  Displaying External Net Link States(Area 1)
Link ID           ADV Router      Age      Seq#          Checksum
3.0.0.0           155.187.240.2   1681     0x800009D2    0xA2B8
4.0.0.0           155.187.241.2   1681     0x80002CFB    0x69BC
```

Note that in this sample output, the ASBR–summary-LSA (type 4) lists the router-IDs of ASBRs 1 and 2, whereas the AS-external-LSA (type 5) shows the two external networks that were advertised by these ASBRs, respectively.

The Backbone Area

All roads lead to Rome. This saying is modeled in OSPF with the creation of the backbone area. All areas that need to communicate with each other must connect to this particular area to have their OSPF and non-OSPF traffic forwarded throughout the internetwork. The distinction here between OSPF and non-OSPF traffic is an important one when considering the inter-area flow of these two classes of traffic. Non-OSPF traffic comprises the usual network application traffic that travels from one destination to another, whereas OSPF inter-area traffic comprises primarily type 3, type 4, and type 5 LSA updates. Both classes of traffic must traverse the backbone; however, the manner in which they do so differs.

Consider first non-OSPF data flows. When a host application generates a packet destined for a remote area, the host forwards this packet to its default gateway. The default gateway (router) will, in turn, forward the packet on a path toward its area's ABR. Once the ABR has received the packet, the ABR will issue a lookup in its routing table to discover the next hop along the path toward the destination network. The ABR will then forward the packet onto a path in the backbone area that will subsequently lead to the destination area's ABR. This ABR would then forward the packet into its area, and the packet will eventually reach its final destination.

Now, consider how an OSPF routing update makes its way across the internetwork. A routing update that occurs within an area will be received by the area's ABR. The ABR will then determine if the update is related to a route that is contained in a summary route or that rather stands as a single nonsummarized route in the ABR's topological database. If the update is for a summarized route, then the ABR will *not* generate a type 3 LSA update. If the update is for a nonsummarized route, then the ABR will update its network-summary-LSA, package the LSA in an LSU, and then flood the LSU out all backbone and area interfaces except the interface from which the update was learned.

There are certain circumstances in which a type 3 LSA will not be flooded out an ABR's interface. They are as follows:

➤ If a neighbor is in a state below the *exchange* state, for example, the *init* or *exstart* state, then the neighbor will not receive the summary LSA.

➤ If an interface is connected to a totally stub area, then the summary LSA will not be forwarded out to this area.

➤ The summary LSA will not be forwarded to the area in which the update occurred.

Now, once the summary LSA has been flooded throughout the entire backbone, each ABR will then take this LSU and flood it out to all attached areas except the backbone area (because this is the area from which it received the update). All internal routers would subsequently add the LSA entry to their topological databases and would go through the usual process of recalculating the routing table.

Note: When a router receives both intra-area and inter-area routing updates, the router will first calculate its routing table for the intra-area routes and then calculate for the inter-area routes.

Because the backbone is the center of the OSPF routing domain, it is extremely critical that routers residing within the backbone be very reliable and very available. Just like routers in the core layer of Cisco's three-layer model, OSPF backbone routers are responsible for providing an optimized transport structure that must facilitate the flow of routing information for the entire network. If connectivity in this layer is compromised, either due to uncontrollable congestion or link failure, inter-area communication could be cut off entirely. It is therefore very important to always reduce the amount of unnecessary traffic crossing the backbone. As we have seen, this can be achieved by configuring route summarization on ABRs. But there is another way this goal can be achieved: through the designation of stub areas.

Stub Areas

A stub area does not accept ASBR-summary-LSAs (type 5), which is the type that originates from an ASBR and describes routes in external autonomous systems. When an ABR for a stub area receives this LSA, the ABR will not forward it.

Because internal routers in a stub area have no knowledge of external routes, the ABR will *automatically* advertise a default route to the stub area. With a default route, a router always has a path to a destination network that is not found in the routing table. This default route is represented in the routing table with a 0.0.0.0 address, as seen in the following entry for an internal stub router:

```
O*IA  0.0.0.0  0.0.0.0  [110/129]  via  10.250.137.1,  00:14:39,  Serial 0
```

The O indicates that this is an OSPF-derived route. The asterisk indicates a default route, and IA denotes an inter-area route; together, these two parameters signify a default route that was advertised in a type 3 LSA by an ABR. The 0.0.0.0 0.0.0.0 parameters denote the standard default-route address and subnet mask, respectively. The bracket values indicate, respectively, OSPF's advertised distance and the cost to the default route. Following these two values comes the router ID of the router from which this default route was learned. And next comes the routing entry's age followed by the interface used to get to the default route.

Note that a default route does not represent any one destination network, per se. Rather, the default route represents all networks that the router does not have listed in its routing table. Whenever a router receives a packet that has an unknown destination address, the router will forward the packet out the interface specified in the default route entry (in the above example, serial 0) and will let the next router deal with the packet. In the case of a stub router, any unknown networks will most likely be external AS networks.

The benefit to designating an area stub is once again a reduction in resource consumption. Routing tables and topological databases will be liberated from the maintenance of all external routes.

There are, however, some design restrictions imposed on stub areas. One of these restrictions states that a stub area should have only one gateway (ABR) to other areas. Having multiple gateways would possibly lead internal routers to select suboptimal paths to external destinations. To see why, consider Figure 6.4.

In Figure 6.4, ABRs 1 and 2 advertise a default route into the stub area. These routes are advertised with an initial default cost of 1 plus the cost of the link on which the

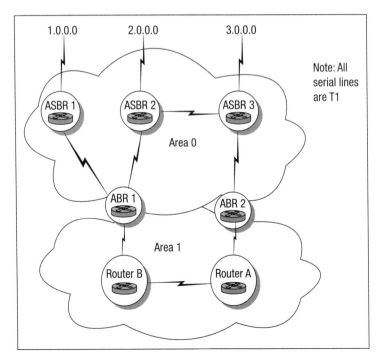

Figure 6.4   Path selection in a stub area.

advertisement occurs. This means that ABR 1 advertises a cost of $1 + 128 = 129$ to Router B, and ABR 2 advertises the same cost to Router A. Router B would then advertise the default route to Router A with a cost of $129 + 128 = 257$, and Router A would advertise its own default route to Router B with the same cost. Both routers now have two default routes in their topological database. However, because both default routes carry different costs (129 and 257), the router must choose only the least-cost path to put in its routing table. Therefore, Router A chooses the default route learned through ABR 2 and Router B chooses the one learned from ABR 1.

Suppose that Router A receives a packet destined for the unknown network 1.0.0.0. It will subsequently send the packet to ABR 2. In Figure 6.4, you can see the very circuitous path that this packet would then take from ABR 2 to network 1.0.0.0. The most optimal path would have been through ABR 1, which connects directly to the ASBR that leads to this external network. However, because Router A chose the default route through ABR 2, Router A must always use ABR 2 when routing to unknown destinations.

Other restrictions imposed on stub areas include (1) not allowing an ASBR to connect to a stub area without connecting to a nonstub area, (2) not allowing a virtual link to run across the stub area, and (3) not allowing the backbone area to be a stub area. Violating any of these three restrictions would prevent type 5 LSAs from being flooded to the areas where these LSAs must be allowed to be accepted.

Configuration of a Stub Area

The following command is used to configure an area as stub:

```
Router(config-router)#area area-id stub
```

The *area-id* parameter identifies the area that is to be stub.

The above command must be issued on all routers within the stub area because all stub routers within the area will exchange hello packets indicating that they are residing in a stub area. Recall that one of the parameters that neighbors must agree on before they establish neighborship is the hello packet's stub indicator. This parameter must match on both routers if they are to become neighbors and route to each other. If a router does not contain the stub indicator (because it was not configured with the **area stub** command), the router will therefore be effectively cut off from the rest of the stub area.

The next command is used to specify the cost for the default route that is advertised into the stub area by an ABR. It is optional:

```
Router(config-router)#area area-id default-cost cost
```

The *area-id* parameter once again denotes the stub area. The *cost* parameter is a value that indicates the cost of the default route (default is 1).

This command is used only on the stub ABR. It cannot be used on internal stub area routers.

To understand when this command would be of use, recall the restriction that only one gateway (ABR) should be used in a stub area. If you were to use multiple ABRs, then, as we have seen, some routers may choose a suboptimal default path to external destinations. Using the **area default-cost** command, however, could in some instances resolve this problem. To see how, again consider Figure 6.4.

In Figure 6.4, Router A chose to take a default route through ABR 2 because ABR 2 advertised a default route with a lesser cost than did ABR 1. To make Router A's default path go through ABR 1, we would need to configure ABR 2 with a high enough default-cost that Router A would choose ABR 1's default route. Because ABR 1's default route reaches Router A with a cost of 257, we could configure ABR 2 with a default-cost of 130 or greater. Why 130 or greater? Because the value of 130 will be added to the cost of the T1 link, which is 128. Router A would therefore receive a default route advertised with a cost of at least 258 and would subsequently go with the lesser cost of 257.

If we were to do this, however, Router A may no longer have an optimal path to network 3.0.0.0. This is exactly why the restriction of a single ABR is imposed on stub areas.

Stub Area Configuration Example

The following example shows the configuration of the stub area depicted in Figure 6.5.

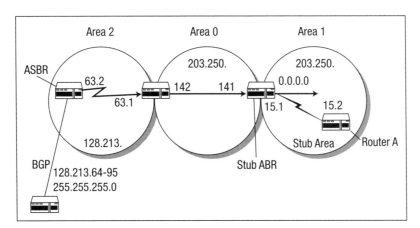

Figure 6.5   A stub area.

The stub area shown in Figure 6.5 has only one gateway. This ABR is configured as follows:

```
ABR(config)#interface ethernet 0
ABR(config-if)#ip address 203.250.14.1 255.255.255.0
ABR(config-if)#interface serial 1
ABR(config-if)#ip address 203.250.15.1 255.255.255.252
ABR(config-if)#exit
ABR(config)#router ospf 10
ABR(config-router)#network 203.250.15.1 0.0.0.0 area 1
ABR(config-router)#network 203.250.14.1 0.0.0.0 area 0
ABR(config-router)#area 1 stub
```

Router A's configuration:

```
Router_A(config)#interface serial 1
Router_A(config-if)#ip address 203.250.15.2 255.255.255.252
Router_A(config-if)#exit
Router_A(config)#router ospf 10
Router_A(config-router)#network 203.250.15.0 0.0.0.255 area 1
Router_A(config-router)#area 2 stub
```

Router A's routing table after being configured stub would be as follows:

```
Router_A#show ip route
 Codes: C - connected, S - static, I - IGRP, R - RIP, M - mobile, B-BGP
        D - EIGRP, EX - EIGRP external, O - OSPF, IA - OSPF inter-area
        E1 - OSPF external type 1, E2 - OSPF external type 2, E - EGP
        i - IS-IS, L1 - IS-IS level-1, L2 - IS-IS level-2,
        * -  CANDIDATE default

Gateway of last resort is 203.250.15.1 to network 0.0.0.0

    203.250.15.0 255.255.255.252 is subnetted, 1 subnets
C    203.250.15.0 is directly connected, Serial 1
O IA 203.250.14.0 255.255.255.0 [110/74] via 203.250.15.1, 00:26:58,
     Serial 1
    128.213.0.0 255.255.255.252 is subnetted, 1 subnets
O IA 128.213.63.0 255.255.255.0 [110/84] via 203.250.15.1, 00:25:59,
     Serial 1
O*IA 0.0.0.0 0.0.0.0 [110/65] via 203.250.15.1, 00:26:59, Serial 1
```

Note that the external route 128.213.64.0 has been substituted with the default route 0.0.0.0. Also note that the cost of this route is 65, which is equal to the default cost (1) plus the cost of the link (64) between the ABR and Router A.

Totally Stub Areas

The totally stub area takes the concept of a stub area one step further by not accepting any types of inter-area LSAs, including types 3, 4, and 5. As a result, a totally stub area must also be injected with a default route.

The advantage to making an area totally stub as opposed to just stub is one of decreased resource consumption. Unlike stub routers, which eliminate only type 5 routes from their routing repositories, totally stub routers eliminate type 3, 4, and 5 routes, which means that totally stub routers work with reduced CPU utilization and more available memory.

Totally stub areas still share the same restrictions, however. That is, a totally stub area must still recognize the rules of using a single gateway, not allowing any internal ASBRs or any virtual links, and not being used as a backbone area. There is additionally one more restriction. All routers in a totally stub area must be Cisco routers because this type of area is proprietary to Cisco and is not an open standard that all vendors must recognize.

Configuration of a Totally Stub Area

The command for configuring a totally stub router is as follows:

```
Router(config-router)#area area-id stub no-summary
```

The *area-id* parameter denotes the area that is turning totally stub.

Note that this command is nearly identical to the **stub area** command. The only difference is the **no-summary** appendage, which tells the ABR that no summary LSAs (types 3, 4, and 5) are to be allowed into the totally stub area.

This command is issued only on the ABR. The rest of the routers in a totally stub area will be configured as normal stub routers, although configuring the rest of these routers as totally stub (by appending the **no-summary** parameter) is permissible. It is just customary not to use the **no-summary** parameter on internal routers in a totally stub area.

The **area default-cost** command may also be used in a totally stub area.

Totally Stub Area Configuration Example

The following example shows how an area becomes totally stub. The diagram for this example is pictured in Figure 6.6.

In Figure 6.6, area 1 is configured as a totally stub area. The configuration on the ABR is as follows:

```
ABR(config)#interface serial 1
ABR(config-if)#ip address 203.250.15.1 255.255.255.252
```

```
ABR(config-if)#exit
ABR(config)#router ospf 1
ABR(config-router)#network 203.250.14.0 0.0.0.255 area 0
ABR(config-router)#network 203.250.15.1 0.0.0.0 area 1
ABR(config-router)#area 1 stub no-summary
```

Router A's configuration:

```
Router_A(config)#interface serial 1
Router_A(config-if)#ip address 203.250.15.2 255.255.255.252
Router_A(config-if)#exit
Router_A(config)#router ospf 1
Router_A(config-router)#network 203.250.15.0 0.0.0.255 area 1
Router_A(config-router)#area 1 stub

Router_A#show ip route
Codes: C - connected, S - static, I - IGRP, R - RIP, M - mobile, B-BGP
       D - EIGRP, EX - EIGRP external, O - OSPF, IA - OSPF inter-area
       E1 - OSPF external type 1, E2 - OSPF external type 2, E - EGP
       i - IS-IS, L1 - IS-IS level-1, L2 - IS-IS level-2,
       * -  candidate default

 Gateway of last resort is 203.250.15.1 to network 0.0.0.0

     203.250.15.0 255.255.255.252 is subnetted, 1 subnets
 C   203.250.15.0 is directly connected, Serial 1
 O*IA 0.0.0.0 0.0.0.0 [110/65] via 203.250.15.1, 00:03:49, Serial 1
```

Note that all summary routes have been exterminated from the routing table and replaced with the default route 0.0.0.0.

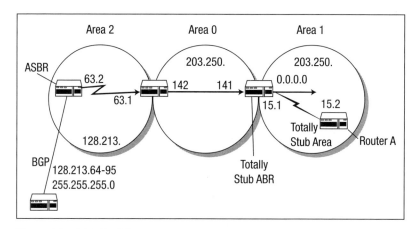

Figure 6.6 A totally stub area.

Not-So-Stubby Areas

Not-so-stubby areas do not accept AS-external-LSAs (type 5) and therefore are similar in this regard to a stub area. Unlike stub areas, however, NSSAs were created to allow certain external routing information into a stub area. Many times, a stub area will connect to routers within the same OSPF domain that are running a different routing protocol, such as RIP or EIGRP (see Figure 6.7). For the stub area and the rest of the OSPF internetwork to learn about these networks, one router from the stub area must redistribute (translate) the RIP or EIGRP routes into OSPF. Any time redistribution occurs, however, a router automatically becomes an ASBR and must propagate the redistributed routing information via type 5 LSAs. This situation is unacceptable to stub areas. After all, this area was made stub for the purpose of shielding it from all routes that it did not need to know about. As a result, the NSSA was defined to allow an ASBR the means of importing external routes into the stub area without having to use type 5 LSAs to do so. The tool used by NSSA ASBRs to achieve this task was the type 7 LSA.

This new link-state advertisement, the type 7 LSA, allows an ASBR to redistribute external routing information learned from a different routing protocol into OSPF and distribute this information via type 7 LSAs into the NSSA. This type of LSA would not, however, be flooded outside the NSSA. Instead, internal routers would flood the type 7 LSAs only throughout the NSSA. Once the type 7 LSA had been received by the NSSA ABR, the latter would translate the type 7 LSA into a type 5 LSA and would then flood the translated LSA throughout the backbone. Other ABRs would subsequently receive and forward the AS-external-LSA to their respective areas (see Figure 6.8).

In addition to being used to connect non-OSPF networks within the OSPF AS, NSSAs are also used by Internet Service Providers (ISPs) to connect OSPF corporate sites with remote sites that are running a different routing protocol. In this scenario,

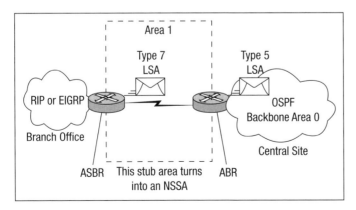

Figure 6.7 Connecting a non-OSPF network to a stub area.

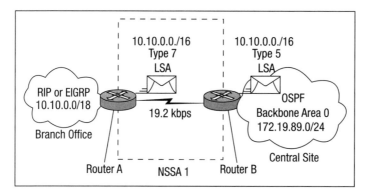

Figure 6.8 The NSSA and type 7 LSA.

the ISP's autonomous system would be configured as an NSSA transit area for the corporate and remote sites.

Configuration of a Not-So-Stubby Area

The command we use to configure an NSSA is as follows:

```
Router(config-router)#area area-id nssa
```

This command must be issued on all routers that are to participate in the NSSA.

An example of an NSSA configuration for the topology in Figure 6.8 follows:

```
Router_A(config)#router ospf 1
Router_A(config-router)#network 162.143.19.0 0.0.0.255 area 0
Router_A(config-router)#network 162.143.22.1 0.0.0.0 area 4
Router_A(config-router)#area 4 nssa

Router_B(config)#router ospf 1
Router_B(config-router)#redistribute rip subnets
Router_B(config-router)#network 162.143.22.2 0.0.0.0 area 4
Router_B(config-router)#area 4 nssa
```

In this configuration, we see that Router A has been set up to redistribute RIP-learned routes into OSPF so that OSPF can advertise these routes to the NSSA. In this case, the NSSA comprises two routers connected via a serial link. When Router A receives the type 7 LSAs, Router A will automatically translate them into type 5 LSAs and flood the backbone area. No extra configuration is needed for this translation to occur.

OSPF Route Summarization

Route summarization is the consolidation of multiple network addresses into one single network address. It is one of the most effective tools for reducing the sizes of routing tables and topological databases in an OSPF multi-area environment.

The two types of route summarization are:

➤ Inter-area route summarization

➤ External route summarization

Inter-Area Route Summarization

When an ABR generates a network-summary-LSA (type 3), the ABR will list in this LSA all the inter-area routes that are known for that area. To reduce resource consumption and minimize the impact of topology changes, an ABR can be configured to summarize these routes and advertise them to the OSPF internetwork. This is referred to as inter-area route summarization, and is illustrated in Figure 6.9.

In Figure 6.9, ABR 1 is configured to summarize the subnetworks ranging from 129.213.64.0 /24 through 129.213.95.0 /24 by using the summary address 129.213.64.0 /19. ABR 1 will generate a type 3 LSA containing this summary route and will forward it to the backbone router. After receiving this inter-area LSA from the backbone router, ABRs 2 and 3 will then enter the LSA into their databases and advertise it to their respective areas. Subsequently, each internal router would also make an entry in its topological database and forward the LSA out any adjacent segments. Finally, each router would, in addition, run its SPF algorithm to calculate the best path to the summary route.

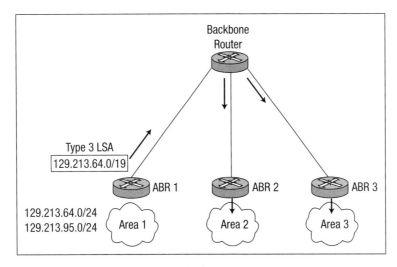

Figure 6.9   Inter-area route summarization.

Configuration of Inter-Area Route Summarization

To perform inter-area route summarization, issue the following command on the ABR:

```
Router(config-router)#area area-id range ip-address mask
```

The *area-id* parameter identifies the area whose routes are being summarized. The *ip-address* and *mask* parameters together denote the summary address that the ABR will advertise for this area.

The following is an example of how inter-area route summarization would be configured on ABR 1 in Figure 6.9:

```
ABR1(config)#router ospf 1
ABR1(config-router)#network 129.213.100.0 0.0.0.2555 area 0
ABR1(config-router)#network 129.213.70.0 0.0.0.255 area 1
ABR1(config-router)#area 1 range 129.213.64.0 255.255.224.0
```

The range specified here consolidates networks 129.213.64.0 /24 through 129.213.95.0 /24. The prefix mask of 255.255.224.0 /19 indicates that the network host boundary has been moved from the 24th bit to the 19th bit. With 19 bits representing the classless network number 129.213.64.0 /19, a prefix mask of 255.255.224.0 would denote the network range 129.213.64.0 /24 through 129.213.95.0 /24.

This example shows how summarization can occur in the direction of the backbone, but summarization can also occur in the other direction. That is, routes in the backbone area can be summarized and advertised by an ABR into the ABR's area. This practice would have the effect of once again reducing the number of routing entries with which internal routers would need to contend. However, summarizing backbone routes is usually not recommended, particularly when an area has multiple ABRs. With multiple ABRs configured to summarize backbone routes, an internal router may end up selecting a suboptimal path to one of these routes because the route (and its cost) would not be explicitly stated in the routing table.

An example of this scenario is depicted in Figure 6.10.

In Figure 6.10, ABRs 1 and 2 have been configured to summarize the backbone routes ranging from 145.36.64.0 /24 through 145.36.95.0 /24 by using the summary address 145.36.64.0 /19. The configuration for one of the ABRs is shown next:

```
ABR_2(router-config)#network 145.36.94.0 0.0.1.255 area 0
ABR_2(router-config)#network 145.36.121.1 0.0.0.0 area 1
ABR_2(router-config)#area 0 range 145.36.64.0 255.255.224.0
```

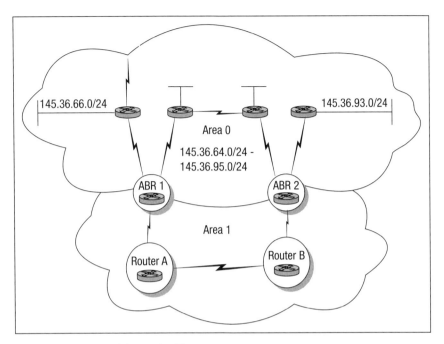

145.36.66.0/24

145.36.93.0/24

Area 0

145.36.64.0/24 -
145.36.95.0/24

ABR 1

ABR 2

Area 1

Router A

Router B

6

Figure 6.10   Summarizing the backbone area.

Now, both ABRs will advertise the backbone summary route with the same cost. Routers A and B will subsequently use the closest ABR in reaching the summary route. Therefore, when Router B needs to reach network 145.36.66.0 /.24 (which is summarized in 145.36.64.0 /19), Router B will use ABR 2. As Figure 6.10 shows, the path through ABR 2 to network 145.36.66.0 /24 is less optimal than the path through ABR 1. Likewise, the same suboptimal path selection would occur when Router A forwards traffic to network 145.36.93.0 /24.

Interestingly, if you were to reverse the area IDs in Figure 6.10 (making the backbone area 1, and area 1 the backbone) the same problems with suboptimal route selection would still occur. It is therefore best to use inter-area route summarization only when the area has a single ABR.

External Route Summarization

External route summarization is the other type of summarization that occurs in a multi-area internetwork. With this type, an ASBR can summarize external routes that the ASBR learns of via redistribution. These external summary routes would then be advertised throughout the OSPF internetwork via type 5 LSAs. Upon receiving these AS-external LSAs, OSPF routers would subsequently add them to their topological databases and run the SPF algorithm to calculate the best path to each external summary route advertised in the LSA. As was the case with inter-area route summarization, summarizing external networks causes a reduction in resource consumption and shields the OSPF internetwork from external topology changes.

However, as was also the case with inter-area route summarization, configuring multiple ASBRs with the same summary routes may lead to suboptimal path selection. Because summarized external routes and costs would not be explicitly stated in a router's routing table, the router would have no way of discerning the best path to one of these implicit routes.

External route summarization occurs only on ASBRs. Configuring it on any other router will have no effect. In addition, external route summarization applies only to external routes that are redistributed into OSPF. This means that ASBRs cannot summarize OSPF routes and then redistribute these routes into another routing protocol. Chapter 13 covers OSPF redistribution and the alternatives.

Configuration of External Route Summarization

The following command is used on an ASBR to summarize external routes:

```
Router(config-router)#summary-address ip-address mask
```

The *ip-address* and *mask* parameters together signify the range of addresses that are being summarized. Note that the *mask* is a wildcard mask.

Figure 6.11 shows an OSPF internetwork in which ASBRs 1 and 2 are redistributing BGP routes into OSPF.

ASBR 1 is redistributing networks 150.239.64.0 /24 through 150.239.95.0 /24, and ASBR 2 is redistributing networks 150.239.96.0 /24 through 150.239.127.0 /24. Both of these autonomous system boundary routers are configured to summarize their contiguous routes with the following commands:

```
ASBR_1(config-router)#summary-address 150.239.64.0 255.255.224.0
```

```
ASBR_2(config-router)#summary-address 150.239.96.0 255.255.224.0
```

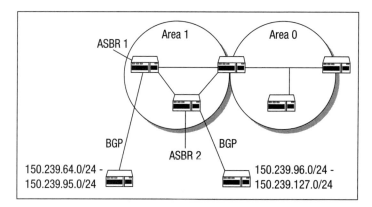

Figure 6.11 Summarizing external routes.

ASBR 1 will consequently advertise to the OSPF domain a type 5 LSA that contains the external summary route 150.239.64.0 /19, whereas ASBR 2's AS-external-LSA will read 150.239.96.0 /19.

Note that even though we are summarizing at multiple ASBRs, the summary routes are different. What this means is that any traffic destined for any of ASBR 1's summarized routes goes through ASBR 1, and any traffic that is destined for any of ASBR 2's summarized routes goes through ASBR 2. Because neither of these two ASBRs is sharing any common external routes, suboptimal path selection is not an issue.

At this point, it would be useful if we could cover the reasoning that a router employs in matching packets with routing table addresses. Consider the previous example. When an internal router receives a packet destined for the address 150.239.103.10 /24, the router will search its routing table for an address whose network bits most closely match 150.239.103.10 /24.

With the following addresses in its routing table:

```
216.39.87.8  /29
107.50.101.0 /24
107.50.98.0  /24
150.239.64.0 /19
150.239.96.0 /19
```

the OSPF router immediately sees that 150.239.64.0 /19 and 150.239.96.0 /19 are possible matches for 160.239.103.10 /24. To see which of these two networks gets selected let us convert the addresses to binary:

```
150.239.64.0  = 10010110.11101111.01000000.00000000
150.239.96.0  = 10010110.11101111.01100000.00000000
150.239.103.10 =10010001.11101111.01100111.00001010
```

The router bases its selection on whichever address shares the most network bits with 150.239.103.10 /24 (the network bits are identified with the prefix mask; 150.239.103.10 /24 has 24 network bits, whereas the other two addresses have 19 network bits). The address, however, would not need to share the same prefix mask with 150.239.130.0 /24. We therefore see that 150.239.96.0 /19 shares the most network bits in common with 150.239.103.10 /24, with a total of 19 matching network bits. On the other hand, network 150.239.64.0 /19 shares only 18 matching network bits.

Summary of OSPF Route Summarization

OSPF employs two types of route summarization: inter-area and external. Inter-area route summarization applies only to routes within an area and is configured only on ABRs. External route summarization applies only to routes injected into OSPF via redistribution and is configured only on ASBRs.

OSPF Cost Calculation

We have thus far seen examples of how cost plays a factor in influencing route selection. The next sections explain exactly how these costs are calculated for both the summary routes and external routes. As we will see, the nature of both these types of routes necessitates a somewhat different approach to cost calculation than the usual approach of adding up the cost of each link in a path.

Cost Calculation for Summary Routes

Inter-area route summarization creates a summary route that gets advertised in a type 3 LSA by an ABR. Multiple routes are consolidated into the summary route, and each of these consolidated routes consequently loses its identity. Not only does a route's identity get taken in this Borg assimilation (Star Trek reference), the route's cost is lost as well. However, before all of the route costs are completely assimilated, the router will use them in calculating the cost for the new summary route. The cost for this new summary route becomes the smallest cost out of all the consolidated routes that are being summarized. For example, if the consolidated routes 133.16.1.0, 133.16.2.0, and 133.16.3.0 each had costs 64, 128, and 6, respectively, the summary route would have a cost of 6.

At this point the cost calculation process would resume its usual operation. That is, the router will increment the summary route cost by an amount equal to the cost of the backbone interface and will then advertise the summary LSA to the rest of the OSPF internetwork. Every router, upon receiving this summary route, would increment the cost by an amount equal to the cost of the interface on which the summary route would next be forwarded.

Figure 6.12 illustrates the steps in the process of calculating summary routes.

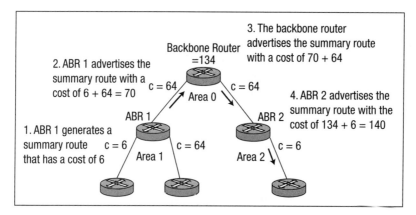

Figure 6.12   The steps in the process of calculating summary routes.

Cost Calculation for External Routes

External routes can be categorized as either type 1 or type 2. This categorization is based on how the cost for an external route is calculated. The cost for a type 1 external route is calculated just as it would be for any given area route, meaning that the cost for a type 1 external network gets incremented at each router hop. The cost for a type 2 external route, however, always stays equal to the cost of the external network and therefore does not get incremented at each hop. Figure 6.13 illustrates the process of external route calculation.

In Figure 6.13, the ASBR has been configured to redistribute external network 10.20.0.0 /16 as a type 1 route. As a result, this route gets advertised with a cost of $x + y$. Router A would then advertise a cost of $x + y + z$. However, if the ASBR was configured to redistribute 10.20.0.0 /16 as a type 2 external route, then the cost advertised to Router A would just be x. Router A would then advertise a cost of x to Router B.

It is best to use type 1 external routes when you have multiple ASBR advertising routes to the same external network. This is because using type 2 external routes in a multi-ASBR setting may lead to suboptimal path selection by internal routers. Therefore, try to use type 2 external routes only when you have one ASBR advertising an external route.

Advertising an External Default Route

While redistribution is the primary method of advertising external routes to the OSPF domain, sometimes an ASBR will also be configured to advertise a default

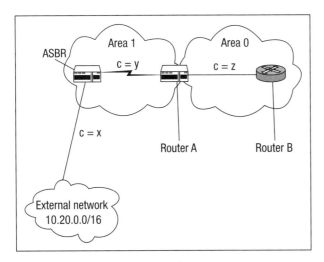

Figure 6.13   Calculating the costs for external routes.

route. This may be the case when there are just too many external networks from the outside world for the ASBR to keep track of. A default route is therefore useful when an internal router does not have explicit routing information on external networks listed in its routing table. By utilizing a default route, an internal router that receives a packet destined for an unknown network will be able to forward the packet to its ASBR. The ASBR would then forward the packet out to an external destination if the ASBR itself had a default route. Note, however, that if a router does not have a default route, then it will not be able to forward an unknown packet and must consequently drop the packet.

By default, an ASBR will not generate a default route and advertise it into the OSPF domain. The ASBR must be configured to do so with the following command:

```
ASBR(config-router)#default-information originate [always]
  [metric metric-value] [metric-type metric-type]
```

The *metric-value* parameter specifies the cost of the default route. The *metric-type* parameter specifies whether the default route is a type 1 (E1) or type 2 (E2) external route. The default metric-value is 10, and the default metric-type is 2.

There are two ways in which the **default-information originate** command can be used by an ASBR to advertise a default route into the OSPF domain. The first way is to omit the **always** parameter when issuing this command. By omitting the **always** parameter, the ASBR will advertise only 0.0.0.0 (the default route) if there is already a default route in the ASBR's routing table. This could occur, for instance, when an external AS running a different routing protocol or OSPF process advertises its default route to the OSPF domain. Figure 6.14 illustrates such a scenario.

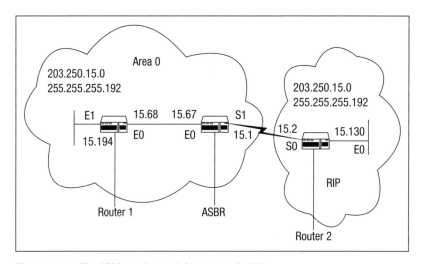

Figure 6.14 The ASBR receives a default route via RIP.

In Figure 6.14, Router 2 advertises 0.0.0.0 in a RIP update. Because the ASBR is running RIP, 0.0.0.0 is entered into the ASBR's routing table as a RIP-derived route. The following output depicts what the routing table would show:

```
ASBR#show ip route
Codes: C - connected, S - static, I - IGRP, R - RIP, M - mobile, B -BGP
       D - EIGRP, EX - EIGRP external, O - OSPF, IA - OSPF inter-area
       E1 - OSPF external type 1, E2 - OSPF external type 2, E - EGP
       i - IS-IS, L1 - IS-IS level-1, L2 - IS-IS level-2, * - candidate
default

 Gateway of last resort is 203.250.15.2 to network 0.0.0.0

     203.250.15.0 255.255.255.192 is subnetted, 4 subnets
 C       203.250.15.0 is directly connected, Serial1
 C       203.250.15.64 is directly connected, Ethernet0
 R       203.250.15.128 [120/1] via 203.250.15.2, 00:00:17, Serial1
 O       203.250.15.192 [110/20] via 203.250.15.68, 2d23, Ethernet0
 R*   0.0.0.0 0.0.0.0 [120/1] via 203.250.15.2, 00:00:17, Serial1
              [120/1] via 203.250.15.68, 00:00:32, Ethernet0
```

In addition, the ASBR has been configured to redistribute RIP into OSPF. However, the default route will not get translated into OSPF until the **default-information originate** command is issued:

```
ASBR(config-router)#default-information originate metric 10 metric-type 2
```

This command now tells the ASBR to generate (in OSPF language) and advertise a default route to the OSPF domain, but only if the ASBR has a default route. In this scenario, the ASBR has received a default route from Router A. The ASBR can therefore advertise 0.0.0.0 in an AS-external-LSA (type 5) to the OSPF domain.

A sample of Router A's routing table after it receives the default route follows:

```
Router_A#show ip route
Codes: C - connected, S - static, I - IGRP, R - RIP, M - mobile, B - BGP
       D - EIGRP, EX - EIGRP external, O - OSPF, IA - OSPF inter-area
       E1 - OSPF external type 1, E2 - OSPF external type 2, E - EGP
       i - IS-IS, L1 - IS-IS level-1, L2 - IS-IS level-2, * - candidate
default

 Gateway of last resort is 203.250.15.67 to network 0.0.0.0

     203.250.15.0 255.255.255.192 is subnetted, 4 subnets
 O       203.250.15.0 [110/74] via 203.250.15.67, 2d23, Ethernet0
 C       203.250.15.64 is directly connected, Ethernet0
```

```
O E2    203.250.15.128 [110/10] via 203.250.15.67, 2d23, Ethernet0
C       203.250.15.192 is directly connected, Ethernet1
O*E2  0.0.0.0 0.0.0.0 [110/10] via 203.250.15.67, 00:00:17, Ethernet0
```

Note that the default route is designated type 2 (E2). This means that the route will always be advertised without cost incrementation. We see that this is the case here because 0.0.0.0 still has a cost of 10 even though the route was advertised.

As mentioned earlier, there are two ways in which the **default-information originate** command can be used to propagate a default route into the OSPF domain. We have just covered the first way. The second way is by including the **always** parameter in the command. The inclusion of this parameter instructs the router to always advertise 0.0.0.0 to the OSPF domain regardless of whether this router has a default route. Due to this unconditional advertisement, you need to make sure that the ASBR does in fact have a default path; otherwise, any unknown packets will be dropped.

Virtual Links

OSPF's hierarchical solution would not be complete without the virtual link. There are times when an OSPF area is being added to the internetwork but cannot directly attach to the backbone area. Other times, two merging OSPF internetworks will require that their backbone areas be connected without being directly attached. Situations also arise for which a redundant connection is needed as a safeguard against a backbone area that splits in half due to router failures.

In all these situations, the virtual link stands as the solution for connecting a disconnected area to the backbone. Figure 6.15 shows an example of a virtual link topology.

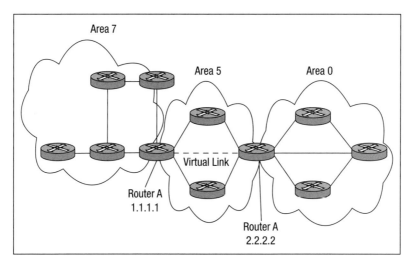

Figure 6.15 Virtual links connect disconnected areas to the backbone area.

The area through which a virtual link traverses is known as the *transit area*. This area can already exist or it can be created. It must not, however, be any type of stub area because it needs to maintain full routing information. In addition, the virtual link cannot traverse multiple areas because this would violate the rule that all inter-area traffic must go through the backbone.

Many OSPF network designers recommend that virtual links not be incorporated into the initial network design because OSPF traffic is best optimized to traverse areas that are directly attached to the backbone. In addition, virtual links preclude backbone area routes from being summarized.

Configuring Virtual Links

Virtual links are point-to-point connections between two routers. Configuration of a virtual link amounts to issuing the following command on both of these routers:

```
Router(config-router)#area area-id virtual-link router-id
```

The *area-id* parameter denotes the area that will serve as the virtual link's transit area. The *router-id* identifies the router that is on the other end of the virtual link.

The following example shows what the configuration would be for the virtual link pictured in Figure 6.15:

```
Router_A(config-router)#area 5 virtual-link 2.2.2.2
```

```
Router_B(config-router)#area 5 virtual-link 1.1.1.1
```

Note that Router A's configuration specifies the router ID of Router B, whereas Router B's configuration specifies the router ID of Router A. Area 5 denotes the transit area for this virtual link.

OSPF in a Multi-Area Nonbroadcast Environment

A challenge may arise in implementing and designing OSPF areas in a nonbroadcast network such as Frame-Relay. To therefore maximize the efficiency with which OSPF operation occurs in such networks, it is best to configure OSPF over a partial mesh topology. This is because a full mesh topology will likely generate quite a bit of OSPF overhead traffic due to the number of active and potentially failed links.

Depending on the network's design, it can also be beneficial to configure the nonbroadcast network in its own area. As we have witnessed in the multi-area broadcast networks, this type of OSPF design would reduce resource consumption on routers and would help centralize traffic within areas. If the design permitted, it can also be of added benefit to designate the nonbroadcast area as stub (or totally stub or NSSA).

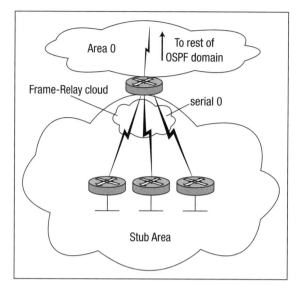

Figure 6.16 OSPF in a nonbroadcast stub area.

Figure 6.16 shows an example of a topology in which OSPF is configured in a partial-mesh nonbroadcast stub network.

Verification of OSPF in a Multi-Area Environment

In addition to the verification commands covered in the previous chapter, two new commands allow you to monitor certain OSPF statistics in a multi-area environment. These **show** commands are:

➤ **show ip ospf border-routers**

➤ **show ip ospf virtual-links**

The **show ip ospf border-routers** Command

The **show ip ospf border-routers** command allows you to view all of the ABRs and ASBRs that an internal router knows of. The output for this command is:

```
Router# show ip ospf border-routers

OSPF Process 109 internal Routing Table

Destination       Next Hop        Cost   Type    Rte Type  Area     SPF No

160.89.97.53      144.144.1.53    10     ABR     INTRA     0.0.0.3  3
160.89.103.51     160.89.96.51    10     ABR     INTRA     0.0.0.3  3
160.89.103.52     160.89.96.51    20     ASBR    INTER     0.0.0.3  3
160.89.103.52     144.144.1.53    22     ASBR    INTER     0.0.0.3  3
```

Table 6.4   Explanation of show ip ospf border-routers command.

Field	Description
Destination	Router ID of the ABR or ASBR
Next Hop	Next-hop router toward the destination
Cost	Cost to reach the destination
Type	Indicates whether the destination is an ABR or ASBR
Rte Type	Route type; can be either an intra-area or inter-area route
Area	Area ID of the area that this route is learned from
SPF No	SPF calculation number that installs this route

Table 6.4 explains what each field represents.

The **show ip ospf virtual-links** Command

The **show ip ospf virtual-links** command is used to verify the configuration of a virtual link. This command identifies such statistics as whether the link is up, the link's state, the area ID of the transit area, and the value of timer intervals.

The output from the **show ip ospf virtual-links** command is:

```
Router# show ip ospf virtual-links

Virtual Link to router 160.89.101.2 is up
Transit area 0.0.0.1, via interface Ethernet0, Cost of using 10
Transmit Delay is 1 sec, State POINT_TO_POINT
Timer intervals configured, Hello 10, Dead 40, Wait 40, Retransmit 5
Hello due in 0:00:08
Adjacency State FULL
```

Chapter Summary

In a single-area environment, OSPF encounters several problems when attempting to scale. These problems have to do with resource consumption on both routers and media and include:

➤ Increased CPU utilization

➤ Decreased memory availability

➤ Increased bandwidth utilization

Degradation of network efficiency and reliability ensues when these problems go unchecked. OSPF's hierarchical solution addresses each of these scalability issues by dividing a single area into multiple areas and providing several tools that have the effects of centralizing OSPF traffic and reducing resource consumption. One of these tools, route summarization, achieves this by consolidating multiple routes into one or more summary routes, which can then be advertised to the OSPF domain. There are two types of OSPF route summarization: inter-area and external.

Area designation is another hierarchical tool used in multi-area environments. An area can be designated as either standard, backbone, stub, totally stub, or NSSA. These designations are allocated by configuring the routers for the areas in which they will reside. This configuration subsequently classifies routers as one of several types: standard, backbone, ABR, ASBR, and specialty. An area designation also influences which OSPF traffic types the area will receive and forward. These traffic types are embodied in several types of LSAs. The inter-area LSAs include LSA types 3, 4, and 5.

The virtual link is a hierarchical component that provides a means to connect areas that are disconnected from the backbone area.

This concludes our discussion on OSPF. We are now aware that the Internet's premier IGP is indeed a highly efficient and powerful routing protocol that can rise admirably to meet the requirements of scalable internetworks. But there is another routing protocol that is challenging OSPF's championship title. This contender is EIGRP, the subject of our next chapter.

Review Questions

1. Which of the following is not a warning sign that indicates a single area is outgrowing its environment?

    a. The topological database is getting large.

    b. The routing table is getting large.

    c. The SPF algorithm is being frequently executed.

    d. The router fails to establish any adjacencies.

2. What are some of the benefits of OSPF's hierarchical solution? Choose two.

    a. It centralizes OSPF traffic.

    b. It allows all areas to maintain the same topological databases.

    c. It eliminates the DR election.

    d. It reduces resource consumption.

3. What is route summarization?

   a. The advertisement of only variable-length subnet masks (VLSMs).

   b. The process of combining a router's interface addresses into a single interface address.

   c. The consolidation of multiple contiguous routes into a single summary route.

   d. The consolidation of multiple noncontiguous routes into a single summary route.

4. Which of the following are benefits of OSPF route summarization? [Choose the two best answers]

   a. Reduces the sizes of routing tables.

   b. Keeps non–OSPF traffic from traveling to summarized routes.

   c. Reduces the frequency of the SPF algorithm calculation.

   d. Allows internal routers to generate summary routes.

5. Which one of the following areas does not accept type 3, 4, and 5 LSAs?

   a. Backbone area

   b. Stub area

   c. Standard hybrid area

   d. Totally stub area

6. What does the backbone area do?

   a. It prevents type 5 LSAs from being forwarded to standard areas.

   b. It maintains topological databases for only standard areas.

   c. It connects all areas.

   d. It floods all LSAs to NSSAs.

7. What is a network-summary-LSA?

   a. An LSA that describes reachability to ASBRs.

   b. An LSA that describes reachability to routes within an area.

   c. An LSA that must utilize route summarization.

   d. An LSA that is generated only by ASBRs.

8. Explain the path that a routing update follows throughout the OSPF domain (assume that no route summarization is in effect).

   a. (1) An internal router floods a topology update throughout its area, (2) the ABR receives the update and floods it out only nonbackbone interfaces, (3) ABRs receive the update and flood it to their respective areas.

   b. (1) An ABR queries internal routers for topology changes, (2) the ABR then floods an update to the backbone area, (3) ABRs receive the update and flood it to their respective areas.

   c. (1) An internal router floods a topology update throughout its area, (2) the ABR receives the update and floods it to the backbone area, (3) ABRs receive the update but do not flood it to their respective areas.

   d. (1) An internal router floods a topology update throughout its area, (2) the ABR receives the update and floods it to the backbone area, (3) ABRs receive the update and flood it to their respective areas.

9. What must stub, totally stub, and NSSA areas have in order to reach destinations that are restricted to these areas?

   a. A rogue ABR that does not recognize its area's status

   b. A default route

   c. Type 8 LSAs

   d. These areas can never reach restricted destinations

10. Which command configures a totally stub area?

    a. **router(config)#area 1 range 136.14.200.0 0.0.0.255**

    b. **router(config)#area 1 stub no-summary**

    c. **router(config-router)#stub area 1 no-summary**

    d. **router(config-router)# area 1 stub no-summary**

11. Which of the following is not a restriction imposed on stub areas?

    a. Virtual links cannot traverse the stub area.

    b. Static routes must be used.

    c. The stub area cannot be a backbone area.

    d. An ASBR cannot lay internal to the stub area.

12. Why is it important for stub areas to have only one gateway (ABR) ?

    a. Because having multiple gateways could lead internal routers to select suboptimal paths

    b. Because internal routers only choose one gateway anyway

    c. Having only one gateway facilitates security policies

    d. Having multiple gateways precludes the propagation of type 3 LSAs

13. What is inter-area route summarization?

    a. The consolidation of type 3 LSA routes into a single summary route

    b. The consolidation of external routes into a single summary route

    c. An activity that occurs only on ASBRs

    d. The summarization of type 1 routes

14. Choose the appropriate command for external route summarization.

    a. **router(config-router)#area 1 range 132.16.64.0 0.0.63.255**

    b. **router(config-router)#area 1 summary 132.16.64.0 0.0.63.255**

    c. **router(config-router)#summary address 132.16.64.0 0.0.63.255**

    d. **router(config-router)#summary-address 132.16.64.0 255.255.192.0**

6

15. How does a router match a packet's destination address with a routing table entry?

    a. The router sees which routing table entry shares the same prefix mask with the packet's address.

    b. The router sees which routing table entry shares the most network bits in common with the packet's address.

    c. The router does a Boolean AND.

    d. The router chooses the routing table entry with the longest prefix mask.

16. How are costs calculated for summary routes?

    a. The cost of a summary route is equal to the greatest cost of an inter-area route.

    b. The cost of a summary route is equal to the average of all costs that are being consolidated.

    c. The cost of a summary route is equal to the cost of the link on which the summary route will be advertised.

    d. The cost of a summary route is equal to the smallest cost of an inter-area route that is consolidated within the summary route.

17. What is the difference between a type 1 and type 2 external route?

    a. The cost of a type 1 external route always remains equal to the cost of the external routes, no matter where it gets advertised in the OSPF domain.

    b. The cost of a type 2 external route always remains equal to the cost of the link on which the external route gets advertised.

    c. The cost of a type 1 external route is equal to the cost of the external route. When this route is advertised, its cost gets incremented by the cost of the link on which the advertisement occurs.

    d. The cost of a type 2 external route gets incremented at each router hop.

18. What command causes an ASBR to advertise a default route only if the ASBR already has a default route?

    a. **router(config)#default-information originate**

    b. **router(config)#default information originate**

    c. **router(config-router)#default-information originate**

    d. **router(config-router)#default information originate**

19. What does a virtual link not do?

    a. Connect disconnected areas with the backbone

    b. Connect external autonomous systems with the ASBR

    c. Merge two disconnected backbone areas

    d. Provide redundancy

20. What does the **show ip ospf border-routers** command indicate?

    a. The link-state of known ABRs and ASBRs

    b. The areas in which the known ABRs and ASBRs reside

    c. The router IDs of known ABRs and ASBRs

    d. The interfaces used to reach known ABRs and ASBRs

Real-World Project

A single-area OSPF network is no longer capable of sustaining a company's technical requirements for efficiency and reliability. As a result, you have been contracted to provide a solution that will adequately resolve the scalability issues this company is facing. After completing your analysis of the network's current operation, you conclude that the single area should be divided into three separate areas. One area would be the backbone, another would be a totally stub area, and the last one would be an NSSA. Figure 6.17 shows the logical topology of this new multi-area inter-network.

Your task now is to configure the routers for their appropriate areas. Your associate has already configured all the internal routers and Router E. You are therefore left with Router D, Router C, and the ASBR.

Configuring Router C:

1. After completing the initial configurations for Router C, enter router configuration mode.

```
Router_C(config)#router ospf 1
```

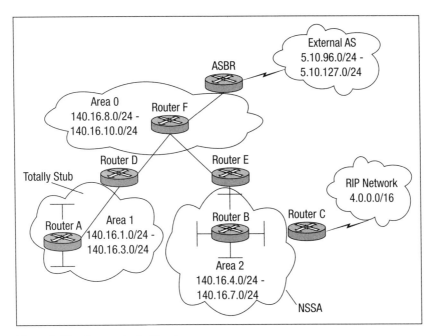

Figure 6.17   The new logical topology.

2. In router configuration mode, specify the interfaces that will be participating in area 2.

```
Router_C(config-router)#network 140.16.7.0 0.0.0.255 area 2
```

This command specifies that any interface that matches 140.16.7.0 0.0.0.255 will be placed in area 2.

3. In the same configuration mode, redistribute RIP subnets into OSPF.

```
Router_C(config-router)#redistribute rip subnets
```

This command allows RIP-learned routes to be injected into the OSPF domain.

4. In the same configuration mode, configure Router C as an NSSA router.

```
Router_C(config-router)#area 2 nssa
```

Router C will subsequently use type 7 LSAs to redistribute and advertise RIP routes.

Configuring Router D:

1. After having completed Router D's initial configuration, enter router configuration mode and specify the interfaces that are to participate in area 1.

```
Router_D(config)#router ospf 1
Router_D(config-router)#network 140.16.1.0 0.0.0.255 area 1
```

2. Summarize networks 140.16.1.0 /24 through 140.16.3.0 /24 with the summary route 140.16.0.0 /22.

```
Router_D(config-router)#area 1 range 140.16.0.0 255.255.252.0
```

Router D will subsequently advertise a type 3 LSA containing the summary route 140.16.0.0 /22.

3. Configure area 1 as totally stub.

```
Router_D(config-router)#area 1 stub no-summary
```

Router D will no longer forward any inter-area OSPF traffic to area 1. Recall, however, that a totally stub ABR will still advertise summary LSAs to the rest of the OSPF domain.

Configuring the ASBR:

1. After completing the ASBR's initial configuration, enter router configuration mode and specify the interfaces that are to participate in area 0.

```
ASBR(config)#router ospf 1
ASBR(config-router)#network 140.16.7.1 0.0.0.0 area 0
```

2. Configure the ASBR to redistribute BGP routes.

```
ASBR(config-router)# redistribute bgp subnets
```

This command causes the ASBR to inject BGP-learned routes into the OSPF domain.

3. Configure the ASBR to always generate and advertise a default route to the OSPF domain.

```
ASBR(config-router)#default-information originate always
```

The ASBR will subsequently advertise a type 2 default route to the OSPF domain via a type 5 LSA.

4. Configure the ASBR to summarize external networks 5.10.96.0 /24 through 5.10.127.0 /24 by using the summary route 5.10.96.0 /19.

```
ASBR(config-router)#summary-address 5.10.96.0 255.255.224.0
```

The ASBR will subsequently advertise the external summary route 5.10.96.0 /19 to the OSPF domain via a type 5 LSA.

6

CHAPTER SEVEN

Enhanced Interior Gateway Routing Protocol

After completing this chapter you will be able to:

✓ Describe the key features of Enhanced Interior Gateway Routing Protocol (EIGRP)

✓ Describe how EIGRP builds neighbor relationships and discovers routes

✓ Explain how the Distributed Update ALgorithm (DUAL) chooses primary and backup routes

✓ Explain the differences between a successor and feasible successor

✓ Explain how EIGRP convergence occurs during a topology change

✓ Configure basic EIGRP operation

✓ Verify basic EIGRP operation

✓ Given a set of network requirements, configure an EIGRP environment and verify proper operation

T his chapter presents a detailed overview of the enhanced version of the Interior
Gateway Routing Protocol (IGRP) operation and basic configuration within a
broadcast environment. In this chapter, we discover that this advanced distance-vector
routing protocol offers a scalable solution to growing multiprotocol internetworks.
Like its link-state counterpart, Open Shortest Path First (OSPF), EIGRP incorporates a hierarchical routing solution that has the effects of minimizing resource
consumption and expediting convergence. However, before we can delve into the
full extent of EIGRP's hierarchical routing solution, we must first become thoroughly
familiar with this protocol's operation within a nonoptimized broadcast environment.
Only after seeing how EIGRP operates within such an environment can we proceed
knowledgeably to the next chapter, which presents the tools that EIGRP uses to
facilitate routing optimization. This chapter presents a thorough coverage of EIGRP's
essential features and functions, and lays the foundation for Chapter 8.

Overview

Enhanced Interior Gateway Routing Protocol is a Cisco proprietary routing
algorithm that was designed to be an enhanced version of IGRP. EIGRP therefore
incorporates many of the same distance-vector features found in IGRP, such as the
metric, but also differs significantly by incorporating link-state features that dramatically increase operating efficiency. These enhanced features include the following:

➤ *Rapid convergence*—The mechanism that EIGRP uses to achieve rapid convergence and a loop-free topology is the Distributed Update ALgorithm. It is the
DUAL's function to perform all route computations. Whenever a topology
change occurs, DUAL finds an alternative loop-free path in the router's topology
table. If there is no alternative path available, EIGRP sends out queries to
discover if any neighbors may have an alternative path that the router can use.
These queries are propagated throughout the internetwork, subsequently
allowing all routers involved with the topology change to synchronize at
the same time.

➤ *Reduced resource consumption*—EIGRP multicasts incremental updates instead of
periodic updates. This means that instead of updates being sent out at regular
intervals, updates are sent out only when a topology change occurs. Furthermore,
instead of transmitting the entire routing table, EIGRP updates contain information pertaining only to the topology change itself. Lastly, these topology
updates are received only by those routers that need to be informed (through
the use of certain hierarchical tools that will be the subject of the next chapter).
Together these features minimize bandwidth usage, free up router memory, and
reduce router CPU utilization levels.

➤ *Support for multiple routed protocols*—Unlike OSPF version 2, which supports
only IP, EIGRP also supports AppleTalk and Novell IPX. Each one of these

network protocols has a different set of requirements that EIGRP addresses through the use of protocol-dependent modules (PDMs). For example, the IP-IPX PDM sends and receives EIGRP packets encapsulated in IPX. The IP-IPX PDM is also responsible for communicating the information that the DUAL needs to make routing decisions for IPX.

➤ *Advanced metric*—Like IGRP, its predecessor, EIGRP uses a composite cost-calculation metric that can take into account bandwidth, delay, reliability, load, and maximum transmission unit (MTU). Also like IGRP, only bandwidth and delay are used by default in the cost-calculation formula. However, unlike IGRP, which uses a 24-bit metric, EIGRP's metric is 32 bits, which means that it can more accurately assess the feasibility of a route when determining the best path.

➤ *Flexible route summarization*—Unlike OSPF, EIGRP route summarization can be done manually on any router and on any interface. As shown in a later section of this chapter, this unique ability greatly facilitates EIGRP's hierarchical operation. Contiguous addressing is still a requirement.

➤ *Support for VLSM*—Route summarization is not possible without variable-length subnet masks (VLSMs). With VLSM support, summary routes can be propagated along with their prefix masks and can subsequently be understood by the receiving EIGRP router. This behavior is known as Classless Inter-Domain Routing (CIDR).

➤ *Unequal-cost load-balancing*—Unlike many other routing protocols, EIGRP supports unequal-cost load-balancing. This feature allows all types of traffic to be distributed across multiple paths that lead to the same destination and that meet certain feasibility requirements. The **variance** command is used to config-ure unequal-cost load-balancing.

➤ *Support for various topologies*—Like OSPF, EIGRP can run over various local area network (LAN) and wide area network (WAN) topologies, such as broadcast, nonbroadcast (e.g., nonbroadcast multiaccess, or NBMA), and point-to-point topologies. As will be seen in Chapter 8, the primary concern with EIGRP's operation within a WAN topology is the amount of bandwidth that is available for EIGRP traffic.

Terminology

This section covers some of the common EIGRP terms prevalent throughout this chapter and the next. These terms may be classified under the following categories:

➤ Information tables

➤ Operation

➤ Packet types

EIGRP's Information Tables

Like OSPF, EIGRP maintains three unique information repositories:

➤ Neighbor table

➤ Topology table

➤ Routing table

Neighbor Table

Enhanced IGRP's neighbor table is very similar to that of OSPF. Newly discovered neighbors get listed in the neighbor table along with other information such as the hello interval and holdtime. The hello interval states how often EIGRP sends hello packets to maintain bidirectional communication between directly connected (adjacent) neighbors. Holdtime is a value that states how many seconds a router can wait without hearing from a neighbor before that neighbor is considered dead (just like OSPF's dead-interval timer). There is a neighbor table for each protocol that EIGRP is configured to support.

The neighbor table also maintains certain information required by the Reliable Transport Protocol (RTP). This information includes sequence numbers, neighbor lists, and transmission lists.

Topology Table

Enhanced IGRP's topology table is similar to OSPF's topological database. The topology table contains all routes that have been learned from neighbor advertisements. These destinations can be either summary routes or individual routes. Listed for each topology table entry are (1) the destination network and subnet mask; (2) the network's state (e.g., passive or active); (3) how many successors the network has; (4) the best feasible distance (i.e., best cost) to reach the network; (4) which neighbors, if any, are advertising the network; (5) the feasible distance through each of these neighbors; (6) the cost that each neighbor is advertising; and (7) the interfaces used to reach the network. EIGRP maintains a topology table for each configured network protocol.

Routing Table

Like OSPF's routing table, Enhanced IGRP's routing table contains the best paths. By default, EIGRP's routing table maintains up to four equal-cost paths. Unequal-cost paths may also be maintained in this repository by using the **variance** command.

An EIGRP routing table entry contains such items as (1) the destination network and subnet mask; (2) whether this is an external, internal, or summary route; (3) the route's administrative distance; (4) the route's feasible distance; (5) the next-hop address; (6) the time since the last update; and (7) the interface used to reach the next-hop. A routing table exists for each configured network protocol.

Terms of EIGRP Operation

Several terms are used in explaining EIGRP operation. Some of the more common ones are the following:

➤ *Successor*—A successor is the next-hop router along the *best* path to a given destination. "Best" is defined here as least cost. Successors are listed in both the topology and routing tables. Multiple successors can be listed in the routing table if they satisfy certain requirements.

➤ *Feasible successor*—A feasible successor is the next-hop router along an *alternative* path to a given destination. To become a feasible successor, a router must meet certain requirements. Feasible successors are listed only in the topology table.

Note: Successors and feasible successors can also denote the routes, as opposed to just denoting the routers. These two denotations are interchangeable.

➤ *Distributed Update ALgorithm*—The DUAL is a finite-state machine that performs all route computations and guarantees a loop-free topology. Using a composite metric based on bandwidth and delay (by default), the DUAL calculates successors and feasible successors for each destination network listed in the topology table. Successors are placed in the routing table. Whenever a successor goes down, the DUAL must evaluate the topology table for any feasible successors. The best feasible successor that is found in the topology table is then placed in the routing table.

➤ *Route evaluation*—The route evaluation process occurs whenever a topology change is detected. In this process, the DUAL evaluates the router's topology table to discover all the best routes (successor routes) that can no longer be used because of the topology change. For each unusable successor route, the DUAL evaluates the router's topology table to discover whether an alternative route (feasible successor route) is currently listed. If the DUAL finds a feasible successor route, the DUAL will immediately replace the unusable successor route with it. In this instance, the route recomputation process would not occur.

➤ *Route recomputation*—If the DUAL does not find a feasible successor route, the DUAL must then begin the route recomputation process. During this process, the router will send out *query* packets to ask neighbors if they have an alternative route for the network in question. The route recomputation process ends once all neighbors have replied to the router and the router has finished either (1) adding an alternative route to its topology and routing tables, or (2) removing the queried route from its topology and routing tables.

➤ *Active state*—During a route recomputation, the routes lost due to a failed successor are said to be in an active state. The active state ends when a lost route has been restored or removed.

➤ *Passive state*—All routes that are not in the process of route recomputation are said to be in a passive state. This is the normal state for a route.

7

EIGRP Packet Types

Enhanced IGRP uses the following types of packets:

➤ *Hello*—Hellos are used for neighbor discovery and thereafter for maintaining bidirectional neighbor relationships. These packets are unreliably multicast.

➤ *Update*—Updates are used to notify neighbors of a route that has been either added to or removed from the topology and routing tables. In this case, the updates are multicast. Update packets are also used during neighbor initialization when topology tables are being built. In this latter case, the updates are unicast. All update packets are transmitted reliably.

➤ *Query*—A query packet is reliably multicast during the route recomputation process. The query packet asks neighbors whether they have an alternative route to an unreachable network.

➤ *Reply*—A reply is sent in response to a query. The reply indicates whether there is an alternative route to an unreachable network. Replies are always unicast reliably.

➤ *Acknowledgment*—The acknowledgment packet is used to acknowledge receipt of a reliable packet.

The Reliable Transport Protocol

Update, query, and reply packets are transmitted reliably. This means that these packets are guaranteed to be delivered accurately and in a timely manner. The machine responsible for always ensuring the guaranteed and accurate delivery of reliable packets is the Reliable Transport Protocol. Each time a reliable packet is generated, RTP assigns a sequence number x to the packet and includes a flag, which indicates that the packet must be acknowledged. When a neighbor receives the packet, it will look inside and see that an acknowledgment is expected. The neighbor subsequently proceeds to generate an acknowledgment packet that contains the sequence number $x + 1$. For instance, if a reliable packet is transmitted with a sequence number of 1, then the acknowledgment's sequence number will be $1 + 1 = 2$. Sequence numbers are assigned so that RTP can detect out-of-order packets. For instance, in this case, if RTP were to receive an acknowledgment of anything other than 2, then RTP would know that an acknowledgment was still due. RTP knows which neighbors still need to send acknowledgments because RTP maintains a *transmission list* that keeps track of neighbors who have been sent reliable packets. This transmission list is stored in the router's *neighbor* table. If a neighbor does not respond to a reliable transmission within a given amount of time, then RTP will retransmit the packet, up to a maximum of 16 times. After 16 times, the router will give up and just drop the packet. The router would then reestablish its neighbor relationship with this unresponsive neighbor.

It should be noted that a reliable packet requires an acknowledgment from *all* neighbors before the next reliable packet can be sent. Consequently, on a multiaccess network, an unresponsive neighbor would pose a significant threat to the timely flow of EIGRP operation by delaying routers from proceeding with their next transmissions. RTP, however, has been designed to handle these situations by retransmitting the non-acknowledged multicast packet as a *unicast* packet to the unresponsive neighbor. This solution allows routers to proceed with their usual operations.

EIGRP Operation

EIGRP operation comprises the following five stages:

➤ Building neighbor relationships

➤ Discovering routes

➤ Choosing the best routes

➤ Maintaining routes

➤ Removing routes

These stages do not necessarily occur sequentially. For instance, the first two stages occur at the same time, whereas the stage of choosing the best routes occurs also in the stage of maintaining routes.

Building Neighbor Relationships

When a router is first configured with EIGRP, it will multicast hello packets to directly connected routers. A router that receives a hello will establish bidirectional communication with its neighbor if the hello packet indicates that both routers are in the same autonomous system (AS) and are running the same network protocol. In addition, both routers must have matching *K values*, or EIGRP metric weights. Any mismatch in AS, protocol, or K value precludes the establishment of neighbor relationships. However, unlike OSPF, neighborship is still formed even though the hello and holdtime intervals may not match.

Hello packets are then transmitted every five seconds to verify that the neighbor relationship remains active. This five-second interval is default for all broadcast media (Ethernet, Token Ring, and FDDI), all point-to-point serial links (PPP, HDLC, and so forth), and all multipoint links with bandwidth greater than T1 (ISDN PRI, Frame-Relay, SMDS, and so forth). On multipoint links with bandwidth less than T1 speed (ISDN BRI, Frame-Relay, SMDS, and so forth), the default hello interval is 60 seconds. A neighbor that does not respond to a hello within a certain amount of time—the holdtime—is considered dead. Neighborship with this dead router is subsequently terminated and all topology table routes learned from it go into an active state.

Neighbor relationships are listed in a router's neighbor table. The neighbor table contains such information as the neighbor's address, the interface used to reach a neighbor, and the holdtime. EIGRP maintains a neighbor table for each network protocol (IP, IPX, AppleTalk) with which it is configured.

A sample of a router's neighbor table follows:

```
Router#show ip eigrp neighbors

IP-EIGRP Neighbors for process 77
ADDRESS           Interface   Holdtime  Uptime    Q       Seq   SRTT   RTO
                              (secs)    (h:m:s)   Count   Num   (ms)   (ms)
160.89.81.28      Ethernet1   13        0:00:41   0       11    4      20
160.89.80.28      Ethernet0   14        0:02:01   0       10    12     24
160.89.80.31      Ethernet0   12        0:02:02   0       4     5      20
```

Table 7.1 explains the fields in the neighbor table.

Discovering Routes

The process of discovering routes occurs at the *same* time that neighbor relationships are established. The following steps describe the route discovery process (see Figure 7.1):

1. Router A comes online and multicasts hello packets out all interfaces that have been configured to participate in EIGRP routing. The EIGRP multicast address is 224.0.0.10.

2. Directly connected routers receive the hello packet and reply with unicast update packets that contain all the routes they have in their routing tables.

Table 7.1   The neighbor table lists all neighbor relationships.

Field	Description
Address	The interface IP-address of the neighbor.
Interface	The interface used to reach this neighbor.
Hold	The number of seconds left before a neighbor is considered dead. Any EIGRP packet received from the neighbor resets the hold value to the holdtime value (15 seconds on broadcast media).
Uptime	Indicates how old the neighbor relationship is.
SRTT	Smooth Round Trip Timer; indicates the average time (in milliseconds) it takes to send a packet to and receive a reply from the neighbor.
RTO	Retransmission Timeout; indicates how long the router will wait without receiving an acknowledgment to a reliably transmitted packet before retransmitting the packet.
Q	Queue; the number of EIGRP packets waiting to be sent.
Seq	Sequence number; the sequence number that was last received from a neighbor.

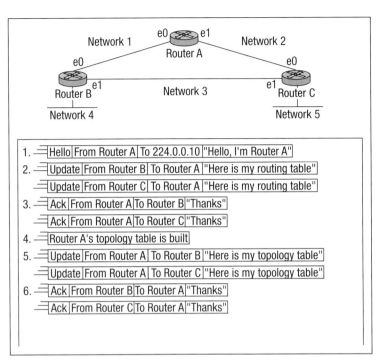

Network 1   e0 ⊠ e1   Network 2

Router A

e0

e0

e1

Router B   Network 3   e1 Router C

Network 4   Network 5

1. ═══ Hello From Router A To 224.0.0.10 "Hello, I'm Router A"
2. ═══ Update From Router B To Router A "Here is my routing table"
   ═══ Update From Router C To Router A "Here is my routing table"
3. ═══ Ack From Router A To Router B "Thanks"
   ═══ Ack From Router A To Router C "Thanks"
4. ═══ Router A's topology table is built
5. ═══ Update From Router A To Router B "Here is my topology table"
   ═══ Update From Router A To Router C "Here is my topology table"
6. ═══ Ack From Router B To Router A "Thanks"
   ═══ Ack From Router C To Router A "Thanks"

Figure 7.1   Route initialization is an efficient process for EIGRP.

3. Router A receives the unicast update packets and replies to each neighbor with a unicast Ack (acknowledgment) packet.

4. Router A then places all the update packets into its topology table.

5. Once its topology table has been built from the update packets received by all directly connected neighbors, Router A proceeds to unicast update packets to each of these neighbors. This update packet contains Router A's topology table.

Note: Any route learned from a neighbor will be included in the update packet sent to that neighbor. However, the route will be sent with a maximum metric (poison route). Like Split Horizon, route poisoning is a loop prevention mechanism.

6. All neighbors receive Router A's topology table and reply with an Ack packet.

At this point, Router A's topology table contains all the routes that neighbors have in their routing tables. Even though these routes are certainly the best routes that neighbors have to offer, Router A is able to utilize only one route for any given destination. (Having multiple *unequal-cost* paths to a network is not permissible unless the router is configured to load-balance, although the router may utilize multiple *equal-cost* paths.) However, the router will still keep all received routes in its topology table to have alternative paths available for whenever the primary path goes down. Both types of paths are distinguished based on their computed metrics.

In this example, it would now be necessary for Router A's DUAL to compute the best routes (successors) and alternative routes (feasible successors) for each network that is listed in Router A's topology table.

Choosing Primary and Backup Routes

The DUAL finite state machine is responsible for choosing EIGRP's best and alternative routes. It does this by first computing the metric for each route in the topology table using the following default formula:

metric = 256[(10,000,000/**min bandwidth**)+ **sum of delays**]

where **min bandwidth** equals the minimum bandwidth of all interfaces along the path and **sum of delays** equals the sum of all interface delays along the same path. For instance, in Figure 7.2, the path from Router 1 to network D going through Router 4 has a minimum bandwidth of 56Kbps, whereas the sum of all delays along this path is 2,000 + 100 + 100 = 2,200.

*Note: The delay value of an interface can be seen with the **show interface** command. However, before using the delay value from this command in the default formula, make sure to divide it by 10 because the default formula expresses delay in tens of microseconds. The **show interface** delay value is in microseconds only. For example, if the delay seen in the **show interface** command is 1,000, divide it by 10, yielding 100. Then 100 is the value you would use in the metric formula.*

In Figure 7.2, Router 1 has just built its topology table and is about to run the DUAL on it to discover the best alternative paths for each listed destination. Let us see how it computes the best path for network D:

Path to network D through Router 2:

256[(10,000,000/56) + 2,200] = 256 [178,571 + 2,200] = 256x180,771 = 46,021,376

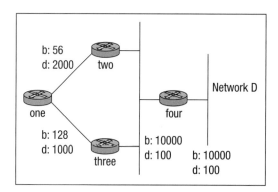

Figure 7.2 Calculating the metric using bandwidth and delay.

Path to network D through Router 3:

$256[(10,000,000/128) + 1,200] = 256 [78,125 + 1,200] = 256 \times 79,325 = 20,307,200$

The cost to reach network D through Router 3 is less than the cost to reach network D through Router 2. The DUAL therefore chooses its best route to network D as the one going to Router 3. Router 3 becomes Router 1's successor for network D. Network D is subsequently entered into the routing table with a cost of 20,307,200. This cost is referred to as the *feasible distance*, defined as the cost to reach a destination.

· Once the DUAL has calculated the successor, it must then calculate the feasible successor (alternate route). The technical definition of a feasible successor is a router whose advertised distance is *less* than the feasible distance through the successor. For example, in Figure 7.2, Router 1 has an alternative path to network D going to Router 2. To see whether Router 2 qualifies as a feasible successor, the DUAL compares the cost advertised by Router 2 with the feasible distance that was just calculated. Let us see what cost Router 2 advertised to Router 1:

Router 2's feasible distance to network D:

$256[(10,000,000/10,000) + 200] = 256[1,000 + 200] = 256 \times 1,200 = 307,200$

Because 307,200 is less than 20,307,200, Router 1's DUAL subsequently tags Router 2 as a feasible successor for network D. The feasible successor will not be placed in the routing table; however, it remains in the topology table.

Figure 7.3 shows another topology in which the DUAL is calculating successors and feasible successors. In Figure 7.3, Router 1 has two paths to network A: The path through Router 2 has a feasible distance of 46,789,476, whereas the path through Router 4 has a feasible distance of 20,307,200. Router 1 subsequently chooses Router 4 as its successor for network A. Router 2 is not chosen as a feasible successor because its advertised distance is 46,277,486, which is greater than 20,307,200. It is important to note that the route to network A through Router 2 is still kept in the topology table.

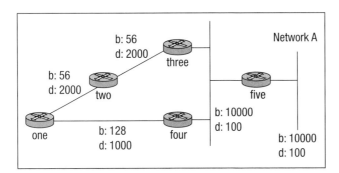

Figure 7.3   Another example of choosing routes.

Maintaining Routes

Network topology changes are inevitable. New networks come up, old routes fail, new routers come online, and router interfaces go offline. EIGRP has been designed to handle all these situations with an efficiency and quickness that allow businesses and corporations to continue operating reliably with minimal downtime and minimal cost. EIGRP is even considered better than OSPF at handling volatile networks because of the minimal resource consumption that EIGRP uses to converge on topology changes. That is, EIGRP expedites convergence by limiting the impact of certain topology changes to only those routers that need to be informed. OSPF, on the other hand, must inform all neighbors in an area of a topology change, which subsequently leads to increased CPU utilization. For a topology that is in a constant state of flux, an entire OSPF area would constantly be required to execute the SPF algorithm and consequently would find convergence always short-lived.

The following subsections discuss the fundamentals behind EIGRP convergence. Chapter 8 explains how convergence can be optimized to meet a network's needs for scalability, performance, and responsiveness.

EIGRP Convergence When a New Router and Network Come Online

A new router that comes online in a production environment will immediately send hello packets out all of its EIGRP interfaces to establish neighborship with directly connected routers. This is the same neighbor discovery process previously discussed. The new router will also inform its newly discovered neighbors of any new networks that have come online due to the router's addition. This process was previously discussed in the section "Discovering Routes," wherein neighbors exchange updates to build their topology tables.

Upon being informed of the new router, the new router's neighbors would subsequently multicast updates to inform their own neighbors of the new networks that have just come online. Neighbors receiving these multicast updates would in turn (1) add the new networks to their topology tables; (2) run the DUAL to calculate successors and feasible successors; (3) add the successors to the routing table; and (4) multicast an update to additional neighbors. In this manner, all routers in an EIGRP internetwork learn of newly added networks (assuming route summarization, filtering, or some other such mechanism is not in place).

Figure 7.4 illustrates a topology that we will use in outlining the steps that EIGRP takes to converge on a new router and new networks. Router 1 has just been installed. A new Ethernet segment (10.1.10.0 /24) was attached, and EIGRP has been configured to be the routing protocol. The following steps now occur:

1. Router 1 multicasts hello packets out both Ethernet interfaces.

2. Because there are no other routers on 10.1.10.0 /24, no reply is received from this network. However, when Router 2 receives the hello, it enters Router 1

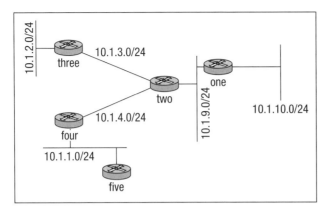

Figure 7.4   Converging on a new router and new networks.

into its neighbor table and sends a hello back to Router 1 along with an update packet that contains Router 2's routing table.

3. Router 1 receives this information, acknowledges it, and subsequently proceeds to enter Router 2 into its neighbor table. Router 1 then builds its topology table and unicasts it to Router 2. At this point, Router 1's topology table contains all networks in the AS. The DUAL is subsequently run on the topology table.

4. While Router 1's DUAL is running, Router 2 analyzes the new router's topology table and notices that there is a new entry, network 10.1.10.0 /24. Router 2 proceeds to enter this network into its topology table and run the DUAL for this route. This computation is practically instantaneous because there is only one way to get to 10.1.10.0 /24. After entering the new network in its routing table, Router 2 then generates an update that contains this new routing entry and multicasts it to Routers 3 and 4. At this point, convergence has completed on Routers 1 and 2.

5. After acknowledging the update, Routers 3 and 4 proceed simultaneously to add the new network to their topology tables, run the DUAL, and make a routing table entry. Router 3 is now done converging, whereas Router 4 is done converging once it generates an update and multicasts it to Router 5.

6. Router 5 processes the new network and converges. Although convergence is not *exactly* simultaneous, it is nonetheless very near to being simultaneous. The EIGRP convergence sequence can be likened to a set of dominoes lined up in a beautifully intricate array. When one domino is struck, they all fall down sequentially and in parallel. Similarly, when an EIGRP router sets off a topology change, all routers quickly converge in a sequential and parallel fashion. To the human eye, this process might indeed appear instantaneous.

7

Converging on a Failed Route—Route Evaluation

We have seen how convergence occurs when new EIGRP components come online. Now we will look at how convergence occurs when one of these components fails. Link failure is the most common form of network component failure. A router that loses a link will also lose its best means of reaching certain destinations. Furthermore, other routers that depended on this failed link would likewise lose their best means of reaching certain destinations. Convergence in this case proceeds through a sequence of events in which routers must first analyze their topology tables in an attempt at determining whether there are any alternative routes (feasible successors) to a destination that can no longer be reached through the best means. Once a router has found an alternative and valid means of reaching the lost destination, it must then inform its neighbors that it has converged on a new route. The neighbors would, in turn, proceed through the same steps of (1) determining which routes are no longer valid and which routes need to be replaced, and (2) then informing their own neighbors of the topology change. In this manner, an entire EIGRP internetwork is apprised of a failed link (once again assuming that there are no mechanisms in place that would artificially limit the extent of topology change notifications). Although convergence in this case may appear to be a complex process, to the routers executing this process it is "just another day on the job." The mechanical efficiency and expediency with which routers perform their duties belies the complexity that human intelligence may at times ascribe to such mechanical processes.

Figure 7.5 illustrates a scenario in which Router 2's link to network B has failed. Table 7.2 shows a summary of Router 2's topology table prior to the failure of this link.

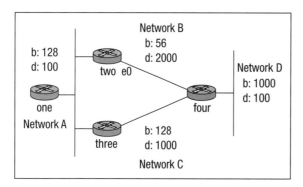

Figure 7.5 Converging on a failed route.

Table 7.2 Router 2's topology table prior to the link failure.

Network	Successor	Feasible Successor	Feasible Distance (Through Successor)	Advertised Distance (From Feasible Successor)
C	Router 3	Router 4	20281600	20256000
D	Router 4	Router 3	46251886	20281600

Note: Networks A and B would show up as directly connected.

The following steps now occur:

1. Router 2 detects the link failure and begins the process of evaluating its topology table to discover which successors are no longer reachable. The DUAL discovers that Router 4 is no longer a reachable successor.

2. As a result, Router 2 must determine which networks are reached via Router 4—these networks must be reached another way. The DUAL discovers that the only network that is reached via Router 4 is network D.

3. The DUAL must now determine if this unreachable network has a feasible successor. By looking in the topology table, the DUAL finds that Router 3 is a feasible successor.

4. The DUAL promotes Router 3 to successor for network D and places the new route in its routing table.

5. Router 2 multicasts an update out to Routers 1 and 3. This update specifies that networks B and D are no longer reachable via Router 2 (technically, Router 2 poisons networks B and D).

6. Routers 1 and 3 subsequently go through the same process of determining if Router 2 is a successor for any networks and, if so, which networks are no longer reachable via this failed successor.

Any feasible successors for these unreachable networks are consequently used and promoted to successor status. For instance, Router 3 was originally using Router 2 as its successor to network B. When Router 3 receives Router 2's update indicating that network B is no longer reachable, Router 3 finds that it has a feasible successor (Router 4) in its topology table. Router 4 becomes the successor for network B. Router 3 subsequently generates an update indicating that network B is no longer reachable via itself (the network is poisoned). This update is multicast only to Router 4 (Split Horizon rule). Because Router 4 is not using Router 3 as a successor for network B, Router 4 is unaffected by this update.

So, how is Router 4 apprised of Router 2's failed link? One likely way is through the expiration of the holdtime. When Router 4 fails to hear anything from Router 2 within 15 seconds (the default holdtime interval), Router 4 would go through the same route evaluation process that its peers went through.

Converging on a Failed Route—Route Recomputation

It is important to note that when the DUAL finds a feasible successor in the topology table, as was the case in our previous step-by-step scenario, the *route evaluation* process does not transition into the *route recomputation* process. This latter activity occurs only when there is no feasible successor to replace a failed successor. In this situation, the router that finds no feasible successor must query its neighbors to determine if they have an alternative route. If a queried neighbor *does* have a valid alternative route, it will reply with its feasible successor for this route. If, however, the queried neighbor *does not* have a feasible successor for this route, then it will send its own queries to all neighbors out all interfaces (except out the interface on which the query was received). This query process continues to flood the AS until each router that sends a query receives a reply.

Only after receiving all replies to a query can the router proceed to finish recomputing the topology table. If the router receives a feasible successor, it will add it to its database and make a new entry in the routing table. If, on the other hand, all replies come back indicating that there are no known alternative and valid routes to the network in question, the router must subsequently remove the questioned route from its topology and routing tables.

In all above cases, after receiving all replies, the router that sent the original query will generate an update that is flooded throughout the internetwork. The purpose of this multicast update is to inform the internetwork of the routes the router has subsequently either removed from or added into its topology and routing tables. All other routers in the internetwork would, in turn, be able to either add or remove routes to or from their topology and routing tables. Once the last router in the internetwork has finished this final stage in the route recomputation process, the internetwork is said to have converged.

Route Recomputation—No Success

Figure 7.6 illustrates a scenario in which Router 5's link to network F has just failed. EIGRP will go through the following steps to achieve convergence:

1. Router 5 evaluates its topology table to determine if there is a feasible successor for network F. Upon finding none, Router 5 will (a) mark the network as

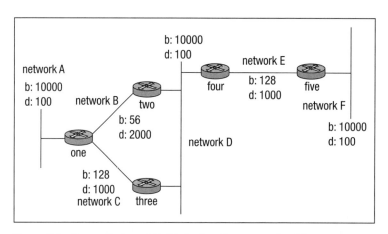

Figure 7.6 Converging on a failed link when there are no feasible successors.

unreachable (by poisoning the network with an infinite metric); (b) flag the network as *active* (signifying that the network is in the route recomputation process); and (c) send a query to Router 4. The query sent to Router 4 advertises network F as unreachable and asks whether there is another way to get to this unreachable component. RTP tracks the query in the neighbor table so that Router 5 knows from whom it can expect to receive a reply.

2. Upon receiving the query, Router 4 evaluates its topology table to determine if it has a feasible successor for network F. It does not because it has only one route (through the successor). Router 4 will consequently (a) mark the network as unreachable; (b) mark the network as active; and (c) multicast a query packet to Routers 2 and 3. The query indicates the same information: Network F is unreachable and another route is required. Router 4 tracks this query.

3. Routers 2 and 3 evaluate their topology tables and find no feasible successor for network F. Both routers mark the network as unreachable/active and multicast queries to Router 1.

4. Router 1 receives both queries indicating that network F is no longer reachable via either Router 2 or Router 3. Router 1 has no other routes to network F. Nor does Router 1 have anyone to query (it cannot send queries out the same interface from which it received them). Router 1 must therefore unicast a reply to both Routers 2 and 3 indicating that there is no other route to network F.

5. Routers 2 and 3 receive the reply and subsequently mark network F as passive (indicating route recomputation for *this* network is over). However, network F is not removed from the topology or routing tables just yet. Routers 2 and 3 then unicast replies to Router 4 indicating that they have no other route to network F.

6. Router 4 marks the network as passive and unicasts a reply to Router 5.

7. Upon receiving the reply, Router 5 removes network F from its topology and routing tables. Router 5 then multicasts an update packet to Router 4 specifying that network F no longer exists.

8. Router 4 proceeds to remove network F from its topology and routing tables and multicasts an update that subsequently allows the rest of the routers to remove this network as well.

Once all the routers have finished removing network F from their topology and routing tables, the internetwork is said to have converged.

Note: Any router that sends a query and does not receive a reply within the default interval of 180 seconds (active interval) will consider whichever router that failed to reply dead. The route evaluation process would subsequently ensue.

Route Recomputation—Success!

The previous step-by-step example illustrates a scenario in which the query process resulted in the removal of routes. The next example presents a scenario in which the query process results in the discovery of an alternative path.

Figure 7.7 should look familiar. Earlier, we saw how Router 2's failed link to network B resulted in the immediate identification of a feasible successor in Router 2's topology table. No route recomputation was therefore necessary for network D. However, a route recomputation *is* necessary for network B. To see why, consider Router 2's topology table, shown in Table 7.3.

What this topology table says is that Router 2's best path to network B is through its directly connected Ethernet0 interface, which has a cost of 46,226,286. There is, however, more to the topology table not shown in Table 7.3. Router 3 is advertising a route for network B via Router 4. This route is placed in Router 2's topology table as a *potential* feasible successor, or PFS (the route is from Router 2 to Router 3 to Router 4). Table 7.4 shows what the entry for this route would be.

Router 3 is advertising a cost of 46,482,286 to get to network B. Router 2 does not choose the PFS as a feasible successor because Router 3's advertised distance (46,482,286) is greater than Router 4's feasible distance (46,226,286).

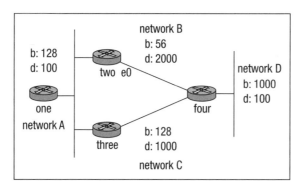

Figure 7.7   Querying for network B.

Table 7.3   A summarized representation of Router 2's topology table.

Network	Successor	Feasible Successor	Feasible Distance (Through Successor)	Advertised Distance (From Feasible Successor)
B	Router 2	—	46226286	—

Table 7.4   A potential feasible successor entry in Router 2's topology table.

Network	Potential Feasible Successor	PFS's Advertised Distance
B	Router 3	46482286

Therefore, when Router 2's link to network B fails, a query is multicast to Routers 1 and 3. Router 1 searches its topology table for a feasible successor and finds only a potential feasible successor, Router 3. Router 1 subsequently replies to Router 2 with an indication that there is no viable alternative route to network B. Note that Router 1 is restricted from sending a query to Router 3 because of Split Horizon, which states that a query cannot be sent out the same interface on which it was received.

Router 3, on the other hand, searches its topology table and finds a feasible successor (FS) for network B, Router 4 (Table 7.5).

Router 3 will subsequently respond to Router 2's reply with an indication that network B is reachable via a feasible path.

Now that Router 2 has received both replies, it can proceed to recalculate its topology table for network B. Router 3 consequently becomes the successor for this network. The routing table is modified accordingly. Thereafter, Router 2 multicasts an update packet out to Routers 1 and 3. This update allows both of these routers to converge on the new route to network B.

Summary of EIGRP Convergence

This section summarizes the events that occur when a link fails.

The router that detects the link failure goes through a route evaluation process to determine which successor routes have become inaccessible. Any and all feasible successors in the topology table for these unreachable networks are promoted to successor without a route recomputation. The routing table is modified to reflect these new routes.

Any unreachable network that does not have a feasible successor will be queried. The query is flooded throughout the EIGRP internetwork. A queried router that does *not* have an alternative path *and* is either (1) not on the AS border or (2) not configured with a relevant summary will generate queries and flood them out all interfaces (except the interface on which the original query was received). A queried router that *does* have an alternative path will send a reply, whereas a queried router that does *not* have an alternative path *and* is either (1) on the AS border or (2) configured with a relevant summary route will also send a reply.

The router that originated the original query packet waits for all replies to come in before either (1) *removing* the queried network from its topology and routing tables

Table 7.5   Router 3's toplogy table for network B.

Network	Successor	Feasible Successor	Feasible Distance (Through Successor)	Advertised Distance (From FS)
B	Router 2	Router 4	46251886	46226286

(which is the case when the replies come back with no alternative path) or (2) *adding* an alternative path for the queried network to its topology and routing tables (which is the case when a reply does comes back with an alternative path).

The router has subsequently converged. It will generate an update and multicast it out all interfaces. This update contains information on what paths the router has either added to or removed from its topology and routing tables.

Each router that receives the update will modify its topology and routing tables accordingly. At this point, the EIGRP internetwork has converged.

Configuring EIGRP

Basic EIGRP configuration entails starting the EIGRP routing process on the router and identifying which interfaces and networks EIGRP will be routing for.

The following command enables the EIGRP routing process:

```
Router(config)#router eigrp AS-number
```

The *AS-number* parameter identifies the autonomous system. All routers that are configured with the same AS number will reside in the same AS. Two different EIGRP autonomous systems communicate with each other via redistribution.

Note: An IGRP AS with the same AS number is automatically redistributed into the EIGRP AS (and vice versa).

The following command identifies which classful networks EIGRP will be routing for:

```
Router(config-router)#network network-number
```

The *network-number* parameter identifies the directly connected major network on which EIGRP will send and receive routing updates. An interface that belongs to the major network will participate in this routing process.

Warning: The major network you specify must be directly connected to the router (the same caveat applies to RIP and IGRP).

Whereas the previous command uses classful networks, the following command allows you to specify *classless* networks:

```
Router(config-router)#network ip-address wildcard-mask
```

The *ip-address* and *wildcard-mask* together allow you to specify networks at any level of granularity you desire. For instance, specifying a host address (e.g., 110.123.239.32 0.0.0.0) prompts the router to route only for those interfaces whose IP addresses match the configured host address, whereas specifying a regular subnet number (e.g., 136.17.49.0 0.0.0.255) allows you to match only those interfaces that are within the configured subnetwork.

The classless **network** command is similar to OSPF's **network** command. Both share the same objective of specifying the interfaces that are to participate in the routing protocol process. However, EIGRP's version of this command does not share the OSPF objective of identifying the areas in which interfaces reside. Instead, the EIGRP **network** command specifies (by implication) the *autonomous system* in which interfaces reside. To specify that an interface reside in a certain AS you would simply specify the **network** command under the appropriate routing process.

So, what are the benefits of using classless network statements? The primary benefit is not having to designate any interfaces as passive. With the classful **network** command you could specify only a major network number and then would need to designate all interfaces passive that you did not want routing EIGRP.

*Note: The classless EIGRP **network** command is available beginning in Cisco IOS release 12.0.*

Example Configuration

Figure 7.8 shows the topology for an EIGRP internetwork composed of two autonomous systems.

We will configure Router A for major network 2.0.0.0 and for classless network 1.4.0.0. /16. Both will reside in AS 1. We will configure classless network 1.1.0.0 /16 in AS 2.

```
Router_A(config)#router eigrp 1
Router_A(config-router)#network 2.0.0.0
Router_A(config-router)#network 1.4.0.0 0.0.255.255
Router_A(config-router)#router eigrp 2
Router_A(config-router)#network 1.1.0.0 0.0.255.255
```

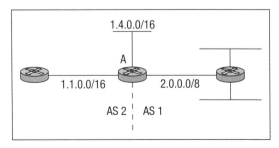

Figure 7.8   Diagram of an EIGRP internetwork.

Note that we were allowed to mix classless network statements with classful ones. Any interface that resides in either major network 2.0.0.0 or classless network 1.4.0.0 /16 will participate in the EIGRP routing process for AS 1. Any interface that resides in classless network 1.1.0.0 /16 will participate in the EIGRP routing process for AS 2.

The wildcard mask used in this configuration prompts the router to match up the first two bytes of any of its interface IP addresses with the first two bytes of 1.4.0.0 (for AS 1) and 1.1.0.0 (for AS 2). Any interface on Router A whose first two IP address bytes match the first two bytes of either 1.4.0.0 (for AS 1) or 1.1.0.0 (for AS 2) will subsequently be allowed to participate in the appropriate EIGRP routing process.

Verifying EIGRP

There are several commands useful in monitoring EIGRP operation and configuration, as well as in troubleshooting problems therewith. Some of the more common of these commands are as follows:

➤ **show ip eigrp neighbors**

➤ **show ip eigrp topology**

➤ **show ip eigrp traffic**

➤ **show ip route eigrp**

We have already covered the **show ip eigrp neighbors** command in the section "EIGRP Operation." We will therefore exclude its coverage here.

The **show ip eigrp topology** Command

The **show ip eigrp topology** command shows the router's topology table. We have up until now seen depictions of the EIGRP topology table; now, we get to see how the router's IOS depicts it:

```
Router_A#show ip eigrp topology table

IP-EIGRP Topology Table for process 68
Codes: P - Passive, A - Active, U - Update, Q - Query, R - Reply,
       r - Reply status
P 192.150.42.120 255.255.255.248, 1 successors, FD is 2172416
         via 192.150.42.9 (2172416/2169856), Fddi0
P 192.150.42.8 255.255.255.248, 1 successors, FD is 28160
         via Connected, Fddi0
```

```
P 192.150.42.48 255.255.255.248, 1 successors, FD is 2560515840
        via 192.150.42.9 (2560515840/2560513280), Fddi0
P 192.150.42.16 255.255.255.248, 1 successors, FD is 281600
        via Connected, Ethernet0
P 192.150.42.40 255.255.255.248, 1 successors, FD is 2560026880
        via 192.150.42.9 (2560026880/2560001280), Fddi0
P 192.150.42.32 255.255.255.248, 1 successors, FD is 2560026880
        via 192.150.42.9 (2560026880/2560001280), Fddi0
```

The fields presented in the **show ip eigrp topology** command are described in Table 7.6.

Consider the typology table entry P 192.150.42.120 255.255.255.248, 1 successors, FD is 2172416 via 192.150.42.9 (2172416/2169856), Fddi0. This is a topology table entry for a network whose successor is 192.150.42.9. The feasible distance through this successor is 2172416. The values enclosed within parentheses are the feasible distance and advertised distance, respectively. The advertised distance is *equivalent* to the feasible successor's feasible distance to 192.150.42.120. Fddi0 is the interface to reach the successor.

The EIGRP AS shown in Figure 7.9 is reflected in the IP-EIGRP topology table. Note that Router A has one and the same successor for all destinations. This successor is Router B (192.150.42.9).

Table 7.6 Explanation of the output of the show ip eigrp topology command.

Field	Description
IP-EIGRP Topology Table for process 68	This field indicates that this is an IP topology table for AS 68.
Codes	There are six codes: Passive, Active, Update, Query, Reply, and Reply Status. The Passive and Active codes refer to the DUAL state of the network. The Update, Query, and Reply codes refer to the type of packet that is being sent to the network.
	Passive (P): The network is not in the process of route recomputation.
	Active (A): The network is in the process of route recomputation.
	Update (U): An update packet concerning the network has been sent to a neighbor.
	Query (Q): A query packet concerning the network has been sent to a neighbor.
	Reply (R): A reply packet concerning the network has been sent in response to a neighbor's query.
	Reply status (r):This field tracks the neighbors that must reply to the router's query.

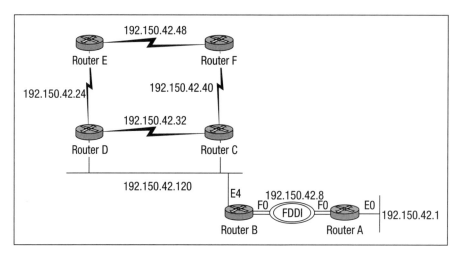

Figure 7.9 Diagram of an EIGRP internetwork.

The **show ip eigrp traffic** Command

The **show ip eigrp traffic** command shows the type and number of EIGRP packets sent and received from the router. Following is the output from this command:

```
Router#show ip eigrp traffic

IP-EIGRP Traffic Statistics for process 77
  Hellos sent/received: 218/205
  Updates sent/received: 7/23
  Queries sent/received: 2/0
  Replies sent/received: 0/2
  Acks sent/received: 21/14
```

Table 7.7 explains the fields in the **show ip eigrp traffic** command.

Table 7.7 Explanation of the output of the **show ip eigrp traffic** command.

Field	Description
IP-EIGRP Traffic Statistics for process 77	Indicates that this is a display of traffic statistics for IP-encapsulated EIGRP packets being sent and received from AS 77
Hellos sent/received: 218/205	Number of hello packets that the router has sent/received
Updates sent/received: 7/23	Number of update packets that the router has sent/received
Queries sent/received 2/0	Number of query packets that the router has sent/received
Replies sent/received: 0/2	Number of reply packets that the router has sent/received
Acks sent/received: 21/14	Number of acknowledgment packets the router has sent/received

The **show ip route eigrp** Command

The **show ip route eigrp** command is used to view EIGRP entries in the router's routing table. Following is a sample of the output for this command:

```
Router_A#show ip route eigrp

. . .

192.150.42.0 is subnetted (mask is 255.255.255.248), 7 subnets
D       192.150.42.120 [90/729600] via 192.150.42.9, 0:01:16, Fddi0
D       192.150.42.48  [90/757760] via 192.150.42.9, 0:01:16, Fddi0
D       192.150.42.40  [90/755200] via 192.150.42.9, 0:01:16, Fddi0
D       192.150.42.32  [90/755200] via 192.150.42.9, 0:01:16, Fddi0
D       192.150.42.24  [90/732160] via 192.150.42.9, 0:01:16, Fddi0
C       192.150.42.16 is directly connected, Ethernet0
C       192.150.42.8 is directly connected, Fddi0
```

This is the routing table for Router A in Figure 7.9. The D indicates an EIGRP-derived internal route. The first bracketed value is the administrative distance (90 is the default administrative distance for an internal EIGRP route). The second bracketed value is the feasible distance for the network. 192.150.42.9 is the router (successor) from which the network advertisement was received. Fddi0 and Ethernet0 are the interfaces used to reach respective networks.

7

Chapter Summary

EIGRP is an advanced distance-vector routing protocol that was designed by Cisco to meet the scalability requirements that its predecessor, IGRP, could not. As an advanced routing algorithm that incorporates link-state features, EIGRP offers several advantages over traditional distance-vector algorithms, such as (1) faster convergence; (2) multiprotocol support; and (3)support for optimization features such as route summarization and VLSM.

One of EIGRP's primary components is the Distributed Update ALgorithm. The DUAL is responsible for calculating primary and backup loop-free routes, as well as synchronizing convergence within the EIGRP internetwork.

Topology changes result in a process that involves recalculating topology and routing tables. Convergence within an EIGRP internetwork is complete once all appropriate routers within the autonomous system have been notified of the topology changes and the appropriate routes have been either added to or removed from the routers' topology and routing tables.

This concludes our discussion on the fundamentals of EIGRP. Chapter 8 will explain how an EIGRP internetwork can be optimized through the use of hierarchical features such as route summarization and EIGRP packet suppression. It will also examine how Enhanced IGRP optimizes bandwidth utilization over WAN topologies, particularly Frame-Relay, where the variety of link configurations makes bandwidth configuration a critical step in ensuring EIGRP operates reliably and efficiently in the WAN environment.

Review Questions

1. Which one of the following is not a function of the DUAL?

   a. Perform route computations

   b. Find loop-free paths

   c. Ensure fast convergence

   d. Establish neighbor relationships

2. Which two metrics does EIGRP use in calculating the best path?

   a. Hops

   b. Bandwidth

   c. Ticks

   d. Delay

3. Which one of the following is not a feature of EIGRP?

   a. Multiprotocol support

   b. Unequal-cost load-balancing

   c. Support for multiple areas

   d. Fast convergence

4. What is the purpose of EIGRP's neighbor table?

   a. Maintains information on bidirectional neighbor relationships

   b. Maintains all routes in the internetwork

   c. Contains the best routes in the internetwork

   d. Stores information on only IP neighbors

5. Which one of the following does the topology table not contain?

   a. Feasible successor

   b. Potential feasible successor

   c. Uptime for all networks

   d. Feasible distance through successor

6. What is a successor? Choose two.

    a. The next-hop router along the best path to a given destination

    b. The feasible distance for the best path

    c. The route with the smallest bandwidth

    d. The route with the smallest cost to a given destination

7. What criterion must a router meet to be considered a feasible successor?

    a. The router must be close to a given destination.

    b. The router's advertised distance must be less than the feasible distance through the successor.

    c. The router's advertised distance must be greater than the successor's feasible distance.

    d. The router's advertised distance must be less than or equal to the feasible distance through the successor.

8. Which one of the following is not an EIGRP packet?

    a. Query

    b. Update

    c. Hello

    d. DUAL

9. When does the route evaluation process occur?

    a. Whenever a topology change occurs

    b. When the router has no feasible successor in its topology table

    c. When a router adds a route to its topology and routing tables

    d. Whenever a neighbor sends a hello packet

10. When does the route recomputation process first occur?

    a. When the router has no feasible successor in its topology table

    b. As soon as the router sends a query packet

    c. As soon as a topology change occurs

    d. When the router must send a reply packet

11. How does EIGRP build neighbor relationships?

    a. By exchanging topology tables

    b. By exchanging routing tables

    c. By exchanging hello packets

    d. The router is configured with neighbors. Topology tables are then exchanged.

7

12. How does a router that has just initialized discover routes?

    a. The router receives topology tables from neighbors.

    b. The router receives neighbor tables from neighbors.

    c. The router receives routing tables from neighbors.

    d. The router must send query packets to discover routes. Neighbors then respond with their routing tables.

13. What is feasible distance?

    a. The cost to reach a given destination.

    b. A value that specifies the router's cost to a successor.

    c. A value that indicates how reliable a path is.

    d. The cost to reach the feasible successor.

14. Which routes are placed in the routing table?

    a. Feasible successor routes

    b. Potential feasible successor routes

    c. Successor routes

    d. Both successor and feasible successor routes

15. What does a router do when one of its interface links fails?

    a. It removes all networks that were reached through the failed link.

    b. It goes into the route recomputation process.

    c. It evaluates the successor routes that are no longer reachable and determines whether any of these routes have feasible successors.

    d. It evaluates its topology table to determine which feasible successor routes are no longer reachable.

16. When does a network go into an active state? Choose two.

    a. When a router loses its successor for the network and has no feasible successor for the network.

    b. When a router immediately detects that the network is no longer reachable.

    c. When a router goes into the route recomputation process.

    d. When a router goes into the route evaluation process.

17. How does a router that has sent a query know when it has received all replies?

    a. The Reliable Transport Protocol (RTP) keeps track of all queried neighbors in the router's topology table by maintaining a neighbor and transmission list.

    b. Each neighbor sends a copy of the query back to the router. This lets the router know which neighbors have received the query and therefore lets the router know which neighbors must be replying.

     c. The Reliable Transport Protocol (RTP) keeps track of all queried neighbors in the router's neighbor table by maintaining a neighbor and transmission list.

     d. The router assumes that it has received all replies once 180 seconds have elapsed.

18. What occurs when a router adds or removes a route to or from its topology and routing tables?

     a. The router sends a reply packet indicating what it has added or removed.

     b. The router will multicast a routing update to the internetwork.

     c. The router must multicast a query packet to the internetwork.

     d. Nothing occurs.

19. What command enables the EIGRP routing process?

     a. **Router(config-if)#ip network eigrp 1**

     b. **Router(config)#router eigrp 1**

     c. **Router(config)#eigrp router 1**

     d. **Router(config)#ip eigrp router 1**

20. What does the **show ip eigrp traffic** command tell you?

     a. The amount of EIGRP congestion on all interfaces

     b. The type and number of EIGRP packets sent and received from the router

     c. Which networks are being routed to

     d. Which neighbors are successors and feasible successors

Real-World Project

For this hands-on project, we configure EIGRP Router 1 in Figure 7.10. We then follow the DUAL in calculating this router's successor and possible feasible successor for network 10.1.6.0 /24. Finally, we verify that Router 3's configuration was successful.

Configuring Router 1:

1. After completing Router 1's initial configuration, enable the EIGRP routing process. Use autonomous system number 1.

```
Router_1(config)#router eigrp 1
```

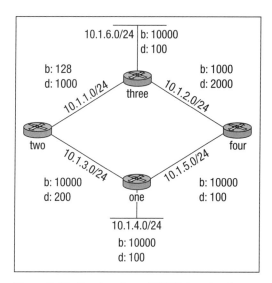

Figure 7.10 Topology for an EIGRP internetwork.

2. In router configuration mode, specify that EIGRP is to route for classful network 10.0.0.0.

```
Router_1(config-router)#network 10.0.0.0
```

All interfaces on Router 1 will be sending and receiving EIGRP traffic.

Determining Router 1's successor for network 10.1.6.0 /24:

1. For Router 1's path going through Router 2 to network 10.1.6.0 /24, calculate the feasible distance using the formula 256[(10,000,000/**min bandwidth**) + **sum of delays**].

In Figure 7.10, the minimum bandwidth for this particular path is 128Kbps. The sum of all delays is 200 + 1,000 + 100 = 1,300. The feasible distance is then:

256[(10,000,000/128) + 1,300] = 256(78,125 + 1,300) = 256(79,425) = 20,332,800

2. Calculate the feasible distance for the path through Router 4.

In Figure 7.10, the minimum bandwidth for this particular path is 1,000Kbps. The sum of all delays is 100 + 2,000 + 100 = 2,200. The feasible distance is then:

256[(10,000,000/1,000) + 2,200] = 256(10,000 + 2,200) = 256(12,200) = 3,123,200

3. Compare the two costs and choose the lesser of the two. This will be Router 1's feasible distance to 10.1.6.0 /24.

20,332,800 versus 3,123,200

The path through Router 4 is subsequently chosen as Router 1's successor route.

Determining Router 1's feasible successor:

1. To see if Router 2 is a feasible successor, calculate its advertised distance using the formula 256[(10,000,000/Min Bandwidth) + Sum of Delays].

Router 2's advertised distance for 10.1.6.0 /24 is equal to its feasible distance for this network. With a minimum bandwidth of 128 and a total delay of 1,100, its feasible distance is:

256[(10,000,000/128) + 1,100] = 20,281,600

This is therefore Router 2's advertised distance.

2. If Router 2's advertised distance is less than Router 1's feasible distance for 10.1.6.0 /24, then Router 2 can become a feasible successor.

20,281,600 is greater than 3,123,200

Router 2 cannot be a feasible successor. It will be placed in Router 1's topology table as a potential successor.

Verifying Router 1's configuration:

1. Issue the command that allows you to view Router 1's EIGRP neighbors.

```
Router_1#show ip eigrp neighbors

IP-EIGRP Neighbors for process 1
ADDRESS     Interface   Holdtime    Uptime Q   Seq   SRTT   RTO
10.1.3.2    Ethernet0   13          0:00:41    0     11     4     20
10.1.5.2    Ethernet1   14          0:02:01    0     10     12    24
```

2. From the output of the **show ip eigrp neighbors** command, we see that Router 1 has established bidirectional neighbor relationships with Routers 2 and 4. Issue the command that allows you to view Router 1's topology table.

```
Router_1#show ip eigrp topology

IP-EIGRP Topology Table for process 1
Codes: P - Passive, A - Active, U = Update, Q - Query, R - Reply,
       r - Reply status
P 10.1.4.0 255.255.255.0, 1 successor, FD is 281600
     via Connected, Ethernet2
P 10.1.3.0 255.255.255.0, 1 successor, FD is 307200
     via Connected, Ethernet0
P 10.1.5.0 255.255.255.0, 1 successor, FD is 281600
     via Connected, Ethernet1
P 10.1.1.0 255.255.255.0, 1 successor, FD is 20307200
     via 10.1.3.2 (20307200/20256000), Ethernet0
```

```
P 10.1.2.0 255.255.255.0, 1 successor, FD is 3097600
        via 10.1.5.2 (3097600/3072000), Ethernet1
P 10.1.6.0 255.255.255.0, 1 successor, FD is 3123200
        via 10.1.5.2 (3123200/793600), Ethernet1
```

3. From the output of the **show ip eigrp topology** command, we see that all networks show up in Router 1's topology table. Our configuration was successful.

CHAPTER EIGHT

Optimizing EIGRP

After completing this chapter, you will be able to:

✓ Describe the benefits of EIGRP route summarization

✓ Explain how route summarization occurs in a scalable EIGRP internetwork

✓ List and explain the methods that EIGRP uses to limit the range of EIGRP traffic

✓ Describe how load-balancing occurs in a scalable EIGRP internetwork

✓ Explain the reasons for optimizing EIGRP bandwidth utilization in a Frame-Relay environment

✓ Given an interface-configuration specification, configure EIGRP to utilize the appropriate amount of bandwidth

Now that we have established a foundation for understanding Enhanced IGRP's operation within a nonoptimized broadcast environment, we can move on to learn how this advanced routing algorithm can scale to meet the needs of expanding networks that are concerned with minimizing resource consumption and improving network performance. As we will see, several features allow EIGRP to devise a hierarchical routing solution that can sufficiently address the scalability requirements of even the most demanding internetwork environments. These hierarchical features include route summarization, load-balancing, traffic-bounding, bandwidth optimization, and other such instruments whose engineering has helped catapult EIGRP to a status as one of the Internet's most valued distance-vector routing protocols.

EIGRP Route Summarization

Route summarization is the first major component of EIGRP's hierarchical routing solution. With this feature, routers can advertise a group of contiguous network addresses as a single route—a summary route. Advertising a summary route, as opposed to advertising a set of individual routes, has the advantage of reducing the sizes of the topology and routing tables. Smaller tables not only free up router memory and reduce router CPU utilization, they also allow routers to make faster routing computations and therefore achieve faster convergence.

In addition, routers are no longer impacted by topology changes in which the summary route masks the event's occurrence. This benefit is due to the fact that remote routers are not aware of topology changes that occur to networks contained within a summary route; they are aware of only the summary route itself.

In addition to the benefit of reducing the impact and extent of topology changes, route summarization also has the benefit of reducing the impact and extent of query packets. Route summarization has the effect of creating *query boundaries*, which stop queries from being propagated outside a summarized region (actually, they are propagated outside a summarized region but are immediately replied to).

Another advantage to route summarization within an EIGRP internetwork is the decrease in network bandwidth utilization. As will be seen in the section "EIGRP Bandwidth Optimization," this last advantage is extremely relevant to wide area network (WAN) environments seeking to optimize performance over bandwidth-hungry circuits.

Types of Route Summarization

EIGRP recognizes two types of route summarization:

➤ Automatic route summarization

➤ Manual route summarization

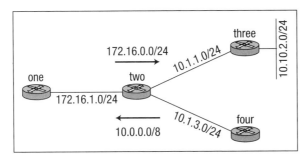

Figure 8.1 EIGRP automatically summarizes networks at major network boundaries.

Automatic Route Summarization

Route summarization occurs automatically on major network boundaries. At this boundary, the router summarizes all subnetworks into a single major network number. For example, Figure 8.1 shows a topology in which Router 2 resides on the boundary between two major networks, 172.16.0.0 and 10.0.0.0.

In Figure 8.1, Router 2 will summarize 172.16.1.0 /24 to 172.16.0.0 /16 and will forward this summary route to Routers 3 and 4. Likewise, Router 2 will summarize 10.1.1.0 /24, 10.1.3.0 /24, and 10.10.2.0 /24 to 10.0.0.0 /8 and will advertise this summary route to Router 1.

Automatic route summarization is a relic of classful distance vector algorithms (such as RIP and IGRP), which would not advertise subnets across major network boundaries because they could not send a subnet mask with the advertisements. Recall that subnet masks are used to define the subnet numbers. Without a subnet mask, all the router sees is a major (classful) network, such as 172.16.0.0 or 10.0.0.0. Therefore, without the ability to inform its neighbor residing in a different major network of the subnet mask being used in its own major network, a router's classful routing protocol would have no choice but to summarize all of its routes into one major network number before advertising them to its neighbor. Classful routing protocols cannot disable this feature.

Now that classless routing algorithms have stormed into the routing paradigm, the need for automatic route summarization is no longer the result of a router's inability to send subnet masks. Instead, classless protocols may need to preserve the automatic route summarization feature for purely resource-related reasons. That is, minimizing bandwidth utilization and reducing router workload are in many situations the reasons for not disabling automatic route summarization, which classless routing protocols (such as EIGRP) have the capacity to do.

However, if there are no issues with resource consumption, then it is in some circumstances best to disable automatic route summarization. Disabling this feature may even be a requirement, for instance, when there is a need to support discontiguous subnets (subnets of the same major network that are separated by a different major network). Figure 8.2 illustrates such a scenario.

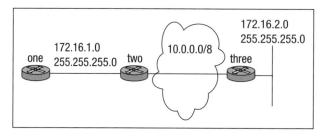

Figure 8.2 Support discontiguous subnets by disabling automatic route summarization.

Automatic route summarization is enabled by default. The IOS command that *disables* automatic route summarization for EIGRP follows:

```
Router(config-router)#no auto-summary
```

Manual Route Summarization

EIGRP has the unique ability to summarize routes at arbitrary network boundaries. What this means is that summarization can be configured on the interface of any router within the internetwork. This capability is one advantage that EIGRP has over Open Shortest Path First (OSPF), which is able to summarize routes only at specific network boundaries, namely at the area border router (ABR) and Autonomous System Boundary Router (ASBR). EIGRP, however, must still abide by the rule that summarized routes must be contiguous.

The following command configures EIGRP manual route summarization:

```
Router(config-if)#ip summary-address eigrp AS-number ip-address mask
```

The *AS-number* identifies the autonomous system whose networks are being summarized. The *ip-address* and *mask* together represent the summary route that consolidates a range of network numbers. Note that this command is an interface configuration subcommand, not a router configuration subcommand.

Figure 8.3 shows an autonomous system (AS) in which Router 2 summarizes the contiguous networks 190.1.1.0 /24, 190.1.2.0 /24, and 190.1.3.0 /24 into the summary route 190.1.0.0 /22 on its Ethernet 0 interface. Router 2 subsequently advertises this summary route to Router 1.

Router 2's configuration is as follows:

```
Router_2(config-if)#interface ethernet0
Router_2(config-if)#ip-address 10.2.50.1 255.255.255.0
Router_2(config-if)#ip summary-address eigrp 100 190.1.0.0 255.255.252.0
```

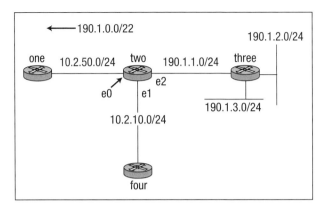

Figure 8.3   EIGRP can summarize routes at arbitrary network locations.

Manual summarization for 190.1.0.0 /22 has been configured only on Ethernet 0, but the same configuration also could have been applied on Ethernet 1. However, the same summarization could *not* have been done on Ethernet 2 because this is the interface that the summary route attaches to. You cannot successfully summarize networks on the interfaces to which the summarized networks are attached.

Router 2's topology table after summarization has been configured follows:

```
Router_2#show ip eigrp topology
IP-EIGRP Topology Table for process 1

Codes: P - Passive, A - Active, U - Update, Q - Query, R - Reply,
       r - Reply status

P 10.2.10.0/24, 1 successors, FD is 45842176
        via Connected, Loopback0
P 10.2.50.0/24, 1 successors, FD is 2169856
        via Connected, Serial0
P 190.1.1.0/24, 1 successors, FD is 10511872
        via Connected, Serial1
P 190.1.0.0/22, 1 successors, FD is 10511872
        via Summary (10511872/0), Null0
P 190.1.3.0/24, 1 successors, FD is 10639872
        via 190.1.1.1 (10639872/128256), Serial1
P 190.1.2.0/24, 1 successors, FD is 10537472
        via 190.1.1.1 (10537472/281600), Serial1
```

Note the entry for summary route 190.1.0.0 /22 specifies the null 0 interface. This simply indicates that there is no specific interface that leads to 190.1.0.0 /22. The null interface does not mean, however, that packets destined for any network contained within 190.1.0.0 /22 will be dropped. When a packet destined for a host in this summarized network is received, Router 2 matches the packet's destination IP-address with the routing table entry whose network bits most closely match that of the packet. Because Router 2's routing table contains entries that have a /24 mask, the packet is most certainly to be matched with one of these /24 networks, instead of being matched with 190.1.0.0 /22. (If, however, a packet was for some reason able to match 190.1.0.0 /22, then it *would* be dropped.)

The topology table for Router 1 once it has received the summary route from Router 2 follows:

```
Router_1#show ip eigrp topology

 IP-EIGRP Topology Table for process 1

Codes: P - Passive, A - Active, U - Update, Q - Query, R - Reply,
       r - Reply status

P 10.2.10.0/24, 1 successors, FD is 46354176
        via 10.2.50.1 (46354176/45842176), Serial0
P 10.2.50.0/24, 1 successors, FD is 2169856
        via Connected, Serial0
P 190.1.0.0/22, 1 successors, FD is 11023872
        via 10.2.50.1 (11023872/10511872), Serial0
```

In Router 1's topology table, we see that the summary route 190.1.0.0 /22 shows up with Router 2 as the successor. Any packet destined for a network in 190.1.0.0 /22 will be matched with this summary route and transmitted out serial 0 to Router 2.

Whenever a network contained within a summary route fails, the router that is configured with the summary route makes a note that the network is no longer valid. However, the *summary route* still remains valid. When *all* networks contained within the summary route have become invalid, the router removes the summary route from its topology and routing tables and notifies the internetwork that the summary route has been removed.

Limiting the Range of EIGRP Traffic

Limiting the range of EIGRP traffic is the next component to EIGRP's hierarchical routing solution. In many networks, requirements for scalability are such that an internetwork must periodically assess its operations to determine if technical requirements for scalability and optimization are being met. When an assessment of the network reveals that such requirements are not being met, network administrators must work on providing solutions that can ensure that scalability and optimization issues are handled effectively and efficiently. In an EIGRP environment, this may mean having to reduce the impact and range of EIGRP traffic.

Several tools are available to limit the range and impact of EIGRP traffic, particularly query and routing update traffic. As we will see, each of these tools offers a unique solution to dealing with the scalability and optimization issues faced by many of today's internetworks.

Limiting the Query Range

A router that sends out queries must wait for all replies to come back before its Distributed Update ALgorithm (DUAL) can proceed with the route recomputation process. When all but one router (or several routers) reply, the querying router must continue to wait for the reply. This condition, known as "stuck-in-active," refers to the fact that the querying router is in an active state with respect to the destination. Stuck-in-active status lasts for 180 seconds (the default "active time") and will eventually lead the querying router to go active for all the destinations for which the unresponding neighbor is a successor.

The stuck-in-active condition may be due to several causes, the most common of which is a resource consumption or malfunction issue. Directly related to this cause is the extent to which query packets are allowed to traverse the EIGRP internetwork. A very wide query range increases the probability that on its journey a query packet will encounter unforeseen congestion or a link failure.

One remedy to the stuck-in-active condition is therefore to limit the range of queries. Limiting the query range will reduce the likelihood that a link failure or link congestion will prevent the successful delivery of both queries and replies.

Several ways exist to limit the query range:

➤ Route summarization

➤ Autonomous system boundaries

➤ Stub designation

We will cover the first two methods, route summarization and autonomous system boundaries, next. We will cover the last method, stub designation, in the section "How Stub Designation Limits the Range of Queries and Routing Updates."

How Route Summarization Limits the Query Range

Earlier, we mentioned that one advantage of route summarization is its ability to limit the impact that queries have on routers that lay outside a summarized region. To see how this process actually occurs, consider the internetwork depicted in Figure 8.4. In this figure, automatic route summarization is occurring on Routers 2 and 3, who are advertising 10.0.0.0 to Router 4. Router 4 will subsequently have an entry in its topology and routing tables for 10.0.0.0 /8.

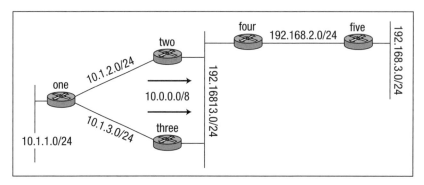

Figure 8.4 Route summarization limits the range of query packets.

Now, say that Router 1's link to network 10.1.1.0 /24 goes down. Because Router 1 finds no feasible successor in its topology table, Router 1 multicasts a query packet to Routers 2 and 3 (Figure 8.5).

Routers 2 and 3 have no feasible alternative paths to 10.1.1.0 /24. These routers will therefore multicast queries to each other and to Router 4 (Figure 8.6).

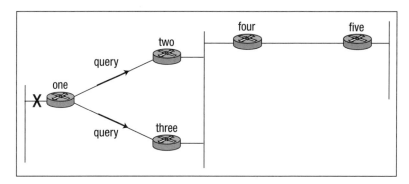

Figure 8.5 Router 1 multicasts a query to Routers 2 and 3.

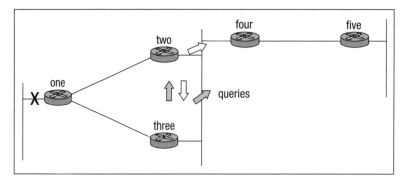

Figure 8.6 Routers 2 and 3 multicast queries.

Upon receiving the queries from Routers 2 and 3, Router 4 checks its topology table to see what it has listed for the network in question. Router 4 finds only 10.0.0.0 /8, but it does not in any way interpret this network as identical to 10.1.1.0 /24. Router 4 consequently has no knowledge of network 10.1.1.0 /24 and therefore no feasible path to it. As a result, Router 4 sends a reply packet back to Routers 2 and 3, informing them that there is no alternative path to network 10.1.1.0 /24. Router 4 will not query Router 5 because 10.1.1.0 /24 is not an entry in Router 4's topology and routing tables. Only if it had an entry for this network would it send out a query. (Recall that queries are sent out *only* when a router finds that it has no *feasible* successor for a network; a network must therefore already exist in the topology table before a query is sent for it.)

The query range in this example is bounded by Router 4, whose lack of knowledge of the summarized network prevents a query from being sent for it to Router 5. Note that the query range is not bounded by Routers 2 and 3, even though they are configured with summary routes that mask network 10.1.1.0 /24, because Routers 2 and 3 *do* have network 10.1.1.0 /24 listed in their topology tables, and they must therefore generate queries for it when they discover that this network has no feasible successor.

8

How Autonomous System Boundaries Limit the Query Range

Figure 8.7 illustrates an internetwork that is divided into two autonomous systems, AS 1 and AS 2. Router 1 is in AS 1, Router 3 is in AS 2, and Router 2 is in both ASes.

Consider what happens when Router 3's link to network C fails. Router 3 queries Router 2 for a feasible successor for network C (Figure 8.8).

Now, upon receiving the query, Router 2 checks its topology table and discovers it has no alternative route to network C. Because this is the edge of the AS, Router 2 subsequently replies to Router 3. However, at the same time that Router 2 sends its reply, it will also send a query to AS 1. Router 1 would then reply to Router 2.

In this scenario, the original query was bound by the AS border on Router 2. Although this had the effect of limiting the query range for AS 2, it did *not* prevent

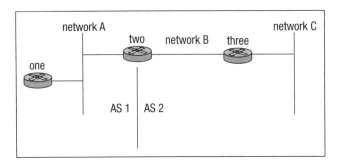

Figure 8.7   Router 2 serves as the AS boundary.

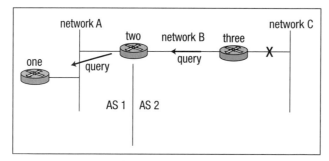

Figure 8.8 Router 3 queries for network C.

a new query for network C from being launched into AS 1. However, even though a new query is generated, for the purpose of addressing the stuck-in-active condition this technique of query suppression is still a viable solution because the *original* query packet cannot be propagated outside the AS boundary.

Limiting the Update Range

For large internetworks, it is often not necessary for remote routers to have full knowledge of nor be updated by all networks. Depending on the scalability and optimization requirements that an internetwork is looking to address, a router can be configured to advertise and accept only certain routing information, thereby precluding the internetwork from being inundated with nonessential routing update packets.

Several features aim toward achieving this goal of limiting the extent and impact of routing updates:

➤ Route summarization

➤ Distribution lists

➤ Stub designation

How Route Summarization Limits the Range of Routing Updates

We have already mentioned how route summarization limits the extent of routing updates. By consolidating several contiguous routes into a single summary route, the number of routing updates is diminished, and the impact of topology changes is not felt far outside the summarized region in which the topology change occurs.

For example, consider Figure 8.9, in which Router 2 is configured to automatically summarize at the major network boundary. Now, consider what occurs when Router 3's link to network 10.10.2.0 /24 fails. Router 3 sends a query to Router 2. Router 2 then sends a query to both Routers 1 and 4 (recall that a summarized region will still send out queries). Both send back replies indicating that they have no alternative path to 10.10.2.0 /24. Router 2 subsequently replies to Router 3

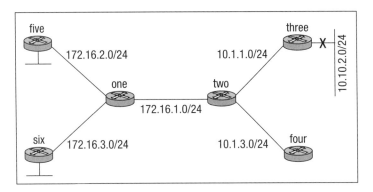

Figure 8.9   Router 2 is performing automatic route summarization.

with the bad news. Router 3 therefore removes the network from its topology and routing tables and sends a routing update to Router 2 indicating the removal of 10.10.2.0 /24. Router 2 removes the network from its own topology and routing tables and sends a routing update to Router 4. A routing update will be sent to Router 1 as well (EIGRP logic dictates that a router that has just modified its topology and routing tables must multicast a routing update out all interfaces except the interface from which the topology change was learned). However, upon receiving the routing update, Router 1 looks in its topology table and finds that it has no listing for network 10.10.2.0 /24. There is a listing for 10.0.0.0 /8, but 10.0.0.0 /8 is *not* 10.10.2.0 /24 (the router must actually see an entry for 10.10.2.0 /24). As a result, Router 1 makes no modifications to its topology and routing tables and therefore does not send any update to Routers 5 and 6.

An update boundary for the summarized region 10.0.0.0 /8 has subsequently been established at Router 1. Note that this boundary is geographically identical to the query boundary. In fact, many times an update boundary and a query boundary will exist together.

While the above example illustrates a scenario in which automatic route summarization created the update and query boundaries, it should be noted that EIGRP *manual* route summarization has the capacity to affect the same results.

How Distribution Lists Limit the Range of Routing Updates

A distribution list is a routing filter that prevents certain routing information from being either sent or received. In the context of EIGRP, a distribution list is applied on an outbound interface to restrict the router from advertising certain networks. These routers are usually connected to a remote network and are not required to be transit points for other routers. Figure 8.10 illustrates such a scenario.

In Figure 8.10, Router 1 is connected to a stub network (i.e., a network with only one exit point) and has been configured with an outbound distribution list. This particular distribution list has been configured to prevent Router 1 from advertising

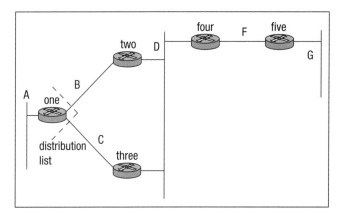

Figure 8.10 Router 1 is configured with an outbound distribution list.

networks that are not directly connected. Router 1 will therefore advertise only network A to Routers 2 and 3. This means when Router 2 advertises networks D, E, and F to Router 1, Router 1 will not turn and advertise these networks to Router 3. Likewise, upon receiving these same networks from Router 3, Router 1 will not turn and advertise them to Router 2.

In this example, an outbound distribution list consequently has the effect of limiting the range of routing updates by preventing the router from advertising networks that are not local. Note, however, that the Router 1 still has knowledge of remote networks because it still places received advertisements into its topology and routing tables. The outbound distribution list affects only what is sent, not what is received.

To see if Router 1's distribution list affects the way it responds to the occurrence of remote topology change, consider Figure 8.10 again. If Router 5's link to network F fails, a query is propagated all the way to Router 1. Upon receiving the query for network F from both Routers 2 and 3, Router 1 checks its topology table and discovers that it has no feasible successor. As a result, Router 1 generates a reply and unicasts it to Routers 2 and 3 (note that the distribution list had no effect on the reply being sent). Router 5 eventually receives a reply and removes network F from its topology and routing tables. It then forwards a routing update that eventually reaches Router 1. Router 1 subsequently removes the network from its topology and routing tables and is then said to have converged.

Note in this example that the distribution list was *not* a factor in limiting the range of routing updates. Router 1's distribution list therefore has no effect on its convergence.

How Stub Designation Limits the Range of Queries and Routing Updates

The previous section discussed how distribution lists address the issue of limiting the update range. However, this discussion did not resolve the fact that queries would still be sent out to any routers, even though they happened to be configured with distribution lists. To solve this issue, we would need to configure the remote non-transit routers with a *stub designation*. A stub designation has the effect of preventing queries from being sent to routers that are configured as stub.

For example, consider Figure 8.11, in which Router 3 has been designated stub. Router 3 will consequently advertise in its hello packet that it is a stub router. As a result, Routers 1 and 2 will make a note not to send queries to Router 3.

Designating routers as stub can certainly save a large and active EIGRP internetwork from making considerable resource expenditures. This benefit is most clearly seen in redundant topologies, where stub designations have the capacity to cut down tremendously on bandwidth and CPU utilization. In addition, convergence is expedited.

Figure 8.12 shows a redundant topology in which a partial mesh exists between two distribution-layer routers and three access-layer routers. Because the access-layer

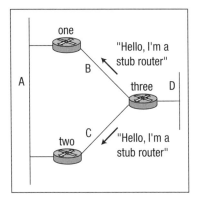

Figure 8.11   Designating a router stub.

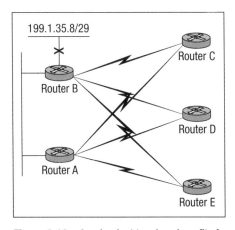

Figure 8.12   A redundant topology benefits from stub designation.

routers in Figure 8.12 have no need of being transit points for Routers A and B, the access-layer routers have been designated stub. The stub designation will prevent Routers A and B from sending any queries out their serial interfaces. As a result, if Router B's link to 199.1.35.8 /29 happened to go down, it would send a query only to Router A instead of also sending a query to Routers C, D, and E. Furthermore, Router A would send an immediate reply to Router B instead of querying the same access-layer routers.

In fact, the query process in this topology could get quite complicated if the access-layer routers were *not* designated stub because the access-layer routers would send queries back over the serial links. The result would be similar to a broadcast storm.

For example, consider a scenario in which the access-layer routers in Figure 8.12 are not designated stub. When Router B's link to 199.1.35.8 /29 goes down, the following sequence of events would occur:

1. Router B proceeds to query all neighbors. Assume that Routers C, D, and E receive B's query simultaneously.

2. Routers C, D, and E proceed to query Router A, who has already received B's query.

3. Before Router A receives the queries from the access-layer routers, it sends a query to them. Router A will then send the access-layer routers a reply because its topology table indicates that network 199.1.35.8 /29 is inaccessible.

4. The access-layer routers receive Router A's query, followed in turn by Router A's reply. The access-layer routers proceed to reply to Router A because their topology tables indicate that 199.1.35.8 /29 is inaccessible as well. The access-layer routers then proceed to send a reply to Router B.

5. Upon receiving the replies from the access-layer routers, Router A proceeds to send a reply to Router B. All replies have now been received by Router B. Because nobody had an alternative path to network 199.1.35.8 /29, Router B removes the network from its topology and routing tables and proceeds to send a multicast update out to all its neighbors. Once again, though, Router A and the access-layer routers would send the update back over the serial lines.

As this scenario shows, it would be in the internetwork's best interest (in fact, in everyone's best interest) to use the stub feature.

Note: *The EIGRP stub feature is currently available only in certain revisions of IOS release 12.0. Consult Cisco's Web site for more information.*

EIGRP Load-Balancing

Load-balancing is another component to EIGRP's hierarchical routing solution. This feature allows a router to distribute traffic across multiple paths that lead to the same destination. The benefits of being able to load-balance equates to a more efficient use of network bandwidth as well as an optimization of application response times. There are two types of load-balancing:

➤ Equal-cost load-balancing

➤ Unequal-cost load-balancing

Equal-Cost Load-Balancing with EIGRP

Equal-cost load-balancing refers to load-balancing that occurs over paths whose distances to a network are the same. For example, in Figure 8.13, Router E has three ways to get to network Z. The path through Router B has a cost of 20, and the paths through Routers C and D have a cost of 20 as well. All paths to network Z are subsequently placed in Router E's routing table.

Equal-cost load-balancing is enabled by default on the router. You cannot disable it.

Unequal-Cost Load-Balancing with EIGRP

Whereas every routing protocol supports equal-cost load-balancing, only a subset supports unequal-cost load-balancing. With the latter type, paths do not have to have the same cost.

By default, EIGRP uses up to four paths for equal-cost load-balancing. However, EIGRP can be configured to load-balance over unequal cost paths as well. This is made possible through the **variance** command:

```
Router(config-router)#variance multiplier
```

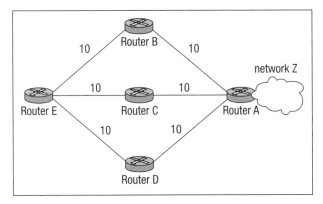

Figure 8.13   Equal-cost load-balancing.

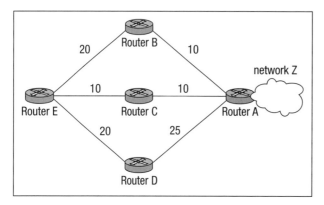

Figure 8.14 Load-balancing over unequal cost paths.

This command tells the router that it can load-balance only over paths that have a cost smaller than the cost of the best path multiplied by the *multiplier*, which is a value from 1 to 128. To see how the **variance** command works, consider Figure 8.14.

In Figure 8.14, Router E has three potential paths to network Z. The costs for these paths are:

➤ Through Router B: 30

➤ Through Router C: 20

➤ Through Router D: 45

Obviously, Router E's best path to network Z is through Router C. If we wanted Router E to use the path through Router B as well, then we would need to issue the following command on Router E:

```
Router_1(config-router)#variance 2
```

With this command, Router E is able to load-balance only over those paths whose costs are smaller than 20×2 = 40. Router 1 can therefore load-balance over the path through Router B. The path through Router 4, however, cannot be used because it has a cost of 45, which is not less than 40.

There is one more criterion an EIGRP path must meet to become a successful candidate for unequal-cost load-balancing: The path must be a feasible successor.

In this example, Router B is a feasible successor because its advertised distance is 10, which is less than the feasible distance of 20. Router B is therefore considered a valid candidate for unequal-cost load-balancing.

EIGRP Bandwidth Optimization

With some routing protocols, the process of converging on a topology change may end up resulting in the consumption of a low-speed link's entire bandwidth. This is particularly true for WAN links, such as those of Frame-Relay, ATM, and ISDN. EIGRP solves this problem by using only a configured portion of a link's bandwidth for transmitting EIGRP traffic.

A link's bandwidth is configured with the following command:

```
Router(config-if)#bandwidth bandwidth
```

where *bandwidth* is expressed in kilobits per second (Kbps).

Enhanced IGRP will by default use up to no more than 50 percent of a link's configured bandwidth. For instance, if a link had a bandwidth of 256Kbps, EIGRP could by default use up to only 128Kbps for transmitting EIGRP traffic (such as queries, updates, and so forth). Note that this percentage restriction applies only to EIGRP traffic; user traffic can consume as much bandwidth as it needs. As a result, congestion would still occur if user data packets were to compete with EIGRP packets for a link's bandwidth. However, the field would be tilted in favor of user traffic because EIGRP traffic is the one that would be constrained by the above percentage restriction.

Moreover, Enhanced IGRP can be configured to utilize any percentage of a link's bandwidth. Opting for a custom percentage as opposed to going with the default percentage may be necessary when network applications require certain amounts of bandwidth availability at all times. Modifying the percentage may also be necessary when EIGRP traffic itself requires certain levels of bandwidth availability.

The technical requirements for both types of traffic must be carefully weighed to make a determination as to how to appropriate the correct amount of network bandwidth for each traffic type. Once these requirements have been analyzed, there are two commands that may then be used to tell EIGRP what percentage of the link's bandwidth it is allowed to use:

➤ **bandwidth**

➤ **ip bandwidth-percent eigrp**

Customizing EIGRP Bandwidth Utilization with the **bandwidth** Command

As mentioned earlier, EIGRP defaults to using up to 50 percent of a link's configured bandwidth. But what if we needed EIGRP to use either more or less than what the default permits? The answer comes with the **bandwidth** command. With this command, an interface can be configured with an *artificial* bandwidth, that is, a bandwidth that does not actually represent the interface's true link speed. By specifying an artificial bandwidth, we can shape the amount of a link's bandwidth that EIGRP will be allowed to appropriate.

For example, suppose we have an interface with a capacity to handle 64Kbps. By default, EIGRP will acquisition up to 50 percent of this. However, if we needed EIGRP to utilize, say, only 16Kbps, then we would assign the interface a bandwidth of 32Kbps. EIGRP would, as a result, acquisition up to 50 percent of 32Kbps (16Kbps).

The following configuration illustrates this example:

```
Router(config-if)#interface serial0
Router(config-if)#bandwidth 32
```

Whatever value is specified with the **bandwidth** command, EIGRP always takes 50 percent of it (by default).

Using the **bandwidth** command may appear as if it would cause the router to influence its rate of transmitting user traffic, but in actuality the effect would be directed only toward EIGRP traffic (e.g., queries, updates, replies, and so forth). This is because the **bandwidth** command is used only by the routing protocol, in this case, EIGRP; the router itself does not use this command for any other purpose. As a result, the command restricts only the traffic that is generated by the routing protocol itself.

Customizing EIGRP Bandwidth Utilization with the ip bandwidth-percent eigrp Command

The second way of modifying EIGRP's bandwidth consumption is with the following command:

```
Router(config-if)#ip bandwidth-percent eigrp AS-number percent
```

where the *AS-number* denotes the interface's autonomous system, and *percent* denotes the percentage of the interface's configured bandwidth that EIGRP may utilize.

For example, the following configuration allows EIGRP to use up to 80 percent of a 56Kbps link:

```
Router(config-if)#interface serial 0
Router(config-if)#bandwidth 56
Router(config-if)#ip bandwidth-percent eigrp 2 80
```

The specified percentage can also be configured above 100 percent. This may be necessary when network policy dictates that the bandwidth for an interface be configured lower than what the actual link speed (also referred to as the committed information rate, or CIR) may be. For instance, the next example shows a configuration in which a 256Kbps link (CIR = 256) has been configured with an artificial bandwidth of 128Kbps. EIGRP is then configured to use 150 percent of this artificial bandwidth:

```
Router(config-if)#interface serial 0
Router(config-if)#bandwidth 128
Router(config-if)#ip bandwidth-percent eigrp 2 150
```

EIGRP traffic will use up to 192Kbps (150 percent of 128) of the 256Kbps link.

Although both the **bandwidth** and **ip bandwidth-percent eigrp** commands may be used to influence EIGRP's rate of bandwidth consumption, only the **bandwidth** command is recommended. If the link's bandwidth cannot be modified (for instance, due to policy reasons), use the **ip bandwidth-percent eigrp** command.

Earlier we mentioned that EIGRP's bandwidth-adaptation capability was useful for WAN links. Due to cost factors, WAN links are usually provisioned with the minimum amount of bandwidth necessary to support the traffic load that uses these links. Additionally, sometimes WAN circuits are purposefully configured to support either more or less bandwidth than that with which they have actually been provisioned. Other times, WAN circuits may be provisioned in a multipoint topology in which the bandwidth for each link varies.

In these and other circumstances, EIGRP must be able to adapt to the WAN environments in which it operates. This adaptation is generally a matter of selecting the correct percentage of bandwidth for EIGRP to use in each unique network setting. Although the steps to this analysis of network requirements are beyond the scope of this book, we present here some general rules to use when determining how to assign bandwidth for Frame-Relay circuits. With this knowledge in hand, we will be able to see how EIGRP's bandwidth utilization adapts itself to its surroundings and helps both user and routing protocol traffic flow optimally.

Bandwidth Utilization over Frame-Relay Point-to-Point Interfaces

On a point-to-point Frame-Relay interface (or subinterface), the bandwidth is, by default, 1544Kbps (1.544Mbps). On these types of interfaces, set the bandwidth to match the CIR for the interface's link.

For example, the following configuration shows a point-to-point subinterface that has been configured with a bandwidth that matches the link's CIR of 64Kbps:

```
Router(config-if)#inteface serial0.1 point-to-point
Router(config-if)#bandwidth 64
```

With this configuration, EIGRP traffic consumes 32Kbps (50 percent of 64Kbps).

If there are several point-to-point subinterfaces on a major interface, then still configure each subinterface to match the CIR for each subinterface link. However, the total bandwidth for all subinterfaces should not exceed the actual speed of the access line.

Figure 8.15 shows a Frame-Relay topology in which the central router has a T1 access line (1.544Mbps) hooked up to its serial 0 interface. The T1 line has been fractionalized into 10 logical circuits that are each on a separate subinterface. Each of these circuits has been provisioned with a capacity of 256Kbps. However, the central router's T1 line (also referred to as an access line) has the capacity to support only 1544Kbps. The access line is said to be oversubscribed (the amount of over-subscription in this case is [256×10] − 1544 = 1016Kbps).

When an interface is oversubscribed, as it is in Figure 8.15, the general rule is to divide the access line speed equally across each of the subinterfaces. Therefore, in this example, the access line speed of 1544Kbps would be divided by 10 to give 154Kbps. This value of 154Kbps is what you would configure on each subinterface, as shown next:

```
Router(config-if)#interface serial 0
Router(config-if)#interface frame-relay
Router(config-if)#interface serial0.1 point-to-point
Router(config-if)#bandwidth 154
Router(config-if)#interface serial0.2 point-to-point
Router(config-if)#bandwidth 154
Router(config-if)#interface serial0.3 point-to-point
Router(config-if)#bandwidth 154
. . .
Router(config-if)#interface serial0.10 point-to-point
Router(config-if)#bandwidth 154
```

EIGRP subsequently uses up to 77Kbps (50 percent of 154Kbps) on each subinterface.

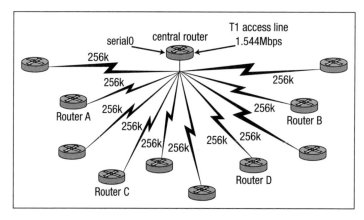

Figure 8.15 Configuring the bandwidth for Frame-Relay point-to-point subinterfaces.

Bandwidth Utilization over Frame-Relay Multipoint Interfaces

On a multipoint interface (or subinterface), EIGRP divides the interface's configured bandwidth by the number of neighbors on the interface to determine the amount of bandwidth that is to be associated with each neighbor's link.

In Figure 8.16, for example, EIGRP will by default divide the bandwidth configured on serial 0 by four to determine the bandwidth available for each link. For instance, a bandwidth of 756Kbps will tell EIGRP that it is to associate 756Kbps/4 = 189Kbps with each link. EIGRP would then utilize up to 94Kbps (50 percent of 189Kbps) for each link.

Make sure, however, that the specified bandwidth does not overload the circuits. In the previous example, using a bandwidth of 756Kbps would not be a good idea if, for instance, each of the four circuits had a CIR of only 64Kbps. Using 756Kbps in this situation would cause EIGRP to use the entire bandwidth on each circuit, likely causing EIGRP packets to be dropped. Instead, the proper action would be to use the sum of the circuits' actual capacities (CIRs) in determining the interface's bandwidth. In our continuing example, this would mean configuring the interface with a bandwidth of 64Kbps×4 = 256Kbps.

The following configuration is correct:

```
Router(config-if)#interface serial 1
Router(config-if)#ip address 148.33.45.17 255.255.255.240
Router(config-if)#encapsulation frame-relay
Router(config-if)#frame-relay map ip 198.33.45.18 100 broadcast
Router(config-if)#frame-relay map ip 198.33.45.19 200 broadcast
Router(config-if)#frame-relay map ip 198.33.45.20 300 broadcast
Router(config-if)#frame-relay map ip 198.33.45.21 400 broadcast
Router(config-if)#bandwidth 256
```

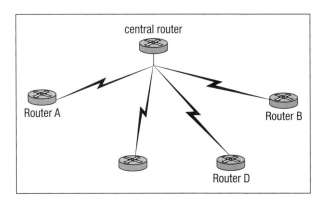

Figure 8.16   Diagram of an EIGRP Frame-Relay internetwork.

The serial 1 interface has been configured with a bandwidth of 256Kbps. EIGRP sees that there are four links on this interface, so it will divide 256Kbps by 4 to get 64Kbps. EIGRP will subsequently use up to 32Kbps (50 percent of 64Kbps) for each link.

Bandwidth Utilization over Multipoint Frame-Relay Interfaces—Varying CIRs

Many times, a Frame-Relay topology is composed of several links that have varying CIRs. In this case, a new formula for calculating the bandwidth for multipoint interfaces is required: *Configure the bandwidth to represent the minimum CIR times the number of links.* For example, consider the topology shown in Figure 8.17, which indicates that there are three virtual circuits with capacities (CIRs) of 256Kbps, and one virtual circuit with a CIR of 56Kbps. The central router's access line is T1. Using the above formula for bandwidth calculation, we find that the bandwidth on Router A's serial 0 interface should be 56Kbps×4 = 224Kbps. With this configured bandwidth, EIGRP will subsequently utilize up to 50 percent of each 56Kbps link.

Although such a configuration ensures that the link with the CIR of 56Kbps will not be overdriven, it does not allow EIGRP traffic to effectively utilize the three 256Kbps links. A more efficient strategy is therefore required in this scenario, as well as in other similar scenarios.

Bandwidth Utilization over Hybrid Frame-Relay Interfaces

The best solution to a topology with differing CIRs is to use both multipoint and point-to-point subinterfaces on the same major interface. With this hybrid approach, links with differing capacities can be placed on point-to-point subinterfaces, and links with equal capacities could be placed on multipoint subinterfaces. Each point-to-point subinterface can then be configured with a bandwidth that matches its respective link's CIR, whereas each multipoint subinterface can be configured with

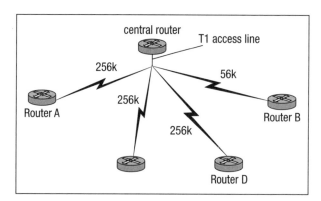

Figure 8.17 A multipoint Frame-Relay network with differing CIRs.

a bandwidth that equals the total capacity of its multipoint links. As a result, no links would be in danger of being *overutilized* by EIGRP, nor would any links be *underutilized*.

In Figure 8.18, Router A has 10 virtual circuits leading into an E1 line (2.048Mbps) on its serial 0 interface. Three of the circuits have CIRs of 384Kbps, four have CIRs of 128Kbps, and the remaining have CIRs of differing values. To optimize EIGRP bandwidth utilization, the 384Kbps and 128Kbps links have been placed on multi-point subinterfaces, whereas the three links with varying CIRs have each been placed on separate point-to-point subinterfaces. The relevant configuration for the topology is shown as follows:

```
Router_A(config-if)#interface serial0
Router_A(config-if)#encapsulation frame-relay
Router_A(config-if)#interface serial0.1 multipoint
Router_A(config-if)#ip-address 112.37.1.1 255.255.255.0
Router_A(config-if)#bandwidth 1152
Router_A(config-if)#interface serial0.2 multipoint
Router_A(config-if)#ip-address 112.37.2.1 255.255.255.0
Router_A(config-if)#bandwidth 512
Router_A(config-if)#interface serial0.3 point-to-point
Router_A(config-if)#ip-address 112.39.3.5 255.255.255.252
Router_A(config-if)#bandwidth 320
Router_A(config-if)#interface serial0.4 point-to-point
Router_A(config-if)#ip-address 112.39.3.9 255.255.255.252
Router_A(config-if)#bandwidth 192
Router_A(config-if)#interface serial0.5 point-to-point
Router_A(config-if)#ip-address 112.39.3.13 255.255.255.252
Router_A(config-if)#bandwidth 64
```

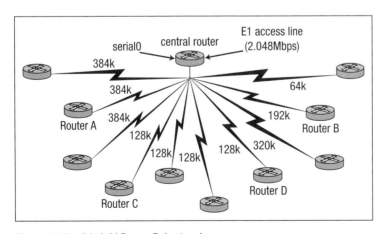

Figure 8.18   A hybrid Frame-Relay topology.

In this configuration, the three circuits with CIRs of 384Kbps are on serial 0.1, whereas the four circuits with CIRs of 128Kbps are on serial 0.2. On these multipoint subinterfaces, EIGRP will divide the bandwidth by the number of links to determine what amount of bandwidth is available to each link. EIGRP will then use up to 50 percent of each link's bandwidth. But what if we needed EIGRP to utilize either more or less bandwidth?

The first option, as we have been doing, is to make the modifications using the **bandwidth** command. However, if policy reasons prevent this option, the next option would be to use the **ip bandwidth-percent eigrp** command.

For example, in the preceding scenario, let us say that EIGRP needs to use 70 percent instead of 50 percent of the bandwidth on serial 0.1. The modified configuration for this multipoint subinterface would look like the following:

```
Router_A(config-if)#interface serial0.1 multipoint
Router_A(config-if)#bandwidth 1152
Router_A(config-if)#ip bandwidth-percent eigrp 70
```

EIGRP traffic will now be allowed to utilize up to 268Kbps (70 percent of 384Kbps) on each link for serial 0.1.

Summary of Bandwidth Utilization over Frame-Relay Interfaces

Several types of interface configurations are possible with Frame-Relay. We have covered the following:

➤ Point-to-point interface

➤ Multipoint interface

➤ Hybrid interface

Configure the bandwidth on a point-to-point interface or subinterface to match the link's actual speed (CIR). Likewise, if there are multiple point-to-point subinterfaces, configure each subinterface's bandwidth to match its link's CIR.

Configure the bandwidth on a multipoint interface or subinterface to match the total speed of all the links. However, if this value exceeds the access line speed, then configure the bandwidth to match the latter. Furthermore, if the links have differing CIRs, then one option is to configure the bandwidth to match the lowest CIR times the number of links. EIGRP divides the configured bandwidth on the multipoint interface or subinterface by the number of links on the interface to determine the bandwidth allocation of each link.

Another option to configuring a topology in which the links are of varying speeds is to create a hybrid interface. Links with matching CIRs could be placed on multiple subinterfaces, whereas links with differing CIRs could be placed on separate point-to-point subinterfaces. This type of interface configuration has the advantage of allowing EIGRP to make the most efficient use of all the links' bandwidths.

In all of these types of interface configurations, EIGRP will by default use up to 50 percent of each link's available bandwidth, as configured with the **bandwidth** command. To specify a different percentage, use the **ip bandwidth-percent eigrp** command.

Building Scalable EIGRP Internetworks

Now that we have seen some of the components that EIGRP uses to support the requirements of large growing networks, let us examine how all of these components can work together to bring about a supremely scalable EIGRP internetwork. Before we do this, however, we should first analyze the technical goals that scalable EIGRP internetwork strives toward achieving.

Goals of EIGRP Scalability

The goals of EIGRP scalability can be categorized as the following:

➤ *Reliability and availability*—An Enhanced IGRP internetwork seeks to minimize the downtime caused by topology changes. When topology changes occur, EIGRP routers must be available to communicate the topology changes accurately and expediently.

➤ *Responsiveness*—An Enhanced IGRP internetwork must respond quickly and accurately to topology changes. Remember that routing infrastructures exist to support the end user and his or her applications. An EIGRP internetwork that is slow to converge will have a negative effect on user traffic as well as on the user.

➤ *Efficiency*—An Enhanced IGRP internetwork that achieves its operation goals with minimal work is said to be efficient.

➤ *Adaptability*—An Enhanced IGRP internetwork that can efficiently and adequately support network growth and modification is said to be *adaptable*.

Design Prerequisites for a Scalable EIGRP Internetwork

To achieve these scalability goals, EIGRP asks that a couple of crucial design requirements first be met:

➤ *Hierarchical network infrastructure*—The internetwork must be designed hierarchically. In Cisco terms, this means following the three-layer model discussed in Chapter 1. This design model seeks to centralize the traffic that occurs at each layer for the purposes of meeting the requirements of a scalable internetwork.

➤ *Hierarchical addressing scheme*—The internetwork must use an addressing scheme that allocates contiguous blocks of address space to each area of the internetwork. Meeting this design requirement allows for the successful occurrence of Classless Inter-Domain Routing (CIDR) and route summarization. It is perhaps important to note that a hierarchical addressing scheme depends on a hierarchical network infrastructure. Without a tiered network foundation, CIDR and route summarization would be difficult, if not impossible, to implement.

Presenting the Scalable EIGRP Internetwork

Figure 8.19 presents a diagram of an EIGRP internetwork that has been built with a hierarchical network infrastructure and a hierarchical addressing scheme. This diagram incorporates most of the components of an EIGRP hierarchical routing solution.

The first component we find in Figure 8.19 is route summarization. Router A is performing automatic route summarization, whereas Routers B, C, and D have

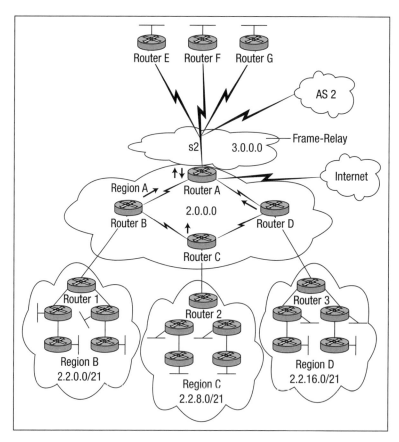

Figure 8.19 Topology of a well-built EIGRP internetwork.

been manually configured to summarize regions B, C, and D, respectively. Router B summarizes region B with the address 2.2.0.0 /21 and advertises it to Routers A and C; Router C summarizes region C with the address 2.2.8.0 /21 and advertises it to Routers B and D; Router D summarizes region D with the address 2.2.16.0 /21 and advertises it to Routers A and C; lastly, Router A automatically summarizes regions A, B, C, and D with the address 2.0.0.0 /8 and advertises it to network 3.0.0.0 /8. Furthermore, Router A also summarizes 3.0.0.0 and advertises it to 2.0.0.0.

The next hierarchical component we may discover in Figure 8.19 is traffic-bounding. Both query and update packets have been limited in range by the route summarization occurring on Routers A through D and by the stub designations assigned to Routers E, F, and G. Queries sent from region B receive an immediate reply from Routers A and C; queries sent from region C receive an immediate reply from Routers B and D; and queries sent from region D receive an immediate reply from Routers A and C.

Another hierarchical component we find in Figure 8.19 is load-balancing. Router C has been configured with unequal-cost load-balancing so as to use Routers B and D to get to 3.0.0.0 or the Internet.

The last hierarchical component in Figure 8.19 is EIGRP bandwidth optimization on the Frame-Relay network. Router A has a fractionalized access line leading into the Frame-Relay cloud. The three links to Routers E, F, and G each have a capacity of 768Kbps. Router A subsequently places the three 128Kbps links on a multipoint subinterface with a bandwidth of 384Kbps, and places the 868Kbps link on a point-to-point subinterface with a bandwidth of 768Kbps.

Chapter Summary

EIGRP optimization is an integral feature of any EIGRP internetwork that seeks scalability at minimal cost to network resources. EIGRP optimization comprises several hierarchically engineered features, including route summarization, traffic-bounding, load-balancing, and WAN bandwidth optimization.

The first hierarchical feature of an EIGRP internetwork, route summarization, has several benefits, including reducing resource consumption and expediting convergence after the occurrence of topology changes. There are two types of route summarization: automatic and manual. Automatic route summarization is performed by default at major network boundaries. Manual route summarization is done at any location where addressing is contiguous.

Traffic-bounding is EIGRP's next hierarchical component. Route summarization, stub designation, AS boundaries, and distribution lists are all traffic-bounding features that prevent query and routing update packets from inundating an EIGRP environment.

Another hierarchical component to EIGRP is load-balancing. There are two types of load-balancing: unequal-cost and equal-cost. Being able to distribute traffic across multiple unequal-cost or equal-cost paths is highly useful for minimizing delay and increasing throughput for user traffic.

Bandwidth optimization is the last major feature of a scalable EIGRP internetwork. With this feature, Enhanced IGRP has the capacity to use a configurable percentage of a link's configured bandwidth. This feature is used heavily in WAN environments, such as Frame-Relay, where router interfaces must be configured with the appropriate bandwidth.

This concludes our discussion on the Enhanced Interior Gateway Routing Protocol. As we have seen, EIGRP is a highly scalable routing protocol with tremendous potential in the global routing industry. It may be only a matter of time before this algorithm becomes the Internet's standard for IGP routing. Until then, EIGRP will continue to rise in popularity as it continues to offer what many internetworks around the world seek most—scalability.

Review Questions

1. Where does manual route summarization occur in EIGRP internetworks?

    a. Only at major network boundaries

    b. At any location where there is contiguous addressing

    c. Only on stub routers

    d. At locations where there is no contiguous addressing

2. Which one of these is not an advantage of route summarization?

    a. Limits the impact of topology changes

    b. Reduces the size of routing tables

    c. Allows routers to support discontiguous addressing

    d. Sets query boundaries

3. Why may it be necessary to disable automatic route summarization?

    a. Because there are issues with resource consumption

    b. To support discontiguous subnets

    c. Because EIGRP does not support variable-length subnet masks (VLSMs)

    d. To support contiguous subnets

4. Which command is used for manual route summarization?

   a. **ip summary-address eigrp**

   b. **ip summary address eigrp**

   c. **ip eigrp summary address**

   d. **ip eigrp summary-address**

5. How does route summarization limit the query range?

   a. By preventing queries from being propagated outside the AS.

   b. By preventing queries from being generated whenever a topology change occurs in a summarized region.

   c. By preventing routers that are configured with route summarization from propagating the queries.

   d. Queries that are sent outside of a summarized region receive an immediate reply.

6. What is meant by "stuck-in-active?"

   a. A condition in which a router must wait for a reply from a router before proceeding with route recomputation.

   b. A condition in which a router must wait to send a query to a router before proceeding with route recomputation.

   c. A condition in which a topology change forces routers to remove networks from their topology and routing tables.

   d. The router that fails to reply to a query is considered to be in this condition.

7. Which one of these is not a way to limit the query range?

   a. Route summarization

   b. AS boundaries

   c. Stub designations

   d. Load balancing

8. What happens when a router that lays on the border of two ASes receives a query?

   a. The router drops the query.

   b. The router sends a reply and then forwards a new query into the other AS.

   c. The router does not send any reply but still forwards a new query into the other AS.

   d. The router will send a reply without forwarding a new query to the other AS.

9. How do outbound distribution lists limit the range of routing updates?

   a. By preventing a router from advertising certain networks.

   b. By keeping the router from receiving certain routing updates.

   c. Outbound distribution lists do not limit the range of routing updates; they limit the query range.

   d. By preventing a router from advertising neighbors.

10. What are two benefits to designating a router stub?

    a. It prevents queries from being sent to the stub router.

    b. It reduces resource consumption.

    c. It allows stub routers to become transit points.

    d. It prevents neighbor discovery.

11. What requirements must be met for unequal-cost load-balancing to occur?

    a. The **variance** command must be issued, the router must have multiple paths to the destination, and the paths must all be successor routes.

    b. The **variance** command must be issued, the router must have only up to four paths to the destination, and the paths must all be feasible successor routes.

    c. The **variance** command must be issued, the router must have multiple paths to the destination, and the paths must be either successor or feasible successor routes.

    d. The **variance** command must be issued, the router must have multiple paths to the destination, and the paths must be listed in the routing table.

12. What does the **bandwidth** command do?

    a. It tells the router how much user traffic can be placed on a link.

    b. It specifies the bandwidth of an interface (in bps).

    c. It tells the router how much bandwidth is not available for load-balancing.

    d. It specifies the bandwidth of an interface (in Kbps); this value is then used by EIGRP to determine how much bandwidth is available for EIGRP traffic.

13. What percentage of a link's bandwidth does EIGRP use by default?

    a. 25

    b. 50

    c. 75

    d. 100

14. What should you configure the bandwidth on a point-to-point interface or subinterface to be?

    a. The actual link speed (CIR)

    b. Twice the actual link speed

    c. The configured bandwidth of the router's slowest interface

    d. The amount of bandwidth you want EIGRP to consume

15. What does the **ip bandwidth-percent eigrp** command do?

    a. It tells EIGRP what percentage of the link's configured bandwidth to use.

    b. It tells EIGRP how much user traffic to send.

    c. It tells EIGRP what percent of user traffic to send.

    d. It allows EIGRP to determine what the link's CIR is.

16. How does the EIGRP calculate the bandwidth available for each link on a multipoint interface (or subinterface)?

    a. The configured bandwidth is divided by the number of links on the multipoint interface.

    b. EIGRP senses the speed of each link.

    c. The configured bandwidth for each link on the multipoint interface is divided by the number of links on the multipoint interface.

    d. It does not do any bandwidth calculation in this case because you are supposed to configure the bandwidth for each link on the multipoint interface.

17. What should the configured bandwidth of a multipoint interface (or subinterface) be if the access line is oversubscribed *and* all links on the multipoint interface have identical CIRs?

    a. Half the bandwidth of the sum total of all CIRs

    b. The access line speed

    c. The speed of the slowest link

    d. The sum total of all the links' CIRs divided by the number of links on the multipoint interface

18. What should the configured bandwidth of multipoint interface (or subinterface) be if not all links on the multipoint interface have identical CIRs? (Assume you cannot use a hybrid interface.)

    a. The access line speed

    b. The speed of the slowest link

    c. The speed of the slowest link multiplied by the number of links on the multipoint interface

    d. The access line speed divided by the number of links

8

19. Which design prerequisites are necessary for building a scalable EIGRP internetwork?

    a. Hierarchical network structure, powerful routers

    b. Multiple protocols, hierarchical addressing scheme

    c. Hierarchical network structure, multiple protocols

    d. Hierarchical network structure, hierarchical addressing scheme

20. Which one of the following is not a hierarchical component of EIGRP?

    a. Route summarization

    b. Traffic-bounding

    c. Area designation

    d. Bandwidth optimization

Real-World Project

For this hands-on project, we will configure the EIGRP internetwork presented in Figure 8.19 and reshown in Figure 8.20.

Actually, we will configure only Routers A and C using the knowledge we have acquired from both this chapter and Chapter 7. On Router A, we will focus on the configurations for optimizing EIGRP bandwidth. On Router C, we will focus on configuring manual route summarization.

Configuring Router A:

1. After completing the initial configurations for Router A, enable the EIGRP routing process for AS 1:

```
Router_A(config)#router eigrp 1
```

2. In router configuration mode, specify that EIGRP will be routing for classful networks 2.0.0.0 and 3.0.0.0.

```
Router_A(config)#network 2.0.0.0
Router_A(config)#network 3.0.0.0
```

Router A will be performing automatic route summarization in both directions. Network 2.0.0.0 /8 will be advertised to network 3.0.0.0, and, likewise, network 3.0.0.0 /8 will be advertised to network 2.0.0.0.

3. Go into Router A's serial 2 interface and enable Frame-Relay.

```
Router_A(config-if)#interface serial2
Router_A(config-if)#encapsulation frame-relay
```

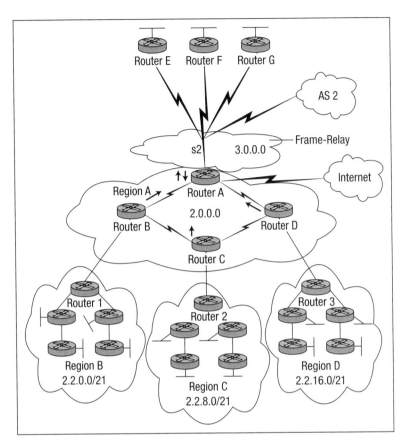

Figure 8.20   Diagram of our scalable EIGRP internetwork.

4. Specify that the three links leading to Routers E, F, and G are to be on a multipoint subinterface. Also specify that the link to AS 2 is to be on a point-to-point subinterface.

```
Router_A(config-if)#interface serial2.1 multipoint
Router_A(config-if)#ip address 3.1.1.1 255.255.255.248
Router_A(config-if)#interface serial2.2 point-to-point
Router_A(config-if)#ip address 3.1.1.9 255.255.255.252
```

The multipoint subinterface is on one subnet. It contains the links to Routers E, F, and G. The point-to-point subinterface is on its own subnet and contains the link to AS 2.

5. Specify that the bandwidth for serial 2.1 is 384Kbps, and that the bandwidth for serial 2.2 is 768Kbps.

```
Router_A(config-if)#interface serial 2.1 multipoint
Router_A(config-if)#bandwidth 384
Router_A(config-if)#interface serial2.2 point-to-point
Router_A(config-if)#bandwidth 768
```

On Router A, EIGRP will subsequently see that each link on the multipoint sub-interface has an available bandwidth of 128Kbps. EIGRP will also see that it can utilize up to 384Kbps on the point-to-point subinterface.

Configuring Router C:

1. After completing the initial configurations for Router C, enable the EIGRP routing process for AS 1:

```
Router_C(config)#router eigrp 1
```

2. Specify that EIGRP will be routing for classful network 2.0.0.0.

```
Router_C(config-router)#network 2.0.0.0
```

3. Configure the summary route 2.2.8.0 /21 on Router C's serial 0 and serial 1 interfaces.

```
Router_C(config-if)#interface serial 0
Router_C(config-if)#ip summary-address eigrp 2.2.8.0 255.255.248.0
Router_C(config-if)#interface serial 1
Router_C(config-if)#ip summary-address eigrp 2.2.8.0 255.255.248.0
```

Router C will subsequently advertise the summary route to Routers B and D. These routers would in turn advertise the route to their respective regions and to Router A. Because Router A is already summarizing at the major network boundary, it will not propagate Router C's summary route to 3.0.0.0.

CHAPTER NINE

Border Gateway Protocol

After completing this chapter, you will be able to:

✓ Describe Border Gateway Protocol (BGP) features and operation

✓ Explain how BGP peering functions

✓ Explain how BGP policy-based routing occurs

✓ Characterize common BGP attributes

✓ Describe BGP synchronization

✓ Justify when BGP should be used and discuss BGP alternatives

✓ Configure and verify BGP operation

✓ Given a set of network requirements, configure a BGP environment and verify proper operation (within described guidelines)

This chapter explores the operation and basic configuration of the Border Gateway Protocol. BGP's essential features and functions are introduced, followed by an overview of BGP's role in *policy-based routing*. Policy-based routing is a distinguishing BGP component that allows network administrators to define the conditions under which traffic may flow across an autonomous system. These conditions are defined by what are known as *path attributes*, which, like the technical metrics of interior gateway protocols (IGPs), influence a router's path selection process. A large portion of this chapter is therefore devoted to examining the path attributes used in BGP policy-based routing. Upon sufficiently addressing this topic, this chapter then presents a look at some fundamental commands necessary for BGP operation and verification.

This chapter lays the groundwork for Chapter 10, which focuses on scaling BGP through the application of policy-based features whose purpose it is to facilitate controlled routing in a BGP internetwork.

BGP Features and Operation

BGP Features

The Border Gateway Protocol is a highly powerful interdomain routing protocol designed to exchange routing and reachability information between autonomous systems (ASes). Developed as a replacement for its predecessor, exterior gateway protocol (EGP), BGP is the standard exterior routing protocol for today's global Internet. Within the Internet, BGP is used extensively to connect corporate enterprises to Internet Service Providers (ISPs) as well as to connect ISPs with each other. In fact, the Internet would not be the pervasive and ubiquitous entity that it is today without the likeness of a highly scalable interdomain routing algorithm such as BGP.

The current version of BGP is BGP4, defined in RFC 1771.

Although BGP is essentially known as an exterior routing protocol used between ASes, it can be used *within* an AS as well. An autonomous system is, according to RFC 1771, "a set of routers under a single technical administration, using an interior gateway protocol and common metrics to route packets within the AS, and using an exterior gateway protocol to route packets to other ASes." BGP can simultaneously fulfill the roles of both an IGP and EGP. However, as we will see later, BGP's lack of flexibility as an IGP leads many ASes to run additional routing protocols, such as Routing Information Protocol (RIP) or Open Shortest Path First (OSPF), within their autonomous systems. Figure 9.1 depicts the use of both IGPs and EGPs within and between autonomous systems.

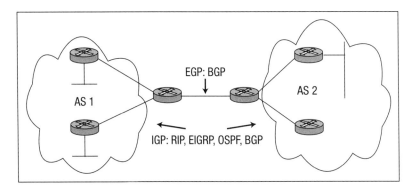

Figure 9.1 IGPs operate within an AS, and EGPs operate between ASs.

When BGP is run between ASes, it is called External BGP (EBGP). When BGP is run within an AS, it is called Internal BGP (IBGP). A router running IBGP will exchange BGP routing information only with other routers within the same AS, whereas a router running EBGP will exchange routing information only with routers residing in different ASes.

Note: *The terms IBGP and EBGP are not separate standards. These terms are instead used to refer only to the manner in which BGP operates with respect to an AS.*

A router can run IBGP exclusively as the AS's only interior routing protocol or it can run IBGP in conjunction with other interior routing protocols. When IBGP is the only operant IGP, all routers within the AS should be directly connected to each other. When operating with other routing protocols within the AS, IBGP routers are not required to be directly connected.

A router running EBGP should be directly connected with another EBGP neighbor that is residing in the neighboring AS. Although this is not an absolute requirement, it is generally considered the recommended procedure for connecting EBGP neighbors.

Figure 9.2 illustrates the differences between EBGP and IBGP in a multi-AS environment.

In Figure 9.2, Routers A and B are directly connected and have established an EBGP session, and Routers C and D have also established an EBGP session. Routers B and C, on the other hand, have established an IBGP session. Notice that Routers B and C are not directly physically connected. They are instead connected via Router E, with whom they are exchanging RIP updates. Routers B and C are therefore said to have established a *logical* IBGP connection with each other.

9

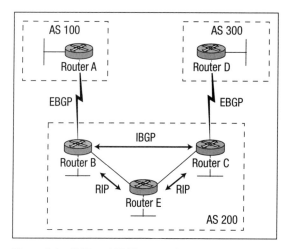

Figure 9.2 IBGP and EBGP connections.

BGP Operation

BGP uses the Transmission Control Protocol (TCP) as its layer 4 transport protocol (port 179). This means that BGP is a connection-oriented routing protocol that allows its routers to establish reliable connections with each other and transmit reliable routing information. When a BGP router first initializes, it establishes a TCP connection with a directly connected BGP router. Both routers are said to be peers, or neighbors. In Figure 9.2, for example, Routers A and B are EBGP peers, and Routers B and C are IBGP peers.

Once the TCP connection is established between two BGP peers (whether they are directly connected or not), the first message that each side transmits is an *open* message. The purpose of this message is to negotiate and confirm BGP connection parameters between the two peers. Some of the connection parameters that are established are the following:

➤ *BGP version number*—The current version is 4. If a peer happens to be running an earlier version, both peers can negotiate to use this earlier version.

➤ *AS number*—This is the sender's autonomous system number.

➤ *Holdtime*—This is the maximum number of seconds that may elapse without receiving an update or keepalive message from a neighbor. Like the Enhanced Interior Gateway Routing Protocol (EIGRP) and OSPF holdtimes, an expired holdtime indicates that the neighbor is dead. Two peers use the smallest of their configured holdtimes.

➤ *BGP router ID*—This is the sender's router ID. It is chosen in exactly the same way that OSPF chooses it; that is, the router ID is the highest active interface IP address, or the highest loopback interface IP address (if configured).

Once both peers have accepted each other's open message, the BGP connection is reliably established and both peers may then proceed to exchange routing information. Initially, both peers will exchange their BGP routing tables. The BGP routing table contains all of a router's best routes. This routing table is separate from the IP routing table, which is what the AS's IGP uses. However, despite the separation, both routing tables may be dependent on each other's information. As a result, the router can be configured to exchange information between the two tables.

The following output shows what a BGP routing table looks like:

```
Router#show ip bgp

BGP table version is 716977, local router ID is 193.0.32.1
Status codes: s suppressed, * valid, > best, i - internal
Origin codes: i - IGP, e - EGP, ? - incomplete

Network          Next Hop        Metric  LocPrf   Weight Path
*>i3.0.0.0        193.0.22.1      0       100      0 1800 1239 ?
*>i6.0.0.0        193.0.22.1      0       100      0 1800 690 568 ?
*>i7.0.0.0        193.0.22.1      0       100      0 1800 701 35 ?
*>i8.0.0.0         93.0.22.1      0       100      0 1800 690 560 ?
```

The BGP routing table output is explained in Table 9.1.

BGP routing tables are exchanged only during neighbor initialization. Thereafter, incremental routing updates are the only routing information that gets exchanged.

Table 9.1 The fields of a BGP routing table.

Field	Description
BGP table version	Indicates the version number of the BGP table. This value is incremented any time the table changes due to a topology or router configuration change.
Local router ID	The router's router ID.
Status code	Indicates the entry's status. The status can be one of the following values: s—suppressed, *—valid, >—best path, i—IBGP-learned entry.
Origin code	Indicates the entry's origin. It is found at the end of each entry. The origin can be one of the following values: i—IGP origin, e—EGP origin, ?—Unknown (redistributed from an IGP).
Network	The network IP address.
Next hop	The next hop's IP address.
Metric	Path attribute, also known as the MED.
LocPrf	Local preference.
Weight	Weight of the route.
Path	AS-path attribute.

These updates are used to notify the BGP internetwork of a topology change, and they convey the following information fields:

➤ *Network reachability*—A BGP update message contains all the networks that are reachable via a single path. Multiple paths require multiple update messages. Networks are listed along with their prefix masks. Consequently, classless network addresses and summary routes may be included in the BGP update.

➤ *Path attributes*—Most routing algorithms associate a metric with each network. For instance, in the case of RIP, the metric associated with each network is hop count. With BGP, however, each network is associated with multiple metrics known as path attributes. These path attributes are listed along with each network in the BGP update.

➤ *Unreachable (withdrawn) networks*—The BGP update also indicates the routes that are no longer reachable and have been withdrawn from service.

Because BGP does not send periodic routing updates, a BGP peer must have some way to ensure that other peers remain alive and reachable. The message suited specifically for the purpose of keeping a peer relationship active is the keepalive message. Keepalive messages have the effect of resetting the holdtime timer and are sent often enough to keep it from expiring.

Note: If a peer's holdtime is zero, then the peer will not send any keepalives. Neither will the peer on the other side send any keepalives. This is because both peers will use the smallest holdtime configured between them, which in this case is zero.

Whereas keepalive messages are sent to keep BGP connections open, notification messages are sent to close BGP connections. These latter messages are sent only when an error condition is detected, such as when a packet error occurs or the holdtime expires.

Summary of BGP Features and Operation

BGP is an exterior routing algorithm that allows ISPs and corporate enterprises to exchange network reachability information between autonomous systems. As an Internet standard, BGP supports the following features:

➤ Fast convergence

➤ Robust metrics called path attributes

➤ Unsurpassed scalability

➤ Support for Classless Inter-Domain Routing (CIDR) and route summarization

➤ Reliable and incremental routing updates

BGP routers that establish a TCP connection with each other are called peers, or neighbors. Peers can establish either an intra-AS connection, known as an Internal

BGP, or an extra-AS connection, known as an External BGP. BGP connection peers initially exchange their full BGP routing tables and thereafter exchange only routing updates triggered by topology changes or router configuration changes. BGP operation involves transmission of the following message types:

➤ *Open message*—After establishing a TCP connection, BGP peers send each other an open message to negotiate and verify BGP connection parameters.

➤ *Update message*—Routing updates contain such information as network reachability, path attributes, and withdrawn routes.

➤ *Keepalive message*—Keepalives ensure that a peer relationship remains open and active.

➤ *Notification message*—Notifications are sent whenever an error condition is detected. The BGP connection is subsequently terminated.

The next section explores one of BGP's most fundamental and distinguishing trademarks, policy-based routing.

Policy-Based Routing

As a policy-based routing protocol, BGP makes routing decisions based not on technical metrics (such as cost or hop count), but rather on network policy decisions. Network policy decisions define exactly how BGP routing information should be controlled as it passes from one AS to another. For example, consider Figure 9.3.

Figure 9.3 depicts a BGP environment comprising four ASes, each under separate administration and using different network policies. Consider AS 100's network

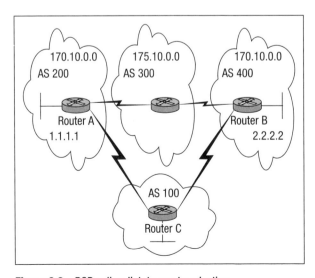

Figure 9.3   BGP policy dictates route selection.

policy regarding the other ASes. Network administrators in AS 100 have laid out the following guidelines (policies) for defining how traffic is to flow through this AS:

1. Accept traffic from AS 200 only if it originates from network 170.10.0.0.

2. Accept traffic from AS400 that does not originate from network 190.10.0.0 /16.

3. Do not notify AS 200 of reachability to AS 400.

4. Use the path through AS 200 to reach AS 300.

Each of these rules is a component of a network policy that determines how traffic is to enter and leave AS 100. A network administrator would translate the policies into the appropriate BGP commands. Once the commands have been issued on the appropriate routers, BGP is said to have implemented policy-based routing.

Policy-based routing is therefore defined as an activity in which policies, or rules, are set for the purpose of defining how traffic is routed through an AS.

Although BGP can potentially support many policies, BGP is usually able to support only those that abide by the *hop-by-hop routing paradigm*. This paradigm, which is used in the current Internet, basically states that a router can advertise to another AS only those routes that the router itself uses. In other words, if a router's routing table does not list a certain route, then that route can be neither used nor advertised. We are, in fact, familiar with this type of routing paradigm because it is the one used by all routing protocols mentioned in this book.

BGP Path Attributes

The previous section stated that BGP uses policy-based routing to influence its route selection decision-making process and that these policies are translated into BGP commands. What exactly is the language BGP uses to represent and implement network policy? It is the language of path attributes.

Path attributes can best be understood when compared and contrasted to the metrics that characterize our usual routing protocols. For instance, RIP uses a metric called hop count. BGP uses a similar metric (path attribute) called AS-path, which represents the number of ASes used to reach a given destination. Both metrics can be used by their respective routing algorithms in determining the best path. However, whereas RIP hop count is the only means of selecting the best path, AS-path is but one of many means of choosing the best path.

RIP's definition of best path is lowest hop count; OSPF's definition of best path is least-cost path, based on media bandwidth; and EIGRP's definition of best path is the path with the smallest feasible distance, a function of media bandwidth and delay. BGP's definition of best path depends on the routing policy and on the path attributes being used to implement the policy. If, for instance, there was a policy that required a network to be reached through the shortest possible route, then the best path to this network would be the path with the least number of AS hops. In this case, the AS-path attribute determines the best path.

Although the AS-path attribute is a good introduction to the concept of BGP policy-based routing, most other BGP path attributes differ dramatically from the routing protocol metrics with which we have become accustomed. Before we explore each of these unique path attributes, however, it would be prudent to analyze their general characteristics.

Attribute Characteristics

Path attributes fall into four characterizing categories:

➤ Well-known mandatory

➤ Well-known discretionary

➤ Optional transitive

➤ Optional nontransitive

The following sections explore these classifications in detail.

Well-Known Path Attributes

Well-known path attributes are attributes that are recognized by all BGP autonomous systems that are compliant with RFC standards. These attributes are propagated in routing updates to BGP peers.

Well-known attributes are divided into two classes: well-known mandatory and well-known discretionary. Well-known mandatory attributes are required to appear in routing updates, whereas well-known discretionary attributes are not required to appear in routing updates.

Well-known mandatory path attributes include the following:

➤ AS-path

➤ Next hop

➤ Origin

Well-known discretionary path attributes include the following:

➤ Local preference

➤ Atomic attribute

9

Optional Path Attributes

Unlike well-known attributes, optional attributes are *not* necessarily recognized by all compliant BGP autonomous systems. Those optional path attributes that *are* recognized are propagated in routing updates to BGP neighbors.

Like well-known attributes, optional attributes are divided into two classes: optional transitive and optional nontransitive.

Optional transitive attributes that are not recognized by a BGP router are marked as *partial* and propagated to BGP peers. The unrecognized attribute is in this case propagated without having any effect on the router's path selection process. Examples of attributes in this class include the following:

➤ Aggregator

➤ Communities

Optional nontransitive attributes that are not recognized by a BGP router are immediately discarded. In this case, the router does not propagate the attribute. The following is an example of an optional nontransitive path attribute:

➤ Multiexit discriminator (MED)

Note: The multiexit discriminator is also commonly referred to as the metric.

The next sections amplify the following path attributes:

➤ AS-path

➤ Next hop

➤ Local Preference

➤ MED (metric)

➤ Origin

➤ Weight

Chapter 10 covers the rest of the path attributes and shows how all path attributes can be configured as part of any scalable policy-based routing implementation.

AS-Path Attribute

The AS-path attribute is a well-known mandatory attribute that is used to list the ASes on the path toward a given destination. A router that generates a routing advertisement will prepend its AS number to the advertisement before transmitting it to the neighboring AS. An AS that receives the advertisement will, in turn, prepend its own AS number and will then forward the advertisement to the next AS, and the process will repeat. The AS-path attribute is therefore the list of AS numbers that a routing update has traversed to reach a destination. This list can be sequentially ordered (an AS-set) or it can be unordered (an AS-sequence). This last point will be relevant later.

For an example of how the AS-path attribute is used, consider Figure 9.4. In this figure, network 180.10.0.0 is advertised by Router B in AS 200. Before transmitting the update, Router B will prepend the AS number 200. Upon receiving the update, Router C will in turn prepend its own AS number, 300, and send the update to Router A in AS 100. The AS-path attribute that Router A consequently sees in the update for network 180.10.0.0 is (300, 200). Router A now knows that to get to this network it must go through two ASes, AS 300 and AS 200.

The same scenario applies for the other networks as well. Router B's AS-path attributes for both networks would be (300, 100) and (300), respectively. Router C's AS-path attributes for networks 150.10.0.0 and 180.10.0.0 would be (100) and (200), respectively.

One of the reasons the AS-path attribute is mandatory is that it is a loop-extermination mechanism. A router that receives an AS-path attribute that includes its own AS number will know the update was generated by its own AS and will subsequently discard the update. For example, suppose that in Figure 9.4 there is a serial link between Routers A and B. If Router C in AS 300 sends an update to Router A, who sends it to Router B, who in turn sends it back to Router C, the AS-path attribute will read (300, 100, 200). Router C would notice that this update is in a loop and would immediately discard it.

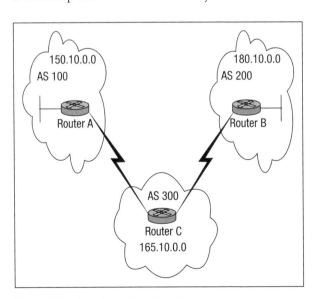

Figure 9.4 AS-path attribute in action.

Next Hop Attribute

The next hop attribute is another well-known mandatory path attribute. This attribute indicates the next hop IP address that a router should use to reach a destination contained in the update message.

If an EBGP router is sending the update, the next hop attribute will specify the EBGP router's own IP address. In Figure 9.5, Router C advertises network 150.10.0.0 to Router A with a next hop IP address of 10.10.20.2. Likewise, Router A advertises its AS's networks to Router C with a next hop IP address of 10.10.20.1.

Now, an interesting rule in BGP states that the "next hop advertised by EBGP should be carried into IBGP." This means that the next hop IP address of an EBGP peer is forwarded into an AS unchanged. For example, in Figure 9.5, we saw that Router A received an advertisement from Router C with a next hop of 10.10.20.2. When Router A forwards the advertisement to Router B, the next hop IP address does not become 170.10.30.1 (as you might expect it would), but instead remains 10.10.20.2. Router B will therefore think that network 150.10.0.0 has a next hop IP address of 10.10.20.2.

It would be wise to make sure that Router B actually had a path to 10.10.10.0; otherwise, Router B would drop any packets it received that were destined for network 150.10.0.0. One way that Router B could learn of 10.10.10.0 is through an IGP that advertises for this network. Another way would be to configure a static route.

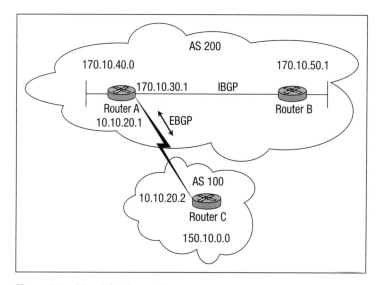

Figure 9.5 Advertising the next hop.

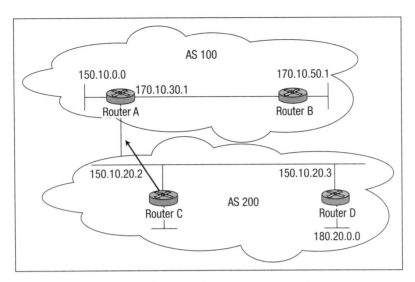

Figure 9.6 Working the next hop attribute on a multi-access network.

Multi-access Networks

On a broadcast multi-access network, such as Ethernet, the next hop attribute follows the same BGP rule, which states again that the next hop advertised by EBGP should be carried into IBGP. In Figure 9.6, for example, Routers A, C, and D are all sharing an Ethernet segment.

Assume that Router D is a non-BGP router communicating with Router C via an IGP. Upon receiving an advertisement for network 180.20.0.0 from Router D, Router C would inject this information into BGP and advertise it to Router A. But Router C would not specify its own IP address in the next hop attribute; instead, Router C would specify Router D as the next hop. Upon receiving the update for network 180.20.0.0 from Router C, Router A would therefore see that this network is reachable via 150.10.20.3.

On a multi-access network, a next hop address would refer to the originator of a network advertisement as opposed to referring to the router that propagates the advertisement simply because it makes more sense to use the most direct route. In Figure 9.6, the most direct path from Router A to network 180.20.0.0 is via Router D.

NBMA Networks

On an NBMA network, such as Frame-Relay, the next hop attribute is transmitted in exactly the same manner as it is on a broadcast multi-access network. In Figure 9.7, for example, Routers A, C, and D are connected in a full mesh Frame-Relay environment. Router C will advertise 180.20.0.0 to Router A with a next hop of 150.10.20.3.

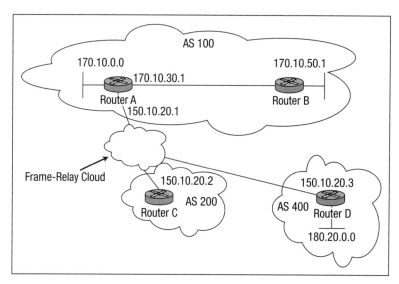

Figure 9.7 Full mesh Frame-Relay wide area network.

There is a potential problem with this configuration, however. If the virtual circuit between Routers A and D failed or if no circuit was ever established between them, Router A would not be able to reach network 180.20.0.0 even though this network could otherwise be reached via Router C.

One solution to this problem is to prevent Router C from using Router D as the next hop. Router C would instead be configured to use its own address as the next hop for network 180.20.0.0.

Local Preference Attribute

The local preference attribute is a well-known discretionary attribute that indicates to an AS the preferred path in exiting the AS to reach a given destination. This attribute is expressed in a numerical value; the higher the value, the more preferred the path. Local preference is configured on the router and is propagated in routing updates to all BGP routers in the same AS. BGP routers receiving an update with the local preference attribute set will subsequently know which is the preferred exit point in reaching the network specified in the update. As an example, consider Figure 9.8.

Figure 9.8 presents a configuration in which Routers C and D are receiving updates about network 150.10.0.0 from AS 100 and AS 300, respectively. Router C has been configured with a local preference of 150, and Router D has been configured with a local preference of 200. Both routers exchange routing updates that contain their respective local preferences for network 150.10.0.0. Consequently, both routers will see that this network is best reached through Router D, whose local preference attribute reads 200. Furthermore, because local preference is an attribute that gets

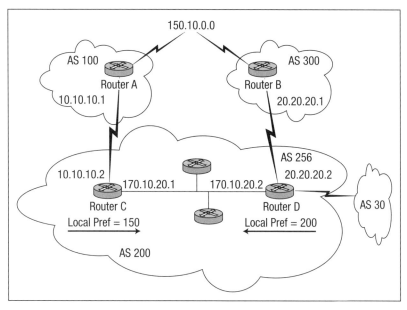

150.10.0.0

AS 100

Router A

10.10.10.1

AS 300

Router B

20.20.20.1

AS 256

10.10.10.2   170.10.20.1   170.10.20.2   20.20.20.2

Router C   Router D   AS 30

Local Pref = 150   Local Pref = 200

AS 200

Figure 9.8   Setting local preference on Routers C and D.

sent throughout the entire AS, all routers would know to use Router D instead of Router C to reach network 150.10.0.0.

MED Attribute

The multi-exit discriminator attribute is an optional nontransitive path attribute, which means that this attribute will be recognized by *some* BGP ASes but not neces-sarily by *all*. When it is recognized, it will be propagated to BGP peers; when it is not recognized, it will be dropped. The MED is also referred to in BGP4 as the *metric* (and in BGP3 as the *inter-AS attribute*).

The function of the MED path attribute is to indicate to external neighbors the preferred path into an AS. If an AS has multiple entry points, this attribute will have the effect of influencing the path that other ASes take to enter that AS. Like local preference, the MED is a numeric value that is configured on a router. Unlike local preference, however, the *lowest* value signifies the most preferred path. Moreover, the MED is exchanged between ASes. When an EBGP peer sends the metric into another AS via a routing update, the update or metric gets propagated throughout the AS but does *not* leave the AS without the MED being reset to 0, which is the default value.

Figure 9.9 depicts an example in which AS 100 is receiving updates for network 180.10.0.0 from Routers B, C, and D. Because these three routers have also been configured with MEDs, Router A subsequently receives each of their metrics as well. Router B has sent a metric of 100; Router C, a metric of 150; and Router D, a metric of 200.

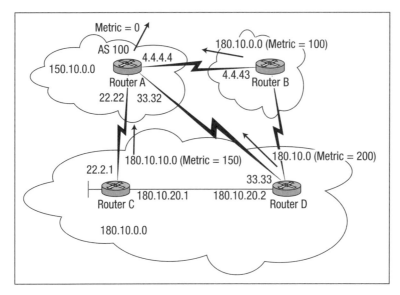

Figure 9.9 Metrics (MEDs) are sent to other ASes.

Now, by default, a router compares only MEDs coming from neighbors in the same AS. As a result, Router A will compare only the metrics coming from AS 200, and Router B's metric will therefore not be a factor in Router A's path selection for network 180.10.0.0. This is unfortunate because Router B has the lowest MED (100) compared to Router C (150) and Router D (200). Router A will therefore choose Router C as the next best hop toward network 180.10.0.0.

Origin Attribute

The origin attribute is a well-known mandatory path attribute that defines the origin of the path information. This path attribute can be one of three possible values:

➤ *IGP*—This value indicates the route is interior to the AS that originated it. This occurs when either (1) the BGP **network** command is used, or (2) IGP information is redistributed into BGP. In both cases, the BGP routing table will indicate the path origin as an "i" (for IGP).

➤ *EGP*—This value indicates the route was learned via the EGP and is indicated in the BGP routing table with an "e" (for EGP).

➤ *Incomplete*—This value indicates the route is from an unknown source or is learned via some other means, such as when a static route is redistributed into BGP. An incomplete origin is designated in the BGP routing table with a "?".

Weight Attribute

The weight attribute is a path attribute that is proprietary to Cisco. The weight attribute is similar to local preference in that they both are used to influence the path that routers take to external destinations. A router chooses the path with the highest weight.

The value of this attribute can range anywhere from 0 to 65,535, with 0 being the least preferred weight. By default, paths that are originated by a router have a weight of 32,768, and all other paths have a weight of 0.

Unlike all other path attributes, weight is not propagated to any other routers, but instead remains local to the router on which it is configured.

As an example of how the weight path attribute works, consider Figure 9.10. In this figure, Routers A and B advertise network 175.10.0.0 to AS 100. Router C subsequently has two ways to reach this network and must decide which path to choose. Because in this instance network policy dictates that Router B should prefer paths going through AS 200, Router C is configured to set the weight of updates coming from Router A higher than the weight of updates coming from Router B. Specifically, any update for network 175.10.0.0 coming from Router A will be set with a weight of 200, and any update for the network coming from Router B will be set with a weight of 100. Router C therefore chooses the path going through Router A.

9

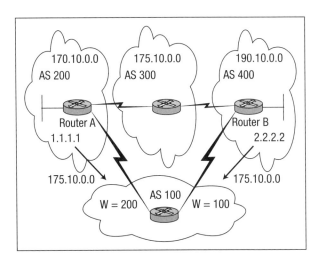

Figure 9.10   Working with the weight path attribute.

Summary of BGP Path Attributes

BGP's path selection decision-making process is based on network policy and is implemented through the application of BGP path attributes. BGP path attributes can be classified into four major characterizations:

➤ *Well-known mandatory*—AS-path, next hop, origin

➤ *Well-known discretionary*—local preference, atomic aggregate

➤ *Optional transitive*—aggregator, communities

➤ *Optional nontransitive*—multi-exit discriminator

Well-known path attributes are understood by *all* BGP ASes, whereas optional path attributes are *not* necessarily understood by all BGP ASes.

AS-path is an attribute that lists the set of ASes that a routing update takes to reach a given destination network. *Next hop* is an attribute that identifies the IP address of the next router along a path to a given destination network. *Origin* is an attribute that identifies the source of a routing update, which can be either (1) IGP (i), (2) EGP (e), or (3) incomplete (?). *Local preference* is an attribute that is used to influence the path a router takes to reach an external network. Lastly, the *multi-exit discriminator (MED, or metric)* is an attribute used to influence the path that routers in external ASes take to enter the local AS.

Furthermore, attributes can be characterized by how they are propagated or carried within routing updates to other BGP routers residing both within and outside the originating AS. For example, local preference attributes are propagated only *within* the AS, whereas MED attributes are carried into another AS. Cisco's weight attribute, in contrast, is propagated neither inside nor outside the AS, but instead always remains stationary on the router.

The BGP Path Selection Algorithm

When BGP has multiple paths to an external network, only one path can be selected. As we have seen, BGP bases its decision on the path attributes used for implementing routing policy. When a BGP router receives multiple updates advertising the same destination with the same path attribute (but not the same value), the BGP router will compare the path attributes and choose the best path based on how their values are weighted.

But what if the path attributes are different? For example, what if the router received two advertisements regarding the same network, where one update contained just the well-known mandatory attributes (AS-path, next hop, origin) and the other carried in addition the MED attribute? To top it off, imagine also that the router had a weight configured for this same network. We can see, then, that the router needs some way of assigning preferences to path attributes because, unlike EIGRP or Interior Gateway Routing Protocol (IGRP), there is no way to create a composite path attribute that could take into consideration all possible attributes. What is needed instead is something akin to the *administrative distance* concept. With administrative distances, preferences are assigned to routing protocols so that when a router learns of a network via two or more different routing protocols, the router can choose the path learned via the routing protocol with the highest preference (lowest administrative distance).

BGP has adopted a strategy similar to the administrative distance concept. However, instead of assigning numerical preference values to attributes (for example, 1 for weight, 5 for local preference, 100 for MED, and so forth), BGP tosses the attributes onto a numbered list and tells routers to start at the top of the list (highest preference) and move down until a match is made. The following numbered list presents this decision-making algorithm for choosing the best path.

1. First, if an internal path is not synchronized and synchronization is enabled (explained in the next section, "Understanding BGP Synchronization"), do *not* consider the path.

2. If the next hop address specified in the next hop path attribute is not reachable, then do *not* consider the path.

3. Prefer the path with the highest weight.

4. If weight is irrelevant or if multiple paths have the same weight, prefer the path with the highest local preference.

5. If local preference is irrelevant or if multiple paths have the same local preference, prefer the path originated by the local router. (A *locally originated path* is a path that the router learns through the BGP **network** command or through redistribution from an IGP).

6. If the local router did not originate the path, prefer the path with the shortest number of AS hops (as indicated in the AS-path attribute).

7. If multiple paths have the same AS length, prefer the path with the lowest origin value: IGP < EGP < Incomplete.

8. If multiple paths have the same origin, prefer the path with the lowest metric (MED). (Recall that MEDs are compared only if they are coming from the same AS.)

9. If MED is irrelevant, or if multiple paths have the same MED, prefer EBGP-learned paths over IBGP-learned paths.

10. If none of the paths were learned via EBGP (that is, if only local paths remain), and synchronization is disabled, then prefer the path with the lowest IGP metric to the BGP next hop.

9

11. If, on the other hand, only EBGP paths remain and load-balancing conditions are met, then prefer the paths equally and load balance over them.

Note: BGP load-balancing is not an objective of this book.

12. If load balancing conditions are not met, then prefer the path whose next hop has the lowest BGP router ID.

Any match with one of the above steps causes the path that is decided on to be placed in the BGP routing table and advertised to all BGP peers.

Note that the first numbered entry in the above algorithm states that a path must be synchronized before its path attributes can be considered in the route selection process. Synchronization is another important feature of BGP operation and is explained in the next section.

Understanding BGP Synchronization

Consider Figure 9.11. In this figure, Router D in AS 200 is advertising network 150.10.0.0 via EBGP to Router A. Routers A and C have established an indirect IBGP connection and are exchanging BGP routing updates with each other. Router B is not configured to run BGP and is instead running only an IGP. Additionally, Routers A and C are not redistributing any BGP routes into the IGP. Router B is therefore unaware of any external BGP networks, including network 150.10.0.0.

Now, upon receiving an advertisement for network 150.10.0.0 from Router A, Router C propagates the update to Router E in AS 400. Router E will subsequently

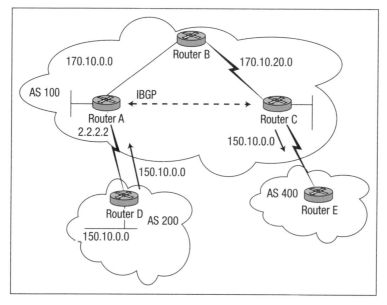

Figure 9.11 Router B is unaware of network 150.10.0.0.

proceed to send traffic for this network to Router C, who will, in turn, relay the traffic to Router B. However, upon receiving traffic destined for network 150.10.0.0, Router B will discover that it has no entry for this route in its IGP routing table. The traffic for this network is therefore dropped, creating what is referred to as a "black hole." Router C is aware that its IGP neighbor is dropping packets (thanks to ICMP messages) but is powerless to do anything about it (artificial intelligence is not within the routers' capabilities). Because Router C still considers the path to network 150.10.0.0 to be viable, it will continue to send traffic for this destination to Router B.

BGP's solution to this problem is *synchronization*. Synchronization can be defined by the following rule: If your AS is being used as a transit system for other ASes, do not advertise routes via BGP to these ASes until all routers in your AS have listed the routes in their IP routing tables. This means that a router must wait until its IGP has learned of a route before the route can be either used or advertised via BGP. Once the router's IGP has learned of the route (we will see how this occurs in a moment), the router may then use *and* advertise the route to external ASes.

Besides learning of routes through itself, there are three other ways in which an IGP learns of routes that BGP can advertise. The first way is simply through the route being local to the router (i.e., directly connected). For example, in Figure 9.11, Router C's link to Router B (network 170.10.20.0), is listed automatically in Router C's IGP routing table as directly connected. Because the network is in the IGP routing table (IGP has "learned" the route), Router C can advertise it to Router E as a BGP route.

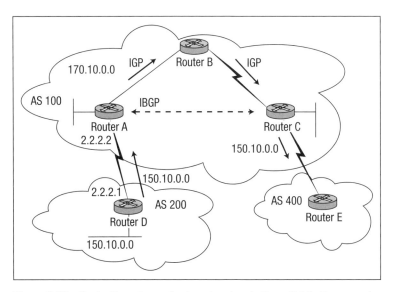

Figure 9.12   Router B can learn of external routes via the redistribution occurring on its neighbors.

Another way in which an IGP receives routing information in a BGP environment is through redistribution. This learning method is especially significant if the route is being learned via BGP only. In this case, the router that is originating the routing information would redistribute the information from BGP into IGP and would then advertise it to IGP neighbors (Figure 9.12).

Figure 9.12 is a continuation of our discussion on how the black hole problem on Router B can be resolved. Upon receiving BGP updates for network 150.10.0.0 from Router D, Router A could redistribute this information into its IGP. The IGP would then advertise network 150.10.0.0 to Router B, who would then advertise the network to Router C via the IGP. Recall that the synchronization rule requires a router to hold off advertising a route to an external AS until its IGP has learned the route. Because Router C's IGP has just learned network 150.10.0.0, Router C can now advertise it to Router E.

There is, moreover, an alternative to BGP redistribution: static routes. If, in Figure 9.12, Router B was configured with a static route to network 150.10.0.0, then it would have a route to the network and would not drop packets destined to it. However, Router B would still need to communicate this static route to Router C, which is waiting patiently to advertise it to Router E. Router B would therefore need to redistribute the static route into its IGP so the IGP could relay network 150.10.0.0 to Router C.

Synchronization is enabled on BGP routers by default. In certain cases you may not need this feature. If, for instance, your AS will not be used as a transit AS for other ASes, synchronization can be disabled. You can also disable this feature when all routers in your AS are running BGP. In this latter instance, all routers would be aware of external networks so there would be no reason to make each router hold off on advertising routes.

Understanding When to Use BGP

As an interautonomous routing protocol, BGP is used primarily to connect enterprise networks with Internet Service Providers and to connect ISPs with each other.

In an ISP, BGP is a necessity. To find out why, consider the conditions in which an ISP operates. First, the ISP must carry full Internet routing tables that maintain upward of at least 50,000 routes. This requires a classless routing protocol that is scalable enough to support such massive routing databases and at the same time maintain sufficient performance standards.

Within this type of ISP, RIP and IGRP cannot meet these scalability requirements because RIP is a classful routing protocol whose maximum hop count is 15 and IGRP is a classful routing protocol whose maximum hop count is 255. We are therefore left with three common choices for a scalable ISP routing protocol: EIGRP, OSPF, and BGP.

Consider the next operational conditions for an ISP. It must have multiple connections with other ISPs and must allow traffic from each of these ISPs to transit through its own AS. These conditions require exchanging network reachability information with multiple ASes. Although BGP is especially designed for routing of this type, OSPF and EIGRP also have exterior routing capabilities. We must therefore move on to considering the next operational requirement of an ISP.

The next ISP condition requires that traffic be controlled as it passes through the ISP. ISPs have to devise and implement extensive routing policies to meet technical requirements for performance, accessibility, and security. This therefore necessitates a routing protocol that is flexible enough to execute this style of policy-based routing and at the same time maintain adaptability to future policy changes. EIGRP and OSPF are *not* policy-based routing protocols, which means that they are not suited to the type of inter-AS routing that ISPs expect. BGP is, however, as we have seen in this chapter, the best policy-based routing protocol known to the Internet.

The conditions we have just covered are not relevant to all Internet ASes. Corporate non-ISP enterprises, for instance, may meet only one or a few conditions that still enjoin network engineers within these companies to recommend a BGP implementation. Decisions *always* depend ultimately on the company's goals and technical requirements. But, in general, BGP is a viable option for a corporate enterprise whenever at least one of the following conditions is relevant:

1. The enterprise is a transit AS for other ASes, and traffic going to and coming from these ASes must be controlled.

2. The enterprise has active connections to multiple ISPs or ASes.

3. The enterprise's routing policies differ from its ISP or another AS.

4. Enterprise resources have the capacity to support BGP.

5. The enterprise has a solid understanding of BGP operation and configuration.

The following sections discuss these conditions in more detail.

The Transit AS

One condition that may qualify an enterprise network for BGP is that the enterprise's AS is used as a transit system for other ASes. An enterprise that wishes its AS to be used as a transit system must communicate its transit availability to other ASes via either an exterior routing protocol such as BGP or via the application of static routes in these other ASes. With static routes, however, there is no sophisticated method of controlling the traffic transiting the AS. For corporate enterprises that deal with many external networks and establish various trusts therewith, the requirement for being able to filter and modify traffic coming from external sources would therefore make policy-based BGP the more appropriate solution.

Multihoming the Internet Connection

The next condition that may qualify an enterprise network for BGP is that the enterprise has a multihomed connection to the Internet. This involves connecting the enterprise's AS to multiple ASes, whether they be ISPs or other corporate entities. It is a common misconception that a multihomed Internet connection automatically necessitates BGP. In actuality, the need for BGP in a multihomed environment is always dependent on the enterprise's unique requirements and on the other ASes' routing policies.

Differing Routing Policy

Whenever the enterprise's routing policy differs from that of its neighboring AS, BGP is highly recommended and may in fact be a necessity. This is because routers in both ASes must be able to communicate their routing policies to each other to facilitate the types of policy-based routing that both ASes want implemented. If one of the ASes did not communicate its policy, then it would be bound by the other AS's policy. If both ASes happened to use the same routing policy, however, BGP's advantage would be greatly diminished. In fact, in this case, two viable alternatives to BGP exist: static and default routes. We will explore these two alternatives in the section "Alternatives to BGP—Static and Default Routes."

Resource Capacity

Another condition in our list of criteria for implementing BGP has to do with resource capacity. Due to the potentially high number of routing entries in a typical BGP routing table, enterprise routers should have sufficient memory and processing power to maintain this information and at the same time react swiftly and efficiently to the potential number of topology changes that can result. In addition, there must be enough bandwidth between the enterprise and its neighboring ASes to accommodate the transfer of sizable BGP routing tables.

BGP Understanding

One final BGP implementation condition is often neglected—understanding BGP. Obviously, BGP is a highly complex technology, due mostly to its policy-based functionalities. Therefore, when an enterprise network embarks on a mission to devise, implement, and maintain a BGP internetwork, the corporation would best be advised to make sure that its technical staff is knowledgeable and skilled in this protocol's operation and configuration. Generally, an enterprise will have a few senior technical engineers that are experienced and resourceful enough to handle the more complex issues involved with running BGP. It is up to these engineers to coordinate with other engineers and with corporate management to ensure that the policies devised and implemented for the enterprise are in harmony with the enterprise's business and technical goals and requirements.

Alternatives to BGP—Static and Default Routes

As previously mentioned, static and default routes can be used as alternatives to BGP when two ASes share the same network policy. Figure 9.13 illustrates how this could occur.

In Figure 9.13, Enterprise C is running an IGP within its AS, and the ISP is running IBGP within its AS. Both ASes share the same network policy. As a result of meeting this condition and meeting certain other technical requirements, network engineers within Enterprise C have decided that BGP is not necessary between their AS and the ISP. Instead, Enterprise C has opted to employ a default route that would be propagated to its AS and point toward the ISP. The purpose of the default route being propagated throughout the enterprise AS is to inform internal routers that they have a route to any unknown destination. This action is necessary in this case because Router C is not advertising the ISP to Enterprise C via its IGP. Internal routers would therefore have no idea how to reach the ISP if they did not have a default route leading to this external AS.

Whereas Enterprise C learns of the ISP via a default route, the ISP learns of Enterprise C via static routes. Specifically, Router I is manually configured with static routes that define all of Enterprise C's networks. The static routes are then *redistributed* into Router I's IGP, which is IBGP. BGP will carry the static routes throughout and beyond the ISP's domain. As a result, all ISP routers would know specifically of any network in Enterprise C.

Note in Figure 9.13 that no routing protocol is running between Routers C and I. Router C has made its serial interface passive, and Router I has done the same. This serial link is therefore devoid of any routing protocol traffic (not user traffic).

9

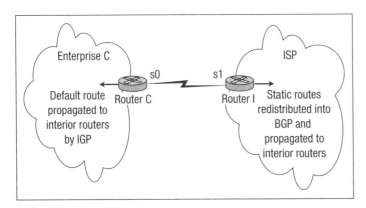

Figure 9.13   Using default and static routes between two ASes.

Configuring a Static Route

The **ip route** command is a routing protocol-independent command used to define a static route entry in the IP routing table. The command's syntax is as follows:

```
Router(config)#ip route prefix prefix-mask {address|interface}
  [administrative distance]
```

Note: The braces { } indicate that the parameter is required. The vertical bar | indicates that only one of the parameters can be chosen. Brackets [ ] indicate an optional parameter.

Table 9.2 explains the meaning of the **ip route** command parameters.

Example Static Route Configuration

Figure 9.14 once again shows the familiar diagram of Enterprise C and its ISP.

The ISP will configure a static route to 168.20.0.0 using the following command on Router I:

```
Router_I(config)#ip route 168.20.0.0 255.255.0.0 10.10.10.1
```

Table 9.2   Explaining the ip route command.

Parameter	Explanation	Example
prefix	The network IP address that you want to input into the router's routing table	172.16.0.0
prefix-mask	The network's subnet mask	255.255.255.0
address	The next hop router's IP address	172.16.85.224
interface	The router's own interface used to reach the next hop	serial 0
administrative distance	The static route's assigned administrative distance	205

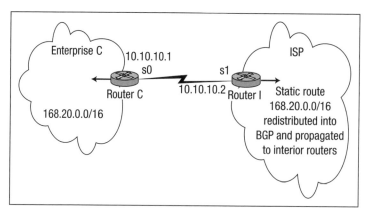

Figure 9.14   Using a static route to learn about Enterprise C.

Router I would then redistribute this static route into BGP and advertise it to the rest of the ISP domain. It is in this manner that an ISP becomes aware of the neighboring AS without running BGP on the external connection between them.

Using the Administrative Distance Feature with Static Routes (Optional)

When a router learns of a network via two different routing protocols, the router uses the network learned via the protocol with the lowest administrative distance (AD). Table 9.3 presents the default administrative distances of common routing protocols and static routes.

A static route that uses the *address* parameter in the **ip route** command has a default AD of 1, whereas a static route that uses the *interface* parameter in the same command has a default AD of 0.

The reason for wanting to modify the AD of a static route is to be able to use the static route as a backup to a dynamically learned route. Because the static route will by default have a lower AD than that of any dynamic routing protocol, the static route would be used as the primary route unless its AD was modified to be higher than the routing protocol's AD. For example, if you wanted to back up a RIP-learned route by configuring a static route for it, then you would need to specify an administrative distance of more than 120; otherwise, the static route would preempt RIP's path as the primary path.

Table 9.3   Administrative distance table.

IP Route Learned Via	Default Administrative Distance
Connected interface	0
Static route using a connected interface	0
Static route using an IP address	1
EIGRP summary route	5
External BGP (EBGP)	20
Internal EIGRP	90
IGRP	100
OSPF	110
IS-IS	115
RIP	120
EGP	140
External EIGRP	170
Internal BGP (IBGP)	200
Unknown source	255

Tip: A static route whose AD is higher than the routing protocol's AD is called a *floating static route*. The corresponding dynamic route always overrides a floating static route.

Configuring a Default Route

Default routes can be configured in a number of ways. Each routing protocol handles default routes a little differently, depending on how they are configured. The following sections explore how the interior gateway protocols RIP, EIGRP, and OSPF can each be configured with default routes. In each example, we will use Figure 9.14 and focus on configuring Router C in Enterprise C.

RIP Default Route Configuration

The following command is used to configure a *default static route* on Router C:

```
Router_C(config)#ip route 0.0.0.0 0.0.0.0 s0
```

The route 0.0.0.0 0.0.0.0 is a default route that is placed in Router C's routing table. Whenever a packet with an unknown destination address is received, the 0.0.0.0 entry in Router C's table will match the address and cause the packet to be forwarded out the serial 0 interface toward Router I. This is an example of a default static route, so named because it incorporates the default function in a static route format.

Default static routes are automatically propagated by RIP. This means that Router C will advertise the 0.0.0.0 route to Enterprise C. Upon receiving this route, all internal routers in this AS will insert 0.0.0.0 into their routing tables with the next hop address indicating the router from whom the route was received.

The following output shows what the routing table of a router laying deep inside Enterprise C might look like:

```
Router_X(config)#show ip route
R168.20.14.0 /24 [120/1] via 168.20.13.2, 00:00:05, Ethernet0
R168.20.39.0 /24 [120/3] via 168.20.38.2, 00:00:47, Ethernet1
R0.0.0.0 /0 [120/7] via 168.20.13.2, 00:00:05, Ethernet0
```

Router X received the default route originally sent by Router C and placed it in its routing table. Router X received the entry from a neighbor with an IP address of 168.20.13.2. Note that the update for 0.0.0.0 took seven hops to reach Router X.

EIGRP Default Route Example

EIGRP, like RIP, can also use a default static route to create a default route in its routing table. However, unlike RIP, the default route is not automatically propagated into the AS but must instead be redistributed into EIGRP. EIGRP would then propagate the route into the AS, just as it is in RIP. Router C would be configured to do this with the following command output:

```
Router_C(config)#ip route 0.0.0.0 0.0.0.0 10.10.10.2
Router_C(config)#router eigrp 1
Router_C(config-router)#redistribute static
```

The only difference between configuring a default route on EIGRP and configuring one on RIP is that with EIGRP you have to redistribute the default route before it can be propagated. The **redistribute static** command tells the router to advertise the default route 0.0.0.0 via EIGRP.

In this example, Router C will advertise the default route to Enterprise C, which will have the desired effect of giving all internal routers a way to reach the ISP.

OSPF Default Route Example

Although OSPF can also use the default **static route** command to create a default route, it will not automatically propagate the route into the OSPF domain. The following command must be used:

```
Router(config-router)#default-information originate [always]
```

The *always* parameter is an optional parameter that tells the ASBR to *always* advertise the default route 0.0.0.0 to the OSPF domain. If this parameter is omitted, the ASBR will advertise 0.0.0.0 only if the ASBR already has the default route in its routing table. This would occur if the ASBR was configured with a default static route or if the default route was received from an external neighbor via a routing update.

As the ASBR for Enterprise C, Router C's configuration would look like the following:

```
Router_C(config)#ip route 0.0.0.0 0.0.0.0 so
Router_C(config)#router ospf 1
Router_C(config-router)#default-information originate always
```

Router C would subsequently advertise 0.0.0.0 to Enterprise C via OSPF.

Configuring BGP

Configuration of BGP begins with the **router bgp** command:

```
Router(config)#router bgp AS-number
```

The *AS-number* identifies the autonomous system number and is a value between 1 and 65,535.

Note: If you are going to be connecting your AS to the Internet, then you must request an AS number from the Internet Assigned Numbers Authority (IANA).

Once the BGP routing process has been enabled with the **router bgp** command, the next configuration task is to identify the router's BGP-speaking neighbors. This occurs with the following command:

```
Router(config-router)#neighbor ip-address remote-as AS-number
```

The *ip-address* parameter specifies the neighbor's interface IP address. This is generally the IP address of the interface that the neighbor uses to reach your router. The *AS-number* identifies the autonomous system that the neighbor is in. If this value happens to be the same as the local router's, then an IBGP connection is established. If the values are not the same, the neighbor is in a different AS and therefore an EBGP connection is established.

For example, in Figure 9.15, Routers 1 and 3 are speaking BGP whereas Router 2 is instead running only an IGP. Routers 1 and 3 will establish an IBGP connection with each other using TCP when they both specify each other's reachable interface IP addresses using the **neighbor remote-as** command.

The following command output shows the configurations on Routers 1 and 3:

```
Router_1(config)#router bgp 1
Router_1(config-router)#neighbor 168.10.11.1 remote-as 1

Router_3(config)#router bgp 1
Router_3(config-router)#neighbor 168.10.10.1 remote-as 1
```

The next step in the BGP configuration is to specify which networks the router is to originate or advertise. This is accomplished with the following command:

```
Router(config-router)#network prefix [mask prefix-mask]
```

The *prefix* parameter identifies the network address, and *prefix-mask* is an optional parameter that indicates the network's prefix mask. As a result, the advertised network can be either a classful or a classless network number.

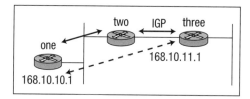

Figure 9.15 Establishing IBGP neighborship.

The BGP **network** command differs from the **network** command of an IGP. In an IGP, the **network** command is used to identify the interfaces on which the IGP is allowed to receive and advertise network routes. In BGP, this command is used only to indicate which networks within the router's AS are to be *originated*—that is, advertised as originating from the router's AS.

As a result, networks within the AS that are not directly connected can be specified in the BGP router's **network** statements.

There is one more important consideration to take into account before issuing the BGP **network** command in a production environment: *The network must already be in the router's IP routing table.* This rule is a relic of the BGP synchronization rule. Recall that synchronization forces routers to hold off on advertising a network to external peers until the network has been matched in the IP routing table. This is meant as a way of ensuring internal IGP-only routers are in sync information-wise with BGP routers (and vice versa). With respect to the BGP **neighbor remote-as** command, this rule is therefore meant to make sure that BGP routers do in fact have routes to internal destinations before they start advertising these internal destinations to external ASes.

Recall from the discussion on synchronization that routes are placed in the routing table in one of three ways:

1. Via being directly connected
2. Via being statically configured with the **ip route** command
3. Via being learned by a dynamic routing protocol

Consequently, any network advertised with the BGP **network remote-as** command must have already been learned in the IP routing table through one of these three methods. If the command is applied without a matching IP routing table entry, then the router will not allow the network to be advertised.

*Note: The **network remote-as** synchronization rule is relevant only when BGP synchronization is enabled. If BGP synchronization is disabled, then the **network remote-as** command will work regardless of whether the IP routing table has matching entries.*

Figure 9.16 provides a diagram in which Routers A and B have established an IBGP connection with each other. Both routers have enabled synchronization and are redistributing EBGP-learned routes into their IGP. Router E, which is running only the IGP, is aware of all external routes.

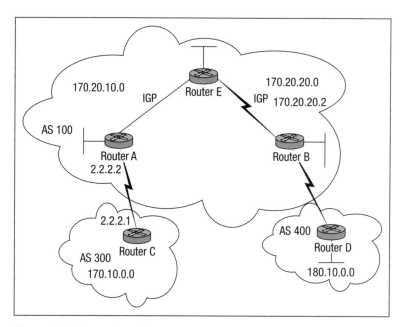

Figure 9.16 Routers A and B have established an IBGP connection across Router E.

The following command output shows how Router A's configuration would appear:

```
Router_A(config-router)#router bgp 100
Router_A(config-router)#neighbor 170.20.20.2 remote-as 100
Router_A(config-router)#neighbor 2.2.2.1 remote-as 300
Router_A(config-router)#network 170.20.10.0 mask 255.25.255.0
Router_A(config-router)#network 170.20.20.0 mask 255.255.255.0
Router_A(config-router)#network 2.0.0.0
```

Router A's configuration has specified two neighbors. Router B is an IBGP neighbor, and Router C is an EBGP neighbor. No neighbor statement was configured for Router E because this router is not speaking BGP (neighborship would be established with Router E via the IGP instead). Nor was a neighbor statement configured for Router D. In this case, the reason is that Router D is not a connected BGP peer, like Router C is.

We also see in Router A's configuration how the network statements were applied. Router A's directly connected networks are specified, as well as the nonconnected network 170.20.20.0 /24. Router A is able to advertise these networks (excluding network 2.0.0.0, due to Split Horizon) to AS 300 because these networks are listed in its IP routing table. Networks 2.0.0.0 and 170.20.10.0 are listed because they are directly connected, whereas network 170.20.20.0 is listed because it was learned dynamically from Router E (*through the IGP*).

Note that Router A did not specify a **network** statement for any of the external networks in AS 300 and AS 400. This is simply because Router A does not *need* to originate its own advertisements for these routes on top of passing them along as they are received from these ASes. Recall that the BGP **network** command is used only to specify which networks the router is to originate and advertise. When an update for, say, network 180.10.0.0 in AS 400 is received, Router A will simply forward the update to AS 300 and thereby would allow AS 300 to learn of that route. However, if Router A is to also specify this network in the **network** command, then it would originate its own advertisements for this network on top of propagating whatever advertisements were received for it. Consequently, this situation creates duplicate advertisements.

Interestingly, in Figure 9.16, Router A learns of network 170.20.20.0 dynamically via an IGP advertisement from Router E (Router B was forbidden from advertising this network via IBGP because of Split Horizon). Router A redistributes this IGP-learned network into its BGP routing process so that the network can be advertised via EBGP to AS 300 (this configuration doesn't show any redistribution commands, but assume they are there). We applied a **network** statement for 170.20.20.0, but this was, in fact, redundant because redistribution is a process that automatically causes redistributed routes to be advertised without the need for specifying **network** statements. This point will be addressed when we cover BGP redistribution in greater depth in Chapter 10.

9

Optional BGP Configuration Commands

This section covers some optional BGP configuration commands that are relevant to previous topics covered thus far in this chapter. The following optional BGP commands will be explored here:

➤ **no synchronization**—Used to disable BGP synchronization

➤ **aggregate-address**—Used to create and advertise a summary route

➤ **neighbor update-source**—Used to tell the router to use its loopback interface to establish an IBGP connection with a neighbor

➤ **neighbor next-hop-self**—Used to force the BGP router to use its own interface IP address as the next hop

➤ **bgp always-compare-med**—Used to allow the router to compare metrics coming from neighbors in different ASes

This chapter has covered the path attributes of BGP policy-based routing; Chapter 10 will show how they are configured individually.

Disabling BGP Synchronization

As mentioned previously, the BGP synchronization rule states that a route must hold off on advertising a route to external BGP peers until the router's IGP has had a chance to learn the route and place it in the router's IP routing table. The purpose of this rule is to ensure that all internal routers have paths to networks before the EBGP routers start advertising the paths to external ASes, figuring that all peers within the originating AS can successfully route packets for these ASes.

In certain cases, however, this feature may be unnecessary and even a hindrance to performance. If, for instance, an AS will not be used as a transit system for other ASes, synchronization can be disabled. Also, if all routers in an AS are running BGP, there is no need to ensure that they are all aware of advertised paths, and hence synchronization may be disabled.

BGP synchronization is enabled by default. To disable it, issue the following command:

```
Router(config-router)#no synchronization
```

Omitting the **no** parameter reenables synchronization.

Configuring BGP Route Summarization

BGP3 did not permit Classless Inter-Domain Routing (CIDR). BGP4 *does* permit CIDR, which, as a result, allows networks to be summarized and advertised as a single route (a supernet). Like OSPF and EIGRP, the route summarization feature has the advantages of reducing the sizes of routing tables and of minimizing bandwidth consumption, not to mention speeding up network convergence and minimizing the impact of topology changes. The following command is used to implement BGP route aggregation:

```
Router(config-router)#aggregate-address ip-address mask
```

The *ip-address* and *mask* together indicate the summary route that is to be created and advertised to external peers.

This command allows the summary route to be advertised; however, it should be noted that *all* of the routes that have been consolidated in the summary route will be advertised as well. For example, if you are creating a summary route for network 168.10.10.0 /24 and 168.10.20.0 /24, both the summary route *and* these two networks will be advertised together.

To prevent the advertisement of consolidated networks along with the summary route, you would need to issue the following variation of the **aggregate-address** command:

```
Router(config-router)#aggregate-address ip-address mask summary-only
```

The **summary-only** appendage will prevent the router from advertising the summary route's consolidated networks.

It should also be noted that the **summary-only** appendage will not have any effect if the router is summarizing networks that it originates. That is, if the router is summarizing networks that are specified by the **network** command, the networks *will* be advertised along with the summary route. For example, consider Figure 9.17.

In Figure 9.17, Router B is configured to summarize network 170.10.10.0 /24 with the summary route 170.10.0.0 /16. Router B's configuration is as follows:

```
Router_B(config)#router bgp 200
Router_B(config-router)#neighbor 3.3.3.1 remote-as 300
Router_B(config-router)#network 170.10.10.0 mask 255.255.255.0
Router_B(config-router)#aggregate-address 170.10.0.0 255.255.0.0 summary-only
```

What happens here is that Router B will create and advertise the summary route 170.10.0.0 /16 and will also advertise network 170.10.10.0 /24 along with it to AS 300. Router C in AS 300 will subsequently advertise both routes to its BGP peers.

One solution to this problem is to not use the **network** and **aggregate-address** commands at all, but to instead use the **ip route** command to create the sum-mary route. A static route that signifies the summary route would then need to be redistributed into BGP so that it could be advertised to AS 300. Router B could implement this solution by the following configuration:

```
Router_B(config)#ip route 170.10.0.0 255.255.0.0 null0
Router_B(config)#router bgp 200
```

9

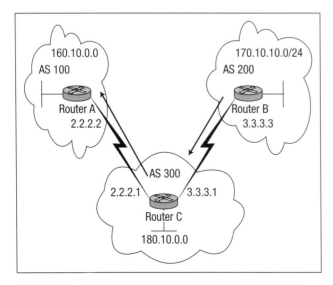

Figure 9.17 Router B is configured to summarize 170.10.10.0.

```
Router_B(config-router)#neighbor 3.3.3.1 remote-as 300
Router_B(config-router)#redistribute static
```

In this configuration, Router C has created a static summary route for 170.10.0.0 / 16 and is redistributing it into BGP. The static summary route will be advertised to Router C in AS 300. Router C would, upon receiving this advertisement, propagate it to its BGP peers.

Note that the static summary route has the **null0** appendage. All this does is place the route into the IP routing table with an interface of null 0.

In the next example, shown in Figure 9.18, Router C is receiving updates about networks 160.20.0.0 and 160.10.0.0 from Routers A and B, respectively. When Router C originates an advertisement for network 160.0.0.0 /8, Router C will advertise it to AS 400 and will indicate in the advertisement an AS path attribute of (300). This is the default behavior because whenever an aggregate route is propagated, it will have the AS number of the router that is propagating it.

But what if we did not want Router C to use its own AS number as the origin for the summary route, and instead want it to keep the AS numbers of the routes that were being summarized? The answer comes with the following command:

```
Router(config-router)#aggregate-address address mask as-set
```

The **as–set** appendage forces a router to propagate a summary route with the AS numbers of the originating ASes.

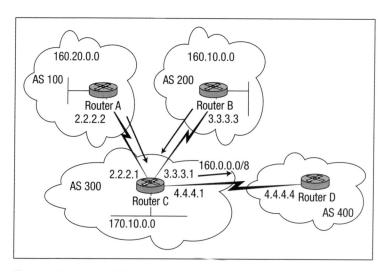

Figure 9.18   Summarizing networks 160.20.0.0 and 160.10.0.0 into 160.0.0.0 /8.

Therefore, in this example, we would issue the following configuration on Router C:

```
Router_C(config)#router bgp 300
Router_C(config-router)#neighbor 2.2.2.2 remote-as 100
Router_C(config-router)#neighbor 3.3.3.3.remote-as 200
Router_C(config-router)#neighbor 4.4.4.4 remote-as 400
Router_C(config-router)#network 170.10.0.0 mask 255.255.0.0
Router_C(config-router)#aggregate-address 160.0.0.0 255.0.0.0 as-set
```

Router C will send an update to Router D about 160.0.0.0 /8 with the following AS path attribute listed in the update: (100, 200, 300).

Note: The AS-set is a list that includes the ASes of routes that are not omitted in the AS-path attribute when the routes are summarized. In this example, the AS-set is (100, 200).

Configuring a Loopback Interface on BGP Routers

Loopback interfaces provide a safeguard against losing reachability between two communicating routers. This is due to the fact that loopback interfaces are virtual interfaces that exist only in software and therefore cannot go down because of interface hardware failure. In BGP, loopback interfaces are used primarily for IBGP connections in which redundant network paths exist. Figure 9.19 provides an illustration of a loopback interface.

In Figure 9.19, Routers A and B have established a TCP connection via the link through 180.10.20.0. Router A has established the IBGP connection with Router B's loopback interface. If Router B's Ethernet 0 interface were to become unavailable, the only connection that would need to be reestablished is the TCP connection. Both routers would then be able to reach each other via the link passing through Router C.

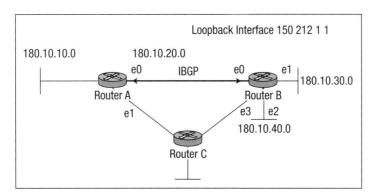

Figure 9.19   Using a loopback interface with BGP.

The following commands are used to configure a loopback interface:

```
Router(config)#interface loopback number
Router(config-if)#ip address ip-address subnet-mask
```

The loopback interface is configured just like any other interface. That is, it has a number (e.g., loopback 1) and an IP address.

The following BGP command is used to tell the router to use its loopback interface to establish an IBGP connection with a neighbor:

```
Router(config-router)#neighbor ip-address update-source loopback number
```

The *ip-address* indicates the neighbor's interface IP address and the *number* is the loopback interface number.

The following configuration shows how these commands work on Router B in Figure 9.19:

```
Router_B(config)#interface loopback 1
Router_B(config-if)#ip address 150.212.1.1 255.255.255.0
Router_B(config-if)#exit
Router_B(config)#router bgp 100
Router_B(config-router)#neighbor 180.10.20.2 update-source loopback 1
```

In this configuration, we see that Router B has configured a loopback interface with an IP address of 150.212.1.1 and is using it to establish a peering session with Router A.

The following output shows how Router A's neighbor statement would appear:

```
Router_A(config-router)#neighbor 150.212.1.1 remote-as 100
```

Manipulating the Next Hop

Earlier in this chapter, we saw that when a router in a multi-access environment receives an update from a neighbor on the same multi-access media, the router will propagate the update using that neighbor's IP address as the next hop listed in the next hop path attribute. In Figure 9.20, for example, Router C receives an update for network 180.20.0.0 from Router D and propagates the update to Router A with the next hop pointing to Router D's IP address.

However, we also saw that if the link between Routers A and D were to fail, Router C would continue to advertise network 180.20.0.0 to Router A with a next hop that still pointed to Router D. To prevent this occurrence, the following command would need to be issued:

```
Router(config-router)#neighbor ip-address next-hop-self
```

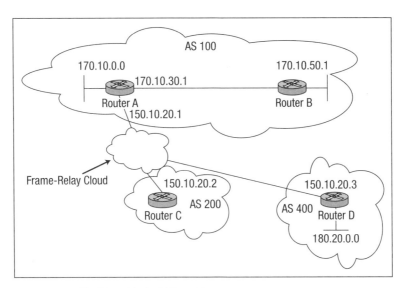

Figure 9.20   Working with the BGP next hop.

This is another variation of the BGP **neighbor** command. The **next–hop–self** appendage tells the router to advertise itself as the next hop instead of using another neighbor's address. Subsequently, we see that Router C would be able to resolve the next hop issue with the following configuration:

```
Router_C(config)#router bgp 200
Router_C(config-router)#neighbor 150.10.20.3 remote-as 400
Router_C(config-router)#neighbor 150.10.20.1 remote-as 100
Router_C(config-router)#neighbor 150.10.20.1 next-hop-self
```

Note the **neighbor next–hop–self** command specifies Router A, not Router D. Whenever Router C sends an update to Router A, the next hop will be Router C's interface IP address (150.10.20.2).

Verifying BGP

Verification of BGP's operation and configuration involves the following commands:

➤ **show ip bgp**—Used to view the router's BGP routing table

➤ **show ip bgp summary**—Used to view the status of BGP connections

➤ **show ip bgp neighbors**—Used to view statistics on BGP neighbors

➤ **clear ip bgp**—Used to cause router configuration changes to take effect

The following sections discuss these commands.

Using the **show ip bgp** Command

The **show ip bgp** command is used to view the router's BGP routing table. It displays such information as the status of network entries, destination network address, next hop IP address, and the values of various path attributes. The following output shows a sample BGP routing table:

```
Router#show ip bgp

BGP table version is 716977, local router ID is 193.0.32.1
Status codes: s suppressed, * valid, > best, i - internal
Origin codes: i - IGP, e - EGP, ? - incomplete

   Network          Next Hop          Metric LocPrf Weight Path
*>i3.0.0.0          193.0.22.1             0    100      0 1800 1239 ?
*>i6.0.0.0          193.0.22.1             0    100      0 1800 690 568 ?
*>i7.0.0.0          193.0.22.1             0    100      0 1800 701 35 ?
*>i8.0.0.0          193.0.22.1             0    100      0 1800 690 560 ?
```

The primary fields of this command are explained in Table 9.1, in the section "BGP Features and Operation."

Using the **show ip bgp summary** Command

The **show ip bgp summary** command is used to display the status of all the router's BGP connections. Other information garnered from this command includes the total number of BGP paths the router knows of and the number of BGP messages sent to and received from BGP neighbors. The output is as follows:

```
Router#show ip bgp summary

BGP table version is 717029, main routing table version 717029
19073 network entries (37544 paths) using 3542756 bytes of memory
691 BGP path attribute entries using 57200 bytes of memory

Neighbor     V    AS  MsgRcvd MsgSent  TblVer  InQ OutQ Up/Down State/PfxRcd
193.0.16.1   4  1755    32642    2973  717029    0    0 1:27:11
193.0.17.1   4  1755     4790    2973  717029    0    0 1:27:51
193.0.18.1   4  1755     7722    3024  717029    0    0 1:28:13
.
.
. (more...)
```

Table 9.4 explains the output of the more significant fields from the **show ip bgp summary** command.

Table 9.4   Significant fields from the show ip bgp summary command.

Field	Description
Neighbor	The IP address of the BGP neighbor.
V	Version; the BGP version number spoken to the neighbor.
AS	The neighbor's autonomous system number.
MsgRcvd	Indicates the number of BGP messages received from the neighbor. These messages can include open, update, notification, and error messages.
MsgSent	Indicates the number of BGP messages sent to the neighbor.
TblVer	Table version; the last version of the BGP database that was sent to the neighbor.
InQ	Input queue; the number of BGP messages from the neighbor that are waiting to be processed.
OutQ	Output queue; the number of BGP messages that are waiting to be sent to the neighbor.
Up/Down	The length of time that the BGP session has been up, or the current state if it is not up.
State/PfxRcd	Indicates the current state of the BGP session/the number of prefixes (advertised networks) the router has received from the neighbor.

Using the **show ip bgp neighbors** Command

The **show ip bgp neighbors** command is used to display information about the TCP and BGP connections to neighbors. It can be used with a variety of keywords to display information such as the state of each BGP connection and the neighbor's router ID.

The output from the **show ip bgp neighbors** command is as follows:

```
Router#show ip bgp neighbors

BGP neighbor is 171.69.232.178,  remote AS 10, external link
  Index 1, Offset 0, Mask 0x2
   Inbound soft reconfiguration allowed
   BGP version 4, remote router ID 171.69.232.178
   BGP state = Established, table version = 27, up for 00:06:12
   Last read 00:00:12, hold time is 180, keepalive interval is 60 seconds
   Minimum time between advertisement runs is 30 seconds
   Received 19 messages, 0 notifications, 0 in queue
   Sent 17 messages, 0 notifications, 0 in queue
   Inbound path policy configured
   Route map for incoming advertisements is testing
   Connections established 2; dropped 1
More...
```

One important item to note in this output is the BGP state. In this example, the BGP state is Established, which means that the local router and its neighbor have established a successful TCP and BGP connection with each other.

Using the **clear ip route** Command

Whenever you change a BGP filter, weight, distance, version, or timer, or you make some other type of configuration change, you need to reset the BGP connection for the configuration change to take effect and for peer routers to be informed. Use either of the following commands to reset BGP connections:

> ➤ **clear ip bgp** ★—This command resets all BGP connections in the BGP routing table.

> ➤ **clear ip bgp** *address*—This command resets the BGP connection only with the specified neighbor.

Chapter Summary

The Border Gateway Protocol is an exterior gateway protocol whose primary function is to exhange routing and reachability information between BGP autonomous systems. Although BGP was designed to facilitate inter-AS communication, it can also be used within the AS as an interior gateway protocol.

When two BGP peers initialized, a TCP connection is established and full routing tables are exchanged. Thereafter, only incremental updates are sent whenever a topology change occurs. To ensure that BGP peers remain active, a keepalive message is exchanged periodically.

BGP is a policy-based routing protocol, which means that it bases its routing decision not on technical IGP metrics, but rather on policy-based metrics called path attributes. The purpose of policy-based routing is to ensure that inter-AS traffic is controlled.

BGP employs several policy-based attributes to control the traffic that is allowed to pass through an AS. These attributes can be categorized according to how they are recognized and propagated in a BGP implementation. Examples of path attributes include local preference, weight, origin, and next hop.

Review Questions

1. What is an Interior Gateway Protocol (IGP)?

   a. A routing protocol that exchanges network routing information with other autonomous systems

   b. A derivative of IGRP

   c. A routing protocol that exchanges network routing information within an autonomous system

   d. A protocol that allows IP, IPX, and AppleTalk to work together

2. Which one of the following is not a feature of BGP?

   a. Connection-oriented

   b. Policy-based routing

   c. Superior scalability

   d. Periodic updates

3. What is the first BGP message exchanged between two routers?

   a. Open

   b. Update

   c. Notification

   d. Error

4. What type of BGP connection is established between autonomous systems (ASes)?

   a. IBGP

   b. IGP

   c. EGP

   d. EBGP

5. How often do BGP peers exchange routing information after initializing?

   a. Every 30 minutes.

   b. Only as often as the network administrator specifies.

   c. Whenever topology changes occur.

   d. Only when polled by each other.

6. Which one of the following items would a BGP update message not contain?

   a. Network reachability information

   b. Holdtime counter

   c. Path attributes

   d. Withdrawn routes

7. What is policy-based routing?

   a. A type of routing process that uses technical metrics such as hop count and bandwidth to forward traffic.

   b. The use of various routing protocols to support complex networks.

   c. A method of ensuring routing protocol traffic gets authenticated by an AAA server before being allowed to enter an AS.

   d. The use of network policy to define how traffic is controlled as it passes through an AS.

9

8. Which of the following are characteristics of a well-known path attribute? [Choose the two best answers]

   a. Recognized by only certain BGP ASes

   b. Dropped when not supported

   c. Recognized by all BGP ASes

   d. Always supported

9. Which of the following are classified as optional transitive path attributes?

   a. Atomic aggregate

   b. Communities

   c. Local preference

   d. Aggregator

10. How is the AS-path attribute used?

   a. Whenever a route update passes through an AS, the AS number is prepended to the list of ASes in the update.

   b. Whenever an update is prevented from entering an AS, the AS-path attribute marks the AS unreachable.

   c. It is used to ensure that route updates carry security protocols to prevent neighboring ASes from learning about certain ASes.

   d. It is used to list the number of networks traversed along a path within the AS.

11. What does the next hop path attribute indicate?

   a. The local router's outbound interface IP address

   b. The next hop router's IP address

   c. The neighboring AS's atomic ID

   d. The metric received from an EBGP peer

12. What is the local preference path attribute used for?

   a. Influencing the path that intra-AS routers take to external destinations

   b. Influencing the path that intra-AS routers take to internal destinations

   c. Giving the local router higher priority to use network bandwidth

   d. Giving the local router preference in communicating with external destinations not listed in the routing table

13. Which of the following are characteristics of the MED attribute? [Choose the two best answers]

    a. Exchanged only within the AS

    b. Paths with the lowest MED are most preferred

    c. Influences the path external neighbors take to reach the local AS

    d. Optional transitive path attribute

14. Which one of the following is not a possible value for the origin path attribute?

    a. IGP (i)

    b. Default (d)

    c. EGP (e)

    d. Incomplete (?)

15. Which of the following are characteristics of the weight path attribute? [Choose the two best answers]

    a. Exchanged between neighboring ASes

    b. Paths with the highest weight are most preferred

    c. Cisco proprietary

    d. RFC defined

16. Which path attribute do Cisco BGP routers prefer most when there are multiple path attributes for the same destination?

    a. MED (metric)

    b. Origin

    c. Weight

    d. Local preference

17. What does the BGP synchronization rule state?

    a. Peer EBGP routers should synchronize their routing tables with each other before communicating.

    b. IBGP routers must wait to establish BGP connections with each other until they all have synchronized routing information with external ASes.

    c. BGP routers should hold off on advertising routes to external peers until the routes have been matched in the IP routing table.

    d. BGP routers should synchronize their BGP routing tables with all peers within the AS before exchanging updates with external peers.

18. Under which of the following conditions could BGP be recommended for an enterprise network? [Choose the three best answers]

   a. Traffic allowed to transit the AS must be controlled.

   b. Single connection to another AS that is using the same routing policy.

   c. Lack of memory and processor power on the routers.

   d. When routing policy differs with the neighboring AS.

   e. When multihoming the Internet connection.

19. How would static and default routes be used as an alternative to running BGP between a corporate AS and ISP?

   a. Static routes would be configured within the corporate AS, and the ISP would have a default route to the corporate AS.

   b. The corporate AS would have to be configured with static routes and a default route to reach the ISP, and the ISP would use an IGP to learn about the corporate AS.

   c. The corporate AS would have a default route to the ISP, and the ISP would learn of the corporate AS via static routes.

   d. BGP is always required whenever a corporate AS must communicate with an ISP.

20. Which command enables BGP route summarization?

   a. **aggregate-address bgp** *ip-address mask*

   b. **summary-route bgp** *ip-address mask*

   c. **aggregate-route** *ip-address mask*

   d. **aggregate-address** *ip-address mask*

21. What command is used to establish BGP neighborship?

   a. **neighbor** *ip-address* **bgp as-number** *as-number*

   b. **bgp neighbor** *ip-address* **neighbor-as** *as-number*

   c. **neighbor** *ip-address* **remote-as** *as-number*

   d. **neighbor** *ip-address* **bgp remote-as** *as-number*

22. Why would you want to disable BGP synchronization?

   a. If your AS was multihomed to the Internet

   b. If BGP policy required EBGP neighbors to share only certain networks with each other

   c. When all internal routers within your AS speak BGP

   d. When you have an IGP working together with BGP

23. What is one consideration to take into account when using the BGP **network** command?

    a. When BGP synchronization is enabled, the network you are going to configure must be matched in the IP routing table.

    b. Nonconnected networks cannot be specified.

    c. The **network** command allows you to specify which interfaces will be able to run BGP.

    d. External routes must have neighbor statements.

24. Which BGP verification command would you use to view the BGP routing table?

    a. **show ip bgp**

    b. **show ip bgp summary**

    c. **show ip bgp neighbor**

    d. **show ip bgp table**

25. Why would you need to use the **clear ip bgp** command?

    a. To disable the router's BGP process

    b. To minimize traffic congestion caused by BGP messages

    c. To remove BGP routes from the IP routing table

    d. To reset BGP neighbor connections after a configuration change

Real-World Projects

Figure 9.21 presents a diagram of an internetwork in which BGP is to be configured as the exterior gateway protocol. In the figure, AS 300 is an ISP that has recently acquired new contracts with three corporate enterprises. These clients are grouped into three autonomous systems: AS 100, AS 200, and AS 400. BGP is to be run over the serial links between the ISP and AS 100 and AS 200. Between the ISP and AS 400, BGP is not to be configured. In this latter case, the ISP will configure a static route to AS 400, which will be using a default route to connect to the ISP.

As one of the ISP's network engineers, it is your task to configure Router C in AS 300 according to the guidelines set forth above. This is how you would proceed:

Project 9.1
To configure BGP between the ISP and AS 100 and AS 200:

1. Enable the BGP routing process on the ISP's router for AS 300, Router C:

```
Router_C(config)#router bgp 300
```

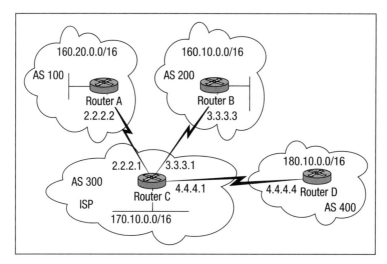

Figure 9.21 An ISP AS and three corportate client ASs.

2. In router configuration mode, specify the neighbors in AS 100 and AS 200 that will be speaking BGP with Router C:

```
Router_C(config-router)#neighbor 2.2.2.2 remote-as 100
Router_C(config-router)#neighbor 3.3.3.3 remote-as 200
```

The neighbors that you have specified will be establishing an EBGP relationship with Router C.

3. Configure Router C to originate and advertise network 170.10.0.0 /16.

```
Router_C(config-router)#network 170.10.0.0 mask 255.255.0.0
```

Router C will subsequently generate an update for network 170.10.0.0 /16 and advertise it to Routers A and B. The following path attributes will appear automatically in the update:

➤ AS-path: (300)

➤ next hop: 2.2.2.1 (for the update sent to Router A) or 3.3.3.1 (for the update sent to Router B)

➤ origin: EGP

4. Allow Router C to summarize all of AS 200's networks with the address 160.10.0.0 /16 and advertise *only* this route (assume that AS 200 contains more routes than are pictured in Figure 9.21):

```
Router_C(config-router)#aggregate-address 160.10.0.0 255.255.0.0
    summary-only
```

This command allows Router C to create a summary route for AS 200 and advertise it to AS 100. The **summary-only** appendage instructs Router C to not advertise the individual networks contained within that summary route. As a result, Router A will receive an update for AS 200 that contains only one network, 160.10.0.0 /16.

To allow the ISP to learn of AS400:

➤ On Router C, specify a static route for network 180.10.0.0 /16 using the next hop address of Router D:

```
Router_C(config)#ip route 180.10.0.0 255.255.0.0 4.4.4.4
```

This command will place an entry for network 180.10.0.0 /16 in Router C's IP routing table. However, the entry will not be placed in its BGP routing table and, consequently, will not be advertised by BGP unless we redistribute the static route.

To redistribute the static route into BGP:

➤ On Router C, go into the BGP routing process and enter the command that allows you to redistribute static routes:

```
Router_C(config)#router bgp 300
Router_C(config-rouer)#redistribute static
```

The **redistribute static** command causes all of a router's static routes to be advertised by the routing protocol. In this case, there is only one static route, network 180.10.0.0, and it will be advertised by BGP to all of Router C's BGP peers.

Whereas the ISP and the BGP ASes are now aware of AS 400, AS 400 is not yet aware of any of these external entities. As the ISP's network engineer, you have been assigned the task of configuring AS 400 with a default route to the ISP. AS 400 is using RIP.

Project 9.2

To configure a default route for AS 400:

➤ On Router D in AS 400, create a default static route that points to network 170.10.0.0 /16 (the ISP) using the next hop address of Router C:

```
Router_D(config)#ip route 0.0.0.0 0.0.0.0 4.4.4.1
```

This default static route will be placed in Router D's IP routing table. Because Router D is running RIP, the default static route will be advertised automatically to AS 400. All routers within AS 400 would subsequently have a default route to the ISP (and beyond).

9

Implementing BGP in Scalable ISP Networks

After completing this chapter, you will be able to:

✓ Describe the scalability problems associated with Internal Border Gateway Protocol (IBGP)

✓ Explain and configure Border Gateway Protocol (BGP) route reflectors

✓ Describe and configure policy control in BGP using prefix filters

✓ Describe and configure policy control in BGP using route maps

✓ Describe and configure BGP communities and peer groups

✓ Describe methods to connect to multiple Internet Service Providers (ISPs) using BGP

✓ Explain how BGP uses redistribution to advertise routes

✓ Given a set of network requirements, configure a multihomed BGP environment and verify proper operation (within described guidelines)

In our last chapter, we introduced you to the fundamentals of BGP policy-based routing. In this chapter, we will continue to explore this defining feature by presenting some of the tools employed in its implementation. These tools, as we will see, are based on the path attributes introduced in the last chapter and are the mechanisms by which scalable ISP networks and corporate BGP enterprises create the policies that control the flow of inter-AS routing information. In particular, the following routing policy tools will be covered:

➤ Route reflectors

➤ Prefix filters

➤ Route maps

➤ Communities

➤ Peer groups

This chapter also covers how BGP policy can be applied to multihomed ASes, wherein the issues of performance, reliability, and scalability have a direct impact on exactly how BGP policy is implemented in these types of environments. As will be seen, BGP's unparalleled flexibility as a policy-based routing protocol makes it the ideal choice for any network exterior gateway protocol (EGP) solution, especially those of ISPs.

Scalability Issues with IBGP

Chapter 9 presented a few rules that BGP implementations are required to follow, such as the synchronization and next hop rules. Another rule that BGP specifies is the BGP Split Horizon rule: *A route learned via IBGP cannot be propagated to other IBGP peers.* Figure 10.1 clarifies this rather surprising specification. Upon receiving an IBGP update from Router A, Router B will not forward it to its IBGP peer, Router C.

The purpose of the BGP Split Horizon rule is to prevent routing loops from starting within the AS. Necessarily, then, all BGP routers within an AS must be fully meshed

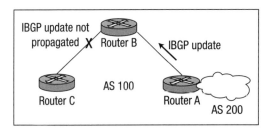

Figure 10.1   The BGP Split Horizon rule.

logically. A full logical mesh between BGP routers allows each peer to establish a direct relationship with each and every other peer in the AS. With this configuration, no IBGP peer would need to forward routes from one IGP peer to other IBGP peers, thus upholding the Split Horizon edict.

However, as you can imagine, a full mesh in a large-scale network is definitely not a scalable solution to the BGP Split Horizon rule. This is because the more routers there are, the more Transmission Control Protocol (TCP) and BGP sessions that would need to be established and maintained. The number of router resources such a scenario demands is potentially enormous, as Figure 10.2 illustrates.

Not only would this scenario put an excessive amount of strain on the routers, it would also result in a substantial increase in network traffic. As each fully meshed BGP speaker generated multiple updates for each of its links, the resulting bandwidth consumption could end up congesting links that were not meant to handle such heavy loads.

There are two scalable solutions to our BGP Split Horizon dilemma:

➤ Confederations

➤ Route reflectors

The first of these—confederations—is not a Building Scalable Cisco Networks (BSCN) objective; therefore, we will take a closer look at the latter one, route reflectors.

10

BGP Route Reflectors

Route reflectors are BGP routers that are allowed to propagate routes learned from one IBGP peer to other IBGP peers (see Figure 10.3).

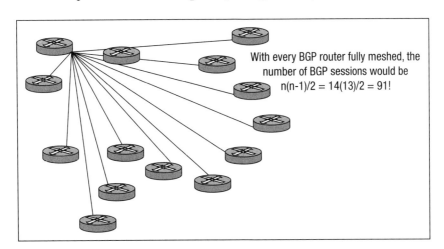

With every BGP router fully meshed, the number of BGP sessions would be n(n-1)/2 = 14(13)/2 = 91!

Figure 10.2   Logical full mesh between IBGP peers.

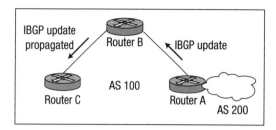

Figure 10.3 Route reflectors solve Split Horizon scalability issues.

Route reflectors obviate the need for a logical full mesh between IBGP peers. When a route reflector receives an IBGP update, it simply forwards it to its neighboring peers. As a result, the number of TCP BGP connections is substantially reduced, along with the amount of traffic necessary to establish and maintain so many connections.

Route reflectors are used primarily by ISPs, which generally have a need for such an instrument whenever the number of neighbor statements increases too much. Within these environments, multiple route reflectors are common to further optimize peer relationships and for redundancy purposes.

Understanding Route Reflector Terminology

Several terms describe route reflector associations, such as the following:

➤ Client

➤ Cluster

➤ Nonclient

➤ Originator ID

➤ Cluster ID

A route reflector establishes peering relationships with routers that are known as *clients*. Clients are the routers that send routing information to the route reflector so that the route reflector may propagate the information to its neighboring peers. In Figure 10.3, for example, Routers A and C are clients of Router B, which is the route reflector. Clients must abide by the BGP Split Horizon rule.

Together, route reflectors and clients form what is called a *cluster*. For example, in Figure 10.3, Routers A, B, and C form one cluster.

Only route reflectors have clients. If an IBGP peer of the router reflector is not a client, it is called a *nonclient*.

The *originator ID* is a BGP path attribute that identifies the client or nonclient in the local AS who originates an update and sends it to the route reflector. The route reflector is the creator of this attribute, not the client or nonclient. Besides identifying the originator of a route, the originator ID also serves as a loop-suppression mechanism. When an update happens to loop back to its originator, the originator knows there is a loop and will consequently drop the update.

Another designation associated with route reflectors is the *cluster ID*. Generally, the router ID of the cluster's route reflector identifies the cluster. However, when a cluster has multiple route reflectors (due to redundancy and improved performance, for example), each route reflector in the cluster is configured with a cluster ID. This identifies the cluster and also allows route reflectors in the same cluster to recognize updates from each other.

Understanding Route Reflector Design

In an ISP, where route reflectors are most often employed, multiple clusters exist. Each cluster contains at least one route reflector and usually at least a couple of clients. Moreover, all route reflectors in the AS must be fully meshed (logically) with BGP. This requirement ensures that route reflectors forward client updates to all other nonclient route reflectors (this last point is clarified in the next section). Figure 10.4 is an example of an ISP network that has incorporated route reflectors.

In this figure, Routers A, B, and C have been configured as route reflectors. Router B's clients are Routers D, E, and F, whereas Router C's clients are Routers G and H. Router A, however, does not have any clients and is therefore in its own cluster. As a result, there are three clusters in the ISP. Routers B, D, E, and F form one cluster; Routers C, G, and H form another cluster; and Router A forms its own cluster.

10

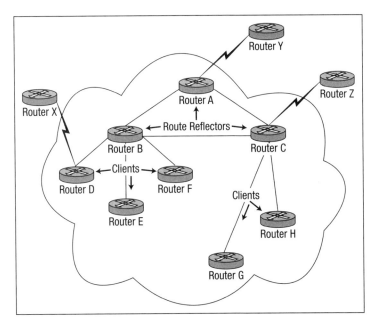

Figure 10.4   Route reflectors in an ISP.

Furthermore, all the route reflectors have nonclients. Router B's nonclients are Routers A and C, Router C's nonclients are Routers A and B, and Router A's nonclients are Routers B and C. Recall that the definition of a nonclient is an *IBGP* peer of a route reflector that is not a part of the same cluster. Therefore, *none* of the external routers (Routers X, Y, and Z) are considered nonclients because they are EBGP peers rather than IBGP peers.

In this ISP network, the physical connections within ISP 100 are not shown; only the IBGP connections are shown. The physical connections may therefore differ somewhat from Figure 10.4. However, the physical connections are still important factors in the route reflector decision, particularly in deciding where route reflectors and clients should be placed. When designing a route reflector network, always follow the physical topology in deciding where to place these devices. This design tip ensures that packet forwarding paths are not affected and that routing loops do not form.

Note: For more information on designing route reflector networks, consult a dedicated text on BGP network design.

Understanding Route Reflector Operation

Route reflector operation is somewhat straightforward. Upon receiving an update, a route reflector takes one of the following actions:

➤ If the update is from a *client* peer, the route reflector propagates the update to both its client and nonclient peers.

➤ If the update is from a *nonclient* peer, the route reflector propagates the update to only its client peers.

➤ If the update is from an EBGP peer, the route reflector propagates the update to both its client and nonclient peers.

Recall that *route reflectors* must be fully meshed logically to ensure the propagation of client updates. The reason for this is that when a route reflector receives a client update (or EBGP update), the update is passed along to other route reflectors that are in different clusters. Because these route reflectors have received an update from a nonclient peer, the update is not passed along to any other nonclients, which means that if the route reflectors were partially meshed, only some of these would receive the updates.

In Figure 10.5, for example, Routers A, B, and C are all route reflectors in a partial IBGP mesh. When Router A receives an EBGP update, it forwards it to its nonclient peer, Router B. Router B, however, will not forward the update to Router C because updates received from nonclient peers are not propagated to other nonclients. A full IBGP mesh would therefore be required between the route reflectors.

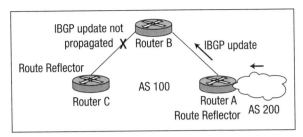

Figure 10.5   Why a full BGP mesh is required between route reflectors.

Configuring BGP Route Reflectors

Route reflector configuration occurs with the following command issued on the prospective route reflector:

```
Router(config-router)#neighbor ip-address route-reflector-client
```

The *ip-address* identifies the BGP peer who will be a client of the route reflector.

The following command output configures a router to be a route reflector and configures the specified neighbors to be its clients:

```
Router(config)#router bgp 200
Router(config-router)#neighbor 172.16.13.1 remote-as 200
Router(config-router)#neighbor 172.16.13.1 route-reflector-client
Router(config-router)#neighbor 172.16.15.1 remote-as 200
Router(config-router)#neighbor 172.16.15.1 route-reflector client
```

Note that the **neighbor route-reflector-client** command is used in conjunction with the **neighbor remote-as** command, not as a substitute for it. As you will see throughout this chapter, the **neighbor remote-as** command is always required in BGP configurations.

Verifying BGP Route Reflectors

Verification of a route reflector's status and of its clients occurs with the **show ip bgp neighbor** command. This command identifies which BGP peers are clients of the route reflector.

The following output illustrates route reflector verification:

```
Router#show ip bgp neighbor

 BGP neighbor is 171.69.232.178,  remote AS 10, external link
 Index 1, Offset 0, Mask 0x2
  Route-Reflector Client
  BGP version 4, remote router ID 171.69.232.178
```

```
BGP state = Established, table version = 27, up for 00:06:12
Last read 00:00:12,hold time is 180, keepalive interval is 60 seconds
Minimum time between advertisement runs is 30 seconds
Received 19 messages, 0 notifications, 0 in queue
Sent 17 messages, 0 notifications, 0 in queue
Inbound path policy configured
Route map for incoming advertisements is testing
Connections established 2; dropped 1
```

BGP Prefix Filters

Any routing policy that requires filtering routing information based on network number (prefix) will use prefix filters. With prefix filters, you can restrict routing information that a BGP peer advertises to and receives from specified BGP neighbors. This can be accomplished in one of two ways:

➤ Distribute list

➤ Prefix list

The following sections explore in depth these two routing policy tools.

Distribute Lists

Distribute lists use access lists to filter updates sent to and received from BGP peers. When filtering incoming updates, the distribute list has the effect of preventing certain networks from being learned in the BGP and IP routing tables. When filtering outgoing updates, the distribute list prevents certain networks from being advertised to certain neighbors. For example, in Figure 10.6, Router B is advertising network 180.10.0.0 to Router C. To prevent this network from being advertised to

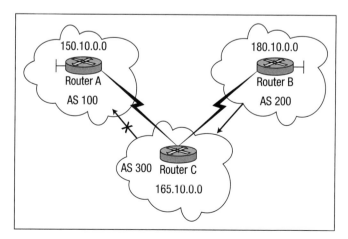

Figure 10.6   Router C filters network 180.10.0.0 on the outbound.

AS 100, Router C applies an outbound distribute list that denies network 180.10.0.0 from being sent in an update to Router A.

The following command is used to create a distribute list and associate it with an access list:

```
Router(config-router)#neighbor {ip-address|peer-group}
    distribute-list access-list-number in|out
```

The braces {} indicate a required parameter and the vertical bar | indicates that only one parameter is to be chosen.

Table 10.1 explains the meaning of the **neighbor distribute-list** command syntax.

Let us now see how this command would be used to configure Router C (in Figure 10.6) to prevent network 180.10.0.0 from being advertised to Router A (150.10.20.2):

```
Router_C(config)#router bgp 300
Router_C(config-router)#network 165.10.0.0
Router_C(config-router)#neighbor 180.10.20.2 remote-as 200
Router_C(config-router)#neighbor 150.10.20.2 remote-as 100
Router_C(config-router)#neighbor 150.10.20.2 distribute-list 1 out
Router_C(config-router)#exit
Router_C(config)#access-list 1 deny 180.10.0.0 0.0.255.255
Router_C(config)#access-list 1 permit 0.0.0.0 255.255.255.255
```

This configuration first tells us that Router C is advertising 165.10.0.0 and that Routers A and B are BGP peers of Router C. The **neighbor distribute-list** statement tells us that Router C will be applying access list 1 to all updates sent to Router A. This standard access list indicates that any prefix starting with 180.10 will be denied. The last **access-list** statement is the familiar **permit any**, which allows all other prefixes to be advertised to Router A. This is necessary because all access lists have an implicit **deny any** at the end.

Table 10.1   The neighbor distribute-list command.

Parameter	Meaning
ip-address	The IP address of the BGP neighbor for which routes are to be filtered.
peer-group	The name of a BGP peer group (covered in the section entitled "BGP Peer Groups").
access-list-number	Represents either a standard or extended access list and can range in value from 1 to 199.
in	Indicates that incoming advertisements from the specified BGP neighbor will be filtered.
out	Indicates that outgoing updates to the specified BGP neighbor will be filtered.

Although standard access lists can filter specific network numbers, they cannot filter aggregated routes (summary routes). To see why, consider a scenario in which a router wishes to allow the aggregate route 150.10.0.0 /16 to be advertised, but not any of the routes summarized within it. Using a standard access list, the output would appear as follows:

```
Router(config)#access-list 1 permit 150.10.0.0 0.0.255.255
```

This command permits *all* networks whose first two bytes are 150.10. As a result, any network contained in the summary route 150.10.0.0 /16 would be matched and subsequently advertised.

Extended access lists resolve this problem. Extended access lists can successfully filter any classless prefix that is using any prefix mask.

However, before we delve into using the extended access list as part of a distribute list configuration, we must first understand how the extended access list works with distribute lists because, as we will see, there are differences between normal extended access lists and BGP extended access lists.

Understanding BGP Extended Access List Usage

The following output compares the syntax of a normal extended access list with that of an extended access list that would be part of a BGP distribute list:

➤ Normal extended access list:

```
access-list <number> permit|deny ip <source address>
   <source wildcard> <destination address> <destination wildcard>
```

➤ BGP extended access list:

```
access-list <number> permit|deny ip <source address>
   <source wildcard> <destination address> <destination wildcard>
```

As you can see, the syntax of both types of extended access lists is exactly the same. However, there is a difference in the *meanings* of the last two parameters, the destination parameters. Whereas the source parameters still specify the network address/mask that is to be filtered, the destination parameters no longer specify the destination address/mask. Instead, the destination parameters specify the exact *prefix mask* that is to be matched.

To explain, consider the previous example, in which the aggregate route 150.10.0.0 /16 was to be advertised without its consolidated networks. Using an extended access list, the following command would be issued to accomplish that task:

```
Router(config)#access-list 100 permit ip 150.10.0.0 0.0.255.255
   255.255.0.0 0.0.0.0
```

The access list permits a network whose first two bytes match 150.10 and whose prefix mask is 255.255.0.0. The 0.0.0.0 parameter is a wildcard parameter that indicates how many bits in the prefix mask are relevant. In this case, all the bits in 255.255.0.0 are relevant. As a result of this access list, only the aggregate route 150.10.0.0 /16 would be advertised; networks consolidated within, such as networks 150.10.20.0 /24 and 150.10.30.0 /24, would not be advertised.

Prefix Lists

Prefix lists are the second way in which routing information can be filtered based on prefix. Introduced in IOS Release 12.0, prefix lists can provide an attractive alternative to access lists in many route-filtering policies. Some of the advantages of using prefix lists are as follows:

➤ Increased performance in list processing.

➤ Support for incremental editions to the prefix list; this is unlike access lists, which cannot be modified incrementally.

➤ More user-friendly command-line interface; compared to extended access lists, the prefix list is easier to understand and use.

➤ Greater flexibility in specifying match conditions.

Prefix lists filter in much the same way that access lists do. That is, filtering involves matching the network number and prefix mask of an update with what is listed in the filter list. When there is a match, the route is either permitted or denied.

Specifically, the rules for matching a route can be stated as follows:

➤ *Empty prefix lists permit all routes.* This is the same rule that access lists follow. That is, access lists applied on an interface without specifying matching conditions will imply that all routes are permitted.

➤ *The first match causes the route to exit out of the prefix list.* This rule is the same as that for access lists, wherein a match causes the route to exit out of the access list testing process (i.e., stop being processed) and be either permitted or denied.

➤ *Processing begins at the "top" of the prefix list.* With access lists, the "top" is the first statement in the list. With prefix lists, however, the top is the **prefix list** statement with the lowest sequence number (explained in the following discussion).

➤ *An implicit **deny any** exists at the end of every prefix list.* This feature is shared by access lists. Any route that does not form a match with a prefix list will be denied and dropped.

10

In a prefix list, each statement is assigned a sequence number. This value is used to determine the order in which statements are processed during the matching process. A route will be matched first with the **prefix list** statement that has the lowest sequence number.

By default, prefix list sequence numbers are generated automatically. If you disable this automatic feature, you must manually specify the sequence number for each statement. In addition, by default, sequence numbers that are generated automatically will have values in increments of five. For instance, the first statement in a prefix list would be 5, the second would be 10, the third would be 15, and so forth. If you are manually specifying the sequence numbers, and for some reason you leave out a sequence number from a statement, the statement will be assigned a sequence number equal to the current maximum value plus 5.

Lastly, you may delete an individual prefix list statement without having to specify its sequence number.

Here, then, are the commands used in configuring prefix lists:

```
Router(config)#ip prefix-list name [seq seq-value] deny|permit
    network/len [ge ge-value] [le le-value]
Router(config-router)#neighbor {ip-address|peer-group}
    prefix-list name in|out
```

Table 10.2 explains the syntax of the **ip prefix-list** command.

The *le* and *ge* values are optional parameters that can be used to specify the range of the prefix length to be matched. When these values are omitted, an exact match with *network/len* is assumed. For example, the following command permits the prefix 70.0.0.0 /8:

```
Router(config)#ip prefix-list cisco permit 70.0.0.0/8
```

Table 10.2 The ip prefix-list command.

Parameter	Meaning
name	Prefix list name. Each prefix list has a name instead of a number. In addition, there is no concept of a standard or extended prefix-list.
seq-value	Sequence number. Determines the order in which statements are matched.
deny|permit	The action to take when a match occurs.
network/len	Network/length. The prefix to be matched and the length of the prefix.
ge-value	Used to specify the range of the prefix length to be matched for prefixes that are more specific than for *network/len*. The range is from *ge-value* to 32 if the *ge* parameter is stated alone.
le-value	Used to specify the range of the prefix length to be matched for prefixes that are more specific than for *network/len*. The range is from *len* to *le-value* if the *le* parameter is stated alone.

This command tells the router to permit an update only if its address is 70.0.0.0 /8. The network length value of 8 says that eight bits in 170.0.0.0 are required to match, whereas the omission of the *le* and *ge* values indicate that *all* bits are required to match. This would mean that addresses such as 70.10.0.0 /16, 70.193.58.0 /24, or 60.0.0.0 /8 would not be matched.

Note that the preceding **prefix-list** statement is well suited for matching aggregate routes (summary routes). Usually, you would not want to match a group of prefixes contained within an aggregate route, but rather only the aggregate route itself; the **ip prefix-list** command is a quick and useful tool for accomplishing exactly this task.

The next command in the configuration of prefix lists is the **neighbor prefix-list** command, whose syntax was presented earlier. This command is used to filter routing information for a particular neighbor and to associate the prefix list with that neighbor. Table 10.3 explains the output of this command's syntax.

*Note: Although the **neighbor prefix-list** command and the **neighbor distribute-list** command both have the same purpose of filtering routing information, you cannot use them both when filtering for the same neighbor.*

Example Prefix List Configuration

In the following example (Figure 10.7), Router C is to be configured with a prefix list that allows it to accept only the prefix 180.10.0.0 /16 from Router B. All other routes from Router B are not to be accepted.

The following output shows how this configuration takes place on Router C:

```
Router_C(config)#router bgp 300
Router_C(config-router)#neighbor 10.10.10.2 remote-as 200
Router_C(config-router)#neighbor 10.10.20.2 remote-as 100
Router_C(config-router)#neighbor 10.10.10.2 prefix-list voyager in
Router_C(config-router)#exit
Router_C(config)#ip prefix-list voyager permit 180.10.0.0/16
```

Consequently, upon receiving updates from Router B (neighbor 10.10.10.2), Router C applies a prefix list called "voyager" to determine which updates are accepted and

Table 10.3   Explaining the neighbor prefix-list command.

Parameter	Meaning
ip-address	IP address of the BGP neighbor for which routes are to be filtered
peer-group	Name of a BGP peer group (covered in the section entitled "BGP Peer Groups")
name	The prefix list name
in	Specifies that the prefix list will be applied to incoming updates from the specified neighbor
out	Specifies that the prefix list will be applied to outgoing updates to the specified neighbor

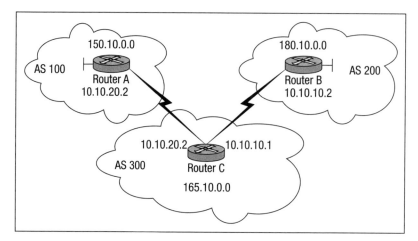

Figure 10.7 Router C is to be configured with a prefix list.

which are dropped. Any prefix that *exactly* matches 180.10.0.0 /16 will be accepted. The implicit **deny any** causes the rest to be dropped.

Note in the **ip prefix-list** statement that we did not specify a sequence value. As a result, with the automatic sequence generation feature enabled, the sequence number assigned to the **prefix list** statement would be 5. This automatic sequence feature may be disabled with the **no ip prefix-list sequence-number** command in router configuration mode.

In addition, you can delete a prefix list with the **no ip prefix-list** *name* router configuration command, where *name* is the name of the prefix list you wish to delete. To delete a specific **prefix list** statement, use the **no ip prefix-list seq** *seq-value* router configuration command, where *seq-value* is the sequence number of the statement you wish to delete.

Verifying Prefix Lists

To see which prefix lists are configured on your router, the following commands are available:

➤ **show ip prefix-list detail**

➤ **show ip prefix-list summary**

The **show ip prefix-list detail** command displays information on all prefix lists. This includes the prefix lists' descriptions and hit counts.

The following output is a sample from this command:

```
Router#show ip prefix-list detail
Prefix-list with the last deletion/insertion: voyager
ip prefix-list voyager:
```

```
Description: filters routes from Router B
count: 1, range entries: 0, sequences: 5 - 5, refcount: 1
seq 5 permit 180.10.0.0/16 (hit count: 3, refcount: 1)
```

This output is from Router C in our earlier example. The name of the prefix list is "voyager", and the hit count indicates that a match with the prefix list occurred three times.

The **show ip prefix-list summary** command omits the description and hit count fields, but still shows all the prefix lists that are configured.

There are several other **show ip prefix-list** commands that allow you to display only certain information about prefix lists. The more common of these commands are the following:

➤ **show ip prefix-list [details | summary]** *name*—Displays the prefix list with the associated name.

➤ **show ip prefix-list** *name* **[***network/len***]**—Displays the prefix list associated with a specific network.

➤ **show ip prefix-list** *name* **[seq** *seq-num***]**—Displays the prefix list associated with a specific sequence number.

Summary of BGP Prefix Filters

Prefix filters are routing policy tools that control the routing information sent to and received from BGP neighbors. The two types of BGP prefix filters are distribute lists and prefix lists. The former use standard and extended access lists to filter networks, and the latter use prefix lists.

Prefix lists are usually preferred over access lists because of their flexibility and improved performance, as well as other attractive features. However, prefix lists still share many of the same features as access lists, including a similar matching process and the implicit **deny any**.

BGP Route Maps

BGP route maps are an indispensable tool for any BGP routing policy. Route maps serve various purposes and can be used in different capacities on the router. In BGP, route maps are used for the following major purposes:

➤ As a method of controlling and modifying routing information.

➤ As a method of defining the conditions by which routes are redistributed between BGP and other routing protocols.

In our discussion on route maps here, we focus only on the first of these two purposes.

Route Map Fundamentals

Route maps are complex access lists. Like access lists, route maps attempt to match routing updates with certain conditions; if a match is made, an action is taken. The manner in which route maps perform these tasks differs significantly from that of access lists. Specifically, route maps match not only prefixes but also *path attributes*. In addition, route maps not only permit and deny routing updates, they also modify the path attributes contained within the updates. These two distinguishing functions characterize route maps and make them an extraordinarily agile tool for implementing BGP policy.

Table 10.4 presents the similarities and differences between route maps and access lists.

The following three commands are used to configure a route map:

```
Router(config)#route-map name permit|deny [sequence-number]

Router(config-route-map)#match {conditions}

Router(config-route-map}#set {actions}
```

The first of these commands is explained in Table 10.5.

Table 10.4 Comparing access lists with route maps.

Access List Feature	Corresponding Route Map Feature
One access list	One route map.
One access list statement	One route map statement.
An access list number	A route map name.
Match criteria comprise only network addresses and masks	Match criteria can comprise, in addition, path attributes and other routing information.
Statements cannot be individually edited or deleted	Statements are sequentially numbered, which means they can be individually edited or deleted.
Only action is to either deny or permit a route	Can deny and permit routes and also modify routes' path attributes using **set** commands.
Implicit **deny any**	Implicit **deny any**.

Table 10.5 The route-map command.

Parameter	Meaning
name	The route map's name.
permit|deny	The action to be taken if the **match** conditions are met.
sequence-number	Indicates the order in which statements are processed, similar to the prefix list sequence number.

All route map statements that have the same name belong to the same route map list. In addition, each statement has a different sequence number. For example, the following two route map statements belong to a route map list named "RM":

```
Router(config)#route-map RM permit 10
Router(config-route-map)#(the first set of match conditions goes here)
Router(config-route-map)#(the first set of set actions goes here)
!
Router(config)#route map RM permit 20
Router(config-route-map)#(the second set of match conditions goes here)
Router(config-route-map)#(the second set of set conditions goes here)
```

Like prefix lists, route maps process statements from the top down, starting with the statement that has the lowest sequence number. In this example, the first statement that would be processed is the one with sequence number 10.

The first set of **match** conditions that are met will cause the specified **set** actions to be taken on the routing update. Some of the **match** and **set** parameters that can be configured in a route map are the following:

➤ **match as-path**

➤ *match community*

➤ **match interface**

➤ *match ip address*

➤ **match ip next-hop**

➤ **match ip route-source**

➤ **match metric**

➤ **match route-type**

➤ **match tag**

➤ **set as-path**

➤ **set automatic-tag**

➤ *set community*

➤ **set interface**

➤ **set default interface**

➤ **set ip default next-hop**

➤ **set level**

10

➤ *set local-preference*

➤ *set metric*

➤ **set metric-type**

➤ **set next-hop**

➤ **set origin**

➤ **set tag**

➤ *set weight*

Note: *The ones in italic are used most in this chapter.*

As an example of how the **match** and **set** commands are used, consider our route map named "RM". With this route map, we could define a match condition that checks to see if a routing update possesses the next hop address 10.10.10.1. The configuration would appear as follows:

```
Router_C(config)#route-map RM permit 10
Router_C(config-route-map)#match ip next-hop 10.10.10.1
```

At this point, a routing update that matched this next hop condition would be permitted. If there were nothing more to this **route-map** statement, the routing update would be either advertised or accepted, depending on another command that we will soon present. But we could also choose to make some modifications to the permitted update before either its transmission to or acceptance from the BGP neighbor. Continuing with our example, then, we could define a **set** action that changes the MED (multi-exit discriminator, or metric) of the update to, say, 5. This configuration would appear as follows:

```
Router_C(config-route-map)#set metric 5
```

As a result, once the metric had been modified, the update would continue on its journey.

What would have happened, though, if the next hop condition in our example was not matched? Whenever a match does not occur with the first set of match conditions, the second set of match conditions is checked, and if these conditions don't form a match, then the third set of conditions is checked, and so forth, until there are no more **route-map** statements in the route list. If an update proceeds through the entire list and does not get matched, the update is discarded. This is the route map's implicit **deny any**.

Another possible action that could be taken on routing updates is the following: If the match criteria are met and the **route-map** command specifies **deny**, then the route will *not* be controlled or modified and the update is denied (dropped).

Table 10.6   The neighbor route-map command.

Parameter	Meaning
ip-address	The BGP neighbor to which you want to apply the route map
peer-group	BGP peer-group name (covered in the section entitled "BGP Peer Groups")
name	The same route map name configured in the **route-map** command
in	Tells the router to apply the route map to all updates received from the specified neighbor
out	Tells the router to apply the route map to all updates sent to the specified neighbor

There is one more command necessary in a route map configuration:

```
Router(config-router)#neighbor {ip-address|peer-group}
   route-map name in|out
```

This command applies the route map to routing updates being sent to or received from the specified neighbor. Table 10.6 explains the meaning of its syntax.

*Note: You cannot use a route map to filter inbound BGP updates when using a "match" on the **ip address**. You would need to use a prefix filter instead.*

Example Route Map Configuration

Similar to prefix filters, route maps can be used to filter routing updates coming from or being advertised to certain neighbors. However, route maps do not generally permit or deny updates as a means in itself. That is, route maps will usually match updates only because the router has been instructed to *modify* the updates' path attributes; hence, the purpose for matching a network address using the route map. If you wanted to match the address simply for the purpose of restricting it, then you should use a distribute list or prefix list instead, because this is what they were meant for.

The following **route-map** configuration command is used to match an IP address:

```
Router(config-route-map)#match ip address {ip-address|access-list-number}
```

If you specify an IP address instead of using an access list, the router will match the exact IP address. For example the following command matches the host address 10.10.10.1:

```
Router(config-route-map)#match ip address 10.10.10.1
```

If you wanted to specify a group of network addresses, you could use a standard access list, as follows:

```
Router(config-route-map)#match ip address 1
!
Router(config)#access-list 1 permit 10.10.0.0 0.0.255.255
```

10

The first of these commands tells the router to match an update whose IP address forms a match with access list 1. Access list 1 permits any address whose first two bytes begin with 10.10. But what would occur if an address didn't meet the access list criteria? Then there would be no match for the address, and the update would move on to the next **route-map** statement to be matched against the next set of match conditions. Note, therefore, that the access list's implicit **deny all** would not cause the update to be dropped (denied).

Continuing with our example, say that we wanted to modify an update that passed the previous match condition by changing its metric to 10. The following command would execute this task:

```
Router(config-route-map)#set metric 10
```

With this command, any update that meets the match conditions will have its metric attribute changed to 10. The purpose of this route map statement has thus been fulfilled.

Figure 10.8 illustrates an example in which we can see a **route-map** in action. In this figure, Router C is to be configured with a route map that lets it set the weight of networks coming from network 180.10.0.0 to 100. All other routes received from Router B are to have a weight of 1.

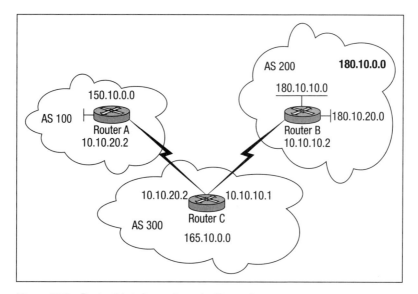

Figure 10.8 Router C is to be configured with a route map.

The following configuration is applied on Router C in this example:

```
Router_C(config)#router bgp 300
Router_C(config-router)#neighbor 10.10.10.2 remote-as 200
Router_C(config-router)#neighbor 10.10.10.2 route-map voyager in
Router_C(config-router)#exit
Router_C(config)#route-map voyager permit 10
Router_C(config-route-map)#match ip address 1
Router_C(config-route-map)#set weight 100
Router_C(config-route-map)#exit
Router_C(config)#access-list 1 permit 180.10.0.0 0.0.255.255
Router_C(config)#route-map voyager permit 20
Router_C(config-route-map)#set weight 1 (note there is no match condition
    in this route-map statement; this implies that all routes are accepted)
```

The access list in this configuration allows addresses whose first two bytes are 180.10 to be matched with the **route-map** statement and allows for their weights to be set to 100. If an address didn't form a match with 180.10, then the update would move on to statement 20, which does not have any **match** conditions, only a **set** action. Whenever there is no **match** condition in a **route-map** statement, the implication is to **permit any**. In this example, therefore, any update that was matched with route **map-statement** 20 would be permitted and would have its weight set to 1.

Warning: Always remember that any updates that fail to meet route map conditions will be dropped due to the implicit **deny any**. Therefore, always make sure your route map configuration takes this eventuality into account.

10

BGP Communities

Communities are another major tool used in a BGP routing policy. The primary purpose of the community attribute is to allow destinations to be grouped together so that routing decisions can be applied to the group (called a community) instead of to each individual destination. This ability to group destinations into communities is very useful for ISPs and other enterprise networks that must configure a routing policy for a large number of BGP routers. Within these networks, the community attribute allows a BGP router to make a routing decision (e.g., a filtering, preference, or redistribution decision) based upon the value of the community attribute received in a routing update. Because the attribute is shared by multiple destinations, the router subsequently ends up making a routing decision simultaneously for multiple destinations. This is usually an effective strategy because all destinations in a community share common properties, which therefore facilitates a routing policy that can be applied successfully to the entire community.

Each destination can be a member of more than one community. By default, all destinations belong to the Internet community, which is a predefined well-known community that includes every single router in every AS.

The community attribute is an optional transitive path attribute, which means that if a router does not recognize the attribute, it will be marked as "partial" and transmitted to the next BGP peer without being modified in any way. A router that does recognize the update's community attribute will be able to make routing decisions using that attribute and will subsequently be allowed to propagate it to neighboring peers. However, a BGP router must be configured to propagate communities; otherwise, these attributes will by default be stripped from updates before being propagated.

The community attribute value is a 32-bit number in the range of 1 to 4,294,967,200. The high-order 16 bits identify the AS number of the attribute's origin, whereas the low-order 16 bits are a locally defined community number. By default, the community value is entered as one decimal number; however, you may enter it in the format *AS:nn*, where *AS* is the AS number and *nn* is the low-order 16-bit local community number.

Creating the Community Attribute

Before a community can be used in a BGP policy, the community must first be manually set. This task is accomplished with a route map by using the following command:

```
Router(config-route-map)#set community {community-value [additive]}|none}
```

Table 10.8 explains the parameters of the **set community** command.

The result of the community attribute's creation is that any routing update that matches the associated route map condition will cause the update to be *tagged* with the community value. For example, in the following configuration, Router A is

Table 10.8   The set community command.

Parameter	Meaning
community-value	A number from 1 to 4,294,967,200 or one of the predefined well-known values listed later in this section
additive	Specifies that the community value will be added to the already existing communities listed in the update's community attribute
none	Removes the community from the prefixes that pass the route map

configured to match updates whose next-hop is 10.10.10.1 and to set their community attribute to 100:

```
Router_A(config)#route-map voyager permit 10
Router_A(config-route-map)#match ip next-hop 10.10.10.1
Router_A(config-route-map)#set community 100
```

The community value in the preceding configuration is a decimal number. However, it may also be one of the *predefined well-known* values. These values are as follows:

➤ **no-export**—A router that receives an update tagged with this community value will not propagate the update to *EBGP* peers.

➤ **no-advertise**—A router that receives an update tagged with this community value will not propagate the update to *any* BGP peers.

With these values, a router is able to influence another peer's actions. We will see in a moment how this can occur.

The next command used in community configuration is the familiar **neighbor route-map** command, repeated here:

```
Router(config-router)#neighbor {ip-address|peer-group}
   route-map name in|out
```

Because the community attribute is set in a route map, it must always be applied to neighbor updates with this command.

In addition, to propagate community attributes to neighbors, the following command must be used:

```
Router(config-router)#neighbor {ip-address|peer-group} send-community
```

The *ip-address* identifies the neighbor to whom you want the community attribute sent. If you do not issue this command, the attribute will not be sent.

Example Community Configuration

We now put all these community commands together to see how they can actually be used in BGP policy decisions.

In our first example, illustrated in Figure 10.9, Router B wants to prevent all networks in its AS from being advertised to AS 100. Router B therefore needs to tell Router C, to whom updates are being sent, not to propagate AS 200's networks to AS 100.

10

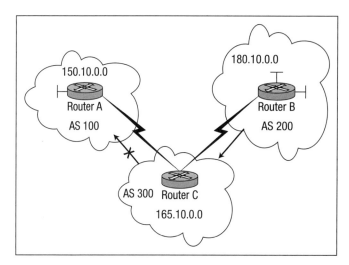

Figure 10.9 Router C is not allowed to export AS 200's networks to AS 100.

The following output shows how Router B implements this policy:

```
Router_B(config)#router bgp 200
Router_B(config-router)#neighbor 10.10.10.1 remote-as 300
Router_B(config-router)#neighbor 10.10.10.1 send-community
Router_B(config-router)#neighbor 10.10.10.1 route-map voyager out
!
Router_B(config)#route-map voyager permit 10
Router_B(config-route-map)#match ip address 1
Router_B(config-route-map)#set community no-export
!
Router_B(config)#access-list 1 permit 0.0.0.0 255.255.255.255
```

In the preceding output, Router B has been configured with a route map named "voyager". This route map, which will be applied to all routing updates being sent to Router C (neighbor 10.10.10.1), states that any IP address matching access list 1 will be tagged with a community attribute of **no-export**. Because access list 1 permits all networks, Router B will subsequently tag all network advertisements with the **no-export** attribute. In addition, the **neighbor send-community** command has been issued to send this attribute to Router B.

Upon receiving updates from Router B, Router C will note that they all carry the **no-export** attribute. This tells Router C not to propagate these updates to external BGP peers. As a result, the updates would always remain local to Router B's AS, AS 300.

In the next example, illustrated in Figure 10.10, Router D in AS 300 is sending updates about its networks to Router C in AS 200. Router C, however, notices upon

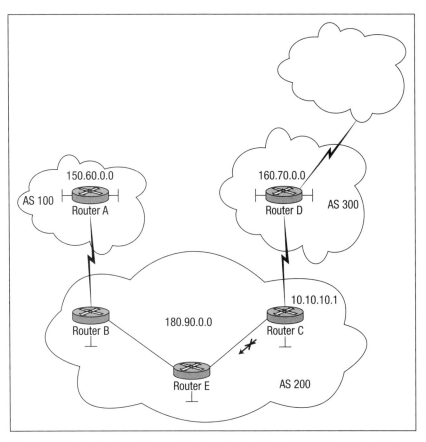

150.60.0.0
AS 100
Router A

160.70.0.0
AS 300
Router D

180.90.0.0
Router B

10.10.10.1
Router C

Router E   AS 200

10

Figure 10.10   Router C receives updates from Router D tagged with the **no-advertise** attribute.

receiving these updates that they are tagged with the **no-advertise** community attribute. As a result, Router C does not propagate the updates concerning Router D's networks to its IBGP peer, Router E.

The following output shows us how Router D's configuration would appear:

```
Router_D(config)#router bgp 300
Router_D(config-router)#neighbor 10.10.10.1 remote-as 300
Router_D(config-router)#neighbor 10.10.10.1 route-map voyager out
!
Router_D(config)#route-map voyager permit 10
Router_D(config-route-map)#match ip address 1
Router_D(config-route-map)#set community no-advertise
!
Router_D(config)#route-map voyager permit 20
Router_D(config-route-map)#set community 300
!
Router_D(config)#access-list 1 permit 160.70.0.0 0.0.255.255
```

Notice in Router D's configuration that any update whose routes do not match the first two octets of 160.70.0.0 will be tagged with a community attribute of 300. Based on this particular community value, Router C can subsequently choose how it responds to these updates, depending, of course, on how Router C is configured. For instance, Router C may be configured with a route map that matches updates with attribute 300 so that routing information in these updates can be modified according to a given policy and then propagated to neighboring peers. Or Router C may be configured with a routing policy that controls how it accepts (as opposed to how it transmits) updates that are tagged with this attribute.

In all cases such as those just described, the community attribute is a tool that can be used to control which routing information a router accepts, prefers, or advertises. The following section explores how these routing decisions can be configured using the community attribute.

Using the Community Attribute in BGP Policy

The following command is often issued to enforce a routing policy based on the community attribute:

```
Router(config)#ip community-list community-list-number
   permit|deny community-value
```

This command creates what is called a *community list*. Building on the concept of grouping destinations to create a community, community lists allow you to group communities together to create a *macrocommunity* to which routing decisions can then be applied.

The community list is used with a route map, which will match an update's community attribute with the list and apply set actions if the update meets the list's conditions (this is the same process we explored earlier). The following **match** command is used in this situation:

```
Router(config-route-map)#match community community-list-number [exact]
```

Table 10.7 explains the fields in both the **ip community-list** and **match community** commands.

Just like the **set community** command, the **ip community-list** command can specify predefined well-known community values. The following are those that can be matched with the community list:

➤ **no-export**—A router that receives an update tagged with this community attribute value will not propagate the update to external BGP peers.

➤ **no-advertise**—A router that receives an update tagged with this community attribute value will not propagate the update to *any* BGP peers.

Table 10.7   The meanings of community parameters.

Parameter	Meaning
community-list-number	The number that identifies the community list and distinguishes it from other community lists. In the route map statement, this number tells the router which community list to use when matching an update's community attribute.
community-value	The community value, originally created with the **set community** command.
exact	This parameter from the **match community** command tells the router that the community attribute must match exactly with the community list. That is, all the community values listed in an update's community attribute must be specified in the community list; otherwise, there is no match.

➤ **internet**—A router that receives an update tagged with this community attribute value will propagate the update to *all* BGP peers.

Figure 10.11 presents a scenario in which Router D in AS 300 is transmitting updates to Router C in AS 200. Router D's updates are configured to carry community attributes. Router C will be configured to use these attributes to set the weight of incoming updates based on their community values.

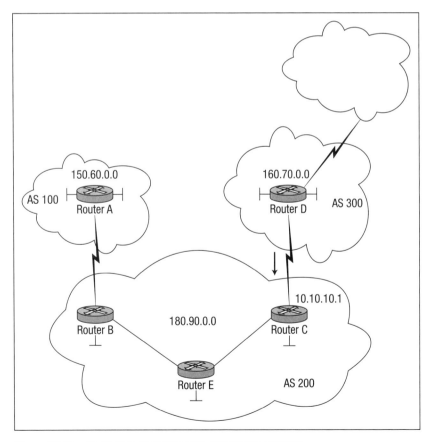

Figure 10.11   Router D tags updates with community attributes.

First, we present Router D's configuration, annotated:

```
Router_D(config)#router bgp 300
Router_D(config-router)#neighbor 10.10.10.1 remote-as 200
Router_D(config-router)#neighbor 10.10.10.1 send-community
   (allows the community attribute to be sent to Router C)
Router_D(config-router)#neighbor 10.10.10.1 route-map voyager out
   (the voyager route map will be applied to all routing updates sent
   to Router C)
!
Router_D(config)#route-map voyager permit 10
Router_D(config-route-map)#match ip address 1
   (match the update's routes with access list 1)
Router_D(config-route-map)#set community 100 200 additive
   (for matching routes, append their community attributes with the
   community values 100 and 200)
!
Router_D(config)#access-list 1 permit 0.0.0.0 255.255.255.255
   (permit any address)
```

In this configuration, we see that all updates being sent to Router C are being appended with the community values 100 and 200. The **additive** keyword is necessary; otherwise, community values 100 and 200 would replace any community values already listed in the update's community attribute. (The community attribute is just a list of community values that have been appended to it, similar to the **as–path** attribute.)

Now we present Router C's configuration, annotated:

```
Router_C(config)#router bgp 200
Router_C(config-router)#network 180.90.0.0
Router_C(config-router)#neighbor 180.90.10.2 remote-as 200
Router_C(config-router)#neighbor 10.10.10.2 remote-as 300
Router_C(config-router)#neighbor 10.10.10.2 route-map enterprise in
   (the enterprise route map is applied to all routing updates received
   from Router D)
!
Router_C(config)#route-map enterprise permit 10
   (permit an update that matches the route map condition in
   this statement)
Router_C(config-route-map)#match community 1
   (match a route's community attribute with community list 1)
Router_C(config-route-map)#set weight 30
   (for matching routes, set their weight to 30)
!
```

```
Router_C(config)#route-map enterprise permit 20
  (permit an update that matches the route map condition in
  this statement)
Router_C(config-route-map)#match community 2 exact
  (match a route's community attribute exactly with community list 2)
Router_C(config-route-map)#set weight 10
  (for matching routes, set their weight to 10)
!
Router_C(config)#route-map enterprise permit 30
  (permit an update that matches the route map condition in
  this statement)
Router_C(config-route-map)#match community 3
  (any updates that do not form a match with any of the previous route
  map conditions will be matched with community list 3)
!
Router_C(config)#ip community-list 1 permit 100
  (permit a community attribute with the value 100 listed in it)
Router_C(config)#ip community-list 2 permit 200
  (permit a community attribute with the value 200 listed in it)
Router_C(config)#ip community-list 3 permit internet
  (permit a community attribute with any community value)
```

In Router C's configuration, any route received from Router D that has a community attribute with a value of 100 will be set with a weight of 30, whereas any route with a value of 200 (and *only* 200, as indicated by the **exact** parameter) will be set with a weight of 10. All other routes end up matching community list 3, whose **internet** keyword permits all routes with any community value. Note, however, that routes received from Router D *without* a community attribute will be denied. This is because community list 3 requires *at least* one community value to be able to permit a community attribute and the attribute's associated route.

BGP Peer Groups

BGP peer groups are the next major tool in implementing a routing policy. In many cases, multiple BGP neighbors are configured with the same update policies. For instance, they may share the same prefix filters, the same outbound route maps, or perhaps the same route preferences. In these situations, the BGP *neighbors* could be grouped into a peer group or a group of BGP neighbors that share the same update policies. Policies could then be assigned to peer groups rather than to individual peers. Such an approach has the following advantages:

➤ *Reduces resource consumption*—CPU utilization decreases and available memory increases.

➤ *Simplifies BGP configurations*—There is no longer a need to replicate the same policies for every individual BGP peer whose update policy is the same.

➤ *Improves performance*—Routing updates are sent only once for each peer group. These updates are replicated and sent to each peer group member.

Even though each member in a peer group will be required to have the same outbound update policies (as specified by the prefix filter or route map), each peer group member is not required to share the same inbound update policies. This means that upon being assigned inbound and outbound routing policies (after joining the peer group), the peer group member may be configured to override any inbound policy statements with which the peer disagreed.

Like the weight path attribute, the peer group is a nontransitive path attribute, which means that it always remains local to the router on which it was configured instead of being propagated to other BGP routers.

Note: If you are using an IOS release prior to 11.1(18) CC, additional peer group requirements must be adhered to. Consult Cisco's online documentation for more information on this issue.

Peer Group Configuration

The following command is used to create a BGP peer group:

```
Router(config-router)#neighbor peer-group-name peer-group
```

The *peer-group-name* identifies the name of the peer group to be created.

The following command assigns a BGP peer to the peer group:

```
Router(config-router)#neighbor ip-address peer-group peer-group-name
```

The *ip-address* identifies the router's BGP neighbor that is to be assigned to the peer group.

You can also *clear* a BGP peer group by issuing the following command:

```
Router#clear ip bgp peer-group peer-group-name
```

This command has the effect of clearing all connections to a peer group.

Peer Group Configuration Example

In Figure 10.12, all IBGP peers within AS 100 have the same routing update policies. All EBGP peers, including Routers A, E, F, and G, have the same update policies as well. Moreover, the two sets of policies are not the same.

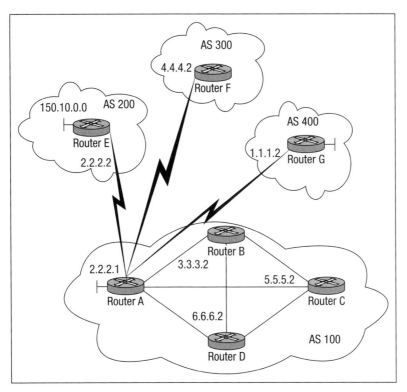

Figure 10.12   Router A is to be configured with BGP peer groups.

10

Router A in AS 100 has subsequently been configured with two peer groups, one for its IBGP peers and the other for its EBGP peers. The following output (once again annotated) shows Router A's configuration for its first peer group, called "intra":

```
Router_A(config)#router bgp 100
Router_A(config-router)#neighbor intra peer-group
   (defines the peer group called "intra")
Router_A(config-router)#neighbor intra remote-as 100
   (establishes a peer relationship with the intra peer group in AS 100)
Router_A(config-router)#neighbor intra route-map voyager out
   (applies the voyager route-map to all routing updates sent to the
   intra peer group)
Router_A(config-router)#neighbor intra prefix-list enterprise in
   (applies the enterprise prefix-list to all routing updates coming
   from the intra peer group)
Router_A(config-router)#neighbor 5.5.5.2 prefix-list cisco in
   (applies the cisco prefix-list to all routing updates coming from
   Router C)
Router_A(config-router)#neighbor 3.3.3.2 peer-group intra
Router_A(config-router)#neighbor 5.5.5.2 peer-group intra
Router_A(config-router)#neighbor 6.6.6.2 peer-group intra
```

In Router A's configuration, we see that the peer group named "intra" is created and is assigned neighbors from AS 100. We also see that two routing policies were created and applied to the peer group, and that one inbound policy was created and applied only to Router C. Recall that only *inbound* peer group policies can be overridden.

The next output shows how Router A was configured with a policy for its other peer group, called "delta":

```
Router_A(config)#router bgp 100
Router_A(config-router)#neighbor delta peer-group
Router_A(config-router)#neighbor 2.2.2.2 remote-as 200
Router_A(config-router)#neighbor 2.2.2.2 peer-group delta
Router_A(config-router)#neighbor 4.4.4.2 remote-as 300
Router_A(config-router)#neighbor 4.4.4.2 peer-group delta
Router_A(config-router)#neighbor 1.1.1.2 remote-as 400
Router_A(config-router)#neighbor 1.1.1.2 peer-group delta
Router_A(config-router)#neighbor 1.1.1.2 prefix-list ether in
Router_A(config-router)#neighbor delta route-map giga out
```

The preceding configuration for Router A shows us that Routers E, F, and G belong to the peer group called "delta." The route map called "giga" is applied to updates sent to this peer group, whereas the prefix list called "ether" is applied only to updates received from Router G.

Note in this example that we were unable to specify the **neighbor remote-as** command for the peer group, as we were able to do in Router A's first peer group configuration. This is because Router A's EBGP neighbors reside in different ASes, which requires us to configure separate **neighbor remote-as** statements.

Summary of BGP Routing Policy Tools

BGP routers can use several major tools to implement an administratively defined routing policy:

➤ *Route reflectors*—A route reflector is a router that can propagate IBGP-learned routing updates to IBGP peers. This tool may be necessary in a BGP environment that is unable to scale with a full IBGP mesh.

➤ *Prefix filters*—Prefix filters are used to restrict network advertisements from being either sent to or received from certain BGP neighbors. Distribute lists and prefix lists are examples of prefix filters.

➤ *Route maps*—BGP route maps are complex access lists that are used to control and modify routing information as well as to define the conditions in which redistribution occurs. These policy tools consist of match conditions and set actions.

➤ *Communities*—Communities are another way to control and modify routing information. A community is a group of *destinations* to which routing decisions (such as preference, acceptance, and redistribution) can be applied. This tool is created and associated with a route map.

➤ *Peer groups*—A peer group is a group of *BGP peers* that share the same update policies. All BGP peers that are assigned to a peer group inherit the peer group's inbound and outbound update policies.

Multihoming with BGP

Chapter 9 explored how enterprise networks could be connected to an ISP without using BGP. This type of connection is accomplished by employing static and/or default routes within both the corporate network and the ISP. Moreover, we also explained some of the conditions in which this BGP-less connection might be recommended. One of these conditions stated that static or default routes could be used as an alternative to an external BGP connection when only one connection existed between the corporate enterprise and another AS, such as an ISP. In this situation, if the routing policy was the same for both ASes, and if other administrative conditions were met, then using BGP would not be necessary.

However, we also saw that you would most likely want to have BGP running between your AS and the ISP whenever you had active connections to multiple ISPs. In this event, the reason for opting for BGP is likely because the routing policies of your AS and the ISPs would differ and possibly because your AS may need to serve as a transit system for trusted external traffic.

In this chapter, we therefore explore how a corporate enterprise can use BGP to make connections with multiple ISPs and at the same time integrate some of the alternative connection methods introduced in Chapter 9. The result of this integration, as we shall see, facilitates a highly efficient and cost-effective means for your AS to connect to its ISPs at peak performance and with optimal scalability.

Multihoming Solutions

Multihoming describes the situation when an AS connects to more than one ISP. Frequently, the AS's technical requirements are such that the AS needs to have a highly reliable and available Internet connection. Other times, an AS's technical requirements dictate the need for improved performance with respect to traffic coming from and going to the Internet connection. Both of these are reasons a network would choose to multihome its Internet connection.

10

Multihoming can occur in three common ways, based on how the ISPs use BGP to inform the corporate AS of the ISPs' routes. These multihoming methods are as follows:

➤ All connected ISPs use BGP to forward only default routes to the AS.

➤ All connected ISPs use BGP to forward default routes *and* certain selected routes to the AS.

➤ All connected ISPs use BGP to forward *all* their routes to the AS.

We explore each of these multihoming solutions in the following sections.

Forwarding Default Routes

Figure 10.13 presents an example of the first multihoming method. In this figure, both ISP 1 and ISP 2 are propagating default routes via EBGP to AS 200.

Upon receiving these default routes, Routers B and C in AS 200 would each enter the route, denoted by 0.0.0.0, into their routing tables and would then propagate it to Router E. Router E would subsequently have two default routes to choose from. As a result, Router E's IGP will choose the default route that has the lowest

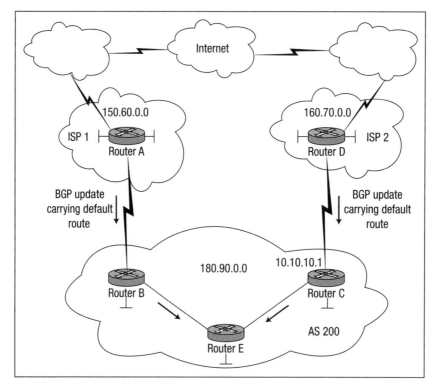

Figure 10.13 Forwarding default routes to an AS via BGP.

IGP metric. For instance, if OSPF were being used, and both routes were received with different costs, Router E would choose the route with the lowest cost. If Routing Information Protocol (RIP) were used as the AS's IGP, then the default route with the lowest hop count would be chosen.

As seen in the preceding example, and as shown in Chapter 9, an AS uses the default route to reach unknown external destinations. This is how the AS learns of the outside world. How, though, would the *ISPs* learn of the AS's routes? The answer lies with EBGP. EBGP peers in the AS propagate all the AS's routes to the ISPs.

The benefit to using the default route method to connect an AS to multiple ISPs is the reduction in resource consumption on both the AS's routers and media. ISPs generally have an enormous number of routes listed in their routing tables. To propagate all these routes to the AS would consume a massive amount of bandwidth (particularly on slow-speed serial links) and would increase router central processing unit (CPU) utilization levels and decrease available memory substantially. Therefore, sending only a single default route to the AS would be the best multihoming solution if these types of issues were of particular relevance to the AS.

Forwarding Default Routes and Selected ISP Routes

Sometimes, simply having a default route is not a sufficient solution for meeting an AS's performance requirements. This would be the case when AS routers frequently exchange traffic with certain external destinations. The AS routers need to be able to reach these destinations using the quickest and most efficient means while at the same time being able to implement any policies associated with them. As a result, the appropriate multihoming solution in this type of scenario would be for the ISPs to forward both default routes *and* selected external routes to the AS. The AS would, in turn, forward all its own intra-AS routes to the ISPs.

When communicating with known external destinations, the AS will usually choose the shortest AS path. This is the default action when no specific path attributes, such as local preference, are used in determining the "best" route. For all unknown destinations, the AS bases its path selection on the default route with the lowest IGP metric.

Figure 10.14, for example, presents a scenario in which ISP 1 and ISP 2 are connected to each other and exchange full routing information between each other. ISP 1 is sending to AS 200 only a default route, whereas ISP 2 is sending to AS 200 both the default route and network 12.0.0.0.

Assuming that no specific path attributes have been set in AS 200, Router C will choose the path to network 12.0.0.0 that has the shortest number of AS hops. Given that Router C has only one path to this network (because ISP 1 is sending only a default route), the AS path factor is in this case irrelevant.

10

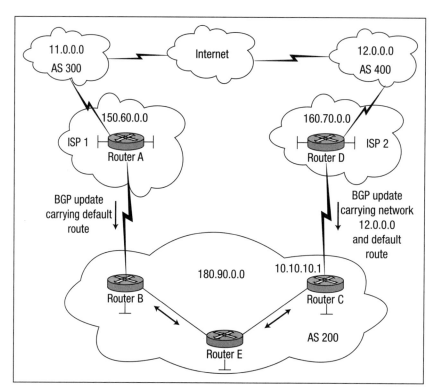

Figure 10.14 Forwarding default routes and a selected route.

Router C has also received two default routes, one from its EBGP peer and the other from Router E (who received it from Router B). When Router C needs to reach an unknown destination, it will use the default route that has the lowest IGP metric within the AS. For instance, if RIP were the IGP within AS 200, Router C would receive a default route from Router E with a hop count of 2, whereas the default route from ISP 2 would be directly connected. As a result, Router C would always choose the default route through ISP 2 when transmitting to unknown destinations.

Forwarding All ISP Routes to the AS

The third multihoming method occurs when the ISPs forward all their routes to the AS. This method is usually the least preferred due to the tremendous amount of resources required to receive, process, and store all the ISP routes. If using this solution, the AS must make sure that its EBGP routers have enough processing power and enough available memory to handle full ISP routing tables, which usually range between 50,000 and 100,000 routes. The bandwidth consumption levels on serial links must also be considered.

As usual, the AS sends all its routes to the ISPs, which then forward some or all of the routes (depending upon the mutually established policy between the ISP and the AS with regard to this matter) to the Internet after applying the appropriate policy configurations.

Just as in the previous multihoming scenario, AS routers will by default choose paths to known external destinations based on the AS path advertised in their updates. Of course, the AS always has the option of creating a routing policy to influence path selection. The decision to go with either the default policy or a custom-tailored policy is, as previously stated, a function of the AS's goals and requirements.

Figure 10.15 presents an example of the third multihoming scenario. Here, ISPs 1 and 2 are exchanging full routing information with each other and with AS 200. AS 200 is forwarding its local routes to both ISPs.

Note that, in this situation, if AS 200 forwards routes learned from ISP 1 to ISP 2, and likewise routes learned from ISP 2 to ISP 1, AS 200 would end up becoming a potential transit system for the Internet. This is because ISP 1 and ISP 2 would know that they could reach each other's Internet routes by going through AS 200. Although such a path may not appear optimal, remember that "optimal" is most often defined in BGP according to routing policy and not according to media metrics (such as hop count, load, cost, and so forth). As a result, the ISP's BGP policy may be such that AS 200 is the preferred path for certain Internet destinations.

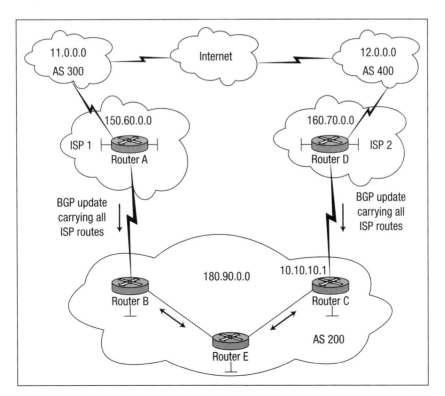

Figure 10.15 Forwarding all routes to the AS.

To prevent your AS from becoming a transit system for unwanted Internet traffic, you would configure the AS's EBGP peers with prefix filters (if you wanted to filter based just on prefix) or community or route map filters (if you wanted to filter based on various path attributes, such as weight, origin, or community). There are, in fact, many options, as we have seen thus far, and the best option may not be the most obvious. Familiarity and experience with a routing protocol as complex as BGP are of tremendous benefit to the success of any BGP implementation.

Additional Path Attribute Configurations

This chapter has already shown how route maps are used to configure some path attributes, such as metric and weight. In the coming sections, we explore some additional commands for configuring BGP path attributes and present some examples of their application in BGP policy.

Revisiting Weight

Weight, as previously stated, is a nontransitive path attribute that influences the path that intra-AS routers take to reach external destinations. We have seen that this Cisco-proprietary attribute is configured with BGP route maps, but there is, in fact, another way to configure it. The following command may be used:

```
Router(config-router)#neighbor {ip-address|peer-group} weight weight
```

This command is used in assigning a weight to a neighbor connection. All routes that are received from the neighbor will have the same weight. This approach to configuring weight may not be flexible enough for some policies, however, particularly when these policies need to be able to apply different weights to routes received from the neighbor. In such situations, a route map would be the preferable configuration method.

Figure 10.16 presents a scenario in which Router C in AS 100 is receiving advertisements from Routers A and B in AS 200 and AS 400, respectively. Both sets of advertisements include network 175.10.0.0 in AS 300, as well as certain Internet routes.

Router C has been configured to set the weight of all routes coming from Router A to 200. For network 175.10.0.0, however, Router C wishes to use the path through AS 400. Therefore, Router C uses a route map to set a higher weight for this network and applies it to Router B's updates. The following shows Router C's configuration:

```
Router_C(config)#router bgp 100
Router_C(config-router)#neighbor 2.2.2.2 remote-as 400
Router_C(config-router)#neighbor 1.1.1.1 remote-as 200
```

```
Router_C(config-router)#neighbor 1.1.1.1 weight 200
Router_C(config-router)#neighbor 2.2.2.2 route-map voyager in
!
Router_C(config)#route-map voyager permit 10
Router_C(config-route-map)#match ip address 1
Router_C(config-route-map)#set weight 1500
!
Router_C(config)#access-list 1 permit 175.10.0.0 0.0.255.255
Router_C(config)#route-map voyager permit 20
```

In the preceding configuration, Router C sets the weight of network 175.10.0.0 to 1500. Because the path with the highest weight is preferred, Router C will subsequently choose to reach this network via AS 400 rather than via AS 200.

Local Preference

Like weight, local preference is a tool for influencing the path that intra–AS routers take to reach external destinations. Unlike weight, however, this path attribute may be propagated to IBGP routers within the AS.

The two ways to configure local preference are as follows:

➤ The **bgp default local-preference** command

➤ A route map

10

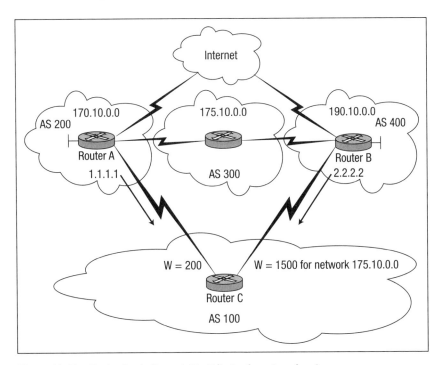

Figure 10.16 Router C sets the weight attributes for external routes.

Configuring a Default Local Preference

The first method used to configure local preference occurs by changing the default local preference value of 100 to a different value. This task is accomplished with the following command:

```
Router(config-router)#bgp default local-preference value
```

where *value* is the local preference value to be configured.

For example, in Figure 10.17, Routers C and D have been configured with default local preferences of 150 and 200, respectively. Because local preference is sent to IBGP peers within the AS, both routers exchange updates containing their respective default local preference values. For instance, Router C propagates an update for network 150.10.0.0 to Router D with a local preference of 150, whereas Router D propagates the same network to Router C with a local preference of 200. Upon receiving Router D's local preference, Router C sees that the best path to network 150.10.0.0 is via Router D because this router has the highest local preference for this route.

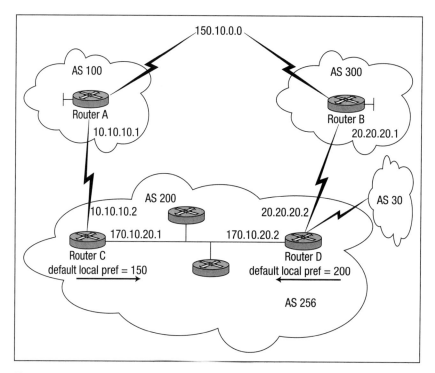

Figure 10.17 Configuring and forwarding the default local preference.

The following output shows the relevant configurations for Routers C and D:

```
Router_C(config)#router bgp 200
Router_C(config-router)#neighbor 170.10.20.2 remote-as 200
Router_C(config-router)#bgp default local-preference 150

Router_D(config)#router bgp 200
Router_D(config-router)#neighbor 170.10.20.1 remote-as 200
Router_D(config-router)#bgp default local-preference 200
```

Note in Figure 10.17 that if Router D was to receive updates from Router B in AS 300 concerning routes in AS 100 and was to propagate these routes to Router C, Router C would subsequently be required to reach any network in AS 100 by going through Router D—definitely not a desirable path.

Several possible solutions exist for this route selection problem. One solution would be to prevent Router B in AS 300 from advertising routes for AS 100 to Router D. This may not be acceptable, though, because if the link between Router C and AS 100 failed, AS 200 would then be unaware of the route through AS 300 (unless AS 200 had a default route pointing to AS 300—but assume this is not the case).

Another possible solution would be to prevent Router D from advertising AS 100's routes to its IBGP peers. But again, as in the previous solution, it would be desirable for all AS 200 routers to have an alternative route to AS 300 just in case the link between Router C and AS 100 becomes unavailable.

Perhaps the most effective solution to this problem would be to configure a route map on Router C that sets the local preference for AS 100's networks to a value higher than Router D's. With this approach, all BGP routers in AS 200 would be informed that the best route to AS 100 would be via Router C, not Router D. Moreover, AS 200 would still be receiving advertisements for AS 100 from Router D, so in case Router C's serial link became unavailable, AS 200 would be aware of the alternative route.

Consequently, route maps are a second method of configuring local preference.

Configuring Local Preference by Using a Route Map

As we have just seen, route maps have greater flexibility when configuring local preference. This flexibility affords a network's technical administrators the capability to custom fit a BGP routing policy that most accurately meets the network's goals and requirements.

The following command is used to configure local preference using a route map:

```
Router(config-route-map)#set local preference value
```

where *value* is the local preference number assigned to a route that meets the **route-map** statement **match** condition.

The following output is for Router C in the previous example. It has been designed to allow AS 200's requirements for redundancy and optimal path selection to be met with a BGP policy that uses a route map to configure local preference. Once again, the configuration is annotated:

```
Router_C(config)#router bgp 200
Router_C(config-router)#neighbor 10.10.10.1 remote-as 100
Router_C(config-router)#neighbor 10.10.10.1 route-map BSCN in
    (applies the BSCN route map to all routing updates coming from Router A)
!
Router_C(config)#route-map BSCN permit 10
    (permits any update that meets the match condition for this route map
    statement)
Router_C(config-route-map)#match as-path 1
    (tells the router to match routes with AS path access-list 1.
    AS path access lists are just like normal access lists, except
    that AS numbers replace network addresses)
Router_C(config-route-map)#set local-preference 500
    (sets the local preference of matching routes to 500)
!
Router_C(config)#route-map BSCN permit 20
    (since this is an empty route map statement, all routes that did
    not meet the above match condition will be permitted)
!
Router_C(config)#ip as-path access-list 1 permit ^100$
    (This is the AS path access list referred to in the preceding match
    condition. It tells the router to permit routes whose AS path attribute
    starts with 100 [as indicated by the ^ symbol] and ends with 100 [as
    indicated by the $ symbol]. In other words, a route is permitted only
    if it originated in AS 100.)
```

Note: AS path access lists and BGP regular expressions (such as ^ and $) are not test objectives. We used these items in the preceding configuration only because they happened to present a more efficient means of matching all routes in AS 100.

In the preceding configuration, Router C sets the local preference of all routes originating in AS 100 to 500. Router C propagates these routes to its local AS along with their local preference attribute. Routers in AS 200 would therefore use Router C to reach AS 100, whereas all other routes to external destinations would go through Router D.

BGP Redistribution

Redistribution is the process of translating routing information from one routing protocol into another. In this section, we discuss how BGP redistribution can be used as a means of learning and advertising network routes.

How BGP Advertises Routes via Redistribution

BGP advertises networks that it learns of in its BGP routing table in one of the following three ways:

➤ The **network** command

➤ Redistributing static routes into BGP

➤ Redistributing dynamic routes into BGP

Chapter 9 already covered how the first of these three methods can be used to advertise routes. We therefore focus here only on the latter two methods.

Advertising via Redistribution of Static Routes

Whenever static routes are redistributed into BGP, BGP automatically advertises the routes without requiring the **network** command. Generally, this type of redistribution is utilized only when an aggregate route (summary route) is to be created and advertised via EBGP. By using a static route to create the aggregate route, an EBGP router can summarize its AS and then redistribute the route into its BGP routing process so as to advertise it to external peers. Consequently, this is one manner in which BGP route summarization occurs.

To create an aggregate static route that will be redistributed into BGP, the following command would be used in conjunction with the **redistribute static** command:

```
Router(config)#ip route address mask null0
```

The static route is created here just like it normally would be. That is, the *address* identifies the network, and the *mask* indicates the network's subnet mask. The only difference with this version of the **ip route** command is the **null0** appendage.

The **null0** parameter is required in order to place the aggregate static route into the IP routing table. Before a route can be successfully redistributed into BGP (whether the route is static or dynamic), the route must already be known in the IP routing table, due to the BGP synchronization rule. Using the **null0** parameter allows this synchronization requirement to be met by making the router believe that there is actually a route for the aggregate static route (the router sees the **null0** interface just like any normal interface), which subsequently causes the router to place the aggregate static route into the IP routing table.

10

You may be wondering, though, why the aggregate route could not have been created by the router's IGP. Actually, it could have. If this were the situation, the router would simply redistribute the IGP into its BGP process. No aggregate static route would need to be created, and there would be no synchronization issue because the aggregate route would already be in the IP routing table.

Redistributing a static route or an IGP into BGP are two methods of causing the router to advertise an aggregate route. There is yet another method, one that does not require redistribution. This alternative method occurs through the **aggregate-address** command.

We covered the **aggregate-address** command in Chapter 9, so we will not explain it here again. Note, however, that this method of advertising an aggregate route is preferred over redistribution of an aggregate static route. The reason for this has to do with how each method responds to the aggregate route when all the networks that are being consolidated within it have gone down or become unavailable (for whatever reason). With the static redistribution method, the router will continue to advertise the aggregate route, creating a potential black hole within the network. With the **aggregate-address** command, however, the router will detect that all the aggregated networks are no longer reachable, and it will subsequently stop advertising the aggregate route. See Figure 10.18 for an example of this scenario.

In Figure 10.18, Router A is configured with an aggregate static route for network 160.10.0.0 /16, whereas Router B is configured with an aggregate route for network 170.50.0.0 /16 using BGP's **aggregate-address** command. When Router A's aggregated networks go down, it continues to advertise the aggregate route to Router C in AS 200. However, when Router B's aggregated networks go down, the networks are removed from Router B's BGP table and the aggregate route does not get advertised.

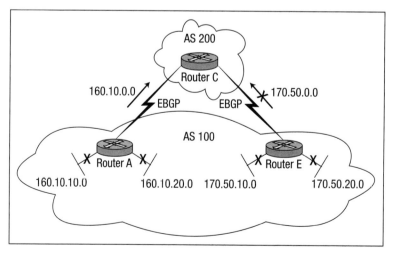

Figure 10.18 Router A continues to advertise the aggregate route when both its networks fail.

Advertising via Redistribution of Dynamic Routes

The other way in which BGP can advertise routing information is via redistributing dynamically learned routes. Generally, routes within the AS will be learned dynamically from an IGP. These IGP routes would be redistributed into the BGP routing process and advertised to BGP peers.

However, although redistributing routes from a *BGP* into an *IGP* is an acceptable practice, redistributing routes from an *IGP* into a *BGP* is not recommended. One reason is that any change in the IGP topology will cause BGP updates to be generated, possibly resulting in unstable BGP routing tables. Another reason is that routing loops could result when prefix filters are not applied with complete awareness of areas in the network where routes redistributed from BGP into the IGP are being redistributed back into BGP. Figure 10.19 shows an example of when this latter problem would occur.

In Figure 10.19, Router C in AS 300 is redistributing external routes from BGP into IGRP so that Routers B and D, who are not running BGP, can learn of the external networks. In addition, Router C is redistributing IGRP routes into BGP. However, Router C is not configured with any filter that prevents it from advertising external routes that were originally injected into IGRP and then reinjected back into BGP.

For instance, Router C injects (redistributes) external network 160.10.0.0 into IGRP and advertises it to Router B. Router B, in turn, advertises it via IGRP to Router D,

10

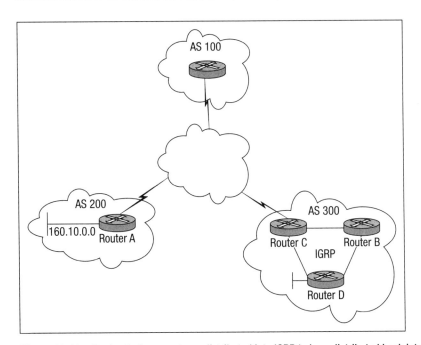

Figure 10.19   Router C allows routes redistributed into IGRP to be redistributed back into BGP.

which, in turn, passes it back via IGRP to Router C. Router C injects this external network into BGP and advertises it to its EBGP peers. Whereas AS 200 would ignore the update for this network (because the update's AS path attribute would already list AS 200), AS 100 might possibly think that it has a viable route to this network through AS 300. A routing loop would subsequently ensue if AS 100 were to start using this route.

In Chapter 13, we learn how such problems with redistribution can be handled in the most effective and efficient manner possible.

Chapter Summary

Implementing BGP in scalable ISP networks and in corporate enterprise networks is a highly involved process that requires a carefully designed and well-executed BGP routing policy. This chapter has examined several policy tools that aid scalable BGP implementations in configuring a policy that meets their networks' specific goals and requirements for controlling interdomain traffic flow.

One policy tool is the BGP route reflector, which is a router that is allowed to propagate IBGP-learned routing information to other IBGP peers. Route reflectors are used primarily in ISP ASes to counteract scalability problems caused by having to support a full IBGP logical mesh as a solution to the BGP Split Horizon rule.

The next BGP policy tool is the prefix filter. Prefix filters are used to restrict network advertisements from either being sent to or received from certain BGP peers. Distribute lists are one type of prefix filter that use standard and extended access lists, and prefix lists are another type of prefix filter that offer a more flexible and effective method of restricting updates based on prefix numbers.

Route maps are policy tools used to control and modify routing information and to define the conditions under which redistribution occurs. In relation to BGP, route maps are a highly flexible means for allowing an AS to filter routing information, create and modify BGP path attributes, and facilitate the use of communities. These and other tasks are accomplished through the configuration of route map lists, which are complex access lists that define the conditions for matching routes and specify the actions to be taken when a condition is matched.

Route maps are used to create communities, which are groups of destinations that share common attributes. Routing decisions, such as preference, acceptance, and redistribution, can be applied to communities based on their commonly shared community path attribute. The benefit of using communities comes from the fact that policy decisions can be configured for the community rather than for each individual destination contained within it.

Just as communities group destinations together, peer groups group BGP peers together. Peers that share the same update policies, such as filtering, advertising, and redistribution, can be configured as members of a peer group. The primary benefit of using peer groups is the ability to apply policies to groups of BGP neighbors without having to apply the same policy for each individual neighbor.

This chapter also presented various ways in which a corporate AS could multihome its Internet connection using BGP. These methods are classified according to how the multihomed ISPs advertise their routes via BGP to the corporate AS. One way is for the ISPs to send default routes into the AS; another way is for the ISPs to send both default routes *and* selected routes (for instance, routes that the corporate AS uses often) to the AS; and a third way is for ISPs to send *all* their routes to the AS. In all such multihoming methods, the corporate AS will send its own routes to the ISPs via BGP.

Finally, this chapter presented a short look at how BGP can use redistribution to advertise routes. This involves redistribution of either static routes, which are usually aggregate static routes, or of dynamic routes learned via an IGP.

Review Questions

1. What is the major scalability problem with IBGP?

   a. Supporting a full logical mesh between IBGP peers

   b. Running IBGP with an IGP that does not support redistribution

   c. Using route reflectors with IBGP

   d. Sustaining adequate routing policies

2. What does the BGP Split Horizon rule state?

   a. All BGP routers in an AS must be fully meshed physically.

   b. The number of TCP connections must not rise above a sustainable level.

   c. A route learned via IBGP cannot be propagated to other IBGP peers.

   d. Route reflectors must be used.

3. What is the difference between a client and a nonclient?

   a. A client can have more BGP neighbors than a nonclient.

   b. Nonclients are not BGP routers, whereas clients are.

   c. Unlike a client, a nonclient cannot establish a peering session with a route reflector.

   d. A client is an IBGP peer of a route reflector that resides within the same cluster, whereas a nonclient is an IBGP peer of a route reflector that resides in a different cluster.

10

4. Which of the following is a major design requirement for route reflector networks?

    a. Multiple clusters must exist.

    b. All route reflectors in the AS must be fully meshed logically.

    c. A cluster must contain only one route reflector.

    d. The physical topology should not be followed when designing a route reflector network.

5. Which one of the following does not accurately describe route reflector operation?

    a. If the update is from a client peer, the route reflector propagates the update to both its client and nonclient peers.

    b. If the update is from a nonclient peer, the route reflector propagates the update to only its client peers.

    c. If the update is from an EBGP peer, the route reflector propagates the update to both its client and nonclient peers.

    d. If the update is from an IGP peer, the route reflector propagates the update to only nonclients.

6. Choose the command that configures a route reflector client:

    a. **neighbor 183.120.20.32 route-reflector**

    b. **neighbor 183.120.20.32 route-reflector-client**

    c. **neighbor 183.120.20.32 client-route-reflector**

    d. **neighbor 183.120.20.32 reflector**

7. What do prefix filters do?

    a. They filter routing advertisements based on the next-hop address.

    b. They modify updates' prefixes.

    c. They filter routing updates based on prefix.

    d. They filter and modify routing updates based on prefix.

8. Which command successfully applies an outbound distribution list to a neighbor?

    a. **neighbor 150.93.39.2 permit ip distribute-list out**

    b. **neighbor 150.93.39.2 ip distribute-list 1 out**

    c. **neighbor 150.93.39.2 1 distribute-list out**

    d. **neighbor 150.93.39.2 distribute-list 1 out**

9. When configuring distribute lists, what is one advantage to using an extended access list rather than a standard access list?

   a. The ability to filter only an aggregate route.

   b. The ability to match network addresses that are using various protocols.

   c. Unlike standard access lists, extended access lists can filter based on community.

   d. Standard access lists can filter only on the outbound.

10. Which of the following are advantages to using prefix lists instead of access lists? [Choose the two best answers]

   a. With prefix lists, there is no **implicit deny any**.

   b. Support for incremental modifications.

   c. The ability to match routes based on various path attributes.

   d. Greater flexibility.

11. In what order do prefix lists match routes?

   a. Starting with the first prefix list statement

   b. Starting with the statement with the lowest sequence number

   c. Starting with the first statement that has the lowest address

   d. Starting with the statement configured with the highest priority name

12. Which of the following commands successfully configures a prefix list?

   a. **ip prefix-list permit 185.16.82.0 voyager out**

   b. **prefix-list 185.16.82.0 voyager out permit**

   c. **ip prefix-list 185.16.82.0 /24 voyager permit out**

   d. **ip prefix-list voyager permit 185.16.82.0/24**

13. What does the **neighbor prefix-list** command do?

   a. It applies the prefix list to updates received from or sent to a neighbor.

   b. It specifies which neighbors are not to be sent any routing updates.

   c. It prevents the neighbor from advertising routes.

   d. It applies the prefix list only to updates sent to a neighbor.

14. Which command displays information about a prefix list, including the description and hit count?

   a **show ip prefix-list summary**

   b. **show ip prefix-list name**

   c. **show ip prefix-list detail**

   d. **show prefix-list**

10

15. What are two reasons for using BGP route maps?

    a. To filter networks

    b. To modify path attributes

    c. To create peer groups

    d. To develop a map of the network topology

16. Which of the following features are shared by both access lists and route maps? [Choose the two best answers]

    a. The ability to make incremental modifications to the list

    b. Permitting and denying routes

    c. The implicit **deny any**

    d. A number that identifies the list

17. What occurs when a route passes through a route map without forming a match?

    a. The route is permitted.

    b. The route is stored until it can form a match.

    c. The route is denied.

    d. The route is modified and then denied.

18. Which set of commands successfully configures a route map?

    a. `Router(config)#route-map voyager permit 10`
       `Router(config-route-map)#match address 1`
       `Router(config-route-map)#set weight 30`

    b. `Router(config)#route-map permit voyager 10`
       `Router(config-route-map)#match ip address 1`
       `Router(config-route-map)#set weight 30`

    c. `Router(config)#route-map voyager permit 10`
       `Router(config-route-map)#match ip address 1`
       `Router(config-route-map)#set weight 30`

    d. `Router(config)#route-map voyager 10 permit`
       `Router(config-route-map)#match address ip 1`
       `Router(config-route-map)#set weight 30`

19. What is the correct interpretation of the following command:

```
Router(config)#access-list 1 permit 10.10.0.0 0.0.255.255
```

    a. Permit a route whose address matches 10.10.0.0 exactly.

    b. Permit a route whose address matches 10.10.0.0 and whose subnet mask is 255.255.0.0.

    c. Permit a route whose address matches the first two bytes of 10.10.0.0.

    d. Permit a route whose address matches the first two bytes of 10.10.0.0 and whose subnet mask is 255.255.0.0.

20. What is a BGP community used for?

    a. Grouping destinations so that routing decisions can be applied to the group rather than to individual destinations

    b. Implementing a routing policy in which BGP peers are grouped

    c. Creating a route map

    d. Grouping destinations that have different attributes so that one policy can be applied to the group instead of to each individual destination

21. What does the **no-export** community attribute specify?

    a. Not to advertise an update tagged with this community value to any IBGP peers

    b. Not to advertise an update tagged with this community value to any BGP peers

    c. Not to advertise an update tagged with this community value outside the AS

    d. A BGP peer that is not allowed to communicate with external neighbors in certain ASes

10

22. What is a BGP peer group?

    a. A group of BGP peers that share the same update policies

    b. A group of EBGP peers that are to use the same community value

    c. A compilation of all routes that have certain path attributes that are the same

    d. A cluster that contains multiple route reflectors

23. Which one of the following is a requirement for peer groups?

    a. Peer groups must always have members that reside within the same AS.

    b. Members must not be configured with different outbound update policies.

    c. Members of a peer group must be fully meshed logically.

    d. Peer groups must be designed with fewer than 100 members.

24. Choose the correct peer group configuration:

    a. `Router(config-router)#neighbor voyager peer-group permit`

       `Router(config-router)#peer-group voyager neighbor 10.10.10.1`

    b. `Router(config-router)#neighbor voyager peer-group`

       `Router(config-router)#neighbor 10.10.10.1 voyager`

    c. `Router(config)#neighbor voyager peer-group permit`

       `Router(config-router)#neighbor 10.10.10.1 voyager`

    d. `Router(config-router)#neighbor voyager peer-group`

       `Router(config-router)#neighbor 10.10.10.1 peer-group voyager`

25. Which of the following is not a common multihoming solution?

    a. All connected ISPs use BGP to forward only default routes to the AS.

    b. All connected ISPs use an IGP to forward static routes to the AS.

    c. All connected ISPs use BGP to forward default routes and certain selected routes to the AS.

    d. All connected ISPs use BGP to forward all their routes to the AS.

Real-World Projects

In the following real-world projects, we examine a corporate AS's routing policy and choose the appropriate tools that will allow us to implement this policy with maximal effectiveness and minimal work.

Company XYZ is looking to scale its BGP enterprise to include a multihomed Internet connection and a routing policy that will control transit routing information from the two ISPs to which it connects. Figure 10.20 shows the logical topology.

The following policies were drafted by the company's technical administrators:

➤ Configure Router E in AS 200 as a BGP route reflector and specify its IBGP peers as clients.

➤ On Router C in AS 200, prevent routing updates for any network in 12.0.0.0 from being accepted from Router D in ISP 2.

➤ Allow Router B in AS 200 to advertise only a summary route for network 180.90.0.0 /16 to Router A in ISP 1.

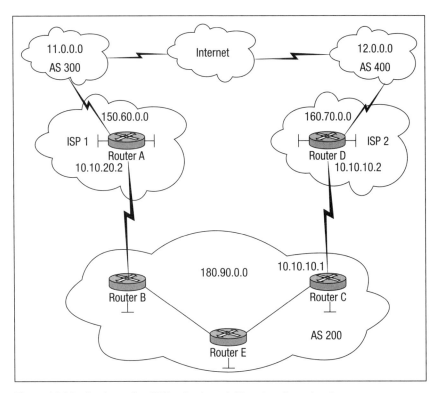

Figure 10.20   Implementing BGP policy in scalable enterprise networks.

10

➤ Make AS 200 prefer the path to network 11.0.0.0 that goes through ISP 1.

➤ Based on the community attribute received from Router D in ISP 2, allow Router C in AS 200 to accept a routing update from this neighbor only if the update's community value originates from ISP 2.

As one of the technical administrators for the company, it is your task to configure the above policies on the appropriate routers by using the most effective and efficient means you have learned from reading this chapter.

Using this chapter and Cisco's online documentation as reference guides, you decide to start first with Router C.

Project 10.1

To prevent routing updates for any network in 12.0.0.0 from being accepted from ISP 2's Router D (policy 2):

1. Go into router configuration mode and specify that Router D is an EBGP neighbor:

```
Router_C(config)#router bgp 200
Router_C(config-router)#neighbor 10.10.10.2 remote-as 2
```

Router C will subsequently establish an EBGP peering session with Router D.

2. Apply a standard distribute list to all routing updates received from Router D:

```
Router_C(config-router)#neighbor 10.10.10.2 distribute-list 1 in
```

Access list 1 must now be created.

3. Create an access list that denies network 12.0.0.0 but permits all other networks:

```
Router_C(config)#access-list 1 deny 12.0.0.0 0.255.255.255
Router_C(config)#access-list 1 permit 0.0.0.0 255.255.255.255
```

The first **access-list** statement forms a match with any route whose first byte is 12. These routes are denied. The second **access-list** statement permits all other routes, which includes any route whose first byte is not 12.

The last policy that you need to configure on Router C is policy 5.

To allow Router C in AS 200 to accept a routing update from Router D
only **if the update's community value originates from ISP 2 (policy 5):**

1. In router configuration mode, apply a route map named "picky" to all routing updates received from Router D:

```
Router_C(config)#neighbor 10.10.10.2 route-map picky in
```

Router C will subsequently apply the picky route map to all updates received from Router D.

2. In route-map configuration mode, create a match condition that allows Router C to match an update's community attribute *exactly* with community list 1:

```
Router_C(config)#route-map picky permit 10
Router_C(config-route-map)#match community 1 exact
```

The first line in this **route-map** statement tells the router to permit any update that forms a match. The second line forces the update to be matched exactly with community list 1. If the update forms a match with this community list, the update will exit out of the route map process.

3. Create a community list that permits a community attribute that has the value 2 listed in it:

```
Router_C(config)#ip community-list 1 permit 2
```

Any update with a community attribute value of 2 will be permitted. Because the earlier match condition appends the **exact** keyword, the update will form a match with the **route-map** statement if and only if its community attribute specifies just one community value, 2.

4. Let the implicit **deny any** that exists at the end of the route map prevent all other updates from being accepted from Router D.

This will have the effect of preventing all routing updates that originate outside of ISP 2 from being accepted from Router D. In addition, any update received from Router D without a community attribute (even if originating from ISP 2) will be denied.

This concludes the policy configuration on Router C. You decide to next configure Router D.

Project 10.2

To allow Router B to advertise *only* a summary route for network 180.90.0.0 /16 to ISP 1's Router A (policy 3):

1. Enter router configuration mode and specify that Router A is to be a BGP peer:

```
Router_B(config)#router bgp 200
Router_B(config-router)#neighbor 10.10.20.2 remote-as 1
```

Router B in AS 200 subsequently establishes an EBGP peer relationship with Router A in ISP 1.

2. Create a prefix list named "ISP1a" that allows only the summary route 180.90.0.0 /16 to be permitted.

```
Router_B(config)#ip prefix-list ISP1a permit 180.90.0.0/16
```

The absence of the *le* and *ge* parameters implies an exact match will try to be formed with 180.90.0.0 /16. The implicit **deny any** will deny any route that does not form an exact match with 180.90.0.0 /16.

3. Apply the ISP1a prefix list to all routing updates sent to Router A:

```
Router_B(config-router)#neighbor 10.10.20.2 prefix-list ISP1a out
```

As a result of the preceding configurations, the only route that will be advertised to Router A is 180.90.0.0 /16.

The last policy you will configure on Router B is policy 4.

10

To make AS 200 prefer the path to network 11.0.0.0 through ISP 1 (policy 4):

1. In global configuration mode, specify a route map named "ISP1b" that permits updates that form a match with succeeding match conditions:

   ```
   Router_B(config)#route-map ISP1b permit 10
   ```

2. After entering route map configuration mode, specify a match condition that tells the router to match updates with access list 1:

   ```
   Router_B(config-route-map)#match ip address 1
   ```

3. Next, specify a set action that will give matching updates a local preference of 400:

   ```
   Router_B(config-route-map)#set local-preference 400
   ```

   Any route that forms a match with the above access list will acquire a local preference of 400.

4. In global configuration mode, create a standard access list that matches updates whose first byte begins with 11:

   ```
   Router_B(config)#access-list 1 permit 11.0.0.0 0.255.255.255
   ```

   Routes that do not form a match with this access list will move on to the next **route-map** statement

5. Specify an empty **route-map** statement for the ISP1b route map:

   ```
   Router_B(config)#route-map ISP1b permit 20
   ```

   An empty **route-map** statement implies that all updates that do not form a match with the preceding match conditions are permitted. As a result, Router B limits the routing policy only to network 11.0.0.0. All other networks remain totally unaffected by what has transpired here with this route map configuration.

6. Apply the ISP1b route map to all updates received from Router A:

   ```
   Router_B(config-router)#neighbor 10.10.20.2 route-map ISP1b in
   ```

   Upon receiving an update from Router A in ISP 1, Router B applies the ISP1b route map to it. If the update contains an advertisement for any network in

11.0.0.0, Router B sets the network's local preference to 400. Because local preference is propagated within an AS, Router B propagates the network along with its local preference. Because routes with the highest local preference are preferred, all BGP routers within AS 200 will subsequently see that the best path to networks in 11.0.0.0 are via Router B and via ISP 1.

This concludes policy configuration for Router B. If you have not already delegated this task of configuring BGP policy to somebody else (always a smart option, right?), your last project is to configure Router E's policy.

Project 10.3

To configure Router E in AS 200 as a BGP route reflector and specify its IBGP peers as clients (policy #1):

1. In router configuration mode, specify that neighbors 180.90.10.2 and 180.90.20.2 (Routers B and C, respectively) are BGP neighbors:

```
Router_E(config)#router bgp 200
Router_E(config-router)#neighbor 180.90.10.2 remote-as 200
Router_E(config-router)#neighbor 180.90.20.2 remote-as 200
```

Router E subsequently establishes an IBGP peer relationship with both Router B and Router C.

2. Specify that Router E's IBGP neighbors are to become route reflector clients:

```
Router_E(config-router)#neighbor 180.90.10.2 route-reflector-client
Router_E(config-router)#neighbor 180.90.20.2 route-reflector-client
```

Note there is no specific command that makes Router E a route reflector. It becomes a route reflector when it establishes clients.

Your policy configuration is complete. Well done.

10

CHAPTER ELEVEN

Managing Network Traffic and Congestion

After completing this chapter, you will be able to:

✓ Understand what causes network congestion

✓ Identify ways to reduce network traffic

✓ Describe the functions of access lists

✓ Describe how routing updates can be optimized

There is no question that day by day the load on computer networks increases. But put on hold the purchasing decision to acquire a whole new set of network equipment because there are many things that you can do to curb the outflow of cash. Not only that, throwing money at the problem to purchase faster and more efficient equipment doesn't necessarily guarantee results.

It turns out that there is much more to network traffic than just running your network applications. In fact, much of the traffic may be due to overhead in just keeping the network happy and functioning. This chapter details what causes this overhead and shows how to analyze a situation to reduce or eliminate some of this overhead.

Congestion Overview

Network congestion occurs whenever the traffic exceeds available bandwidth. This is analogous to our typical highway system. If the roads can handle 10,000 cars in an hour and there are 15,000 cars, then there is congestion. It is unlikely that the roads will be able to handle those 15,000 cars in an hour.

The highway analogy drops off rapidly because traffic patterns for networks are very different. For instance, roads typically handle traffic in one direction, whereas network media often handle traffic in two directions. This is referring to the same "pavement" and not to a two-direction road. In addition, network traffic has a very "bursty" nature, and it has the ability to "throw away" packets (you can't toss cars off a road despite the frequent desire to do so sometimes). Still, the highway model does provide some very good insights into the way that we must deal with congestion in a computer network.

Traffic in an IP Network

There are many sources of traffic in an IP network. This is not an exhaustive list, nor is it broken down in typical OSI fashion, but rather these are the types of applications and/or devices that might actually create the traffic.

➤ High-level user applications

➤ Low-level applications

➤ Routing protocol updates

➤ Encapsulated protocol transport

Figure 11.1 shows the types of traffic that must compete for the available bandwidth of a link.

High-Level User Applications
The traffic generated by user applications is the familiar client/server model and nearly always has a mapping with a desktop application. Much of this traffic falls

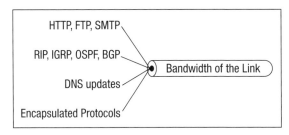

Figure 11.1   IP traffic to travel along a link.

into these protocols: HTTP (Web browsing), FTP (file transfer), SMTP (electronic mail), NNTP (news), and even Telnet (terminal). Many other applications (such as audio and video) embed themselves into one of these streams.

Low-Level Applications

The world has a word-based, rather than numbers-based, language. The Domain Naming System (DNS) mapping of names to numbers (or host/domain to machine) as well as numbers to names generates a significant amount of IP traffic in one of the world's largest fully distributed database systems. Most of the updates between primary and secondary name servers happen outside of the user's knowledge (although if they fail, the users definitely know about it).

In addition, protocols designed for diagnostics, monitoring, or statistics gathering, such as ICMP packets or SNMP packets, can create a fair amount of traffic just to keep things humming along.

Routing Protocol Updates

Whenever a network topology changes, or when time-to-live counters expire, routers transmit their routing information to other routers. This keeps networks humming along and minimizes packet loss due to no-route-to-host errors.

Encapsulated Protocol Transport

Depending on network topology, some traffic may be encapsulated into another protocol and transmitted across a large IP network, such as the Internet. This is often true in Novell or AppleTalk networks, or networks that are somewhat less scalable and less prevalent. Typically, border or near-border devices transparently embed the associated packets (such as IPX and AppleTalk) into IP packets, enabling less scalable and extendable protocols to travel the larger domain of IP networks—likely the Internet. The border devices often generate a substantial amount of traffic to keep their logical links up.

Encrypted traffic, or the use of a Virtual Private Network (VPN), is an encapsulation method. In this case, one could encapsulate IP as well as any other protocol with

11

some level of security such that when the traffic passes through a public network such as the Internet, the information is safe from "prying eyes."

Traffic in a Mutliprotocol Network

IP may be king for large-scale networks, but there are still plenty of small to medium businesses that do not use IP. Also, IP is a relative newcomer as a deployed network protocol. Yes, it is winning favor and will likely defeat the other protocols in the long run, but plenty of shops are migrating or in a plan-to-migrate stage. This is particularly true when you consider the entire world. Although the Internet has drawn North America into the TCP/IP family, much of the rest of the world uses other protocols, such as IPX/SPX.

Protocols such as IPX and AppleTalk each have layers that match or somewhat match the OSI network model, just as IP does. Each of these protocols has its own associated network overhead. In fact, one of the nice things about IP is its minimization of chat. One simply has to put a sniffer on an IPX or AppleTalk network (or even a segment that has NetBEUI) to see how much traffic goes by even if presumably there is no user traffic.

The following items in these protocols (in addition to IP) generate their own overhead and contribute to the consumption of the precious network bandwidth:

➤ *Service broadcasts*—The availability of resources such as printer servers or file servers

➤ *Address Resolution Protocol (ARP)*—The mapping of physical addresses to logical addresses

➤ *Keepalives*—For connection-based protocols

➤ *Time-to-live (TTL) updates*—To minimize the storage requirements on both the source and destination ends

Figure 11.2 shows some of the network protocols, including IP, that may travel along a network link.

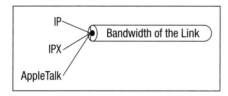

Figure 11.2   Multiprotocol network.

Managing Congestion

What can be done when network congestion is present? Obviously, the network cannot transmit more than it is capable of. At some point, traffic (or traffic requirements) must be reduced or rescheduled. Some mechanisms to do just this follow:

➤ Filter broadcasts

➤ Filter application traffic

➤ Change or increase timers for updates

➤ Switch tables from dynamic to static

➤ Control router overhead

Filter Broadcasts

Periodic broadcasts, such as Service Advertisement Protocols (SAPs), broadcast continuously at specified intervals. Often, these types of broadcasts should be limited to a specific segment of a network, and shouldn't be transmitted elsewhere. After all, is it that useful to broadcast worldwide a printer physically located in Germany? Other times, it is more useful to lengthen the time between broadcasts because indeed sometimes it is useful to advertise services across segments, just not so frequently.

Note: If you increase the intervals for broadcasts, there is increased latency between the time that a device may change its service offerings and the time that the broadcast actually occurs. Depending on the robustness of applications, this could prove sticky to track down. Application code should have the ability to fail-over if resources cannot be attached that are obviously broadcast as available—but we all know how well some network software is written.

Filter Application Traffic

Sometimes it is necessary to filter or block application traffic. Access lists can be implemented to limit traffic by service so that a particular type of traffic cannot pass through critical links.

Some corporations allow HTTP traffic (often Web-based) on an after-hours basis but not during the business day. This type of policy, although well-intentioned, will likely crumble over time as more and more business-to-business applications come online. Originally, this restriction was intended to prevent employees and other personnel from "surfing the Web" to places such as ESPN or stockbroker sites. Now, it is a matter of blocking sites rather than traffic—a task for a proxy of sorts, not a border router.

11

Change or Increase Timers for Updates

Some protocols periodically transmit information to their peers, clients, or servers. The intervals between these transmissions can be lengthened, thus reducing traffic and therefore the bandwidth requirements. SAP notifications are one such example. You can adjust the time interval between these updates.

Switch Tables from Dynamic to Static

Routers utilize routing protocols to periodically transmit information to their neighbors or distant routers so that traffic flow is maintained, adaptable, and efficient. However, in many scenarios the traffic is well known, so there is little need to have a dynamic nature. Embedding static routes eliminates the need to dynamically advertise network routes across certain links. A combination of this type of management as well as reducing the intervals for dynamic links can drastically improve performance over a slow link such as a serial or dial-up line.

By converting from dynamic to static, you also lose the benefits of having a dynamic network. Often, static routes are very difficult to maintain because it sometimes requires having a very up-to-date network map and a bird's-eye view of the "world." As long as you are confident that this will not be an issue, it is fine. But remember that performance degradation due to the existence of dynamic routing packet overhead is infinitely preferable over downtime due to routing problems.

The other side of this coin is that an error in a dynamic route can quickly propagate to other areas of the network—carried by routing protocols. Although this is easier to fix because the correction is just as easily transmitted, it still can wreak a lot of havoc in the meantime.

Control Router Overhead

Some routing protocols are more efficient in maintaining information than others. For instance, neither RIPv1 nor IGRP transmit the subnet mask—they rely on the class information intrinsic to the network address. By not transmitting this information with router updates, the overhead is measurably less than a routing protocol such as Open Shortest Path First (OSPF), especially with very large routing tables. This works very well in very small networks, but there is a price to pay with large networks.

As already demonstrated in earlier chapters, large networks can have very large routing tables. A distance-vector-based routing protocol would have all participating routers transmit their entire routing tables to every neighboring router in the internetwork. Converting to a link-state routing protocol (for many other reasons as well), limits the amount of traffic generated because only deltas or link changes are sent, rather than the whole table. Consider a routing table of 1,000 entries with 200 routers. Even if an entry is only a few bytes in length, there are still several orders of magnitude in data not transmitted with a route change. Remember also that distance-vector protocols transmit everything at periodic intervals as short as 30 seconds, so large amounts of data are not only transmitted, they are transmitted all of the time.

The point here is that you can somewhat control the overhead by choosing the right class of routing protocol. Keep in mind that the class may choose your network before you choose the routing protocol. If your network is very large, you will probably need a link-state protocol. Otherwise, all the cons of a distance-vector protocol will rear their ugly heads.

IP Access Lists

It may seem odd, but Cisco introduced access lists as a security measure—hence the name "access list." These lists determine whether an incoming packet had access or authorization to be forwarded to a destination through an interface. It was, and still is, a mechanism for authorizing people to remotely log in to the router for configuration. So although security continues to have a presence, access lists are used more frequently to control traffic flow in an overall network.

From our list of mechanisms for managing congestion, two can be controlled using access lists. These are the abilities to filter broadcasts and to filter application traffic. Access lists are good at filtering traffic—in fact, that is what they do.

Filtering Traffic

When filtering traffic, or implementing access lists, two key points are important to understand. Like any other process, one that is implemented poorly can yield equally poor results. Worse, the symptoms may not show up until either traffic increases dramatically, or the network design is scaled accordingly. This time period may be weeks or months down the road. The key points to understand are the following:

➤ Access control list (ACL) processing requirements

➤ Application requirements

Access Control List Processing

The CPU behind a Cisco IOS router must execute instructions at a high level in an orderly fashion. The presence of an ACL creates more work for the CPU, and therefore a router with an ACL will be less efficient at processing packets than a router without an ACL. An ACL is a set of rules that the router explicitly follows. Knowledge of these rules and an understanding of how to take advantage of them are key to routing and network performance.

For instance, it is important to know that IOS processes use *short-circuit evaluation*. As the CPU goes through its list of rules, once it finds a rule that explicitly allows traffic it no longer traverses the access list, it just passes the traffic. This efficiency can turn a long ACL into a short list for a good percentage of the traffic. So even though you may have some really obscure rules that get invoked on maybe 0.001 percent of the packets, it is best if the CPU didn't actually have to test for them each and every time that it processed a packet. Therefore, obscure rules for allowing traffic should go to the bottom of the ACL, whereas the most common rules for denying traffic should go to the top of the ACL.

Note: Actual details of the processing are covered in Chapter 12.

It is clear that ACLs require both memory and CPU cycles to process. The ACL requirements will sometimes dictate the model and accessories (such as the memory capacity) of a router.

Tip: "Getting a bigger gun" is not always the way to go. That is, if you see performance issues in a router, getting a bigger, faster, smarter model is not the way to go. Often, looking at the way the router processes information can save thousands of dollars in what would be minimal gains. A 2x performance in optimizing rules is definitely going to be cheaper than purchasing a router that has 2x the CPU horsepower. The results may be the same, but your pocketbook (or your company's) will definitely feel it.

Application Requirements

You should know a bit about your network and how traffic flows. This isn't evident in the physical makeup of a network. You want to validate traffic as it enters a corporate environment, or the perimeter, before passing it through. This isn't just for security measures. Often, traffic that doesn't belong on a network inadvertently (or sometimes not so inadvertently) clogs the network. This is particularly true in environments that use CSMA/CD such as Ethernet. Collisions cause delays and retransmits and even more congestion. So, traffic not bound for a destination should be removed at the earliest entry point.

Note: Early denial of service (DoS) attacks have preyed on layers 2 and 3. By creating ICMP traffic over and over, valid traffic simply couldn't get through. A reasonable way to eliminate the traffic, therefore, was to eliminate the request at the perimeter. That way, the DoS packets could not do their damage on the inside.

When to Use Access Lists

Access lists need not be used everywhere. As stated earlier, the mere presence of an access list will diminish the performance of a router. The complexity of the rule set determines by how much. Discussion of these common reasons to use access lists follows:

➤ At Internet access points

➤ To protect subnets

➤ To restrict application traffic

➤ To trigger dial-on-demand routing

➤ To prioritize and custom queue

➤ For route filtering

Internet Access Points

Most companies would prefer that people on the Internet not be able to access their networks. Certainly, key personnel occasionally (perhaps traveling and on the road) need to enter via the Internet, but for the most part, access from the outside is a big no-no. Figure 11.3 shows a perimeter router that is essentially between the corporate network and the Internet.

Many connection-based protocols, such as HTTP, FTP, and Telnet, have to be initiated from one host. The target host is often on the other side of a router. A router can detect which interface initiates the connection and determine whether traffic should pass. By using this information, an administrator can establish an ACL that prevents passing of traffic that is initiated on the *outside* interface or is attached to the Internet, while allowing traffic that is initiated on the *inside* interface or the corporate network. Access lists do provide a basic level of logging denied as well as accepted packets. Figure 11.4 shows this particular design, where the rules are logical rather than actual.

Much as people would like to think so, a router is not a great security device even though it can be loosely called a firewall. Most firewalls do not act as routers as they statefully examine each packet at the service protocol level. Although access lists do provide logging, they do not do so at the level that a proxy firewall would.

11

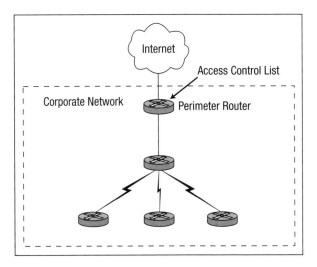

Figure 11.3 Perimeter router to the Internet.

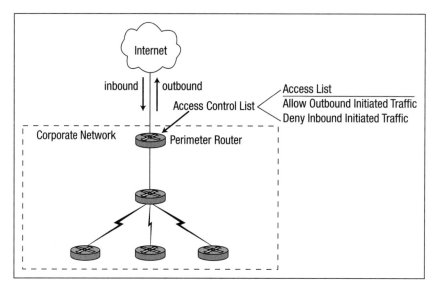

Figure 11.4 Perimeter router with simple access control list.

In addition, from a forensic point of view, putting an access control list on a perimeter router prior to the firewall can hinder analysis of all the data because an access control list explicitly denies certain types of traffic. The logging of this traffic can be invaluable in determining the techniques of a hacker. For instance, port scanning is the first stage of an attack. Yet, if the perimeter router blocked all but one or two service protocols, the downstream firewall would not be able to detect port scanning.

Do not construe this as extra security similar to a "belts and suspenders" action. A firewall is meant as a security device, whereas a router is meant to pass packets. Having a router do double duty is fine for small installations, but it probably is inadequate for a large or scaled installation.

In any case, a proper corporate management security policy—something that is mandated and approved by management, not IT—will dictate the implementation. However, it is an IT professional's job to educate management.

Protecting Subnets

The larger a corporation grows, the more people, and thus departments, start to specialize. Finance, research and development, marketing, sales, engineering, and executive staff start to take advantage of networking resources. Subnets and nets start to partition themselves along these corporate lines.

For practical reasons, it is unlikely that engineering staff have anything to do with the finances of the company aside from following budgetary constraints. They have little need, therefore, to access resources on that subnet. Internal corporate *trust* can be set up and implemented on a series of routers throughout the organization

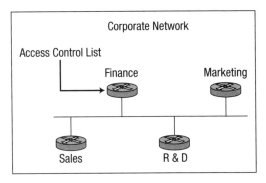

Figure 11.5   Guarding the finance subnet.

much in the same fashion as was done to protect the Internet from the corporate network. In this fashion, for example, engineering, or any other division, is blocked from accessing servers on the finance side. Figure 11.5 illustrates this setup.

Restricting Application Traffic

Some segments can be set up with the whole idea that they will be carrying only one or two types of traffic—say, NNTP news or SMTP mail. Router filters and access lists can be established to prevent any other traffic from entering that particular zone. These access lists focus not only on the source and destination of the packets, but also on the service field. TCP services have a designated service field; the most common of these are listed in Table 11.1. Chapter 12 covers these services in greater detail.

Triggering Dial-on-Demand Routing

An access list can monitor for specific types of traffic or, in fact, any kind of traffic to trigger a modem or an ISDN terminal adapter to connect to a remote system. These events are useful in the following types of situations:

➤ When costs for links are prohibitively expensive for permanent leased lines, such as international dialing

➤ When leased lines are unavailable, such as in remote areas

Table 11.1   Common services and their TCP ports.

Service Name	Common Name	TCP Ports
FTP	File Transfer Protocol	20, 21
Telnet	Telnet, Remote Terminal	23
SMTP	Electronic Mail	25
POP3	POP Mail	110
NNTP	Network News	119

➤ When primary links are down and a backup link is required

➤ When extra bandwidth is required during peak periods

Prioritizing and Custom Queuing

Many customers still use virtual terminal (Telnet) access for their legacy databases. Even though graphical user interface applications are very appealing, hundreds if not thousands of applications still exist, and it seems most of them are in the realm of large legacy database applications. End user primary access is Telnet, remote shell (rsh), 3270-emulation, or ssh (secure shell). When the same media (Ethernet, leased serial lines, dial-up modem, FDDI, and Token Ring, for example) are used to carry this type of traffic in addition to HTTP, video applications, audio applications, electronic mail, and so on, drastic congestion problems can result. In that case, all the protocols suffer equally.

Because these legacy database applications are often the heart of the business (if these systems go down, the business goes down)—typically representing customer information, billing, invoicing, inventory management, and so forth—this traffic must have priority over, say, an employee listening to a RealAudio playback of a baseball game. Policy violation issues aside, some protocols can have priority over other protocols. The routers can rate the service protocols to allow mission-critical applications to run more smoothly than nonmission applications. This is a good example of the benefit of establishing a finer granularity of control with access lists.

Route Filtering

Distribution lists and route maps provide different methods for determining what should go into a routing update. Access lists can control and filter the attributes within a routing update for route maps. For a distribution list, access lists can be used to control the contents of a routing update. This is detailed in the next section.

Reducing Routing Update Traffic

There are several ways to reduce routing update traffic. Reducing the traffic allows the transport media to more effectively handle data traffic, which is most likely the reason for the network in the first place. Some methods to reduce traffic are as follows:

➤ Changing routing protocols from distance-vector to link-state

➤ Using static and default routes

➤ Using summary routes

➤ Filtering content of updates

Changing Routing Protocols from Distance-Vector to Link-State

You can radically reduce routing update traffic by switching from a distance-vector protocol to a link-state protocol—moving from RIPv1 to OSPF, for instance. When a distance-vector protocol sends updates, it sends the entire contents of the routing table. Link-state protocols, on the other hand, transmit only incremental updates concerning a single route. The savings can be immense, depending on the complexity of the network or the size of the routing table.

Using Static and Default Routes

Default routes can represent one of the most effective ways to handle traffic—especially at an end node of a network, or where there is little choice but to travel beyond a network through a single router. Rather than store information on where traffic should be forwarded, simply pass it to an upstream router to handle it. Default routes are also used to send traffic upstream to much larger networks, such as the Internet.

Static routes can be used to augment a system that has a limited number of paths to other places. Static routes are simple and elegant. On the other hand, they are also often overlooked and difficult to manage in a dynamic network, a network that is in transition, or one that changes frequently. Many times the dependency on static routes bites IT professionals when the topology changes.

Neither static routes nor default routes accompany other route information when performing route updates. So, keeping in mind the downsides, when the opportunity presents itself, you should consider this as yet another way to minimize traffic in the routing updates.

Using Summary Routes

The use of summary routes, covered in Chapter 3, can also reduce the amount of information sent in a routing update. Effectively, a group of networks organized hierarchically under a common prefix can be consolidated into a single advertised route. Depending on the implementation of the design and how hierarchical the system, the cost savings can be enormous. Subnetting a single network by five bits, for example, can reduce the number of routing table entries by 31 (32 routes can be reduced to 1). Add this to the data portion that a routing protocol transmits, and a substantial amount of information *doesn't* get transmitted.

Filtering Content of Updates

The Cisco IOS has two commands, **route-map** and **distribute-list**, that can be used to control the amount of information included in a routing update.

Filtering Routing Updates Outbound

We have discussed how to reduce the traffic in routing protocols in general. Now let us shift the discussion to optimization on an individual router in the form of what gets transmitted to neighboring routers. This section and the previous section may overlap a bit, mostly due to overlap of the general with the specific. These optimizing solutions are:

➤ Static route

➤ Summary route

➤ Passive interface

➤ Outbound route filter

Static Route

Static routes are important only on the router where they were created. These routes are not included in any router updates and are not propagated to any neighboring routers. It is possible, however, to explicitly mark them for redistribution. For the most part, because these routes are not propagated, they do not contribute to the size of the route table and thus do not contribute to any increase in traffic.

Summary Route

Although a summary route has little effect on the routing table of the router where the summarization occurs (because it still has all of the routes for all the networks in the subnetted network), there is a dramatic effect upstream. By definition, the summary takes many networks and consolidates them into a single route (or a handful of routes). Sending, say, 1 route instead of the 50 routes that are represented in a summary can drastically alter the traffic due to any routing update.

Passive Interface

You can prevent a router from generating regularly scheduled routing updates on a specific interface that is configured as a passive interface. The router will accept routing updates on that interface, but it will not generate traffic bound for that subnet, nor destined for nets downstream. Because this occurs on an interface-by-interface basis, routing updates can occur on some interfaces but not others.

Outbound Route Filter

You can add a special outbound route filter to selectively remove routes from a transmitted routing update. This is done by the use of the **distribute-list** command. The routing table will have more routes than are transmitted to neighboring routers. As with the passive interface, the **distribute-list** command can be applied on an interface-by-interface basis.

Decreasing the Routing Table

The basic optimization on the routing table is to shrink it. After all, a small routing table implies several advantages:

➤ Less CPU processing is used to find a match.

➤ Routing updates are smaller.

➤ It is easier to understand.

So, it is advisable to do whatever is necessary to keep the size of these tables down. This can be done by the following methods:

➤ Applying a route filter inbound

➤ Using a default route

Applying a Route Filter Inbound

With **distribute-list** statements, an inbound route filter will selectively remove routes from an arriving route update. If route redistribution is occurring, the **distribute-list** can be applied to the routing process receiving the routes, or it can be applied to an arriving interface.

Using a Default Route

The default route concept is fairly easy. It is not necessary to populate a route table with every route in the system if the bulk of the routes go to a specific neighboring router. Simply designating this router as the default route and then eliminating all the rules that would have traffic travel to it eliminates the bulky routes. The remaining routes go to other destinations.

11

Chapter Summary

As a network grows, like any other system, it can encounter traffic congestion. Although we don't cover here all of the elements that can cause the congestion (that is likely the topic for an entirely new set of books because it spans the entire OSI model), we do discuss the contributing factors.

Numerous means of limiting congestion exist; we discuss here all of the ways that pertain to network design. However, the routing protocol, surprisingly, can generate a substantial amount of traffic. Of all the types of traffic, this is one over which the network engineer has direct control and very real abilities to help contain.

We introduce the concept of access lists and how they can be used to reduce and block unnecessary traffic. Chapter 12 goes into the actual configuration of these access lists.

Review Questions

1. Which of the following contribute to traffic in an IP network?

    a. An encrypted tunnel between routers

    b. Routing protocol updates

    c. Route table caches

    d. High-level user network applications

2. Which of the following solutions is a reasonable mechanism to reduce traffic on a network?

    a. Add routers to isolate traffic.

    b. Switch routing tables from static to dynamic.

    c. Separate networks into logical groups.

    d. Filter broadcasts.

3. What are some of the features of an access list?

    a. A list of rules that control whether packets are denied or allowed

    b. A security measure for the router

    c. A method of determining whether a route table is applied

    d. An authentication method for end users

4. Which of the following will make an access list more efficient?

    a. Put obscure deny rules at the top of the list.

    b. Put frequent or common deny rules at the top of the list.

    c. Put obscure allow rules at the top of the list.

    d. Put frequent or common allow rules at the top of the list.

5. Which of the following are reasons to employ access lists?

    a. To protect subnets

    b. To prioritize and custom queue

    c. To filter routes

    d. To freely enable all traffic

6. Which of the following can be restricted using an access list?

    a. Electronic mail from a specific user

    b. Electronic mail from a specific host

    c. Electronic mail

7. Which of the following solutions are reasonable mechanisms to reduce routing update traffic?

   a. Switch from a link-state routing protocol to a distance vector protocol.

   b. Make use of default routes.

   c. Make use of static routes.

   d. Make use of access lists.

8. How do static routes reduce the routing update traffic?

   a. Static routes do not propagate as part of the routing protocol.

   b. Static routes minimize the route table.

   c. Static routes employ mechanisms to prevent routes on an interface from being propagated.

9. What are ways to decrease the size of an individual router's route table?

   a. Use a default route.

   b. Use static routes.

   c. Apply a route filter outbound.

   d. Apply a route filter inbound.

Real-World Project

Because this chapter has no configuration options, this project covers the diagnostic thought process rather than actually working on physical equipment. Also, because the diagnostic process is the process of elimination, we do not necessarily go down each path—only a specific path. However, knowledge of the decisions used to choose a path is far more important than the details of the path itself.

11

Project

Gadget, Inc., is faced with a problem. It has a network application that is incredibly slow. Its entire business operates on this application because it handles ordering, provisioning, purchasing, inventory, and other related business items. Six months ago, the network performance was acceptable. Lately, the delays have been unbearable.

Gadget also uses the Internet as a transport for its Virtual Private Networks for all of its remote sites—30 of them in total.

Because this is a networking course, we start off with this problem being a network problem. Otherwise, we would start off determining whether it was a networking problem, which would be pointless in this book.

1. Find out how the application uses the network.

It turns out that the network application uses TCP/IP.

2. Find out which service ports the network application uses.

The network application uses TCP ports 7780 and 7781.

3. Monitor the traffic on your network and determine what else uses the network. You may be required to use profiling tools. Some can interrogate a router to determine the traffic broken down by TCP port. Other products, such as a network sniffer, can do the same.

There seems to be a fair amount of HTTP and FTP traffic in addition to traffic on 7780 and 7781. For the purposes of this example, let us call it BUZ.

4. Find out how important HTTP and FTP are to your organization. It may turn out that HTTP is crucial to your organization, or it may not be important at all. Also find out where the traffic goes.

All FTP traffic goes to the Internet. A fair amount of HTTP traffic goes to the Internet, although a substantial amount of internal HTTP traffic exists (an intranet, perhaps). It turns out that HTTP traffic is crucial but not critical. FTP traffic is neither crucial nor critical.

Because FTP is not that important, and HTTP is important but probably not as important as the custom business application, it is best to prioritize the protocols (the actual process is covered in Chapter 12).

Because Gadget uses the Internet as a transport for traffic to its remote sites, you cannot merely diminish access to the Internet. So, by increasing the priority for all traffic on the BUZ TCP port or by decreasing the priority for the HTTP and FTP protocols, you effectively ensure that the BUZ application traffic goes through at the expense of the other protocols.

You could also lower the priority of FTP in relation to HTTP. This would give better performance to people that use Web-based applications now that you have reduced their priority relative to the BUZ traffic.

You could also have purchased a bigger pipe to the Internet, but that would have cost money. The savings here is that you have improved performance despite the network restraints.

CHAPTER TWELVE

Managing Network and Device Access

After completing this chapter, you will be able to:

✓ Configure Internet Protocol (IP) standard and extended access lists

✓ Limit virtual terminal, Hypertext Transfer Protocol (HTTP), and Simple Network Management Protocol (SNMP) access

✓ Verify access list operation

✓ Explain reflexive, context-based, and dynamic access list types

✓ Given a set of network requirements, configure an access list to limit access to your network and verify proper operation (within described guidelines) of your routers

✓ Configure an alternative to using access lists (Null Port)

✓ Explain the use of Cisco Easy IP

✓ Explain how Domain Name System (DNS) and Dynamic Host Configuration Protocol (DHCP) are used to manage IP addresses

✓ Configure an IP helper address to manage broadcasts

A ccess lists have been introduced and discussed in earlier chapters. In this chapter, we look at using access lists and non-access list features to manage access to network features and devices that allow the administrator to increase security and manage bandwidth. One of the most critical functions of managing IP traffic is balancing the need to eliminate unwanted traffic with facilitating appropriate user access to necessary resources. We need to be sure that a solution to one problem does not create another problem for a different group of users.

The Cisco IOS offers a rich set of tools for reducing unwanted traffic (often broadcasts) while assisting necessary broadcasts to navigate through the network.

Access List Basics

Access control lists (ACLs) are the basic tools for managing IP traffic. An *access list* is a sequentially processed collection of **permit** and **deny** statements that filter data packets based on source addresses or upper-layer protocols. The two types of IP access lists are *standard* and *extended*. Standard IP access lists filter all IP traffic based exclusively on source address. Extended IP access lists offer more control by filtering based on source address, destination address, or protocol characteristics.

Creating an access list is a two-part process. First, the list is created—one condition per line—in *global configuration* mode, and then it is applied in *interface configuration* mode. A wide variety of options exist for the syntax of an access list, the basic one being the following:

```
Router(config)#access-list [list number] [permit|deny] [conditions defined]
--after last access line is a nondisplayed "deny everything else" command--
Router(config-if)#ip access-group [list number] [in|out]
```

An implicit **deny any** ends every access list; therefore, the list must contain at least one **permit** statement to specify what can pass through, or everything will be blocked (denied). The following is a simple standard access list that will block all IP traffic from network 192.168.1.0 from exiting interface e0.

```
Router#config t
Router(config)#access-list 50 deny 192.168.1.10 0.0.0.255
Router(config)#access-list 50 permit any
Router(config)#int e0
Router(config-if)#ip access-group 50 out
```

We will look at the wildcard (0.0.0.0) and the keyword (**any**) in the next two sections. The first access list line defines the network to be denied. The second line allows all traffic from any other networks or the Internet. The last two lines select the interface and direction of traffic to be filtered. Figure 12.1 shows the above access list.

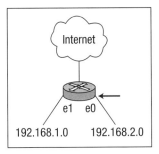

Figure 12.1 Simple standard access list.

By applying the access list to Ethernet0 as an outbound list, we do not prevent network 192.168.1.0 from accessing the Internet, as we would have had we applied it to Ethernet1 as an inbound list.

Wildcard Masks

Wildcard masks in both standard and extended IP access lists are the inverse of *subnet masks*. Like an IP subnet mask (or IP address), a wildcard mask is a 32-bit value written in dotted-decimal format. Address bits corresponding to wildcard mask "1" bits are ignored; address bits corresponding to wildcard mask "0" bits are used in comparisons.

Remember that subnet masks are all binary ones from left to right and then all zeros indicating the boundary between network and host address. Wildcard masks are just the opposite—all binary zeros from left to right and then all ones with the zero(s) indicating the host address range. For this reason, 1 bits in the mask are referred to as "don't care" bits. If no mask is specified, the mask is assumed to be 0.0.0.0. Table 12.1 shows some examples of wildcard masks.

Mask Keywords

Two keywords, **any** and **host**, can be used to define IP addresses with masks in either standard or extended access lists. The keyword **any** matches all addresses and is equal to 0.0.0.0 255.255.255.255. The keyword **host** causes the address that follows

Table 12.1   Access list wildcard mask examples.

Address	Mask	Matches
0.0.0.0*	255.255.255.255	All addresses
141.100.1.16/16	0.0.255.255	Entire network 141.100.0.0
141.100.1.16/16	0.0.0.0	Only host 141.100.1.16
141.100.1.16/21	0.0.7.255	141.100.0.0 to 141.100.7.255

* This could actually be any IP address.

12

it to be treated as if it were specified with a mask of 0.0.0.0. The following is a simple standard access list that demonstrates each keyword.

```
Router#config t
Router(config)#access-list 50 deny 192.168.1.10 0.0.0.0
Router(config)#access-list 50 permit 0.0.0.0 255.255.255.255
Router(config)#access-list 90 deny host 192.168.1.10
Router(config)#access-list 90 permit any
```

Access list 50 uses full coding, whereas list 90 uses the keyword.

Access List Processing

When creating access lists, order is very important. You should create the condition line entries in order from specific to general. The router processes the conditions from top to bottom until a match is found or no conditions apply. The first condition match determines whether the router permits or denies the packet. Because the router stops processing conditions after the first match, the order of the list is critical. If no conditions match, the router denies the packet, that is, discards it. This is an important concept to remember when creating access lists. The last "invisible" entry in every access list is what is known as an implicit **deny any**. Traffic not explicitly permitted is implicitly denied.

To filter a specific host address and then permit all other addresses, for example, make sure your entry about the specific host appears first.

The following code, although overly simple, would permit all traffic at the first access list line and would therefore never process the second command. Network 192.168.1.0 would meet the conditions of the first line.

```
Router#config t
Router(config)#access-list 50 permit any
Router(config)#access-list 50 deny 192.168.1.10 0.0.0.0
Router(config)#int e0
Router(config-if)#ip access-group 50 out
```

Access List Numbering

Access lists are numbered to indicate the type of access list and to help in list management. Each filter criteria line in a particular list shares the same list number, and that number is used when applying the list to an interface. Table 12.2 shows the most common types of access lists and the available list number ranges. The range 300 to 699 has been omitted; it is used to support older protocols such as AppleTalk, XNS, and DECnet.

Table 12.2   Common access lists and number ranges.

Range	Access List Type
1-99	IP standard access list
100-199	IP extended access list
200-299	Protocol type-code access list
700-799	48-bit Appletalk address access list
800-899	IPX standard access list
900-999	IPX extended access list
1000-1099	IPX Service Advertisement Protocol (SAP) access list
1100-1199	Extended 48-bit MAC address access list
1200-1299	IPX summary address access list
1300-1999	IP standard access list (expanded range)
2000-2699	IP extended access list (expanded range)

Among the uses for access lists are the following:

➤ To control the traffic of packets on a router interface

➤ To access virtual terminal connections

➤ To restrict contents of routing updates

➤ To determine the "interesting" traffic that initiates a dial-on-demand routing (DDR) connection

➤ To filter input traffic to other technologies, such as priority and custom queuing

Access lists can be applied to a network interface or a virtual terminal line. When access lists are applied to one or more interfaces, they can filter either inbound traffic or outbound traffic, depending on the configuration. To the extent that inbound access lists can preserve router resources, they are generally considered to be more efficient and are preferred over outbound lists. This is because a router with an outbound access list must fully process and switch every packet before it uses the access list criteria to determine whether to forward or discard the packet.

Inbound Access List Processing

For inbound access lists, upon receiving a packet, the router checks it against the access list condition. If the access list condition permits the packet, the router exits the access list and continues to process the packet. If the access list condition denies the packet, the router discards the packet and returns an Internet Control Message Protocol (ICMP) *Admin Denied* message. If the list condition does not apply, the next list condition is tested until a condition has been met or the packet is discarded. Figure 12.2 diagrams how an inbound access list is processed.

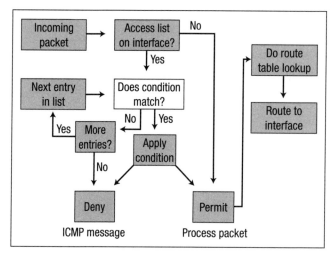

Figure 12.2 Inbound access list processing.

Any packets discarded at this point do not use any router resources such as central processing unit (CPU) time or buffer space for switching to an outbound port.

Outbound Access List Processing

After receiving, processing, and switching a packet to a controlled interface, the router checks the packet against the access list condition. If the access list condition permits the packet, it is transmitted. If the access list condition denies the packet, the router discards it and returns an ICMP *Admin Denied* message. If the list condition does not apply, the next list condition is tested until a condition has been met or the packet is discarded. Figure 12.3 diagrams how an outbound access list is processed.

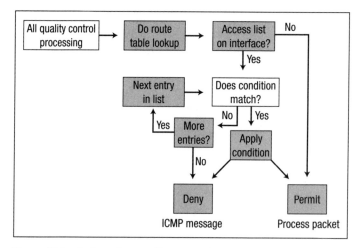

Figure 12.3 Outbound access list processing.

Documenting Numbered IP Access Lists

Cisco IOS version 12.0 introduced the **remark** keyword for documenting both standard and extended access lists. The keyword appears immediately after the access list number and is followed by the comment or remark. An example might look like the following code:

```
Router(config)#access-list 50 remark block traffic from sales network
Router(config)#access-list 50 deny 192.168.1.10 0.0.0.255
Router(config)#access-list 50 remark allow traffic from other networks
Router(config)#access-list 50 permit any
Router(config)#int e0
Router(config-if)#ip access-group 50 out
```

Using Named Access Lists

Since Cisco IOS release 11.2, you can use a text name for access lists, which allows you to create more than 99 standard and 100 extended access lists. The benefits of using named access lists are:

1. The name can be meaningful and indicative of the list's purpose. This is a particularly important feature for documentation and maintenance purposes, and it will also benefit anyone who has to support your ACLs later.

2. It is possible to selectively delete specific lines within a named access list, which cannot be done with numbered lists.

You should consider the following points before creating named access lists:

➤ Named access lists are not compatible with older IOS releases (before release 11.2).

➤ A standard access list and an extended access list cannot have the same name. This rule really means no two access lists can have the same name—not an unusual requirement.

➤ Names must begin with an alphanumeric character and are case sensitive. Within the name almost any character can be included.

➤ Only access lists for packet filters and route filters on interfaces—not all types of access lists—can use a name.

Named access lists have a different format than other access lists. The initial line establishes the type and name of the list. This access list statement is followed by one or more **permit** or **deny** statements. The following is an example of a named standard access list:

```
Router(config)#ip access-list standard accounting_access
Router(config-std-nacl)#permit 192.168.3.0 0.0.0.255
Router(config-std-nacl)#permit 192.168.4.0 0.0.0.255
```

```
Router(config-std-nacl)#permit 192.168.5.0 0.0.0.255
Router(config-std-nacl)#permit host 192.168.6.50
Router(config-std-nacl)#interface serial 0
Router(config-if)#ip access-group accounting_access out
```

The following is how the preceding access list looks if you show the running configuration. Note the change in the order and the removal of the wildcards.

```
!
ip access-list standard accounting_access
 permit 192.168.6.50
 permit 192.168.3.0
 permit 192.168.4.0
 permit 192.168.5.0
!
```

Next is an example of a named extended access list:

```
Router#configure terminal
Router(config)#ip access-list extended server-screen
Router(config-ext-nacl)#permit tcp any host 192.168.2.20 eq 80
Router(config-ext-nacl)#permit tcp host 192.168.1.151 host 192.168.2.20
Router(config-ext-nacl)#int s1
Router(config-if)#ip access-group server-screen out
```

The following is how this access list looks if you show the running configuration. Note that the TCP port 80 was replaced with the acronym **www**.

```
!
ip access-list extended server-screen
 permit tcp any host 192.168.2.20 eq www
 permit tcp host 192.168.1.151 host 192.168.2.20
!
```

Editing an Access List

It is not possible to reorder access list items or to edit them in place. A possible solution to this problem follows. First, create a new access list with a different access list number. This could be as simple as copying and pasting the existing list into Notepad and, while making your edits, changing the access list number. Then paste the new list back into the global configuration.

Second, use the **ip access-group** command to apply the new access list to the router interface. Because there can be only one per direction (per network protocol), the new access list replaces the old one. Be aware that you will not have filtering on that interface while the router replaces the old access list. If this few seconds creates an unacceptable security breach, use the **ip shutdown** command to stop IP traffic during the changeover. The following code is an example of applying access list 151 to replace 150:

```
config term
interface ethernet 0
ip shutdown
ip access-group 151
no ip shutdown
```

Access List Rules and Suggestions

The mixture of rules and suggestions in the following descriptions will help you to create access lists that will have the intended results.

Top-Down Processing

Because access lists are evaluated sequentially from top down, organize your list so that the more specific references within a network or subnet appear before the more general ones. To improve performance, frequently occurring conditions should always appear before less frequently occurring conditions if possible. For example, because IP packets include Transmission Control Protocol (TCP), User Datagram Protocol (UDP), and Internet Control Message Protocol (ICMP), it makes sense to filter those protocols before filtering IP so that you don't "throw the baby out with the bath water."

Standard List Filtering

Because standard lists are limited to blocking all IP traffic based on source address, you may find that standard lists are of somewhat limited usefulness. If you need any finesse at all, you will probably require an extended access list.

New Lines Always Append to the End

Planning is crucial. Any new lines are always added to the end of the access list. You cannot change the order of the list or selectively insert or remove lines when using numbered access lists. When using IP named access lists (Cisco IOS release 11.2 and later), you can remove specific lines but you still cannot reorder the lines.

Implicit Deny Any

Unless you add an explicit **permit any** to the end of your list, it will by default deny *all* traffic that fails to match any of the access list permit lines. You must therefore have at least one permit statement or you will block all traffic. You are defining what traffic you want to permit—but sometimes it is easier to define what traffic you do not want.

12

Undefined Access List Means **permit any**

Since Cisco IOS release 10.3, if you apply an access group to an interface before any access list lines have been created, the result will be an implicit **permit any**. In earlier releases, an undefined access list caused everything to be denied—an implicit **deny any**. The conservative approach would be to create your access list before you apply it to an interface.

List Application

Apply the access list with the **access-group** command in the interface configuration mode. Until you do, there is no filtering.

Access List Placement

In general, place *extended access lists* as close to the source as possible to reduce the router resources required to process the packet. Why route a packet all the way through the network only to kill it off later? Place *standard access lists* close to the destination—this is necessary (although not desirable) due to the limitation of being able to filter only on the source address. Obviously, if the access list can be placed closer to the source without introducing unintended results, that is a bonus.

Inbound vs. Outbound Lists

When determining whether an access list should be inbound or outbound, always assume you are standing in the middle of the router. The direction is relative to the router, not the network. The default is outbound if you do not specify **in**.

Router-Generated Packets

Router-generated packets, such as routing table updates, cannot be acted upon by an outbound access list. Therefore, they must be filtered on an inbound access list.

Fragmented Packets

IP permits fragmentation of large packets into smaller ones (fragments) in order to cross networks that support only smaller packet sizes. Therefore, extended access lists check only the initial fragment of a fragmented packet set. Additional fragments are permitted without testing, which creates a potential problem if you are using access lists as a security tool.

Standard Access Lists

Standard access lists filter based exclusively on the source address of the packet. The IP standard access list number range is 1 to 99. These lists can be applied to a router interface or to a virtual terminal connection to limit Telnet sessions into the router. The two basic access list commands are **access-list** and **ip access-group**.

Creating a Standard Access List

The **access-list** command is used to create each condition of the list using one condition per line. The lines are processed sequentially and cannot easily be reordered once they are in place. The syntax for each line in the list is:

```
access-list access-list-number (permit | deny)
  [source [source-wildcard] | any] [log]
```

The **access-list** keyword must be hyphenated and must begin each statement. The **access-list-number** range for IP standard access lists is 1 to 99. The **permit** or **deny** choice determines whether the list allows or discards the packet—there is no default, you must choose one. The **source** or **any** option allows you to specify an IP address, with or without the optional **wildcard** mask, or you can use the keyword **any**, which allows all addresses.

The **log** option (since version 11.3) results in logging packets that meet the condition. How logging occurs is controlled with the **logging console** command. Generally, the first event is logged and then every 5 minutes a summary is logged. A sample logging might look like this:

```
list 50 permit 192.168.1.10 1 packet
```

Five minutes later, it might look like this:

```
list 50 permit 192.168.1.10 73 packets
```

The lines are added to the router configuration and processed in order of entry. New lines are always appended to the bottom of the list. It is not possible to insert or remove lines from the access list. Generally, it is good practice to configure your access lists using a separate text editor such as Notepad rather than directly to the router interface, particularly for longer, more complex access lists. You will still use the router interface for some access lists, particularly in isolating problems during troubleshooting.

Watch out for common errors found in access list lines, such as the following, which are probably configuration errors:

➤ `access-list 70 permit 142.98.0.0`

➤ `access-list 70 permit 0.0.0.0`

The first address is a network address and would never be assigned to a host, so no packets would ever pass. Networks and subnets are always specified with explicit masks. It was probably supposed to be:

```
access-list 70 permit 142.98.0.0 0.0.255.255
```

12

The second mistake is probably missing the host address. The 0.0.0.0 by itself is not a valid host address and does not mean all networks, so no packets would ever pass.

Applying a Standard Access List

The **ip access-group** command links an existing access list to an interface. Each interface may have one inbound and one outbound access list for each network-layer protocol supported. The syntax for each line in the list is:

```
ip access-group access-list-number (in | out)
```

The **ip** indicates the protocol. The **access-group** keyword must be hyphenated and follows the IP statement. The **access-list-number** range indicates which list is to be applied to the interface. **In** or **out** determines whether the list checks inbound or outbound packets—**out** is the default if you do not specify one. Always view this decision as if you are standing in the center of the router—it is in to the router not in to an adjacent subnet.

A single access list may be applied to more than one interface on a router at a time by using the **ip access-group** command in interface configuration mode for each interface. All interfaces in the group will implement the **access-list** statements.

Removing a Standard Access List

To remove the entire list, type **no access-list access-list-number** in global configuration mode, or you can unapply the list by typing the **no ip access-group access-list-number** command while in the interface configuration mode. The following code demonstrates both techniques.

```
Router#config t
Router(config)#no access-list 50
Router(config)#int e0
Router(config-if)#no ip access-group 50
```

If you remove the list but leave the **access-group** command on newer versions of the IOS, the result is the same as if there was a single **permit any** list item. Older versions defaulted to a **deny any** and would therefore block all traffic.

Location of Standard Access Lists

Generally, you want to place standard access lists as close to the destination router as possible in order to exercise the most control. Figure 12.4 shows a simple network with two subnets, 192.168.1.0 and 192.168.2.0.

If we want to prevent users in 192.168.1.0 (or even a single host) from accessing the server in 192.168.2.0, we could apply an outbound list on e0 or an inbound list on e1. By applying it to the e0 interface, the 192.168.1.0 users can still access the

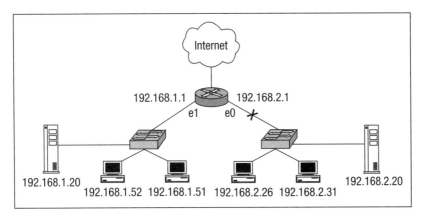

Figure 12.4 A two-subnet network with an access list.

Internet; that would not be true if we applied it to e1. The following code would block the entire network:

```
Router#config t
Router(config)#access-list 50 deny 192.168.1.10 0.0.0.0
Router(config)#access-list 50 permit any
Router(config)#int e0
Router(config-if)#ip access-group 50 out
```

Similarly, the following code would block a single host from the network:

```
Router#config t
Router(config)#access-list 60 deny host 192.168.1.52
Router(config)#access-list 60 permit any
Router(config)#int e0
Router(config-if)#ip access-group 60 out
```

Standard Access List Example

The information in Figure 12.5 shows a simple network with two subnets, 192.168.1.0 and 192.168.2.0, and an Internet connection.

The following code represents the access lists applied to our router in this example:

```
Router(config)#access-list 10 permit host 195.168.2.20
Router(config)#access-list 10 permit 195.168.1.20 0.0.0.255
Router(config)#access-list 20 deny 195.168.2.26 0.0.0.255
Router(config)#access-list 20 permit host 195.168.2.20
Router(config)#access-list 20 permit any
Router(config)#int s0
Router(config-if)#ip access-group 10 out
Router(config)#int e1
Router(config-if)#ip access-group 20 out
```

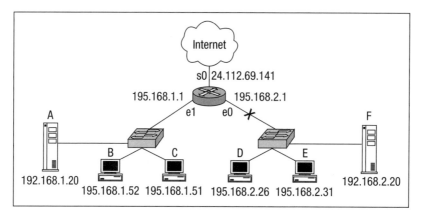

Figure 12.5 A two-subnet network with an Internet connection.

Who can access the Internet?

➤ User F is explicitly allowed by line 1 of access list 10.

➤ Users A, B, and C are allowed implicitly by line 2 of access list 10.

➤ Users D and E are denied by the implied **deny any** for access list 10.

Who can access Server A (195.168.1.20)?

➤ Users B and C—they have the same subnet and no filtering.

➤ Users D, E, and F are denied implicitly by line 1 of access list 20.

➤ Any Internet users are allowed implicitly by line 3 of access list 20.

Why doesn't line 2 of access list 20 allow Server F (195.168.2.20) to reach Server A (195.168.1.20)?

➤ Line 1 of access list 20 has already killed off the packet.

Extended Access Lists

Standard access lists are relatively easy to configure, and they use minimal CPU resources because each list is based on a single criterion—the source address of the packet. As such, an extended access list is very similar to a security guard at a building site—if you have a badge, you get in; if not, you don't. Extended access lists provide a higher level of control by being able to filter based on the session-layer protocol, source and/or destination IP address, and application port number. These features make it possible to limit traffic based on the uses of the network. Figure 12.6 shows a simple network with two subnets, 192.168.1.0 and 192.168.2.0.

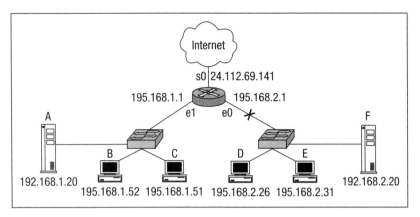

Figure 12.6   A two-subnet network with an access list.

With the standard access list, we can only block all IP traffic from a single user or all addresses from the 192.168.1.0 network. With an extended access list, we can block a user (or all addresses) in the 192.168.1.0 network from accessing the File Transfer Protocol (FTP) services on the 192.168.2.20 server while still allowing other services.

Creating an Extended Access List

As with standard lists, the **access-list** command is used to create each condition of the list—using one condition per line. The lines are processed sequentially and cannot easily be reordered once in place. The IOS version 12.x syntax for each line in the list is:

```
access-list access-list-number (permit | deny)
  (protocol | protocol keyword) (source source-wildcard | any) [source
port]
  (destination destination-wildcard | any) [destination port] [options]
```

The **access-list** keyword must be hyphenated and must begin each statement. The **access list-number** range for IP extended access lists is 100 to 199. The **permit** or **deny** option determines whether the list allows or discards the packet—because there is no default, you must choose one.

The **protocol** entry defines the protocol to be filtered, such as IP, TCP, UDP, or ICMP, for example. Because IP headers transport TCP, UDP, and ICMP, it is important to specify the protocol or you could end up inadvertently filtering more than

12

you want to. The **protocol** keyword could include **eigrp**, **gre**, **icmp**, **igmp**, **igrp**, **ipnip**, **nos**, or **ospf**, among others.

The **source source-wildcard | any** functions the same as for standard access lists, including the keywords **host** and **any**. The optional **source port** can be specified as a port number, such as 80, or as a mnemonic or acronym, such as HTTP.

The **destination destination-wildcard | any** functions the same as the source address, including the keywords **host** and **any**. The optional **destination port** can be specified as a port number, such as 80, or as a mnemonic or acronym, such as HTTP. The options for TCP, UDP, and ICM are covered in the following sections.

The optional **options** feature includes the **log** feature discussed earlier in the standard access lists section. Another option is **established**, which filters TCP to restrict traffic to only one direction by searching the TCP packet to see if the ACK (acknowledge) or RST (reset) bit is set.

With extended access lists, every condition listed in the **access-list** statement must match for the statement to match and the **permit** or **deny** condition to be applied. As soon as one condition fails, the next line in the access list is compared. Figure 12.7 shows how each line of an extended access list is processed.

So many options are available for filtering with extended access lists that you should use the question mark (**?**) **help** feature to look at all of the possibilities. We cover the most common ones in the next sections.

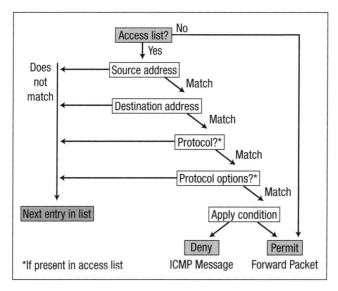

Figure 12.7 Extended access list processing.

TCP Syntax

The access list **tcp** option supports both source and destination ports. You can access each by using either the port number or a mnemonic or acronym. Keyword relational operators such as those shown in the following code output precede these.

```
2504Router(config)#access-list 101 deny tcp any ?
  A.B.C.D  Destination address
  any      Any destination host
  eq       Match only packets on a given port number
  gt       Match only packets with a greater port number
  host     A single destination host
  lt       Match only packets with a lower port number
  neq      Match only packets not on a given port number
  range    Match only packets in the range of port numbers
```

After choosing an option such as **eq**, you specify a mnemonic (or acronym) or port number, such as those shown in the following code output for the TCP port names.

```
2504Router(config)#access-list 101 deny tcp any eq ?
  <0-65535>     Port number
  bgp           Border Gateway Protocol (179)
  chargen       Character generator (19)
  cmd           Remote commands (rcmd, 514)
  daytime       Daytime (13)
  discard       Discard (9)
  domain        Domain Name Service (53)
  echo          Echo (7)
  exec          Exec (rsh, 512)
  finger        Finger (79)
  ftp           File Transfer Protocol (21)
  ftp-data      FTP data connections (used infrequently, 20)
  gopher        Gopher (70)
  hostname      NIC hostname server (101)
  ident         Ident Protocol (113)
  irc           Internet Relay Chat (194)
  klogin        Kerberos login (543)
  kshell        Kerberos shell (544)
  login         Login (rlogin, 513)
  lpd           Printer service (515)
  nntp          Network News Transport Protocol (119)
  pim-auto-rp   PIM Auto-RP (496)
  pop2          Post Office Protocol v2 (109)
  pop3          Post Office Protocol v3 (110)
```

12

```
smtp          Simple Mail Transport Protocol (25)
sunrpc        Sun Remote Procedure Call (111)
syslog        Syslog (514)
tacacs        TAC Access Control System (49)
talk          Talk (517)
telnet        Telnet (23)
time          Time (37)
uucp          Unix-to-Unix Copy Program (540)
whois         Nicname (43)
www           World Wide Web (HTTP, 80)
```

Using the **?** in place of the port number when typing the command allows you to verify the port number associated with a protocol name. Other port names can be found in RFC 1700.

TCP's Established Option

The **established** option is available only with TCP because it uses the connection-oriented attributes of the TCP. The **established** option is true only when the TCP ACK or RST bits are set. Because it matches an already established connection, it must have been precipitated by the source host, not an outsider. Note, however, that it is possible that **SYNchronize** messages used to establish a new connection from the outside can then be explicitly or implicitly denied. This could help reduce a common type of hacker attack that buries a host in **SYN** requests, preventing the host from handling normal business.

Consider the three-step "handshake" that TCP uses to establish a connection. Figure 12.8 demonstrates this process.

Assume that the objective is to stop Host B from initiating a TCP connection with Host A while still permitting A to initiate connections with B. If you create a standard access list to block IP packets from B, it will in fact stop B from initiating a TCP

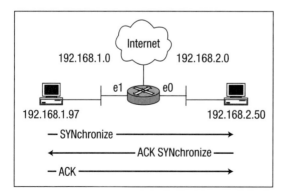

Figure 12.8 Establishing a TCP connection process.

session, but it will also block any TCP session initiated by A because the acknowledge (**ACK SYNchronize**) from B will never be allowed back.

Because the packet being blocked is coming from Host B, it isn't possible for the router to send an ICMP message to Host A. Host A will then appear to hang until it gets a TCP time-out.

A possible solution, using the **established** option might look like this:

```
access-list 150 permit tcp host 192.168.2.50 host 192.168.1.97 established
access-list 150 deny tcp host 192.168.2.50 host 192.168.1.97
```

The **established** keyword permits sessions to be initiated in one direction but not the other—without it, TCP time-outs may occur. Since Cisco IOS version 10.3, the **established** option can be configured on statements with ports specified. Earlier versions allowed only the established option on TCP access list statements without specific port numbers.

Note: Source port filtering, the process of filtering data on the source port of a packet, is not secure because a hacker could change a source port. A hacker could easily create a packet with a different source port that could pass through the filter.

UDP Syntax

The access list **udp** option (RFC 768), like **tcp**, supports both source and destination ports. Using either the port number or mnemonic (or acronym) can access each. Keyword relational operators such as those shown in the following code output precede these.

```
2504Router(config)#access-list 101 permit udp any ?
  A.B.C.D  Destination address
  any      Any destination host
  eq       Match only packets on a given port number
  gt       Match only packets with a greater port number
  host     A single destination host
  lt       Match only packets with a lower port number
  neq      Match only packets not on a given port number
  range    Match only packets in the range of port numbers
```

After choosing an option, such as **eq**, you specify a mnemonic (or acronym) or port number such as those shown in the following code output for the UDP port names.

```
2504Router(config)#access-list 101 permit udp any eq ?
  <0-65535>  Port number
  biff       Biff (mail notification, comsat, 512)
  bootpc     Bootstrap Protocol (BOOTP) client (68)
```

12

```
bootps         Bootstrap Protocol (BOOTP) server (67)
discard        Discard (9)
dnsix          DNSIX security protocol auditing (195)
domain         Domain Name Service (DNS, 53)
echo           Echo (7)
isakmp         Internet Security Association and Key Management Protocol
               (500)
mobile-ip      Mobile IP registration (434)
nameserver     IEN116 name service (obsolete, 42)
netbios-dgm    NetBios datagram service (138)
netbios-ns     NetBios name service (137)
netbios-ss     NetBios session service (139)
ntp            Network Time Protocol (123)
pim-auto-rp    PIM Auto-RP (496)
rip            Routing Information Protocol (router, in.routed, 520)
snmp           Simple Network Management Protocol (161)
snmptrap       SNMP Traps (162)
sunrpc         Sun Remote Procedure Call (111)
syslog         System Logger (514)
tacacs         TAC Access Control System (49)
talk           Talk (517)
tftp           Trivial File Transfer Protocol (69)
time           Time (37)
who            Who service (rwho, 513)
xdmcp          X Display Manager Control Protocol (177)
```

ICMP Command Syntax

The access list **icmp** option (RFC 792) allows filters on **icmp-type**, **icmp-code**, and **icmp-message**. After designating **permit/deny** and the source and destination addresses, include the ICMP code or type (numbers 0 to 255). Since Cisco IOS version 10.3, you can use symbolic names to make configuration and understanding complex lists easier. You no longer need to use cryptic message numbers such as 0 to filter the ping **echo-reply**.

The following code includes the symbolic names you can use:

```
2504Router(config)#access-list 101 permit icmp any any ?
  <0-255>                      ICMP message type
  administratively-prohibited  Administratively prohibited
  alternate-address            Alternate address
  conversion-error             Datagram conversion
  dod-host-prohibited          Host prohibited
  dod-net-prohibited           Net prohibited
  echo                         Echo (ping)
  echo-reply                   Echo reply
  general-parameter-problem    Parameter problem
```

host-isolated	Host isolated
host-precedence-unreachable	Host unreachable for precedence
host-redirect	Host redirect
host-tos-redirect	Host redirect for TOS
host-tos-unreachable	Host unreachable for TOS
host-unknown	Host unknown
host-unreachable	Host unreachable
information-reply	Information replies
information-request	Information requests
log	Log matches against this entry
log-input	Log matches against this entry, include input interface
mask-reply	Mask replies
mask-request	Mask requests
mobile-redirect	Mobile host redirect
net-redirect	Network redirect
net-tos-redirect	Net redirect for TOS
net-tos-unreachable	Network unreachable for TOS
net-unreachable	Net unreachable
network-unknown	Network unknown
no-room-for-option	Parameter required but no room
option-missing	Parameter required but not present
packet-too-big	Fragmentation needed and DF set
parameter-problem	All parameter problems
port-unreachable	Port unreachable
precedence	Match packets with given precedence value
precedence-unreachable	Precedence cutoff
protocol-unreachable	Protocol unreachable
reassembly-timeout	Reassembly timeout
redirect	All redirects
router-advertisement	Router discovery advertisements
router-solicitation	Router discovery solicitations
source-quench	Source quenches
source-route-failed	Source route failed
time-exceeded	All time exceededs
timestamp-reply	Timestamp replies
timestamp-request	Timestamp requests
tos	Match packets with given TOS value
traceroute	Traceroute
ttl-exceeded	TTL exceeded
unreachable	All unreachables
<cr>	

12

RFC 1812 dictates that traffic denied by filtering (ACL) will display an ICMP *Administratively Prohibited* message to the sender, using the sender's address as destination and the filtering router interface address as source. This may not always be good security practice. It might be better not to send this message back to external users because of the implication that when there is filtering there is something worth protecting or hacking, depending on your point of view. You likely would want to deny ICMP *Administratively Prohibited* messages outbound at the external interface. If you ping **www.microsoft.com**, you should see this policy in effect.

Location of Extended Access Lists

Because extended access lists can filter on more than the source address, location is much more flexible. Placement can now be dictated by network strategy and performance objectives. Moving the placement closer to the source will minimize traffic congestion and maximize performance by reducing router resources. Having extended access lists more centrally located allows you to maintain tighter control over them as part of your network security strategy.

Consider these guidelines in determining placement of extended access lists:

➤ Keep denied traffic, or traffic to be inevitably denied, off the network backbone.

➤ Place access list as close to the source as possible to reduce the impact on such network resources as router CPU usage and network bandwidth. Why route a packet through an entire network (maybe over large geographical area) only to kill it and then send an ICMP message back?

➤ What impact will this placement decision have on network growth in the future?

➤ If you have a choice, select the router with the appropriate CPU resources.

➤ What are the impacts on other interfaces and access to services?

➤ How are access list management and security impacted?

Limiting Access to Services and Features

In this section, we look at various access list examples to see how we manage access to network services and features. We look at filtering to deny or permit access to virtual terminal (Telnet) sessions, ping attacks (ICMP echo requests and ICMP echo replies), Internet mail (Simple Mail Transport Protocol, or SMTP), Hypertext Transfer Protocol (HTTP), Simple Network Management Protocol (SNMP), and Domain Name System (DNS) servers.

Limiting Access to Virtual Terminals

Just as we can add filtering to the physical interfaces, such as Ethernet0 and serial 1, we can use a special form of the standard access list to filter the virtual ports, thereby limiting Telnet access to our routers. Although standard and extended access lists will block packets from going through the router, they are not designed to block packets that originate within the router, such as router-initiated Telnet sessions.

Five virtual ports, or *vty lines*, designated as vty 0 through vty 4, allow up to five Telnet sessions to be established. Because you cannot control which virtual port will be accessed (first available), you should set identical restrictions on all vty lines at one time.

An *inbound* access list will control access to that particular router. An *outbound* access list will control users that have successfully Telneted into the router from being able to use it as a platform to access other devices. We look at this situation in Figure 12.8.

Access lists for virtual terminals use the number range 1 through 99 and the **access-class** command, which is identical to **access-group** except that it can be used only for this purpose. The following code demonstrates this:

```
Router-A(config)#access-list 10 permit 192.168.1.0 0.0.0.255
Router-A(config)#access-list 11 deny any
```

First, we created two access lists with a single line each. The first permits all hosts within the 192.168.1.0 network—it could have been a host if we had chosen. The implicit **deny any** will block all other traffic. Even those allowed to pass through will need to supply any required passwords. The second list denies all traffic.

Our configuration of the virtual terminals looks like the following:

```
Router-A(config)#line vty 0 4
Router-A(config-line)#access-class 10 in
Router-A(config-line)#access-class 11 out
Router-A(config-line)#password cisco
Router-A(config-line)#login
```

The **line vty 0 4** applies the lines to all five virtual ports; had we used **line vty 0 2**, it would have covered only the first three, or **line vty 3 4** only the last two. The **password** command sets the password, and the **login** command requires every access to furnish the password.

The following code shows the result when Router B tries to Telnet into Router A.

```
Router-B>telnet Router-A
Trying Router-A (192.168.10.1)...
% Connection refused by remote host
Trying Router-A (192.168.12.1)...
% Connection refused by remote host
```

This code uses the hostname **Router-A**, so Telnet attempted all interfaces, but attempts to Telnet to an IP address yield the same result.

The following display demonstrates that the **show line vty** command lists the access lists that are applied. You should run this command to verify that your access lists are, in fact, applied to all virtual terminals.

```
Router-A#show line vty
  Tty Typ   Tx/Rx   A Modem  Roty AccO AccI  Uses   Noise  Overruns   Int
    2 VTY     -       -        -   11   10     0       0      0/0       -
    3 VTY     -       -        -   11   10     0       0      0/0       -
    4 VTY     -       -        -   11   10     0       0      0/0       -
    5 VTY     -       -        -   11   10     0       0      0/0       -
    6 VTY     -       -        -   11   10     0       0      0/0       -
```

The following code shows the result of a permitted user (who cleared access–list 10 and supplied the password) trying to Telnet on to another router. Note that it blocked both an Ethernet interface *e0* (192.168.100.100) and the serial interface *s0* (192.168.10.2).

```
Router-A>telnet Router-B
Trying Router-B (192.168.100.100)...
% Connections to that host not permitted from this terminal
Trying Router-B (192.168.10.2)...
% Connections to that host not permitted from this terminal
Router-A>
```

Alternative to Using Access Control Lists

An alternative to using access lists can block all Telnet access to a router. The advantages to this alternative are that there is no CPU usage and a standard access list number is preserved. Remember, though, that *you* are included in the "all" that will be blocked. This technique is very simple in that you require a login but then don't set a password to authenticate the access.

```
Router-A(config)#line vty 0 4
Router-A(config-line)#no password
Router-A(config-line)#login
```

The following shows what the users will see when they attempt to Telnet in.

```
Router-B> Router-A
Trying Router-A (192.168.10.1)... Open

Password required, but none set
[Connection to Router-A closed by foreign host]
```

Hindering Ping Attacks

If you want to prevent users from pinging one or more of your router interfaces, you can use the ICMP echo and echo-reply ports on an extended access list. The following commands demonstrate this feature; you would undoubtedly want to add other features.

```
Router-A(config)#access-list 101 deny icmp any any echo
Router-A(config)#access-list 101 deny icmp any any echo-response
Router-A(config)#access-list 101 permit ip any any
Router-A(config)#int s1
Router-A(config-if)#ip access-group 101 in
```

The result of pinging the interface from another router is as follows:

```
Router-B>ping 192.168.12.1
Type escape sequence to abort.
Sending 5, 100-byte ICMP Echos to 192.168.12.1, timeout is 2 seconds:
U.U.U
Success rate is 0 percent (0/5)
```

The result of pinging the interface from a workstation at the command or DOS prompt is as follows:

```
ping 192.168.12.1
Pinging 192.168.12.1 with 32 bytes of data:Reply from 192.168.12.1:
Destination net unreachable.Reply from 192.168.12.1: Destination net
unreachable.Reply from 192.168.12.1: Destination net unreachable.Reply from
192.168.12.1: Destination net unreachable.
Ping statistics for 192.168.12.1:    Packets: Sent = 4, Received = 4, Lost
= 0 (0% loss),Approximate round trip times in milli-seconds:    Minimum =
0ms, Maximum =  0ms, Average =  0ms
```

Providing Internet Mail

The following example shows some possible commands that would allow our servers to initiate TCP sessions over the Internet. The keyword **established** prevents Internet users from establishing TCP sessions with the servers. The third and fourth lines allow Internet TCP packets to reach the servers only if they are SMTP packets.

```
access-list 105 permit tcp any host 195.168.2.20 established
access-list 105 permit tcp any host 195.168.1.20 established
access-list 105 permit tcp any host 195.168.2.20 eq smtp
access-list 105 permit tcp any host 195.168.1.20 eq smtp
interface serial 0
  ip access-group 105 in
```

Figure 12.9 shows our simple network design.

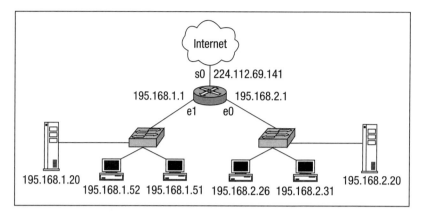

Figure 12.9 Simple network to demonstrate TCP and SMTP access.

Limiting Access to Hypertext Transfer Protocol

Using Figure 12.9, let us assume we want to block network 195.168.1.0 from being able to surf the Web while we still want to allow other services such as FTP. We also do not want to interfere with network 195.168.2.0 users in any way. The code would be the following:

```
access-list 106 deny tcp 195.168.1.20 0.0.0.255 any eq www
access-list 106 permit ip any any
interface ethernet 1
  ip access-group 106 in
```

Limiting Access to Simple Network Management Protocol

Again using Figure 12.9, let us assume we want to allow network 195.168.2.0 to be able to send and receive SNMP packets. The code would be as follows, and there would probably be other lines to control other features.

```
access-list 108 permit udp any any eq snmp
interface ethernet 0
  ip access-group 108 in
```

Allowing Access to Domain Naming System Servers

Whereas DNS typically uses a UDP transport, it can use TCP when large quantities of data are involved. We need **permit** filters for DNS over both TCP and UDP. Using Figure 12.9, let us assume we want to allow network 195.168.2.0 to be able to receive SNMP packets. The code would be as follows, and there would probably be other lines to control other features.

```
access-list 110 permit udp any eq domain 195.168.2.0 0.0.0.255
access-list 110 permit tcp any eq domain 195.168.2.0 0.0.0.255
interface ethernet 0
  ip access-group 110 out
```

Verify Access List Operation

Several basic commands allow the user to view existing access lists. Each offers its own strengths and weaknesses. You should be familiar with each of these commands, which are described in the following sections.

show access-list

The **show access-list** command is used to display any access lists from all protocols. The following display shows a standard and extended access list. You will note that this command displays the number of filtered packets for each line.

```
show access-lists
xtended IP access list 145
    deny tcp any host 195.168.2.20 eq telnet (7 matches)
    deny tcp any host 195.168.1.20 eq telnet (4 matches)
    permit ip any any (317 matches)
show access-list
Standard IP access list 50
    deny   210.93.105.10 (2 matches)
    permit any (91 matches)
```

show ip access-list [access-list-number]

The **show ip access-list** command displays only the IP access lists. Adding the optional **access-list-number** displays only the one list; without it, all IP access lists are displayed. Note the display information is identical to the **show access-list** display.

```
show ip access-list
Extended IP access list 130
    deny   tcp 223.8.151.0 0.0.0.255 host 210.93.105.11 eq www (8 matches)
    permit tcp any any (4 matches)
show access-list
Extended IP access list 130
    deny   tcp 223.8.151.0 0.0.0.255 host 210.93.105.11 eq www (8 matches)
    permit tcp any any (4 matches)
```

12

clear access-list counters [access-list-number]

The system automatically counts how many packets meet the condition for each line of an access list; the counters are displayed with the **show access-list** command. Use the **clear access-list counters** command in EXEC mode to clear the counters of an access list so you can start fresh after making changes. Adding the optional **access-list-number** will clear only the one counter; without it, all counters are cleared.

show line

The following display demonstrates that the **show line** command lists the access lists that are applied to the virtual terminals. The default displays all interfaces; adding vty 2 4 would only include the specified ports. You should run this command to verify that your access lists are in fact applied to all virtual terminals.

```
Router-A#show line vty 0 4
 Tty Typ   Tx/Rx  A Modem  Roty AccO AccI   Uses   Noise  Overruns   Int
   2 VTY     -    -    -     -   11   10      0      0     0/0        -
   3 VTY     -    -    -     -   11   10      0      0     0/0        -
   4 VTY     -    -    -     -   11   10      0      0     0/0        -
   5 VTY     -    -    -     -   11   10      0      0     0/0        -
   6 VTY     -    -    -     -   11   10      0      0     0/0        -
```

show running-config

Although not very specific or high tech, the **show running-config** command does show the access lists and the interfaces. The following is a partial display of the current configuration.

```
!
interface Ethernet0
 ip address 223.8.151.1 255.255.255.0
 ip access-group 130 in
!
interface Serial1
 ip address 204.204.7.2 255.255.255.0
 ip access-group 50 out
 ip access-group 105 in
 no logging event subif-link-status
!
 - - lines ommitted by author - -
!
access-list 10 permit 192.168.1.0 0.0.0.255
access-list 11 deny any
access-list 50 deny 210.93.105.10
access-list 50 permit any
```

```
access-list 105 permit tcp any host 195.168.2.20 established
access-list 105 permit tcp any host 195.168.1.20 established
access-list 105 permit tcp any host 195.168.2.20 eq smtp
access-list 105 permit tcp any host 195.168.1.20 eq smtp
access-list 130 deny   tcp 223.8.151.0 0.0.0.255 host 210.93.105.11 eq www
access-list 130 permit tcp any any
!
line vty 0 4
 access-class 10 in
 access-class 11 out
 password cisco
 login
!
```

show interface vs. show ip interface

Comparing the **show interface** and **show ip interface** commands, only the **show ip interface** command tells you about the access list(s). Adding an interface designation such as **e0** to the command shows only the specified interface—see the following display. The **show ipx interface** displays IPX access list information as well.

```
Lab-C#show ip interface e0
Ethernet0 is up, line protocol is up
  Internet address is 223.8.151.1/24
  Broadcast address is 255.255.255.255
  Address determined by setup command
  MTU is 1500 bytes
  Helper address is not set
  Directed broadcast forwarding is enabled
  Multicast reserved groups joined: 224.0.0.9
  Outgoing access list is not set
  Inbound  access list is 130
  Proxy ARP is enabled
  Security level is default
```

Dynamic Access Lists

Traditional access lists (standard and extended) are pretty much cast in stone. What they filter the day you build them is what they will filter forever. But what if you need some flexibility—the ability to change with the circumstances. In a nutshell, that is what dynamic access lists can offer you. With dynamic access lists, you can literally create temporary openings to your network based on a predefined user authentication process for designated users whose IP traffic would normally be blocked at a router.

Dynamic access lists can be used in conjunction with other standard access lists and static extended access lists. The user must first Telnet to the router where the device automatically attempts to authenticate the user. Once authenticated, the user then gains temporary access through the router and is able to reach designated destination hosts. Afterwards, dynamic access list can reconfigure the interface back to its original state.

As with standard lists, the **access-list** command is used to create each condition of the list, one condition per line. The lines are processed sequentially and cannot easily be reordered once in place. The IOS version 12.x syntax for each line in the list is:

```
access-list access-list-number dynamic (name) [timeout n]
  (permit | deny) (protocol) any (destination IP) (destination-wildcard)
```

The **access-list** keyword must be hyphenated and must begin each statement. The **access-list-number** range for dynamic access lists is 100 to 199. The **name** entry is an alphanumeric name for the dynamic access list. The optional **timeout** parameter creates an absolute life (time-out) for dynamic entries. The **permit** or **deny** features are the same as before.

The **protocol** entry defines any traditional protocol to be filtered, such as IP, TCP, UDP, ICMP, and so forth (because you can only have one dynamic access list entry per access list, it is common to use IP or TCP as the protocol). The source IP address is always replaced by the authenticating host IP address, so you should *always* use the keyword **any** for the source IP address. The **destination destination-wildcard | host | any** functions are the same as for extended access lists (for security reasons, be conservative and use hosts or subnets to limit your exposure).

How Dynamic Access Lists Work

The following steps describe the dynamic access list process:

1. User opens a Telnet session through a virtual terminal port to a border router configured with a dynamic access list.

2. The Cisco IOS software prompts for a password (or user ID and password) and performs the user authentication. If the authentication session fails, no change occurs to the list and therefore no access is allowed. The router, a central access security server such as Cisco's TACACS+ or Remote Access Dial-In User Service (RADIUS), can do authentication. Once authenticated, the Telnet session is closed and the IOS creates a temporary entry in the dynamic access list.

3. The user can access data through the router.

4. The IOS deletes the temporary access list entry when the idle time-out or absolute time-out is reached, or when the system administrator manually clears it. The temporary access list entries are *not* automatically deleted when the user ends the session.

Properly configured, dynamic access lists provide the same benefits as standard and static extended access lists with the additional security benefits of authenticating users and thereby reducing the opportunity for network break-ins by hackers. You can create temporary access through a firewall without compromising your security restrictions.

When configuring dynamic access lists, remember the following points:

➤ You cannot assign the same dynamic name to another named access list.

➤ You cannot create more than one dynamic access list for any one extended access list. Even though it might appear to work, only the first dynamic access list will function.

➤ Assign any parameters, such as port numbers, to the dynamic access list the same as you do for any static access list. The temporary list entries will inherit these parameters.

➤ Configure Telnet access first so that users must Telnet into the router to be authenticated before they gain access to the router.

➤ Use the log option and check your log regularly to look for suspicious activity.

➤ You must define either an idle time-out with the **timeout** keyword in the **autocommand**, or define an absolute time-out in the **access-list** command; otherwise, the access list entry will remain configured indefinitely until removed manually by an administrator. You can configure both idle and absolute time-outs—just remember that the idle time-out value must be less than the absolute time-out value.

➤ You cannot specify the order of temporary access list lines. Additions to the dynamic list always appear at the beginning of the list.

➤ Dynamic access list temporary entries are never saved to NVRAM.

Three Methods of Authentication

The three basic methods for configuring an authentication query process are discussed in the following sections. Cisco recommends that you use Cisco's TACACS+ server to provide authentication, authorization, and accounting (AAA) services, as well as protocol support, protocol specification, and a centralized security database.

The **username** and **password** Options

Use the **username** command in global configuration. This method is somewhat effective because authentication can be determined on a per-user basis. The **local** option tells the router to look for the username/password line at the global configuration level—without it, it will expect to find the password, as you will see in the next example.

```
username name password password
line vty 0 4
  login local
```

The **password only** Option

Use the **password** and **login** commands under **line vty 0 4**. This method is less effective because the password is port-specific; all users use the same password. Any user knowing the password can authenticate. Do not add **local** to the **login** command, or you will need to use the **username/password** option from the preceding example.

```
line vty 0 4
  password password
  login
```

Configure a Security Server

For the best security and for ease of security database updating, use a network access security server such as Cisco's TACACS+ server or RADIUS. This method requires additional configuration steps on the TACACS+ server, but allows for stricter authentication queries and more sophisticated tracking capabilities.

```
line vty 0 4
  login tacacs
```

Sample Dynamic Access List with Local Authentication

We will use our simple two-subnet example from earlier in this chapter. Figure 12.10 shows our simple network design.

The following abbreviated output from the **show run** command demonstrates the basic configuration. Only pertinent lines have been included.

```
username bscn password cisco
!
interface serial 0
  ip address 24.112.69.141 255.255.255.0
  ip access-group 110 in
!
```

```
access-list 110 permit tcp any host 24.112.69.141 eq telnet
access-list 110 permit udp any eq 53 any gt 1023
access-list 110 permit tcp any eq www any gt 1023 established
access-list 110 permit tcp any eq 20 195.168.1.0 0.0.0.255 gt 1023
access-list 110 permit tcp any eq 21 195.168.1.0 0.0.0.255 gt 1023 estab-
lished
access-list 110 dynamic bscn timeout 60 permit ip any host 195.168.1.20 log
!
line vty 0 2
  login local
  autocommand access-enable host timeout 10
line vty 3 4
  login local
  rotary 1
```

The first line sets the **username** (**bscn**) and **password** (**cisco**) that will have to be furnished by the external user. We could have eliminated this line and added **password cisco** and replaced **login local** with just **login** under the **line vty** section to have a port-specific password only, but this is less secure.

The interface configuration is fairly straightforward; we assigned our IP address and applied our access list as an inbound list on serial 0.

The first **access-list** line allows any outside host to establish a Telnet session with our router. If we had a small number of outside users with known IP addresses, we might have made this line more specific, but most users working with an Internet Service Provider (ISP) will not have a permanent IP address.

The second **access-list** line allows all internal users to get DNS replies from outside. Because it is a UDP packet, we cannot use the established option (but we will use it in the next example).

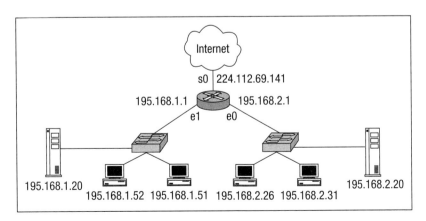

Figure 12.10   Simple one-router network to demonstrate the dynamic access list.

The third **access-list** line allows all internal users to get HTTP replies from outside if the session originated from within our network (**established**).

The fourth and fifth **access-list** lines allow only users from network 195.168.1.0 to use FTP services.

The sixth **access-list** line sets up our dynamic access list parameters. The name (**bscn**) matches the username in our configuration. We are granting full IP access to server 195.168.1.20, although we could have set more parameters to allow access only to, say, email or browsing our intranet. Our absolute time-out is set to 60 minutes, which means the connection will be broken at that point, and reauthentication will need to occur. User access requirements and your security needs will dictate this time-out value. We will also be logging each session.

The **autocommand** line is second only to the dynamic **access-list** command in importance. Without it in the **line vty** section, you have nothing. The **host** parameter must appear just as you see it, or the IP address of the authenticated outside user will not be substituted and any outside user would be allowed access. The **timeout 10** entry sets the idle time limit to 10 minutes. This time limit is reset to 10 every time a packet matches the dynamic **access-list** entry. Its job is breaking the connection after a period of inactivity. The absolute **timeout** set up in **access-list** line 6 does not get reset—when it is reached, the connection is broken with no exceptions.

Note that we applied the **autocommand** only to line **vty 0 2**. If we have a console connection to the router, we would probably have configured all five virtual ports the same. But what if we have to Telnet into that router for administration purposes? The router is going to authenticate us and then close the Telnet session just like it does to everyone else. Setting the **rotary 1** command under virtual terminals 3 and 4 enables Telnet access on port 3001. This means that you can now Telnet in using the following command: **telnet 24.112.69.141 3001**, and bypass the dynamic **access-list**.

Sample Dynamic Access List with TACACS+ Authentication

The configuration and use of the TACACS+ server is beyond the scope of the book and the requirements of the certification exam. Our last configuration would look like the following listing if we were using an authentication server.

```
aaa authentication login default tacacs+ local
aaa authorization exec tacacs+
!
username bscn password cisco
!
```

```
interface serial 0
  ip address 24.112.69.141 255.255.255.0
  ip access-group 110 in
!
access-list 110 permit tcp any host 24.112.69.141 eq telnet
access-list 110 permit udp any eq 53 any gt 1023
access-list 110 permit tcp any eq www any gt 1023 established
access-list 110 permit tcp any eq 20 195.168.1.0 0.0.0.255 gt 1023
access-list 110 permit tcp any eq 21 195.168.1.0 0.0.0.255 gt 1023 estab-
lished
access-list 110 dynamic bscn timeout 60 permit ip any host 195.168.1.20 log
!
tacacs-server host 195.168.1.21
tacacs-server key bscnkey
!
line vty 0 2
  login authentication default
line vty 3 4
  login local
  rotary 1
```

The first line actually allows us to validate locally if the TACACS+ server is unavailable. In this case, the **username bscn password cisco** command creates the values that will be needed for authentication.

Displaying Dynamic Access Lists

Displaying a temporary access list is very much like displaying any other access list. You use the **show access-list [access-list-number]** or **show ip access-list [access-list-number]** from Privilege Exec mode—the optional **access-list-number** shows only that one access list. The trick is that you can see the temporary access list lines only when they are in use. After the absolute or idle **timeout** parameter has activated, the temporary entries are cleared. The number of matches displayed indicates the number of times the **access-list** entry was used.

To manually delete a temporary **access-list** entry, type **clear access-template [access-list-number | name] [source] [destination]**.

Issues to Consider

As with all tools, dynamic access lists are not perfect, nor are they simple to correctly configure. You should always consider the following points:

➤ Dynamic access lists use IP extended access lists, so make sure you have a solid understanding of how extended access lists are used to filter traffic. Dynamic access lists employ user authentication and authorization as implemented in the Cisco AAA paradigm. You should be familiar with how to configure AAA user authentication and authorization.

12

➤ Cisco IOS releases prior to release 11.1 are not compatible with dynamic access lists and could cause you severe security problems.

➤ Dynamic access lists allow an external event (a Telnet session) to place a dynamic opening in the router security (firewall) by temporarily reconfiguring an interface to allow user access. During this time, another host might spoof the authenticated user's address to gain access behind the firewall. This feature does not cause the address-spoofing problem; it is a problem inherent to all access lists. To reduce exposure to spoofing, you could configure network data encryption so that traffic from the remote host is encrypted at a secured remote router, and decrypted locally at the router.

➤ When the dynamic access list forces an access list rebuild, additional access list entries are created on the router interface. This list will grow and shrink dynamically. Larger, more complex access lists can reduce packet-switching performance.

Reflexive Access Lists

Properly configured, the **established** parameter for extended access lists is very helpful in our efforts to secure our network when we are using TCP, a connection-oriented protocol. We create an outbound connection through a TCP port, and the responding device can respond back to us through the same port. This connection remains open as long as packets coming in have the ACK bit set to indicate they are a part of an ongoing communication, or until a packet comes through with the FIN bit set to indicate the end of the session. Any packets originating from the outside trying to establish a connection are rebuffed.

But what about other protocols, such as UDP and ICMP, that are not connection-oriented and do not have a predefined end of message bit. A similar problem exists with TCP applications that send on one port and receive on another. Either way, the established feature doesn't work.

Cisco has developed a process—really a feature of IP named *extended access lists*—called *reflexive access lists* to provide what is referred to as *reflective filtering*. Without getting into the details, it basically means that any specified IP packet going out of a filtered port will create a temporary access list item inbound on an inbound port. This temporary access list item mirrors what would have been an access list item for the original packet with the source and destination information reversed. This temporary opening remains active until a TCP FIN packet or a time-out timer expires. The time-out is critical for protocols that do not have a session-ending message.

Continuing with our simplified overview, let us assume our host 195.168.1.52 wants to use TCP port 1045 to establish a Telnet session with 201.1.1.123 in another network through its TCP 23 (Telnet) port. The access list statement to allow this, if we had to create one, would be:

```
permit tcp host 195.168.1.52 eq 1045 host 201.1.1.123 eq 23
```

What actually gets created is a reflected inbound entry that looks like the following:

```
permit tcp host 201.1.1.123 eq 23 host 195.168.1.52 eq 1045
```

Reflexive Access List Network Basics

Reflexive access lists can filter network traffic based on IP upper-layer protocol "session" information. They create temporary entries in a temporary access list that permit IP traffic for sessions originating from within the network, but they deny IP traffic for sessions originating from outside. They use reflexive filtering defined within named extended IP access lists only. Although you can use reflexive access lists in conjunction with either standard or static extended access lists, you cannot create them within numbered, standard-named IP, or any other protocol access lists.

Reflexive access lists can be an important part of securing your network against spoofing and certain denial-of-service attacks. They can be a major component in a firewall defense strategy. These lists are relatively simple to use and provide greater control than basic access lists over which packets enter your network.

What Is a Reflexive Access List?

Reflexive access lists are similar to other access lists in that they contain condition statements for permitting IP packets that are evaluated sequentially until a match occurs or no more statements exist. The biggest difference from other types of access lists is that they are temporary access lists containing only temporary entries that are automatically created when a new IP session begins and then automatically removed when the session ends or a time-out timer expires.

Reflexive access lists are not applied directly to an interface, but are instead "nested" into an extended named IP access list that is applied to an interface. Due to the concept of nesting, reflexive access lists do not have the usual implicit **deny any** at the end of the list.

As discussed earlier, TCP session filtering using the **established** keyword filters packets based on whether the ACK or RST bits are set. The assumption is that this indicates that the packet is not the first in the session and therefore belongs to an established session. Unfortunately, setting these bits is not a difficult task for a hacker. Reflexive access lists, on the other hand, offer session filtering that is more difficult to spoof because more criteria must be matched before a packet is permitted through. You can require that source and destination addresses and port numbers—not just the ACK and RST bits—are checked. Because the session filtering uses only temporary entries that are removed when a session is over, the hacker is limited to a smaller window of opportunity.

Network Topology Issues

Before we get into the details of creating reflexive access lists, we need to discuss the two common network designs that will use these as well as which interface to place them on. Reflexive access lists are generally applied to a border router connecting your internal network to the big, bad external world. Determining which topology is most like your network helps you decide whether to apply the reflexive access lists to an internal or external interface.

The first topology is displayed in Figure 12.11. The border router separates the external world on serial 0 and our internal network on Ethernet0. In this case, our reflexive access lists would be configured on the external interface serial 0. This would prevent unwanted IP traffic from entering the internal network unless it is part of a session established from within our network. There is no real reason that there could not be multiple interfaces (such as two Ethernet ports) to either the internal or external network as long as we can separate them as to internal versus external.

The second topology (Figure 12.12) shows our border router with external and internal (private) interfaces but also an additional internal (public) interface for servers to which we would like the outside world to have relatively free access. Never missing an opportunity for the flamboyant, this internal public network is often referred to as the Demilitarized Zone (DMZ). With this topology, your reflexive access lists are configured for the internal interface Ethernet1. This allows external

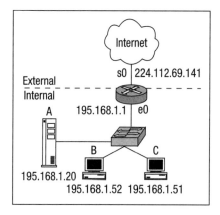

Figure 12.11 Simple network to demonstrate internal and external interfaces.

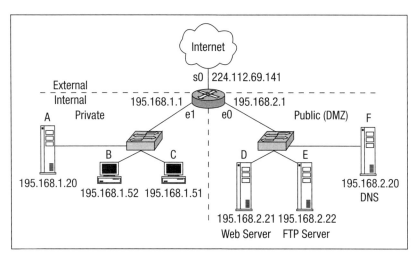

Figure 12.12 Network with internal public, internal private, and external interfaces.

traffic to access the services in the public server network, such as WEB or FTP servers, but limits IP traffic to your internal network unless the traffic is part of a session established from within the internal network.

Note: *The external interface is sometimes referred to as "untrusted" or "dirty" (as in the dirty side of the router), whereas the internal interface is referred to as "trusted" or "clean."*

Configuring Reflexive Access Lists

Before you can configure reflexive access lists, you must decide whether to configure reflexive access lists on an internal or external interface. You should also be sure that you have a basic understanding of the IP protocol and of access lists; specifically, you should know how to configure extended IP named access lists.

Two primary commands need to be configured in building reflexive access lists: the **permit** and the **evaluate** statements.

The permit Statement

The **permit** statement is the primary configuration entry in an extended IP named access list. The syntax is:

```
permit protocol source destination reflect name [timeout seconds]
```

The **protocol** can be any TCP/IP protocol that can use extended IP named access lists. The **source** and **destination** entries are like any other access list source and destination, including the keywords **host** and **any** as well as wildcard masks and, where appropriate, port numbers. The **name** entry is the name of the temporary reflexive access list that will be created when packets start matching the criteria. The optional **timeout** represents an idle timer for this line only. When set (in seconds), this timer overrides the default time-out (300 seconds) set with the **ip reflexive-list timeout** command in global configuration.

The keyword **reflect** in a **permit** statement is the key to creating the temporary access list entries in the partner access list. The **reflect** statement in an outbound extended IP named access list creates the entries in the inbound extended IP named access list when packets matching the condition(s) are recognized.

The extended IP access list that contains the reflexive access list **permit** statement can also contain regular **permit** and **deny** statements. They can be created before or after the reflexive **permit** statements. Be careful though—as with all access lists, the order of entries is critical. When a packet reaches the interface, it will be evaluated sequentially by the access list until a match occurs. If a match occurs before reaching the reflexive **permit** statement, the packet will be processed and will not trigger a temporary entry to be created for the reflexive access list.

The **evaluate** Statement

The **evaluate** statement is the final configuration entry in another extended IP named access list that partners with the **permit** access list statements just discussed. The syntax is:

```
evaluate name
```

The **name** entry is the name of the temporary reflexive access list that was specified in the **permit** statements, and will be created when packets start matching the criteria. See the "Viewing Reflexive Access Lists" section of this chapter to see how they appear.

Let us engage in some oversimplification for a moment. In the following code, we applied two access lists, **test-out** and **test-in**, to the serial interface:

```
Internet serial 0
  ip access-group test-out out
  ip access-group test-in in
!
ip access-list extended test-out
  permit tcp any any eq 53 reflect newlist-packets
  permit tcp any any eq 80 reflect newlist-packets
!
ip access-lst extended test-in
  evaluate newlist-packets
```

First, we created **test-out** with a couple of normal-looking **permit** statements, except that the **reflect** keyword in each says, "When we get a match, I want you to create an entry in a temporary access list named newlist-packets that reverses all of the source and destination designations of the original packets that launched this session. Then you help those nice returning packets find their way through our security." Now we know what we are going to do.

Second, we created **test-in**. It happens to have just the one statement, although there could be regular static access list entries as long as they appear before the **evaluate newlist-packets** statement—it is nested at the bottom. The command is saying, in essence, "If that nice test-out finds any matching packets, I've agreed to make room for his temporary access list right below us."

Note: We applied both access lists to the same interface, but there is no reason we couldn't have our outbound access list on Ethernet0 and our inbound access list on serial 0. The IOS will build the temporary access list with entries properly following the inbound access list.

External Interface

The following steps are basic to configure reflexive access lists for an external interface, the type we might apply to a simple network with only internal and external considerations—that means no internal public server networks (such as in Figure 12.11).

➤ Define the reflexive access list(s) in an outbound IP named extended access list.

➤ Nest the reflexive access list(s) in an inbound IP named extended access list.

➤ Set a global timeout—not required, but be aware of the default.

The outbound reflexive access list evaluates traffic traveling out the interface. When the reflexive access list criterion is matched, temporary entries are created in the inbound nested access list. These entries will apply to inbound traffic arriving in your network.

As each packet matches a reflexive access list, the time-out timer gets reset. If no new matching packets are detected before the time-out timer expires, then the temporary list items are removed. The global time-out value (default 300 seconds) sets the default time-out. Changing the global default value will change all reflexive access lists, or you can specify a time-out for a particular reflexive access list entry when you define the reflexive access list. To change the global time-out value, type the following in global configuration mode:

```
ip reflexive-list timeout [new value in seconds]
```

12

A simple example allowing the 195.168.1.0 users from Figure 12.11 access to the Internet and DNS servers might look like the following:

```
ip reflexive-list timeout 120
!
Interface serial 0
  ip access-group f1211-out out
  ip access-group f1211-in in
!
ip access-list extended f1211-out
  permit tcp any any eq 53 reflect f1211-packets
  permit tcp any any eq 80 reflect f1211-packets
!
ip access-1st extended f1211-in
  evaluate f1211-packets
```

The first line changes the global time-out value to 2 minutes. This will impact all reflexive access list entries on this router that do not specify their own time-out value (see the next example).

Internal Interface

The following steps are basic to configure reflexive access lists for an internal-private interface, the type we might apply to a network with internal private, internal public, and external considerations, such as shown in Figure 12.12.

➤ Define the reflexive access list(s) in an inbound IP named extended access list.

➤ Nest the reflexive access list(s) in an outbound IP named extended access list.

➤ Set a global timeout—not required, but be aware of the default.

The inbound reflexive access list evaluates traffic traveling out the internal private network. When the reflexive access list criterion is matched, temporary entries are created in the outbound nested access list. These entries will apply to inbound traffic arriving into your internal private network. If this seems backwards, remember, whether an access list is inbound or outbound is determined from the router's perspective—we are sending initial packets out of the internal private network (inbound to the router) and filtering packets coming into internal private network (outbound to the router).

As each packet matches a reflexive access list, the time-out timer gets reset. If no new matching packets are detected before the time-out time, then the temporary list items are removed. The global time-out value (default 300 seconds) sets the default time-out—see the preceding example. Changing the global default value will change all reflexive access lists, or you can specify a time-out for a particular reflexive access list entry when you define the reflexive access list.

A simple example allowing the 195.168.1.0 users from Figure 12.12 access to the Internet and DNS servers might look like the following:

```
Interface ethernet 1
  ip access-group f1212-in in
  ip access-group f1212-out out
!
ip access-list extended f1212-in
  permit tcp any any eq 53 reflect f1212-packets timeout 120
  permit tcp any any eq 80 reflect f1212-packets timeout 180
!
ip access-lst extended f1212-out
  evaluate f1212-packets
```

The two **permit** entries set their own time-outs as 2 and 3 minutes. Any that do not have a setting will be governed by the global default of 300 seconds.

Alternative External Interface Example

The following configuration is for a reflexive access list on an external interface for the simple internal/external network shown previously in Figure 12.11. Just as before, we are allowing the 195.168.1.0 users access to the Internet and DNS servers outside the network.

```
ip reflexive-list timeout 240
!
Interface serial 0
  ip access-group bscn-out out
  ip access-group bscn-in in
!
Ip access-list extended bscn-out
  permit tcp 195.168.1.0 0.0.0.255 any eq 80 reflect bscn-packets timeout
180
  permit tcp 195.168.1.0 0.0.0.255 any eq 53 reflect bscn-packets
!
Ip access-list extended bscn-in
  permit icmp any 195.168.1.0 0.0.0.255 echo-response
  permit tcp any host 195.168.1.20 eq 80
  permit bgp any any
  permit eigrp any any
  evaluate bscn-packets
```

Our inbound list allows ping echo responses only to our network and allows outsiders HTTP access to our Web server 195.168.1.20. In addition, we allow both BGP and EIGRP routing updates. In the first line, we changed the default time-out to 4 minutes but applied a more restrictive 3 minutes on our reflexive list allowing Web access.

Viewing Reflexive Access Lists

Like all access lists, the reflexive access lists can be displayed using the **show access-list** command while in the privilege mode. If the command is executed before any reflexive access sessions have been initiated, the command could display the following:

```
Extended IP access list bscn-in
  permit icmp any 195.168.1.0 0.0.0.255 echo-response
  permit tcp any host 195.168.1.20 eq 80 (2 matches)
  permit bgp any any (3 matches)
  permit eigrp any any
  evaluate bscn-packets
Extended IP access list bscn-out
  permit tcp 195.168.1.0 0.0.0.255 any eq 80 reflect bscn-packets timeout
180
  permit tcp 195.168.1.0 0.0.0.255 any eq 53 reflect bscn-packets
```

Notice that no reflexive access list entries appear because no traffic has triggered the reflexive access list—the list is still empty.

After a couple of HTTP sessions are initiated from within the network to an outside host, the **show access-list** command could display the following:

```
Extended IP access list bscn-in
  permit icmp any 195.168.1.0 0.0.0.255 echo-response
  permit tcp any host 195.168.1.20 eq 80 (7 matches)
  permit bgp any any (4 matches)
  permit eigrp any any
  evaluate bscn-packets
Extended IP access list bscn-out
  permit tcp 195.168.1.0 0.0.0.255 any eq 80 reflect bscn-packets timeout
180
  permit tcp 195.168.1.0 0.0.0.255 any eq 53 reflect bscn-packets
Reflexive IP access list bscn-packets
  permit tcp host 201.37.14.127 eq www host 195.168.52 eq 80 (5 matches)
  (time left 140 seconds)
```

The reflexive access list is actually a separate temporary list created just below the named access list that "nested" the **evaluate** command. If there were any other open sessions, there would be additional entries in this new table.

Temporary Reflexive Access List Entries

Temporary access lists with their temporary entries (filters) can be rather mysterious and somewhat difficult to observe without real traffic, so you should be aware of the following attributes of these temporary entries. The list is not exhaustive, and there is no significance to the order.

➤ The temporary entry will always be a permit entry.

➤ The entry always uses the same protocol as the original outbound packet.

➤ The entry always uses the same source and destination addresses as the original outbound packet, except that the source and destination addresses are swapped.

➤ For TCP and UDP packets, the entry always specifies the same source and destination port numbers as the original outbound packet, except that the source and destination port numbers are swapped.

➤ Inbound traffic is evaluated against any temporary entries in sequential order until the temporary entry expires. Any packets matching a temporary entry are allowed into your network.

➤ With all protocols, if no packets matching the temporary entry are processed before the time-out timer expires, the entry will expire and be removed from the temporary access list. Matching packets reset the time-out timer.

➤ For TCP sessions, the temporary entries are removed at the end of a TCP session. Two events can terminate a TCP session. First, two TCP packets with the FIN bit set indicates that the session is about to end; the software then waits five seconds to allow the session to close. Second, a TCP packet with the RST bit set indicates an abrupt and unexpected session close.

Reflexive Access List Caveats

Some applications, such as FTP, allow port numbers to be changed during a session, meaning that the port numbers of returning packets are not the same as those of the originating packet. Reflexive access lists cannot resolve this, and the return packet will be denied—even if it is part of the same session. Sometimes an alternative such as passive FTP will work with reflexive access lists.

Reflexive access lists cannot examine data in the packet beyond the layer 4 (OSI model) information, such as TCP and UDP port numbers and the related IP addresses. They cannot follow the application as we just saw with the FTP discussion in the preceding paragraph. If you need to filter based on higher level (application) information, then look at context-based access control (CBAC), discussed in the next section.

12

CBAC and Other New Tools

Constantly changing technologies, ever-growing feature lists, and the increasing sophistication of hacker attacks make it very difficult to feel confident that the system you just configured is still secure. Cisco has developed and continues to develop many tools that appear in the latest release of the Cisco IOS. Even though the following features are not objectives on the certification exam, you should at least be aware of their existence and the fact that resources are available to learn more about them.

Context-based access control is an advanced traffic-filtering functionality for network firewalls that, unlike access lists, is not limited to examining packets at the network or even transport layer. CBAC does examine at both of these layers, but it also examines the application-layer protocol data to monitor the state of a given TCP or UDP session. This means that as multiple channels are created or used by applications such as SQL*Net, FTP, and RPC, CBAC can respond by creating temporary openings in the firewall access lists to allow return traffic and additional data connections for specified sessions that originated from within the protected network. This application layer awareness and ability to evolve with the traffic are beyond the capabilities of access list technologies.

CBAC has the ability to detect and prevent certain types of network attacks such as SYN flooding, in which a hacker floods a server with a barrage of requests for connections (SYNchronize packets) but has no intention to complete the connection. The resulting half-open connections can bury the server under attack, leading to diminished ability or inability to meet valid requests. This is a common denial-of-service (DoS) attack.

Additionally, CBAC can guard against other types of DoS attacks by monitoring for unusually high rates of new connections, IP packet fragmented attacks, and packet sequence numbers in TCP connections to see if they are within expected ranges.

CBAC offers features for Microsoft NetShow, Cisco IOS Intrusion Detection System (IDS), Java and HTTP (Java blocking), CU-SeeMe (only the White Pine version), RealAudio, VDOLive, StreamWorks, FTP, TFTP, SMTP, H.323 (NetMeeting, ProShare, etc.), UNIX R-commands (such as **rlogin**, **rexec**, and **rsh**), Sun RPC, and Microsoft RPC.

What CBAC Cannot Do

CBAC does not provide intelligent filtering for all protocols—only for the protocols that you specify for inspection. If you fail to specify a protocol for CBAC inspection, temporary openings will not be created, and returning packets will be filtered. If you don't specify it, then it is out—unless your access lists allow it.

Generally, CBAC cannot protect your network from attacks from within. CBAC detects and protects only against attacks that travel through the firewall, which would generally exclude most internal traffic.

This Cisco IOS firewall feature set is supported on most router platforms that use release 12.

Other Resources

You might want to look at "Time-Based Access Lists." Because version 12.0 of the IOS allows you to construct access lists based on time ranges, the filtering is allowed to run on a time-based schedule. Great for those middle-of-the-night jobs or weekends.

"TCP Intercept" has been around since version 11.3 to help fend off SYN flood attacks. This is not actually an access list, but it works closely with the access list features.

Cisco Encryption Technology (CET) is a proprietary technology that secures IP traffic between routers using encryption. IPSec is a suite of standards-based technologies that allow any vendor's IPSec-compliant devices to communicate using cryptography.

The Null Port Feature

Access lists, by definition, contribute to router overhead—the longer and more complex, the greater the impact. The router (CPU) processes every line of an access list until a match is found or the packet is ultimately discarded. On heavily used production routers, any overhead (CPU cycles) that can be conserved is worth considering. One alternative to using access lists is to use the null interface feature of the IOS.

The null interface is a virtual interface with no connection to any network. Traffic directed to the null interface using a static route disappears—it is effectively discarded. You can use the **ip route** command to create a static route to the null interface. The syntax is as follows:

```
ip route address subnet-mask null 0
```

Assume we have a two-location network such as the one depicted in Figure 12.13. We want remote network 195.168.4.0 to be able to access the Internet and our server farm on the 195.168.2.0 network. There is no reason for those users to access the local user network (195.168.1.0) at the main location.

On Router A, then, we configure a static route that looks like the following:

```
ip route 195.168.1.0 255.255.255.0 null 0
Router RIP
  Network 195.168.4.0
  Network 195.168.5.0
```

The routing protocol information is included to force us to recognize that the two routers will undoubtedly exchange information that will show another route to the 195.168.1.0 network. The good news is that it won't matter because the static route will have the lower metric and will trump anything the routing protocols can provide.

It is important to consider the location of the null interface because any time a packet comes into the router to the defined destination, it will be dropped. Consider what

12

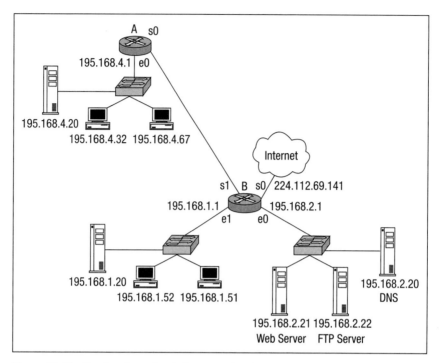

Figure 12.13 Two-location network demonstrating the null interface.

would happen if we had a similar interest in blocking user access from network 195.168.1.0 to the remote network 195.168.4.0 and we added the following static route to Router-B:

```
ip route 195.168.4.0 255.255.255.0 null 0
```

Although it would meet our primary objective, it would also block all other traffic to 195.168.4.0 from the Internet or 195.168.2.0. Note that the result would be as bad if we had placed it on Router A. This would be a job for an access list.

ip helper-address

By default, routers block broadcasts and prevent broadcast storms. Large flat networks are notorious for problems with broadcast storms. Client hosts often rely on broadcasts to establish initial connections with a variety of network servers, such as domain name servers (DNS), BOOTP/Dynamic Host Configuration Protocol (DHCP) servers, or TFTP servers. Everything is fine if the client and server are on the same network—the server can respond to the client's broadcast request and the client can learn the IP address of the server from the reply.

If the server is not on the same network as the client, problems arise. The destination IP broadcast address (255.255.255.255) is sent in a layer 2 broadcast packet (FFFFFFFFFFFF), which by default the routers (RFC 1812) will not forward. Because localizing or segmenting broadcast traffic was probably a primary reason for implementing the routers in the first place, removing the feature is generally not an option. So what do we do now?

The Cisco IOS supports an *IP helper address* feature to change a UDP packet's broadcast destination address to a specific destination or subnet address. The packet can now be routed.

The helper address is configured on an incoming interface so that it can hear the broadcasts on that subnet. The syntax is:

```
Router(config-if)#ip helper-address (destination-address)
```

The **destination-address** can be a host or subnet address. It is also possible to define multiple helper addresses—one for each target device. Any supported broadcast will then be forwarded to each destination.

Eight default UDP ports are automatically forwarded if you define an **ip helper-address**:

➤ Time (37)

➤ TACACS (49)

➤ DNS (53)

➤ BOOTP/DHCP server (67)

➤ BOOTP/DHCP client (68)

➤ TFTP (69)

➤ NetBIOS name service (137)

➤ NetBIOS datagram service (138)

Consider the design shown in Figure 12.14, where all users are located in the 195.168.1.0 network and all server support is in 195.168.2.0 except for a single file/print server 195.168.1.20.

Let us look at a couple of possible helper address examples. The following example shows a single helper to the DHCP server (and, as a side benefit, TFTP and DNS services):

```
interface Ethernet 1
  ip address 195.168.1.1 255.255.255.0
  ip helper-address 195.168.2.22
```

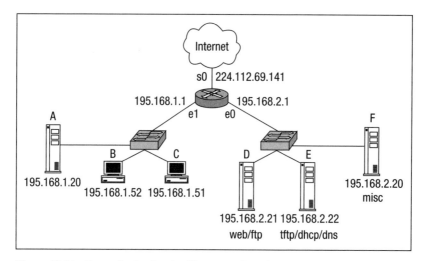

Figure 12.14 Two-subnet network with a server farm for support services.

The following example shows three helper addresses—one for each of the servers. With this scenario, each server will receive DHCP requests, DNS requests, and so on.

```
interface Ethernet 1
   ip address 195.168.1.1 255.255.255.0
   ip helper-address 195.168.2.20
   ip helper-address 195.168.2.21
   ip helper-address 195.168.2.22
```

The following example shows single helper addresses directed to the subnet. All servers will now see all supported packets. This option would support more servers being added to the subnet without any additional configuration.

```
interface Ethernet 1
   ip address 195.168.1.1 255.255.255.0
   ip helper-address 195.168.2.255
```

ip forward-protocol

When the helper address alone won't meet your needs, the **ip forward-protocol** command allows you to select and deselect the types of broadcasts that will be forwarded by the **helper** command. This feature is defined in global configuration mode and therefore applies to the entire router (all ports). The syntax of this command is:

```
ip forward-protocol (UPD [port] | nd | sdns)
```

The optional parameters are:

```
Router-A(config)#ip forward-protocol ?
  nd              Sun's Network Disk protocol
  sdns            Network Security Protocol
  spanning-tree   Use transparent bridging to flood UDP broadcasts
  turbo-flood     Fast flooding of UDP broadcasts
  udp             Packets to a specific UDP port
```

Selecting the **UDP** option and requesting help show that you can be very specific as to which broadcast packets you want forwarded.

```
Router-A(config)#ip forward-protocol udp ?
  <0-65535>     Port number
  biff          Biff (mail notification, comsat, 512)
  bootpc        Bootstrap Protocol (BOOTP) client (68)
  bootps        Bootstrap Protocol (BOOTP) server (67)
  discard       Discard (9)
  dnsix         DNSIX security protocol auditing (195)
  domain        Domain Name Service (DNS, 53)
  echo          Echo (7)
  isakmp        Internet Security Association and Key Management Protocol
                (500)
  mobile-ip     Mobile IP registration (434)
  nameserver    IEN116 name service (obsolete, 42)
  netbios-dgm   NetBIOS datagram service (138)
  netbios-ns    NetBIOS name service (137)
  netbios-ss    NetBIOS session service (139)
  ntp           Network Time Protocol (123)
  pim-auto-rp   PIM Auto-RP (496)
  rip           Routing Information Protocol (router, in.routed, 520)
  snmp          Simple Network Management Protocol (161)
  snmptrap      SNMP Traps (162)
  sunrpc        Sun Remote Procedure Call (111)
  syslog        System Logger (514)
  tacacs        TAC Access Control System (49)
  talk          Talk (517)
  tftp          Trivial File Transfer Protocol (69)
  time          Time (37)
  who           Who service (rwho, 513)
  xdmcp         X Display Manager Control Protocol (177)
  <cr>
```

12

Consider the possibility of the following two commands being added in the configuration of your router.

```
ip forward-protocol udp snmp
no ip forward-protocol udp tftp
```

You can now forward SNMP packets and prevent TFTP packets from being forwarded by the **ip helper-address** command. A series of these **no** statements could reduce the number of UDP packets being forwarded and reduce the congestion on the network and stress on servers.

Cisco Easy IP

Cisco IOS contains a full DHCP server implementation, Cisco Easy IP, which assigns and manages IP addresses from specified address pool(s) within the router to DHCP hosts. This DHCP server supports many DHCP options, as defined in RFC 2132. Cisco Easy IP enables transparent and dynamic IP address allocation for hosts via DHCP, reduces router configuration tasks via dynamic PPP/IPCP address negotiation, conserves IP addresses via Port Address Translation (PAT), and minimizes Internet access costs for remote offices.

Chapter Summary

This chapter looked at using access lists and non-access list features to manage access to network features and devices that allow the administrator to increase security and manage bandwidth. Our goal is balancing the need to eliminate unwanted traffic with facilitating appropriate user access to necessary resources. The Cisco IOS offers a rich set of tools for filtering traffic while creating pathways for necessary traffic to maneuver through the system.

Access control lists are still the basic tools for managing network traffic. An access list is a section of the router configuration containing a sequentially processed collection of **permit** and **deny** statements. The two types of IP access lists are *standard* and *extended*. Standard IP access lists filter all IP traffic based exclusively on source address. Extended IP access lists offer more control by filtering based on source address, destination address, or protocol characteristics.

Creating an access list is a two-part process. First, the list is created—one condition per line—in *global configuration mode*, and then it is applied in *interface configuration mode*.

Without access lists, the interface can pass all packets unrestricted. Access lists carry the assumption that you now want to control what will pass. Therefore, implicit in each access list is a **deny any** statement at the end. Each interface can have only one inbound and one outbound access list of any type for each network layer protocol.

The ranges of access list numbers are 1–99 for standard and 100–199 for extended. Since Cisco IOS release 11.2, you can use alphanumeric names for access lists, which allows you to create more than 99 standard and 100 extended access lists. The benefits of using named access lists are:

➤ The name can be meaningful and indicative of the list's purpose. This is a particularly important feature for documentation and maintenance purposes. This will also benefit anyone having to support your ACLs later.

➤ It is possible to selectively delete specific lines within a named access list, which cannot be done with numbered lists.

➤ Some advanced filtering features will work only with named access lists.

In addition to controlling traffic such as HTTP or SNMP through router interfaces over an external interface, access lists can be used to limit access to the virtual terminals by filtering Telnet session requests. The following code demonstrates standard, extended, and named access lists, as well as access class to secure the virtual terminals.

```
interface serial 0
  ip access-group accounting_access out
interface Ethernet 1
  ip access-group 106 in
interface Ethernet 0
  ip access-group 50 out
access-list 10 permit 192.168.1.0 0.0.0.255
access-list 11 deny any
access-list 50 remark block traffic from sales network
access-list 50 deny 192.168.1.10 0.0.0.255
access-list 50 remark allow traffic from other networks
access-list 50 permit any
access-list 106 permit tcp 195.168.1.20 0.0.0.255 any eq www
access-list 106 permit udp any any eq snmp
access-list 106 permit ip any any
ip access-list standard accounting_access
  permit 192.168.3.0 0.0.0.255
  permit host 192.168.6.50
!
line vty 0 4
  access-class 10 in
  access-class 11 out
  password cisco
  login
```

12

Two basic topologies are explored for looking at our border routers (Figure 12.15). In topology #1, the routers represent the boundary between the external ("untrusted,"

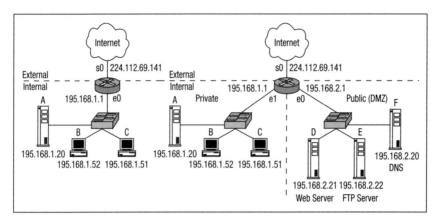

Figure 12.15 Network with internal public, internal private, and external interfaces.

or "dirty") world and our internal ("trusted," or "clean") world. We then define the interfaces as external or internal based on the above. Topology #2 assumes the above plus a third connection, or interface(s) to our internal public network, where our "open" resources, such as Web, DNS, and FTP servers, might be located.

The **established** parameter for extended access lists is very helpful in securing our network when we are using TCP, a connection-oriented protocol. We create an outbound connection through a TCP port, and the responding device can respond back to us through the same port. This connection remains open as long as packets coming in have the ACK bit set, indicating they are a part of an ongoing communication, or until a packet comes through with the FIN bit set, indicating the end of the session. Any packets originating from the outside trying to establish a connection are rebuffed.

Dynamic access lists can create temporary openings to a network based on a predefined user authentication process for designated users whose TCP traffic would normally be blocked at a router. The outside user must first Telnet to the router to be authenticated. Once authenticated, the user gains temporary access through the router to reach predefined destination hosts. Afterwards, a dynamic access list can reconfigure the interface back to its original state.

Dynamic access lists will not work with UDP and ICMP that are not connection-oriented and with TCP applications that send on one port and receive on another. Cisco has developed reflexive access lists to provide what is referred to as reflective filtering. Basically, any specified IP packet going out of a filtered port will create a temporary access list item on an inbound port. This temporary access list item mirrors what would have been an access list item for the original packet with the source and destination information reversed. This temporary opening remains active until a TCP FIN packet is received or a time-out timer expires. The time-out is critical for protocols that do not have a session-ending message.

Context-based access control is an advanced traffic filtering functionality for network firewalls that is not limited like access lists to examining packets at the network or even transport layer. CBAC examines both of these layers, and it also examines the application-layer protocol data to monitor the state of a given TCP or UDP session. This means that as multiple channels are created or used by applications such as SQL★Net, FTP, and RPC, CBAC can respond by creating temporary openings in the firewall access lists to allow return traffic and additional data connections for specified sessions that originated from within the protected network. This application layer awareness and ability to evolve with the traffic are beyond the capabilities of access list technologies.

CBAC has the ability to detect and prevent common denial-of-service attacks by monitoring for SYN flooding, unusually high rates of new connections, IP packet fragmented attacks, and packet sequence numbers in TCP connections to see if they are within expected ranges.

CBAC offers features for Microsoft NetShow, Cisco IOS Intrusion Detection System, Java and HTTP, CU-SeeMe (only the White Pine version), RealAudio, VDOLive, StreamWorks, FTP, TFTP, SMTP, H.323 (NetMeeting, ProShare, etc.), UNIX R-commands (such as **rlogin**, **rexec**, and **rsh**), Sun RPC, and Microsoft RPC.

We can verify the presence of access lists with the **show access-list** and **show ip access-list** commands, the latter being more restrictive by showing only IP lists. Additional tools are **show line** for showing the line vty configuration and, of course, the **show running-config** to see the entire current configuration including ACLs and interface application info.

Some non-access list features or tools addressed in this chapter include:

➤ The Cisco **IP helper address** feature can change a certain UDP packet's broadcast destination address to a specific destination or subnet address. The packet can then be routed to the appropriate host or subnet.

➤ The **ip forward-protocol** command, related to the **helper address** command, allows you to add or remove UDP broadcast protocols from the initial pool of eight that will be forwarded by the **helper** command.

➤ Cisco IOS contains a full DHCP server implementation, Cisco Easy IP, which provides transparent and dynamic IP address allocation for hosts via DHCP, reduces router configuration tasks via dynamic PPP/IPCP address negotiation, conserves IP addresses via Port Address Translation, and minimizes Internet access costs for remote offices.

Although they are not exam requirements, other resources you might want to look at include Time-Based Access Lists, which allow you to construct access lists based on time ranges, thus allowing filtering to run on a time-based schedule—great for those middle of the night jobs or weekends.

12

TCP Intercept has been around since version 11.3 to help fend off SYN flood attacks. This is not actually an access list, but it works closely with the access list features.

Cisco Encryption Technology is a proprietary technology that secures IP traffic between Cisco routers using encryption. IPSec is a suite of standards-based technologies that allow any vendor's IPSec-compliant devices to communicate using cryptography.

Review Questions

1. True or false: A subnet mask and wildcard mask are basically opposites. The first identifies the network portion of an address, whereas the latter identifies the hosts.

    a. True

    b. False

2. What do the following statements do?

   ```
   access-list 50 deny 192.168.1.10 0.0.0.255
   access-list 50 permit any
   int e0
     ip access-group 50 out
   ```

    a. Block all traffic to network 192.168.1.10

    b. Block all traffic to host 192.168.1.10

    c. Block all traffic from network 192.168.1.10

    d. Block all traffic from host 192.168.1.10

3. What do the following statements do?

   ```
   access-list 50 deny 192.168.1.10 0.0.0.255
   access-list 50 deny 192.168.2.10 0.0.0.255
   access-list 50 deny 192.168.3.10 0.0.0.255
   access-list 50 permit any
   int e0
     ip access-group 50 out
   ```

    a. Deny traffic from three subnets through the router

    b. Deny traffic from three subnets out the Ethernet0 interface only

    c. Block all traffic out the Ethernet0 interface

    d. Block all traffic through the Ethernet0 interface

4. True or false: Named access lists can be either standard or extended.

   a. True

   b. False

5. True or false: The extended access list feature works with TCP and UDP traffic.

   a. True

   b. False

6. Which of the following statements are true about the null 0 feature? (Choose two)

   a. It is an option to be used with extended named access lists.

   b. It is used with a **GOTO** statement.

   c. It is a virtual port that is not connected to a physical network.

   d. It is used with a static route.

7. Which of the following statements are true about the **helper-address** statement? (Choose two)

   a. It assists hosts to contact resources they might otherwise be cut off from by routers.

   b. Only one can be applied to a particular interface in either direction.

   c. It converts certain broadcast packets to unicast packets.

   d. It is difficult to set up and should be tried only by the company's IT manager.

8. Which of the following can provide an IP address to a host device?

   a. IP helper address

   b. IP forward protocol

   c. Cisco Easy IP

   d. Reflexive access lists

9. When working with a border router, we often say it is the border between which two networks?

   a. Internal public and external

   b. Internal and external

   c. Internal private and internal public

   d. Clean and trusted

12

10. When working with a border router, we often say it is the border of which three networks? (Choose three)

    a. Internal private

    b. The IP Null Port

    c. Internal public (DMZ)

    d. External

11. Which one of the following does not create a temporary path for a communications session established within your network?

    a. Reflexive access list

    b. Dynamic access list

    c. Standard access list

    d. Extended access list using the **established** command

12. Which statements are false relative to the access list tool? (Choose two)

    a. They are a list of **permit** and **deny** statements that are processed sequentially.

    b. There must be at least one **deny** statement in each access list.

    c. They can be applied to a virtual terminal (**line vty**) to create a temporary Ethernet port.

    d. Extended access lists offer greater filtering capabilities than standard access lists.

13. If properly applied to an interface, what will the following command do?

    ```
    access-list 105 permit tcp any host 195.168.2.20 established
    ```

    a. Allow any machine to start a TCP session with our server 195.168.2.20

    b. Open a channel for any TCP session that was initiated by our server 195.168.2.20

    c. Create a reflexive access list

    d. Fail because no specific TCP port was defined

14. Which one of the following requires an outside user to authenticate using Telnet before a predefined access to the network is enabled?

    a. Reflexive access list

    b. Extended IP named access list

    c. Dynamic access list

    d. Extended access list with the **established** option

15. What do the following statements do?

```
line vty 0 4
#no password
login
```

a. Allow anyone to log in to the router through a Telnet session without a password

b. Set the virtual terminal password to **no**

c. Prevent everyone from Telnetting into a router

d. Tell the router to use the **enable secret** password.

Real-World Project

For this project, you are asked to configure a reflexive access list for the network presented in Figure 12.16.

You want to allow the users on network 195.168.1.0 to be able to establish HTTP, DNS, and Telnet sessions outside the network. At the same time, you want sessions to network 195.168.1.0 initiated from the outside to be blocked while still allowing outside users to be able to access the servers in network 195.168.2.0. You are concerned that if one of your servers in network 195.168.2.0 is compromised, it could be used for an attack on 195.168.1.20.

Strategy

To define your topology, 195.168.1.1 connects your internal private network, 195.168.2.1 connects your internal public network, and 24.112.69.141 is your

12

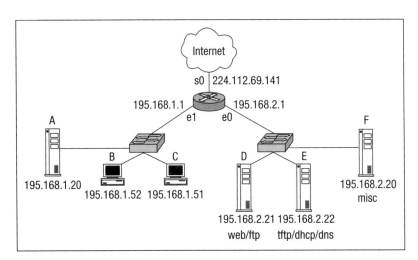

Figure 12.16   Diagram of a sample network.

external connection. You will use a reflexive access list in which you will filter traffic out the external (serial 0) connection, looking for the three types of traffic originating in 195.168.1.0. You will apply the inbound filter to Ethernet1 because applying it to serial 0 would interfere with traffic heading to your public network. You will add static access list commands to meet the rest of the objectives.

Configuring Router:

1. Configure serial 0 as follows:

```
Router(config)#Interface serial 0
Router(configif)# ip access-group outbound out
```

2. Configure Ethernet1 as follows:

```
Router(config-if)#Interface Ethernet 1
Router(configif)# ip access-group inbound out
```

The traffic will be inbound to the user network but outbound on the Ethernet interface.

3. Create your outbound access list next.

```
Router(config)#ip access-list extended outbound
Router(config-ext-nacl)#permit tcp 195.168.1.1 0.0.0.255 any eq 80
   reflect keep-data
Router(config-ext-nacl)#permit tcp 195.168.1.1 0.0.0.255 any eq 53
   reflect keep-data
Router(config-ext-nacl)#permit tcp 195.168.1.1 0.0.0.255 any eq 23
   reflect keep-data
Router(config-ext-nacl)#permit tcp 195.168.2.1 0.0.0.255 any
Router(config-ext-nacl)#permit udp 195.168.2.1 0.0.0.255 any
Router(config-ext-nacl)#permit icmp 195.168.2.1 0.0.0.255 any
!
Router(config-ext-nacl)# ip access-list extended inbound
Router(config-ext-nacl)#permit tcp 195.168.2.1 0.0.0.255 any
   established
Router(config-ext-nacl)#evaluate keep-data
```

4. To verify your access lists, use:

```
Router(config)#show ip access-list
```

To see the reflexive access list, you will need to wait until there are some sessions with the outside world initiated by your user network.

CHAPTER THIRTEEN

Optimizing Routing Update Operation

After completing this chapter, you will be able to:

✓ Select and configure the different ways to control routing update traffic

✓ Configure route redistribution in a network that does not have redundant paths between dissimilar routing processes

✓ Configure route redistribution in a network that has redundant paths between dissimilar routing processes

✓ Configure policy-based routing using route maps

✓ Resolve path selection problems that result in a redistributed network

✓ Verify route redistribution

✓ Given a set of network requirements, configure redistribution between different routing domains and verify proper operation

✓ Given a set of network requirements, configure policy-based routing within your network and verify proper operation

This chapter explores route redistribution in a multirouting protocol environment. It presents issues with implementing redistribution, as well as methods for facilitating a successful redistribution environment.

This chapter also explores some of the methods that can be used to optimize routing update operation for networks in which redistribution may or may not be occurring. The methods covered include default static routes, route filtering, administrative distance modification, and passive interfaces.

Standard policy-based routing is introduced as a way of influencing the flow and precedence of selected network traffic. Policy-based routing is shown to be a tremendously useful means of balancing optimal network performance with the scalability and accessibility requirements that characterize so many of today's truly successful internetworks.

Overview of Multirouting Protocol Networks

Networks commonly run multiple routing protocols within a single autonomous system. As we saw in Chapter 10, Border Gateway Protocol (BGP) implementations are among the types of networks that use multiple routing protocols within autonomous systems (ASes). In BGP, the main reason for running multiple routing protocols is to allow an interior gateway protocol (IGP) to handle the AS's internal routing update operations and to let BGP handle the AS's external routing update operations.

Scenarios other than BGP employ multiple routing protocols. The following data points outline some of these other situations:

➤ *Migrating from an older IGP to a newer one*—As networks scale to meet business needs and technical goals and requirements, IGPs must be able to offer a viable routing solution that is scalable enough to meet the networks' new needs. For a network whose IGP cannot scale with the network, a new IGP is required to replace the old one. In such a situation, both IGPs will coexist until the older protocol has been phased out.

➤ *Backward compatibility*—Some applications may use protocols that are not compatible with a network's new routing protocol. In this situation, the older protocol must be kept to ensure backward compatibility with these applications.

➤ *Multivendor environment*—Often, some routers in a network will employ proprietary routing protocols, such as Interior Gateway Routing Protocol (IGRP) and Enhanced IGRP (EIGRP), whereas other routers in the same network will employ nonproprietary protocols.

➤ *Efficiency*—Depending on the network's characteristics and requirements, one routing protocol may work better than another in one part of the network, whereas the opposite could be true in a different area of the same network. In this situation, a multirouting protocol network benefits performance.

➤ *Administrative boundaries*—In some networks, administration is distributed rather than centralized. In these types of environments, certain areas of the network may be using different protocols and technologies.

In all of these situations, redistribution may be necessary.

Understanding Redistribution

Redistribution is the process of distributing routing information discovered through one routing protocol into the update messages of another routing protocol. In Figure 13.1, for example, Router 2 is redistributing EIGRP-learned routes into its IGRP process and then advertising them via IGRP to Router 3.

Another definition of redistribution is the capacity for Autonomous System Boundary Routers (ASBRs) to exchange and advertise routes learned from one AS to the next. In this context, an AS simply denotes a group of networks using the same routing protocol. In Figure 13.1, Router 2 is an ASBR that is receiving routes from the EIGRP AS and advertising them via redistribution to the IGRP AS.

The following output shows how Router 3's routing table would look after receiving the redistributed routes:

```
Router_B#show ip route
Codes: C - connected, S - static, I - IGRP, R - RIP, M - mobile, B - BGP
       D - EIGRP, EX - EIGRP external, O - OSPF, IA - OSPF inter-area
       E1 - OSPF external type 1, E2 - OSPF external type 2, E - EGP
       i - IS-IS, L1 - IS-IS level-1, L2 - IS-IS level-2, * -candidate
default

 172.16.0.0/24 is subnetted, 4 subnets
I   172.16.2.0 [100/293200] via 172.16.13.1, 00:00:32, Ethernet0
I   172.16.3.0 [100/239900] via 172.16.13.1, 00:00:32, Ethernet0
C   172.16.13.0 is directly connected, Ethernet0
C   172.16.14.0 is directly connected, Ethernet1
```

This table tells us that networks 172.16.2.0 and 172.16.3.0 were learned via IGRP.

This example demonstrates a case in which the router is practicing *unidirectional redistribution*. Unidirectional redistribution is redistribution that occurs from routing protocol **x** into routing protocol **y**, but not from routing protocol **y** into routing protocol **x**. Router 2 is redistributing EIGRP into IGRP but not IGRP into EIGRP.

13

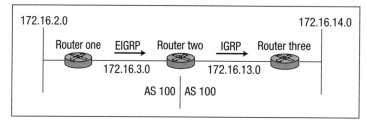

Figure 13.1   Redistribution occurs on a router.

Bidirectional redistribution, on the other hand, is redistribution that occurs in both directions; routing protocol **x** is redistributed into routing protocol **y**, and routing protocol **y** is redistributed into routing protocol **x**. Figure 13.2 presents an example of this scenario.

In Figure 13.2, Router 2 is redistributing EIGRP routes from network 10.0.0.0 into IGRP and advertising them to Router 1. Router 2 is also redistributing IGRP routes from network 172.16.0.0 into EIGRP and advertising them to Routers 3 and 4.

The following routing table is for Router 4:

```
Router_4#show ip route
Codes: C - connected, S - static, I - IGRP, R - RIP, M - mobile, B - BGP
       D - EIGRP, EX - EIGRP external, O - OSPF, IA - OSPF inter-area
       E1 - OSPF external type 1, E2 - OSPF external type 2, E - EGP
       i - IS-IS, L1 - IS-IS level-1, L2 - IS-IS level-2, * -candidate
default

 10.0.0.0/24 is subnetted, 3 subnets
C    10.1.3.0 is directly connected, Ethernet0
E    10.1.1.0 [90/8903] via 10.1.3.2, Ethernet0
E    10.10.2.0 [90/39200] via 10.1.3.2, Ethernet0
E EX 172.16.0.0 [170/43200] via 10.1.3.2, Ethernet0
```

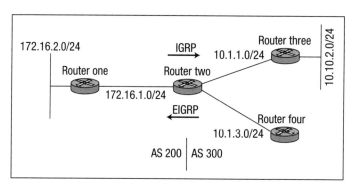

Figure 13.2   Bidirectional redistribution occurring on Router 2.

The *EX* in the last routing table entry indicates that the route is external. Whenever a route is redistributed into EIGRP and advertised to an EIGRP router in another AS, the route will be tagged with an *EX* in the routing table. These routes will also have a default administrative distance of 170, as shown in this routing table.

We see here that Router 4 has acquired the external route 172.16.0.0 from Router 2, who is doing the redistribution between EIGRP and IGRP. Note in this example that the external route is a summary route. This is because route summarization occurs automatically at major network boundaries, unless it is disabled. As a result, Router 4, as well as Router 3, are unaware of the more specific routes in network 172.16.0.0.

Redistribution and Administrative Distance

A router in a multirouting protocol environment will inevitably learn of a destination from more than one routing protocol. In these environments, a router must be able to choose which of the routing protocols would offer the best route. The tool that lets a router make this decision is the *administrative distance*.

Administrative distances, as we have seen in Chapter 2, are assigned to routes learned from different sources and are used to rate the believability of the sources. Sources with lower administrative distances are preferred over those with higher administrative distances. As a result, when a router receives the same route from two different routing protocols, the router chooses the route that comes from the routing protocol with the lower administrative distance. Table 13.1 presents the common default administrative distances.

Table 13.1   Common administrative distances ranked smallest to largest.

Routing Information Source	Default Distance
Connected routes	0
Static routes for local interface	0
Static routes to next-hop router	1
EIGRP summary route	5
External BGP derived routes	20
EIGRP derived routes	90
IGRP derived routes	100
OSPF derived routes	110
RIP (v1 & v2) derived routes	120
IS-IS derived routes	115
EGP derived routes	140
External EIGRP derived routes	170
Internal BGP derived routes	200
Unknown	255

13

We mention administrative distances here because in a redistribution environment it may be necessary to modify the administrative distance for certain routes to prevent the problem of suboptimal path selection. Later sections of this chapter discuss this issue, along with other issues that are related to a redistribution environment.

Understanding Metric Redistribution

A router uses metrics to determine the best path to a destination. When routes are redistributed from one routing protocol into another routing protocol, so are the metrics. However, because metrics are not the same for two different routing protocols (except for IGRP and EIGRP), the router must be able to translate the metric of the received routing protocol into the metric of the other routing protocol. For instance, if a router received a Routing Information Protocol (RIP) route and redistributed it into Open Shortest Path First (OSPF), the route's hop count would be translated into cost. Moreover, this route (and any other route) would be assigned a cost that was configured on the router. The metric value that gets assigned to redistributed routes is called the *default*, or *seed*, metric.

The default metric is used within the AS in exactly the same manner that the AS's routing protocol uses the metric. This means that when the default metric for a route is advertised, the metric gets incremented. This is the default behavior for redistributed routes.

Major Issues with Redistribution

Implementing redistribution in large networks can be quite a challenge because each routing protocol has its own unique way of operating, and not all routing protocols work smoothly with each other. Some major issues with implementing redistribution are the following:

➤ *Routing feedback loops*—Routing feedback loops is a problem in which routers send routing information learned from one AS back into that same AS. This usually occurs when redistributing at multiple points in the network (see Figure 13.3).

➤ *Suboptimal path selection*—Different routing protocols use different metrics to calculate the best path. Because the metric for one routing protocol cannot be accurately translated into the metric of another routing protocol, suboptimal path selection may occur.

➤ *Unsynchronized convergence*—Because different routing protocols respond to topology changes at various rates, faster converging protocols will synchronize before slower converging protocols. The result is an inconsistent view of the topology from the routers' perspectives.

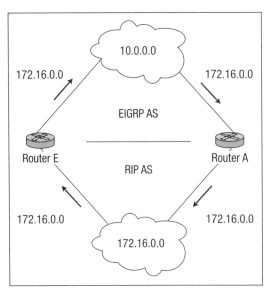

Figure 13.3 Network 172.16.0.0 is redistributed back into the RIP AS.

Major Guidelines to Follow when Redistributing

To prevent issues such as those just described from militating against a successful redistribution implementation, Cisco offers the following design guidelines:

➤ *Know your network's features*—Be extremely familiar with your network's features, including its topology and traffic patterns. Redistribution is a powerful tool that can be wielded to influence user traffic to either the network's benefit or its detriment. Therefore, being thoroughly familiar with your environment is necessary to make sure that redistribution is occurring where and how it *should* be occurring.

➤ *Establish routing protocol boundaries*—Routing protocol boundaries allow the network to keep different routing protocol operations separate from each other. This makes administration a lot easier and improves network performance.

➤ *Use unidirectional redistribution*—To prevent the problem of routing feedback loops, you should try to redistribute in only one direction. In the other direction, the alternatives to redistribution would be to use default or static routes.

➤ *Control bidirectional redistribution*—When two-way redistribution is a necessity, you must control how redistribution occurs to prevent problems with routing feedbacks and suboptimal path selection. Later sections of this chapter explain how this type of control can be accomplished using such tools as route filters and administrative distance modification.

13

Configuration of Redistribution

Cisco supports the redistribution of all common routing protocols. Fortunately, all routing protocols are configured to be redistributed with one command, the **redistribute** command. However, not all protocols are redistributed with the exact same *parameters*. In addition, you should still always consult Cisco IOS documentation to determine if any special issues need to be taken into account with the routing protocols you are planning to redistribute. This will help ensure that your network does not encounter any hidden problems that could have been prevented by simply consulting the IOS literature.

The following steps outline the process of configuring route redistribution:

1. Locate the router on which redistribution will be occurring.

2. Enter the routing process into which routes are to be redistributed. This will be known as the "core" routing process.

3. Issue the **redistribute** command to redistribute a protocol into the core routing process. This injects the protocol's routes into the core routing process so the core protocol can advertise the routes.

At this point, unidirectional redistribution is established.

The following sections explore how these steps work. We use OSPF and EIGRP as examples.

Redistributing into OSPF

The following command is used in the second step, entering the routing process:

```
Router(config)#router ospf process-id
```

The routing process is OSPF, which will also be known as the core routing process, or core protocol. This is the protocol into which routes will be injected.

The following command is used in the third step, issuing the **redistribute** command:

```
Router(config-router)#redistribute protocol [process-id|AS-number]
   [metric metric-value] [metric-type type-value] [route-map map-tag]
   [subnets] [tag tag-value]
```

Notice that quite a few optional parameters are available with OSPF redistribution. Table 13.2 explains all of them.

We now take a look at how the OSPF **redistribution** command works in an OSPF example scenario.

Table 13.2 Explaining the OSPF **redistribute** command.

Parameter	Meaning
protocol	Protocol that is being redistributed. Possible protocols include: **connected**, **bgp**, **eigrp**, **egp**, **igrp**, **isis**, **iso-igrp**, **mobile**, **odr**, **ospf**, **static**, or **rip**.
process-id/AS-number	Process ID or AS-number of the protocol being redistributed.
metric-value	The default (seed) metric that will be assigned to the redistributed routes. This parameter must be configured when redistributing into protocols other than OSPF and when not using the **default-metric** command.
type-value	An OSPF parameter that identifies whether the redistributed protocol's routes should be advertised as type 1 or type 2 external routes. Possible values are therefore **1** for type 1 routes or **2** for type 2 external routes. Type 2 is the default.
map-tag	A route map name. Route maps can be used to specify the conditions in which routes can be redistributed.
subnets	An OSPF parameter that allows subnets to be redistributed into OSPF. The default behavior is *not* to redistribute subnets.
tag-value	32-bit decimal number attached to external routes. If this value is not specified, then the remote autonomous system number is used for routes from BGP and EGP; for other protocols, zero (0) is used.

Example OSPF Redistribution Scenario

Figure 13.4 illustrates a network topology in which Router E is running OSPF and Router A is running RIP. Router C is redistributing RIP routes into OSPF and advertising them to Router E.

The following output shows the initial configuration for Router C:

```
Router_C(config)#router rip
Router_C(config-router)#network 203.250.15.0
!
Router_C(config)#router ospf 1
Router_C(config-router)#network 203.250.15.1 0.0.0.0 area 0
```

At this stage, Router C is configured to advertise and receive RIP updates on *both* its Ethernet and serial interfaces (RIP is advertised to Router E, but Router E runs

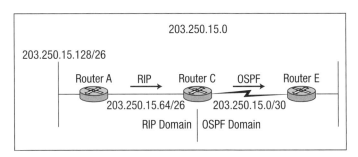

Figure 13.4 Unidirectional redistribution is occurring only on Router C.

only OSPF). Its serial interface is also placed in area 0 and will be advertising and receiving only OSPF. There are no OSPF updates being sent to Router A.

The following command now configures redistribution on Router C:

```
Router_C(config-router)#redistribute rip metric 10 subnets
```

Router C will subsequently redistribute RIP-learned routes into its OSPF routing process and will advertise them to Router E with a cost of 10. Note that because the **metric-type** parameter was omitted from the command, the routes will be type 2 external routes and will always have a cost of 10, no matter where they are carried in the OSPF domain.

Note also that the **subnets** keyword was specified. This is necessary for Router C to be able to redistribute 203.250.15.128 /26, which is a subnet of network 203.250.15.0 /24. If the **subnets** keyword were omitted, 203.250.15.128 /26 would *not* be redistributed.

The following configuration shows us how Router E's routing table appears after receiving the redistributed routes from Router C:

```
Router_E#show ip route
Codes: C - connected, S - static, I - IGRP, R - RIP, M - mobile, B - BGP
       D - EIGRP, EX - EIGRP external, O - OSPF, IA - OSPF inter-area
       E1 - OSPF external type 1, E2 - OSPF external type 2, E - EGP
       i - IS-IS, L1 - IS-IS level-1, L2 - IS-IS level-2, * -candidate
default

 203.250.15.0 is variably subnetted, 3 subnets, 2 masks
C    203.250.15.0 255.255.255.252 is directly connected, Serial0
O    203.250.15.64 255.255.255.192 [110/74] via 203.250.15.1, 00:08:37,
Serial0
O E2 203.250.15.128 255.255.255.192 [110/10] via 203.250.15.1, 00:8:37,
Serial0
```

The second entry in Router E's routing table indicates that network 203.250.15.64 /26 is an OSPF intra-area route. This route was not redistributed because Router A never advertised it to Router C (due to Split Horizon).

The third entry in this routing table indicates that network 203.250.15.128 is an OSPF type 2 external route. This is the route that Router C redistributed. Note that the route's cost is 10.

Redistributing into EIGRP

The following command is used to redistribute routing protocols into EIGRP:

```
Router(config-router)#redistribute protocol [process-id|AS-number]
  [match {internal|external1|external2}] [metric metric-value]
  [route-map map-tag]
```

Table 13.3 explains the parameters used in this command.

The next section presents an example of EIGRP redistribution.

Example EIGRP Redistribution Scenario

Figure 13.5 presents a diagram of an EIGRP internetwork that comprises two ASes, AS 1000 and AS 2000. In this illustration, both ASes are using the same routing protocol, EIGRP. Router 2 is configured to redistribute Router 3's routes from AS 1000 and advertise them to Router 1.

Note here that automatic route summarization will occur at Router 2 unless this feature is disabled. If it is not disabled, Router 2 will advertise redistributed routes at the major network boundary.

Table 13.3   Explaining the EIGRP redistribute command.

Parameter	Meaning
Protocol	Protocol that is being redistributed into the routing process. Possible protocols include: **connected, bgp, eigrp, egp, igrp, isis, iso-igrp, mobile, odr, ospf, static,** or **rip.**
process-id/AS-number	Process ID or AS-number of the protocol being redistributed.
match	For OSPF, the criteria by which OSPF routes are redistributed into other routing domains: **Internal** specifies that routes that lay internal to a specific AS may be redistributed; **external1** specifies that external type 1 routes may be redistributed; **external2** specifies that external type 2 routes may be redistributed.
metric-value	The default (seed) metric assigned to the redistributed routes. This parameter must be configured when redistributing into protocols other than OSPF and when not using the **default-metric** command.
map-tag	A route map name. Route maps can be used to specify the conditions in which routes can be redistributed.

13

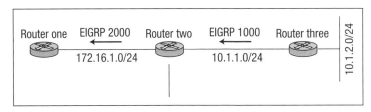

Figure 13.5   Unidirectional redistribution occurring on Router 2.

The following output shows us how Router 2 was configured:

```
Router_2(config)#router eigrp 1000
Router_2(config-router)#network 10.0.0.0
Router_2(config-router)#no auto-summary

!
Router_2(config)#router eigrp 2000
Router_2(config-router)#network 172.16.0.0
Router_2(config-router)#redistribute eigrp 1000
Router_2(config-router)#no auto-summary
```

In this configuration, Router 2 will be redistributing EIGRP routes that come from AS 1000 into EIGRP AS 2000. The **no auto-summary** feature prevents both routing processes from summarizing their routes at the major network boundary.

As a result, upon receiving an advertisement for network 10.1.2.0 /24 from Router 3, Router 2 redistributes the route into AS 2000 and advertises it to Router 1. The following topology table would appear on Router 1:

```
Router_1#show ip eigrp topology 10.1.2.0 255.255.255.0

IP-EIGRP topology entry for 10.1.2.0/24
  State is Passive, Query origin flag is 1, 1 Successor(s), FD is 46763776
  Routing Descriptor Blocks:
  20.1.1.1 (Serial0), from 20.1.1.1, Send flag is 0x0
      Composite metric is (46763776/46251776), Route is External
      Vector metric:
        Minimum bandwidth is 56 Kbit
        Total delay is 41000 microseconds
        Reliability is 255/255
        Load is 1/255
        Minimum MTU is 1500
        Hop count is 2
      External data:
        Originating router is 10.1.2.1
        AS number of route is 1000
        External protocol is EIGRP, external metric is 46251776
        Administrator tag is 0 (0x00000000)
```

The topology table indicates that this route is external and gives additional information about the route.

Note in this example that we did not specify a default metric for the redistributed routes. When redistributing into protocols other than OSPF, if the default metric is not specified (either within the **redistribute** command or by using the **default-metric** command), the default metric is 0 and routes *cannot* be redistributed. In actuality, therefore, the redistribution shown for Router 2 could never have taken place unless it had a default metric for the redistributed routes.

The following command can be used to configure a default-metric for routes redistributed *into* EIGRP (and IGRP):

```
Router(config-router)#default-metric bandwidth delay reliability loading mtu
```

Each of the parameters in this command is used by EIGRP and IGRP to compute the composite metric for routes that they redistribute.

Table 13.4 presents an explanation of the **default-metric** command parameters.

As an example, let us configure Router 2 from our scenario with a default metric:

```
Router_2(config)#router eigrp 2000
Router_2(config-router)#default-metric 10000 2000 255 1 1500
```

Consequently, all routes that are redistributed into EIGRP AS 2000 will be assigned a metric that will be calculated from the **default-metric** values configured for Router 2.

There is also another command used to set the default metric. This command is used for redistributing routes into OSPF, RIP, EGP, or BGP:

```
Router(config-router)#default-metric number
```

where *number* is the value of the metric.

13

Table 13.4   Explaining the EIGRP/IGRP default-metric command.

Parameter	Meaning
bandwidth	Minimum bandwidth of the route in Kbps.
delay	Route delay integer in tens of microseconds.
reliability	A measure of the reliability of a route; expressed as a value from 0 to 255, where 255 indicates the highest reliable route.
loading	A measure of the load on a route; expressed as a value from 1 to 255, where 255 indicates the route is completely loaded.
mtu	Maximum Transmission Unit (MTU). The MTU is the maximum packet size accepted on a route; expressed as an integer value.

For example, the following command assigns a default metric to routes that are redistributed into OSPF:

```
Router(config-router)#default-metric 100
```

where the number *100* indicates a cost of 100.

Bidirectional Redistribution and Alternatives

Thus far we have explored how unidirectional redistribution occurs. But now we need to address how the other routing process, the one that is being redistributed into the core, will learn of the core's routes. Several redistribution techniques allow the "edge" routing process (as it is called) to learn of the core's routes. The following methods may be employed:

➤ Distribute a default route into the edge routing process

➤ Redistribute static routes into the edge routing process

➤ Redistribute all routes into the edge routing process and use route filters

➤ Redistribute all routes into the edge routing process and modify the administrative distance for selected routes

Distributing a Default Route

Distribution of a default route into the edge routing process is an alternative to bidirectional redistribution. This method of informing the edge AS about the core AS's routes is a way to prevent routing feedback loops and other redistribution issues from affecting the network's stability and performance.

The command used to configure a default route depends on the routing protocol being used. With RIP, for example, the default route is created by the **ip default-network** command. This command allows a directly connected network to be advertised to the RIP domain as the default route 0.0.0.0 /0. Upon receiving the route, an internal RIP router will use it to forward any packets addressed to unknown destinations.

The syntax for the **ip default-network** command is as follows:

```
Router(config-router)#ip default-network network-number
```

where *network-number* is the directly connected network for which a default route will be advertised. The network number must also be configured via the **network** command in the routing process that will be advertising the default route.

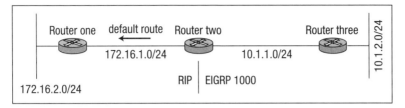

Figure 13.6   Distributing a default route to the RIP domain.

For example, in Figure 13.6, Router 2 is the ASBR for RIP and EIGRP. EIGRP is learning of the RIP domain via redistribution of the latter's routes into the former, whereas RIP is learning of the EIGRP AS via distribution of a default route into the RIP domain.

The following output shows Router 2's configuration for RIP:

```
Router_2(config)#router rip
Router_2(config-router)#network 172.16.0.0
Router_2(config-router)#network 10.0.0.0
Router_2(config-router)#ip default-network 10.0.0.0
```

This configuration tells us that RIP is advertising for network 172.16.0.0 and 10.0.0.0. The **ip default-network** statement indicates that RIP is also to advertise a default route (0.0.0.0) for network 10.0.0.0. This route will be advertised to network 172.16.0.0, the RIP domain in Figure 13.6.

*Note: The **ip default-network** command does not cause a default route to be forwarded into the network specified in this command. That is, Router 2, for example, would not forward the default route into network 10.0.0.0.*

The following output shows us how Router 1's routing table would look after receiving the default route from Router 2:

```
Router_1#show ip route

<output omitted>

 172.16.0.0/16 is subnetted, 2 subnets
C    172.16.1.0 255.255.255.0 is directly connected, Ethernet0
C    172.16.2.0 255.255.255.0 is directly connected, Ethernet1
R*   0.0.0.0 0.0.0.0 [120/1] via 172.16.1.1, 00:00:06, Ethernet0
```

The asterisk * symbol denotes that the route is a default route. Whenever Router 1 receives a packet whose destination network is not listed in its routing table, Router 1 matches the packet with 0.0.0.0 and forwards it out its Ethernet0 interface to Router 2.

13

Redistributing Static Routes

Distributing a default route is one way to inform an AS of another AS; redistributing static routes is the other alternative. Static routes allow manual specification of a destination network without requiring a dynamic routing protocol to learn it. However, in most cases, the static routes must be redistributed into the routing protocol if the static routes are to be advertised.

The following command is used to create a static route:

```
Router(config)#ip route prefix mask address|interface
    [administrative-distance] [tag tag] [permanent]
```

Table 13.5 explains the parameters of the **ip route** command.

Example Static Route Redistribution Scenario

The previous example (Figure 13.6) showed how Router 2 was distributing a default route into the RIP domain. In this new example, the same router is now creating a *static* route for the EIGRP AS and redistributing it into the RIP domain. RIP-learned routes are still being redistributed into Router 2's EIGRP process.

The following configuration for Router 2 tells us that Router 2 is redistributing network 10.0.0.0 /8 into RIP and advertising it to network 172.16.0.0:

```
Router_2(config)#router rip
Router_2(config-router)#network 172.16.0.0
Router_2(config-router)#redistribute static
!
Router_2(config)#ip route 10.0.0.0 255.0.0.0 ethernet0
```

Table 13.5   Explaining the ip route command.

Parameter	Meaning
prefix	The destination route prefix (network number)
mask	The destination's prefix mask
address	The IP address of the next-hop router along the destination's path
interface	The local interface used to reach the destination
administrative-distance	Used to create a floating static route (a route that can be dynamically overridden by a routing protocol)
tag	Route map tag
permanent	Indicates that the route will not be removed from the routing table even if the interface associated with the route becomes unavailable

The following output shows how Router 1's routing table would look after it received the static route from Router 2:

```
Router_1#show ip route

<output omitted>

 172.16.0.0/16 is subnetted, 2 subnets
C    172.16.1.0 255.255.255.0 is directly connected, Ethernet0
C    172.16.2.0 255.255.255.0 is directly connected, Ethernet1
R    10.0.0.0 [120/1] via 172.16.1.1, 00:00:03, Ethernet0
```

The last entry in this routing table indicates that Router 1 learned of network 10.0.0.0 via a RIP update from Router 2. Router 1 consequently has a route to the EIGRP AS.

Default Static Routes

The default static route incorporates the features of both static and default routes. In a redistribution environment, this hybrid feature is generally used by routing protocols for which the **ip default-network** command does not work effectively, such as with EIGRP. In EIGRP, using the **ip default-network** command will not cause a default route to be advertised; instead, a default static route must be created to achieve this purpose.

Default static routes are also used to reduce the number of static route entries that get redistributed. Instead of redistributing numerous static routes, a router could simply create and advertise a default static route. This route would hence emulate a default route.

So, why not just advertise a default route? You could. But with certain routing protocols, such as RIP, default static routes have an advantage over normal default routes: automatic advertisement. Default static routes are automatically advertised, unlike normal default routes, which must be specified in **network** statements.

The following command configures a default static route:

```
Router(config)#ip route 0.0.0.0 0.0.0.0 address|interface
```

where *address* is the next-hop IP address, and *interface* is the local interface used to reach the default route.

Example Default Static Route Configuration

In Figure 13.7, Router 2 is connected to a non–RIP network, 180.17.0.0. To inform the RIP domain of a path to this network, Router 2 is configured to advertise a default static route to Router 1.

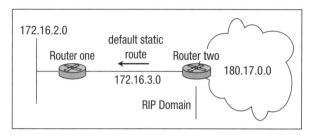

Figure 13.7 Advertising a default static route.

The following output shows the relevant configuration for Router 2:

```
Router_2(config)#router rip
Router_2(config-router)#network 172.16.0.0
!
Router_2(config)#ip route 0.0.0.0 0.0.0.0 180.17.3.2
```

Router 2 will automatically advertise the default route 0.0.0.0 to network 172.16.0.0. Upon receiving this route, Router 1 will subsequently be able to reach any unknown destination.

Controlling Routing Protocol Operation

In a multirouting protocol environment, occasionally you will not want certain routing information to be propagated or accepted. For example, when using a wide area network (WAN) connection, the best choice is to propagate only the minimum amount of information required to ensure reachability between the local and remote networks. In another instance, you may want to control routing information to prevent routing loops in a redistribution environment.

Whatever the reason for controlling routing update traffic, several techniques can accomplish this task:

➤ *Passive interface*—This feature prevents all routing updates for a routing protocol from being advertised on an interface.

➤ *Route update filtering*—This feature allows certain routing updates to be restricted.

➤ *Administrative distance modification*—This technique is used to prevent suboptimal path selection in a redistribution environment.

Passive Interfaces

Passive interfaces prevent a routing protocol's updates from being sent out a particular interface, but do not prevent the routing updates from being received on that interface.

The following command configures a passive interface:

```
Router(config-router)#passive-interface type number
```

where *type* and *number* are the interface type and interface number, respectively.

When using the **passive-interface** command on a link-state routing protocol, be aware that the command prevents neighbor relationships from being established. This is because hello packets, which are used to establish neighbor adjacencies, cannot be sent out a passive interface. Therefore, without being able to send a hello to another neighbor, the bidirectional neighbor relationship could never begin.

Example Passive Interface Configuration

In some of the earlier examples in this chapter, RIP was advertising on networks that did not use the same protocol. In such cases, passive interfaces should be configured to prevent RIP from wasting network resources (Figure 13.8).

In Figure 13.8, Router 2 is advertising a default route to its RIP domain. Because it is using the **ip default-network** command to accomplish this, Router 2 has to specify a network statement for network 10.0.0.0, even though this network is not using RIP (it is running only EIGRP). However, no RIP advertisements will be sent to this network because Router 2's Ethernet1 interface has been made passive for RIP.

The following configuration shows us how this occurred:

```
Router_2(config)#interface ethernet 1
Router_2(config-if)#ip address 10.1.1.1 255.255.255.0
!
Router_2(config)#router rip
Router_2(config-if)#network 172.16.0.0
Router_2(config-if)#network 10.0.0.0
Router_2(config-if)#ip default-network 10.0.0.0
Router_2(config-if)#passive-interface ethernet 1
```

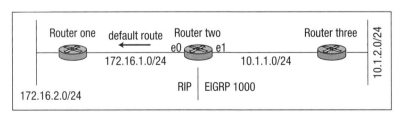

Figure 13.8 Router 2 is configured with a passive interface for Ethernet1.

Route Filters

Route filtering is another method for controlling routing update traffic. This technique allows a router to restrict certain network advertisements from being either accepted or received. The tool used to accomplish this filtering process is the distribute list, which uses access lists to match network advertisements with specified criteria. Specifically, the following steps describe how this filtering process occurs:

1. An update is received or about to be sent on an interface.

2. The router determines whether a route filter is associated with the interface.

3. If a filter is associated with the interface, the update is matched against the access list. If a filter is not associated with the interface, the update is not controlled and is processed as usual.

4. If the update forms a match with the access list, the update is controlled accordingly. If the update goes through the access list without forming a match, the update is dropped by the **implicit deny any**.

Route Filtering Configuration

Route filtering is configured by creating an access list and applying it to a routing protocol via the **distribute-list** command. To filter outbound updates, the following **distribute-list** command would be used:

```
Router(config-router)#distribute-list number|name out
  [interface-name | routing-process | AS-number]
```

Table 13.6 explains the **distribute-list out** command, which is used to filter routing updates that the router *sends*.

To filter routing updates that the router receives, use the following **distribute-list** command:

```
Router(config-router)#distribute-list number|name in [interface]
```

Table 13.6   Explaining the distribute-list out command.

Parameter	Meaning
number/name	Standard access list number or name.
out	Applies the standard access list to updates sent from the router.
interface-name	Interface name and number on which the route filter will be applied.
routing-process	Routing process name, or the **static** or **connected** keyword. The **static** keyword specifies that the route filter will be applied only to redistributed static routes, whereas the **connected** keyword specifies that the route filter will be applied only to redistributed connected routes.
AS-number	Autonomous system number.

Table 13.7   Explaining the **distribute-list in** command.

Parameter	Meaning
number\name	Standard access list number or name.
in	Applies the standard access list to all routing updates received by the router.
interface	Interface name and number on which the route filter will be applied.

Table 13.7 explains the syntax for the **distribute-list in** command.

Example Route Filtering Scenarios

The following sections explore some examples in which the **distribute-list** command is used to control routing update traffic.

Route Filtering Example 1

In Figure 13.9, Router 2 is advertising networks from 10.0.0.0 to Router 1 via EIGRP. However, Router 2 does not want Router 1 to learn about network 10.10.2.0 /24. Therefore, Router 2 applies an outbound route filter to all EIGRP updates sent to Router 1.

The following output describes how route filtering occurred on Router 2:

```
Router_2(config)#router eigrp 1
Router_2(config-router)#network 10.0.0.0
Router_2(config-router)#network 172.16.0.0
Router_2(config-router)#distribute-list 5 out e0
!
Router_2(config)#access-list 5 deny 10.10.2.0 0.0.0.255
Router_2(config)#access-list 5 permit 0.0.0.0 255.255.255.255
```

In the preceding configuration, Router 2 is configured with a distribute list that gets applied to all EIGRP routing updates sent out Ethernet0, which is the inter-

13

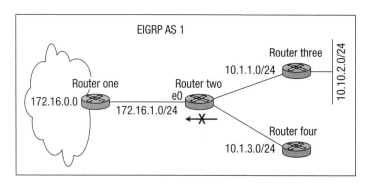

Figure 13.9   Router 2 is filtering network 10.10.2.0 /24 from all EIGRP updates sent to Router 1.

face leading to Router 1. This distribute list uses access list 5, which states that all addresses whose first three bytes match 10.10.2 will be denied, and all other routing updates will be accepted.

The reason we choose not to filter network 10.10.2.0 /24 on the inbound is because we want Router 4 to be able to accept updates for that network. If an inbound filter is applied on Router 2, Router 4 will be unable to receive updates for 10.10.2.0 /24.

Route Filtering Example 2

In the next route filtering example, shown in Figure 13.10, Router 2 is connected to Router 3 via a serial link on which EIGRP is *not* configured. Router 2 is therefore configured with static routes for networks 190.1.2.0 /24 and 190.1.3.0 /24, which are redistributed into Router 2's EIGRP process and advertised to Routers 1 and 4.

However, what if we did not want network 190.1.2.0 /24 advertised to Routers 1 and 4? Then we would need a distribute list. With a distribute list applied to Router 2's advertised *static* routes, we could prevent that network from being propagated via EIGRP to Routers 1 and 4.

The following configuration (annotated) shows us how this could occur:

```
Router_2(config)#ip route 190.1.2.0 255.255.255.0 serial0 (creates a static
route for network 190.1.2.0 /24)
Router_2(config)#ip route 192.1.3.0 255.255.255.0 serial0 (creates a static
route for network 190.1.3.0 /24)
!
Router_2(config)#router eigrp 100
Router_2(config-router)#network 10.0.0.0 (EIGRP works only in network
10.0.0.0)
Router_2(config-router)#default-metric 10000 100 255 1 1500 (assigns the
default metric to routes redistributed into EIGRP)
Router_2(config-router)#redistribute static (injects static routes into
EIGRP)
Router_2(config-router)#distribute-list 1 out static (applies access-list 1
only to static routes that are advertised outbound)
!
Router_2(config)#access-list 1 deny 190.1.2.0 255.255.255.0 0.0.0.255 (any
route whose first three bytes match 190.1.2 will be denied)
Router_2(config)#access-list 1 permit 0.0.0.0 255.255.255.255 (permits all
other routes)
```

The preceding configuration shows us that Router 2 will be applying access list 1 to the static routes that are set to be advertised by EIGRP. Because access list 1

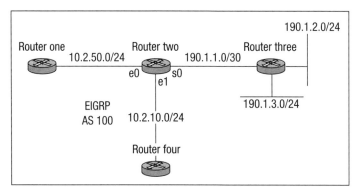

Figure 13.10 Router 2 is configured with static routes for Router 3's networks.

specifies that only networks whose first three bytes do not match 190.1.2. will be permitted, Router 2 ends up advertising just network 190.1.3.0 /24 to Routers 3 and 4.

Administrative Distance Modification

As mentioned earlier, administrative distance modification is a tool used to prevent suboptimal path selection in a redistribution environment. Suboptimal path selection occurs when a router chooses to accept routes from a routing protocol that has a better administrative distance than another routing protocol advertising the same routes, but a worse path than the other routing protocol. In this case, the reason the chosen path would be less desirable would be because of bidirectional redistribution at multiple locations in the internetwork.

To see how such a problem could occur, consider Figure 13.11.

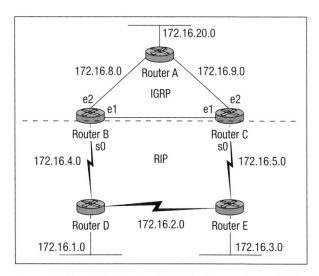

Figure 13.11 Bidirectional redistribution is occurring on Routers B and C.

In Figure 13.11, network 172.16.0.0 is split into two autonomous systems, the RIP AS and the IGRP AS. Routers B and C are performing redistribution between both routing protocols. That is, in both routers, IGRP is being redistributed into RIP, and RIP is being redistributed into IGRP.

The following configurations (annotated) are for Routers B and C, respectively:

```
Router_B(config)#router rip
Router_B(config-router)#network 172.16.0.0
Router_B(config-router)#passive-interface ethernet1 (RIP will not advertise
out Ethernet 1)
Router_B(config-router)#passive-interface ethernet2 (RIP will not advertise
out Ethernet 2)
Router_B(config-router)#default-metric 3 (a hop-count of 3 is assigned to
all routes redistributed into RIP)
Router_B(config-router)#redistribute igrp 100 (all IGRP routes in AS 100
are redistributed into RIP)
!
Router_B(config)#router igrp 100
Router_B(config-router)#network 172.16.0.0
Router_B(config-router)#passive-interface serial0 (IGRP will not advertise
out serial 0)
Router_B(config-router)#default-metric 10 100 255 1 1500 (a metric calcu-
lated from these values is assigned to all routes redistributed into IGRP)
Router_B(config-router)#redistribute rip (all RIP routes are redistributed
into IGRP)

Router_C(config)#router rip
Router_C(config-router)#network 172.16.0.0
Router_C(config-router)#passive-interface ethernet1
Router_C(config-router)#passive-interface ethernet2
Router_C(config-router)#default-metric 3
Router_C(config-router)#redistribute igrp 1
!
Router_C(config)#router igrp
Router_C(config-router)#network 172.16.0.0
Router_C(config-router)#passive-interface serial0
Router_C(config-router)#default-metric 10 100 255 1 1500
Router_C(config-router)#redistribute rip
```

In these configurations, Routers B and C are both employing passive interfaces to keep routing protocols from advertising out interfaces where their advertisements would not be understood.

Let us now take a look at the routing table for Router B:

```
Router_B#show ip route
<output omitted>

 172.16.0.0/24 is subnetted, 9 subnets
C   172.16.4.0 is directly connected, Serial0
C   172.16.7.0 is directly connected, Ethernet1
C   172.16.8.0 is directly connected, Ethernet2
I   172.16.1.0 [100/307200] via 172.16.7.2, 00:00:22, Ethernet1
I   172.16.2.0 [100/307200] via 172.16.7.2, 00:00:22, Ethernet1
I   172.16.3.0 [100/307200] via 172.16.7.2, 00:00:22, Ethernet1
I   172.16.5.0 [100/307200] via 172.16.7.2, 00:00:22, Ethernet1
I   172.16.9.0 [100/281600] via 172.16.8.2, 00:01:07, Ethernet2
I   172.16.20.0 [100/281600] via 172.16.8.2, 00:01:07, Ethernet2
```

What happened? Why are there no RIP routes in Router B's routing table? The answer is that when *Router C* redistributes all RIP routes into IGRP and advertises them to Router B, Router B ends up having to make a choice between these routes and the same routes learned via RIP from Router D. Because the choice is made in favor of the routing protocol with the lower administrative distance, which in this case is IGRP, Router B subsequently chooses all RIP routes that are learned via IGRP from Router C. (Figure 13.12 shows a copy of the previous diagram for your convenience.)

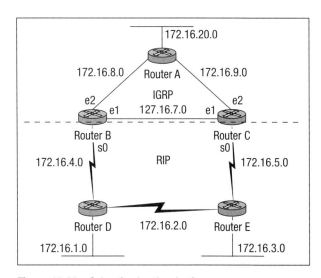

Figure 13.12   Suboptimal path selection.

13

Note that Router B is using a rather circuitous route for network 172.16.1.0. Assuming that the serial lines are all T1 speed and all the Ethernet links are 10Mbps, Router B would definitely want to choose the route for this network from Router D instead of from Router C, all things being equal.

The same problem is true for Router C. Router C would not want to use the path through Router B to reach network 172.16.3.0 because the best path would be through Router E (again, all things being equal).

To resolve this issue of suboptimal path selection, we would need to modify the administrative distance for certain RIP routes received from IGRP. Specifically, for Router B, our goal would be to make it prefer network 172.16.1.0 from RIP rather than from IGRP. This would be accomplished by issuing the **distance** command on Router B, as follows:

```
Router_B(config)#router igrp 100
Router_B(config-router)#distance 130 0.0.0.0 255.255.255.255 1
!
Router_B(config)#access-list 1 permit 172.16.1.0
```

This configuration indicates that an administrative distance of 130 will be applied to routes that form a match with access list 1. Access list 1, in turn, indicates a match is made only with 172.16.1.0 (note that the absence of the wildcard indicates an exact match); any other route will receive the usual IGRP administrative distance of 100.

As a result, upon receiving an IGRP advertisement for network 172.16.1.0 from Router C, Router B assigns the network an administrative distance of 130. When Router B receives the advertisement for this network via RIP from Router D, Router B will see that the administrative distance for the RIP-learned route is lower than what was assigned for IGRP. The RIP route for 172.16.1.0 is therefore selected and placed in the routing table.

We could also issue a similar configuration on Router C to make it prefer RIP-learned 172.16.3.0 over IGRP-learned 172.16.3.0.

Warning with Modifying Administrative Distance

Modifying the administrative distance for routes is a procedure that must be handled carefully and with enough forethought to know exactly what the effects will be on route selection. Not being able to accurately project how the network will respond to administrative distance modification for certain routes and protocols may end up causing your network even worse problems with suboptimal path selection than what you were originally trying to resolve.

Verifying Redistribution

After configuring your network with redistribution, always verify that the redistribution operation is occurring as expected. The following tips will help you in this process:

➤ Understand the network's topology, traffic patterns, and redistribution requirements.

➤ Analyze routing tables on a subset of internal and ASBR routers to determine if optimal paths are in fact being selected.

➤ Run a **trace** on routes to determine if the shortest routes are being taken.

➤ If you suspect that there may be problems with feedback loops or suboptimal path selection, narrow the source of the problem and then use the **trace** and **debug** commands to examine how routing protocol traffic is being affected.

Policy-Based Routing

Policy-based routing is the use of rules, or policies, to influence the path that selected traffic takes. Introduced in Cisco IOS release 11.0, policy-based routing allows a network to devise a routing policy that best meets the network's requirements for security, performance, and availability. This feature may also be used with such Quality of Service (QoS) tools as Type of Service (ToS) routing and IOS queueing, both of which are methods for prioritizing selected traffic.

The following data points highlight some of the benefits of policy-based routing:

➤ *Cost savings*—Network traffic can be directed to use high-cost links only for short-duration high-volume file transfers, whereas the rest of the network's traffic can be directed to use low-cost links. This is of particular benefit to high-cost WAN links, where usage costs are generally based on the amount of time the links are in use.

➤ *Load-balancing*—Traditional load-balancing distributes traffic across multiple paths on a per destination basis. With policy-based routing, traffic can be load-balanced across multiple paths based on the traffic's *characteristics*.

➤ *Quality of Service*—This feature allows networks to provide better service to selected network traffic. Using ToS routing and IOS queuing, networks can restrict bandwidth consumption for selected applications and ensure that higher priority applications receive optimal treatment.

➤ *ISP traffic control*—Based on network policy, ISPs can direct traffic originating from their customers through different Internet channels. In addition, using policy-based routing, ISPs can offer custom-tailored grades of service to selected customers.

13

How Policy-Based Routing Works

Policy-based routing uses route maps to test *incoming* packets. With route maps, incoming packets can be permitted or denied based on such characteristics as the packets' address, associated application, protocol, and size.

The route maps employed in policy-based routing are similar to the ones used in BGP policy. Both route maps use **match** conditions to define the criteria for a packet's permission or denial, and both route maps use **set** actions to define how the packet should be controlled once it has met the matching criteria.

However, BGP and non-BGP route maps do have a few differences. For instance, with BGP route maps, if a match condition is met and the route map specifies **deny**, the routing update is dropped. With standard policy-based route maps, however, the packet is allowed to be forwarded as it normally would be, without being controlled or denied. In addition, the **implicit deny any** at the bottom of BGP route maps drops packets, whereas the **implicit deny any** at the bottom of standard policy-based route maps permits the packet to be forwarded as it normally would be, without being controlled or denied.

Finally, with policy-based route maps, each route map statement may have multiple sets of **match** conditions and **set** actions. When this is the case, all **match** conditions in the route map statement must be met before the **set** actions are applied to the packet.

Route Map Configuration

The following commands are used to implement policy-based routing:

```
Router(config)#route-map route-map-name permit|deny [sequence-number]
```

```
Router(config-route-map)#match {conditions}
```

```
Router(config-route-map)#set {actions}
```

Note that these commands are the same as those introduced in the discussion on BGP route maps in Chapter 10.

The following sections explore some of the common **match** and **set** commands employed in a policy-based routing environment.

The **match ip address** Command

One of the **match** commands we used quite often in Chapter 10 was the **match ip address** command. This particular command is also commonly used in standard policy-based routing. This command is presented as follows:

```
Router(config-route-map)#match ip address {access-list-number | name}
  [. . . access-list-number | name]
```

The access list can be either standard or extended. The former can match only a packet's source address, whereas the latter can match the source and destination address, application, protocol type, ToS value, and precedence.

Note that in this command you can specify multiple access lists to test incoming packets. Only one access list would need to match in order to meet the route map statement criterion.

The **match length** Command

Another common **match** command is the **match length** command. This command is presented as follows:

```
Router(config-route-map)#match length min max
```

This command is used to specify the range of a packet's size to be matched. The *min* parameter identifies the minimum layer 3 packet length, and the *max* parameter identifies the maximum layer 3 packet length, inclusive. This means that if a packet's layer 3 length (specified as a numeric value in the packet's length field) falls anywhere between the minimum and maximum values allowed, the packet will form a match.

The **set ip next-hop** Command

The **set ip next-hop** command is used to specify the next-hop router to which a matching packet will be forwarded. This command is presented as follows:

```
Router(config-route-map)#set ip next-hop ip-address [. . . ip-address]
```

where *ip-address* indicates the IP address of the next-hop router to which matching packets are to be forwarded.

Multiple IP addresses can be specified. The first IP address that is active will be used as the next-hop.

13

The **set ip interface** Command

The **set ip interface** command is used to specify the interface from which a matching packet will be forwarded. This command is presented as follows:

```
Router(config-route-map)#set interface interface [. . . interface]
```

where *interface* identifies the local router's interface from which matching packets are to be forwarded.

Multiple interfaces can be specified. The first active interface will be used to forward the matching packet.

*Note: If **set interface** and **set ip next-hop** commands are in the same route map statement, the **set ip next-hop** command will take precedence.*

The **set ip default next-hop** Command

The **set ip default next-hop** command is used to specify the next-hop router to which a packet will be forwarded if there is no explicit route listed in the routing table for the packet's destination address. This command is presented as follows:

```
Router(config-route-map)#set ip default next-hop ip-address
  [. . . ip-address]
```

where *ip-address* is the next hop to which matching packets without an explicit route to the destination are to be forwarded.

Multiple next-hop addresses can be specified. The first one listed will be used.

The **set ip default interface** Command

The **set ip default interface** command is used to specify the interface from which a packet will be forwarded if there is no explicit route listed in the routing table for the packet's destination address. This command is presented as follows:

```
Router(config-route-map)#set default interface interface [. . . interface]
```

where *interface* is the default interface to which matching packets with no explicit destination routes are to be forwarded.

Multiple default interfaces can be specified. The first active one listed is used.

Additional **set** Commands

Additional common **set** commands employed in a policy-based environment are the following:

➤ **set ip tos**—Used to set the IP ToS value in a matching packet's ToS field

➤ **set ip precedence**—Used to set the IP precedence in a matching packet's IP precedence field

Applying the Route Map to an Interface

Once the route map has been configured, it must then be applied to an interface with the following command:

```
Router(config-if)#ip policy route-map route-map-name
```

where *route-map-name* is the route map's name. This command applies the specified route map to *all* packets received on the associated interface. It does not, however, have any effect on packets that are sent out that interface.

Enabling Fast-Switched Policy Routing

Cisco routers are capable of using various methods to switch received packets from inbound to outbound interfaces. These methods are known as *switching paths*, the most common of which are the following:

➤ Process switching

➤ Fast switching

➤ Distributed switching

➤ Netflow switching

Policy-based interfaces use the process-switching path by default. With process switching, each received packet is processed by the router's central processing unit (CPU). Depending on the router's hardware capabilities and the sizes of packets, typical speeds for this type of switching path range from 1,000 to 10,000 packets per second (pps).

However, this switching rate is not fast enough for many policy-based environments for which high switching performance is a requirement. As a result, Cisco now allows policy-based interfaces to perform fast switching. With fast switching, packet-per-second-throughput is dramatically increased because only the first packet in a flow is process-switched; the rest of the packets in the flow are switched without being sent to the router's CPU.

Fast-switched policy routing is disabled by default. To enable this feature, issue the following command *after* policy routing has been configured on the router:

```
Router(config-if)#ip route-cache policy
```

*Note: Although fast-switched policy routing supports all **match** commands, it does not support certain **set** commands. Consult Cisco's IOS documentation for more information on this issue.*

13

Example Policy-Based Routing Scenario

Figure 13.13 presents an internetwork in which policy-based routing has been configured on Router A. Specifically, Router A has two policies that it implements. These routing policies are stated as follows:

1. If a packet arrives from 172.16.0.0 with a packet size that falls within 64 and 128 bytes, direct the packet to Router C.

2. If a packet arrives from Routers B, C, or D with an unknown destination address, direct the packet to Router A's default interface to 172.16.0.0.

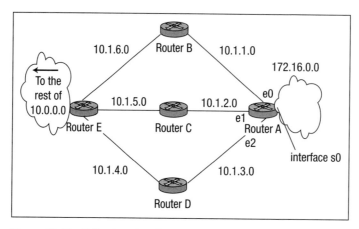

Figure 13.13 Policy-based routing.

The following output (annotated) shows the configuration for Router A's first policy:

```
Router_A(config)#interface serial0
Router_A(config-if)#ip address 172.16.1.2 255.255.255.0
Router_A(config-if)#ip policy route-map voyager (applies a policy-based
route map named "voyager" to all packets received on interface serial0)
!
Router_A(config)#route-map voyager permit 10 (specifies matching packets
will be policy routed)
Router_A(config-route-map)#match ip address 1 (applies access list 1 to the
packet)
Router_A(config-route-map)#match length 64 128 (matches packets that fall
within the specified layer 3 packet size range)
Router_A(config-route-map)#set interface ethernet1 (directs matching pack-
ets out ethernet1 to Router C)
!
Router_A(config)#access-list 1 permit 172.16.0.0 0.0.255.255 (permits a
packet whose source address matches the first two bytes of 172.16.0.0)
```

The preceding configuration tells us that packets coming from 172.16.0.0 with an IP packet size anywhere between 64 and 128 bytes will form a match with the voyager route map and be sent to Router C. Note that both match conditions would need to be met for the packets to be policy-routed; otherwise, the packets would just be forwarded as usual.

The following configuration (annotated) shows Router A's configuration for its second policy:

```
Router_A(config)#interface ethernet0
Router_A(config-if)#ip policy route-map enterprise
Router_A(config-if)#interface ethernet1
```

```
Router_A(config-if)#ip policy route-map enterprise
Router_A(config-if)#interface ethernet2
Router_A(config-if)#ip policy route-map enterprise
!(The policy route map named "enterprise" is applied to all packets re-
ceived on Router A's Ethernet interfaces)
Router_A(config)#route-map enterprise permit 10 (specifies matching packets
will be policy routed)
Router_A(config-route-map)#set ip default interface serial0 (directs all
matching packets with an unknown destination address to serial0)
```

In this configuration, Router A has applied a policy route map named "enterprise" to all of its Ethernet interfaces. The **route–map** specifies that any received packets whose destination address is not listed in Router A's routing table are to be forwarded out serial0, the default interface. Note that the route map statement has no **match** condition, which implies that all packets are matched (although, again, only those packets whose destination address is unknown will be sent to serial0).

Policy Routing Verification

Verification of policy-based operation on the router occurs with the following commands:

➤ **show ip policy**—Displays the names and associated interfaces of all route maps configured on the router

➤ **show route-map**—Shows the contents of all route maps configured on the router. If a route map name is specified with this command, then only that route map's contents will be displayed

➤ **debug ip policy**—Displays IP policy routing activity on the router

In addition to these commands, **ping** and **trace** are commonly used policy verification commands that are used when verifying the paths that packets take, as well as host and network reachability.

Using the **show ip policy** Command

The following output is taken from the **show ip policy** command issued on Router A (in the previous policy routing scenario):

```
Router_A#show ip policy

Interface       Route map
Ethernet0       enterprise
Ethernet1       enterprise
Ethernet2       enterprise
Serial0  voyager
```

Using the **show route-map** Command

The following output is taken from the **show route-map** command issued on Router A (in the previous policy routing scenario):

```
Router_A#show route-map

route-map voyager, permit, sequence 10
  Match clauses:
    ip address (access-lists): 1
    length 64 128
  Set clauses:
    interface ethernet1
  Policy routing matches: 0 packets, 0 bytes
route-map enterprise, permit, sequence 10
  Match clauses:
  Set clauses:
    default interface serial0
  Policy routing matches: 144 packets, 15190 bytes
```

This output presents the contents of both the voyager and enterprise route maps. *Match clauses* are the **match** conditions, and *Set clauses* are the **set** conditions. *Policy routing matches* indicate how many packets and bytes were policy-routed for each route map.

Debugging IP Policy

The **debug ip policy** command is used to view the IP policy routing activity occurring on the router. This verification and troubleshooting command should always be used after configuring IP policy to verify that the policy is working successfully. The following output (taken from Router A in the previous policy routing scenario) shows what this command does:

```
Router_A#debug ip policy

IP: s=172.16.232.150 (serial0), d=10.1.29.182, len 100, policy match
IP: route map voyager, item 10, permit
IP: s=172.16.232.150 (serial0), d=10.1.29.182, (Ethernet1), len 100,
  policyrouted
IP: Serial0 to Ethernet1 10.1.2.2
IP: s=172.16.232.150 (serial0), d=172.16.2.75, len 200,
  policy rejected — normal forwarding
```

The first IP line in this output tells us that Router A received a packet on its serial0 interface from a source whose address was 172.16.232.150, whose destination was 10.1.29.182, and whose packet length was 100. This packet matched the policy on serial0.

The second IP line indicates which voyager **route-map** statement the packet matched. In this instance, it was the statement with sequence number 10 (item 10).

The third IP line indicates that the packet was set to be **policy-routed** out Ethernet1.

The fourth IP line in the output tells us that the packet was routed out Ethernet1 to the next-hop router, whose address was 10.1.2.2 (Router C, see Figure 13.13).

Last, the final line in the debug output indicates that a packet received on serial0 with a length of 200 bytes was not **policy-routed** and was instead forwarded normally. (The reason it was rejected from being **policy-routed** was that the policy we configured earlier accepted packet lengths only in the range of 64 bytes to 128 bytes.)

Chapter Summary

Redistribution is a process that allows routing information discovered through one routing protocol to be distributed or injected into the update messages of another routing protocol. Route redistribution can be implemented in various ways, but issues with routing feedback loops, suboptimal path selection, and unsynchronized convergence need to be taken into account when planning a redistribution policy.

Any redistribution policy would also do well to employ certain routing optimization tools to meet the network's requirements for performance and scalability. Such tools as passive interfaces, route filters, administrative distance, and static and default routes are tremendous aids in facilitating successful route redistribution environments.

In addition to achieving a successful redistribution operation, it is often necessary to control the flow of traffic in certain areas of the internetwork. One of the best ways to accomplish this task is with policy-based routing, which is a process that utilizes filtering methods and QoS techniques to shape the flow of selected packets and prioritize them in accordance with the network's goals and requirements.

13

Review Questions

1. Which one of the following is not a reason for running multiple routing protocols in a network?

   a. Migrating from an older IGP to a newer one

   b. Backward compatibility

   c. Multivendor environment

   d. Using various network media

2. What is redistribution?

   a. A process that allows routing information discovered through one routing protocol to be distributed or injected into the update messages of another routing protocol

   b. A process in which multiple network layer protocols interact with multiple routing protocols to facilitate the exchange of network reachability information

   c. A process that involves injecting routing information into a network layer protocol and advertising it to neighboring routers

   d. A process in which static and default routes are used to create a routing table

3. How does unidirectional redistribution occur on a router? [Choose the two best answers]

   a. One routing protocol is distributed into another routing protocol.

   b. Multiple routing protocols are redistributed into each other.

   c. Static routes are redistributed into a routing protocol.

   d. Static routes are redistributed into routing protocol **x** and a default route is redistributed into routing protocol **y** on the same router.

4. How does a router determine which routing protocol is most believable?

   a. Static routes

   b. Switching paths

   c. Administrative distance

   d. Whichever protocol is learned first

5. What is the default, or seed, metric?

   a. The metric that gets assigned to the routing protocol that redistributes another routing protocol

   b. The lowest-cost metric

   c. The metric that is assigned to the routing protocol that is being redistributed

   d. A value that is unique to every redistributed route

6. Which of the following are specific issues with redistribution? [Choose the two best answers]

   a. Routing feedback loops

   b. Communication between network layer protocols

   c. Unsynchronized convergence

   d. Traffic congestion

7. Which of the following are guidelines to follow when implementing redistribution? [Choose the two best answers]

   a. Familiarity with the network

   b. Uncontrolled bidirectional redistribution

   c. Avoiding redistribution of BGP

   d. Establishing routing protocol boundaries

8. What is the meaning of the *metric-value* parameter in the following command?

   ```
   Router(config-router)#redistribute protocol [process-id|AS-number]
     [metric metric-value] [metric-type type-value] [route-map map-tag]
     [subnets] [tag tag-value]
   ```

   a. The metric's type value, either OSPF type 1 or type 2

   b. A value that must be matched for the route to be redistributed

   c. A value that is assigned to routes that do not have metric when they are redistributed

   d. The metric value that is assigned to all redistributed routes for the specified protocol

9. In the **redistribute** command in question 8, what is the **subnets** keyword used for?

   a. Prevents OSPF subnets from being redistributed

   b. Allows OSPF to redistribute subnets

   c. Specifies only OSPF subnets are to be redistributed

   d. Allows subnets to be redistributed only if route map conditions are met

10. What does the following configuration do?

   ```
   Router(config)#router ospf 1
   Router(config-router)redistribute rip metric 10
   ```

   a. Redistributes OSPF into RIP and assigns RIP a hop count of 10

   b. Redistributes RIP into OSPF and assigns RIP a hop count of 10

   c. Redistributes RIP into OSPF only if the route's metric is 10

   d. Redistributes RIP into OSPF and assigns RIP a cost of 10

13

11. What does the following configuration do? [Choose the two best answers]

```
Router_2(config)#router eigrp 2000
Router_2(config-router)#network 172.16.0.0
Router_2(config-router)#redistribute eigrp 1000
Router_2(config-router)#no auto-summary
```

  a. Redistributes EIGRP into EIGRP AS 2000 and assigns the routes a metric of 1000

  b. Redistributes routes from EIGRP AS 1000 into network 172.16.0.0

  c. Turns off automatic route summarization

  d. Allows EIGRP routes to be redistributed into 172.16.0.0 only if the routes are summarized

12. True or False: All redistributed routes must be assigned a default metric.

  a. True

  b. False

13. What command is used to configure a default metric for routes redistributed into EIGRP?

  a. Router(config)#**metric** *bandwidth delay reliability loading mtu*

  b. Router(config)#**metric default** *bandwidth delay reliability loading mtu*

  c. Router(config)#**default metric** *bandwidth delay reliability loading mtu*

  d. Router(config)#**default metric** *mtu loading reliability delay bandwidth*

14. After redistributing into the core routing process, which of the following is an acceptable redistribution method for the edge routing process? [Choose the two best answers]

  a. Redistribute static routes into the edge routing process

  b. Redistribute all core routes into the edge routing process

  c. Redistribute all core routes into the edge routing process and modify the administrative distance for selected routes

  d. Never redistribute into the edge routing process

15. What command does RIP use to distribute a default route?

  a. **ip default-network**

  b. **redistribute default rip**

  c. **router default route**

  d. **default-network rip**

16. Which one of the following is a correct **static route** command?

    a. Router(config)#**static route** *172.16.0.0 192.16.5.1 ethernet0*

    b. Router(config-router)#**static route** *172.16.0.0 255.255.0.0 ethernet0*

    c. Router(config)#**ip route** *172.16.0.0 192.16.5.1*

    d. Router(config)#**ip route** *172.16.0.0 255.255.0.0 ethernet0*

17. Which one of the following is not a benefit of configuring a default static route?

    a. Can work with EIGRP

    b. Can be a more efficient approach to redistributing static routes

    c. Can be automatically advertised by some routing protocols

    d. Can be advertised without running any routing protocol on the router

18. Which of the following are routing update optimization tools? [Choose the two best answers]

    a. Passive interface

    b. Integrated routing and bridging

    c. Route filtering

    d. Queueing

19. How do passive interfaces work?

    a. Prevent routing updates from being sent and received on an interface

    b. Prevent an interface from responding to a hardware failure on another interface

    c. Allow the interface to send and accept all routing updates from all routing protocols

    d. Prevent routing updates from being sent for specified routing protocols

20. What does the **distribute-list in** command do?

    a. Prevents certain routing updates from being sent out an interface

    b. Prevents certain routing updates from being received on an interface

    c. Allows the router to load-balance for incoming packets only

    d. Allows the router to load-balance for outgoing packets only

13

Real-World Projects

Figure 13.14 presents the logical topology for an internetwork in which two routing protocols, RIP and OSPF, are about to be merged on the ASBRs, Routers B and C, via bidirectional redistribution.

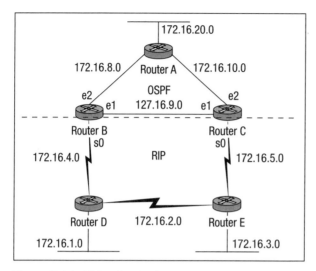

Figure 13.14 Bidirectional redistribution on Routers B and C, and policy routing on Router A.

Because bidirectional redistribution is to occur at multiple locations, technical administrators for the network have come up with a plan for making sure that routing feedbacks and suboptimal path selection do not happen. The plan involves the following steps:

1. On Router B, redistribute OSPF into RIP, and RIP into OSPF; on Router C, redistribute RIP into OSPF, and redistribute static routes into RIP.

2. Use passive interfaces on Routers B and C to prevent routing updates from being needlessly advertised out interfaces where the updates will not be understood by the receiving routing protocol.

3. On Router B, modify the administrative distance for network 172.16.1.0 in order to prefer the route to this network going through Router D instead of the OSPF route going through Router C.

In addition, technical administrators have decided that policy-based routing should occur on Router A so that traffic from network 172.16.20.0 can be directed to Router C. All other traffic is to be forwarded as usual.

As one of the technical administrators for the internetwork, it is your responsibility to make the necessary configurations on the appropriate routers. Using the above guidelines, you decide to begin on Router B.

Project 13.1

To configure bidirectional redistribution between RIP and OSPF on Router B:

1. Enter the OSPF routing process (using process ID 1) and specify that Router B's Ethernet interfaces will be participating in OSPF routing for area 0:

```
Router_B(config)#router ospf 1
Router_B(config-router)#network 172.16.8.0 0.0.248.255 area 0
```

The wildcard mask used here allows all interfaces whose first 21 high-order bits match 172.16.8.0 to be placed in area 0. This means that Router B's Ethernet interfaces, which are on networks 172.16.8.0 and 172.16.9.0, will be routing OSPF, but serial0 will not because its 21st high-order bit is a 0 rather than a 1.

2. Enter the command that redistributes RIP subnets into OSPF with a default metric of 10:

```
Router_B(config)#redistribute rip metric 10 subnets
```

All redistributed RIP routes will be assigned a default metric of 10. The **subnets** keyword allows all RIP subnets to be redistributed into OSPF.

3. Go into the RIP routing process for Router B and specify network 172.16.0.0 as the network for which RIP will be advertising:

```
Router_B(config)#router rip
Router_B(config-router)#network 172.16.0.0
```

Because all of Router B's interfaces are connected to network 172.16.0.0, RIP will be advertising on all interfaces.

4. Redistribute OSPF routes into RIP and assign the routes a default hop count of 3:

```
Router_B(config-router)#redistribute ospf metric 3
```

13

To configure passive interfaces on Router B:

1. In RIP mode, issue the **passive-interface** command for interfaces Ethernet1 and Ethernet2:

```
Router_B(config-router)#passive-interface ethernet1
Router_B(config-router)#passive-interface ethernet2
```

RIP will consequently no longer advertise out Router B's Ethernet interfaces.

The last configuration to be made ensures that network 172.16.1.0 is preferred from RIP rather than from OSPF.

To make Router B prefer the RIP route for network 172.16.1.0:

1. Enter the OSPF routing process and issue a **distance** command that gives all routing updates that match access list 1 an administrative distance of 130:

```
Router_B(config)#router ospf 1
Router_B(config-router)#distance 130 0.0.0.0 255.255.255.255 1
```

The 0.0.0.0 255.255.255.255 parameters indicate that the distance criterion will be applied to any routing source that advertises OSPF.

2. Specify that access list 1 will permit only routes whose first 3 bytes match 172.16.1:

```
Router_B(config)#access-list 1 permit 172.16.1.0 0.0.0.255
```

In conjunction with the **distance** command, **access-list** will assign an administrative distance of 130 to all OSPF updates for network 172.16.1.0. As a result, Router B will prefer the RIP update for that network because RIP's administrative distance of 120 is lower (and hence more preferred) than 130.

Project 13.2

To configure redistribution on Router C:

1. Enter Router C's OSPF routing process and specify that its Ethernet interfaces will be participating in area 0:

```
Router_C(config)#router ospf 1
Router_C(config-router)#network 172.16.8.0 0.0.248.255 area 0
```

The address and wildcard mask allow Router C's Ethernet interfaces to participate in OSPF routing for area 0.

2. Redistribute all RIP routes, including subnets:

```
Router_C(config-router)#redistribute rip subnets
```

You decide next that you would like to configure a default metric rather than let the OSPF routing process assign the default cost of 20.

3. Specify a default metric of 10 for all routes redistributed into OSPF:

```
Router_C(config-router)#default-metric 10
```

This metric value is subsequently assigned to all routes redistributed into OSPF. Note that if any other routing protocol were to be redistributed into OSPF, that protocol's routes would also be assigned a default cost of 10. You therefore see that the **default-metric** command applies to all redistributed routes from *any* routing protocol.

4. Enter the RIP routing process and configure network 172.16.0.0. Make the Ethernet interfaces passive:

```
Router_C(config)#router rip
Router_C(config-router)#network 172.16.0.0
Router_C(config-router)#passive-interface ethernet1
Router_C(config-router)#passive-interface ethernet2
```

Router C will not be advertising RIP out Ethernet1 and Ethernet2.

5. Configure a static route for networks 172.16.10.0 and 172.16.20.0 and redistribute them into RIP:

```
Router_C(config)#ip route 172.16.10.0 255.255.255.0 ethernet2
Router_C(config)#ip route 172.16.20.0 255.255.255.0 ethernet2
Router_C(config)#router rip
Router_C(config-router)#redistribute static
```

As a result, Router C will redistribute networks 172.16.20.0 and 172.16.10.0 into RIP and advertise them to the RIP domain. Internal RIP routers would subsequently have two ways to reach both networks—through either Router B or Router C.

Project 13.3

To configure policy-based routing on Router A:

13

1. Enter Router A's OSPF routing process and specify that all interfaces will be placed in area 0:

```
Router_A(config)#router ospf 1
Router_A(config-router)#network 172.16.0.0 0.0.255.255 area 0
```

In this case, you used a wildcard mask that allows any interface whose first two bytes match 172.16 to be placed in area 0.

2. Configure a route map named "direction" that forwards traffic from network 172.16.20.0 to Router C:

```
Router_A(config)#route-map direction permit 10
Router_A(config-route-map)#match ip address 1
```

```
Router_A(config-route-map)#set ip next-hop 172.16.10.1
Router_A(config-route-map)#exit
Router_A(config)#access-list 1 permit 172.16.0.0 0.0.255.255
```

Any packet whose source address matches the first two bytes of 172.16.0.0 will be policy routed to Router C.

3. Apply the policy to Router A's Ethernet0 interface:

```
Router_A(config)#interface ethernet0
Router_A(config-if)#ip policy route-map direction
```

The direction route map will be applied to all packets that arrive on Router A's Ethernet0 interface, the interface to which network 172.16.20.0 is connected.

Now that your configurations are finished, you will verify that redistribution and policy routing are occurring successfully in the internetwork.

Project 13.4

To verify redistribution operation on Router B:

1. Issue the **show ip route** command to view the routing table:

```
Router_B#show ip route
<output omitted>

C    172.16.4.0 is directly connected, Serial0
C    172.16.8.0 is directly connected, Ethernet2
C    172.16.9.0 is directly connected, Ethernet1
O E2 172.16.2.0 [110/138] via 172.16.9.1, 00:12:03, Ethernet1
O E2 172.16.3.0 [110/138] via 172.16.9.1, 00:12:03, Ethernet1
O E2 172.16.5.0 [110/138] via 172.16.9.1, 00:12:03, Ethernet1
O    172.16.10.0 [110/20] via 172.16.9.1, 00:12:03, Ethernet1
O    172.16.20.0 [110/20] via 172.16.8.2, 00:03:29, Ethernet2
R    172.16.1.0 [120/1] via 172.16.4.2, 00:00:44, Serial0
```

Redistribution is successful on Router B because RIP routes are being redistributed into OSPF (as indicated by the *E2* designation), and network 172.16.1.0 is preferred from RIP instead of from OSPF.

To verify redistribution operation on Router E:

1. View Router E's routing table:

```
Router_E#show ip route
<output omitted>
```

```
C     172.16.2.0 is directly connected, Serial0
C     172.16.3.0 is directly connected, Ethernet0
C     172.16.5.0 is directly connected, Serial1
R     172.16.1.0 [120/1] via 172.16.2.2, 00:00:29, Serial0
R     172.16.4.0 [120/1] via 172.16.2.2, 00:00:29, Serial0
R     172.16.8.0 [120/2] via 172.16.2.2, 00:00:29, Serial0
R     172.16.9.0 [120/2] via 172.16.2.2, 00:00:29, Serial0
R     172.16.10.0 [120/1] via 172.16.5.1, 00:00:13, Serial1
R     172.16.20.0 [120/1] via 172.16.5.1, 00:00:13, Serial1
```

This routing table tells you that Router E is successfully learning OSPF networks via RIP, which means that redistribution is occurring successfully in that direction. The routing table also tells you that Router E is using Router C to reach networks 172.16.10.0 and 172.16.20.0, which means that Router C is successfully redistributing its static routes.

To verify that policy-based routing is occurring on Router A:

1. Check the contents of Router A's route map to see if it is configured properly:

```
Router_A#show route-map

route-map direction, permit, sequence 10
  Match clauses:
    ip address (access-lists): 1
  Set clauses:
    ip next-hop 172.16.10.1
  Policy routing matches: 4 packets, 539 bytes
```

The preceding output indicates that the route-map is configured properly. Four packets have been matched and policy routed.

13

CHAPTER FOURTEEN

Scaling Scenarios

After completing this chapter, you will be able to:

✓ Implement a scalable addressing scheme to cover the various physical parts of a corporate enterprise

✓ Work with and understand how to cope with networks that have different routing protocols

This chapter is a little bit different in that it gives a significant insight into large-scale problem solving—something that the individual chapters do not directly address. The number of scenarios in any network can be likened to the number of variations in snowflakes, so there is no attempt here to cover all types of networks. Rather, these are a set of reasonable and most likely scenarios that any network engineer might encounter.

Implementing an Enterprise IP Numbering Scheme

In the first scenario, we have been given control over the network seen in Figure 14.1. Notice how hierarchically defined the system is? There are regions, campuses, buildings, floors, and finally, hosts. This is a fairly typical large-scale hierarchical organization. It may not be the most practical design with respect to actual wiring, but, in fact, we are working on an addressing scheme, not a trafficking scheme—that comes later. Once everything has a methodological design, then we can work on connecting the various entities.

As with any hierarchical system, it is impractical to show more than two or three levels completely. In a family tree, for example, that would hold true because the number of children and grandchildren grow exponentially. In our hierarchy, we definitely want a scenario in which tens and hundreds of thousands of individual hosts are possible. We only have to figure out how to assign each and every one of them with a unique IP address.

Start with the Requirements

Most networks are not free to choose their starting networks. In fact, if a network engineer sent a letter or message to the InterNIC, Network Solutions, or any other

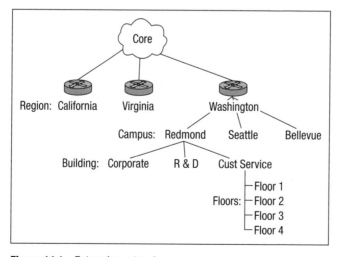

Figure 14.1 Enterprise network.

distribution body, requesting a class A or class B network, the engineer would be laughed at because IP addresses have been gobbled up at an alarming rate. There simply aren't enough to satisfy everyone's appetites. Therefore, we are likely to face one of only two options:

1. Years ago our company had the foresight to acquire a class A or B network.

2. We will use a private addressing scheme.

Item one is really unlikely, and if it is true, we are probably not faced with a numbering scheme problem (although perhaps a renumbering scheme problem). The most likely situation is item two. So, for the purposes of this discussion, we will make one up from the private address pool. Remember, RFC 1918, *Address Allocation for Private Internets,* allocates one class A, 16 class B, and 256 class C networks. For the sake of simplicity, we have been assigned 172.16.0.0/16 class B network (in reality, we are not likely to be assigned this network, but it makes for a nonconflicting example). This allows us to individually address more than 65,000 hosts.

Note: Remember that here is where the classful network discussion ends. We are, in fact, going to subnet the class B network using variable length subnet masks, so it is improper and irrelevant to discuss the networks as classful.

Now we determine the requirements. They are often not in a network engineer's job description; they are more likely a corporate and management decision. However, because a network engineer or administrator is responsible for implementing it, it must be known.

➤ 4 regions

➤ 3 campuses per region

➤ 3 buildings per campus

➤ 4 floors per building

➤ 30 hosts per floor

This calculates to a requirement for as many as 4,320 hosts ($4 \times 3 \times 3 \times 4 \times 30$). In reality, it is very unlikely that a company will grow to its maximum value. More than likely, it will have several two-story buildings, or campuses with one or two buildings. So with the allocation of 4,320 hosts, there will definitely be some unused capacity.

Next, we must ask the following questions:

1. Are these averages?

2. Are these maximums?

3. What are the growth parameters?

The answers to these questions will likely help us come up with an appropriate number scheme. Obviously, we will not be able to predict the future with reference to the third question—only a CEO or a corporate planner can do that. But by the same token, we can do some forecasting to determine whether our addressing scheme can accommodate increases.

*Note: Remember that because this is an enterprise network, we must accommodate for addressing wide area networks (WANs)—a significant part of an enterprise network. WANs consist mostly of point-to-point links, and to use an entire network is likely very wasteful. On the other hand, we can allocate an unused subnet to WAN connections. This is completely acceptable when dealing with private addressing. Alternatively, we can use the **ip unnumbered** command, assuming that Cisco routers are on both ends of the connection.*

Calculate the Subnets

We must consider the subnetting rules that state that there must not be all zeros or all ones in the following:

➤ The network portion of the address

➤ The subnet portion of the address

➤ The host portion of the address

See RFC 950, *Internet Standard Subnetting Procedure,* and RFC 1878, *Variable-Length Subnet Table for IPv4,* for more information.

The number of networks or hosts available, given n bits, is 2^n-2. But only the subnet portion does not have to conform to this rule, for two reasons:

➤ The network portion of the address is often out of our control. In this example, we were assigned the 172.16.0.0/16 network.

➤ The host portion of the address must conform to the subnet rule as defined; otherwise, it is not possible for the router to distinguish between hosts and broadcast addresses. The host cannot use an IP address of all zeros in the subnet address or all ones in the subnet broadcast address.

In reality, the subnet does have to conform to the 2^n-2 networks rule. However, with VLSMs, the entire subnet area, including the original network portion, is considered one subnet (a fact often forgotten). Therefore, the rule needs to be obeyed once, not on each instance of variable subnetting.

Warning: Cisco does provide the utility of **ip subnet-zero**. This command is to be used with the full understanding of the network devices and the knowledge that there is no device that uses the zero broadcast. For the purposes of this discussion, we assume the worst and do not use the zero broadcast. **ip subnet-zero** is the default for Cisco IOS version 12.x, but it can be added to other versions.

In this example, we would choose to conform to the rule in the bits allocated either to the region, campus, or building, but not in each hierarchical layer. It makes the most sense to conform to the rule using the least significant bits. In this case, three bits have been allocated to the access layer, enabling us to identify eight floors. We have no more than four floors to address in any building, however. To obey the rule on this layer makes sense because we reduce the floors that may be addressed to six, which is still an additional 50 percent over what is required.

Let us look at the breakdown in Table 14.1.

Figure 14.2 shows how the 16 bits break down into the new subnet with its components as well as the hosts. The 16 bits in the original network field are not shown.

Note: This hierarchy may seem revolutionary, but it isn't. The U.S. Postal Service (USPS) has been doing something like this for years—not with IP addresses but with ZIP codes. It created the five-digit ZIP code to subdivide the country. We all know that the first digit gives the general region: 9 for the west and 0 for the east, for example. The remaining digits don't seem to be that obvious, but they really are. The USPS added four more digits when it wanted to be more specific. And still later it added two more digits. So with 11 digits, every residence in the United States is represented with a unique number.

Let us now use the Washington region as an example for bit fields. Table 14.2 shows a rough breakdown.

Table 14.1   Bits allocated for each division at minimum.

Division	Requirement	Bits Required	Growth Potential*
Regions	4	3	3 regions
Campuses per Region	3	2	0 campus
Buildings per Campus	3	3	4 buildings
Floors per Building	4	3	3 floors
Hosts per Floor	30	5	0 hosts

*In this example, we start the numbering assuming that the zero broadcast is unavailable.

14

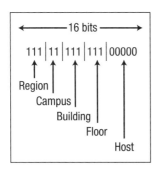

Figure 14.2   Division of bits.

Table 14.2 **Bit fields for the Washington region.**

Name	Description	Bit Value
Region	California	001
	Virginia	010
	Washington	011
Campus	Redmond	01
	Seattle	10
	Bellevue	11
Buildings	Corporate	001
	R&D	010
	Customer Service	011
Floors	Floor 1	001
	Floor 2	010
	Floor 3	011
	Floor 4	100
Hosts	<unnamed>	00001-11110

Table 14.2 doesn't accurately show all items within the hierarchy. Each campus has a set of buildings, and, of course, each building has a set of floors. Each campus will have buildings numbered from 001 to 011—we're taking the uniqueness over the whole address space, not just the bit field for the building.

Now, given a physical location, it is easy to figure out most of an individual IP address. We still need to assign the host portion, so we arbitrarily make it 7, or binary 00111 (it could be anything within the 00001–11110 range). The subnet mask is now very easy. An employee in Washington, working on the Redmond campus in the Customer Service building on the first floor will have the following bit pattern according to Table 14.2, as shown in Figure 14.3.

Add the 16-bit original network of 172.16 (decimal) to the 16 bits of the employee's address, and the resultant IP address is 172.16.107.39 in dotted decimal. Although it isn't immediately obvious where this IP address would physically reside, converting the last two octets to binary would reveal all. The diagrams and tables thus far fully document how to achieve any address within this portion of the enterprise network.

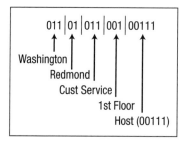

Figure 14.3 Bit fields for a specific employee.

Summarization

Because this network has a hierarchical design, we can take advantage of this ingenious planning—we can use route summarization, which implies that routing tables can be substantially reduced. The top of the hierarchical design has far more generalized subnets in the routing table. Figure 14.4 shows the network with summarized routes for the routers at each stage in this example.

Because the network divisions do not occur on 8-bit boundaries, it is difficult to see where these route summarizations come from. Figure 14.5 shows a complete binary calculation of all the subnets at each stage, making it easy to see where the route summarizations come from.

As mentioned in earlier chapters, reducing the size of the routing table has several advantages. Updates are smaller and require less bandwidth from the network. A small table also requires less memory and less central processing unit (CPU) processing time than a longer list. In addition, network recalculation is substantially reduced from routing updates.

Access List and Non-Access List Scenarios

In the next sections, we explore the configuration of several access list scenarios and a couple of non-access list scenarios to facilitate administering our network. These scenarios will all be based on the two-location local network connected to the larger corporate network at Router B displayed in Figure 14.6.

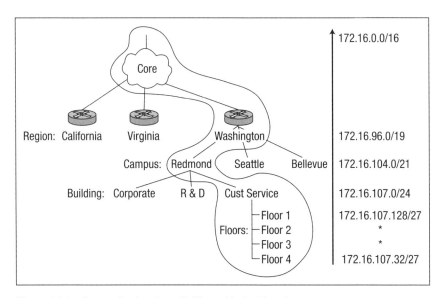

Figure 14.4   Summarized routes with hierarchical addressing.

14

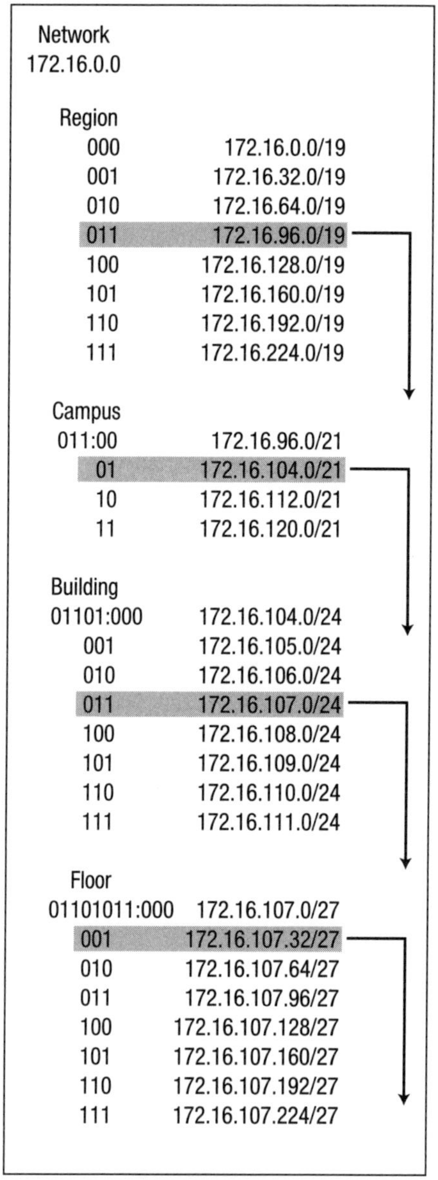

```
Network
172.16.0.0

   Region
      000           172.16.0.0/19
      001           172.16.32.0/19
      010           172.16.64.0/19
      011           172.16.96.0/19 ─┐
      100           172.16.128.0/19 │
      101           172.16.160.0/19 │
      110           172.16.192.0/19 │
      111           172.16.224.0/19 │
                                    │
   Campus                           ▼
   011:00           172.16.96.0/21
      01            172.16.104.0/21 ─┐
      10            172.16.112.0/21  │
      11            172.16.120.0/21  │
                                     │
   Building                          ▼
   01101:000        172.16.104.0/24
      001           172.16.105.0/24
      010           172.16.106.0/24
      011           172.16.107.0/24 ─┐
      100           172.16.108.0/24  │
      101           172.16.109.0/24  │
      110           172.16.110.0/24  │
      111           172.16.111.0/24  │
                                     │
   Floor                             ▼
   01101011:000     172.16.107.0/27
      001           172.16.107.32/27 ─┐
      010           172.16.107.64/27  │
      011           172.16.107.96/27  │
      100           172.16.107.128/27 │
      101           172.16.107.160/27 │
      110           172.16.107.192/27 │
      111           172.16.107.224/27 ▼
```

Figure 14.5   Binary calculation of a hierarchical network.

The Null Port Feature

We want remote network 195.168.4.0 to be able to access the Internet and the corporate network through Router B, but there is no reason for the users to access any of the local resources at the regional office (195.168.1.0 and 195.168.2.0).

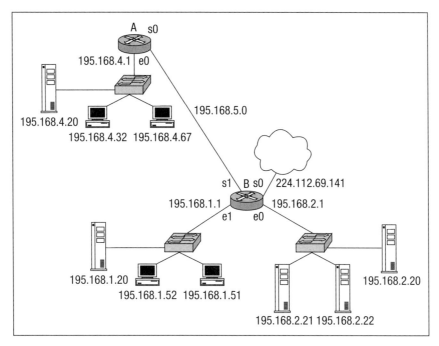

Figure 14.6 Diagram of a two-location local network.

We could easily create an access list to accomplish this, but because we are literally blocking all traffic to those subnets, we can save some CPU resources with a couple of static routes to the null 0 interface (the great void).

On Router A, we configure the two static routes as follows:

```
ip route 195.168.1.0 255.255.255.0 null 0
ip route 195.168.2.0 255.255.255.0 null 0
```

It doesn't matter what routing protocols we use within the network because the routing process will prefer the static route.

ip helper-address and ip forward-protocol

We want to make sure that users in both networks (195.168.1.0 and 195.168.4.0) are able to reach the server network (195.168.2.0) with broadcasts if the local server fails. The basic eight UDP protocols that forward with the **ip helper-address** command (Time, TACACS, DNS, BOOTP/DHCP server, BOOTP/DHCP client, TFTP, NetBIOS name service, and NetBIOS datagram service) can be trimmed, and we need to add SNMP.

14

On Router A we could add:

```
ip forward-protocol udp snmp
no ip forward-protocol udp tacacs
no ip forward-protocol udp tftp
interface ethernet 0
  ip address 195.168.4.1 255.255.255.0
  ip helper-address 195.168.2.255
```

On Router B we could add:

```
ip forward-protocol udp snmp
no ip forward-protocol udp tacacs
no ip forward-protocol udp tftp
interface ethernet 0
  ip address 195.168.1.1 255.255.255.0
  ip helper-address 195.168.2.255
```

Dynamic Access Lists

We have secured Router B somewhat to limit our exposure to outsiders initiating typical sessions within our network. We want to add a dynamic access that will allow corporate administrators (141.19.16.0) access to our server network (195.168.2.0). This example uses local authentication, but it would take only a couple of changes to support a network access security server such as Cisco's TACACS+ or Remote Access Dial-In User Service (RADIUS).

The following abbreviated output from the **show run** command demonstrates the basic configuration for Router B:

```
username RainForest password rocky47
username NightTrain password wally
!
interface serial 0
  ip address 224.112.69.141 255.255.255.0
  ip access-group 110 in
!
access-list 110 permit tcp any host 224.112.69.141 eq telnet
access-list 110 permit udp any eq 53 any gt 1023
access-list 110 permit tcp any eq www any gt 1023 established
access-list 110 permit tcp any eq 20 195.168.1.0 0.0.0.255 gt 1023
access-list 110 permit tcp any eq 21 195.168.1.0 0.0.0.255 gt 1023 estab-
lished
access-list 110 dynamic RainForest timeout 180 permit ip 141.19.16.0
0.0.15.255 195.168.2.0 0.0.0.255 log
```

```
access-list 110 dynamic NightTrain timeout 60 permit tcp any eq www host
195.168.2.21 log
!
line vty 0 2
  login local
  autocommand access-enable host timeout 10
line vty 3 4
  login local
  rotary 1
```

The first line sets the **username** (**RainForest**) and **password** (**rocky47**) that will have to be furnished by the external user. We would probably still use this line with TACACS and configure accordingly as a fallback if the TACACS server was not available. The second line is for noncorporate users.

The first **access-list** line allows any outside host to establish a Telnet session with our router.

The next four **access-list** lines allow our internal users to get DNS, HTTP, and FTP replies from outside. When possible, we use the **established** parameter to allow the session only if it originated from within our network.

The sixth **access-list** line sets up our dynamic access list parameters. The name (**RainForest**) matches the **username** in our configuration. We are granting full IP access to our server network (195.168.2.0) to a limited set of corporate users (141.19.16.0).

The seventh **access-list** line sets up our dynamic access list to allow noncorporate users access only to browsing our intranet. Our absolute time-out is set to 60 minutes, compared to 180 minutes for corporate.

The **autocommand** line is second in importance only to the dynamic **access-list** command. Without it in the **line vty** section, we have nothing. The **host** parameter must appear just as it is here, or the IP address of the authenticated outside user will not be substituted and any outside user would be allowed access. The **timeout 10** entry sets the idle time limit to 10 minutes.

14

We applied the **autocommand** only to **line vty 0 2**. If we had a console connection to the router, we would probably have configured all five virtual ports the same. If we need to Telnet into that router for administration purposes, it is going to authenticate us and then close the Telnet session, just as it does for everyone else. Setting the **rotary 1** command under virtual terminals 3 and 4 enables Telnet access on port 3001. This means that we can now Telnet in using the **Telnet 24.112.69.141 3001** command and bypass the dynamic access list.

Reflexive Access Lists

We are trying to secure our network from outsiders coming through the Internet via serial 0 on Router B. We can use the reflexive access lists feature to create temporary access lists containing only temporary entries; which are automatically created when a new IP session is launched from within our network. These lists are then automatically removed when the session ends or a time-out timer expires.

Reflexive access lists are not applied directly to an interface, but are instead "nested" into an extended named IP access list that is applied to an interface. We want to protect our local user networks (195.168.1.0 and 195.168.4.0) while still providing access to the Web/FTP server (195.168.2.21).

```
ip reflexive-list timeout 240
!
Interface serial 0
  ip access-group filterout out
!
Interface serial 1
  ip access-group filterin out
!
Interface ethernet 1
  ip access-group filterin out
!
Ip access-list extended filterout
  permit tcp 195.168.1.0 0.0.0.255 any eq 80 reflect filterpackets
  permit tcp 195.168.1.0 0.0.0.255 any eq 23 reflect filterpackets
  permit tcp 195.168.1.0 0.0.0.255 any eq 53 reflect filterpackets
!
Ip access-list extended filterin
  evaluate filterpackets
```

We set an absolute access time of two hours.

We tracked three types of packets exiting our external interface serial 0, but we had the IOS build the reflexive access lists on serial 1 and Ethernet1 to allow packets back to the user networks. Note that although they are outbound to the router, they are inbound to the user networks. Had we applied the reflexive lists to serial 0, we would have had limited access to our public area servers.

Routing Protocol Scenarios

In the following sections, we explore the configuration of several routing protocol scenarios. All of these scenarios are based on the diagram presented in Figure 14.7.

In Figure 14.7, an Internet Service Provider (ISP) running Border Gateway Protocol (BGP) connects to four corporate enterprise networks. Two of the enterprise

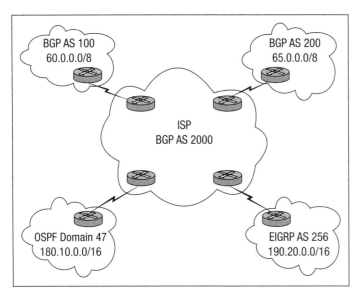

Figure 14.7   Diagram of a multirouting protocol internetwork.

networks, AS 100 and AS 200, are running Internal BGP (IBGP) and External BGP (EBGP), respectively, and the other two enterprise networks, Domain 47 and AS 256, are running strictly Open Shortest Path First (OSPF) and Enhanced Interior Gateway Routing Protocol (EIGRP), respectively.

The OSPF domain is represented by the classless address 180.10.0.0 /16, and the EIGRP AS is represented by the classless address 190.20.0.0 /16. Both addresses are advertised to the Internet by the connected ISP.

Our first configuration begins with the OSPF network.

Overview of OSPF Domain 47

OSPF Domain 47 is designed according to a hierarchical addressing scheme that allows all areas to use VLSMs and route summarization. Domain 47 comprises five areas that are all interconnected via a Frame-Relay WAN. Figure 14.8 shows the logical topology.

The Frame-Relay WAN shown in Figure 14.8 is a point-to-multipoint network containing backbone area 0. This area comprises one Autonomous System Boundary Router (ASBR), which connects the domain to the ISP and performs external route summarization; one internal backbone router; and four area border routers (ABRs).

Each ABR connects to a different type of area: ABR 1 connects to a not-so-stubby area (NSSA), ABR 2 connects to a stub area, ABR 3 connects to a totally stub area, and ABR 4 connects to a standard area. Moreover, each ABR summarizes its respective area.

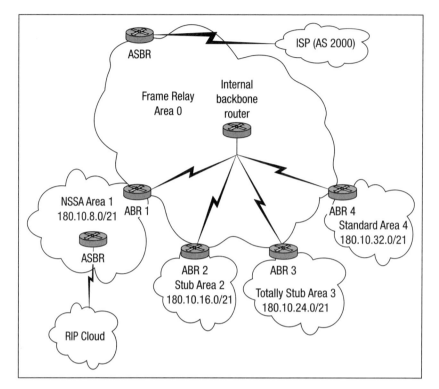

Figure 14.8 OSPF Domain 47 is under a single administration.

Our first configuration for this OSPF internetwork will involve the NSSA.

Configuring the NSSA

Recall from Chapter 6 that an NSSA is usually configured whenever an OSPF stub area must accept external link-state advertisements (LSAs) to connect a non-OSPF network to the OSPF domain. In our scenario, Area 1 is a stub area that has turned into an NSSA to connect a Routing Information Protocol (RIP) network to OSPF Domain 47. This non-OSPF network is sending its routes to the NSSA's ASBR, which is redistributing these routes and advertising them to the NSSA via type 7 LSAs.

The following output presents the NSSA's ASBR configuration, which we have annotated to explain what is occurring at each step:

```
ASBR_NSSA(config)#router ospf 47 (starts the OSPF routing process and
identifies process-id 47, which is similar to an AS designation)
ASBR_NSSA(config-router)#network 180.10.9.1 0.0.0.0 area 1 (identifies the
interface on the router that will be participating in area 1)
ASBR_NSSA(config-router)#area 1 nssa (lets the router know that area 1 is
NSSA)
ASBR_NSSA(config-router)#redistribute rip subnets (lets the router adver-
tise RIP-learned routes to the NSSA)
```

The next configuration is for the NSSA's ABR:

```
ABR1(config)#router ospf 47
ABR1(config-router)#network 180.10.40.2 0.0.0.0 area 0 (identifies the
interface that will be participating in the backbone area)
ABR1(config-router)#network 180.10.9.2 0.0.0.0 area 1 (identifies the
interface that will be participating in area 1)
ABR1(config-router)#area 1 nssa (lets the router know area 1 is NSSA)
ABR1(config-router)#area 1 range 180.10.8.0 255.255.248.0 (explained next)
```

In the preceding configuration for ABR 1, the NSSA is configured to be summarized with the address 180.10.8.0 /21. The addresses consolidated therein range from 180.10.8.0 /24 to 180.10.15.0 /24.

ABR 1 will subsequently generate a type 3 LSA containing this summary route and advertise it to the backbone router in Area 0. In addition to advertising a type 3 LSA to the backbone, ABR 1 will also advertise a type 5 LSA that contains the RIP routes. This LSA is generated when ABR 1 receives the type 7 LSA from the NSSA's ASBR.

Note, however, that the NSSA's ABR is still not allowed to receive type 5 LSAs from the backbone. As a result, the ABR will automatically forward a default route into the NSSA, thus allowing NSSA routers to have a route to unknown external destinations.

Configuring the Stub Area

We now take a look at how the stub area is configured to operate.

Recall from Chapter 6 that stub areas do not accept type 5 LSAs. Consequently, the ABR for this type of area will forward a default route in order to give stub routers a route to unknown external destinations.

The following configuration is for ABR 2, once again annotated:

```
ABR2(config)#router opsf 47 (enables the OSPF routing process and identifies
process-id 47)
ABR2(config-router)#network 180.10.40.3 0.0.0.0 area 2 (identifies the
interface that will be participating in the backbone area)
ABR2(config-router)#network 180.10.17.1 0.0.0.0 area 2 (identifies the
interface that will be participating in area 2)
ABR2(config-router)#area 2 range 180.10.16.0 255.255.248.0 (summarizes area
2 with this address)
ABR2(config-router)#area 2 stub (lets the router know that area 2 is stub)
```

In the preceding configuration, ABR 2 is summarizing the stub area with the address 180.10.16.0 /21. The addresses consolidated therein range between 180.10.16.0 /24 and 180.10.31.0 /24.

14

Configuring the Totally Stub Area

The totally stub area is proprietary to Cisco. Its routers do not accept type 3, 4, or 5 LSAs, requiring the totally stub area to have a default route to any outside destination.

The following configuration presents how ABR 3 is configured to operate in this type of area:

```
ABR3(config)#router ospf 47
ABR3(config-router)#network 180.10.40.4 0.0.0.0 area 0
ABR3(config-router)#network 180.10.25.1 0.0.0.0 area 3
ABR3(config-router)#area 3 stub no-summary (lets the router know that it
resides within a totally stub area)
ABR3(config-router)#area 3 range 180.10.24.0 255.255.248.0 (summarizes area
3 with the this address)
```

In the preceding configuration, ABR 3 is summarizing networks 180.10.24.0 /24 through 180.10.31.0 /24 with the summary route 180.10.24.0 /21. This route will subsequently be advertised to the backbone area and propagated to the other areas.

Configuring the Standard OSPF Area

The standard OSPF area for Domain 47 is summarizing networks 180.10.32.0 /24 through 180.10.39.0 /24 with the summary address 180.10.32.0 /21. As a result, the ABR for this area will generate a type 3 LSA containing this route and advertise it to the backbone area, which will in turn propagate it to all areas except the totally stub area.

The following configuration shows how route summarization occurs on the ABR for the standard area, Area 4:

```
ABR4(config-router)#area 4 range 180.10.32.0 255.255.248.0
```

Configuring the OSPF WAN Network

The WAN network shown in Figure 14.8 is a point-to-multipoint network (in OSPF terms, that is). This simply means that the network is not a full mesh but is instead a partial mesh. Because point-to-multipoint networks do not by default support broadcasts, we must issue the appropriate command to enable this feature. In Chapter 6, we referred to this type of configuration as OSPF in "point-to-multipoint broadcast mode."

The following configuration is for the internal backbone router in Figure 14.8:

```
BBR(config)#router ospf 47
BBR(config-router)#network 180.10.0.0 0.0.255.255 area 0 (all interfaces
whose first two bytes match 180.10 will participate in area 0)
```

```
BBR(config-router)#exit
BBR(config)#interface serial 0
BBR(config-if)#encapsulation frame-relay (enables frame-relay encapsulation)
BBR(config-if)#ospf network point-to-multipoint (configures the OSPF router
in point-to-multipoint broadcast mode)
BBR(config-if)#frame-relay map ip 180.10.41.2 10 broadcast (maps DLCI 10 to
ABR1 and allows broadcasts to be sent on this link)
BBR(config-if)#frame-relay map ip 180.10.41.3 20 broadcast (maps DLCI 20 to
ABR2 and allows broadcasts to be sent on this link)
BBR(config-if)#frame-relay map ip 180.10.41.4 30 broadcast (maps DLCI 30 to
ABR3 and allows broadcasts to be sent on this link)
```

The preceding configuration shows us that all the Frame-Relay neighbors specified with the **frame-relay map ip** command are placed on one subnet, 180.10.41.0 /24. The alternative would be to place each neighbor on a point-to-point link that uses separate subnets. This approach, however, is not scalable for networks in which subnet address space is limited.

Configuring the Backbone ASBR

The backbone ASBR is responsible for connecting the OSPF domain to the outside world. In our scenario, the ASBR in Area 0 is connecting OSPF Domain 47 to the ISP and is forwarding a default route into Area 0. This default route allows all routers in the OSPF domain to reach any unknown destinations that lay external to it.

In addition, the ASBR is summarizing the OSPF domain's routes with the summary address 180.10.0.0 /16. This route is advertised via OSPF to the ISP. The ISP, in turn, redistributes this route into its BGP routing process and forwards it to the rest of the ISP routers.

The following annotated output shows us how the backbone ASBR would be configured in this scenario:

```
Router_ASBR(config)#router ospf 47
Router_ASBR(config-router)#network 180.10.0.0 0.0.255.255 area 0
Router_ASBR(config-router)#network 2.2.2.1 0.0.0.0 area 0 (places the
ASBR's serial interface in area 0)
Router_ASBR(config-router)#summary-address 180.10.0.0 255.255.0.0 (causes
the ASBR to advertise 180.10.0.0 /16 to the ISP)
```

Overview of EIGRP AS 256

The EIGRP AS pictured in Figure 14.9 comprises four regions interconnected by a Frame-Relay network. Route summarization within the AS occurs at each region's exit point. For instance, Router B in Region B is summarizing the networks 190.20.1.0 through 190.20.31.0 with the route 190.20.0.0 /19, whereas Router A of Region A is summarizing all the AS's routes with the address 190.20.0.0 /16 and is forwarding this route to the ISP via EIGRP.

14

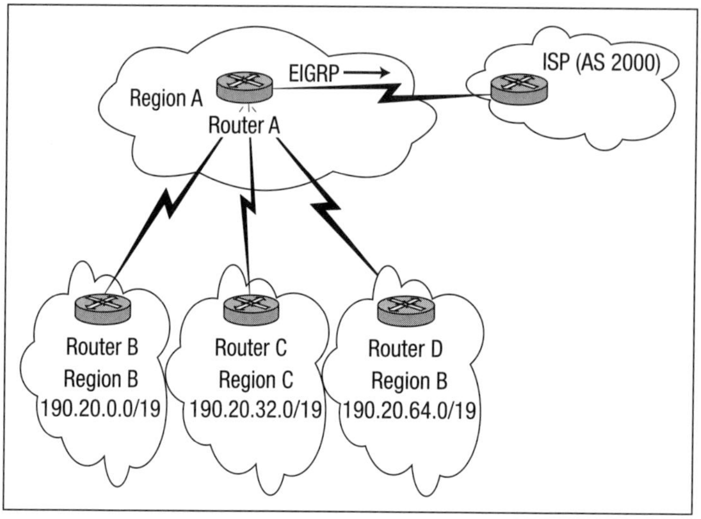

Figure 14.9 EIGRP AS 256.

Our first configuration subsequently begins with Router A.

Advertising the Summary Route to the ISP

Router A is the central congregation point for AS traffic. It has three Frame-Relay links to neighboring EIGRP routers and is the exit and entry point for interdomain traffic.

The following annotated configuration shows us how Router A accomplishes its routing tasks with scalability and performance:

```
Router_A(config)#router eigrp 256 (enables the EIGRP routing process and
identifies AS 256)
Router_A(config-router)#network 190.20.0.0 (identifies the interfaces that
will be routing for AS 256)
Router_A(config-router)#network 3.3.3.1 0.0.0.0 (identifies the serial
interace which will be running EIGRP to the ISP)
Router_A(config-router)#exit
Router_A(config)#interface serial 0 (the interace leading to the ISP
Router_A(config-if)#ip summary-address eigrp 256 190.20.0.0 255.255.0.0
(causes the router to advertise the summary route 190.20.0.0 /16)
```

As we can see from Router A's configuration, network 190.20.0.0 /16 is a summary route that consolidates all of AS 256's networks. This route is advertised via EIGRP to the ISP, which will redistribute it into BGP and advertise it to the BGP routers.

Configuring the EIGRP Internal Routers

The next three configurations are for Routers B, C, and D in Regions B, C, and D, respectively.

Configuring Router B

Router B is the exit point for Region B (the term "Region" is not an official term used in the EIGRP vocabulary). This region is being summarized with the route 190.20.0.0 /19.

The following configuration is for Router B:

```
Router_B(config)#router eigrp 256
Router_B(config-router)#network 190.20.0.0
Router_B(config-router)#exit
Router_B(config)#interface serial 1 (the serial interface leading to Region A)
Router_B(config-if)#ip summary-address eigrp 256 190.20.0.0 255.255.224.0
```

Configuring Router C

Region C comprises EIGRP networks 190.20.33.0 /24 through 190.20.63.0 /24. These networks are summarized with the address 190.20.32.0 /19.

The following configuration is for Router C:

```
Router_C(config)#router eigrp 256
Router_C(config-router)#network 190.20.0.0
Router_C(config-router)#exit
Router_C(config)#interface serial 1 (the serial interface leading to Region A)
Router_C(config-if)#ip summary-address eigrp 256 190.20.32.0 255.255.224.0
```

Configuring Router D

Region D comprises the subnets ranging from 190.20.65.0 /24 through 190.20.95.0 /24. The region has subsequently been summarized with the route 190.20.64.0 /19.

The following configuration is for Router D:

```
Router_D(config)#router eigrp 256
Router_D(config-router)#network 190.20.0.0
Router_D(config-router)#exit
Router_D(config)#interface serial 0 (the serial interface leading to Region A)
Router_D(config-if)#ip summary-address eigrp 256 190.20.64.0 255.255.224.0
```

14

BGP in the Enterprise and ISP

BGP is a highly scalable interdomain routing protocol that supports Classless Inter-Domain Routing (CIDR), variable-length subnet masks (VLSMs), and route summarization. Actually, only BGP 4 supports these scalable addressing features; earlier versions do not. Therefore, whenever incorporating a hierarchical addressing scheme into your BGP implementation, be sure to take this note into account.

In our continuing example based on Figure 14.7, we find that the ISP is running BGP 4 and is incorporating a hierarchical addressing scheme. Specifically, the networks within the ISP's AS (AS 2000) are represented by the Network Information Center (NIC) address 150.10.0.0 /16.

In addition, the ASes that connect to the ISP—AS 100 and AS 200—are also incorporating address scalability features and are each represented by one NIC address. AS 100 is represented by 60.0.0.0 /8, and AS 200 is represented by 65.0.0.0 /8.

The following sections explore how BGP is run between and within these systems.

Running BGP in AS 100

Figure 14.10 presents the logical topology for AS 100. In this diagram, Routers A, B, and C are all running IBGP. Because policy within this network is different from that of the ISP, and because other conditions require that policy be kept separate from that of the ISP, AS 100 is running EBGP between Router B and AS 2000. This allows Router B to control the traffic that is sent to as well as received from external destinations.

In addition, Router B is advertising AS 100 as 60.0.0.0 /8. It does this by creating an aggregate address and forwarding the route via EBGP to the ISP. The ISP, in turn, advertises this route to external destinations, under policy conditions.

The following annotated output shows us the policy running on Router B:

```
Router_B(config)#router bgp 100
Router_B(config-router)#neighbor 60.10.10.2 remote-as 100 (creates an IBGP
peering relationship with Router C)
Router_B(config-router)#neighbor 60.10.20.2 remote-as 100 (creates an IBGP
peering relationship with Router A)
Router_B(config-router)#network 60.10.10.0 255.255.255.252 (allows the
address 60.10.10.0 /30 to be advertised)
Router_B(config-router)#network 60.10.20.0 255.255.255.252 (allows the
address 60.10.20.0 /30 to be advertised)
!(network statements ommitted from display)
Router_B(config-router)#neighbor 5.5.5.2 remote-as 2000 (establishes an
EBGP peer relationship with the ISP's gateway router)
Router_B(config-router)#neighbor 60.10.10.2 route-reflector-client (makes
Router B a route reflector and Router C a client)
Router_B(config-router)#neighbor 60.10.20.2 route-reflector-client (makes
Router A a client)
Router_B(config-router)#neighbor 5.5.5.2 route-map FORTUNE in (applies a
route-map called "FORTUNE" to all routing updates received from the ISP)
Router_B(config-router)#neighbor 60.10.10.1 route-map GATE in (applies a
route-map called "GATE" to all routing updates sent to the ISP)
!
```

```
Router_B(config)#route-map FORTUNE permit 10
Router_B(config-route-map)#match ip address 1 (match a route with access-
list 1)
Router_B(config-route-map)#set community 200 additive (appends community
value 200 to the community attribute of matching routes)
!
Router_B(config)# access-list 1 permit 65.0.0.0 0.255.255.255 (permits all
routes whose first byte matches 65)
!
Router_B(config)#route-map FORTUNE permit 20
Router_B(config-route-map)#set community 300 (replaces the community at-
tribute of all routes that do not match the access-list condition with the
community value 300)
Router_B(config-route-map)#route-map GATE permit 10
Router_B(config-route-map)#match ip next-hop 60.10.10.1 (matches a route's
next-hop address with Router C)
Router_B(config-route-map)#set weight 500 (sets the weight of all routes
comming from Router C to 500)
Router_B(config-route-map)#route-map GATE permit 20 (empty route-map state-
ment implies that all other routes are permitted without being controlled)
!
Router_B(config-router)#aggregate-address 60.0.0.0 255.0.0.0
```

The preceding configuration for Router B allows routes received from Router C to acquire a weight of 500. The default weight given to routes received from a BGP neighbor is 0. As a result, the weight of routes received from Router C will be higher than the weight of routes received from Router A. Because the route with the highest weight is preferred, Router B will subsequently choose paths that go through Router C, that is, whenever Router C and Router A are advertising the same route.

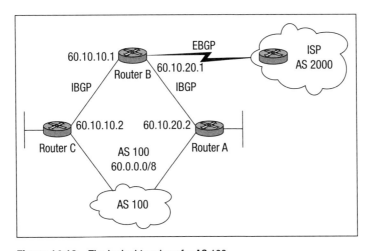

14

Figure 14.10   The logical topology for AS 100.

We also see in the preceding output that Router B is configured with a route map that appends the community value 200 to all routes received from the ISP that have an address whose first byte matches 65. This means that routes originating from AS 200 (as is shown in the next section) will form matches with the aforementioned condition. All other routes whose first byte is not 65 will receive a community attribute of 300, which replaces any community values already listed in the routes' community attribute.

Lastly, we see that Router B has created an aggregate route (60.0.0.0 /8) that summarizes all of AS 100's networks. The address is being advertised to the ISP, which will forward this route (as well as the more specific routes) to the rest of the Internet.

Let us now take a look at how AS 200 is configured to route BGP traffic.

Running BGP in AS 200

Figure 14.11 shows the logical topology for AS 200. In this figure, Router B is advertising IBGP-learned routes to the ISP. These routes, however, are summarized within the aggregate route 65.0.0.0 /8. The ISP is forwarding this route within AS 2000 and to the rest of the Internet.

The following annotated output shows us how AS 200 is configured with a policy that meets the enterprise's goals and requirements.

```
Router_B(config)#router bgp 200
Router_B(config-router)#network 65.0.0.0
Router_B(config-router)# aggregate-address 65.0.0.0 255.0.0.0 summary-only
(allows this aggregate-route to be advertised to the ISP)
Router_B(config-router)#neighbor VOYAGER peer-group (creates a peer group
called "VOYAGER")
Router_B(config-router)#neighbor VOYAGER remote-as 200 (establishes a
peering relationship with the VOYAGER peer group)
Router_B(config-router)#neighbor 65.10.20.2 peer-group VOYAGER (assigns
Router A to the VOYAGER peer group)
Router_B(config-router)#neighbor 65.10.10.2 peer-group VOYAGER (assigns
Router C to the VOYAGER peer group)
Router_B(config-router)#neighbor 6.6.6.2 remote-as 2000 (establishes an
EBGP peer relationship with the ISP router)
Router_B(config-router)#neighbor 6.6.6.2 route-map LOGIC out (applies the
route-map called "LOGIC" to all routing updates sent to the ISP)
Router_B(config-router)#neighbor VOYAGER prefix-list ISP in (applies a
prefix-list called "ISP" to all routing updates received from the VOYAGER
peer group)
!
Router_B(config)#route-map LOGIC permit 10
Router_B(config-route-map)#match ip address 1 (match a route with access-
list 1)
```

```
Router_B(config-route-map)#set local-preference 500 (sets the local-
preference of matching routes to 500)
!
Router_B(config)#access-list 1 permit 150.10.0.0 255.255.0.0 (permits
routes whose first two bytes match 150.10)
Router_B(config)#route-map LOGIC permit 20 (empty route-map statement
permits all)
!
Router_B(config)#ip prefix-list ISP deny 65.10.64.0/24 (denies the address
65.10.64.0 /24 from being accepted by from the VOYAGER peer group)
Router_B(config)#ip prefix-list ISP permit 0.0.0.0/0 (permits all other
routes)
```

The preceding configuration for Router B shows us that all routes from the ISP that match the first two bytes of 150.10.0.0 will be given a local-preference of 500. These routes are actually ISP routes, so Router B is subsequently made the preferential exit point to reach any network within the ISP.

Router B is the only exit point at the moment; however, this configuration takes into account the possibility that future network growth may demand a multihomed Internet connection. In this eventuality, AS 200 wants Router B to remain the preferred exit point to the ISP for ISP networks.

We also note in Router B's configuration that it has created a peer group called "VOYAGER". This peer group is assigned Routers A and C, who both share the same update policies with Router B. Recall from the discussion on BGP (Chapter 10) that peer groups are used to prevent the need for configuring duplicate copies of the same policies for each BGP peer. Although this advantage is not too significant to the present example, such a feature would be of tremendous value to a network in which hundreds of routers were required to have the same update policies.

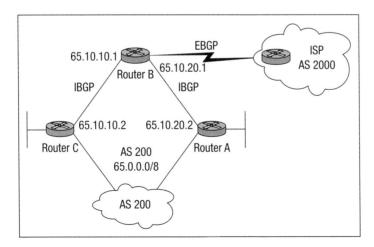

Figure 14.11   Logical topology for AS 200.

CHAPTER FIFTEEN

Sample Test

Question 1

Which of the following statements are typically true of link state routing protocols? [Choose two answers]

❑ a. Establish formal peer relationships using the hello protocol

❑ b. Broadcast routing updates at periodic intervals

❑ c. Maintain routing tables that list all possible routes in the internetwork

❑ d. Support Classless Inter-Domain Routing (CIDR)

Question 2

Which of the following scalability issues do standardized distance-vector routing protocols have? [Choose two answers]

❑ a. Bandwidth utilization

❑ b. Vendor interoperability

❑ c. Support for a large number of routers

❑ d. Support for point-to-point WAN links

Question 3

Which sequence of steps could an OSPF router take after receiving an LSA?

○ a. (1) flood the LSA to the DR/BDR, (2) verify that the LSA is acceptable, (3) copy the LSA to the topological database, (4) check to see if the LSA is already in the topological database

○ b. (1) copy the LSA to the topological database, (2) flood the LSA to the DR/BDR, (3) verify that the LSA is acceptable, (4) check to see if the LSA is already in the topological database

○ c. (1) check to see if the LSA is already in the topological database, (2) verify that the LSA is acceptable, (3) flood the LSA to the DR/BDR, (4) copy the LSA to the topological database

○ d. (1) verify that the LSA is acceptable, (2) check to see if the LSA is already in the topological database, (3) copy the LSA to the topological database, (4) flood the LSA to the DR/BDR

Question 4

In what OSPF state do two OSPF routers exchange DDPs to build their topological databases?

○ a. Init

○ b. Exstart

○ c. Exchange

○ d. Full

Question 5

Which of the following are typical characteristics of an OSPF network that is configured in NBMA mode? [Choose three answers]

❑ a. Occurrence of multicasting

❑ b. Manual configuration of neighbors

❑ c. Occurrence of broadcasting

❑ d. Adjacencies between the DR/BDR and peer OSPF neighbors

❑ e. Partial mesh topology

❑ f. Full mesh topology

Question 6

Which command specifies that OSPF will be in NBMA mode?

○ a. **ip ospf network nbma**

○ b. **ip ospf nbma mode**

○ c. **ip ospf nbma non-broadcast**

○ d. **ip ospf network non-broadcast**

Question 7

In which OSPF mode does dynamic neighbor discovery typically occur? [Choose two answers]

❏ a. NBMA

❏ b. NBMA broadcast (BMA)

❏ c. point-to-multipoint broadcast

❏ d. point-to-multipoint nonbroadcast

Question 8

Which types of route summarization does OSPF support? [Choose two answers]

❏ a. inter-area

❏ b. type 6

❏ c. external

❏ d. hybrid

Question 9

15

Which of the following areas does not accept type 3 LSAs (network-summary LSAs)?

○ a. standard

○ b. stub

○ c. totally stub

○ d. NSSA

Question 10

What do stub, totally stub, and NSSA areas typically use to reach unknown destinations?

○ a. type 6 LSAs

○ b. RIP

○ c. default routes

○ d. virtual links

Question 11

What action is taken by an ABR configured with the following command?

```
Router(config-router)#area 1 range 172.16.0.0 255.255.0.0
```

○ a. Creates a summary route for area 1 and advertises it to another area

○ b. Creates a summary route for another area and advertises it to area 1

○ c. Creates a summary route for area 1 and advertises it to area 1

○ d. Creates a summary route and advertises it only to network 172.16.0.0 /16

Question 12

Which OSPF command can be issued to display the following output?

```
Ethernet 0 is up, line protocol is up

Internet Address 131.119.254.202, Mask 255.255.255.0, Area 0.0.0.0

Process ID 1, Router ID 192.77.99.1, Network Type BROADCAST, Cost: 10

Transmit Delay is 1 sec, State DROTHER, Priority 1

Designated Router (ID) 131.119.254.10, Interface address 131.119.254.10

Backup Designated Router (ID) 131.119.254.28, Interface address
     131.119.254.28

Timer intervals configured: Hello 10, Dead 60, Wait 40, Retransmit 5

Hello due in 0:00:05

Neighbor Count is 8, Adjacent neighbor count is 2

  Adjacent with neighbor 131.119.254.28  (Backup Designated Router)

  Adjacent with neighbor 131.119.254.10  (Designated Router)

Suppress hello for 0 neighbor(s)
```

○ a. **show ip ospf**

○ b. **show ip ospf neighbor**

○ c. **show ip ospf interface**

○ d. **show ip ospf database**

Question 13

Which of the following are advantages that EIGRP has over IGRP? [Choose three answers]

❏ a. Multiprotocol support

❏ b. Faster convergence

❏ c. Unequal-cost load-balancing

❏ d. Support for multiple areas

❏ e. Support for route summarization

15

Question 14

In EIGRP, what is a feasible successor?

○ a. The second best route to a particular destination network

○ b. A router whose feasible distance is greater than twice the feasible distance through the successor

○ c. The best route to a particular destination network

○ d. The route taken by query packets when there is no successor in the topology table

Question 15

What is the correct sequence of events an EIGRP router goes through when it first comes online?

○ a. (1) builds the topology table, (2) builds the routing table, (3) builds the neighbor table

○ b. (1) builds the routing table, (2) builds the neighbor table, (3) builds the topology table

○ c. (1) builds the neighbor table, (2) builds the topology table, (3) builds the routing table

○ d. (1) builds the topology table, (2) builds the routing table

Question 16

Which statement is true for EIGRP operation?

○ a. A query packet is sent whenever the router loses a successor and discovers that there is a feasible successor in the topology table for the lost successor.

○ b. Feasible distance is the cost used to reach the next-hop router along an alternative path to a particular destination network.

○ c. Topology changes occur only when a link fails.

○ d. The route evaluation process begins before the route recomputation process.

Question 17

Which one of the following is not a function of the EIGRP Distributed Update ALgorithm (DUAL)?

○ a. Establishes a loop-free topology.

○ b. Performs all route computations.

○ c. Chooses successors and feasible successors and places them in the topology table.

○ d. Tracks all queried neighbors in the neighbor table.

Question 18

Which of the following features allow EIGRP to limit the range of query packets? [Choose two answers]

❑ a. Outbound distribute lists

❑ b. Route summarization

❑ c. Autonomous system boundaries

❑ d. Unequal-cost load-balancing

Question 19

What does the **variance** command do?

○ a. Allows EIGRP to use the metrics reliability, loading, and MTU in the composite metric calculation

○ b. Allows route summarization to occur on any EIGRP router in the internetwork

○ c. Configures stub routers

○ d. Enables unequal-cost load-balancing

15

Question 20

If a Frame-Relay multipoint interface is configured with three 64Kbps links, and the interface is not oversubscribed, what should the configured bandwidth be for the interface?

○ a. `Router(config-if)#bandwidth 64`

○ b. `Router(config-if)#bandwidth 128`

○ c. `Router(config-if)#bandwidth 192`

○ d. `Router(config-if)#bandwidth 22`

Question 21

What is EBGP?

○ a. A type of BGP protocol used specifically to exchange error messages between BGP peers

○ b. A BGP session between two BGP peers residing in different autonomous systems

○ c. A method that BGP uses to poll neighbors that do not respond to keepalive messages

○ d. A protocol that allows the exchange of network reachability information between internal BGP peers

Question 22

What is the purpose of the BGP *open* message?

○ a. Establishes a BGP connection between two peers

○ b. Opens a TCP connection between two peers

○ c. Used to negotiate which path attributes will be accepted

○ d. Used periodically to verify connectivity between two BGP peers

Question 23

Which two of the following statements are true?

❏ a. Well-known path attributes are recognized by some, but not all, standard BGP implementations.

❏ b. Optional transitive path attributes that are not recognized are dropped.

❏ c. Well-known discretionary attributes are not required to be sent in routing updates.

❏ d. An example of a well-known path attribute is local preference.

Question 24

Which of the following BGP path attributes are used specifically to influence the path a router takes to reach a destination in another AS? [Choose two answers]

❏ a. Origin

❏ b. Local preference

❏ c. Weight

❏ d. Next-hop

Question 25

Which one of the following BGP path attributes is typically used to influence the path that external networks take to reach the local AS?

○ a. Weight

○ b. Local preference

○ c. MED

○ d. Atomic aggregate

15

Question 26

Which of the following path attributes is preferred most in a Cisco-based BGP implementation?

- ○ a. Weight
- ○ b. Local preference
- ○ c. MED
- ○ d. Origin

Question 27

Under which of the following conditions would BGP not likely be recommended? [Choose two answers]

- ❑ a. Traffic transiting the AS must be controlled
- ❑ b. Single connection to another AS that is using the same routing policy
- ❑ c. Lack of memory and processor power on the routers
- ❑ d. When routing policy differs with the neighboring AS
- ❑ e. Multihomed Internet connection

Question 28

How does a BGP router distinguish between its EBGP and IBGP neighbors?

- ○ a. The BGP router exchanges open messages with its peers.
- ○ b. The BGP router must wait until its peers have sent routing updates.
- ○ c. The **neighbor remote-as** command.
- ○ d. There is no need for the BGP router to distinguish between EBGP and IBGP neighbors.

Question 29

Why must a route be matched in the IP routing table before the route can be advertised with the BGP **network** command?

○ a. Because IP routing tables are preferred over BGP routing tables

○ b. To prevent a route that is not supported by the IP routing table from being advertised by BGP

○ c. Because BGP must always learn internal routes through an IGP

○ d. To prevent black holes in the local AS, which could result if the IP routing table and BGP routing tables are not synchronized

Question 30

Which command would you use to display the following output?

```
BGP table version is 716977, local router ID is 193.0.32.1

Status codes: s suppressed, * valid, > best, i - internal

Origin codes: i - IGP, e - EGP, ? - incomplete


   Network          Next Hop          Metric LocPrf Weight Path
*>i3.0.0.0          193.0.22.1             0    100      0 1800 1239 ?
*>i6.0.0.0          193.0.22.1             0    100      0 1800 690 568 ?
*>i7.0.0.0          193.0.22.1             0    100      0 1800 701 35 ?
*>i8.0.0.0          193.0.22.1             0    100      0 1800 690 560 ?
```

○ a. **show ip bgp**

○ b. **show ip bgp summary**

○ c. **show ip bgp neighbor**

○ d. **show ip bgp table**

15

Question 31

What is a BGP *route reflector*?

○ a. A router that uses prefix filters to restrict routing updates from being propagated to IBGP peers

○ b. A type of access list that prevents certain routes from being advertised to BGP peers

○ c. A router that is allowed to propagate IBGP-learned routes to IBGP neighbors

○ d. A BGP feature that allows unequal-cost load-balancing to occur

Question 32

Which of the following are not advantages to using prefix lists instead of access lists to restrict routing information? [Choose two answers]

❏ a. With prefix lists, there is no implicit **deny any**

❏ b. Support for incremental modifications

❏ c. The ability to match routes based on various path attributes

❏ d. Greater flexibility

Question 33

What does the following command do?

```
Router(config-router)#neighbor 150.10.20.2 distribute-list 1 out
```

○ a. Applies **access-list 1** to all routing updates received from 150.10.20.2

○ b. Applies **distribute-list 1** to all open messages sent to 150.10.20.2

○ c. Uses **access-list 1** to prevent all routing updates from being sent to 150.10.20.2

○ d. Applies **access-list 1** to all routing updates sent to 150.10.20.2

Question 34

Examine the following output:

```
Router_C(config)#router bgp 300

Router_C(config-router)#neighbor 10.10.10.2 remote-as 200

Router_C(config-router)#neighbor 10.10.10.2 route-map voyager in

Router_C(config-router)#exit

Router_C(config)#route-map voyager permit 10

Router_C(config-route-map)#match ip address 1

Router_C(config-route-map)#set weight 100

Router_C(config-route-map)#exit

Router_C(config)#access-list 1 permit 180.10.0.0 0.0.255.255

Router_C(config)#route-map voyager permit 20

Router_C(config-route-map)#set weight 1
```

Which of the following statements are true regarding the preceding output for Router C? [Choose two answers]

❑ a. All routing updates received from 10.10.10.2 will be matched with access list 1.

❑ b. Access list 1 permits only summary route 180.10.0.0 /16.

❑ c. A route that does not match the first **route-map** statement will be denied.

❑ d. A route that matches the second **route-map** statement will be assigned a weight of 1.

❑ e. The absence of a **match** condition in the second **route-map** statement implies that all routes that do not form a match with the first **route-map** statement will be denied.

15

Question 35

Examine the following output:

```
Router_A(config)#route-map voyager permit 10
Router_A(config-route-map)#match ip next-hop 10.10.10.1
Router_A(config-route-map)#set community 100
```

Which of the following statements are not true regarding the preceding output? [Choose two answers]

❏ a. Routes that match access list 10 will be permitted.

❏ b. The **route-map** statement has a sequence number of 10.

❏ c. Routes with a next-hop address of 10.10.10.1 will form a match.

❏ d. Community list 100 is used.

Question 36

Which of the following are advantages to configuring peer groups in a large BGP implementation? [Choose two answers]

❏ a. Ability to group destination attributes based on shared routing policies

❏ b. Allows routing decisions to be made based upon the community attribute value

❏ c. Reduces the number of BGP neighbor statements

❏ d. Improves performance in BGP policy routing

Question 37

Examine the following output:

```
Router_A(config)#router bgp 100

Router_A(config-router)#neighbor delta peer-group

Router_A(config-router)#neighbor 2.2.2.2 remote-as 200

Router_A(config-router)#neighbor 2.2.2.2 peer-group delta

Router_A(config-router)#neighbor 4.4.4.2 remote-as 300

Router_A(config-router)#neighbor 4.4.4.2 peer-group delta

Router_A(config-router)#neighbor 1.1.1.2 remote-as 400

Router_A(config-router)#neighbor 1.1.1.2 peer-group delta

Router_A(config-router)#neighbor 1.1.1.2 prefix-list ether in

Router_A(config-router)#neighbor delta route-map giga out
```

What can be said about the preceding output? [Choose two answers]

❑ a. The **prefix-list** applied to neighbor 1.1.1.2 will not work.

❑ b. Neighbor 1.1.1.2 is not a member of the delta peer group.

❑ c. All of Router A's neighbors reside in different ASes.

❑ d. A route map called "giga" is applied to all routing updates sent to the delta peer group.

Question 38

What is the common definition of multihoming?

○ a. A process in which an AS router establishes multiple EGP connections to a neighboring AS

○ b. Another term for load-balancing

○ c. Connecting an AS to more than one ISP

○ d. Connecting an AS to one ISP using a default route and an EGP

15

Question 39

Which one of the following tools is the best means to prevent suboptimal path selection in a redistribution environment?

○ a. Unequal-cost load-balancing

○ b. Stub router designation

○ c. Administrative distance modification

○ d. Passive interfaces

Question 40

Examine the following output:

```
Router_2(config)#router rip

Router_2(config-router)#network 172.16.0.0

Router_2(config-router)#network 10.0.0.0

Router_2(config-router)#ip default-network 10.0.0.0
```

Which of the following statements are true regarding the preceding output? [Choose two answers]

❑ a. RIP is redistributing routing updates from network 10.0.0.0.

❑ b. Network 10.0.0.0 is directly connected.

❑ c. RIP is advertising a default route for network 10.0.0.0 to 172.16.0.0.

❑ d. RIP is advertising a default route for network 172.16.0.0 to 10.0.0.0.

Question 41

Why is uncontrolled bidirectional redistribution at multiple locations within the internetwork not recommended?

○ a. It can lead to route feedback loops.

○ b. It causes problems with router compatibility.

○ c. It prevents full routing information from being propagated throughout the internetwork.

○ d. It is not supported by most common routing protocols.

Question 42

Examine the following output:

```
Router_B(config)#router rip
Router_B(config-router)#network 172.16.0.0
Router_B(config-router)#passive-interface ethernet1
Router_B(config-router)#passive-interface ethernet2
Router_B(config-router)#default-metric 3
Router_B(config-router)#redistribute igrp 100
Router_B(config-router)#exit
Router_B(config)#router igrp 100
Router_B(config-router)#network 172.16.0.0
Router_B(config-router)#passive-interface serial0
Router_B(config-router)#default-metric 10 100 255 1 1500
Router_B(config-router)#redistribute rip
Router_B(config-router)#distance 130 0.0.0.0 255.255.255.255 1
Router_B(config-router)#exit
Router_B(config)#access-list 1 permit 172.16.1.0
```

Which of the following statements are true regarding the preceding configuration? [Choose two answers]

❏ a. Certain RIP networks are not being redistributed into IGRP.

❏ b. **Access-list 1** is used to modify the administrative distance for network 172.16.1.0.

❏ c. Only routes that are permitted by access list 1 will be assigned a default metric.

❏ d. Network 172.16.1.0 is assigned an administrative distance of 130 when it is learned from IGRP.

Question 43

Which one of the following is not a characteristic of policy-based routing?

○ a. QoS support

○ b. Load-balancing

○ c. Traffic control

○ d. Prefix lists

15

Question 44

Which one of the following statements is true regarding policy-based route maps?

○ a. They test outgoing packets.

○ b. A packet can be permitted or denied based on such characteristics as the packet's source and destination addresses, application, protocol, size, ToS, and precedence.

○ c. A packet is dropped if it matches a **route-map** statement that specifies a **deny**.

○ d. The implicit **deny any** at the end of the policy route map causes the packet to be dropped.

Question 45

Examine the following output:

```
Router_A(config)#interface serial0

Router_A(config-if)#ip address 172.16.1.2 255.255.255.0

Router_A(config-if)#ip policy route-map enterprise

Router_A(config-if)#exit

Router_A(config)#route-map enterprise permit 10

Router_A(config-route-map)#match ip address 1

Router_A(config-route-map)#match length 64 128

Router_A(config-route-map)#set interface ethernet1

Router_A(config-route-map)#exit

Router_A(config)#access-list 1 permit 172.16.0.0 0.0.255.255
```

What can be said with regard to the preceding routing policy? [Choose two answers]

❏ a. A route map called "enterprise" is applied to all routing updates sent out Router A's serial0 interface.

❏ b. **Access-list 1** permits a packet whose source address matches the first two bytes of 172.16.0.0.

❏ c. A packet is required to form a match with only one **match** condition in order to be policy routed.

❏ d. Packets that meet the route map criteria will be forwarded out Router A's Ethernet1 interface.

Question 46

Examine the following output:

```
ip route 195.168.1.0 255.255.255.0 null 0
```

Which of the following statements are true regarding the above statement? [Choose two answers]

❏ a. Requires fewer router CPU resources than an access list accomplishing the same thing.

❏ b. Is the final statement in a reflexive access list securing network 195.168.1.0.

❏ c. Any packets addressed to server 195.168.1.25 will be discarded.

❏ d. Requires greater router CPU resources than an access list accomplishing the same thing.

Question 47

Examine the following output:

```
ip forward-protocol udp snmp
no ip forward-protocol udp tftp
interface Ethernet 1
  ip address 195.168.1.1 255.255.255.0
  ip helper-address 195.168.2.20
  ip helper-address 195.168.2.21
  ip helper-address 195.168.2.22
```

What can be expected from the above seven statements? [Choose two answers]

❏ a. The router will allow any SNMP broadcast packets to pass through instead of being discarded.

❏ b. Any interface receiving an SNMP broadcast packet will be forwarded to Ethernet 1.

❏ c. A DHCP broadcast packet received by Ethernet 1 will be forwarded as three unicast packets to three host addresses.

❏ d. An SNMP broadcast packet received by Ethernet 1 will be forwarded as a multicast packet to the 195.168.2.0 subnet—probably a server network.

❏ e. The first statement adds SNMP to, and the second removes TFTP from, the pool of UDP broadcast packets that will be forwarded by the **ip helper** command.

❏ f. The first statement adds SNMP to, and the second removes TFTP from, the pool of TCP broadcast packets that will be forwarded by the **ip helper** command.

15

Question 48

Which of the following **access-list** statements, if properly applied to an interface, will block all IP packets from the 192.168.1.0 network?

○ a. `access-list 50 deny 192.168.1.57 0.0.0.0`

○ b. `access-list 50 deny 192.168.1.0 255.255.255.0`

○ c. `access-list 50 deny any 192.168.1.0 0.0.0.0`

○ d. `access-list 50 deny 192.168.1.57 0.0.0.255`

Question 49

Examine the following output:

```
access-list 10 permit 192.168.1.0 0.0.0.255
access-list 11 deny any
line vty 0 4
  access-class 10 in
  access-class 11 out
```

What best describes the result of the above statements?

○ a. They convert the console port to another Ethernet interface.

○ b. Only hosts from the 192.168.1.0 network will be able to Telnet in to this router, and they will not be able to Telnet from this router to other sites within our network.

○ c. The code is in error; the access lists should be applied to router ports such as serial 0.

○ d. No one will be able to Telnet into our router, and console users will only be able to Telnet to the 192.168.1.0 network.

Question 50

Examine the following output:

```
Internet serial 0
  ip access-group test-out out
  ip access-group test-in in
!
ip access-list extended test-out
  permit tcp any any eq 53 reflect newlist-packets
  permit tcp any any eq 80 reflect newlist-packets
!
ip access-lst extended test-in
  evaluate newlist-packets
```

What best describes the result of the last statement?

○ a. Causes **test-out** to reverse itself and effectively block HTTP and DNS traffic coming into serial 0.

○ b. Outbound DNS and HTTP traffic through serial 0 will generate a temporary inbound access list with temporary entries identical to those in **test-out** except that the source and destinations will be reversed.

○ c. It created a log file called newlist-packets reflecting the activity on **test-out**.

○ d. Outbound DNS and HTTP traffic through serial 0 will generate a temporary inbound opening that will allow any DNS and HTTP traffic in through serial 0.

15

Question 51

Examine the following output:

```
Internet serial 0
  ip access-group test-out out
  ip access-group test-in in
!
ip access-list extended test-out
  permit tcp any any eq 53 reflect newlist-packets
  permit tcp any any eq 80 reflect newlist-packets
!
ip access-1st extended test-in
  evaluate newlist-packets
```

Which of the following statements are true about the above configuration? [Choose two answers]

❏ a. They represent examples of named access lists.

❏ b. They demonstrate implementation of dynamic access lists.

❏ c. The names **test-out** and **test-in** could have been replaced by numbers in the range 100-199.

❏ d. They demonstrate implementation of reflexive access lists.

Question 52

Examine the following output:

```
ip helper-address 195.168.2.20
ip forward-protocol udp snmp
```

What can be said with regard to the two statements?

○ a. Both statements are configured at the global configuration mode.

○ b. The first statement is configured at the global configuration mode. The second statement is configured at the interface configuration mode.

○ c. Both statements are configured at the interface configuration mode.

○ d. The first statement is configured at the interface configuration mode. The second statement is configured at the global configuration mode.

Question 53

Examine the following output:

```
Router(config)#access-list 50 deny 192.168.1.10 0.0.0.0
Router(config)#int e0
Router(config-if)#ip access-group 50 out
```

What best describes the result of the above access list and application statements?

○ a. All outbound IP traffic from host 192.168.1.10 through the Ethernet 0 interface will be blocked.

○ b. All outbound IP traffic to host 192.168.1.10 through the Ethernet 0 interface will be blocked.

○ c. All outbound IP traffic through the Ethernet 0 interface will be blocked.

○ d. All outbound IPX traffic from host 192.168.1.10 through the Ethernet 0 interface will be blocked.

Question 54

Examine the following output:

```
line vty 0 4
  no password
  login
```

What best describes the result of the above configuration statements?

○ a. All Telnet sessions will be prompted for their user ID because there is no password.

○ b. The first Telnet session will be prompted to create a password.

○ c. No Telnet sessions can be established with this router.

○ d. All Telnet sessions will be prompted for the router hostname because there is no password.

15

Question 55

Examine the following output:

```
access-list 105 permit tcp any host 195.168.2.20 eq smtp
access-list 105 permit tcp any host 195.168.2.20 established
interface serial 0
  ip access-group 105 in
```

What can be said with regard to the above statements relative to server 195.168.2.20? [Choose two answers]

❏ a. The server will be able to participate only in traffic initiated beyond serial 0.

❏ b. The server can receive email updates from beyond serial 0.

❏ c. TCP traffic sessions with 195.168.2.20 generally cannot be initiated from beyond serial 0.

❏ d. TCP traffic sessions with 195.168.2.20 must be with well-established and trusted hosts.

Question 56

Examine the following output:

```
Extended IP access list 145
    deny tcp any host 195.168.2.20 eq telnet (7 matches)
    deny tcp any host 195.168.1.20 eq telnet (4 matches)
    permit ip any any (317 matches)
Standard IP access list 50
    deny   210.93.105.10 (2 matches)
    permit any (91 matches)
```

Which commands could have created the above display? [Choose two answers]

❏ a. **show access-lists**

❏ b. **show access-lists summary**

❏ c. **show IP access-lists**

❏ d. **show access lists**

Question 57

Which of the following statements, if properly applied, will block all IP traffic to the 192.168.115.0 network? [Choose two answers]

❏ a. `access-list 175 deny 192.168.115.0 0.0.0.255 any`

❏ b. `access-list 100 deny any 192.168. 115.0 0.0.0.255`

❏ c. `access-list 50 deny any 192.168.115.0 0.0.0.255`

❏ d. `ip route 195.168.115.0 255.255.255.0 null 0`

Question 58

Which of the following statements is true regarding the host and network addresses from the following VLSM address: 172.16.17.74/29?

○ a. 74 is the network; 75 through 80 are the host addresses; and 81 is the broadcast address.

○ b. 72 is the network; 73 through 78 are the host addresses; and 79 is the broadcast address.

○ c. 74 is the network; 75 and 76 are the host addresses; and 77 is the broadcast address.

○ d. 72 is the network; 73 and 74 are the host addresses; and 75 is the broadcast address.

Question 59

We are given the following network: 192.168.0.160/27. We want to subnet this network into just four new networks. List them.

○ a. 192.168.0.160/28; 192.168.0.164/28; 192.168.0.168/28; and 192.168.0.172/28.

○ b. 192.168.0.160/29; 192.168.0.164/29; 192.168.0.168/29; and 192.168.0.172/29.

○ c. 192.168.0.160/28; 192.168.0.168/28; 192.168.0.176/28; and 192.168.0.184/28.

○ d. 192.168.0.160/29; 192.168.0.168/29; 192.168.0.176/29; and 192.168.0.184/29.

15

Question 60

Examine these 4 networks:

```
172.16.98.0/25
172.16.98.128/25
172.16.99.0/25
172.16.99.128/25
```

How would they best be summarized?

○ a. 172.16.0.0/16

○ b. 172.16.98.0/23

○ c. 172.16.98.0/24 and 172.16.99.0/24

○ d. 172.16.99.0/23

Question 61

How many hosts are available with a subnet mask of /23?

○ a. 510

○ b. 512

○ c. 254

○ d. 256

CHAPTER SIXTEEN

Answer Key

1. a, d	22. a	43. d
2. a, c	23. c, d	44. b
3. d	24. b, c	45. b, d
4. c	25. c	46. a, c
5. b, d, f	26. a	47. c, e
6. d	27. b, c	48. d
7. b, c	28. c	49. b
8. a, c	29. d	50. b
9. c	30. a	51. a, d
10. c	31. c	52. d
11. a	32. a, c	53. c
12. c	33. d	54. c
13. a, b, e	34. a, d	55. b, c
14. a	35. a, d	56. a, c
15. c	36. c, d	57. b, d
16. d	37. c, d	58. b
17. d	38. c	59. d
18. b, c	39. c	60. b
19. d	40. b, c	61. a
20. c	41. a	
21. b	42. b, d	

Question 1

Answers a and d are correct. Link state routing protocols establish formal peer relationships using the hello protocol, and they support CIDR. Answer b is incorrect because link-state routing protocols multicast routing information. Answer c is incorrect because link-state routing tables maintain only the best possible routes.

Question 2

Answers a and c are correct. As a network scales, its distance-vector routing protocol will consume enormous amounts of network bandwidth by broadcasting routing tables at frequent intervals. In addition, only a limited number of routers can be supported. Answer b is incorrect because vendor interoperability is not an issue with standard distance-vector routing protocols such as RIP. Answer d is incorrect because distance-vector routing protocols support point-to-point WAN links.

Question 3

Answer d is correct. Remember that the first thing an OSPF router does when it receives an LSA is verify the LSA's contents to determine whether it will be accepted.

Question 4

Answer c is correct. During the exchange state, a DR and adjacent OSPF neighbor will exchange database description packets (DDPs) that contain LSA information for building the topological database.

Question 5

Answers b, d, and f are correct. All of these are typical characteristics of a network in OSPF NBMA mode. In NBMA mode, neighbors must be statically defined because multicasts and broadcasts are not supported. Adjacencies occur successfully only when there is a full mesh.

Question 6

Answer d is correct. The **ip ospf network non-broadcast** command tells the router that OSPF will be operating in an NBMA environment, meaning that no broadcasts/multicasts will be supported. This command is enabled by default on NBMA interfaces, such as Frame-Relay.

Question 7

Answers b and c are correct. Neighbor discovery is automatic only when neighbor statements are not used, which is usually the case with networks that support broadcasts/multicasts. A network that is configured in NBMA broadcast mode (also known as BMA mode) supports broadcasts/multicasts, as does a network that is configured in point-to-multipoint broadcast mode. Answers a and d are incorrect because these OSPF modes do not support broadcasts/multicasts and must therefore use **neighbor** statements to discover neighbors.

Question 8

Answers a and c are correct. Inter-area route summarization occurs at the ABR, whereas external route summarization occurs at the ASBR. Answers b and d are incorrect because these are not valid types of route summarization for OSPF.

Question 9

Answer c is correct. Totally stub areas do not accept inter-area LSAs, which include type 3, 4, and 5 LSAs. Answers a, b, and d are incorrect because they accept type 3 LSAs.

Question 10

Answer c is correct. ABRs automatically inject default routes into these types of areas. Answers a, b, and d are incorrect.

Question 11

Answer a is correct. The ABR creates a summary route (172.16.0.0 /16) for area 1 and advertises it to another area. If the ABR was connected to the backbone area (as it usually would be), then the summary route would be flooded throughout that area. Backbone routers would in turn flood the summary route to other areas that are part of the same OSPF domain.

Question 12

Answer c is correct. The **show ip ospf interface** command identifies such items as the interfaces on which OSPF is configured, the identities of DRs and BDRs, and timer intervals.

16

Question 13

Answers a, b, and e are correct. Unlike IGRP, EIGRP supports multiple protocols, route summarization, and faster convergence. Answer c is incorrect because unequal-cost load-balancing is a feature shared by both of these routing protocols. Answer d is incorrect because areas are not an EIGRP feature.

Question 14

Answer a is correct. A feasible successor is the second best route to a particular destination network. Answer b is incorrect because in order to be a feasible successor, a route's advertised distance must be less than the feasible distance through the successor. Answer c is incorrect because a feasible successor is not the best route to a destination network. Answer d is incorrect because query packets do not travel through feasible successors.

Question 15

Answer c is correct. When an EIGRP router initializes, it must first establish neighbor relationships to build the neighbor table. Discovered routes are placed in the topology table, and the best of these routes are placed in the routing table.

Question 16

Answer d is correct. The route evaluation process begins before the route recomputation process. Answer a is incorrect because query packets are sent whenever a feasible successor is not found for a failed successor. Answer b is incorrect because feasible distance is the cost used to reach a particular destination network, not the cost used to reach a next-hop router. Answer c is incorrect because topology changes may also occur in such situations as when a route and/or router are added to the network.

Question 17

Answer d is correct. The DUAL does not track queried neighbors, nor does it have any tracking responsibility whatsoever; this function belongs to the Real Time Transport Protocol (RTP). The DUAL is EIGRP's finite-state machine for calculating the best routes (successors) and second best routes (feasible successors); it also maintains a loop-free topology and guarantees near-instantaneous convergence after a topology change occurs.

Question 18

Answers b and c are correct. EIGRP can limit the range of query packets with route summarization and autonomous system boundaries. Answer a is incorrect because outbound distribute lists do not prevent query packets from being propagated; their only influence is on how replies are sent. Answer d is incorrect because unequal-cost load-balancing has no relevance to the suppression of queries.

Question 19

Answer d is correct. The **variance** command allows unequal-cost load-balancing to occur. In order to qualify for unequal-cost load-balancing, a route must be either a successor or feasible successor. The other answers are wrong.

Question 20

Answer c is correct. On a multipoint interface in which all links are of equal speed (or CIR) and no oversubscription is featured, the interface bandwidth should typically be configured to equal the sum of the links' bandwidths. This is because EIGRP will take the multipoint interface's configured bandwidth and divide it by the number of links on that interface to determine the amount of bandwidth allocated to each link. EIGRP then appropriates up to 50 percent of each link's bandwidth.

Question 21

Answer b is correct. EBGP is a BGP session formed between two external BGP peers. Answer a is incorrect because EBGP is not used specifically to exchange error messages. Answer c is incorrect because polling is not an EIGRP feature. Answer d is incorrect because EBGP is not a protocol that allows for the exchange of network reachability information between internal BGP peers; rather, the BGP peers are required to be external.

Question 22

Answer a is correct. The BGP *open* message is used to establish a BGP connection between two peers. Answer b is incorrect because the TCP connection must already be established before the *open* message can be exchanged. Answer c is incorrect because path attributes are not negotiable in *open* messages. Answer d is incorrect because the *open* message is not used periodically to verify connectivity between BGP peers; that task instead belongs to the BGP *keepalive* message.

16

Question 23

Answers c and d are correct. A well-known path attribute must be recognized by all standard BGP implementations, whereas optional path attributes are not required to be recognized by all standard BGP implementations. Furthermore, unlike well-known mandatory path attributes, well-known discretionary path attributes are not required to be in routing updates. Answer b is incorrect because optional transitive path attributes that are not recognized are marked as "partial" and are propagated to neighboring peers.

Question 24

Answers b and c are correct. The major difference between local preference and weight is that the former is propagated within the AS, whereas the latter remains local to the router on which it is configured; but both are used to influence the path taken to networks in external ASes. Answer a is incorrect because origin is a path attribute used specifically to define the source of routing information. Answer d is incorrect because the next hop attribute is used to identify the next hop router used to reach a destination network.

Question 25

Answer c is correct. The MED (also known as the metric) path attribute is typically used to influence the path that external networks take to reach the local AS. This attribute is exchanged between EBGP peers and is propagated within their local ASes, but is not forwarded to their external ASes. Answers a and b are incorrect because weight and local preference do the opposite of what MED does; that is, they are used to influence the path taken from the local AS to reach external networks. Answer d is incorrect because the atomic aggregate is not used to influence the path that external networks take to reach the local AS.

Question 26

Answer a is correct. In Cisco-based BGP networks, weight is the most preferred of all the path attributes. Because weight is a proprietary path attribute, it is not the most preferred path attribute in networks that do not use Cisco routers. In this latter case, local preference would be the most preferred path attribute.

Question 27

Answers b and c are correct. BGP is not likely to be recommended when the AS has only a single external connection to an AS whose routing policy is identical to the local AS. Answers a, d, and e are incorrect because these are conditions in which BGP would likely be recommended as an external connectivity solution for an AS.

Question 28

Answer c is correct. The **neighbor remote-as** command identifies the peer's AS number. If this AS number is the same as the local router's AS number, then the local router knows that an IBGP session is established. If the AS numbers are different, then the local router knows that an EBGP session is established. Answers a and b are incorrect because the router does not employ these methods to distinguish between EBGP and IBGP peers. Answer d is incorrect because this differentiation is required for the router to be able to perform certain operations and abide by certain rules with respect to its peers.

Question 29

Answer d is correct. The purpose of requiring a route to be in the IP routing table before the route can be advertised with the BGP **network** command is to make sure that black holes do not occur in the local AS. Requiring the BGP router to match routes in the IP routing table has the effect of making sure that all IGP routers in the local AS are working with the same IP routing tables as the BGP router. With this type of synchronization established, no router in the AS will be left unaware of local routes.

Question 30

Answer a is correct. The **show ip bgp** command displays the BGP routing table. Answer b is incorrect because the **show ip bgp summary** command is used to display the status of all BGP connections. Answer c is incorrect because the **show ip bgp neighbors** command is used to display information about the TCP and BGP connections to neighbors. Answer d is incorrect because there is no such command as **show ip bgp table**.

Question 31

Answer c is correct. A route reflector is a router that is allowed to propagate IBGP-learned routes to IBGP neighbors. This is one solution to the scalability problems inherent in maintaining a full IBGP mesh.

16

Question 32

Answers a and c are correct. BGP prefix lists feature an implicit **deny any**, just like access lists. The ability to match routes based on various path attributes is not a function of prefix lists, which can match routes based only on prefix or network number. Answers b and d are incorrect because these are two advantages of prefix lists.

Question 33

Answer d is correct. The command presented in this question applies **access-list 1** to all routing updates sent to 150.10.20.2. Answer a is incorrect because for routing updates to be checked upon reception, the **in** keyword would need to be specified. Answer b is incorrect because **distribute-list** uses access lists and access list numbers; in addition, **distribute-list** is not applied to open messages. Answer c is incorrect because there is not sufficient information to conclude that *all* routing updates would be restricted.

Question 34

Answers a and d are correct. The route map is applied to all routing updates received from neighbor 10.10.10.2. Specifically, the first **route-map** statement applies access list 1 to all routes and forms a match with routes whose addresses match the first two bytes of 180.10.0.0. Routes that are permitted by access list 1 will be assigned a weight of 100, whereas routes that are denied by access list 1 will automatically form a match with the second **route-map** statement. These latter routes would then be assigned a weight of 1. Answer b is incorrect because the access list's wild-card mask permits routes with any combination of low-order 16 bits. Answer c is incorrect because there is a second **route-map** statement for all routes that do not meet the first statement's criteria. Answer e is incorrect because omitted **match** conditions always imply a "match any".

Question 35

Answers a and d are correct. The voyager route map does not use any access lists, nor community lists, to match routes. Routes whose next-hop IP address is 10.10.10.1 will form a match and will be appended with a community attribute value of 100.

Question 36

Answers c and d are correct. Peer groups reduce the number of **neighbor** statements by grouping peers that share the same update policies. Peer groups also improve policy routing performance because routing updates are sent only once for each peer group, as opposed to being generated and sent individually to each peer group member. Answers a and b are incorrect because these are features of communities, not peer groups.

Question 37

Answers c and d are correct. In Router A's configuration, three EBGP peers have become members of the "delta" peer group. A route map named "giga" is applied to all routing updates sent to this peer group. Answer a is incorrect because inbound update policies can be overridden by a peer group member. Answer b is incorrect because neighbor 1.1.1.2 is a member of the delta peer group.

Question 38

Answer c is correct. Multihoming occurs when an AS is connected to multiple ISPs. Answers a and d are incorrect because an AS must be connected to more than one other AS to qualify for the multihoming definition. Answer b is incorrect because load-balancing is not a definition of multihoming.

Question 39

Answer c is correct. The best way to prevent suboptimal path selection in a redistribution environment is to modify the administrative distance of selected routes. Answers a and b are incorrect because load-balancing and stub router designation are irrelevant to the issue of suboptimal path selection. Answer d is incorrect because passive interfaces are used primarily to prevent routing updates from being sent needlessly out interfaces where they will not be understood, nor be accepted.

Question 40

Answers b and c are correct. In Router 2's configuration, RIP is advertising for networks 172.16.0.0 and 10.0.0.0. A default route for network 10.0.0.0 is propagated to network 172.16.0.0. Answer a is incorrect because there is no **redistribute** command in this configuration, nor is there any implication of the occurrence of redistribution. The reason answer b is correct is that RIP requires that all networks transmitting RIP messages be directly connected. Answer d is incorrect because the output does not indicate that RIP is advertising a default route for network 172.16.0.0; the output instead indicates that RIP is advertising a default route for network 10.0.0.0 (and forwarding it to network 172.16.0.0).

Question 41

Answer a is correct. Uncontrolled bidirectional redistribution at multiple locations in the internetwork can lead to routing feedback loops. This would occur because the AS would be redistributing routes back into the routing protocol from which the routes were learned. Answer b is incorrect because router compatibility is unaffected by redistribution. Answer c is incorrect because in order to prevent full routing information from sent, some method of controlling routing updates would be necessary, such as route filters. Answer d is incorrect because all common routing protocols support bidirectional redistribution, whether controlled or not.

16

Question 42

Answers b and d are correct. In Router B's configuration, **access-list 1** is used to assign an administrative distance of 130 to any IGRP-learned route that matches network 172.16.1.0. Answer a is incorrect because there is no indication in Router B's configuration that routes are being filtered upon being redistributed. Answer c is incorrect because only redistributed RIP routes will be assigned the default metric.

Question 43

Answer d is correct. Policy-based routing does not use prefix lists; it uses route maps and access lists instead. Answers a, b, and c are incorrect because these are all attributes of policy-based routing.

Question 44

Answer b is correct. With policy-based route maps, a packet can be permitted or denied based on such characteristics as the packet's source and destination addresses, application, protocol, size, ToS, and precedence. Answer a is incorrect because only *incoming* packets can be tested by policy-based route maps. Answers c and d are incorrect because policy-based route maps never drop a packet under any condition; instead, a packet that does not meet policy criteria is simply forwarded as usual.

Question 45

Answers b and d are correct. In Router A's configuration, any packet that is permitted by **access-list 1** and is between 64 and 128 bytes in length will be policy routed. Answer a is incorrect because the "enterprise" route map is applied to all packets *received* on Router A's serial0 interface. Answer c is incorrect because both **match** conditions need to be met for the packet to be policy routed.

Question 46

Answers a and c are correct. The statement is a static route to the null 0 port, effectively killing off packets addressed to that network (including server 195.168.1.25). Answer b is incorrect because the statement is not an **access list** statement of any kind. Answer d is incorrect because access lists require CPU resources to process, whereas the static route becomes the "best" route to 195.168.1.0 in the routing table and the switching function forwards the packets without evaluation.

Question 47

Answers c and e are correct. The first two statements modify the pool of UDP broadcast packets (including DHCP) that will be forwarded by the **ip helper** command. The last three statements convert any of the pool of UDP broadcast packets received by Ethernet 1 to unicast packets—which can now be routed. Answer a is incorrect at least because it impacts only SNMP packets arriving at an interface with the **ip helper** command—and then it is converted from a broadcast packet. Answer b is incorrect because it is basically backwards. Answer d is incorrect because it creates three unicast packets to specific addresses, not a multicast packet. Answer f is incorrect because UDP, not TCP, broadcasts.

Question 48

Answer d is correct. Answer a is incorrect because it blocks only host 192.168.1.57. Answer b is incorrect because 255.255.255.0 is a subnet mask not a wildcard mask. Answer c is incorrect because while the keyword **any** would apply to any source, the destination is wrong for a standard access list.

Question 49

Answer b is correct. The access lists applied to the virtual terminals allow only hosts from the 192.168.1.0 network to Telnet in to this router; they will not be able to Telnet from this router to other sites within our network—or anywhere else. Answer a is gibberish. Answer c is incorrect because access lists can be applied to the virtual terminals to restrict Telnet access. Answer d is incorrect because **line vty** refers to the virtual terminals, not the console port.

Question 50

Answer b is correct. The reflexive **access list** statements in **test-out** will be triggered by outbound DNS and HTTP traffic through serial 0 and will generate a temporary inbound access list at the **evaluate** statement with temporary entries detected while monitoring **test-out** except that the source and destinations will be reversed.

16

Question 51

Answers a and d are correct. The reflexive access lists are a feature of IP extended named access lists. Answer b is incorrect because it is a reflexive, not a dynamic, access list. Answer c is incorrect because they are a feature only of IP extended named access lists.

Question 52

Answer d is correct. The **ip helper-address** statement is configured at the interface configuration mode. The **ip forward-protocol** statement is configured at the global configuration mode.

Question 53

Answer c is correct. The implicit **deny all** statement ending the list combined with the fact that there are no **permit** statements means all IP traffic will be blocked. Answer a, although true, is not the best (most descriptive) answer. Answer b is incorrect because standard access lists are based on source addresses only, not destination. Answer d is incorrect because the access list number and the source address are not IPX designations.

Question 54

Answer c is correct. The **login** command requires all Telnet users to supply a password, but because no password is created to authenticate the users, no Telnet sessions can be established with this router.

Question 55

Answers b and c are correct. The first statement allows email updates through serial 0, whereas the second blocks sessions in through serial 0 that were not imitated by server 195.168.2.20. Answer a is reversed. Answer d is gibberish.

Question 56

Answers a and c are correct. It happens that the result is the same in this output because we are using only IP protocol. Had we been running IPX and/or AppleTalk in addition, then answer a would have included that data as well. Answers b and d are incorrect because there are no such commands.

Question 57

Answers b and d are correct. Answer b, an extended **access-list** statement, and d, a static route to the null 0 port, will discard all packets destined to the 192.168.115.0 network. Answer a is incorrect because the source and destination are reversed. Answer c is incorrect because the access list number is for a standard access list, which operates on source addresses only.

Question 58

Answer b is correct. A 29-bit subnet mask leaves 3 bits for the hosts—or 6 hosts, 1 network, and 1 broadcast. Answers c and d are incorrect because there are 2 hosts, 1 network, and 1 broadcast. Writing out the binary for 172.16.17.74 indicates that the network is 172.16.17.72, eliminating answer a.

Question 59

Answer d is correct. Adding four new networks would add 2 bits to the subnet mask. This makes answers a and c incorrect. A 29-bit subnet mask leaves 3 bits for the hosts, which means that the networks increment by 8, not 4.

Question 60

Answer b is correct. Write out the bit patterns of the four networks to see that the common bits align on the 23rd bit. This makes the summarization best with 23 bits in the subnet mask. Answer a is correct, but it is not the best answer because there are plenty of other networks that are represented in this summarization, not just the 4. Answer c is also actually correct, but it is not the best answer because it requires two summarizations, not one. Answer d is incorrect because it does not include all networks.

Question 61

Answer a is correct. A 23-bit subnet mask leaves 9 bits for the host field. 2^9 equals 512. However, the two broadcast addresses cannot be used (all zeros and all ones). Therefore, only 510 hosts are available.

16

Appendix A
Answers to Review Questions

Chapter 1 Solutions

1. **b, d,** and **e.** Distribution, Core, and Access.

2. **c.** Unknown IP addresses are forwarded to all segments except the source

3. **a, b,** and **d.** Store-and-forward, fast-forward, and fragment-free

4. **b.** Distribution

5. **a.** Reliability and availability

6. **d.** Adaptability

7. **e.** Accessibility and security

8. **c.** Efficiency

9. **a.** Reliability and availability

10. **c.** Efficiency

11. **d.** Adaptability

12. **c.** Efficiency

Chapter 2 Solutions

1. **b.** 255.255.255.240

   c. 255.255.255.192

2. **a.** 255.255.240224.0

3.

Subnet Value	Subnet Address	Broadcast Value	Host Range
0	171.16.0.0	171.16.31.255	171.16.1.1 = 171.16.31.254
32	171.16.32.0	171.16.63.255	171.16.32.1 = 171.16.63.254
64	171.16.64.0	171.16.95.255	171.16.64.1 = 171.16.95.254
96	171.16.96.0	171.16.127.255	171.16.96.1 = 171.16.127.254
128	171.16.128.0	171.16.159.255	171.16.128.1 = 171.16.159.254
160	171.16.160.0	171.16.191.255	171.16.161.1 = 171.16.191.254

4. **c.** Subnets 16; hosts 4,094

5. routing, switching

6. **c.** Determine the best route from all of the choices in the routing table

7. **a.** The destination network must be known and accessible to the router

   c. The appropriate protocol must be active on the interfaces of the router

   d. The routing table must reflect the best path to the desired network via one of the router's interfaces

8. False

9. False

10. False

11. False

12. True

13. **a.** RIPv1, RIPv2

   b. RIPv1, RIPv2

   c. IGRP, EIGRP

   d. RIPv2, EIGRP, OSPF

   e. IGRP

   f. OSPF

   g. EIGRP, OSPF

   h. RIPv1, RIPv2, IGRP, EIGRP

   i. RIPv1, RIPv2, IGRP

   j. EIGRP, OSPF

   k. RIPv1, RIPv2, IGRP, EIGRP

  l. None

  m. OSPF

  n. RIPv1, IGRP

  o. RIPv2, EIGRP, OSPF

  p. RIPv2, EIGRP, OSPF

14. **c. show ip routes**

15. **b.** IP address of neighbor device

16. **a. show run**

  c. show IP protocols

  d. show interfaces

17. **c. telnet**, **ping**, **trace**, **show interfaces**

Chapter 3 Solutions

1. **a, b,** and **d.** Network Address Translation allows address space to be utilized without allocation from IANA. Hierarchical addressing and CIDR organize addresses in a logical fashion, meaning addresses can be used more efficiently.

2. **c.** Seven networks fit into three bits. Add this to the original 24 to make 27.

3. **a.** Thirty-two bits in an IP address minus 29 bits for the network leaves 3 bits for the host field, or a maximum of eight hosts. However, the two broadcast addresses, all zeros and all ones, subtract this amount by 2. The correct answer is six hosts.

4. **b.** This will give exactly eight nets and 30 hosts.

5. **b, c.** RIPv2 and OSPF support classless routing updates.

6. **a, d.** 172.30.0.0/16 and 172.0.0.0/8 are not in the range provided by the NIC for nonroutable addresses.

7. **a, b, c.** The IANA doesn't actually do any routing. It is an administrative body.

8. **a.** These networks can be summarized using the following single entry, 172.16.20.0/23—admittedly not a great savings.

9. **a, b.** The route tables are reduced and there is increased availability of IP addresses.

10. **a.** The whole idea behind this hierarchical system is to assign multiple netmasks to a network, not just one.

Chapter 4 Solutions

1. **b.** OSPF. EIGRP is technically an advanced distance-vector routing protocol, but it is also referred to as a hybrid protocol because it incorporates both distance-vector and link-state characteristics.

2. **b, d.** Distance-vector protocols typically use hop count and always send out periodic updates.

3. **a, b.** Link state protocols always establish neighbor relationships and send multicasts rather than broadcasts.

4. **b, d.** Contrary to popular belief, a routing protocol is *not* necessary to route a packet. This is because a route could be learned instead with a static route or by being directly connected. In these two cases, a routing protocol is therefore unnecessary.

5. **c.** Note that this is true only when the link failure is directly connected.

6. **d.** Hop count is the number of routers traversed to reach a destination.

7. **b.** Remote topology changes are those that occur without the router's direct awareness. When a router detects a remote topology change via a routing update, it makes a note of it (if it is accepted) and multicasts a routing update to selected neighbors.

8. **c.** Scalability problems associated with distance-vector routing protocols generally involve resource-consumption issues and reachability limitations. However, they could also include other issues, such as performance constraints and security.

9. **c.** The hello protocol is responsible for establishing bidirectional communication (a neighbor relationship) between two link-state routers.

10. **a, c.** Contrary to popular belief, a router that detects a failed link (either directly or via a routing update) does not wait for the next scheduled update to inform its neighbors. Instead, the router immediately broadcasts a triggered update.

11. **b, c, f, g.** These are all features of OSPF.

12. **a, c, g, h.** These are all features of EIGRP.

13. **a.** BGP's primary reason for existing is to exchange network reachability information with other BGP routers, whether they reside within or outside the AS.

14. **c.** Answer d may be true in the future, thanks to continuing research and development of artificial intelligence. Presently, however, routers must be issued the commands to implement network policy.

15. **b.** A TCP connection is always established first.

Chapter 5 Solutions

1. **c.** OSPF v2 does not support any network layer multiple routing protocols besides IP.

2. **a, d.** The hello packet does not contain the LSA type or DR MAC address.

3. **d.** The router first verifies that the LSA is acceptable.

4. **b.** Adjacencies are established and DDPs are exchanged.

5. **c.** An LSR is only sent out when the router needs more info from a DDP.

6. **b.** Broadcasts interrupt all CPUs, whereas multicasts interrupt only selected CPUs.

7. **d.** Routers must be in full state before they can start routing packets.

8. **c.** The path with the least cost is chosen.

9. **a.** The occurrence of multicasting is not a characteristic of NBMA mode.

10. **c.** Whether an NBMA network is configured to support multicasting or not, a full mesh is still required.

11. **d.** Split Horizon does not distinguish between multicasts and broadcasts.

12. **c. ip ospf network**

13. **b.** The main occasion for configuring a point-to-multipoint network is when the full mesh requirement cannot be met.

14. **a.** In point-to-multipoint mode (either broadcast or nonbroadcast), no DR/BDR election occurs.

15. **d.** A partial mesh scales better.

16. **b.** Multicasting occurs when OSPF is in NBMA broadcast mode.

17. **c.** The DR's router ID is not found in the **show ip ospf** output.

18. **d.** The **show ip protocol** command will tell you about the occurrence of redistribution.

19. **b.** Varying neighbor costs indicate that not all neighbors are directly connected.

20. **b.** The configuration indicates that OSPF is in NBMA broadcast mode. We can therefore infer that a full mesh is being used.

Chapter 6 Solutions

1. **d.** A router will still be able to establish adjacencies.

2. **a, d.** Traffic centralization and reduced resource consumption are the two major benefits of OSPF's hierarchical solution.

3. **c.** Routes must be contiguous in order to be allowed to be summarized.

4. **a, c.** Routing table sizes are reduced and the SPF algorithm is calculated less frequently.

5. **d.** Totally stub areas cannot accept inter-area LSAs.

6. **c.** The backbone area's primary function is to interconnect all areas.

7. **b.** A network-summary-LSA is generated only by ABRs.

8. **d.** This describes the correct sequence of events for a topology update.

9. **b.** A default route is necessary.

10. **d. router(config-router)# area 1 stub no-summary**. The totally stub command is issued only on the ABR.

11. **b.** Static routes may be used in stub areas.

12. **a.** Using multiple stub area gateways can lead to suboptimal route selection.

13. **a.** Inter-area route summarization occurs only on ABRs.

14. **d. router(config-router)#summary-address 132.16.64.0 255.255.192.0**.

15. **b.** The entry that shares the most network bits in common with the packet's destination address is the matching entry.

16. **d.** The smallest cost of a summarized route is used.

17. **c.** The cost of a type 1 external route gets incremented at each router hop.

18. **c. router(config-router)#default-information originate**. If the router does not already have a default route, then this command will not cause a default route to be advertised.

19. **b.** A virtual link connects only OSPF areas.

20. **c.** This command states the router IDs of known ABRs and ASBRs.

Chapter 7 Solutions

1. **d.** The DUAL does not establish neighbor relationships.

2. **b, d.** Although EIGRP also supports reliability, load, and MTU, it uses only bandwidth and delay by default.

3. **c.** EIGRP does not use areas.

4. **a.** EIGRP maintains a neighbor table for each configured network protocol.

5. **c.** The routing table indicates the uptime for all networks.

6. **a, d.** Remember that the terms successor or feasible successor can connote the routes.

7. **b.** This is the criterion for a feasible successor.

8. **d.** There is no such packet as a DUAL packet.

9. **b.** The route evaluation process occurs whenever a topology change occurs.

10. **a.** The route recomputation process first occurs when a router finds that it has no feasible successor in its topology table.

11. **c.** Two routers become neighbors when they see each other's hello packets.

12. **c.** It is routing tables that the neighbors send, not topology tables.

13. **a.** Feasible distance is a neutral term that refers to the cost to reach a destination.

14. **c.** Only successor routes are placed in the routing table.

15. **c.** This is the route evaluation process.

16. **a, c.** The route recomputation process begins when a router finds that it has no feasible successor in its topology table.

17. **c.** The neighbor table is used by the RTP to keep track of all neighbors that have been sent reliable packets.

18. **b.** Each time a router converges it sends a multicast update packet to its neighbors.

19. **b. Router(config)#router eigrp 1**.

20. **b.** This command is useful for monitoring EIGRP activity on the router.

Chapter 8 Solutions

1. **b.** Manual route summarization can also be performed on any bit boundary.

2. **c.** Route summarization requires contiguous addressing.

3. **b.** Discontiguous subnets of the same major network are separated by a different major network.

4. **a.** The hyphen is required.

5. **d.** Refer to Figure 8.19. Each summarized region can propagate a query; however, the query receives an immediate reply.

6. **a.** A router must receive all replies to a query before it can proceed with route recomputation.

7. **d.** Load-balancing has nothing to do with limiting the query range.

8. **b.** Contrary to popular belief, the router will still forward a new query into the other AS.

9. **a.** Also contrary to popular belief, outbound distribution lists do not prevent query propagation.

10. **a, b.** These are two main benefits to stub designation.

11. **c.** The next hops must be either successors or feasible successors.

12. **d.** The **bandwidth** command is relevant only to the routing protocol.

13. **b.** EIGRP's default is 50 percent.

14. **a.** The actual link speed can also be referred to as the CIR.

15. **a.** The actual speed of a link cannot be inferred from just this command.

16. **a.** Remember that EIGRP always divides the configured bandwidth of a multipoint interface or subinterface by the number of links on that multipoint interface or subinterface to determine the amount of bandwidth available for each link.

17. **b.** When the links on an oversubscribed multipoint interface (or subinterface) have identical CIRs, configure the multipoint interface with the access line speed. Recall that the access line speed is what the interface can support (the links themselves are causing the oversubscription).

18. **c.** When a hybrid interface is not an option, take the speed of the slowest link on the multipoint interface and multiply it by the number of links on the multipoint interface.

19. **d.** An internetwork must be hierarchically structured and have a hierarchical addressing scheme.

20. **c.** EIGRP does not use the concept of areas.

Chapter 9 Solutions

1. **c.** IGPs function only within ASes. (BGP is an IGP, but it is also an EGP.)

2. **d.** BGP does not send periodic updates.

3. **a.** The open message is sent after the TCP connection is established and before the BGP connection is established.

4. **d.** EBGP connections are established only between ASes.

5. **c.** Postinitialization updates occur only when there is a topology change.

6. **b.** BGP updates do not contain the holdtime.

7. **d.** Policy-based routing defines how traffic is controlled as it passes through an AS.

8. **c, d.** Well-known path attributes are always supported and always recognized.

9. **b, d.** Optional transitive path attributes include the communities and aggregator attributes.

10. **a.** Whenever an update passes through an AS, the AS number is prepended to the list of ASes in the update's AS-path.

11. **b.** The next-hop path attribute indicates the next-hop router's IP address.

12. **a.** The local preference path attribute is used for influencing the path that intra-AS routers take to external destinations.

13. **b, c.** The MED is an optional nontransitive path attribute that is preferred most when its value is least.

14. **b.** The origin path attribute does not contain a value called default.

15. **b, c.** The weight attribute is Cisco-proprietary and paths with the highest weight are most preferred.

16. **c.** Weight is proprietary to Cisco. Naturally, Cisco would want to make this path attribute most preferred.

17. **c.** The BGP synchronization rule states that BGP routers should hold off on advertising routes to external peers until the routes have been matched in the local routers' IP routing tables.

18. **a, d, e.** BGP is recommended for any of these conditions.

19. **c.** The corporate AS would have a default route to the ISP, while the ISP would learn of the corporate AS via static routes.

20. **d. aggregate-address** *ip-address mask*

21. **c. neighbor** *ip-address* **remote-as** *as-number*

22. **c.** BGP synchronization can be disabled when either (1) the AS is not going to be a transit AS, or (2) when all internal routers within your AS speak BGP.

23. **a.** When BGP synchronization is enabled, the network you are going to configure must be matched in the IP routing table. This is to ensure that both IGP and BGP are synchronized with the same intra-AS routing information before the AS starts advertising this information to external neighbors.

24. **a. show ip bgp**

25. **d.** The **clear ip bgp** command is used to reset BGP neighbor connections after a configuration change. This allows the changes to take effect and BGP neighbors to be informed.

Chapter 10 Solutions

1. **a.** The major scalability problem with IBGP is supporting a full logical mesh between IBGP peers.

2. **c.** The BGP Split Horizon rule states that a route learned via IBGP cannot be propagated to other IBGP peers.

3. **d.** A client is an IBGP peer of a route reflector that resides within the same cluster, whereas a nonclient is an IBGP peer of a route reflector that resides in a different cluster.

4. **b.** A major design requirement for route reflector networks is that all route reflectors in the AS must be fully meshed logically. This is to ensure that updates received from nonclients are propagated across the AS.

5. **d.** IGP peers are not considered clients or nonclients. Any update received from these neighbors is propagated according to the rules of the IGP.

6. **b. neighbor 183.120.20.32 route-reflector-client**.

7. **c.** Prefix filters filter routing updates based on prefix.

8. **d. neighbor 150.93.39.2 distribute-list 1 out**.

9. **a.** One advantage to using an extended access list rather than a standard access list is the ability to specify only an aggregate route (as opposed to the aggregate route and all routes summarized within it).

10. **b, d.** Advantages to using prefix lists instead of access lists include incremental modifications and greater flexibility.

11. **b.** Prefix lists match routes starting with the statement with the lowest sequence number.

12. **d. ip prefix-list voyager permit 185.16.82.0/24**.

13. **a.** The **neighbor prefix-list** command applies the prefix list to updates received from or sent to a neighbor.

14. **c. show ip prefix-list detail**.

15. **a, b.** Two reasons for using BGP route maps are to filter networks and to modify path attributes.

16. **b, c.** Features shared by both access lists and route maps include the **permit | deny** function and the implicit **deny any**.

17. **c.** When a route passes through a route map without forming a match, the route is denied (dropped).

18. **c.** Router(config)#route-map voyager permit 10.
    Router(config-route-map)#match ip address 1.
    Router(config-route-map)#set weight 30.

19. **c.** The correct interpretation is: Permit a route whose address matches the first two bytes of 10.10.0.0.

20. **a.** BGP communities are used for grouping destinations so that routing decisions can be applied to the group rather than to individual destinations.

21. **c.** The **no-export** keyword specifies not to advertise an update tagged with this community value outside the AS.

22. **a.** A BGP peer group is a group of BGP peers that share the same update policies.

23. **b.** One requirement for peer groups is that members must not be configured with different outbound update policies; however, they may be configured with different inbound update policies.

24. **d.** Router(config-router)#neighbor voyager peer-group.
    Router(config-router)#neighbor 10.10.10.1 peer-group voyager.

25. **b.** This is not a common multihoming solution. All connected ISPs use an IGP to forward static routes to the AS.

Chapter 11 Solutions

1. **a, b,** and **d.** An encrypted tunnel is essentially an encapsulated protocol transport. Routing protocol updates and high-level network applications all generate traffic. A route table cache happens internally and generates no traffic.

2. **d.** Adding routers may reduce traffic on certain segments, but it in no way reduces traffic. Switching routing tables from static to dynamic will actually increase traffic. Separating networks into logical groups does nothing to

decrease the traffic, although it may isolate the traffic to specific segments. Filtering broadcasts can reduce the traffic due to the broadcasts.

3. **a, b.** An access control list is a set of rules that govern how packets are received and retransmitted. As a subset, it can determine whether the router can be accessed on ports such as Telnet. It has nothing to do with the route table nor is it an end-user authentication mechanism.

4. **b, d.** Any rule that is used commonly should go to the top of the list. Any rule that is not used commonly should go to the bottom of the list. This is because there is an implicit **deny** at the bottom of the list. Because ACLs are processed on a short-circuit basis, rules that execute near the top of the list will automatically stop the list processing.

5. **a, b, c.** Access lists divide traffic into "allow" and "deny" all reasonable methods to reduce and protect traffic. For freely enabled traffic, no access list is required. It actually requires CPU time to enable.

6. **b, c.** Electronic mail, assuming that we know the service TCP ports, such as POP (110) and SMTP (25), can be blocked using an access list. It can also block traffic from a specific host (and likely a domain). But the access lists cannot look into the individual protocols (at the application level) and block mail from a specific user. Also, this assumes that mail travels on well-known ports. It could not block mail that is accessed via Telnet or a virtual terminal because it is a different type of service.

7. **b, c, d.** Switching from link-state to distance-vector protocol may reduce traffic, but only for very small networks. In general, the switch would be the other way around. All the others are good mechanisms, although the use of an access list would have to employ rules to actually affect route traffic.

8. **a.** Static routes don't actually reduce the routing table and have nothing to do with affecting other routes regardless of interface. They themselves are not propagated.

9. **a, d.** Using a default route eliminates the need to store routes because packets are transmitted to a router that presumably does know about routes. Static routes are entries in a route table; they don't decrease or increase anything. An outbound filter filters only routes that are already on the router, but it doesn't change the route table. An inbound filter can prevent the router from adding routes to its route table.

Chapter 12 Solutions

1. **a.** True.

2. **c.** Blocks all traffic from network 192.168.1.10.

3. **b.** Blocks all traffic out the Ethernet 0 interface.

4. **a.** True.

5. **b.** False.

6. **c.** It is a virtual port that is not connected to a physical network.
   d. It is used with a static route.

7. **a.** Assists host to contact resources they might otherwise be cut off from routers.
   c. It converts certain broadcast packets to unicast packets.

8. **c.** Cisco Easy IP.

9. **b.** Internal and External.

10. **a.** Internal Private.
    b. The IP Null Port.
    c. Internal Public (DMZ).
    d. External.

11. **c.** Standard access list.

12. **b.** There must be at least one **deny** statement in each access list.
    c. They can be applied to a virtual terminal (line vty) to create a temporary Ethernet port.

13. **b.** Open a channel for any TCP session that was initiated by our server 195.168.2.20.

14. **c.** Dynamic access list.

15. **c.** Prevents everyone from telnetting into a router.

Chapter 13 Solutions

1. **d.** Using various network media is not a reason for running multiple routing protocols in a network.

2. **a.** Redistribution is a process that allows routing information discovered through one routing protocol to be distributed or injected into the update messages of another routing protocol.

3. **a, c.** Unidirectional redistribution occurs in only one direction.

4. **c.** Administrative distance is a mechanism for rating the believability of routing protocols.

5. **c.** The default or seed metric is assigned to the routing protocol that is being redistributed.

6. **a, c.** Routing feedback loops and unsynchronized convergence are issues with redistribution.

7. **a, d.** Familiarity with the network and establishing routing protocol boundaries are two redistribution guidelines.

8. **d.** The *metric-value* is assigned to all redistributed routes for the specified protocol.

9. **b.** The **subnets** keyword allows OSPF to redistribute subnets.

10. **d.** This configuration redistributes RIP into OSPF and assigns RIP a cost of 10.

11. **b, c.** This configuration redistributes routes from EIGRP AS1000 into network 172.16.0.0 and disables automatic route-summarization.

12. **a.** True. While OSPF does not require the default metric to be configured, it is still assigned to routes that OSPF redistributes.

13. **c.** The **default metric** command is used to configure a default metric for routes redistributed into EIGRP.

14. **a, c.** The core routing process is the first routing process that is redistributed into. The edge routing process is the second routing process that is redistributed into.

15. **a.** RIP uses the **ip default-network** command to redistribute default routes.

16. **d.** The correct **static route** command is: Router(config)#ip route 172.16.0.0 255.255.0.0 ethernet0.

17. **d.** Default static routes must be advertised via a routing protocol.

18. **a, c.** Passive updates and route filtering are two routing update optimization tools.

19. **d.** Passive interfaces work by preventing routing updates from being sent for specified routing protocols.

20. **b.** The **distribute-list in** command prevents certain routing updates from being received on an interface.

Appendix B
Objectives for Exam 640-503

Routing Principles	Chapter(s)
List the key information routers need to route data	2
Describe classful and classless routing protocols	2
Compare distance vector and link-state protocol operation	2
Describe the use of the fields in a routing table	2
Given a preconfigured laboratory network, discover the topology, analyze the routing table, and test connectivity using accepted troubleshooting techniques	2

Extending IP Addresses	Chapter(s)
Given an IP address range, use VLSMs to extend the use of the IP addresses	3
Given a network plan that includes IP addressing, explain if route summarization is or is not possible	3
Configure an IP helper address to manage broadcasts	12

Configuring OSPF in a Single Area	Chapter(s)
Explain why OSPF is better than RIP in a large internetwork	5
Explain how OSPF discovers, chooses, and maintains routes	5
Explain how OSPF operates in a single area NBMA environment	5
Configure OSPF for proper operation in a single area	5
Verify OSPF operation in a single area	5
Given an addressing scheme and other laboratory parameters, configure a single-area OSPF environment and verify proper operation (within described guidelines) of your routers	5
Given an addressing scheme and other laboratory parameters, configure single-area OSPF in an NBMA environment and verify proper operation (within described guidelines) of your routers	5

Interconnecting Multiple OSPF Areas	Chapter(s)
Describe the issues with interconnecting multiple areas and how OSPF addresses each	6
Explain the differences between the possible types of areas, routers, and LSAs	6
Explain how OSPF supports the use of VLSM	6
Explain how OSPF supports the use of route summarization in multiple areas	6
Explain how OSPF operates in a multiple area NBMA environment	6
Configure a multi-area OSPF network	6
Verify OSPF operation in multiple areas	6
Given an addressing scheme and other laboratory parameters, configure a multiple-area OSPF environment and verify proper operation (within described guidelines) of your routers	6

Configuring EIGRP	Chapter(s)
Describe Enhanced IGRP features and operation	7
Explain how EIGRP discovers, chooses, and maintains routes	7
Explain how EIGRP supports the use of VLSM	7
Explain how EIGRP operates in an NBMA environment	7
Explain how EIGRP supports the use of route summarization	7
Describe how EIGRP supports large networks	7
Configure Enhanced IGRP	7
Verify Enhanced IGRP operation	7
Given a set of network requirements, configure an Enhanced IGRP environment and verify proper operation (within described guidelines) of your routers	7
Given a set of network requirements, configure Enhanced IGRP in an NBMA environment and verify proper operation (within described guidelines) of your routers	7

Configuring Basic Border Gateway Protocol	Chapter(s)
Describe BGP features and operation	9
Describe how to connect to another autonomous system using an alternative to BGP, static routes	9
Explain how BGP policy-based routing functions within an autonomous system	9
Explain how BGP peering functions	9
Describe BGP communities and peer groups	10
Describe and configure external and internal BGP	9
Describe BGP synchronization	9
Given a set of network requirements, configure a BGP environment and verify proper operation (within described guidelines) of your routers	9

Implementing BGP in Scalable Networks	Chapter(s)
Describe the scalability problems associated with Internal BGP	10
Explain and configure BGP route reflectors	10
Describe and configure policy control in BGP using prefix lists	10
Describe methods to connect to multiple ISPs using BGP	10
Explain the use of redistribution between BGP and Interior Gateway Protocols (IGPs)	10
Given a set of network requirements, configure a multihomed BGP environment and verify proper operation (within described guidelines) of your routers	10

Optimizing Routing Update Operation	Chapter(s)
Select and configure the different ways to control routing update traffic	13
Configure route redistribution in a network that does not have redundant paths between dissimilar routing processes	13
Configure route redistribution in a network that has redundant paths between dissimilar routing processes	13
Resolve path selection problems that result in a redistributed network	13
Verify route redistribution	13
Configure policy-based routing using route maps	13
Given a set of network requirements, configure redistribution between different routing domains and verify proper operation (within described guidelines) of your routers	13
Given a set of network requirements, configure policy-based routing within your pod and verify proper operation (within described guidelines) of your routers	13

Implementing Scalability Features in Your Internetwork	Chapter(s)
Given a set of network requirements, configure many of the features discussed in the course and verify proper operation (within described guidelines) of your routers	15

Appendix C
Study Resources

There are many resources to assist in your studies or on the job. The following is a compilation of some web sites the authors have found useful in purchasing equipment, preparing for exams, managing networks, and researching IOS features. Please note that there is no attempt at ranking of the sites within each category.

Study and Information Sites

➤ ExamCram.com—**www.examcram.com**

➤ CertificationZone.com—**www.nwfusion.com/**
Lots of networking links and online newsletters on many topics.

➤ GroupStudy.com—**www.groupstudy.com/**
For CCIE™, CCNP™, CCNA™, CCDP™, and CCDA™ candidates, this page is the companion Web site for GroupStudy's mailing list to discuss Cisco® Certifications.

➤ Boson Software—**www.boson.com/**
Practice test simulations written by networking professionals. Each practice test is based on published exam objectives, and loaded with over 200 practice questions!

➤ Cisco Systems—**www.cisco.com/**
A very large site with lots of resources. Use the search feature to get to extensive PDF files on topics like OSPF, BGP, etc.

➤ Cisco Systems In A Nutshell—**http://ciscoinanutshell.com/**
Many links to Cisco and Cisco-related sites. Often easier to navigate than the Cisco site.

➤ Cisco Systems—**www.cisco.com/warp/public/779/smbiz/service/index.html**
Good link directly into the Cisco site with links to Cisco product info, tools, and technical information.

Equipment and Cables

Obviously, you can buy new Cisco routers from a wide variety of vendors, but with a little work you can buy used and/or refurbished equipment from the following sites:

➤ Whirled Routers—**www.whirled-routers.com**
Good selection of devices including student packages.

➤ Grandstore—**www.grandstore.com/**
Good selection of devices including student packages. A Cisco lab available by the hour for practice including: Ethernet on Cisco 7000 with 100 hosts, Token Ring on Cisco 7000 with 40 hosts, Token Ring on Cisco 2515 with 10 hosts, Token Ring on Cisco 2600 with 15 hosts.

➤ Network Hardware Resale, Inc.—**www.networkhardware.com/**
Lots of Cisco Devices, student packages, and online manuals.

➤ NetFix—**www.netfix.com/**
Good selection of devices including student packages.

➤ Pacific Cable—**www.pacificcable.com/**
Huge selection of all types of cables and connectors. They have the 5-foot DCE/DTE single unit cables plus just about any type of Cisco connector combination you could want—really great when you have an older 4000 and a 25xx and want to connect the very different serial interfaces.

➤ eBay—**www.ebay.com/**
For those willing to take a little risk and patience to wait for the killer deal. Watch for the items near the end time—that's really the only time that matters. Make sure you read all terms, payments accepted, shipping costs, and then make sure that you know the "street" value of the items.

Network Diagramming Software

➤ Microsoft Visio 2000—**www.microsoft.com/office/visio/**
Microsoft Visio® 2000 enables you to communicate effectively with easy-to-assemble drawings and diagrams. Create organizational charts and flowcharts; draw technical schematics and annotate CAD drawings; build Web site maps; and manually or automatically work on network, software, and database design. Free Trial offer downloadable from this site.

➤ Pacestar Software—**www.pacestar.com/**
EDGE diagrammer easy-to-use tool for org charts, simple network diagrams, block diagrams, family trees, data flow diagrams, and more. 30-day sample downloadable from the site.

Router Simulations

➤ RouterSim—**www.routersim.com/**
Currently offers CCNA simulation, which allows you to create, configure, and manage a six-router, two-switch, 5 host-simulated network with 29 labs that you can refer to as you configure your network. Watch for CCNP RouterSims.

Networking Tools

➤ Net3 Group, Inc.—**www.net3group.com/**
Nice, free IP Subnet Calculator for Windows to be downloaded. Network analysis and security tools and many great links to related sites.

➤ Pine Mountain Group, Inc.—**www.pmg.com/**
Provider of result-oriented network analysis training and troubleshooting services. Offers several very interesting networking toolkits free.

Network News and Link Site

➤ Internet.com—**www.internet.com**
E-Business and Internet Technology Network is a leading provider of global real-time news and information resources for Internet industry and Internet technology professionals, Web developers, and experienced Internet users.

➤ Webopedia—**http://webopedia.internet.com/**
Online dictionary and search engine for computer and Internet technology.

Appendix C

Glossary

10Base2

10Mbps baseband Ethernet specification using 50-ohm thin coaxial cable. Part of the IEEE 802.3 specification. Has a distance limitation of 185 meters per segment. Sometimes referenced as Thinnet or cheapernet.

10Base5

10Mbps baseband Ethernet specification using 50-ohm thick coaxial cable. Part of the IEEE 802.3 specification. Has a distance limitation of 500 meters per segment.

10BaseFx

10Mbps baseband Ethernet specification for Ethernet over fiber-optic cabling (IEEE). The **x** would indicate a particular variation of the fiber-optic standard; variations include 10BaseFB, 10BaseFL, and 10BaseFP.

10BaseT

The IEEE 802.3 specification for running Ethernet at 10Mbps over shielded or unshielded twisted-pair wiring. The maximum length for a 10BaseT segment is 100 meters (328 feet).

100BaseFX

The IEEE specification for running Fast Ethernet over fiber-optic cable.

100BaseT4

This technology allows the use of Fast Ethernet technology over existing Category 3 and Category 4 wiring, utilizing all four pairs of wires.

100BaseTX

The IEEE 802.3u specification, also known as Fast Ethernet, for running Ethernet at 100Mbps over shielded or unshielded twisted-pair wiring.

100BaseVG (Voice Grade) AnyLAN

The IEEE 802.12 specification that allows data transmissions of 100Mbps over Category 3 (data grade) wiring, utilizing all sets of wires.

1000BaseX

This IEEE 802.3z specification, known as Gigabit Ethernet, defines standards for data transmissions of 1,000Mbps.

56K technology

The serial transfer of data over analog modems at rates of up to 56Kbps. Although 56K technology started as two competing technologies, the x.2 and the K56flex, eventually the V.90 standard was established. Due to telephone industry standards limiting throughput to 53Kbps, the transfer rate of 56Kbps is theoretical and is not a reality in any of these technologies.

ABR

See *area border router.*

access class

A method of restricting Telnet access to and from a router using access lists.

609

access group

When an access list is created, it must be associated with a physical interface. Access-group is the association of the access list to the interface.

access layer

In the Hierarchical Model, the layer where the users connect to the network. It is here that hubs and LAN switches reside, and where workgroups access the network.

access list

List of comparison statements used by Cisco routers to control access (permit/deny) to or from a router interface for a number of services (for example, to prevent packets with a certain IP address from leaving a particular interface on the router). A two-part process: The access list contains the statements, then the access group applies it to an interface and specifies inbound or outbound traffic.

access method

The standards that control the way in which network devices access the network medium.

access router

Any router that exists at the lowest levels of a network hierarchy.

access server

Communications device that connects asynchronous devices to a LAN or WAN through network and terminal emulation software. Performs both synchronous and asynchronous routing of supported protocols, such as modems, TA (ISDN), and T1 lines. Sometimes called a network access server. See *communication server.*

ACK

See *acknowledgment.*

acknowledgment

A transport layer response to the successful receipt of one or more data packets that triggers the next scheduled transmission of packets in a connection-oriented protocol network. TCP and IPX both use acknowledgments. It is sometimes referred to as its IEEE signal, ACK.

active hub

A network device (multiport repeater) that amplifies LAN transmission signals. It can increase the overall length of the network and the number of nodes.

active state

An EIGRP router's state for a destination when it has lost its successor to that destination and has no other feasible successor available. This state occurs only in the route recomputation process and ends when the lost route is replaced or removed. Compare with *passive state.*

active time

In EIGRP, the time a router has to receive a reply for a queried destination. By default, it is 180 seconds.

AD

See *administrative distance.*

adaptive routing

See *dynamic routing.*

address

A set of numbers, usually expressed in binary format, used to identify and locate a resource or device on a network.

address mask

The address mask for an IP address is used to identify the boundary between the network portion and the host portion of the address. For example, IP address 161.150.23.157 and address mask

255.255.0.0 indicate that the first two octets 161.150 are the network and the last two identify the host. Another notation would be 161.150.23.157/16, indicating the mask; therefore, the network is the first 16 bits or 2 octets.

address resolution

The process of determining one address type, such as IP, from another type, such as MAC. The discovery can be done by broadcast packets and the result is stored for future reference. See *ARP*, *RARP*, and *WINS*.

Address Resolution Protocol (ARP)

A method for finding a host's physical address from its IP address. An ARP request is sent to the network, naming the IP address; then, the machine with that IP address returns its physical address so it can receive the transmission.

adjacency

Relationship formed between selected neighboring routers for the purpose of exchanging routing information. Adjacency is based on sharing a common media segment. In OSPF, an adjacency occurs only between a DR/BDR and a directly connected neighbor; directly connected OSPF routers that are not DRs or BDRs establish neighborships instead. Compare with *neighborship*.

administrative distance (AD)

A somewhat arbitrary rating of reliability of the method of how a router learned about a route. It is one of the factors used in selecting a best path. The smaller the administrative distance, the more attractive the method of learning about a route— directly connected routes have no administrative distance. Cisco routers use administrative distance values between 0 and 255.

administrative weight (AW)

A value set by the network administrator to indicate the desirability of a network link. One of four link metrics exchanged by PTSPs to determine the available resources of an ATM network.

administrator

Person responsible for the control and security of the user accounts, resources, and data on a network.

ADSL

See *asymmetric digital subscriber line*.

advanced distance-vector routing protocol

See *hybrid routing protocol*.

advertised distance

In EIGRP, the metric advertised by a directly connected neighbor for a specific destination network.

advertising

Router process in which routing or service updates are sent at specified intervals to other routers on the network so they can update lists of usable routes.

aggregator

An optional transitive path attribute used to inform the neighboring AS of the BGP router ID and AS number of the router that created the aggregate-route. Compare with *atomic aggregate*.

algorithm

A well-defined rule or method for determining a solution to a problem. In networking, algorithms are commonly used to determine the best path for traffic between a source and a destination or to prevent looping within the network.

AllDR/BDR address

The multicast address 224.0.0.6. OSPF routers use it for exclusive communication with their segment's DR/BDR.

Glossary

AllSPFRouters address

The multicast address 224.0.0.5. DRs/
BDRs use it for communicating with all
OSPF routers on a directly attached
segment.

alternate mark inversion

A method of T1/E1 line coding that uses
alternating positive and negative electrical
pulses to transmit digital signals.

American National Standards Institute (ANSI)

An organization that develops many types
of standards, some having to do with
computers, such as programming languages,
properties of diskettes, and so forth. ANSI is
the U.S. member of the International
Standards Organization (see *International
Standards Organization*).

American Standard Code for Information Interchange (ASCII)

A code in which each alphanumeric
character is represented as a number from 0
to 127, translated into a 7-bit binary code
for the computer. ASCII is used by most
microcomputers and printers; thus, text-
only files can be transferred easily between
different kinds of computers. ASCII code
also includes characters to indicate
backspace, carriage return, and other
control characters.

AMI

See *alternate mark inversion*.

analog transmission

Wavelike signal transmissions over wires or
through the air in which information is
conveyed by varying some combination of
signal amplitude, frequency, and phase.

ANDing

The binary process of comparing the bits
of an IP address with the bits in the subnet
mask to determine the boundary between
the network portion and the host portion
of the address.

ANSI

See *American National Standards Institute*.

antivirus

A type of software that detects and removes
virus programs.

any

In access lists, a keyword used to specify the
permission or denial of traffic no matter the
source, destination, protocol, or port.

anycast address

An address used in ATM for shared
multiple-end systems. An anycast address
allows a frame to be sent to specific groups
of hosts (rather than to all hosts, as with
simple broadcasting).

AppleTalk

A LAN protocol suite developed by Apple
Computer for communication between
Apple Computer products and other
computers. Phase 1 of AppleTalk supports a
single physical network that can have only
one network number and be in a single
zone. Phase 2, the more recent version,
supports multiple logical networks on a
single physical network and allows
networks to be in more than one zone.

application layer

The layer of the OSI model that provides
support for end users and for application
programs using network resources.

area

Logical set of network OSPF-based
segments and their attached devices. Areas
are connected via routers to create a single
autonomous system. See also *autonomous
system*.

area border router (ABR)

In OSPF, any router that has interfaces configured to be a part of multiple areas.

ARCnet

Token bus LAN (802.4) technology used in the 1970s and 1980s.

ARP

See *Address Resolution Protocol.*

ARPANET

Advanced Research Projects Agency Network. Packet-switching network established in 1969 and developed in the 1970s by BBN—funded by ARPA (and later DARPA). Later evolved into the Internet.

AS

See *autonomous system.*

ASBR

See *Autonomous System Boundary Router.*

ASBR-summary-LSA

See *LSA Type 4.*

ASCII

See *American Standard Code for Information Interchange.*

AS-external-LSA

See *LSA Type 5.*

AS-path

A well-known mandatory path attribute that includes a list of all autonomous systems across which an update has transited.

AS-sequence

An ordered list of all the AS numbers that an update has traversed. This list is found in the update's AS-path path attribute. The AS-sequence does not contain the AS-set. Compare with *AS-set.*

AS-set

An unordered list of all the AS numbers associated with routes that have been aggregated in a summary-route. The AS-set must be configured to be included in the path attribute; otherwise, the summary-route will be associated only with the AS number of the BGP router that creates the summary-route. Compare with *AS-sequence.*

asymmetric digital subscriber line (ADSL)

A service that transmits digital voice and data over existing (analog) phone lines. It is differentiated from other digital subscriber line technologies in that the transmit speed is often different from the receive speed. Typically, the uplink speed is smaller than the downlink speed.

asynchronous transfer mode (ATM)

International standard used in high-speed transmission media—such as E3, SONET, and T3—for cell relay in which multiple service types (such as voice, video, or data) are conveyed in fixed-length, 53-byte cells.

asynchronous transmission synchronization (ATS)

A process used in serial data transfer in which a start bit and a stop bit are added so the receiving station can know when a particular bit has been transferred. Also known as bit synchronization.

atomic aggregate

A well-known discretionary path attribute used to inform a neighboring AS that it (the neighboring AS) is being sent aggregate-routes. Compare with *aggregator.*

attachment unit interface (AUI)

IEEE 802.3 specification used between a multistation access unit (MAU) and a network interface card.

Glossary

attachment unit interface (AUI) connector

A 15-pin D-type connector sometimes used with Ethernet connections.

attempt state

An OSPF state that is valid only for neighbors in an NBMA environment. "Attempt" means that the router is sending hello packets to the neighbor, but has not yet received any information.

attenuation

The loss of signal that is experienced as data is transmitted across network media.

authority zone

Associated with DNS, It is a section of the domain-name tree for which one name server is the authority. See also *DNS*.

autonomous switching

Cisco-specific feature that allows faster packing processing. The CiscoBus handles the packets independently, thus freeing the system processor to handle other tasks.

autonomous system (AS)

A group of networks under a common administration sharing a common routing strategy. Autonomous systems are subdivided into areas. Each autonomous system must be assigned a unique 16-bit number by the IANA.

Autonomous System Boundary Router (ASBR)

ABR located between an OSPF autonomous system and a non-OSPF network. ASBRs run both OSPF and another routing protocol, such as RIP. ASBRs must reside in a nonstub OSPF area. See also *ABR*, *nonstub area*, and *OSPF*.

average rate

The average rate, in kilobits per second (Kbps), at which a given virtual circuit will transmit.

AW

See *administrative weight*.

B channel

In ISDN, a single 64Kbps link. In BRI implementations, two such B channels exist. In PRI, there are 23.

B8ZS

See *bipolar with eight zero substitution*.

backbone

A high-capacity infrastructure system that provides optimal traffic between separated network segments.

backbone area

An OSPF area that interconnects other OSPF areas and accepts all types of OSPF traffic. All OSPF areas must attach to the backbone area.

backbone router

In OSPF, any router that is connected to Area 0.

backoff

The retransmission delay introduced by MAC protocols. When a collision occurs between two transmitters, both "back off" for a random time period, thus encouraging the line to be free for transmission, assuming that there is no interference from a third party.

backplane

The physical connection between boards, whether processor-based, memory-based, or I/O-based. It is often a chassis with individual slots to handle each device. The chassis may also provide power to all devices.

backup designated router (BDR)

In OSPF, when multiple routers are connected to broadcast media segments (such as an Ethernet), specific routers are elected as representatives (one primary and one backup) of the network to receive and transmit routing updates on that segment. The election is based on priority and/or router ID. The BDR is the backup router on that segment.

backward explicit congestion notification (BECN)

A Frame-Relay network device detecting congestion can set a single address bit in frames traveling in the opposite direction (toward the source of the data). A DTE receiving frames with the BECN bit set to 1 can forward the info on to higher-level protocols to exercise flow control. Compare with *forward explicit congestion notification*.

bandwidth

The rated throughput capacity of a given network protocol or medium. Compare with *throughput*.

base bandwidth

The difference between the lowest and highest frequencies available for network signals. The term is also used to describe the rated throughput capacity of a given network protocol or medium.

baseband

A communications strategy that uses a single carrier frequency over a medium. Ethernet is such an example of baseband signaling. Baseband is often called narrowband. Compare with *broadband*.

basic rate interface (BRI)

An ISDN digital communications line that consists of three independent channels: two bearer (or B) channels, each at 64Kbps, and one data (or D) channel at 16Kbps. ISDN basic rate interface is often referred to as 2B+D.

baud rate

Named after French telegraphy expert J. M. Baudot, this term is used to define the speed or rate of signal transfer.

Bc

See *committed burst*.

BDR

See *backup designated router*.

Be

See *excess burst*.

BECN

See *backward explicit congestion notification*.

Bellman-Ford algorithm

The process by which distance-vector routing protocols exchange updates on a periodic timer. This process is generally characterized by low memory utilization and slow convergence time. It is also known as routing by rumor. The algorithm itself iterates on the number of hops in the route to find a shortest-path spanning tree. It is computationally simpler than a link-state routing algorithm, but is prone to problems such as routing loops.

best-effort delivery

A network system that does not use an acknowledgment system to guarantee reliable delivery of data.

BGP

See *Border Gateway Protocol*.

BGP client

An IBGP peer that is adjacent with a route reflector residing in the same cluster. BGP clients are configured. Compare with *BGP nonclient*.

BGP cluster

The combination of the route reflector and its associated clients.

BGP distribute list

Uses access lists to filter routing information based on prefix. The BGP distribute list is applied to all routing updates that are either sent to or received from specified BGP neighbors. Compare with *BGP prefix list.*

BGP next-hop rule

For EBGP, the next-hop is always the IP address of the neighbor who originated the routing update. For IBGP, the BGP next-hop rule states that the next-hop advertised EBGP should be carried into IBGP. However, the BGP next-hop rule can be overridden.

BGP nonclient

An IBGP peer that is adjacent with a route reflector residing in a different cluster. A nonclient may also be an adjacent peer who is simply not configured as a client of the route reflector. Compare with *BGP client.*

BGP peer group

A group of BGP peers that share the same update policies. A BGP router that joins a peer group inherits the peer group's inbound and outbound update policies. A peer group member can override only inbound update policies; outbound policies must always be identical for each peer group member.

BGP prefix filter

A way of restricting routing information from being sent to or received from BGP peers.

BGP prefix list

Uses prefix lists to filter routing information based on prefix. The BGP prefix list is applied to all routing updates that are either sent to or received from specified BGP neighbors. Compare with *BGP distribute list.*

BGP route map

Complex access lists that are used to control routing information and specify the conditions under which BGP redistribution occurs. BGP route maps consist of route map statements that include match conditions and set actions.

BGP Split Horizon rule

States that an IBGP-learned route cannot be propagated to other IBGP peers. The purpose of this rule is to prevent intra-AS routing loops.

BGP synchronization rule

States that a BGP router should not advertise a route to an external neighbor unless that route is local (directly connected) or is learned from the IGP. The purpose of this rule is to prevent black holes within the AS caused by external neighbors trying to use a path that goes through an area where routers are missing routes.

BGP4

BGP version 4. Version 4 of the predominant interdomain routing protocol used on the Internet. BGP4 supports CIDR and uses route aggregation mechanisms to reduce the size of routing tables.

binary

A Base2 numbering system used in digital signaling, characterized by 1s and 0s.

binding

The process of associating a protocol and a network interface card (NIC).

bipolar violation

A pair of digital pulses that have the same polarity (such as both positive or both negative). This intentional error is introduced to inform the remote end of the link that a string of ones is being sent in place of a string of zeroes.

bipolar with eight zero substitution (B8ZS)

A T1 line coding scheme that utilizes intentional bipolar violations to signify that binary ones should be transmitted across a T1 circuit in place of the eight binary zeroes that were actually supposed to be coded. This is done to keep the clocking in the network consistent.

bit

An electronic digit used in the binary numbering system.

bit-oriented protocol

Class of communications protocols that can transmit frames independent of the frame content. Bit-oriented protocols provide full-duplex operation and are more efficient and reliable than byte-oriented protocols. Bit-oriented protocols live at the data link layer of the OSI model. See also *byte-oriented protocol.*

bit rate

The speed at which bits are transmitted—usually in bits per second (bps).

blackout

A total loss of electrical power.

BOOTP

A protocol used in resolving an IP address based on a layer 2 MAC address.

Border Gateway Protocol (BGP)

An interdomain routing protocol (RFC 1163) that replaces EGP. Exchanges reachability status only with other BGP systems.

bottleneck

Any point in an internetwork where the amount of data being received exceeds the data-carrying capacity of the link. See also *congestion.*

BPDU

See *bridge protocol data unit.*

BRI

See *basic rate interface.*

bridge

A device that connects and passes packets between two network segments that use the same communications protocol. Bridges operate at the data link layer of the OSI reference model. A bridge filters, forwards, or floods an incoming frame based on the MAC address of that frame.

bridge group

In transparent bridging, the designation given to a physical interface (usually Ethernet) to initiate its participation in bridging functions.

bridge priority

The criterion on which a root bridge is elected. The bridge with the lowest priority becomes the root bridge.

bridge protocol data unit (BPDU)

A spanning tree protocol update entity used in path determination between bridges.

bridged virtual interface (BVI)

In IRB, an interface used to translate between routed and bridged traffic. This interface has both a protocol address for the protocol to be routed and a MAC address on which to base bridging decisions.

bridging address table

A list of MAC addresses kept by bridges and used when packets are received to determine which segment the destination address is on before sending the packet to the next interface or dropping the packet if it is on the same segment as the sending node.

broadband

A communications strategy that uses signaling over multiple communications channels. Cable television and cable modems are examples of putting multiple signals onto a single wire. Compare with *baseband*.

broadcast

A packet delivery system in which a copy of a packet is given to all hosts attached to the network.

broadcast address

A special address reserved for transmitted messages to all hosts on a network. Compare with *multicast address* and *unicast address.*

broadcast domain

The collective group of devices that are the designated recipients of a broadcast. The broadcast domain is usually limited to a single segment bounded by a router. This is because routers do not forward broadcasts. However, bridges do forward broadcasts, and therefore the domain usually includes both sides of a bridge.

broadcast storm

An undesirable condition in which broadcasts have become so numerous as to bog down the flow of data across the network.

brouter

A device that can be used to combine the benefits of both routers and bridges. Its common usage is to route routable protocols at the network layer and to bridge nonroutable protocols at the data link layer.

brownout

A short-term decrease in the voltage level, usually caused by the startup demands of other electrical devices.

buffer

Storage space allocated to deal with the inconsistent nature of incoming versus outgoing data. If data comes in faster than a device can push it out, then the data must be stored in a buffer.

bus mastering

A bus accessing method in which the network interface card takes control of the bus in order to send data through the bus directly to the system memory, bypassing the CPU.

bus topology

A path used by electrical signals to travel between the CPU and the attached hardware.

BVI

See *bridged virtual interface.*

byte

A set of bits (usually eight) operating as a unit to signify a character.

byte-oriented protocol

Class of communications protocols that uses a specific character from the user character set to delimit frames. As such, more processing is required and parallel processing is much more difficult. Bit-oriented protocols have pretty much replaced byte-oriented protocols because they are more efficient. Byte-oriented protocols live at the data link layer of the OSI model. See also *bit-oriented protocols.*

cable

Transmission medium of copper wire or glass fiber encased in a protective cover (PVC or Teflon).

cable modem

A modem that provides Internet access over cable television lines.

caching-only server

A server that operates the same way as secondary servers, except that a zone transfer does not take place when the caching-only server is started.

CAM

See *content-addressable memory*.

carrier

An entity that delivers items from one location to another. In telephony, a carrier is referred to as a third-party organization that provides the means to deliver voice and data.

carrier detect (CD)

A signal that indicates that an interface is active. Also, a modem signal that indicates a call has been connected.

carrier sense multiple access with collision avoidance (CSMA/CA)

A contention media-access method that uses collision avoidance techniques (e.g., Ethernet).

carrier sense multiple access with collision detection (CSMA/CD)

A contention media-access method that uses collision detection and retransmission techniques (e.g., AppleTalk).

category 1 cabling

The lowest of the five grades of UTP cabling described in the current EIA/TIA-568 standard. Used for telephone communications. Not suitable for transmitting data.

category 2 cabling

One of five grades of UTP cabling described in the current EIA/TIA-568 standard. Capable of transmitting data at speeds up to 4Mbps.

category 3 cabling

One of five grades of UTP cabling described in the current EIA/TIA-568 standard. Used in 10BaseT networks. Can transmit data at speeds up to 10Mbps.

category 4 cabling

One of five grades of UTP cabling described in the current EIA/TIA-568 standard. Used primarily in Token Ring networks to transmit data at speeds up to 16Mbps.

category 5 cabling

One of five grades of UTP cabling described in the current EIA/TIA-568 standard. Used for Ethernet and Fast Ethernet installations. Can transmit data at speeds up to 100Mbps. Pending the new standards, this is the typical "spec" for data and often phone to allow maximum flexibility down the road.

CCITT

See *Consultative Committee for International Telegraph and Telephone*.

CD

See *carrier detect*.

CDDI

See *copper distributed data interface*.

CDP

See *Cisco Discovery Protocol*.

CDV

See *cell delay variation*.

cell

A fixed-size data unit for ATM switching and multiplexing. Cells include identifiers that specify the data stream to which they belong. Each cell consists of a 5-byte header and 48 bytes of payload.

Glossary

cell delay variation (CDV)

A QoS parameter that measures the difference between a cell's actual transfer delay (CTD) and the expected transfer delay. It can show how closely cells are spaced within a virtual circuit. Multiplexers and switches introduce cell delay variation.

cell error rate (CER)

A QoS parameter that measures the percentage of transmitted cells that have errors when they arrive at their destination.

cell loss priority (CLP)

The field in an ATM cell header that determines the probability of a cell being dropped should the network become congested.

cell loss ratio (CLR)

A QoS parameter that indicates the number of cells lost to the total number of transmitted cells.

cell misinsertion ratio (CMR)

A QoS parameter that measures the number of cells that arrive at their destination out of sequence per second.

cell relay

Network technology based on the use of small, fixed-size packets, or cells. Because cells are of fixed length, they can be processed and switched in hardware at high speeds. Is the basis for such high-speed network protocols as ATM, IEEE 802.6, and SMDS.

cell transfer delay (CTD)

A QoS parameter that shows the average time for a cell to be transferred from its source to its destination over a virtual connection.

central processing unit (CPU)

Device that executes machine instructions. All computing devices have a CPU, although some are more general purpose than others. Cisco routers have general-purpose CPUs, but run a specific operating system, IOS.

CER

See *cell error rate.*

challenge handshake authentication protocol (CHAP)

Security feature supported on lines using PPP encapsulation that prevents unauthorized access to a network by identifying the remote end. The router or access server can then decide whether to allow access. An improvement over the earlier PAP.

channel

A communications path used for data transmission. Several channels can be multiplexed using several techniques to pass simultaneously through a single media.

channel service unit (CSU)

A digital device that connects end-user equipment to the local digital telephone loop. Often referred to together with DSU as CSU/DSU. See *DSU.*

channelized E1

Access link operating at 2.048Mbps that is subdivided into 30 B channels and 1 D channel. Supports DDR, Frame-Relay, and X.25. A European contemporary of the North American T1.

channelized T1

Access link operating at 1.544Mbps. It can be subdivided into 24 channels (fractional T1s) of 64Kbps each. The individual channels or groups of channels can be connected to different destinations. Supports DDR, Frame-Relay, and X.25.

CHAP

See *challenge handshake authentication protocol.*

checksum

Technique for verifying the integrity of received data. A value calculated by the receiving node and compared to one calculated by the sending node and then stored in the frame. The header and data fields can have separate checksums.

CIA

See *classical IP over ATM*.

CIDR

See *Classless Inter-Domain Routing*.

CIR

See *committed information rate*.

circuit

A communications path between points. Most circuits involve two endpoints.

circuit switching

A telephony term indicating the physical switching of a path connecting endpoints of a "call."

Cisco Discovery Protocol (CDP)

Media- and protocol-independent device-discovery protocol that runs on all Cisco-manufactured equipment including routers, access servers, bridges, and switches. With CDP, a device can advertise its existence to other devices and receive information about other devices on the same LAN or on the remote side of a WAN. Runs on all media that support SNAP, including LANs, Frame-Relay, and ATM media.

Cisco IOS software

The operating system that runs on Cisco equipment. IOS is the acronym for *Internetworking Operating System*. Most Cisco hardware loads the IOS into flash memory so that the operating system is retained even during power outages. The IOS is easily updated to new revisions as they are released.

CiscoView

A GUI-based device-management software to provide dynamic status, statistics, and configuration information for Cisco devices. In addition to displaying a physical view of Cisco chasses, it can also provide device monitoring functions and basic troubleshooting. CiscoView can also integrate with other SNMP-based network management devices.

class A network

A TCP/IP network that uses addresses starting between 1 and 126 and supports up to 126 subnets with 16,777,214 unique hosts each.

class B network

A TCP/IP network that uses addresses starting between 128 and 191 and supports up to 16,384 subnets with 65,534 unique hosts each.

class C network

A TCP/IP network that uses addresses starting between 192 and 254 and supports up to 2,097,152 subnets with 223 unique hosts each.

class D network

Any IP address with a first octet value that is between 224 and 239. This class of address is used for multicast operations.

class E network

Any IP address with a first octet value that is between 240 and 247. This class of address is used for research purposes only and is not currently deployed in existing internetworks.

class of service (CoS)

Single byte field in the IP header that defines the abstract parameters precedence, delay, throughput, and reliability. This field is used to manage the priority of any single packet in a network, such that in comparison to other CoS values, it is delivered appropriately. Same as *type of service (ToS)*, as defined in RFC 791.

classful routing

Routing based on information derived from the natural boundaries of the different classes of IP addresses. Routing table information for networks that are not directly connected is kept based on only that natural network because the subnet masks of those remote networks are not contained in the routing update.

classical IP over ATM (CIA)

A specification for running IP over ATM. The specification is defined in RFC 1577.

Classless Inter-Domain Routing (CIDR)

Technique supported by BGP4 based on route aggregation that allows routers to group IP networks under a single address, thereby reducing the number of entries stored in core routers.

classless routing

Routing based on information derived from routing updates that includes subnet mask (such as prefix) information. Routing table information shows all known networks and their accompanying prefix information.

clear channel

The use of B8ZS line coding for T1 circuits. See *bipolar with eight zero substitution*.

CLI

See *command-line interface*.

client

A node that requests a service from another node on a network.

client/server networking

Networking architecture utilizing front-end "client" nodes that request and process data stored by the back-end "server" node.

clock source

The specification of the party responsible for providing clocking for synchronization of a circuit.

CLP

See *cell loss priority*.

CLR

See *cell loss ratio*.

cluster ID

A BGP path attribute that identifies a cluster that has multiple route reflectors. When a cluster has only one route reflector, the cluster is identified by the router ID of its route reflector. Compare with *originator ID*.

CMIP

See *Common Management Information Protocol*.

CMR

See *cell misinsertion ratio*.

CO

Telephone company Central Office. Many services, such as ISDN and DSL, are available only within certain distances from the CO.

coaxial cable

Data cable, commonly referred to as *coax*, made of a solid copper core, which is insulated and surrounded by braided metal and covered with a thick plastic or rubber covering. This is the standard cable used in cable TV and in older bus topology networks.

CODEC

See *coder-decoder*.

coder-decoder (CODEC)

A device that typically uses pulse code modulation to transform analog signals into digital signals and digital signals back into analog signals.

coding

The electrical process that is used to convey digital information.

collapsed backbone

A nondistributed backbone in which all network segments are interconnected by a single internetworking device. Hubs, routers, and switches are examples of devices that collapse a virtual network segment.

collision

The result of two frames transmitting simultaneously in an Ethernet network and colliding, thereby destroying both frames.

collision domain

Segment of an Ethernet network between managing nodes in which only one packet can be transmitted at any given time. Switches, bridges, and routers can be used to segment a network into separate collision domains.

Command-line interface (CLI)

The basic interface for Cisco devices.

committed burst (Bc)

The maximum amount of data that a Frame-Relay network is committed to accept and transmit at the committed information rate. This is a negotiated tariff metric. See also *committed information rate* and *excess burst*.

committed information rate (CIR)

The rate, measured in bits per second, that a Frame-Relay network agrees to make available to transfer information under normal conditions, averaged over a minimum increment of time. CIR and "burst" rates (Bc) are used in negotiating rates.

common carrier

Supplier of communications utilities, such as phone lines, to the general public.

Common Management Information Protocol.

OSI network management protocol created and standardized by ISO for the monitoring and control of heterogeneous networks.

communication

The transfer of information between nodes on a network.

communication port (COM port)

A connection used for serial devices to communicate between the device and the motherboard. A COM port requires standard configuration information, such as IRQ (interrupt request), I/O (input/output) address, and COM port number.

communication server

Communications device that connects asynchronous devices to a LAN or WAN through network and terminal emulation software. Performs only asynchronous routing of IP and IPX. See *access server*.

communities

An optional transitive path attribute that identifies the group of destinations to which routing decisions (such as preference, acceptance, and redistribution) can be applied. This attribute is created using a route map and is advertised to both internal and external peers.

COM port

See *communication port*.

compression

The process of converting a data set or a data stream that reduces the storage or bandwidth requirements, respectively. Typically, to evaluate the data, a reverse process called expansion occurs. See *expansion*.

concurrent routing and bridging

A technology that allows the mixing of routing and bridging on a single device. However, data that arrives at the router through a bridged interface can be dispatched only via another bridged interface. The same is true for routed traffic.

configuration register

Describes how the router behaves when it is powered up. Cisco hardware has a 16-bit configuration register. Typical examples are console baud rates and OEM identification.

congestion

A condition that arises when the data being passed across a circuit exceeds the data-carrying capacity of that circuit.

congestion avoidance

A mechanism by which an ATM network can control traffic entering the network to minimize delays. Lower-priority traffic can be discarded at the edge of the network if the conditions dictate that it cannot be delivered.

connection-oriented communication

Refers to packet transfer in which the delivery is guaranteed.

connectionless-oriented communication

Refers to packet transfer in which the delivery is not guaranteed.

connectivity

The linking of nodes on a network so that communication can take place.

console

A physical port used in the configuration of a router. The console is the default source for configuration information.

Consultative Committee for International Telegraph and Telephone (CCITT)

International organization based in Switzerland that is responsible for the development of communications standards. Now called the *ITU-T*.

content-addressable memory

Memory that is accessed based on its contents, not on its memory address.

contention

The access method in which network devices compete for permission to access a physical medium.

convergence

The exchanging of routing updates by routers that participate in dynamic routing protocol activities to form a consistent perspective of the network. When all routers know of all possible destinations in the network, the network has converged.

copper distributed data interface (CDDI)

Implementation of FDDI protocols over STP and UTP cabling. Uses electrical cable rather than optical cable. CDDI transmits over relatively short distances (up to 100 meters), providing data rates of 100Mbps using a dual-ring architecture to provide redundancy. Based on the ANSI Twisted-Pair Physical Medium Dependent (TPPMD) standard.

core gateway

Primary routers in the Internet.

core layer

The backbone of the network in the Hierarchical Model, designed for high-speed data transmission.

core router

Any router attached to the highest level of network hierarchy, usually the core backbone of the network.

CoS

See *class of service.*

cost

In OSPF, the metric used for route calculation. This calculation is based on the bandwidth of the link in question.

CPE

See *customer premise equipment.*

cps

Cells per second.

CPU

See *central processing unit.*

CRB

See *concurrent routing and bridging.*

CRC

See *cyclic redundancy check.*

crosstalk

Electronic interference caused when two wires get too close to each other.

CSMA/CA

See *carrier sense multiple access with collision avoidance.*

CSMA/CD

See *carrier sense multiple access with collision detection.*

CSU

See *channel service unit.*

CTD

See *cell transfer delay.*

current successor

In EIGRP, the existing best route to a particular destination network.

customer premise equipment (CPE)

Terminating equipment, such as terminals, telephones, modems, TA, and CSU/DSUs supplied by the telephone company, installed at customer sites, and connected to the telephone company network.

custom queuing

A Cisco proprietary strategy for prioritizing traffic output from a router interface, usually a low-speed serial interface.

cut-through packet switching

A switching method that does not copy the entire packet into the switch buffers. Instead, the destination address is captured into the switch, the route to the destination node is determined, and the packet is quickly sent out the corresponding port. Cut-through packet switching maintains a low latency.

cyclic redundancy check (CRC)

Error-checking technique in which a frame recipient performs a calculation on the frame contents and compares the result to a value stored in the frame by the sending node. If the values are different, the frame has been corrupted.

D channel

A digital subscriber service channel to facilitate communication between an ISDN-capable router and the switch to which that router is connected.

D connectors

Connectors shaped like a "D" that use pins and sockets to establish connections between peripheral devices using serial or parallel ports. The number that follows is the number of pins they use for connectivity. For example, a DB-9 connector has 9 pins, and a DB-25 has 25.

Glossary

data communications equipment (DCE)

An EIA term referring to the network end of a communications channel (the other end, DTE, refers to the user end of the communications channel). Provides a physical connection to a network, forwards traffic, and provides a clocking signal used to synchronize data transmissions. Modems and interface cards are typical DCE devices, whereas computers, multiplexers, and protocol translators are DTE devices.

data field

In a frame, the field or section that contains the data.

data-link connection identifier (DLCI)

A value that specifies a permanent virtual circuit (PVC) or a switched virtual circuit (SVC) in a Frame-Relay network.

data link layer

The layer in the OSI model at which hardware signals and software functions are converted. This is also known as layer 2 of the OSI model. This layer is logically subdivided into two parts: the media access control (MAC) sublayer and the logical link control (LLC) sublayer. The MAC portion is where the burned-in hardware address is stored. The LLC discriminates between protocols to ensure proper passage of various network-layer protocol traffic types.

data service unit (DSU)

Device used in digital transmission that adapts the physical interface on a DTE device to a transmission facility such as a T1 or an E1. The DSU is also responsible for such functions as signal timing. Often referred to in conjunction with a CSU.

data terminal equipment (DTE)

Device used at the user end of a user-network interface that serves as a data source, a destination, or both. These devices include computers, protocol translators, and multiplexers. See also *data communications equipment.*

database description packet (DDP)

Used to carry LSA information between two routers involved in the exchange state. See also *exchange state.*

datagram

Information groupings that are transmitted as a unit at the network layer.

DB-9

Connector with 9 pins used for serial-port or parallel-port connection between PCs and peripheral devices.

DB-25

Connector with 25 pins used for serial-port or parallel-port connection between PCs and peripheral devices.

DCE

See *data communications equipment.*

DDP

See *database description packet.*

DDR

See *dial-on-demand routing.*

DE

See *discard eligible.*

de facto standard

Standard that exists because of its widespread use, not necessarily because it is a standard approved by any particular governing body. See also *de jure standard.*

de jure standard

Standard that exists because of approval by an official standards body. See also *de facto standard.*

dead interval

The time that elapses without receiving any communication from a neighbor before that neighbor is considered unavailable. In OSPF, the default dead interval is 40 seconds. Compare with *hello interval*. See also *holdtime*.

debug

Any of the many commands used in diagnosing router problems, or simply watching router operation processes.

DECnet

Group of communications protocols developed and supported by Digital Equipment Corporation (now Compaq Computer Corporation). It supports both OSI protocols and proprietary Digital protocols.

decryption

The process of taking an encrypted stream of information and unencoding it, making it understood by the existing application or a downstream application. See also *encryption*.

dedicated LAN

A network segment dedicated or allocated to a single device. Data collection devices make use of these, as do LAN switching devices.

dedicated line **or** dedicated circuit

Usually used in WANs to provide a constant connection between two points.

default gateway

Normally a router or a multihomed computer to which packets are sent when they are destined for a host that is not on their segment of the network.

default route

A route that signifies a gateway of last resort for traffic destined for remote networks for which a router does not have specific reachability information.

delay

A calculation based on bandwidth of the link to determine the amount of time it takes to transmit data from across that link. This value is an amount of time expressed in milliseconds.

demarc

See *point of demarcation*.

deny

The process of prohibiting the passage of specific traffic.

designated router (DR)

In OSPF, the primary router elected to receive and send link-state updates to all routers that share a broadcast media segment. This election is based on the router priority, using router ID as a tie-breaker if priorities are identical.

destination address

The network address to which the frame is being sent. In a packet, this address is encapsulated in a field of the packet so all nodes know where the frame is being sent.

destination protocol address

The layer 3 address of the intended recipient of a specific packet.

destination service access point (DSAP)

This one-byte field in the frame combines with the SAP (service access point) to inform the receiving host of the identity of the destination host.

DHCP

See *Dynamic Host Configuration Protocol*.

dial backup

A DDR technology used to provide redundancy for a primary circuit to compensate for overload and/or failure of that circuit.

Glossary

dialed number identification service

The method for delivery of automatic number identification using out-of-band signaling.

dialer group

A designation that specifies the association of a dialer list with a specific router interface. Usually used in the definition of interesting traffic.

dialer interface

A logical interface used in the creation of rotary groups. Generally in charge of one or more physical interfaces.

dialer list

A designation used to define interesting traffic that should be allowed to initiate a DDR call to a specific destination.

dialer pool

A group of physical interfaces ordered on the basis of the priority assigned to each physical interface.

dialer profile

A configuration of physical interfaces to be separated from a logical configuration required for a call. Profiles may also allow thelogical and physical configurations to be bound together dynamically, call by call.

dialer string

A telephone number associated with a particular destination.

dial-on-demand routing

A technology generally associated with ISDN in which a data connection is established on an as-needed basis. When not in use, the link automatically disconnects and returns to an idle state.

dial-up line

A communications circuit that is established by a switched-carrier connection using the network of a telephone company.

dial-up networking

Refers to the connection of a remote node to a network using POTS. Also the name of temporary networking under the Microsoft Windows family of operating systems.

digital

In networking technologies, a string of electrical signals that take on the characteristics of one of two discrete binary states.

Digital network architecture (DNA)

A network architecture developed by Digital Equipment Corporation (now Compaq Computer Corporation).

digital subscriber line (DSL)

A public network technology that delivers high bandwidth over conventional copper wiring at limited distances.

directed broadcast

A layer 3 term for a data transmission destined to all hosts in a specific subnet.

discard eligible (DE)

ATM cells that have their cell loss priority (CLP) bit set to 1. If the network is congested, discard eligible traffic can be dropped to ensure delivery of higher-priority traffic. It is also called *tagged traffic*. See also *cell loss priority.*

distance-vector routing algorithm

See *Bellman-Ford algorithm.*

distance-vector routing protocol

Any dynamic routing protocol using the Bellman-Ford algorithm for routing update exchange that employs the use of metric addition to derive a measurement of a route to a particular destination network. Commonly referred to as "routing by rumor."

Distributed Update ALgorithm (DUAL)

An EIGRP finite state machine that performs all route computations and allows all EIGRP routers involved in a topology change to synchronize near-instantaneously on a loop-free topology. Using a composite metric based on such media properties as bandwidth and delay, the DUAL calculates successors and feasible successors for each destination listed in the topology table. Whenever the router detects that a successor has become unavailable for a certain destination, the DUAL performs a route evaluation and possibly a route recomputation. See also *route evaluation* and *route recomputation*.

distribute list

A configuration option that allows the filtering of reachability (such as routing) information using **access-list** commands to permit and/or deny routes.

distribution layer

In the Hierarchical Model, this layer functions as the separation point between the core and access layers of the network. The devices in the distribution layer implement the policies that define how packets are to be distributed to the groups within the network.

distribution router

Any router in an internetwork hierarchy that connects lower-level access routers to the higher-level core routers.

Djykstra's algorithm

The process that many link-state routing protocols employ to keep reachability information in a current state. Generally characterized by high memory usage and very fast convergence time.

DLCI

See *data-link connection identifier.*

DNA

See *digital network architecture.*

DNS

See *domain name system.*

domain

Networking system used worldwide on the Internet and in Windows NT networks to identify a controlled network of nodes that are grouped as an administrative unit.

domain name service (DNS)

The part of the distributed database system responsible for resolving a fully qualified domain name into the four-part IP (Internet Protocol) number used to route communications across the Internet. DNS can also stand for domain name server. See also *domain name system.*

domain name system (DNS)

A hierarchical client/server-based database management system. Was created and is operated by the InterNIC to provide alpha-based names for numeric-based IP addresses. See also *domain name service.*

dot address

A dot address refers to the 32-bit IP address in decimal form. It consists of four octets that are each eight bits in length and converted into decimal. It does *not* refer to a domain name.

down state

The first OSPF neighbor state. It means that no information has been received from a neighbor, but hello packets can still be sent to the neighbor in this state. If a router doesn't receive a hello packet from a neighbor within the dead interval (by default, four times the hello interval), then the neighbor state changes from full to down.

Glossary

DR

See *designated router.*

DRAM

See *dynamic random access memory.*

DS-0

A single 64,000-bit-per-second timeslot, usually associated with a T1 or fractions thereof.

DS-1

A grouping of 24 DS-0s. Refers to the framing methodology of T1 transmissions. However, DS-1 is often incorrectly considered to be synonymous with T1. T1 refers to the line coding methodology.

DS-1/DTI

An interface circuit used for DS-1 application with 24 trunks.

DS-3

Framing specification for transmitting digital signals at 44.736Mbps on T3 equipment.

DSAP

See *destination service access point.*

DSL

See *digital subscriber line.*

DSU

See *data service unit.*

DTE

See *data terminal equipment.*

DUAL

See *Distributed Update ALgorithm.*

dumb terminal

A keyboard/monitor combination that accesses a mainframe computer for data but provides no processing at the local level.

dynamic address resolution

The use of Address Resolution Protocol (ARP) to acquire and store information as needed. See also *Address Resolution Protocol.*

dynamic host configuration protocol (DHCP)

A greatly expanded implementation of the BOOTP protocol used for dynamic assignment of IP addresses on the network. DHCP also provides for gateway, DNS servers, WINS servers, and myriad other network elements.

dynamic random access memory (DRAM)

Variable-state memory that stores information using capacitors. Because capacitors drain, they must continually be "refreshed." DRAMs cannot be accessed during refresh cycles and therefore are slower than SRAMs. SRAMs require no refresh cycle because they maintain information as long as power is applied.

dynamic routing

The routing process that adjusts itself according to routing conditions, congestion, and other factors. In this fashion, packets may take different routes from source to destination at different points in time. Also called *adaptive routing.*

dynamic window

Used in flow control as a mechanism that prevents the sender of data from overwhelming the receiver. The amount of data that can be buffered in a dynamic window varies in size—hence its name.

E1

Wide-area digital transmission scheme, used predominantly in Europe, that carries data at a rate of 2.048Mbps. E1 lines can be leased for private use from common carriers. Compare with *T1.*

E3

Wide-area digital transmission scheme, used predominantly in Europe, that carries data at a rate of 34.368Mbps. E3 lines can be leased for private use from common carriers. Compare with *T3*.

EBGP

See *External Border Gateway Protocol*.

EEPROM

An EPROM that can be erased electronically (instead of using ultra-violet light). Stands for electrically erasable programmable read-only memory. See also *read-only memory*.

EGP

See *Exterior Gateway Protocol*.

EIA

See *Electronics Industry Association*.

EIA/TIA-232

The official name for RS-232 (which has been officially dropped), or the physical layer for the transmission of serial information. The original TIA-232 was far more ambitious than the minimal 3-pin usage, or even the 8-pin usage. Maximum transmission speed in this specification is 64Kbps. The most common usage is for terminals, modems, and console devices.

EIGRP

See *Enhanced Interior Gateway Routing Protocol*.

ELAN

Emulated LAN. An ATM network that mimics either an Ethernet or Token Ring network. Multiple ELANs can exist on a single ATM network.

electromagnetic interference (EMI)

The term used for the external interference of electromagnetic signals that causes reduction of data integrity and increased error rates in a transmission medium.

electronic mail

The application level form of messaging for end users. By far the most prevalent protocol for the transmission of electronic mail is SMTP. However, large organizations use more enterprise-based protocols. See *Simple Mail Transfer Protocol*.

Electronics Industries Association (EIA)

The group that specifies electrical transmission standards. Responsible for many common signaling specifications, such as EIA RS-232, EIA-RS-422, and so on.

EMI

See *electromagnetic interference*.

encapsulation

The technique used by layered protocols in which a layer adds header information to the protocol data unit (PDU) from the layer above.

encapsulation bridging

The encapsulation of transparently bridged frames into the framing type of a serial link (HDLC, Frame-Relay, and so on) in order to cross a WAN.

encryption

The modification of data for security purposes prior to transmission so it is not comprehensible without the decoding method. See also *decryption*.

end system (ES)

An end-user device on a network.

Enhanced Interior Gateway Routing Protocol (EIGRP)

A Cisco proprietary dynamic routing protocol that attempts to combine the positive traits of distance-vector and link-

Glossary

state protocols. EIGRP is sometimes referred to as a hybrid routing protocol or an advanced distance-vector routing protocol.

enterprise network

The collective set of computing and networking devices that provide for the needs of an entire organization. It likely consists of many networking technologies from assorted vendors. Although the desire to standardize on a minimum number of vendors is a goal, it is often unachievable because of the diverse number of platforms.

EPROM

See *read-only memory.*

error control

A process or technique to detect and in some cases correct errors in the transmission of data.

ES

See *end system.*

Ethernet

A framing convention used in CSMA/CD networks.

excess burst (Be)

The amount of data that a Frame-Relay internetwork will attempt to transmit after the committed burst (Bc) is accommodated. In general, the data from excess burst is delivered at a lower probability than the data from committed burst because excess burst data can be marked as discard eligible (DE). See also *committed burst* and *discard eligible.*

exchange state

An OSPF state that indicates that two OSPF routers are exchanging link-state advertisements (LSAs) to discover the link-state topology.

EXEC

The interactive command-line processor in Cisco IOS.

expansion

The process of running a compressed data set or compressed data stream through an algorithm to derive an original data set or data stream that is larger or requires more bandwidth. See also *compression.*

explorer

An SRB term that refers to frames dispatched from a source device in order to locate a suitable pathway to a specific destination device.

exstart state

An OSPF state that occurs after the DR/BDR election and indicates that two adjacent routers are ready to discover the link-state topology by exchanging summarized link-state databases. During this state, the master/slave relationship is defined to determine which of the adjacent routers, either the DR or the adjacent router, initiate the exchange of link-state information.

extended access list

Any access list that is meant to employ more than basic functionality of traffic filtering. In IP, an extended access list can filter on source address, destination address, protocol, and port.

extended superframe

A T1 framing convention that employs the transmission of 24 T1 frames.

exterior gateway protocol

Any generic internetworking protocol that exchanges routing information between two or more autonomous systems. EGP is a specific instance of an exterior gateway protocol, even though they have the same name. The distinction is the same as for *internet* and *Internet*.

Exterior Gateway Protocol (EGP)
An Internet protocol that exchanges routing information between two or more autonomous systems as defined in RFC 904. It has been replaced by BGP. See *BGP*.

exterior router
Router connected to an AURP (AppleTalk Update-Based Routing Protocol) tunnel, responsible for the encapsulation and de-encapsulation of AppleTalk packets in a foreign protocol header (for example, IP).

External Border Gateway Protocol (EBGP)
A BGP implementation that connects external ASes. EBGP peers are usually directly connected physically.

external gateway protocol (EGP)
A dynamic routing protocol that connects two external ASes.

external route
In OSPF, a route received from any source outside of the local area.

Fast Ethernet
IEEE 802.3 specification for data transfers of up to 100Mbps.

fast switching
A Cisco feature used to expedite packet switching through a router by means of a route cache. Compare with *process switching*.

fault tolerance
This is a theoretical concept defined as a resistance to failure. It is not an absolute and can be defined only in degrees.

FCS
See *frame check sequence*.

FDDI
See *fiber distributed data interface*.

FDM
See *frequency division multiplexing*.

feasible distance
In EIGRP, the metric associated with each piece of routing information entered into the routing table.

feasible successor
In EIGRP, the second best route to a particular destination network. The feasible successor is selected only if the advertised distance of the second best route is lower than the feasible distance of the best route. Also refers to the next-hop router along the alternative path to a destination.

FECN
See *forward explicit congestion notification*.

fiber channel, fibre channel
Defines full gigabit-per-second data transfer over fiber-optic cable.

fiber distributed data interface (FDDI)
A high-speed data-transfer technology designed to extend the capabilities of existing local area networks using a dual-rotating ring technology similar to Token Ring.

fiber-optic cable
A physical medium capable of conducting modulated light transmissions. Compared with other transmission media, fiber-optic cable is more expensive, but is not susceptible to electromagnetic interference and is capable of higher data rates. Also known as *fiber-optics* or optical fiber.

fiber-optics
The transmission of energy by light through glass fibers for communication and signaling.

FIFO
See *first-in first-out*.

Glossary

File Transfer Protocol (FTP)

The set of standards or protocols that allow you to transfer complete files between different computer hosts.

filter

A process or a device that screens and separates items. A router, for instance, will filter packets according to a set of rules and allow or deny forwarding accordingly.

firewall

A generic term for a device that filters network traffic. On the low end, it can be a simple router with an access list. On the high end, it can be a device that opens each packet and evaluates it using upper layers of the OSI network model.

firmware

Code that is typically embedded into a ROM, PROM, or EPROM, and delivered with a hardware device. Typically, firmware is the code that the device executes upon power-up. In general, it is not changeable without physically removing and/or replacing the ROM.

first-in first-out (FIFO)

A queuing strategy that dispatches traffic in the order in which it was received. In other words, FIFO is the absence of queuing.

flapping

A problem with routing in which an advertised route keeps switching, or flapping, between two or more paths due to an intermittent network failure.

flash memory

A form of non-volatile memory. It can sustain its contents without power, making it suitable to use flash memory to deliver changeable code, such as Cisco's IOS as well as store configurations.

flash update

The writing of code or data to flash memory. A flash update occurs, for example, when you upgrade the Cisco IOS from 11.2 to 12 on a router. An update occurs also when you save a configuration, although it is not necessarily viewed as a flash update.

flat addressing

A method of addressing that doesn't use any sort of hierarchy to determine location. MAC addresses are flat because there is nothing in the address that indicates location within the internetwork—bridges must broadcast or flood packets to all network segments to deliver any packets to their destinations. Compare with *hierarchical addressing*.

flooding

The process of distributing routing information throughout the network.

flow control

A method used to control the amount of data that is transmitted within a given period of time. There are different types of flow control. See also *dynamic window*.

forward explicit congestion notification (FECN)

A method for the Frame Relay network to deal with congestion. The network can set a single address bit in frames traveling toward their destination. A DTE receiving frames with the FECN bit set to one can forward the info on to higher-level protocols to exercise flow control. Compare with *backward explicit congestion notification*.

FRAD

See *frame relay access device*.

fragment-free

A fast packet-switching method that uses the first 64 bytes of the frame to determine if the frame is corrupted. If this first part is intact, then the frame is forwarded.

frame
Grouping of information transmitted as a unit across the network at the data link layer.

frame check sequence (FCS)
A function performed on inbound frames to determine whether they are valid entities worthy of further processing.

frame check sequence field
This field performs a cyclic redundancy check (CRC) to ensure that all of the frame's data arrives intact.

frame forwarding
The method that frame traffic traverses an ATM network.

frame length field
In a data frame, the field that specifies the length of a frame. The maximum length for an 802.3 frame is 1,518 bytes.

Frame-Relay
Data link layer switching protocol used across multiple virtual circuits of a common carrier, giving the end user the appearance of a dedicated line.

Frame-Relay access device (FRAD)
Device that provides access to Frame-Relay networks with support for a variety of LAN and Legacy protocols. Often includes an integral CSU/DSU or high-speed serial network interface and complies with industry standard RFC 1490 for internetworking with routers.

frame type field
In a data frame, the field that names the protocol that is being sent in the frame.

frequency
The number of cycles of an alternating current signal over a unit of time, expressed in hertz.

frequency division multiplexing (FDM)
Technology that divides the output channel into multiple, smaller bandwidth channels, each using a different frequency range.

FTP
See *File Transfer Protocol*.

full-duplex
The transmission of data in two directions simultaneously.

full mesh
A network topology in which each device in the network has a physical or virtual connection to every other device in the network (or mesh). It is extremely efficient as a delivery mechanism in that there is a route to each device, minimizing any propagation delay. However, it is costly from a growth standpoint because the number of links grows exponentially with each device that is added to the system.

full state
The last OSPF state. In this state, routers are fully adjacent with each other. All the router and network LSAs are exchanged and the routers' databases are fully synchronized within each area. Routing may now occur.

gateway
A hardware and software solution that enables communications between two dissimilar networking systems or protocols. Usually operates at the upper layers of the OSI protocol stack, above the transport layer but can perform at all seven layers.

Glossary

GB
Gigabyte. 1,000,000,000 Bytes or 1,000 Megabytes.

Gb
Gigabit. 1,000,000,000 bits or 1,000 Megabits.

GBps
Gigabytes per second. Note the uppercase B indicates bytes as compared to bits which is represented by a lowercase b.

Gbps
Gigabits per second. Note the lowercase b indicates bits as compared to bytes which is represented by an uppercase B.

generic routing encapsulation (GRE)
A tunneling protocol developed by Cisco to encapsulate a number of protocol packet types inside an IP tunnel. This creates virtual point-to-point links to Cisco routers at remote points over an IP network.

giant
An Ethernet frame in excess of the maximum transmittable unit size of 1,518 bytes.

gigabit (Gb)
Term used to specify one billion bits or one thousand megabits.

Gigabit Ethernet
IEEE specification for transfer rates up to one gigabit per second.

gigabits per second
One billion bits per second.

gigabyte
One billion bytes.

gigabytes per second
One billion bytes per second.

graphical user interface (GUI)
An interface that uses a graphics subsystem instead of a character generator to provide visual display. Modern GUIs use mice, menus, and virtual windows to separate and select content.

GRE
See *generic routing encapsulation*.

group-membership-LSA
See *LSA type 6*.

GUI
See *graphical user interface*.

half-duplex
A circuit designed for data transmission in both directions, but not simultaneously.

handshaking
The initial communication between two modems, during which they agree upon protocol and transfer rules for the session.

HDB3
See *high density bipolar level three*.

HDLC
See *high level data link control*.

header
Control information placed at the beginning of a data stream.

hello interval
The time that elapses between the transmission of two consecutive hello packets. In OSPF the default hello interval is 10 seconds; in EIGRP the default hello interval is 5 seconds. Sometimes referred to as the *keepalive interval*. Compare with *dead interval*.

hello packet
A packet used by some routing protocols to discover and maintain neighbor relationships.

hello protocol
A means of communication between two hosts on a network that require constant and continued connectivity to each other. The two devices exchange these hello messages at a specified interval.

helper address
An address used to forward selected broadcasts by converting them to unicasts or directed broadcasts.

heterogeneous network
A network that consists of dissimilar devices using dissimilar protocols that may provide or support dissimilar functions and/or applications.

hierarchical addressing
An addressing scheme that incorporates contiguous addressing and tools like VLSM in accordance with a hierarchically designed network.

high-density bipolar level three (HDP3)
A line-coding technique employed by users of E1 technologies.

high-level data link control (HDLC)
A Cisco proprietary serial framing convention that allows the use of multiple protocols across a serial link. This is the default encapsulation for serial interfaces on Cisco routers.

high-speed serial interface (HSSI)
A serial interface that must be employed in order to transmit and/or receive at a rate greater than 2Mbps, up to 52Mbps. The network standard for high-speed serial communications over WAN links. It includes Frame-Relay, T1, T3, E1, and ISDN.

holddown
The state entered into by a router that has just received a routing update indicating a failed route. The holddown prevents a router from accepting routing information for the failed route for a predetermined amount of time.

holdtime
A general term that refers to how long a device waits before purging an entry in a routing table, neighbor table, topology table, and so on. Once the holdtime expires, the entry, whatever the type, is purged. In EIGRP, the default holdtime is 15 seconds; in BGP, the default holdtime is 180 seconds. Also referred to as the HoldTime and hold-time.

hop
The crossing of a router in an internetwork.

hop count
The number of routers or hops between a source and a destination.

host
Used generically for any system on a network. In the Unix world, used for any device that is assigned an IP address.

hostname
The NetBIOS name of the computer or node given to the first element of the Internet domain name. It must be unique on the network.

host number
In IP, the decimal number that identifies the host portion of an IP address.

HOSTS file
Similar to LMHOSTS file except that the HOSTS file is most commonly used for TCP/IP name resolution of domain names.

hot standby routing protocol (HSRP)
Allows redundant default gateways.

HSRP
See *hot standby routing protocol*.

HSSI
See *high-speed serial interface*.

HTML
Hypertext markup language. Simple hypertext document formatting language that uses tags to indicate how a given part of a document should be interpreted by a viewing application, such as a WWW browser.

HTTP
See *Hypertext Transfer Protocol*.

hub
A hardware device that connects multiple independent nodes to a shared media. Also known as a concentrator or multiport repeater.

hybrid network
A network made up of more than one type of networking technology.

hybrid routing protocol
A routing protocol that employs the characteristics of both distance-vector and link-state protocols to attempt to exploit the positive aspects of each.

HyperTerminal
A Windows-based communications program that allows you to establish host/ shell access to a remote system.

hypertext transfer protocol (HTTP)
A protocol used by Web browsers to transfer pages and files from the remote node to your computer.

IANA
See *Internet Assigned Numbers Authority*.

IBGP
See *Internal Border Gateway Protocol*.

ICMP
See *Internet Control Message Protocol*.

Inter-domain Policy Routing
Currently an IETF proposal, it is an inter-domain routing protocol that dynamically exchanges policies between autonomous systems. IDPR encapsulates inter-autonomous system traffic and routes it according to the policies of each autonomous system along the path.

IEEE
See *Institute of Electrical and Electronics Engineers*.

IEEE 802.1
Standard that defines the OSI model's physical and data link layers. This standard allows two IEEE LAN stations to communicate over a LAN or WAN. It is often referred to as the "internetworking standard." It also includes the spanning tree algorithm specifications.

IEEE 802.2
Standard that defines the LLC sublayer for the entire series of protocols covered by the 802.x standards. This standard specifies the adding of header fields, which tell the receiving host which upper layer sent the information. It also defines specifications for the implementation of the logical link control (LLC) sublayer of the data link layer.

IEEE 802.3
Standard that specifies physical layer attributes such as signaling types, data rates and topologies, and the media-access method used. It also defines specifications for the implementation of the physical layer and the MAC sublayer of the data link layer, using CSMA/CD, This standard also includes the original specifications for Fast Ethernet.

IEEE 802.4

Standard that defines how production machines should communicate and establishes a common protocol for use in connecting these machines. It also defines specifications for the implementation of the physical layer and the MAC sublayer of the data link layer using Token Ring access over a bus topology.

IEEE 802.5

Standard often used to define Token Ring. However, it does not specify a particular topology or transmission medium. It provides specifications for the implementation of the physical layer and the MAC sublayer of the data link layer using a token-passing media-access method over a ring topology.

IEEE 802.6

Standard that defines the distributed queue dual bus (DQDB) technology to transfer high-speed data between nodes. It provides specifications for the implementation of metropolitan area networks (MANs).

IEEE 802.7

Standard that defines the design, installation, and testing of broadband-based communications and related physical media connectivity.

IEEE 802.8

Standard that defines a group of people who advise the other 802-standard committees on various fiber-optic technologies and standards. This advisory group is called the Fiber-Optic Technical Advisory Group.

IEEE 802.9

Standard that defines the integration of voice and data transmissions using isochronous Ethernet (IsoEnet).

IEEE 802.10

Standard that focuses on security issues by defining a standard method for protocols and services to exchange data securely by using encryption mechanisms.

IEEE 802.11

Standard that defines the implementation of wireless technologies, such as infrared and spread-spectrum radio.

IEEE 802.12

Standard that defines 100BaseVG-AnyLAN, which uses a 1000Mbps signaling rate and a special media-access method allowing 100Mbps data traffic over voice-grade cable.

IETF

See *Internet Engineering Task Force.*

IGP

See *Interior Gateway Protocol.*

IGRP

See *Interior Gateway Routing Protocol.*

industry standards architecture (ISA)

The standard of the older, more common 8-bit and 16-bit bus and card architectures.

infrared (IR)

Wavelength of light (longer than light visible to the naked eye) that is used in many wireless data transmission technologies.

init state

An OSPF state that specifies that a neighbor received a valid hello packet and added the sender's router ID to its neighborship database.

Institute of Electrical and Electronics Engineers (IEEE)

A standards body comprised of electrical and electronics engineers charged with creating physical and data link layer standards.

integrated routing and bridging (IRB)
Integrated routing and bridging is used in Cisco IOS to route a given protocol between routed interfaces and bridged interfaces within a single router.

integrated services digital network (ISDN)
An internationally adopted standard for end-to-end digital communications over PSTN that permits telephone networks to carry data, voice, and other source traffic.

intelligent hubs
Hubs that contain some management or monitoring capability.

inter-area route
In OSPF, any route to a destination outside of the local area.

interdomain routing
Routing that occurs between autonomous systems. Also called inter-autonomous system routing.

interesting traffic
In DDR, the specific traffic types that can initiate an ISDN connection to connect two remote sites.

interface
A device, such as a card or a plug, that connects pieces of hardware with the computer so information can be moved from place to place (e.g., between computers and printers, hard disks, and other devices, or between two or more nodes on a network).

interface processor
The I/O processor for any of the media and protocol adapter boards that operate in the Cisco 7000 series routers.

interference
An entity that delays, prohibits, or otherwise prevents a process from performing its function or within its specified parameters. Electrical interference, for example, may prevent radio signals or wired signals from maintaining their patterns, thus preventing transmission of information.

interior gateway protocol (IGP)
Any routing protocol employed within an AS.

Interior Gateway Routing Protocol (IGRP)
A Cisco proprietary classful, distance-vector routing protocol that functions on a 90-second update timer.

intermediate system-to-intermediate system (IS-IS)
An OSI link-state hierarchical routing protocol based on DECnet routing in which routers exchange routing information based on a single metric to determine network topology.

Internal Border Gateway Protocol (IBGP)
An implementation of BGP between routers inside the same AS. IBGP peers do not have to be directly connected physically with each other, as long as they can reach each other via an IGP or static route.

internal loopback address
Used for testing with TCP/IP, this address—127.0.0.1—allows a test packet to reflect back into the sending adapter to determine if it is functioning properly.

internal router
In OSPF, any router in which all interfaces configured for OSPF operation are in the same area.

International Standards Organization (ISO)
A voluntary organization founded in 1946, comprising the national standards organizations of many countries, and

responsible for creating international standards in many areas, including computers and communications. ANSI (American National Standards Institute) is the American member of ISO. ISO produced OSI (Open Systems Interconnection), a seven-layer model for network architecture.

International Telecommunication Union—Telecommunication Standards Sector (ITU-T)

A body that formally sets standards, specifications, and recommendations. It used to be known as the CCITT, or the Consultative Committee on International Telegraph and Telephone.

Internet

A public IP-based internetwork that facilitates communications on a global scale.

internet

Short for internetwork. See *internetwork*.

Internet Assigned Numbers Authority (IANA)

The organization responsible for Internet protocol addresses, domain names, and protocol parameters.

Internet Control Message Protocol (ICMP)

Network-layer internet protocol, documented in RFC 792, that reports errors and provides other information relevant to IP packet processing.

Internet domain name

Name used on the Internet. Made up of three elements: the computer name, the top-level domain to which the machine belongs, and the root-level domain.

Internet Engineering Task Force (IETF)

A group of research volunteers responsible for specifying the protocols used on the Internet and for specifying the architecture of the Internet.

Internet group management protocol (IGMP)

Protocol responsible for managing and reporting IP multicast group memberships.

Internet layer

In the TCP/IP architectural model, this layer is responsible for the addressing, packaging, and routing functions. Protocols operating at this layer of the model are responsible for encapsulating packets into Internet datagrams. All necessary routing algorithms are run here.

Internet Network Information Center (InterNIC)

The group that provides Internet services, such as domain registration and information, directory, and database services.

Internet Protocol (IP)

Network-layer protocol, documented in RFC 791, that offers a connectionless internetwork service. IP provides features for addressing, packet fragmentation and reassembly, type-of-service specification, and security.

Internet Research Task Force (IRTF)

The research arm of the Internet Architecture Board, this group performs research in areas of Internet protocols, applications, architecture, and technology.

Internet Service Provider (ISP)

A company that specializes in providing individuals, companies, and corporations with access to the public Internet.

internetwork

A group of networks that are connected by routers or other connectivity devices so that the networks function as one network.

internetworking

The process of interconnecting networks using devices, protocols, and technologies for the purpose of communicating information.

Internetwork Operating System (IOS)

Cisco's router operating system software that provides the intelligence and functionality of Cisco routers.

Internetwork Packet Exchange (IPX)

Connectionless network-layer protocol from Novell.

InterNIC

See *Internet Network Information Center.*

interoperability

The capacity for different devices, protocols, or technologies to work together.

intra-area route

In OSPF, a route to a destination network within the local area.

inverse ARP

Method of building dynamic routes in a network. It allows an access server to discover the network address of a device associated with a virtual circuit.

IOS

See *Internetwork Operating System.*

IP

See *Internet Protocol.*

IP address

32-bit number representing a unique designation for a network device. An IP address is represented in decimal dotted octets (i.e., eight bits separated by dots with each octet represented as a decimal number).

IP multicast

A routing technique that allows IP traffic to be propagated from one source to many destinations, or from many sources to many destinations. One packet is sent to a multicast group, which is identified by a single IP destination group address.

IP spoofing

The process of substituting the source IP address on a packet or set of packets to fool a device into allowing it to be forwarded.

IPCONFIG

Windows NT command that provides information about the configuration of the TCP/IP parameters, including the IP address.

IPSec

A protocol designed for virtual private networks (VPNs). Used to provide strong security standards for encryption and authentication.

IPv6

The next generation of IP. Supports a 128-bit address, CIDR, and authentication.

IPX

See *Internetwork Packet Exchange.*

IPX address

The unique address used to identify a node in the IPX network. An IPX address is an 80-bit number, 48 of which identify the MAC address and 32 of which identify the network number.

IR

See *infrared.*

IRB

See *integrated routing and bridging.*

ISA

See *industry standards architecture.*

ISDN

See *Integrated Services Digital Network.*

IS-IS

See *Intermediate System-to-Intermediate System.*

ISO

See *International Standards Organization.*

isochronous transmission

A method of asynchronous transmission requiring a node other than the sender or receiver to provide the clock signaling.

ISP

See *Internet Service Provider.*

ITU-T

See *International Telecommunication Union.*

jabber

An error condition in which a network device continually transmits random, meaningless data onto a network. Under IEEE 802.3, it is a data packet whose length exceeds what is prescribed in the standard.

jam

Describes the collision reinforcement signal output by the repeater to all ports. The jam signal consists of 96 bits of alternating ones and zeros. The purpose is to extend a collision sufficiently so that all devices cease transmitting.

JANET

See *Joint Academic Network.*

jitter

The fluctuation of the data packet with respect to a standard clock cycle. Jitter is undesirable and must be minimized.

Joint Academic Network (JANET)

An X.25 WAN connecting university and research institutions in the United Kingdom.

JPEG

A file format for compressing photo-realistic images. Compression yields are often 10% of original size. For compressing non-photo-realistic images, GIF is the preferred format. It is also a very common type of data found in HTTP streams.

K values

In IGRP and EIGRP, the values of bandwidth, delay, reliability, load, and MTU.

K56flex technology

One of the original two 56Kbps data-transfer technologies designed for modems. They were both replaced by the V.90 standard.

KB

Kilobyte.

Kb

Kilobit.

KBps

Kilobytes per second.

Kbps

Kilobits per second.

keepalive interval

A routing protocol term that refers to how often keep-alive messages are sent to a router to determine if the router is still active and to keep the connection from timing out.

keepalive message

A message passed across a link to keep an active, constant conversation with a node on the remote end.

kerberos

A standard for authenticating network users. Passwords are not transmitted across the network and therefore cannot be decrypted.

Kermit

Kermit is a File Transfer Protocol first developed at Columbia University in New York City in 1981 for the specific purpose of transferring text and binary files without errors between diverse types of computers over potentially hostile communication links. It is a suite of communications software programs from the Kermit Project at Columbia University. Kermit software offers a consistent approach to file transfer, terminal emulation, script programming, and character-set conversion on hundreds of different hardware and operating system platforms, using diverse communication methods.

L2F protocol
See *layer 2 forwarding protocol*.

L2TP
layer 2 tunneling protocol.

LAN
See *local area network*.

LAN Switch
A high-speed switch that forwards packets between data link segments.

LAPB
See *link access procedure balanced*.

LAPD
See *link access procedure D Channel*.

laser
An acronym for *light amplification by stimulated emission of radiation*. A narrow beam of coherent light that is modulated into pulses to carry data. SONET is a form of networking based on laser technology. See also *synchronous optical network*.

last-bit-in-first-out
See *weighted fair queuing*.

LAT
See *local area transport*.

latency
The time used to forward a packet in and out of a device. Commonly used in reference to routing and switching.

layer 1
See *physical layer*.

layer 2
See *data link layer*.

layer 2 forwarding protocol (L2F)
A dial-up VPN protocol designed to work in conjunction with PPP to support authentication standards, such as TACACS+, for secure transmissions over the Internet.

layer 2 tunneling protocol (L2TP)
A dial-up VPN protocol that defines its own tunneling protocol and works with the advanced security methods of IPSec. L2TP allows PPP sessions to be tunneled across an arbitrary medium to a "home gateway" at an ISP or corporation.

layer 3
See *network layer*.

layer 4
See *transport layer*.

layer 5
See *session layer*.

layer 6
See *presentation layer*.

layer 7
See *application layer*.

(LBIFO)
Last-bit-in-first-out. See *weighted fair queuing*.

learning bridge
A bridge that builds its own bridging address table, rather than requiring you to enter information manually.

leased line
A transmission line provided by a communications carrier for private and exclusive use by a customer.

link access procedure balanced (LAPB)

A layer 3 technology associated with X.25 implementations.

link access procedure D Channel (LAPD)

A technology that allows the use of a separate access path for ISDN signaling and call requests.

link state

In OSPF, the status of a link between two routers.

link-state advertisement (LSA) packet

An OSPF packet that describes link-state information, such as the router's operational interfaces, the cost used to send traffic out an interface, the next-hop router ID, and advertised routes. Several types of LSAs exist.

link-state database

See *topological database.*

link-state request (LSR) packet

An OSPF packet used to request missing or outdated LSA information.

link-state routing algorithm

See *link-state routing protocol.*

link-state routing protocol

Any dynamic routing protocol that employs Djykstra's algorithm for passing and maintaining routing information.

link-state update packet

An OSPF packet that contains the LSA packet. Sent when a topology change occurs or in response to an LSR packet.

LLC

See *logical link control.*

LLC2

See *logical link control, type 2.*

LMHOSTS file

A text file that contains a list of NetBIOS host-name-to-IP-address mappings used in TCP/IP name resolution.

LMI

See *local management interface.*

load

A value between 1 and 255 that specifies the saturation level of a link.

load-balancing

In routing, the ability of a router to distribute traffic across all of its interfaces that are the same distance from the destination address. Effective load-balancing occurs when the maximum number of factors (including cost) are built into the equation and links are used to their fullest extent.

loading state

In the loading state, an OSPF router sends a link-state request (LSR) packet to request missing or outdated LSA information. The router receiving this request responds by sending the information in a link-state update (LSU) packet.

local area network (LAN)

A high-speed computer network limited to a relatively small geographic area—typically a small building or floor of an office tower. LANs typically connect workstations, servers, printers, and other office productivity appliances. LAN standards specify signaling and cabling at the physical and data link layers of the OSI networking model. Token Ring, Ethernet, and FDDI are the most common LAN technologies.

local area transport (LAT)

A layer 2 protocol developed by the Digital Equipment Corporation (now Compaq Corporation).

Glossary

local broadcast

A broadcast on the local network that looks for the IP address of the destination host.

local management interface (LMI)

An interface that provides an ATM end-system user with network management information. It is defined by the ITU-T.

local preference

A well-known discretionary path attribute that provides an indication to routers in the AS about which path is preferred to exit the AS. Paths with highest local preference are always preferred. This attribute is propagated within the AS but is not propagated outside the AS.

logical addressing scheme

Refers to the addressing method used in providing manually assigned node addressing.

logical AND

The process of deriving an IP network address by associating the address with a subnet mask and performing this Boolean function on the pair.

logical channel

A communications path between two or more network nodes that is packet switched and nondedicated. Because packet switching is used, multiple logical channels may exist simultaneously on a single physical channel.

logical link control (LLC)

Sublayer of the data link layer of the OSI reference model. Provides an interface for the network layer protocols and the media access control (MAC) sublayer, also part of the data link layer.

logical link control, type 2 (LLC2)

Connection-oriented OSI LLC-sublayer protocol. See also *logical link control*.

longest match

The methodology behind route selection and data forwarding decisions within the router. The more bits a router can match when comparing the destination address and the routing table, the better the chance of reaching that destination.

loop

A continuous circle that a packet takes through a series of nodes in a network until it eventually times out.

loopback plug

A device used for loopback testing.

loopback testing

A troubleshooting method in which the output and input wires are crossed or shorted in a manner that allows all outgoing data to be routed back into the card.

LSA

See *link-state advertisement*.

LSA packet

See *link-state advertisement packet*.

LSA type 1

An intra-area OSPF packet that identifies a router's active interfaces and neighbors. Also called the router-LSA.

LSA type 2

An intra-area OSPF packet that identifies the routers with which a DR has established adjacency. This LSA is originated by the DR. Also called the network-LSA.

LSA type 3

An inter-area OSPF packet that describes reachability to area routes. This LSA is originated by an ABR. Also known as the network-summary-LSA.

LSA type 4

An inter-area OSPF packet that describes reachability to an ASBR. Also called the ASBR-summary-LSA.

LSA type 5

An inter-area OSPF packet that describes reachability to destinations outside the OSPF domain. This LSA is originated by an ASBR. Also called the AS-external-LSA.

LSA type 6

An inter-area OSPF packet that is used in MOSPF to locate multicast group members. Also called the group-membership-LSA.

LSA type 7

An intra-area LSA that is used within a not-so-stubby-area (NSSA) and describes reachability to external destinations that were imported into the NSSA by an NSSA ASBR.

LSR packet

See *link-state request packet*.

LSU packet

See *link-state update packet*.

MAC

See *media access control*.

MAC address

See *media access control address*.

MAC address learning

Function performed by a learning bridge. The source address and also interface of each received packet are stored for future delivery of packets by the learning bridge. Unless the MAC address is known, a bridge must forward packets to every interface instead of the known interface. This enables the bridge to operate efficiently because traffic does not go to unintended locations.

MAN

See *metropolitan area network*.

management information base (MIB)

A network information database installed on an end station that is used and maintained by a network management protocol such as SNMP or CMIP.

mark

In T1/E1 implementations, a binary value of 1. T1-capable devices use ones to maintain proper clocking.

master name server

The supplying name server that has authority in a zone.

match condition

A **route-map** command used to match a routing update based on specified conditions. See also *set action*.

maximum transmission unit (MTU)

The largest packet size, in bytes, that can be forwarded by any given layer 2 encapsulation.

MB

Megabyte. One million bytes. Usually refers to file size.

Mb

Megabit. One million bits. Term used to rate transmission transfer speeds (not to be confused with megabyte).

Mbps

Megabits per second.

MD5

Authentication protocol.

MED

See *multiexit discriminator*.

media

Various physical environments by which data transmission occurs. This is the plural form of *medium*.

media access control (MAC)

In the OSI model, the lower of the two sublayers of the data link layer. Defined by the IEEE as responsible for interaction with the physical layer.

media access control address (MAC address)

A six-octet number that uniquely identifies a host on a network. It is a unique number, burned into the network interface card, so it cannot be changed.

media access unit (MAU)

IEEE 802.3 specification referring to a transceiver. Not to be confused with a Token Ring MAU (multistation access unit), which is sometimes abbreviated MSAU.

media rate

The maximum transmission rate that can occur over a specific media type. Often, specifications are less than the maximum so as to give headroom for manufacturing or installation defects.

memory address

Usually expressed in binary, this is the label assigned to define the location in memory at which the information is stored.

mesh

A connection; can be either partial or full.

message

A portion of information that is sent from one node to another. Messages are created at the upper layers of the OSI reference model.

metric

A unit of measure to facilitate the selection of the best route to a given destination. In BGP, the metric is an optional nontransitive path attribute also known as the *MED*.

metropolitan area network (MAN)

An internetwork implementation that spans across a city, not necessarily large geographic spans.

MHz

Megahertz.

MIB

See *management information base.*

microsegmentation

The process of using switches to divide a network into smaller segments.

Microsoft point-to-point encryption (MPPE)

Microsoft's proprietary, point-to point, secure data encryption method, designed for use with *point-to-point tunneling protocol.*

microwaves

Very short radio waves used to transmit data over 890 MHz.

modem

A device used to modulate and demodulate the signals that pass through it. It converts the direct current pulses of the serial digital code from the controller into the analog signal that is compatible with the telephone network.

MOSPF

See *Multicast Open Shortest Path First.*

MTU

See *maximum transmission unit.*

multiaccess network

Any network that allows multiple devices to communicate simultaneously.

multicast

A single packet transmission from one sender to a specific group of destination nodes. In OSPF, the means by which routing updates are passed. Only OSPF routers respond to OSPF multicasts.

multicast address

An address that specifies a subset of devices on the network—or a group of addresses. Compare with *broadcast address* and *unicast address.*

multicast group

A group of devices that are identified by a multicast address. Network devices join a multicast group when they wish to receive the group's transmissions.

Multicast Open Shortest Path First (MOSPF)

An intradomain multicast routing protocol used in OSPF networks. MOSPF adds extensions to the OSPF unicast protocol to support IP multicast routing.

multicast router

A router that is running a multicast routing protocol and configured to receive multicast traffic.

multiexit-discriminator (MED)

An optional nontransitive path attribute that provides an indication to external routers about the preferred path into the AS. Paths with the lowest MED are preferred most. This attribute is propagated to an external AS and is used within it, but is not carried to the next AS without being set to 0, which is the default MED value. Also called the *metric.*

multihoming

The process of connecting an AS to multiple ISPs.

multilayer switch

A switch that operates at different layers of the OSI model. The most prominent multilayer switches operate at layers 2 and above. Examples of multilayer switches include switch routers and router switches.

multilink PPP

A standardized implementation of PPP that allows for the bonding of multiple B channels to aggregate bandwidth for the duration of a specific call.

multimode fiber

Fiber-optic cabling that supports the propagation of multiple light frequencies. Compare with *single-mode fiber.*

multiplatform

Describes a programming language, technology, or protocol that runs on different types of CPUs or operating systems.

multiplexing

Method of transmitting multiple logical signals across the same channel at the same time.

multiring

In bridging, the use of a bridged network to forward traffic between two layer 3 networks.

multistation access unit (MAU or MSAU)

A hub used in an IBM Token Ring network. It organizes the connected nodes into an internal ring and uses the RI (ring in) and RO (ring out) connectors to expand to other MAUs on the network.

multivendor network

A network that is comprised not only of products from different manufacturers but of different protocols or protocol standards.

mux

A multiplexing device. Combines individual signals into a single signal for transmission over a medium. At the other end, a demux separates the signal back into its original signals.

Glossary

name caching

The storage of name-to-network addresses so that future lookups are not necessary. Name caches are always accompanied with a timeout period wherein future lookups are compulsory.

name resolution

The process of resolving network names to network addresses.

name servers

Contain the databases of name resolution information used to resolve network names to network addresses.

NAP

See *national access provider.*

NAT

See *Network Address Translation.*

national access provider (NAP)

A corporation responsible for larger portions of the public Internet. NAPs are in charge of providing public Internet access to ISPs and to efficiently manage scarce IP address space.

NBMA

Nonbroadcast multiaccess. Refers to multiaccess networks that do not by default support broadcast/multicast traffic. Examples include Frame-Relay, SMDS, and ISDN PRI.

NBNS

See *NetBIOS Name Server.*

NBTSTAT

A command-line utility that displays protocol statistics and current TCP/IP connections using NBT (NetBIOS over TCP/IP).

NDIS

See *Network Driver Interface Specification.*

neighbor

Two routers that exchange routing information with each other. In OSPF, neighbors are routers that have established bidirectional communication. In BGP, neighbors are routers that have established a TCP BGP connection. See also *neighborship* and *adjacency.*

neighbor database

See *neighborship database.*

neighborship

A condition in which routers have established a neighbor relationship with each other. In OSPF, neighborship refers to the relationship formed between two routers that have established bidirectional communication with each other; this includes the relationship between directly connected non-DR/BDR neighbors, as well as the relationship between DRs/ BDRs and directly connected neighbors. Compare with *adjacency.*

neighborship database

An OSPF data repository that contains all of a router's known neighbors within the area. Also called a neighbor database.

neighbor table

In non-distance-vector routing protocols, a listing of routers that share directly connected links. In EIGRP, the neighbor table stores information about adjacent neighbors, including the neighbor's address and local router's outbound interface for the neighbor. The EIGRP neighbor table also stores information required by the Reliable Transport Protocol (RTP), including the transmission list. A topology table exists for each network layer protocol that EIGRP supports.

NetBEUI

See *NetBIOS Extended User Interface.*

NetBIOS

See *Network Basic I/O System*.

NetBIOS Extended User Interface (NetBEUI)

A nonroutable, Microsoft-proprietary networking protocol designed for use in small networks.

NetBIOS Name Server (NBNS)

A central server that provides name resolution for NetBIOS names to IP addresses.

netstat

A command-line utility that displays protocol statistics and current TCP/IP network connections.

network

A term used to describe the interconnectivity of computing devices: workstations, servers, printers, routers, and so forth.

network address

A logical or physical number or name used for identification purposes. For a device to properly communicate with a different device, they must agree and cooperate using a common protocol. A network address is one such element of this protocol and is used to establish identity among devices so that they can ultimately communicate.

Network Address Translation (NAT)

A technology that allows the static and/or dynamic mapping of private, internal IP addresses to a registered public IP address for communication via the public Internet.

network administrator

The role of a network administrator is complicated. At one level it is to organize and implement the care and feeding of a network—to ensure that the network devices can competently, efficiently, and consistently communicate with each other. At another level it is to plan growth and adjust for impending changes as well as to implement any changes.

network analyzer

A device that resides on a network and watches packets as they travel "on the wire." It is used for diagnostics as well as statistical purposes. Sophisticated analyzers are aware of higher-level application protocols and can peel off network layers easily. Originally, network analyzers were single-purpose devices. However, most network analyzers are often very fast PC devices that are able to keep up with gigabit traffic.

Network Basic I/O System (NetBIOS)

A connectionless, data link layer protocol that utilizes broadcasts for communications.

network down

A term used when the clients are unable to utilize the services of the network. This can be administrative, scheduled downtime for upgrades or maintenance, or the result of a serious error.

Network driver interface specification

A Microsoft specification for a generic, hardware- and protocol-independent device driver for NICs that allows binding one or more protocols to one or more NICs.

network ID

The part of the TCP/IP address that specifies the network portion of the IP address. This is determined by the class of the address, which is determined by the subnet mask used.

network information services (NIS)

The user, group, and security information database utilized in a Unix internetwork.

network interface

A logical device for the purpose of receiving and transmitting information. Most network interfaces map directly to physical interfaces such as an Ethernet or serial port. However, network interfaces are often used to distinguish DLCIs in a single physical port into a Frame-Relay network or an encrypted tunnel in a virtual private network.

network interface card (NIC)

Also known as a network adapter, this is the hardware component that serves as the interface, or connecting component, between the network and the node. It has a transceiver, a MAC address, and a physical connector for the network cable.

network interface layer

The bottom layer of the TCP/IP architectural model. Responsible for sending and receiving frames.

network jordanism

Any broadcast protocol that artificially sets ToS for its own packets to something with an elevated level of service in the network in order to gain greater access for low-priority traffic, usually succeeding only in adversely affecting all other traffic flows.

network layer

The third layer of the OSI reference model. This is where routing based on node addresses (IP or IPX addresses) occurs.

network-LSA

See *LSA type 2*.

network management

The entire concept of maintaining, configuring, troubleshooting, and scaling a computer network. Often, hardware and software tools are employed to provide feedback.

Network News Transfer Protocol (NNTP)

An Internet protocol that controls how news articles are to be queried, distributed, and posted.

network number

Part of an IP address that specifies the network to which a particular host belongs.

network operating system (NOS)

An operating system for a computer that provides resources to other entities on a network. Novell NetWare, Linux, and Microsoft Windows NT are examples of general purpose operating systems that provide file and printing resources (as well as others) to workstations on a computer network.

network-summary-LSA

See *LSA type 3*.

network termination 1 (NT1)

An ISDN device that connects the point of demarcation to the CPE.

network termination 2 (NT2)

An ISDN device that performs layers 2 and 3 protocol functions and concentration services.

next-hop

The neighboring router used to reach a destination. In BGP, next-hop is a well-known mandatory path attribute that indicates the next-hop IP address that is to be used to reach a destination. On broadcast and nonbroadcast multiaccess networks, the next-hop will always point to the originator of a routing update, unless this default behavior is overridden.

NIC

See *network interface card*.

NIS

See *network information services*.

NNTP

See *Network News Transfer Protocol.*

node

The endpoint of a network connection. Nodes can be processors, controllers, or a workstation. Also a generic term for a participant on a computer network, or a device that can transmit or receive information utilizing a computer network.

noise

Also known as EMI. See *electromagnetic interference.*

Nonvolatile Random Access Memory (NVRAM)

Static memory space in the router where the router's configuration is stored. As the name implies, NVRAM does not require power to keep its contents in storage.

NOS

See *network operating system.*

notification message

A BGP message sent to inform peers that an error occurred with a routing update. The BGP connection is closed immediately after sending this message.

not-so-stubby area (NSSA)

An OSPF stub area that connects to an external AS via an ASBR. Utilizes LSA type 7 packets. See also *LSA type 7.*

NSSA

See *not-so-stubby area.*

NSSA router

Resides in an OSPF NSSA and does not accept type 5 LSAs. However, to accept certain external routing information, it uses type 7 LSAs.

NT1

See *network termination 1.*

NT2

See *network termination 2.*

null interface

A logical software interface in a router used as an alternative to access lists to deny traffic. Traditionally, a static route is configured to specify the null interface as the outbound interface for traffic destined for the denied network.

NVRAM

See *Nonvolatile Random Access Memory.*

octet

One of four 8-bit divisions of an IP address.

ODI

See *open data-link interface.*

open architecture

Any architecture specification that lies within the public domain. Third-party developers are mandated to license the architecture for their products to anybody. However, strict rules usually exist regarding modifications.

open data-link interface (ODI)

These drivers, heavily used in both Novell and AppleTalk networks, allow the NIC (network interface card) to bind multiple protocols to the same NIC, allowing the card to be used by multiple operating systems. Similar to NDIS.

open message

A BGP message that is sent to open a BGP connection between two neighbors that have just established a TCP connection with one another. The open message contains negotiable parameters, such as the holdtime, and other introductory information, such as the sender router ID.

Open Shortest Path First (OSPF)

A standardized dynamic link-state routing protocol designed to overcome the limitations of RIP by utilizing a hierarchical area structure.

Open Systems Interconnection (OSI) reference model

A seven-layer model created by the ISO to standardize and explain the interactions of networking protocols. In reality, very few implementations of OSI exist. The prevalent models (IP, IPX, AppleTalk, and so forth) span the various layers differently.

optional nontransitive

A class of BGP path attributes that are not necessarily recognized by all standard BGP implementations. If recognized by a BGP router, the router propagates the attribute to neighbors based on the meaning of the attribute. If not recognized by a BGP router, the attribute is dropped.

optional transitive

A class of BGP path attributes that are not necessarily recognized by all standard BGP implementations. If recognized by a BGP router, the router propagates the attribute to neighbors based on the meaning of the attribute. If not recognized by a BGP router, the attribute is marked as partial and propagated to neighbors without affecting the BGP router's policy.

origin

A well-known mandatory path attribute that defines the origin of the path information. The origin can be one of three values, including IGP, EGP, and incomplete. An IGP origin indicates that the path is interior to the originating AS; an EGP origin indicates that the path is learned via the EGP; and an incomplete origin indicates that the path is unknown or is learned via some other means, such as through redistribution into BGP.

originator ID

An optional nontransitive path attribute that is created by the route reflector and indicates the router ID of a route's originator. Compare with *cluster ID*.

OSI

Open Systems Interconnection. See *Open Systems Interconnection (OSI) reference model*.

OSPF

See *Open Shortest Path First*.

packet

A logical piece of information that contains control information as well as data. Control information is usually in the header or less frequently in a trailer.

packet internet gopher (ping)

A TCP/IP protocol-stack utility that works with Internet Control Message Protocol and uses an echo request and reply to test layer 3 connectivity to other systems.

packet-switched network (PSN)

A network that utilizes packet-switching technology for data transfer. Sometimes called a packet-switched data network (PSDN).

packet switching

Networking method in which nodes share bandwidth by dividing the multiple information streams into smaller, more manageable packets. The packets are then transmitted mixed across a medium mixed in with packets from other nodes.

PAP

See *password authentication protocol*.

parallel transmission

Method of data transmission by which bits of data are transmitted simultaneously over a number of channels. Compare with *serial transmission*.

partial mesh
A physical configuration in which not all routers are directly connected.

passive state
An EIGRP router's state for a destination that is not in the route recomputation process. This is the normal state for a route. Compare with active state.

password
A set of characters used with a username to authenticate a user on the network and to provide the user with rights and permissions to files and resources.

password authentication protocol (PAP)
An authentication method that utilizes clear text usernames and passwords to permit and deny access to remote users and/or routers.

patch panel
A device by which the wiring used in coaxial or twisted-pair networks converge, in a central location and is then connected to the back of this panel.

path attributes
Metrics used by BGP to enforce policy-based routing. Path attributes can fall into four separate categories, including well-known mandatory, well-known discretionary, optional transitive, and optional nontransitive. Example, of path attributes include weight, AS-path, next-hop, origin, local preference, atomic aggregate, aggregator, communities, and multiexit discriminator.

payload
The data portion of a packet (i.e., without the control information). See also *packet*.

PBX
See *private branch exchange*.

PDM
See *protocol dependent module*.

PDN
See *public data network*.

PDU
See *protocol data unit*.

peak rate
The maximum rate at which a virtual circuit can transmit data.

peer
A neighbor router. In BGP, a peer is a neighbor that has established a TCP BGP connection with another neighbor. Peers do not have to be directly connected physically for them to exchange routing information.

periodic update
A routing update dispatched at a specified interval.

permanent virtual circuit (PVC)
A logical path—established in packet-switching networks—between two locations. Similar to a *dedicated line*. Known as a permanent virtual connection in ATM terminology. (Not to be confused with private virtual circuit, also known as a PVC.)

physical addressing scheme
Refers to the MAC address on every network card manufactured. Cannot be changed.

physical layer
Bottom layer (layer 1) of the OSI reference model, where all physical connectivity is defined.

ping

A utility that issues ICMP (Internet Control Message Protocol) packets to a host for acknowledgment of receipt. It is one of the most common (although not necessarily the most robust) utilities available to determine connectivity between hosts. See also *packet internet gopher.*

plain old telephone system (POTS)

The current analog public telephone system.

point of demarcation

In telecommunications, the point at which responsibility for the serial link changes from the customer to the telephone company and vice versa.

point-of-presence (POP)

Physical location at which a long-distance carrier or a cellular provider interfaces with the network of the local exchange carrier or local telephone company.

point-to-multipoint connection

A partial mesh.

point-to-point connection

A connection between two routers.

point-to-point protocol (PPP)

A common dial-up networking protocol that includes provisions for security and protocol negotiation and provides host-to-network and switch-to-switch connections for one or more user sessions. The common modem connection used for Internet dial-up.

point-to-point tunneling protocol (PPTP)

A protocol that encapsulates private network data in IP packets. These packets are transmitted over synchronous and asynchronous circuits to hide the underlying routing and switching infrastructure of the Internet from both senders and receivers.

poison reverse updates

A routing update that explicitly indicates that a network or subnetwork is not reachable. Poison reverse updates are sent to default routing loops.

policy-based routing

The setting of policies, or rules, for how traffic flows through an AS. In BGP, policy-based routing involves metrics called path attributes.

polling

The media-access method for transmitting data, in which a controlling device is used to contact each node to determine if it has data to send.

POP

See *point-of-presence* or *Post Office Protocol.*

port number

In IP, a service access point between the transport layer and the upper application layers.

POST

Power-On Self Test.

Post Office Protocol (POP)

A protocol for the delivery and retrieval of electronic mail. In most implementations it is merely a service for the retrieval of electronic mail whereas SMTP is used for delivery. See also *Simple Mail Transfer Protocol.*

POTS

See *plain old telephone system.*

PPP

See *point-to-point protocol.*

PPP multilink

See *multilink PPP.*

PPTP

See *point-to-point tunneling protocol.*

prefix

The bits in an IP address that comprise the network portion.

presentation layer

Layer 6 of the OSI reference model. Prepares information to be used by the application layer.

PRI

See *primary rate interface.*

primary rate interface (PRI)

A higher-level network interface standard for use with ISDN. Defined at the rate of 1.544Mbps, it consists of a single 64Kbps D channel plus 23 (T1) or 30 (E1) B channels for voice or data.

print server

A network device that intercepts print requests and stores (or spools) the data to local storage, thus freeing the transmitting device from managing and maintaining a connection to a physical printer. The print server is then free to retransmit the printing stream to any number of devices at any specified time in any quantity.

priority queuing

A Cisco queuing strategy that allows the prioritization of various traffic based on its importance in the network.

private branch exchange (PBX)

An analog or digital switchboard for telephones located on subscriber premises to connect private and public telephone networks.

private internetwork address space

Any IP addresses that exist in space defined by RFC 1918 (consisting of network 10.0.0.0 through 10.255.255.255, 172.16.0.0 through 172.31.255.255, and 192.168.0.0 through 192.168.255.255).

private virtual circuit (PVC)

Provides a logical connection between locations through a Frame-Relay/ATM cloud. Example: A company has three branch offices. Each location physically connects to the Frame-Relay provider's network through a series of switches, but it appears to the end users as if the three branch offices are directly connected to each other—as if it were an unbroken circuit. (Not to be confused with permanent virtual circuit, also known as PVC.)

process switching

Packet processing without the use of a route cache. Therefore, performance is limited by process level speeds. Compare with *fast switching.*

profile

A template for a user account.

PROM

See *read-only memory.*

propagation delay

The amount of time it takes for information to reach its destination or to reach multiple destinations. Often related to control information and synchronizing rather than raw data.

proprietary

A standard or specification that is created by a single manufacturer, vendor, or other private enterprise.

protocol

A set of rules or standards that control data transmission and other interactions between networks, computers, peripheral devices, and operating systems.

protocol address

A network layer address that consists of a network and a host portion.

protocol converter

A device or procedure to change the language of one system to the language of another system.

protocol data unit (PDU)

OSI term for packet.

protocol dependent module (PDM)

Responsible for EIGRP multiprotocol support. PDMs are responsible for supporting network layer, protocol-specific requirements.

protocol identification field

In a frame, a five-byte field used to identify to the destination node the protocol that is being used in the data transmission.

protocol stack

Two or more protocols that work together, such as TCP and IP, or IPX and SPX. Also known as a protocol suite.

protocol translator

A device or software that converts one protocol to another. The protocols are often at the same or span the same OSI layer. Otherwise, there would be little equivalence between the protocols, and translation would be difficult or impossible.

proxy

An entity or device that performs a function on behalf of another device.

proxy ARP

Variation of the ARP in which an intermediate device such as a router sends an ARP response on behalf of an end node to a requesting host. See also *Address Resolution Protocol*.

proxy server

A program that makes a connection and retrieves information within a computer network on behalf of a client.

PSDN

Packet-switched data network. See *packet-switched network*.

pseudo ring

In source-route translational bridging, the method used to portray an Ethernet segment to Token Ring hosts as simply another Token Ring.

PSN

See *packet-switched network*.

PSTN

See *public switched telephone network*.

public data network (PDN)

A network offered to the public, usually for a fee. PDNs enable small organizations to extend their networks to remote locations without having to purchase long-distance point-to-point links.

public internetwork address space

Any IP addresses that exist outside of the private address space. Public address space is normally under the control of a registration authority in charge of assigning these addresses to companies and/or individuals that require them.

public switched telephone network (PSTN)

A general term referring to all of the telephone networks and services in the world. The same as POTS, PSTN refers to the world's collection of interconnected public telephone networks that are both commercial and government owned. PSTN is a digital network, with the exception of the connection between local exchanges and customers, which remains analog.

PVC

See *permanent virtual circuit* or *private virtual circuit*. Care must be exercised because these two terms do not mean the same thing.

Q.920/Q.921

The ITU-T (formerly the CCITT) specifications for ISDN UNI data link layer.

Q.931

An ISDN call setup protocol that deals with the ISDN network layer between the terminal and switch.

QoS

See *quality of service.*

QoS parameters

The ATM parameters including cell loss ratio (CLR), cell error rate (CER), cell misinsertion rate (CMR), cell delay variation (CDV), cell transfer delay (CTD), and average cell transfer delay.

quality of service

The measurement of performance for a transmission system. This involves both availability of devices or links as well as the ability to perform within specified parameters. In the specific sense, it refers to ATM performance over a virtual circuit.

query packet

An EIGRP packet sent to all neighbors when a router goes into active state for a destination. The query packet asks routers whether they have a valid and alternative path to the destination. A router that has originated a query must wait until all replies are received before the router can proceed with the route recomputation process.

queue

A first-in, first-out list.

queuing

The process of prioritizing traffic output on a serial interface.

queuing delay

The amount of time that an entity enters a queue and when it is released.

R Interface

In ISDN, the interface between the TE2 and TA.

RAM

See *random access memory.*

random access memory

Volatile memory space in a router in which the running configuration is stored. Without power applied, the contents of RAM will be lost.

RARP

See *reverse address resolution protocol.*

read-only memory (ROM)

Read-only memory is a hardware device that can store code and/or data. ROMs cannot be written to by the device on which they are installed; hence, the term read-only. However, programmable read-only memory (PROM) can be programmed using a separate special device. Erasable programmable read-only memory (EPROM) can be written to and erased multiple times.

redistribution

The process of translating routing information from one protocol into another and advertising the translated information to the network See *route redistribution.*

redundancy

The process of providing fail-safe connectivity for hardware and/or software.

reliability

A measurement of dependability of a link on a scale of 1 to 255, with 255 being highly dependable.

reliable transport protocol (RTP)

Responsible for the guaranteed, ordered delivery of EIGRP packets to all neighbors. Uses a transmission list to keep track of all neighbors to which reliable packets have been sent; each neighbor is expected to respond with an acknowledgment.

remote bridge

A bridge that unifies a network via WAN links.

remote node

A node or computer that is connected to the network through a dial-up connection. Dialing in to the Internet from home is a perfect example of the remote node concept.

repeater

A device that regenerates and retransmits the signal on a network. Usually used to strengthen signals going long distances.

reply packet

An EIGRP packet that is sent in response to a query and indicates whether a valid alternative path exists for a destination that is in the route computation process.

request for comments (RFC)

Method used to post documents regarding networking or Internet-related standards or ideas. Some have been adopted and accepted by the Internet Architecture Board as standards.

resource reservation protocol (RSVP)

A protocol that supports the reservation of resources across an IP network. RSVP depends on IPv6.

reverse address resolution protocol (RARP)

A process that dynamically provides addressing information to end clients that know only their MAC address. This process is similar to OOTP and/or DHCP.

RFC

See *request for comments.*

RI

See *ring in.*

ring group

In source-route bridging, the definition of a logical ring that exists inside the bridge to act as a destination ring for a multiport SRB.

ring in (RI)

A connector used in an IBM Token Ring network on a multistation access unit (MAU) to expand to other MAUs on the network. Counterpart to the RO (ring out), the ring-in connector on the MAU connects to the media to accept the token from the ring.

ring out (RO)

A connector used in an IBM Token Ring network on a multistation access unit (MAU) to expand to other MAUs on the network. Counterpart to the RI (ring in), the ring-out connector on the MAU connects to the media to send the token out to the ring.

ring topology

A LAN topology that implements a unidirectional closed loop among nodes. Each node is connected to two and only two neighbors.

RIP

See *routing information protocol.*

RJ-11 connector

Connector used with telephone systems. Can have either four or six conductors. A red/green pair of wires is used for voice and data; a black/white pair is used for low-voltage signals.

RJ-45 connector

An Ethernet cable connector, used with twisted-pair cable, that can support eight conductors for four pairs of wires.

RMON

The remote monitoring standard established in 1992 by RFC 1271 for its usage in Ethernet networks. It provides network administrators with comprehensive network fault diagnosis and performance information.

RO

See *ring out*.

ROM

See *read-only memory*.

root bridge

A bridge in the internetwork that has been configured with the lowest bridge priority value, to make it the highest-priority bridge. All other bridges in the internetwork base path-determination decisions on the cost related to forwarding traffic to the root bridge.

rotary group

In DDR, a number of physical interfaces that have been associated and are under the control of one or more logical dialer interfaces.

route

Information in a router regarding reachability of a particular destination network.

route evaluation

An EIGRP process that occurs whenever an EIGRP router detects a topology change. In this process, the DUAL evaluates the topology table to discover whether there are any new best routes for a given destination. If the topology change is the result of a failed successor for a certain destination, the DUAL would try to find a feasible successor for that destination. If no feasible successor could be found in the topology table, the DUAL would enter route recomputation. See also *route recomputation* and *Distributed Update ALgorithm*.

route filter

A configuration, employing access lists, used to control the networks being advertised out of or into a router.

route map

An IOS feature used to control routing information received from or sent to a neighbor router.

route recomputation

An EIGRP process that occurs whenever the DUAL fails to find a feasible successor in the topology table after a topology change. During this process, the router sends out query packets to ascertain whether EIGRP neighbors have an alternative route for the destination in question. The route recomputation process ends once all neighbors have replied to the router and the router has finished either (1) adding an alternative route for the queried destination to its topology and routing tables, or (2) removing the queried destination from its topology and routing tables. See also *route evaluation* and *Distributed Update ALgorithm*.

route redistribution

The sharing of routing information between two separate routing protocols. Redistributed routes are propagated throughout the network as routes derived by the protocol receiving the shared information.

route reflector

A BGP router that is configured to be allowed to propagate IBGP-learned routes to IBGP peers. See also the *BGP Split Horizon rule.*

route summarization

The process of consolidating a range of contiguous network numbers into a single route and advertising it to the network. Requires VLSM.

routed protocol

Any of the layer 3 protocols that can be implemented on a routed interface. Examples of routed protocols are IP, IPX, AppleTalk, DECnet, and VINES.

router

A device that works at the network layer of the OSI reference model to control the flow of data between two or more network segments.

router-LSA

See *LSA type 1.*

routing

The concept of delivering objects from a source to a destination. Includes the learning of routes to a destination.

routing domain

Group of nodes and intermediate systems that agree on a set of administrative rules for routing. Each domain has a unique addressing scheme.

routing information field

In Token Ring implementations, a field that consists of route control and route descriptor fields that provide pathway information for SRB hosts.

Routing Information Protocol (RIP)

Protocol that uses hop count as a routing metric to control the direction and flow of packets between routers on an internetwork.

routing metric

A quantitative value assigned to a route by an algorithm that indicates reachability. The routing metric is then stored in a routing table. Routers can make decisions to forward packets to a destination by comparing these metrics and choosing the route that has the best value. Some metrics that contributeto a routing metric include bandwidth, communications cost, hop count, delay, MTU, reliability, and load.

routing protocol

Any protocol that builds and maintains network reachability information in a routing table.

routing table

A listing of destination networks, metrics necessary to reach those networks, a next-hop address, and an outbound interface through which to depart the router to reach that destination network.

routing update

Packets sent from a router to other routers to indicate network reachability and associated metrics. The receiving routers use this information to update their routing tables. The content of updates and intervals are protocol specific.

RS-232

The communications standard that defines the flow of serial communications and the particular functions.

RSVP

See *resource reservation protocol.*

RTP

See *Reliable Transport Protocol.*

runt
Any frame transmitted that is smaller than the minimum transmittable unit.

S interface
See *subscriber interface.*

sample
In T1 technologies, a measurement of the height of an analog wave at 125-microsecond intervals, represented by an 8-bit codeword.

SAP
See *service access point* and *service advertisement protocol.*

scalable internetworks
Networks connected by interconnectivity devices that are reliable, secure, accessible, and adaptable to the evolving needs of the network.

SCSI
See *small computer system interface.*

SDLC
See *Synchronous Data Link Control.*

seed router
A router within a network that has fixed addressing rather than dynamic addressing. This allows other routers within the same network to establish network addressing for themselves based on the seed router's address(es). The AppleTalk suite of protocols makes use of seed routers.

segment
A section of a network that is bounded by a router, a bridge, or a switch.

serial interface
Any interface designed to access WAN services. Typical serial interfaces include V.35, EIA/TIA 232, and EIA/TIA 449.

serial line/internet protocol (SLIP)
A method of encapsulation that allows the TCP/IP protocol to be used over asynchronous lines, such as standard telephone lines. Previously used for most Internet access, it has been replaced by PPP because of SLIP's lack of error-checking capabilities.

serial transmission
Method of data transmission by which bits of data are transmitted one-by-one over a single channel. Compare with *parallel transmission.*

server
A node that fulfills service requests for clients. Usually referred to by the type of service it performs, such as file server, communications server, or print server.

server-based application
An application that is run off of a network share, rather than from a copy installed on a local computer.

server-based networking
A network operating system that is dedicated to providing services to workstations, referred to as clients. See *client/server networking.*

service access point (SAP)
This field in a frame tells the receiving host for which protocol the frame is intended.

service advertisement protocol (SAP)
An IPX protocol that provides network clients information about network resources such as file servers or print servers.

service profile identifier (SPID)
A number that identifies the service to which you have subscribed. This value is assigned by the ISDN service provider and

Glossary

is usually a 10-digit telephone number with some extra digits. The SPID can consist of 1 through 20 digits.

session
Refers to the dialog that exists between two computers.

session layer
The fifth layer of the OSI reference model, it establishes, manages, and terminates sessions between applications on different nodes.

set action
A **route-map** command used to control routing updates. In BGP, the set action specifies how matching routes are to be preferred, accepted, advertised, or redistributed. See also *match condition*.

SF
See *superframe*.

shared systems
The infrastructure component routed directly into the backbone of an internetwork for optimal systems access. Provides connectivity to servers and other shared systems.

shielded twisted-pair (STP)
Twisted-pair network cable that has shielding to insulate the cable from electromagnetic interference.

shortest-path routing
Routing that minimizes distance or path cost.

silicon switching
Switching using a silicon-switching engine or processor rather than via embedded software and the main processor. The end result is that routing decisions occur much faster.

silicon switching engine (SSE)
Routing and switching mechanism that compares the header of an incoming packet to a silicon-switching cache and forwards the packet to the appropriate interface. Because the SSE is embedded in the hardware of the silicon switch processor (SSP) of a Cisco 7000, it can perform switching independent of the system processor. Execution of routing decisions occurs much faster than in software.

Simple Mail Transfer Protocol (SMTP)
An Internet protocol used for the transfer of messages and attachments.

Simple Network Architecture (SNA)
A nonroutable IBM protocol usually associated with mainframe connectivity.

Simple Network Management Protocol (SNMP)
A protocol used almost exclusively in TCP/IP networks to do several things: to provide network management devices with a method to monitor and control other network devices; to manage configurations, statistics collection, performance, and security; and to report network management information to a management console.

Simple Network Management Protocol trap (SNMP trap)
An SNMP protocol utility that sends out an alarm notifying the administrator that something in network activity differs from the established threshold, as defined by the administrator.

single-mode fiber
Fiber-optic cabling that operates with a very narrow spectral width. It supports very high bandwidth but requires a light source to operate at the specified frequency. Compare with *multimode fiber*.

single point of failure

Any point in the network that exists without redundancy. If this point fails, much, or all, of the network suffers an outage as well.

sliding window flow control

Method whereby a receiver allows a transmitter to transmit information until a specific window is full. When the window is full, then the transmitter must stop until the receiver advertises a larger window.

SLIP

See *serial link/internet protocol.*

small computer system interface (SCSI)

A technology defined by a set of standards originally published by ANSI for use with devices on a bus known as a SCSI bus.

smart bridge

Builds its own bridging address table, rather than requiring information to be entered manually. Also known as a *learning bridge.*

SMDS

See *switched multimegabit data service.*

SMP

See *symmetrical multiprocessing.*

SMTP

See *Simple Mail Transfer Protocol.*

SNA

See *Simple Network Architecture.*

SNAP

See *subnetwork access protocol.*

snapshot client

A DDR-capable device that runs a distance-vector routing protocol that has frozen its routing table for a specified duration known as a quiet period. When the quiet period expires, the client dials the server router and exchanges routing updates.

snapshot routing

A DDR feature that allows distance-vector routing tables to be frozen for long periods of time known as quiet periods. When the quiet period expires, a client router dials a server router to initiate a period of active routing update exchange.

snapshot server

The router that receives the snapshot call to initiate routing update exchange.

SNMP

See *Simple Network Management Protocol.*

SNMP trap

See *Simple Network Management Protocol trap.*

socket

A logical interprocess communications mechanism through which a program communicates with another program or with a network.

socket identifier

An eight-bit number used to identify the socket. It is used by IPX when it needs to address a packet to a particular process running on a server. The developers and designers of services and protocols usually assign socket identifiers. Also known as a socket number.

SONET

See *synchronous optical network.*

source address

The address of the host who sent the frame is contained in the frame so the destination node knows who sent the data.

source protocol address

The layer 3 address of the originating host.

source-route bridge (SRB)

Used in source route bridging, these bridges send the packet to the destination node through the route specified by the sending node and placed in the packet.

source-route translational bridge (SR/TLB)

A bridge that is capable of forwarding traffic between Ethernet and Token Ring clients by converting the frame type from one to the other and back again.

source-route transparent bridge (SRT)

A Token Ring implementation of bridging between hosts that utilize a RIF and those that do not. The source-route transparent bridge adds or removes the RIF according to the end station's needs.

source service access point (SSAP)

This one-byte field in the frame combines with the SAP to tell the receiving host the identity of the source or sending host.

spanning tree algorithm (STA)

Defined by IEEE 802.1 as part of the spanning tree protocol to eliminate loops in an internetwork with multiple paths.

spanning tree protocol (STP)

Protocol developed to eliminate the loops caused by the multiple paths in an internetwork. Defined by IEEE 802.1.

SPID

See *service profile identifier.*

spike

An instantaneous, dramatic increase in the voltage output to a device. Spikes are responsible for much of the damage done to network hardware components.

Split Horizon updates

A technique used by routers whereby route propagation does not exit an interface where it was learned. This helps eliminate routing loops.

spoofing

The process of representing false information to show connectivity when there is none. In DDR with IPX, spoofing

of watchdogs and SPX keepalives is done to simulate client/server connectivity.

SRAM

See *static random access memory.*

SRB

See *source-route bridge.*

SRT

See *source-route transparent bridge.*

SR/TLB

See *source-route translational bridge.*

SSAP

See *source service access point.*

SSE

See *silicon switching engine.*

standard

Any agreed-upon specification is a standard. Standards may be de facto or de jure. See *de facto standard* and *de jure standard.*

standard access list

An access list of limited functionality, generally used to permit or deny access to/ from hosts and networks. The only criteria considered is the source address of the packet.

standard area

In OSPF, an area that accepts all types of OSPF traffic. Also referred to as a nonstub area.

star topology

A LAN topology by which nodes on the network are connected to a common central switch using point-to-point links. Compare with *bus topology* and *ring topology.*

static IP addresses

IP addresses that are assigned to each network device individually, often referred to as hard-coded.

static random access memory (SRAM)
See dynamic random access memory.

static route
A route that an administrator places in the routing table to override or augment the dynamic routing process.

station IPX address
A 12-digit number that is used to uniquely identify each device on an IPX network.

store-and-forward
A fast packet-switching method, it produces a higher latency than other switching methods because the entire contents of the packet are copied into the onboard buffers of the switch, and the cyclical redundancy check (CRC) calculations are performed before the packet can be passed on to the destination address.

STA
See spanning tree algorithm.

statistical multiplexing
A specific case of multiplexing whereby bandwidth can be dynamically allocated according to need. This makes better use of the bandwidth and it also allows streams to be multiplexed. *See also multiplexing.*

STP
See spanning tree protocol and shielded twisted-pair.

stub area
In OSPF, an area that is allowed only a single point of access. Stub areas know only of the routes within the local area and summary routes to other areas supplied by ABRs. Virtual links cannot be configured across a stub area, and they cannot contain an ASBR.

stub network
Network that has only a single connection to a router.

stub router
Resides in an OSPF stub area. It does not accept type 5 LSAs.

stuck in active
An EIGRP condition in which a router that has sent out a query does not receive one or several replies. The route for which the query was sent will remain in an active state until the active time expires for the query, in which case the neighbors that did not reply are removed from the neighbor table and all their routes are put into active state. *See also active state and active time.*

subinterface
A logical or virtual interface assigned to a single physical interface.

subnet
A logical layer 3 network.

subnet address
The part of an IP address that defines the subnet. It is revealed from the IP address by logically ANDing the IP address with its subnet mask.

subnet mask
A 32-bit address that is used to mask or "screen" a portion of the IP address to differentiate the part of the address that designates the network and the part that designates the host.

subnetting
The process of dividing your assigned IP address range into smaller clusters of hosts.

subnetwork
In an IP network, a subnetwork is part of an existing subnet. Subnetworks provide network administrators with a multilevel,

Glossary

hierarchical routing structure—effectively shielding the entire network structure from other networks.

subnetwork access protocol (SNAP)
An Internet protocol that specifies a standard method of encapsulating IP datagrams and ARP messages on a network.

subscriber interface
In ISDN, the connection between the customer equipment (BRI interface or TA) and an NT1.

successor
The next-hop EIGRP router along the best path to a destination, where "best" is defined as least cost. Can also refer to the best route used to reach a destination, in which case the successor is the path with the least feasible distance. Successors are listed in both the topology and routing tables. See also *feasible successor, feasible distance,* and *advertised distance.*

superframe (SF)
In T1 technology, an entity that consists of 12 T1 frames.

supernetting
The aggregating of IP network addresses and advertising them as a single classless network address.

supernetting mask
Mask—similar to the subnet mask—used in supernetting.

surge
The opposite of a brownout. The voltage increase of a surge is less dramatic than that of a spike, but it can last a lot longer.

surge protectors
Inexpensive and simple devices that are placed between the power outlet and the network component to protect the component from spikes and surges. Also known as surge suppressors.

SVC
See *switched virtual circuit.*

switch
A layer 2 networking device that forwards frames based on destination addresses.

switch type
In ISDN, the model of switch to which the CPE is connected.

switched LAN
A LAN that takes advantage of LAN switches or frame switches.

switched multimegabit data service (SMDS)
Defined by IEEE 802.6. The physical-layer implementation for data transmission over public lines at speeds between 1.544Mbps (T1) and 44.736Mbps using cell relay and fixed-length cells.

switched virtual circuit (SVC)
A virtual circuit that is established dynamically on demand to form a dedicated link and is then broken when transmission is complete. Known as a switched virtual connection in ATM terminology.

symmetrical multiprocessing (SMP)
The utilization of multiple processors on a single system.

synchronization
The agreement of data between two or more devices. In communications, an important synchronization element or data point is common timing.

Synchronous Data Link Control (SDLC)
An IBM proprietary serial encapsulation that is capable of transporting only a single protocol. SDLC is usually associated with mainframe connectivity.

synchronous optical network (SONET)
An ANSI standard for broadband public networks using fiber-optics, initiated by the regional Bell operating companies. With SONET, it is possible for telecommunications products from different vendors to communicate over networks, with data transmission rates from 51.84Mbps to 48Gbps.

synchronous transmission
Digital signal transmission method using a precise clocking method and a predefined number of bits sent at a constant rate.

T Interface
See *trunk interface.*

T1
Digital WAN carrier facility that transmits DS-1-formatted data at 1.544Mbps through the telephone switching network, using AMI or B8ZS coding.

T1 frame
One sample from each of 24 T1 timeslots placed end to end, with one additional bit added for framing.

T3
Digital WAN carrier facility that transmits DS-3-formatted data at 44.736Mbps through the telephone switching network.

TA
See *terminal adapter.*

TACACS
See *terminal access control access control server.*

TACACS+
A Cisco modified and proprietary version of TACACS. The enhancements include authentication, authorization, and accounting.

tagged traffic
See *discard eligible.*

TCP
See *Transmission Control Protocol.*

TCP/IP
See *Transmission Control Protocol/Internet Protocol.*

TDI
See *transparent driver interface.*

TDR
See *time domain reflectometry.*

TE1
See *terminal equipment 1.*

TE2
See *terminal equipment 2.*

telco
Short for telephone company.

telecommunications
Communications over a telephony network. See also *telephony.*

Telecommunications Industry Association (TIA)
An organization that develops standards, with the Electronics Industries Association (EIA), for telecommunications technologies.

telephony
The science and industry devoted to the transmission of sound between endpoints—often for substantial distances. The transmission of data has built upon telephony standards that have existed for decades, which is why telephone companies are the primary implementers of network transport equipment.

Telnet
Standard terminal-emulation protocol in the TCP/IP protocol stack. It is used to perform terminal emulation over TCP/IP via remote terminal connections, enabling users to log in to remote systems and use resources as if they were connected to a local system.

Glossary

terminal

A physical device used to control and/or communicate with a host computer. In early computing, it was always a character-based device such as a cathode ray tube (CRT) and keyboard or a teletype (tty). Also, a program, process, or other device that emulates a physical terminal.

terminal access control access control server (TACACS)

An application used to provide remote authentication services for network access.

terminal adapter

An adapter used in connecting nonnative interfaces to ISDN facilities.

terminal equipment 1 (TE1)

A native ISDN-capable router interface.

terminal equipment 2 (TE2)

A nonnative ISDN interface that must be attached to a TA for ISDN connectivity.

terminal emulator

A character-based program that will mimic the behavior of other terminals, often industry standard hardware devices. The most common emulators are ANSI, VT100, and 3270.

terminal server

A network device that connects physical terminals (see *terminal*) or other asynchronous serial devices to a LAN or WAN, often using TCP/IP, X.25, or LAT protocols.

TFTP

See *trivial file transfer protocol*.

thicknet coaxial

Thick cable most commonly used as the backbone of a coaxial network. It usually comes about 0.375 inch in diameter.

thinnet coaxial

Cable commonly used in older bus topologies to connect the nodes to the network. It is thinner than thicknet, but still about 0.25 inch in diameter.

throughput

The rate at which information passes through a juncture or a device in a network. Compare with *bandwidth*.

TIA

See *Telecommunications Industry Association*.

time domain reflectrometry (TDR)

Method for locating cable lengths, or cable interfaces by sending a signal down the wire and watching for the faint reflections returned at each anomaly in the cable, including the large reflection from the end. Using the known propagation speed in the wire media (approximately 0.7c, for instance, in 10Base2 cable) and timing the reflections yields the distances to each of the sources of reflection. Commonly used for finding cable breaks and length of wire loop in telephony.

timeslot

The space available for a single piece of information from a particular channel in time division multiplexing.

time-to-live (TTL)

Field in an IP header that indicates how long a packet is considered valid. It is also a generic term meant for caches and other temporary storage areas.

token

A frame that provides controlling information. In a Token Ring network, the node that possesses the token is the one that is allowed to transmit next.

Token Ring

IBM proprietary token-passing LAN topology defined by IEEE standard 802.5. It operates at either 4 or 16Mbps in a star topology.

Token Ring adapters

Traditionally ISA or Microchannel devices with 4 or 16Mbps transfer capability, they are used to connect nodes to a Token Ring network.

topological database

An OSPF data repository that stores all known routes in the OSPF internetwork and indicates how these routes are interconnected. All routers in the same area maintain identical topological databases. Also called a *link-state database*.

topology

Defines the shape or layout of a physical network and the flow of data through the network.

topology table

A listing of known destination networks and the number of pathways known to reach those individual destinations. In EIGRP, the topology table stores route entries for all destinations that the router has learned. This includes the destination's address, state, and cost. The topology table contains all successors, feasible successors, and potential successors for each destination. A topology table exists for each network layer protocol that EIGRP supports.

ToS

See *type of service*.

totally-stub area **or** totally stubby area

In OSPF, an area that contains only a single exit point, routes for the local area, and a default route out of the area. No external routes are known to a totally stubby area.

traffic bounding

An EIGRP feature that restricts queries and other routing packets from being propagated outside specific boundaries. EIGRP route summarization, stub designation, AS boundaries, and distribution lists are all hierarchical tools for implementing traffic bounding. Also called EIGRP packet bounding.

traffic management

Any methods employed to avoid congestion in a network. Management also involves the use of hardware and software tools to provide feedback as to the status as well as performance of specific links.

traffic policing

A process used to measure traffic flow across a connection to determine whether action should occur. Where configured limits are breached, then an action such as discarding discard eligible (DE) frames is employed. This occurs in ATM and Frame-Relay networks as well as other similar technologies. See also *discard eligible*.

traffic prioritization

The process of configuring the router to treat differing traffic types as more or less important in consideration for output priority.

traffic profile

A set of ToS attribute values assigned to a port on an ATM switch creating a profile. This profile affects many parameters describing how data should be transmitted from the port (e.g., rate, cell drop eligibility, inactivity timer, and transmit priority).

traffic shaping

The use of buffers to regulate data traffic and ensure that congestion does not occur. ATM, Frame-Relay, and other types of networks make use of traffic shaping.

Glossary

trailer

Any control information that is at the end of a data stream or packet. Compare with *header.*

transceiver

A coined word that combines transmitter and receiver.

Transmission Control Protocol (TCP)

A connection-oriented, reliable data-transmission communication service that operates at the transport layer of the OSI model. Part of the TCP/IP protocol stack.

Transmission Control Protocol/Internet Protocol (TCP/IP)

The suite of protocols combining TCP and IP, developed to support the construction of worldwide internetworks. See *Transmission Control Protocol* and *Internet Protocol.*

Transmission Control Protocol/Internet Protocol (TCP/IP) sockets

A socket, or connection, to an endpoint, used in TCP/IP communication transmissions.

transmission list

See *reliable transport protocol.*

transmit

The process of sending data using light, electronic, or electric signals. In networking, this is usually done in the form of digital signals composed of bits.

transparent bridging

A situation in which the bridges on your network tell each other which ports on the bridge should be opened and closed, which ports should be forwarding packets, and which ports should be blocking them—all without the assistance of any other device.

transport driver interface (TDI)

A kernel-mode network interface that is exposed at the upper edge of all Windows NT transport protocol stacks. The highest-level protocol driver in every such stack supports the TDI interface for still higher-level kernel-mode network clients.

transport layer

Layer 4 of the OSI reference model, it controls the flow of information.

Travan technology

An efficient, low-cost data-backup method for small PCs and laptops, available in TR-1, TR-3, and TR-4 formats. Travan tape drives are available in a wide range of interfaces, such as floppy, parallel, ATAPI, or SCSI.

triggered update

A routing update spawned as a result of a topology change. These updates are not sent out regularly. They go out on an as-needed basis only.

trivial file transfer protocol (TFTP)

A connectionless file-sharing protocol that requires no authentication for uploading and/or downloading of files.

trunk

The physical and logical connections between switches enabled for network traffic.

trunk interface (T interface)

In ISDN, this is usually coexistent with the S interface between the NT1 and the customer equipment.

TTL

See *time-to-live.*

tunnel

A logical configuration of the encapsulation of one layer 3 protocol inside the payload of another layer 3 protocol. Tunnel configuration requires the configuration of the source, destination, and encapsulation modes of the tunnel as well as encapsulated protocol attributes on the logical tunnel interface.

tunnel destination
The termination point of a logical tunnel.

tunnel interface
A logical interface to which encapsulated protocol attributes are assigned. The tunnel's source, destination, and mode are defined here as well.

tunnel mode
The encapsulation method used for a tunnel configuration. The default is **gre-ip**.

tunnel source
The origination point of a logical tunnel.

twinaxial
A type of coaxial cable more commonly found in IBM mainframe environments or used with AppleTalk networks. Contains two insulated carrier wires twisted around each other.

twisted-pair
A type of cable that uses multiple twisted pairs of copper wire.

two-way state
An OSPF state that specifies that two neighboring routers have seen each other's hello packet and established bidirectional communication.

type of service (ToS)
Single byte field in the IP header, which defines the abstract parameters precedence, delay, throughput, and reliability. This field is used to manage the priority of any single packet in a network such that in comparison to other ToS values, it is delivered appropriately. ToS is defined in RFC 791.

U Interface
In ISDN, the connection between the NT1 and the demarc.

UART
See *universal asynchronous receiver/transmitter.*

UDP
See *User Datagram Protocol.*

unicast
A message sent to a single address or network node.

unicast address
The network address of a single network node. Compare with *broadcast address* and *multicast address.*

universal asynchronous receiver/transmitter (UART)
A chip that is responsible for communications carried over a serial port, converting between data bits and serial bits.

universal resource locator (URL)
Standardized addressing scheme for accessing network resources. De facto standard has made it synonymous with Web addresses, although it can refer to protocols other than HTTP.

Unix
An operating system in wide use, with over 100 variations.

unshielded twisted-pair (UTP)
A type of cable that uses multiple twisted pairs of copper wire in a casing that does not provide much protection from EMI. The most common network cable in Ethernet networks, it is rated in five categories.

Glossary

update message

A BGP message that contains network reachability information for a single path with either one or several associated networks; multiple paths require multiple update messages. This message also contains path attributes and paths that have been withdrawn.

User Datagram Protocol (UDP)

A communications protocol that provides connectionless, unreliable communications services and operates at the transport layer of the OSI model. It requires a transmission protocol such as IP to guide it to the destination host.

URL

See *universal resource locator.*

UTP

See *unshielded twisted-pair.*

V.90 standard

The standard that replaced both the K56 flex technology and the x.2 technology as the standard for 56K serial data transfer over phone lines.

variable length subnet mask (VLSM)

A subnet mask that does not remain constant throughout the internetwork for a given classful network.

variance

A multiplier value that allows a router to perform unequal-cost load-balancing. In IGRP and EIGRP, load-balancing can occur only over paths whose cost is smaller than the cost of the best path multiplied by the variance.

versatile interface processor (VIP)

An interface card designed for the Cisco 7000 and Cisco 7500 serious routers. Enables the use of multilayer switching.

VIP

See *virtual IP* or *versatile interface processor.*

virtual circuit

A logical connection setup across a network between a source and destination. The route is fixed and bandwidth is dynamically allocated. See also *permanent virtual circuit.*

virtual connection

A connection established between a source and a destination where packets are forwarded along the same path. Bandwidth is not permanently allocated until it is used.

virtual IP (VIP)

A Cisco Catalyst 5000 running Virtual Networking Services can create logically separated switched IP workgroups across switched ports. This feature is called virtual IP.

virtual LAN (VLAN)

Group of devices located on one or more different LAN segments whose configuration is based on logical instead of physical connections so that they can communicate as if they were attached to the same physical connection. See also *local area network (LAN).*

virtual link

In OSPF, a link that must be configured when a non–Area 0 must be connected directly to another non–Area 0. The virtual link transits the non–Area 0 that is connected to Area 0 to create a logical connection of the new area to Area 0.

virtual private network (VPN)

A network that uses a public network such as the Internet as a backbone to connect two or more private networks. Provides users with the equivalent of a private network in terms of security.

virtual ring

The configuration of a logical ring for implementations of multiport SRBs. The virtual ring must be specified as the destination ring in the SRB configuration of each interface.

virtual terminal (VTY)

A logical port to provide a means of accessing a router through the use of a Telnet session.

VLAN

See *virtual LAN.*

VLSM

See *variable length subnet mask.*

VPN

See *virtual private network.*

VTY

See *virtual terminal.*

WAN

See *wide area network.*

weight

A Cisco-proprietary path attribute used to influence the path that intra-AS routers take to external destinations. Paths with the highest weight are preferred most. This attribute is configured on the router and remains local to it.

weighted fair queuing (WFQ)

A Cisco queuing strategy employed to give low-volume traffic the priority for output consideration. Also called last-bit-in-first-out (LBIFO).

well-known discretionary

A class of BGP path attributes that must be recognized by all standard BGP implementations and do not have to be present in update messages. Examples of path attributes that fall into this class include local preference and atomic aggregate.

well-known mandatory

A class of BGP path attributes that must be recognized by all standard BGP implementations and must be present in all update messages. Examples of path attributes that fall into this class include AS-path, next-hop, and origin.

WFQ

See *weighted fair queuing.*

wide area network (WAN)

Data communications network that serves users across a broad geographical area. Often uses transmission devices such as modems or CSUs/DSUs (channel service units/data service units) to carry signals over leased lines or over common carrier lines.

wildcard mask

A four-octet mask used in the configuration of access lists to specify addresses for permission and/or denial. Also used in defining OSPF area membership.

Windows 95/98

Ubiquitous client operating systems enabling a friendly graphical interface. They have applications in consumer and small business environments but are often unsuitable for corporate networks due to their lack of unified security controls.

Windows 2000

Equivalent of Windows NT 5.0.

Windows Millennium Edition (ME)

The successor to Windows 98.

Windows NT

Ubiquitous corporate network operating system with graphical user interface.

wiring closet

A location within a building, floor, or other convenient place to put cross-connect panels. It is also a place for small network

Glossary

devices, access devices, and remotely managed equipment. It is often not climate controlled and is therefore not suitable for servers or other temperature- and humidity-sensitive equipment.

workgroup

A small group of machines that participate in a logical network. Network service broadcasts are often limited to those participants both to minimize network traffic and to narrow choices for workstations.

World Wide Web

The collective client/server process for retrieving documents that consist of text, graphics, sound, and video over the public Internet. Many of the standards are defined at the W3C consortium (http://www. w3c.org), although many large corporations have done their own standardization.

WWW

See *World Wide Web.*

X terminal

A character-based virtual terminal session within the X-Windows environment. Sometimes referred to as x-term.

X Window System

A client/server model to enable graphical users applications on Unix and Unix-like operating systems. The server is the graphical system and has been adapted for multiple operating systems. The client is almost always Unix or a Unix derivative.

x.2 technology

Developed by US Robotics in 1997, one of the original two 56Kbps data-transfer technologies that were replaced by the V.90 standard.

X.21bis

Physical-layer communications protocol used in X.25. Supports synchronous, full-duplex, point-to-point transmissions with speeds up to 19.2Kbps.

X.25

A WAN technology used in many parts of the world. X.25 is generally a very low-bandwidth serial technology.

Xerox Network Systems

Protocol suite originally designed by Xerox's Palo Alto Research Center (PARC). Many later transport protocols developed by PC vendors, such as Novell, Microsoft (NWLink), 3Com, and Banyan used or currently use a derivation of XNS.

Xmodem

One of the most popular file transfer protocols. It sends data in blocks along with a checksum and waits for an acknowledgment of receipt by the receiver.

XNS

See *Xerox Network Systems.*

Zmodem

A communications protocol similar to Xmodem. However, Zmodem provides better transfer rates and error checking. It achieves faster transmission by allowing larger blocks of data to be transmitted.

Index